FATHER LUIS OLIVARES

A Biography

Father Luis Olivares

A BIOGRAPHY

Faith Politics and the

Origins of the Sanctuary Movement

in Los Angeles

MARIO T. GARCÍA

THE UNIVERSITY OF NORTH CAROLINA PRESS

Chapel Hill

*This book was published with
the assistance of the Thornton H. Brooks Fund
of the University of North Carolina Press.*

Set in Utopia by Tseng Information Systems, Inc.
Manufactured in the United States of America

The University of North Carolina Press has been a
member of the Green Press Initiative since 2003.

Jacket photograph courtesy of Dept. of Special Collections,
Charles E. Young Research Library, UCLA.

Library of Congress Cataloging-in-Publication Data
Names: García, Mario T., author.
Title: Father Luis Olivares, a biography : faith politics and the origins
of the sanctuary movement in Los Angeles / Mario T. García.
Description: Chapel Hill : The University of North Carolina Press, [2018] |
Includes bibliographical references and index.
Identifiers: LCCN 2018010415 | ISBN 9781469643311 (cloth : alk. paper) |
ISBN 9781469643328 (ebook)
Subjects: LCSH: Olivares, Luis, 1934–1993. | Catholic Church—Clergy—
Biography. | Sanctuary movement—California—Los Angeles. | Church work
with refugees—California—Los Angeles. | Social justice—Religious aspects—
Catholic Church. | Political refugees—Central America.
Classification: LCC BX4705.O4838 G37 2018 | DDC 282.092 [B] —dc23
LC record available at https://lccn.loc.gov/2018010415

Something in the subject's life has touched the biographer's own
experience, even though the deed came no closer than a wish. . . .

The biographer has to choose. He cannot write a complete life
of a man without deciding whether he likes him or not, whether he
trusts him or not. Of course, he may decide that, like most human beings,
his hero was a mixture of greatness and weakness, but that also
is an interpretation. . . .

A biography is not an encyclopedia, it is the story of a life.

CATHERINE DRINKER BOWEN,
Biography: The Craft and the Calling

CONTENTS

FIGURES

FATHER LUIS OLIVARES

A Biography

PROLOGUE

*For I was hungry and you gave me food, I was thirsty and you
gave me drink, a stranger and you welcomed me, naked and you
clothed me, ill and you cared for me, in prison and you visited me.*
—Matthew 25:35–36

To know God is to do Justice.
—Jeremiah 20:13–16

*When an alien resides with you in your land, do not molest him.
You shall treat the alien who resides with you no differently than the
natives born among you; have the same love for him as for yourself,
for you, too, were once aliens in the land of Egypt.*
—Leviticus 19:33–34

*You cannot be witness to human suffering and not be convinced
of the existence of social sin. We are all responsible unless we take
a stand and speak up.*
—Fr. Luis Olivares, 1990

On a warm September evening in 1990, a rather large congregation of
people of different ethnic and religious backgrounds gathered to honor
Fr. Luis Olivares, the former pastor of Our Lady Queen of Angeles, better
known as La Placita Church. Tables were arranged in the public open
space by the Plaza bandstand adjacent to the Olvera Street marketplace
in downtown Los Angeles and directly across from La Placita. Dignitaries
such as mayor Tom Bradley, state representatives who had passed a resolution declaring September 5 as "Father Olivares Day," city and county officials who had renamed Olvera Street Fr. Luis Olivares Street for that day,
family members, religious leaders from different denominations, movie
and entertainment figures such as Martin Sheen and Jackson Browne, as
well as friends and colleagues, all came to celebrate the life and accomplishments of this Claretian priest. Also in attendance was the aging icon
of the Chicano Movement and of the farmworkers' struggle, César Chávez.

1

After greeting one another and mingling in the Plaza area and enjoying cocktails, the group sat down to a catered Mexican dinner. Fr. Olivares, looking thinner than usual but still with a charismatic aura about him, sat next to Chávez, symbolizing their close comradeship over many years. As they progressed through the dinner, remarks, and songs by Jackson Browne, some began to notice a growing number of what appeared to be homeless Latinos—Central Americans and Mexicans—who began to gather in front of La Placita and outside the temporary chain link fence placed to shield the banquet from outsiders.

But the outsiders soon noticed Fr. Olivares and began to call out to him. "¡Viva Padre Olivares! ¡Que viva el Padre Olivares! ¡Padre Luis Olivares! ¡Presente! ¡Ven con nosotros! ¡Queremos Padre Olivares! ¡Olivares! ¡Olivares! ¡Olivares!" they shouted in unison.

Jackson Browne, who was singing some of Olivares's favorite songs, upon hearing the shouts for the esteemed guest, stopped singing and said: "I feel it strangely appropriate that I am being accompanied by the voices of people who spend the night in front of the church. . . . I welcome their accompaniment, just as Fr. Luis Olivares welcomes them."

The audience broke out in applause and invited the homeless to share the meal. Capturing the drama of the moment, César Chávez, in his testimony to Olivares, observed in words that could have just as easily been said of him: "You have been with the people in the bad times and in the good times. Your heart is an open temple for those who seek refuge."[1]

Not quite three years later, César again spoke of the goodness of his dear friend and confessor. This time, however, the occasion was the funeral of Fr. Louie, as he was affectionately called. Instead of the scene being La Placita, which for some would have been more appropriate, it was now Mission San Gabriel on a spring day in March, twelve miles northeast of downtown. In a few weeks, César himself would be dead. Fr. Louie had prophesied this, and perhaps that is how it should have been. César Chávez and Luis Olivares, in life and in death, were joined together by their deep Catholic faith and commitment to social justice.

Along with César, some 2,000 mourners, again of different backgrounds and religious faiths, came to honor Olivares one last time. They arrived that late morning in cars and buses. They wanted to be there with enough time to pay their personal respects and goodbyes to Fr. Louie as he lay in state in front of the altar. It took quite a while for the procession of people to make their way to the open casket before the 2 P.M. Mass. "It was like the President of the United States dying," Damaso Olivares, the eldest of the Olivares siblings, later recalled.[2] As the men, women, and some children

Fr. Luis Olivares with César Chávez (left) and Dolores Huerta (right) at dinner honoring Olivares. Actor Charles Haid in back holding sign, Sept. 5, 1990. (Courtesy of the Archival Center/TIDINGS Photo Collection, Archdiocese of Los Angeles)

approached the casket partly covered by a UFW flag, they saw their beloved priest, comrade, and friend looking more gaunt and pale than they had last remembered. He had his glasses on, which he always wore due to his near-sightedness. But he also looked much darker than his normal coloring no doubt due to his illness and the many treatments he had undergone. Still, it was unmistakably, Fr. Luis. As usual, he was dressed as impeccably as a priest can be. With his silk, black suits and Gucci shoes, he once again looked eloquent and dignified in his cassock and collar. As if to one last time remind his people of social action, Fr. Louie also wore on his lapel a United Farm Workers (UFW) button that read in Spanish "No Uvas" (No Grapes).

The people touched the coffin as if to feel, one last time, his radiance and his love for them. Some bent over and tenderly kissed him. Some brought other movement buttons and pinned them on Fr. Louie. Some read "No War in El Salvador," "Economic Justice," "Women's Rights." One in particular that caught the attention of Rev. George Regas of the Episcopalian All Saints' Church in Pasadena read "No Human Need is Illegal."[3] Even in death, they drew on him for faith, commitment, and courage. "He was our conscience," Fr. Matthew DiMaria, a fellow Claretian and longtime friend from their seminary years, told a reporter. "He challenged us. He was a voice for the poor."[4] Dozens of priests concelebrated the Mass of Christian Burial, accompanied by the lyrical waves of Mariachi violins as well as the stirring ones from the Mariachi brass. Speaking for the family, Henry Olivares said of his younger brother: "Whenever Louie was needed, that's where he was. The refugees and immigrants needed him and he rose to the occasion. Wherever there was a need, Louie was willing to do something."[5]

So many had come that the old Mission could not hold them all and many had to strain to hear the liturgy as they spilled outside. "Inside and outside the church on the balmy afternoon," Tom Fox of the *National Catholic Reporter* wrote, "People prayed and sang, many holding back tears."[6] And as they had done at the Olvera Street banquet three years before, many of the Central American refugees as well as others began to spontaneously call out for Olivares right after the consecration. *¡Viva Luis! ¡Viva Luis Olivares! ¡Presente!* For them, Luis Olivares was not only still present, as the calls symbolized, but the priest who had sheltered them was still doing so.[7] They shed tears along with everyone else as Jackson Browne sang, at the end of the service, "You are my hero."[8]

INTRODUCTION

CHICANO/LATINO LEADERSHIP IN HISTORY

As I write this introduction, Donald Trump has been elected president of the United States and is preparing to take the office on January 20, 2017. This is chilling. Trump began his campaign by calling Mexicans rapists and criminals and advocated building a Berlin-like wall between the United States and Mexico and having Mexico pay for it, in order to stem the movement of undocumented immigrants into the United States. He later called for the complete deportation of all 11 million undocumented immigrants—mostly Latinos—from the country. He made other anti-Latino, as well as anti-black and anti-Muslim, comments, as well as misogynous statements. Moreover, Trump exhibits anti-democratic and anti-constitutional tendencies that could threaten American democratic and civil-libertarian principles and practices. There is much fear and apprehension among many Americans, and for good reason. This is certainly true in the Latino communities that may be affected by Trump's anti-immigrant and anti-Latino statements and his deportation threats. These include undoing President Obama's executive order extending protection from deportation to almost 800,000 so-called Dreamers. These are the undocumented children of undocumented parents who were brought into the country as babies or very young children, but who have grown up in the United States, gone to our schools, speak English, and are as American as anyone else, except that they are undocumented. They had no choice about their undocumented status. I have many of them in my classes. But Trump has threatened to deport them as well. I have many other Latino students who were born in this country, but whose parents are undocumented. They fear for their parents. The next four years will, to say the least, be challenging not only for Latinos, but for most Americans.

Why do I say all of this? I say it because history gives us lessons on how, in previous periods in American history, people responded to the challenges of persecution and other forms of exploitation. Challenges to our democratic and civil liberties are not new, but what is also not new is that

Americans have risen to the task and fought back, resisted, and protected their freedoms in nonviolent fashion. My students and this new generation—the Latino and the millennial generation—will do likewise. I am confident of this and I tell my students as much. We may be entering into a new period of intense political resistance in this country, but it will build on earlier such resistance. But the new generation has to be aware of these past struggles, because such knowledge will help empower them and give them the sense that, as César Chávez said "Si se puede": It can be done. The story that I will tell in this book is part of this resistance history. My hope is that it will affect the hearts and minds of many Americans, especially our young people, including Latinos, whom I have called the "voices of the new America." This is the story and biography of a remarkable, courageous, and charismatic individual—Father Luis Olivares, a Catholic priest and a member of the Claretian order, who stood up to authorities who denied Mexican Americans self-determination in their own communities of East Los Angeles and those who in the 1980s persecuted thousands if not millions of political refugees from wars in Central America and those undocumented Mexicans fleeing poverty and lack of a future for their children. Olivares stood up for them and provided powerful leadership and an equally powerful voice. I will tell the story in all its dimensions, exploring Luis Olivares the priest and the man. This is a biography; this is the story of one individual from birth to death. But it is also a collective story—a collective biography—of those who worked and struggled with him to do God's work, that all of his children be treated humanely and with justice.

But telling stories such as that of Fr. Olivares is not something new for me. For many years now, I have been recounting the stories of other brave and dedicated leaders from the Chicano community. It is important that we recognize that Chicanos/Latinos have a history of strong community leadership. It is important that our children, our students, and, indeed, all Americans know that Latinos in this country have been struggling for their civil, labor, cultural, and political rights for decades and that in the process they have made history—American history, as educational leader Sal Castro often said.[1] These are American stories or narratives, and they need to be known. The new generation—the Latino Generation—needs to know about such leadership, in order to inspire them.[2] It's okay to know that we have had Chicano and Latino heroes—both men and women. This is not elitist or top-down history, but a recognition that leadership is organic to communities and that it is indispensable in democratic struggles. I have tried to do this in my biographies, much of them told through oral history testimonios of such leaders as Bert Corona, Sal Castro, Josefina Fierro,

Ignacio López, Raymond Telles, Richard Cruz, Raul Ruiz, Gloria Arellanes, and Rosalio Muñoz, to name just few.[3] The role of leadership has been central to my work, and I continue this focus in my biography of Fr. Olivares.

In these portrayals, I have brought to light various labor, civil rights, and political struggles, including immigrant rights in Chicano history. The role of leadership in community struggles is very rich in this history and much more needs to be documented.[4] In so doing, I have attempted to rewrite American history to include the significant Chicano and Latino contributions. This more integrated history is crucial at a time when we are moving to a minority-majority nation. Everyone's role in American history and every ethnic group's participation must be included in the new American history. This has been my career's work, and it continues with this book. I bring to light the key role of leaders in this history because I want to inspire new leadership among my students and the new generation of young people. They need inspirational and progressive role models—we all do—who are willing to challenge the status quo and to be change makers. If we as historians cannot use history to influence the present and the future, then we are not fulfilling our role as socially responsible historians. The past and the present are intertwined, as E. L. Carr stresses in *What Is History?*, and this could not be clearer than in the link between Fr. Olivares's story and the present challenges facing us.[5]

FAITH AND POLITICS

One aspect of leadership that is important to document is that of religious leadership. Religion and faith are relatively unexplored areas in Chicano history. This is part of an undisclosed past. I noted this in my 2008 book, *Católicos: Resistance and Affirmation in Chicano Catholic History.*[6] I suggested that one reason, perhaps the key reason, for this omission is that Chicano historiography such as that found in Chicano Studies originates from the Chicano Movement of the late 1960s and 1970s that, for the first time, made Chicanos and Latinos into recognized national political actors and forced open many new opportunities for Chicanos and Latinos. Yet this civil rights and empowerment movement saw itself as primarily secular and expressed distrust of religion as a traditional and conservative threat. While the institutional Church in part may well have fit into this category, various faith-based movements did not and in fact represent progressive oppositional social movements. Chicano historiography has to recognize this distinction and incorporate such movements into Chicano history. I agree with Djupe and Olson, who write in general about religious interests in community conflicts, "There is, simply put, an enormous amount of political and social capital stored in individuals and organizations with religious ties."[7] Moreover, even secular aspects of the movement and indeed in Latino politics today, as Roger Gottlieb correctly observes of U.S. history, have been influenced by religious views.[8] The notion that religion and politics represent two separate spheres is not sustainable by the historical record. Various religious movements or religious-influenced movements, as Pierrette Hondagneu-Sotelo documents, have promoted social justice and inclusion of the marginalized.[9] They represent "civil religion," or what Matovina calls "public Catholicism," that in turn stresses the same kind of "communitarianism" that the Chicano Movement aspired to.[10] Religious activists have been part of what it means to be a Chicano or Latino activist. They have been part of achieving what Gottlieb calls "world making" or making the world a better and more just place.[11]

In *Católicos*, for example, I examined in part certain faith-influenced movements such as Católicos Por La Raza and the sanctuary movement in Los Angeles headed by Fr. Olivares. Indeed, my initial interest in Olivares came from researching this earlier study and then deciding to do a full biography of him. Católicos Por La Raza was a short-lived group headed by Richard Cruz that in 1969 challenged the Catholic Archdiocese of Los Angeles, then headed by arch-conservative Cardinal McIntyre, to do more for the Chicano community with respect to sharing its resources with its large number of Chicano Catholic members on education, health, and housing. It called for the Church to have a preferential option for the poor and reminded it of its origins in the Jesus story. Jesus was a poor man who ministered to the poor and oppressed, and he was a migrant. This stress on a preferential option for the poor paralleled that of liberation theology emanating from Latin America beginning in the late 1960s.[12] Católicos forced the resignation of McIntyre and the beginning of a dialogue with the Archdiocese. Of course, as will be noted, Olivares was inspired by liberation theology as well as his own order's missionary orientation plus that of his Catholic family background to reach out to the Central American refugees and declare his parish—La Placita Church in downtown Los Angeles—a public sanctuary in 1985. Two years later, he expanded the sanctuary to include undocumented Mexican immigrants.[13] It is likewise important to stress that the farmworkers' struggle, started in the 1960s and headed by César Chávez, can be considered a faith-based movement due to the strong spiritual leadership of Chávez. You cannot understand Chávez without understanding his deep Catholic faith. Once asked after many years of struggle what kept him going after many ups and downs, the farm-labor leader tellingly responded: "Today I don't think I could base my will to struggle on cold economics or on some political doctrine. I don't think there would be enough to sustain me. For me the base must be faith." That said it all. I consider César Chávez to be one of the great spiritual leaders of the twentieth century in the United States and perhaps the world.[14]

Hence, faith and politics—or faith politics—have not been strangers to Chicano and Latino history, just as they have not been to American history as a whole. Faith politics refers to social movements that are based in the application of religious faith to the movements. Many local community struggles have been headed not only by clergy, both Catholic and Protestant, but by devout laypeople who are inspired by their faith to seek social justice. They represent what Helene Slessarev-Jamir calls "prophetic activism."[15] These include groups such as COPS (Communities Organized for Public Service) in San Antonio and UNO (United Neighborhoods Organization) in Los Angeles in the 1970s and 1980s, as we will learn in Olivares's story, that successfully organized around Catholic parishes to promote new community leadership who became empowered to confront various issues in their barrios and challenge both public and corporate authority in order to bring about progressive changes. Such groups were trained by the Industrial Areas Foundation (IAF) that had been organized in the 1940s by Saul Alinsky, a giant in American labor and community organizing history. There are many other similar movements in various Chicano and Latino communities that bear the influence of churches and faith-oriented individuals and whose stories need to be told. Many of them have been led by women. Faith and politics, or faith politics, have been two sides of the same coin in many cases, and this biography is testimony to this relationship.

Although this is not strictly speaking a study of faith-based movements, it is useful to note some characteristics of such movements that will be revealed in Olivares's story. These include:

1. Religion is shown as a prime motivator for progressive social change for those on society's margins.
2. They envision a new and just relationship between human beings.
3. They are based on nonviolent strategies.
4. They seek to acquire basic human rights and promote an "insurgent citizenship" in support of human rights.
5. They provide a moral voice in support of the oppressed that helps to broaden public support and legitimate efforts to support the cause.
6. They represent a shift from a spiritual focus on individual salvation in the next world to achieving God's kingdom on earth, based on justice.

7. They involve a "subversive reading" of scripture with a focus on justice and peace and thus provide a claim for moral authority.
8. They promote ecumenical (inter-Christian) relations as well as interfaith (Christian, Jewish, and Muslim) relations.
9. They represent social movement from the bottom up, or are grassroots movements.
10. They stress that only the poor and oppressed can change conditions for themselves.
11. They promote clergy as community organizers.
12. They stress the collective self-interests of the community.
13. They note that for clergy there is no division between the struggle for justice and evangelizing; they are one and the same.
14. They are not per se revolutionary movements, but they lead to the empowerment of oppressed communities and the achievement of basic human rights.
15. Finally, the focus and concern is always on social justice.

Having listed such characteristics, let me emphasize again that this is not a sociological study of faith-based movements, which others have done very well—although Olivares's historical importance is fulfilled within such movements or at least those inspired by faith.[16] Instead, this is a full biography of a man—a priest, and one who became converted to struggles of social justice—and of his journey through his personal and social changes. This is historical biography—one that seeks to highlight the role of leadership in history and to understand who become leaders and why. I am in search of the personal and historical Fr. Luis Olivares.

WHO WAS FR. LUIS OLIVARES?

Fr. Luis Olivares is an attractive historical figure who needs to be better known and integrated not only into Chicano history but into American history. He represents one of the foremost clerical leaders of the latter part of the twentieth century in the United States. He is best known for his major leadership in the sanctuary movement in Los Angeles. The sanctuary movement was a national one, spearheaded by churches and Jewish communities to provide a safe haven for the thousands of political refugees fleeing civil wars in Central America in the 1980s, principally from El Salvador and Guatemala. For years, these countries had been led by brutal and repressive dictatorial groups aided and abetted, with military support, by different U.S. administrations as long as they protected American investments (banana republics) and proclaimed their anti-Communist allegiance in the Cold War. Opposition to these regimes led to outright civil wars in the late 1970s and 1980s, especially in El Salvador. Faced with such conflict, in addition to persecution by death squads who suspiciously viewed most citizens as supporters of the insurgents, Salvadorans voted with their feet, and those who could left from both the cities and country-side. In the 1980s about a million Salvadorans entered the United States. They asked for political asylum. However, the administration of President Ronald Reagan refused to grant them such status, for to do so would be to criticize their client states in Central America. Instead, the Reagan admin-istration, to its discredit, labeled the refugees "illegal aliens" who wanted to take jobs from "real Americans." Despite the fact that other countries and the United Nations considered the refugees to be legitimate political refu-gees, the Reagan administration refused to do so.[17]

To counter the Reagan administration, various religious communities came to the aid of the refugees. They helped them cross the border, housed them, fed them, clothed them, got them jobs, and provided legal assis-tance. Of the million Salvadorans who entered, half went to Los Angeles. There they fortunately encountered a priest, Luis Olivares, who embraced them as children of God and who defied the government by providing shel-ter and other assistance. Los Angeles was the Mecca for the majority of Central Americans who entered as refugees and hence it was crucial that the sanctuary movement be present in this location. This is where Olivares and his Mexican American parish, the oldest parish in the city, rose up and headed the most crucial and celebrated sanctuary movement in the coun-try. Olivares became the champion of the refugees, and they loved him. In the most controversial aspect of his sanctuary, he literally housed some of them in the church, where they slept overnight in the pews. As if his embrace of the refugees were not enough, he also embraced and assisted many of the thousands of undocumented Mexican immigrants streaming into Los Angeles, extending sanctuary to them. He challenged the notion that refugees and immigrants did not represent the nation and thus chal-lenged the very meaning of the nation-state and what Cecilia Menjivar calls the "liminal legality" of the Central American refugees.[18] For Olivares, there was no such thing as an "illegal" refugee or immigrant. They were all part of humankind. Olivares promoted what Luis León calls "rehumaniza-tion."[19] In these endeavors, Olivares and the sanctuary movement in gen-eral were not only defying the Reagan administration; they were breaking the law. However, Olivares always said that for him there was a higher law, and that was God's law. God wanted his children protected, not deported to face possible torture and murder in their war-torn countries. Olivares's claim to historical fame, widely covered by local media, might be the sanctuary movement, of which he undoubtedly was the most powerful voice in Los Angeles, the citadel of the refugee diaspora, but it is not his sole claim to fame.

My biography of this remarkable leader is not just focused on the sanctuary movement, although clearly it represents a major part of Olivares's political involvement. I seek to understand and explore his entire life, as far as a biographer can for any subject. Curiously, his personal family history intersected with his later public one on sanctuary. His parents were both political refugees from the Mexican Revolution of 1910. Fleeing to San Antonio, Texas, his parents met and married there and started their family, including Luis, born in 1934, and his six siblings. In San Antonio, his parents and extended family aided and harbored other refugees, especially Catholic clergy fleeing religious persecution by the post-revolutionary government in the 1920s in the Cristero War. The past spoke to the future, since Olivares would carry on this tradition in Los Angeles. I examine his upbringing and how his family's strong Catholic faith influenced him and laid the seed of his later ministry to the poor and oppressed. This ministry began when the young Luis, like his older brother Henry, believed he had a vocation to the priesthood. At age thirteen, with his parents' permission, Luis followed Henry to the Claretian seminary in Compton, California, just outside of Los Angeles. For thirteen years, from 1948, when he first started his seminary years, to his ordination in 1961, Olivares lived apart from his family and embraced the Claretian way of life and his vocation as a priest including the vows of poverty, chastity and celibacy, and obedience. His seminary years revealed a complex young man negotiating his feelings and beliefs in an almost cloistered environment. Through it all, he never seemed to waver in his dedication to becoming a priest.

As a seminarian, Olivares displayed intelligence, leadership qualities, eloquence in speaking, and a charismatic magnetism, to the extent that his Claretian superiors soon marked him as a future leader of the order. After his ordination, he rose quickly through the ranks, and in the mid-1960s was elected treasurer of the order, the second most powerful position next to the Provincial. As treasurer, Olivares managed a multi-million-dollar portfolio, which he invested in the stock market. As such, he was literally wined and dined by Wall Street financiers who wished to obtain the Claretian funds. Olivares learned to love this high lifestyle. He was flown to New York first-class, picked up by a limo, and taken to five-star hotels and restaurants, and Broadway shows. He relished this attention and expertly invested his order's funds, in turn making millions more for the order. He was an economic success and a good company man. Part of this lifestyle included his affinity for nice clothes and nice cars. Can a priest have nice clothes? Well, how about silk black suits, silk shirts, and Gucci shoes? In fact, some in the order referred to him as the "Gucci priest." Olivares would have continued along this path, except that like St. Paul he had a major conversion.

In 1975, Olivares met César Chávez; by his own admission, this was his "conversion." He was drawn to Chávez's own charisma and the power of the farmworkers' movement for dignity and social justice. Olivares became a convert and follower of Chávez and the farmworkers and never looked back. From Los Angeles, he went and ministered to the *campesinos* in the Central Valley and helped organize the grape and lettuce boycotts in the L.A. area. He did whatever Chávez called on him to do, including channeling some of his order's funds to help the union, the United Farm Workers. But his conversion was also personal. He and Chávez became very close; they were political and spiritual brothers. Olivares became César's confessor. They saw in each other—although very different in background and personality—a kinship based on their faith and their commitment to social justice. Meeting César Chávez marked Olivares's conversion to faith politics, but its origins lay with his family background; during the Great Depression, his grandmother Inez helped to feed the poor in the west-side barrio of San Antonio. The roots of Olivares's Mexican American identity also lay in his family background and of his barrio experience, but this was enhanced by his involvement with the mostly Mexican American farmworkers and Chávez's brilliant use of Mexican ethnic symbols, including the banner and image of Our Lady of Guadalupe, the patron saint of Mexico and Mexican Americans.[20]

Olivares's conversion, at the same time, expanded to also include his involvement with a faith-based movement in East Los Angeles. Around the time of his conversion, Olivares requested and was assigned to be pastor of Our Lady of Solitude Church, or La Soledad, in East L.A. He now wanted to do parish work and be closer to the community. Becoming pastor also coincided with an effort to establish a Saul Alinsky–organized community group to help empower Mexican Americans. This became the United Neighborhoods Organization or UNO. Olivares became involved and quickly emerged as one of the key clerical leaders in this grassroots organization to confront key issues in the community involving basic infrastructure improvements, such as street repairs and traffic crosswalks, as well as conditions in the schools and the lack of economic growth in the barrio. Organizing took place at the individual parish level, as all Catholic churches in East L.A. participated along with some Protestant ones. At the same time, UNO also had a community-wide committee that focused on issues that affected all of the parishes, not just individual ones. Together they represented what one scholar refers to as "islands of community," inspired by the Alinsky Industrial Areas Foundation (IAF), that developed community solidarity.[21] UNO, like other faith-based movements, aimed to build community.[22] It utilized the social capital of church-related networks and linked political action to faith beliefs, or what Warren refers to as a "theology of organizing."[23] Social capital meant the existing parish groups, especially those headed by women, who could and did transfer their organizing experience and leadership to UNO.

One key issue that UNO confronted early in its history concerned discriminatory auto insurance rates in East L.A., where Mexican Americans had to pay higher rates than the middle and upper-middle class and the very wealthy in west Los Angeles, including Beverly Hills and Santa Monica. This became UNO's signature issue, and Fr. Olivares became its key leader as head of the group's auto insurance committee. Tackling auto insurance meant taking on the powerful auto insurance companies, as well as county and state governments that had failed to regulate these companies. But it was exactly the kind of issue that UNO wanted to engage, in order to empower its members and to make them realize that people's power could successfully confront institutionalized power. Led by Olivares, who became its key voice and prosecutor of the companies and government, UNO forced the insurance industry to rescind the discriminatory rates and to implement cheaper rates for drivers in the east side. Its victory made UNO into a new and major political player in Los Angeles, and Olivares into a recognized public and media figure. But this was only the beginning of his new ministry.

In 1981, Olivares transferred to La Placita Church to serve as its pastor. This was the hub of Mexican American Catholicism going back to the Spanish colonization of the area. Olivares looked forward to his new assignment, where he could expand UNO's activities. However, this changed when his transfer coincided with the influx of the Central American refugees. Olivares did not hesitate into making his parish into a safe and hospitable space for them. By now, moreover, he had also become a liberationist, or devotee of liberation theology emanating from Latin America and its call for the Catholic Church to prioritize its work with the poor and oppressed. This was the so-called "preferential option for the poor." Olivares applied this theology as a working one by literally aiding the refugees in every way possible. He could not provide for all of them; there were just too many. But he did what he could, despite space and resource limitations at La Placita. If he could not assist all of the refugees, he nevertheless understood the symbolic power of his parish standing up for the refugees and letting others know that there was one Catholic Church that welcomed them. Olivares appreciated the power of symbols especially of a religious nature—"identity markers"—to communicate with Latino refugees and immigrants of primarily Catholic background.[24] He understood that their religious, and predominantly Catholic, faith linked them to Mexican American Catholics and to him. Olivares understood, as Peggy Levitt stresses, that religion is the ultimate "boundary crosser" and that "God needs no passport."[25] Olivares saw ministering to the refugees, and also to Mexican immigrants, as part of a "theologizing experience."[26] After four years of ministering to the refugees and with the help of a core group of assistants such as Fr. Mike Kennedy, a Jesuit priest who had traveled in Central America, Olivares decided that he needed to declare La Placita a public sanctuary. La Placita would become a "haven in a heartless world."[27] This would be not only symbolic, but would openly defy and challenge the Reagan administration, putting it on notice that its policy toward refugees and support for repressive governments in Central America was wrong—it was sinful. Hence on December 12, 1985, the feast day of Our Lady of Guadalupe, Olivares, as pastor of La Placita, and before an ecumenical and interfaith audience and in a "theological drama,"[28] declared public sanctuary with its promise to provide a safe haven for the refugees. This signaled to the federal government that La Placita was out of bounds for immigration and border patrol officials. La Placita became a "counter-space," to use Carbine's term.[29] It was a momentous day, widely covered by local media. Los Angeles had become the Central American refugee capital of the United States, and it was critically important that a Catholic parish, given the largely Catholic background of the refugees, stand up and be counted as a sanctuary church. No other Catholic church in the expansive Los Angeles archdioceses did this, and those few Protestant churches who declared themselves sanctuaries did so only symbolically and not materially. With his leadership, charisma, and articulate voice, Olivares became the heart and soul of the sanctuary movement in the city with the largest Central American refugee population in the country.[30]

But his sympathy for the marginalized did not stop with the refugees. Even more undocumented Mexican immigrants were streaming into Los Angeles to escape poverty and to take care of their families. They were economic refugees and made up the "second wave," as Fr. Alan Deck refers to the "new immigrants" from Mexico and Latin America that entered the United States in the latter part of the twentieth century, to distinguish them from the first wave of primarily Mexican immigrants who entered in large numbers in the first third of the century.[31] Olivares embraced them as well. He housed and cared for as many as he could. After the U.S. Congress passed and Reagan signed the Immigration Reform and Control Act (IRCA) in 1986, which provided amnesty for the undocumented who could prove continued residence in the country up to 1982, Olivares expressed concern over the thousands of undocumented who were not eligible for amnesty since they had arrived after the deadline. They could still be rounded up and deported. Olivares called on other clergy and other Americans to defy the law and to support the undocumented not covered by the law, including by hiring them. To emphasize this, he did what no other sanctuary movement in the country did: in 1987, he extended public sanctuary to Mexican undocumented workers and their families at La Placita. This was unprecedented. Of course, he recognized that this was largely symbolic, but it would still send out a strong message and link the plight of the Central American refugees, almost all who were also not covered by IRCA since they arrived after 1982, with the undocumented Mexicans. They were all children of God, and Americans, including those in the Church, had to assist them even if it meant breaking the law. This is what some scholars refer to as the "spirituality of resistance."[32] Both Central Americans and Mexican undocumented immigrants could be assured that they could find a safe haven at La Placita. Federal authorities would not dare to violate sanctuary.

Olivares's courageous defiance of the federal government and specifically the policies of the Reagan administration brought much criticism from local immigration officials. They considered Olivares to be a rogue priest and a renegade in his own Church. Such criticism did not intimidate Olivares, who continued and expanded his work with the refugees and immigrants. But it was not just federal officials who criticized and opposed Olivares; so, too, did his own Church in the form of then-archbishop and later cardinal Roger Mahony. Mahony and archdiocesan officials did not care for one of their priests to so openly defy the Reagan administration. Mahony and other high church leaders were sympathetic to the refugees and undocumented immigrants, but they did not want to cross the line by openly supporting sanctuary or defying federal law by hiring the undocumented, as Olivares proposed. Indeed, the Catholic Church in the United States as a whole took the same position as Mahony. As a result, subtle and not-so-subtle pressure was put on Olivares by the archdiocese to become less public in his actions and to tone down his criticisms of the Reagan administration. At one point, the Archbishop called in to see Olivares,

Fr. Kennedy, and Fr. Greg Boyle, another of Olivares's key supporters; in a heated exchange, they were told they could no longer speak publicly on these issues. The three priests, derisively referred to as the "three rene-gade priests" by the head of immigration in Los Angeles, refused to do so and continued to voice their concerns about the refugees and immigrants. Nothing was done to them and they were not going to be deterred by their own church.

The drama between Olivares and Mahony is a key part of the Olivares story, bringing together two major Catholic leaders at a time of signifi-cant demographic changes in the L.A. archdiocese and in the Church as a whole in the United States. Latinos were becoming—and in Los Angeles already were—the majority of Catholics, and both men, whether willing or not, were vying for leadership of Latino Catholics. Mahony had supported the farmworkers struggle and had been Bishop of Stockton in the Cen-tral Valley, with its large Mexican American population. When appointed Archbishop of Los Angeles in 1985, he understood that the future of the Church there was Latino Catholics. He hoped to be their champion, only to find that they already had a champion in Fr. Luis Olivares. This rivalry, real but highlighted by the media, characterized this crucial relationship and formed a dramatic backdrop to the sanctuary and immigrant rights movement of the 1980s in Los Angeles.

But Olivares's public activism did not just focus on the plight of Cen-tral Americans and Mexican immigrants, it also involved his participation in the growing protests, in Los Angeles and throughout the country, con-cerning Reagan's interventions in Central America. Millions of Americans called on the United States to stop supporting and arming the repressive governments in El Salvador and Guatemala that were creating the refugee crisis. They also called on the Reagan administration to cease attempting to overthrow the revolutionary government in Nicaragua led by the San-dinistas, who in 1979 had overthrown the long-term dictatorship of the Somoza family, and who were attempting to bring about needed economic and social reforms in their country. Reagan considered them to be Com-munists and puppets of the Soviet Union and Cuba, and armed counter-revolutionaries, the Contras, in the attempt to overthrow the Sandinistas. Olivares became a key leader and voice among the many Central American advocacy groups that sprang up in Los Angeles in protest against Reagan's policies. Fr. Luis's work with the refugees, including leading the sanctu-ary movement, gave him much credibility with these protest groups, who always wanted him to speak at their rallies. In turn, the media constantly sought out Olivares for his opinion on the wars in Central America, the policies of the Reagan administration, and the refugees and undocumented immigrants. He was always on TV and radio and became a media star.[33]

However, in time this public attention and his outspokenness as someone considered a prophet by some began to result in his own order believing that the time had come for Olivares to be reassigned from La Placita. Many believe that the Claretians succumbed to pressures from Mahony and the archdiocese to effect Olivares's removal. This came in 1989, when he was told that he was being transferred to Fort Worth, Texas, and a new pastor was assigned to La Placita who, unfortunately, began to dismantle the sanctuary movement at the church. La Placita would no longer be a sanctuary church. Olivares did not want to leave his parish and the work he had accomplished, but he had no choice. He was bound by his vows to obey his superiors; although he tried everything to stay in Los Angeles, his efforts were to no avail. It appeared that he had become too controversial for both his order and the archdiocese. But Olivares in fact never left Los Angeles. This had nothing to do with his desire to stay, but with his health. In 1990 he was diagnosed with HIV/AIDS and had to be hospitalized. His doctors sadly informed him that he had only a few years left. As his health deteriorated, he moved into the Claretian Provincial House, where the order, his family, and his friends took care of him. He tried to remain active and gave his last public speech in 1992 to celebrate the peace accords in El Salvador, which he had been trying to achieve for many years. The people still loved him and appreciated his contributions and his dedication. But illness took its physical and emotional toll on Olivares. At the same time, he never expressed regrets for what he had done as an activist priest who tried to redefine what it should mean to be a priest and, indeed, the meaning of the Church. For Olivares, it meant being with the people and supporting struggles for social justice and peace. Priests and the Church needed to prioritize this, as he had done. He wished he could have done more and that his activism could have started earlier in his ministry, but he did what he could in the time he had. Fr. Luis Olivares died on March 18, 1993, at age fifty-nine, and was buried at San Gabriel Mission in Los Angeles after a standing-room-only Mass. His supporters, including refugees and immigrants, refused to accept his death. "Presente!" they called out. Fr. Luis was still with them; he was still ministering to them. He still lived.

WHAT IS OLIVARES'S PLACE IN HISTORY?

Although not well known both in Chicano and American history, Fr. Luis Olivares, like many of the other leaders I have worked on, needs not only to be known and appreciated, but integrated into Chicano and American history. Olivares's story is important at different levels. First is his role in Chicano and Latino history: he represents one of the most significant Chicano/Latino religious and political leaders in history of the twentieth century. Like César Chávez and Sal Castro, Olivares accomplished what had never been done before. Chávez's claim to historical fame is that he did what had never been accomplished; he successfully organized farmworkers into a union. Likewise, Sal Castro, for the first time certainly in Chicano history, successfully organized Chicano high-school and middle-school students into perhaps the largest high-school and middle-school strike in American history—the 1968 "blowouts" or walkouts. Olivares, in turn, successfully organized a sanctuary movement among the largest concentration of Salvadoran and other Central American refugees in the country. The greatest achievement of the sanctuary movement in the United States during the 1980s was in Los Angeles, and it was due to Olivares's leadership. In addition, he expanded sanctuary to include Mexican undocumented workers. Olivares's successful work with both refugees and immigrants only reinforces that faith and politics in the Chicano/Latino experience have been significant and hence Chicano Studies and Latino Studies need to integrate this critical relationship and promote research in this area. In taking on both civic and even ecclesiastical power, Olivares represented a radical alternative to the status quo.[34] As such, he represents one of the major Chicano and Latino leaders of his time. The media categorized the 1980s as the "Decade of the Hispanic," suggesting that in this decade Latinos would emerge as a major player in American politics. While this may have been a somewhat premature claim, nevertheless, one can see in the 1980s the evolution of today's Latino political power and part of the origins of the immigrant-rights movement in this country that has become the new area of civil rights. Refugees and immigrants are not the problem, Olivares's legacy stresses. Instead the problem is a political and economic system that exploits them and demonizes them. In the decade of the 1980s, Olivares stands as one of the most significant Latino political leaders, and his importance needs to be acknowledged by other historians and students of Chicano/Latino history. Chicanos and Latinos do not live in a godless world. Olivares epitomizes the fact that religion, as Hondagneu-Sotelo very well puts it, "is a powerful force that enables individuals and organizations to engage in civic and political actions for new immigrants."[35] Religion and churches not only have been important in the protection of Latino refugees and immigrants, but also in assisting them to adjust to American society.[36]

Likewise, Olivares needs to be recognized as a major American religious leader. His leadership in faith-based movements, such as UNO and the sanctuary movement, represented important aspects of grassroots American history. American history is not, or should not, be a top-down history focused on national leaders in Washington, for example. Too much of American history has been portrayed as such, to the exclusion of many other historical actors. American history and certainly all major reforms in this country have come from grassroots movements, from "people power." This was the case with the abolitionist movement, with women organizing to have the right to vote, with workers in the 1930s struggling for the right to organize industrial unions, with the black and Chicano civil rights movements, and with the antiwar and peace movements in the 1960s, to cite just a few examples. So, too, Chicanos in the late 1970s formed community-based organizations such as UNO in Los Angeles to empower themselves and to further the meaning of American democracy; in the 1980s, thousands of Americans, including Chicanos and Latinos, organized in their communities to support the Central American refugees and to assist Mexican undocumented workers. In so doing and inspired by their faith, they aspired to establish what Dr. Martin Luther King Jr. called the "beloved community"—where people are reconciled to live in peace and justice.[37] At the same time, however, the history of the sanctuary movement of the 1980s has significantly omitted Los Angeles. Yet, in my opinion, the most important manifestation of this movement occurred there and was led by Olivares. One cannot fully appreciate or understand the sanctuary movement of that period without considering La Placita. Latinos made history—American history—and in Los Angeles, the second largest city in the country, they made history with the leadership of Fr. Luis Olivares. From a people's view of American history, which is how we need to transform the teaching of this history, Olivares is a giant figure and needs to be recognized as such.

This is equally true in the history of California and Los Angeles. Olivares's story, while very much a Chicano/Latino story and an American story, is also, as writer Rubén Martínez notes, a California and Los Angeles story.[38] Olivares accomplished what he did in Los Angeles, California, and hence he is a major figure in California and Los Angeles history. The critical role of Mexican Americans and Mexican immigrants in this history has for too long been and continues to be sadly neglected, despite the increased production of historical texts and narratives by Chicano historians and others who are attempting to revise this history to include Mexican contributions. I still get many students—both Chicanos and non-Chicanos—

who know little if anything about the significant contributions of Mexican Americans to California history, much less to that of cities such as Los Angeles. I'll never forget an anecdote told to me by a colleague at UC Santa Barbara in 1993 on the death of César Chávez. He informed his students that César had died and what a tragedy this was. One of his students reacted by exclaiming: "This is sad; he was such a great boxer!" The student meant Julio César Chávez—who was a great boxer, but he was not *the* César Chávez. Today, many school districts in California are majority Latino, and Latinos represent the largest ethnic group in the largest state in the union and yet K-12 students in general learn very little if anything about Chicanos and other Latinos. This a dereliction of duty and of responsibility by school boards and school administrators in both our public and private schools. Students need to know about this history and this experience if California and other states with significant Latino populations are to advance in an integrative and just way. Unfortunately, Chicano and Latino students still feel like strangers in their schools because nothing in their curricula speaks to their experiences and backgrounds. They need to know that Chicanos, for example, have contributed mightily to American history. They need to know that they should feel good about themselves. Sal Castro often said—and this is basic pedagogic theory—that for a student to succeed, they must feel good about themselves. Part of this entails recognizing that they are not strangers to or aliens in American history, but major players in that history. Fr. Olivares is someone that they should know about, and hopefully his biography will now be included in a revised curriculum that is inclusive of all ethnic contributions to the history of this country and to states and cities such as California and Los Angeles.

Finally, Fr. Olivares needs to be integrated into the religious and Catholic history of the United States. As a new kind of priest, Olivares represented the continuation of a long history of faith-based movements in this country and of clergy helping to lead social movements for progressive reform. He engaged in a "prophetic praxis" of observing, reflecting on, and acting on the injustices of his time.[39] We are familiar with this in the history of African American clergy—first and foremost with Dr. Martin Luther King Jr. and his and other black ministers' role in the civil rights movement. However, less known is that of Chicano/Latino religious figures, including clergy. In many communities, Chicano and Latino priests and ministers have played important roles in helping to organize against discrimination and prejudice. We are still learning and documenting this history. It is my hope that, in bringing to light the story of Fr. Olivares, this book will further encourage the field of Chicano/Latino religious history to integrate this focus into what we mean by American and Catholic religious history and studies. Today, Latino Catholics represent close to half of all Catholics in the United States and their long history in the Church needs to be better documented and recognized. The Olivares story is also a very Catholic story. But it is a Catholic story of those clergy, such as Olivares, who struggled to define a new and more community-engaged priesthood and Church that would go beyond preaching about people's individual sins and instead confront what liberationists call "social sin": racism, prejudice, exploitation, torture, and wars of choice. Olivares represents a revised story of the priesthood and what the priesthood—and indeed the Catholic Church—should be, and his struggles to accomplish this need to be recognized and integrated into American Catholic history. By the same token, his leadership and the role of Chicano/Latino faith-based movements, such as UNO and the sanctuary movement out of La Placita Church, need to be added to our understanding of the role of faith-based social and political movements in American history. Hopefully, the story of Luis Olivares will help move us in this direction.

Why is the story, the biography, of Fr. Luis Olivares important? It is for all the above reasons and the need to produce a more inclusive history of the United States. Olivares made American history and this contribution needs to be acknowledged and taught. It is not enough for publishers and editors to say, when approached by historians about Chicano/Latino historical figures, "But who is this guy? I've never heard of him or her." That is precisely my point. Why haven't you and other historians, for that matter, heard about a Fr. Olivares or a Sal Castro or a Gloria Arellanes? It is because we have produced and perpetuate a history that does not include all American subjects. This now must change, given the changing demographics of the country. Publishers need to publish these unknown stories, so that they will become known, and so that we can move to that integrative American historical narrative that will hopefully make for a more democratic and just society. I have, over the years, strived for this and this is the latest contribution in this direction.

HOW DO I APPROACH OLIVARES'S STORY?

This is a biography of Fr. Luis Olivares and his role in history and how he made history. As a biography, this is a comprehensive study of his life. I never met Olivares, but knew of him as a result of his involvement and leadership of the sanctuary movement in Los Angeles and his outspoken opposition to Reagan's policies in Central America. He was often the subject of or mentioned in related stories in the *Los Angeles Times*, which I read. When I was writing my *Católicos* book, I decided to include a chapter on Olivares and the sanctuary movement in Los Angeles. This began my research on him including interviews with his family and some of his colleagues in the movement. My research and interviews led to my being invited to participate in a 2003 commemoration at La Placita Church marking the tenth anniversary of his death. That year, I also presented the basis of one of this book's chapter at a lecture I gave at Cal State, Los Angeles sponsored by the Department of Chicano Studies. The more I looked into Olivares, the more attracted I was to him and the more I wanted to know about him. Consequently, I decided to expand my research into a full biography. I expanded my research and my interviews in order to gain a larger portrait of the man. I did not just want to focus on the sanctuary years. I wanted to know the whole story of how he became a liberationist and a community priest. I wanted to know about his roots and his evolution as a priest. This is why I approached him chronologically. I wanted to know the different phases of his life and, more importantly, how he changed as we all change over the life cycle. I also wanted to use my training, skill, and instincts as a historian to do what historians do best: go beyond or into social movements to understand the people, the individuals, involved in movements for social change. Historians go beyond many social scientists who tend to concentrate on the broader issues of such movements or do not study in depth the leaders and members and lose sight that it is individuals who make up these movements. Who are these people? Where do they come from? What motivated them? And how did they affect these movements and the movements affect them? I wanted to know the historical Luis Olivares, but I also wanted to know the personal Luis Olivares.

This is where my previous interest in biography, autobiography, and testimonios influenced my approach to Olivares. If Olivares were still alive, I might have approached him to do a testimonio, or oral history life story, as I did, for example, with Bert Corona and Sal Castro, among others. But Olivares died in 1993 some years before I became interested in him and so there was obviously no way I could do a testimonio. But I could do a biography, and this is what I set out to do. Besides archival research, I did extensive oral histories to try to compensate for my not being able to interview Olivares himself as well as examining some interviews with him. Through this process, I have produced a "biographical testimonio," to coin a new term, in which I contextualize Olivares in all his different phases and yet, as in a testimonio, always keep the focus on him as the main protagonist of this story, his story. In most of my career's work, I have been interested in people who make history and in the role of people acting as historical protagonists and not just victims of history. In Luis Olivares, I found the type of subject who interests me and whose story I want to tell. I mention to my students that if you're going to work on someone's life story, it should be someone that you want to spend a great deal of time with and someone that you can identify with. Why would I want to spend years with someone whose life and politics I differ with? Let someone else do it. I don't have the time or the inclination. I want to reveal key figures in Chicano history, for example, who have made a difference and who can be seen as historical role models. Fr. Olivares fits the bill, and I have not been disappointed.

At a personal level, although as a boy growing up in El Paso, Texas, I never myself wanted to become a priest, but I was raised a Catholic and I received a Catholic education in elementary and high school. I identify as a Catholic, and this was admittedly another attraction to Olivares in addition to his progressive politics, which I share. Moreover, I had already become interested in promoting Chicano Catholic history beginning in the 1990s and so doing a biography of a Catholic priest was in line with that interest. In addition, I have always seen myself as a revisionist historian; part of my interest in writing Chicano Catholic history has been to revise the mistaken notion, espoused by some in Chicano history and Chicano Studies, that religion has not played a progressive political role in this history. This is clearly not the case, and my work in this area—including this book—has aimed to show the important role that religion, especially Catholicism, has played in inspiring and forming faith-based movements among Chicanos and other Latinos. The Olivares story is part of this revision of Chicano history.

UNDERSTANDING LUIS OLIVARES

In writing biography, one of the challenges is how to understand your subject. I had no intention of psychoanalyzing Olivares and yet I obligated to gain a sense of his feelings and thoughts as much as possible. I tried to identify with him and in a sense "get under his skin," while still trying to be as objective as possible as a historian and scholar. One way I attempted to do this was to anticipate how he felt at different times of his life. For example, how did he feel about being removed from his family at age thirteen and being told that he now had a new family, the Claretian order? How did he feel when he finally reached his goal of being ordained a priest? How did he deal, over the years, with having to fulfill his vows especially of chastity and celibacy? And, of course, how must he have felt when informed that he had AIDS? I can't speak to these experiences personally, but at the same time, I tried to imagine how Olivares must have reacted, or how anyone else, including myself, would have reacted. Olivares was a man, a human being, with feelings and emotions like the rest of us, and I had to try to convey as much as possible these sentiments in order to humanize him and link him with readers. Methodologically, it helped that others, such as Professor Denis Lynn Daly Heyck and Fr. Juan Romero, had done extensive interviews with Olivares just prior to his death.[40] Moreover, he was often interviewed by the press and his voice appears there. Unfortunately, it does not appear that he ever kept a diary or journal. In the intervening years since his death, his correspondence with his family in Texas has been lost, and whatever personal letters he had in his possession, he instructed his order to destroy after his death. Instead, what helped me considerably in trying to know Olivares were the more than ninety oral-history interviews that I conducted with a variety of people who knew him: family, such as his siblings; fellow seminarians; fellow Claretian priests; his own seminary students; and colleagues and friends in the faith-based movements that he participated in, such as the farmworkers', UNO, and sanctuary movements. The one glaring omission in these oral histories is the voice of Cardinal Roger Mahony. I requested an interview, only to be told by his personal secretary that the Cardinal was not willing to be interviewed about Fr. Olivares. In part because of my use of oral history, this project might be referred to as a "biographical ethnography."[41] Through these many interviews, in which people shared not only their recollections of Olivares, but also how they thought he reacted to changes in his life, I was able to arrive at some composite of him and weave that into my narrative. I hope that in my study of this remarkable individual, I have been able to present Luis Olivares in all of his facets and changes and to suggest a very complicated and constantly changing human being. In the end, this is a human story which I set out to tell. I hope I have accomplished this.

A LONG ROAD

This project has been a long journey. This is not atypical for historians. To take on a historical topic such as a biography entails much research that can span many years. This is often not well appreciated, for example, by some of my colleagues in Chicano Studies who are more grounded in the humanities, such as literature, where archival and field research are sometimes not necessary or do not take as long. Historians log a lot of miles and spend much time, as I did, doing archival research and interviewing people, especially when dealing with a mid-to-late-twentieth-century subject, for which there are still appropriate living interviewees. As noted, I started this project around 2002, and so it has taken me fifteen years (with some suspensions due to other, more completed projects) to research, organize my research, and write and revise. It is labor intensive, but that's the nature of the work. There are no shortcuts. In my case, because I set out to do an entire life story of Olivares, I had to research his whole life cycle. I should also add, of course, that I was teaching for most of this time with an exception of one sabbatical quarter and so this also prolonged the process. Moreover, unlike bestselling biographers, I didn't have a bevy of research assistants to do some of the research for me. If I did, I would be churning out even more books.

There were two principal areas of research that I engaged with. The first was to locate key archival sources that would shed light on Olivares. Unfortunately, there is no Fr. Luis Olivares Collection anywhere. Ethnic-minority history usually does not have the luxury of established archival holdings, since for many years archives and libraries did not consider Chicano history, for example, to be of much relevance and so did little or nothing about collecting materials about Chicanos. This has been changing over the years and important archival holdings in Chicano history have been and are being organized, but this has been the result of the growth of Chicano political and academic influence and the growing number of Chicano and Latino faculty, administrators including librarians and archivists, as well as students. Unfortunately, this change did not affect my research on Olivares. I had to discover those archives myself, such as they existed. These unofficial archives—unofficial in that they are not part of any professional archives—include a variety of sources. First, I was fortunate to have Henry Olivares provide me with a collection of family items including personal and family photos. One very key source that Henry allowed me to use was the journal and other writings of Arnie Hasselwander, who attended the seminary with Fr. Luis, and who kept a journal for many years and later made a copy for Henry. This source was crucial in helping me to better understand Luis Olivares's seminary years. However, the most overall significant archival materials I found were at three Los Angeles locations. First, I was given access by the Claretians to a number of boxes at their Provincial House belonging to Olivares. They had no idea what was in them. I was able to examine the materials during several trips there. I found newspaper clippings concerning Olivares, and documents and correspondence related to his work. This material was invaluable, and I was able to order copies of anything I wanted. Just as invaluable were two other sources. The first was at La Placita Church where the pastor, Fr. Steve Niskanen, allowed me to look at still more boxes that Olivares had kept there. Again, I found even more materials: newspaper clippings, but also a variety of documents from before and after his becoming pastor at La Placita, including his related work with the sanctuary movement. The second major source was at Dolores Mission Church, in the Boyle Heights barrio, where then-pastor Fr. Mike Kennedy—who as readers will learn was Olivares's main co-leader of the sanctuary movement at La Placita—allowed me to also examine a number of boxes that were not Olivares's, but which had apparently been collected by Fr. Greg Boyle, the pastor of Dolores Mission, during the 1980s. Fr. Boyle was also a collaborator with Olivares in the movement and had, himself, declared his parish a sanctuary church. These boxes contained all sorts of publications and documents pertaining to the sanctuary movement at La Placita and Los Angeles as well as in other parts of the country.

These three unofficial archives were indispensable to me in my research. I did not have the luxury of an Olivares collection in an archive where I could have been aided by an archivist while examining materials. Sometimes historians have to go beyond such nice conditions and literally track down and create their own archival sources, as I had to do in this project. But there are advantages to this type of research, in that you don't have to contend with the bureaucracies of institutionalized archives and libraries. I had free rein in all these locations and I could copy whatever I wanted without limits. Another key advantage was that I was researching in locations, or at least two, that had personal connections to my subject. It was at Provincial House where Olivares had spent his novitiate year of his seminary training in the early 1950s and where his office as treasurer of his order had been located. Moreover, it was at Provincial House where Olivares spend the last three years of his life before his death in 1993. I was in the very place where he studied, worked, and confronted death. I visited what was his room when he was suffering with AIDS. It was a memorable experience. Then at La Placita, of course, I was in the very church and rectory where he proclaimed sanctuary and where he lived and worked. I researched in the conference room where he held meetings and I was given a tour of the living quarters, including Olivares's former room. My research at La Placita also allowed me to spend time in the church and chapel where Olivares said Mass and administered the sacraments, such as baptisms and marriages. I could envision him preaching in the main church, his incredible homilies linking biblical messages to the plight of Central American refugees and Mexican undocumented immigrants. At Dolores Mission, although a Jesuit parish and not a Claretian one, besides researching documents, I had an opportunity to interview Fr. Kennedy as well as former Salvadoran refugees, such as Mario Rivas and Arturo López, who had worked with Olivares. Although this type of research involved various trips to Los Angeles from my home in Santa Barbara, I would not trade it for the world because of the access I had to invaluable materials, plus the sensory experience of literally walking where Olivares walked.

Besides these archival sources, there is no question but that this biography could not have been done without the numerous oral histories that I conducted. I interviewed ninety-three people who shared their memories of Fr. Luis at different stages of his life. Some of these interviews were face-to-face, but many were conducted via telephone. All were recorded and transcribed and on average lasted two hours each. As mentioned, these interviews shed light on various aspects of Olivares's career and were equally illuminating about his personal life. Some interviewees also graciously contributed personal collections of documents pertinent to my story. I am indebted to all those who allowed me to interview them. These interviews were open-ended, although many covered similar topics, depending on which phase of Olivares's life they addressed. All helped me to better understand Fr. Luis.

These key archival sources and oral histories are the two key pillars of my research, but many other sources also were important to me. One such source was the Industrial Areas Foundation holdings at the University of Illinois, Chicago, and the Briscoe Center for American History at the University of Texas at Austin, which both provided me with much information on the formation of UNO and about the Alinsky method used in organizing UNO that Olivares learned and benefitted from. The PADRES Collection at the University of Notre Dame, including a transcript of Fr. Juan Romero's 1992 interviews with Olivares, likewise provided important information on Olivares's involvement with PADRES, a Chicano priest advocacy group in the 1970s and 1980s, of which Olivares became president. Moreover, parish records of La Soledad and La Placita churches at the Los Angeles Chancery Archival Center of the Los Angeles Archdiocese at San Fernando Mission possessed documents pertaining to Olivares's tenure as pastor at both parishes. These are some of the other archival sources that added to my research and rounded out my portrait of Olivares.

Examining all of these sources, including doing the many oral histories, took much time, but it all enriched me in my search for Luis Olivares. In addition, it took me over three years to organize all of my research materials and to write the manuscript. But all this effort has been worthwhile, and I would not trade this experience.

When we choose a historical topic or subject to study, there is usually a link to the present. As Edward Carr correctly observes, we study the past to better know our present. The questions we ask about the past are also questions we have today.[42] How is this relevant to my Olivares biography? It is relevant because his life is a reflection on the making of leadership and how leaders emerge. Leaders are not born; they become leaders. Clearly, Olivares always possessed leadership qualities even as a child and young man, but these qualities grew and flourished only when the context of his life also changed. His leadership qualities emerged after his "conversion" when he encountered César Chávez, but his conversions continued as he engaged in his other struggles, namely UNO and the sanctuary movement. We learn through Olivares's story that leadership in Chicano/Latino communities has always been present and that we always need leaders, but progressive leaders. That is, if leadership is applied, as in Olivares's case, to promote social justice and community empowerment and self-determination against the repressive status quo. We continue to need such leadership among Chicanos and Latinos, but also more broadly against the forces of reaction and regression that would deny people full civil and human rights in order to exploit their labor. We can take comfort in Olivares's story, recognizing that, while he represents a unique figure, there have followed in his wake many others who have risen and are rising to the challenges that face us today. Secondly, Olivares's story is relevant today because, especially in his involvement in UNO and in sanctuary, his story provides a roadmap of how best to organize in the community with the understanding, as UNO had, that in the end people—rank and file—have to produce their own leaders and that it is only they that can bring about positive change in their lives and make history. They are the change makers. Some speak of a new sanctuary movement and, indeed, the New Sanctuary Movement formed in 2007 to assist undocumented immigrants threatened with deportation by the George W. Bush administration, and today with respect to undocumented Central Americans and Mexicans still crossing our southern border in search of economic opportunities and safety from violence in their home countries.[43] But we also don't have to reinvent the wheel. Olivares's story, and that of the historic sanctuary movement out of La Placita Church, can and does provide significant examples of how to organize a sanctuary movement, and we can learn from some of the mistakes that Olivares made. With the threat of increased deportations of the undocumented in our midst, the heroic figure of Fr. Luis Olivares can be a symbol of doing the right thing. Olivares's story is relevant because it reveals how religion and politics can come together to help organize resistance to oppression and to provide a vehicle for prioritizing the needs of the poor and the marginalized in our society. Faith-based movements, especially among contemporary Latino immigrants who bring their faith with them, may be even more relevant today than they were in Olivares's time. Finally, I would say that Olivares is relevant today because of his courage, commitment, tenacity, and his great love for his fellow human beings. We need to emulate this, and we can find no better role model than Fr. Luis.

CONCLUSION

In my estimation, Fr. Luis Olivares is one of the major religious leaders in American history of the latter part of the twentieth century. It would not be fair to compare him to other major religious leaders such as Dr. Martin Luther King Jr. or even to César Chávez, for Olivares must be judged on his own merits. Yet simply because he is not as well-known as King and Chávez does not mean that he does not belong with them. As we revise American history to make room for historical subjects such as Chicanos and Latinos, who have been ignored or sidelined in our understanding and assertion of what we mean by American history, our sense of who has been important to this history will also change. Demographic and new political influences will also shape this, especially with the "browning" of America and the increased role that Latinos are now playing in American society. History, or our understanding of history, will change as the country changes. There will be glitches along the way and perhaps the election of Donald Trump represents a temporary glitch, but it cannot arrest these changes. The United States is not the same country it was fifty years ago or even twenty-five years ago. What we mean by "American history" has to reflect these changes as well. I am confident that, in the continued revision of American history, the role of Fr. Luis Olivares will be more greatly appreciated and that our children and grandchildren of all ethnic backgrounds will come to know who he was and what he did to make this country a better place, one where we truly welcome the stranger and accept everyone as children of God. I am honored and privileged to tell his story. He is still with us—¡Presente!

ONE

San Antonio

How does someone become a figure like Father Luis Olivares? What influences in your life make you into what you become? As a young boy, Luis Olivares did not know that he would become the champion of Central American refugees and undocumented Mexican immigrants. So how can one—or how can I—explain this?

I

In 1917, the revolution in Mexico had been raging for seven years. The dictator, Porfirio Díaz, was overthrown in 1911 after ruling Mexico for over three decades. However, his collapse only inaugurated further conflict, as different revolutionary groups turned on each other and as the remnants of the old Porfirian order attempted to regain power. Thousands of combatants and innocent civilians lost their lives in Mexico's bloodiest civil war. One-tenth of the population—about a million people—perished. To escape this chaos that also ruined the economy, over a million Mexicans had crossed the border into the United States by the end of the 1920s. Many moved into Texas, seeking refuge and a way of sustaining their families.[1]

Damaso Olivares and his wife, Inez, had peacefully lived in the small town of Parras, outside of Saltillo in the northern Mexican state of Coahuila, about 200 miles from the border with Texas.[2] He was a bricklayer and carpenter on the ranch of Francisco Madero, who initially led the revolution against Díaz and was elected President of Mexico, only to be assassinated in 1913. Damaso provided enough for his wife and five children. He was a devout Catholic, as was his wife, and served as the *sacristano* or sacristan at his church: someone who took care of the sacristy where the priest's vestments and the sacred vessels are kept. But the revolution affected every aspect of life, including religion. Many revolutionaries blamed the Catholic Church for its support of the Díaz regime and believed that the Church only favored the rich and powerful. They persecuted the Church and those

31

Catholics who supported it. Some, of course, attacked the Church for more personal and selfish reasons, to acquire its wealth.[3]

Damaso reacted to the anticlericalism of the revolution by sheltering priests who sought protection. He and his family knew many of these priests because they said Mass at the ranch. Damaso helped to hide them by digging a hole in one of the barns until the revolutionaries left.[4] These stories of their grandparents assisting such priests became part of the family lore that would be passed on to Luis Olivares and his siblings. Henry Olivares, one of Luis's older brothers, recalls that Luis always wanted to hear these stories. "Tell me about such and such a priest," he would ask his father or grandmother. "I would say that partly this was an influence on my brother's life," Henry observes.[5]

The anticlericalism of the 1910 Mexican Revolution further came to Parras in 1917 when troops loyal to Venustiano Carranza, one of the major revolutionary figures in northern Mexico and later a president of Mexico, arrested Damaso and demanded that he reveal the location of his church's sacred vessels, which the troops desired for their gold. Damaso refused to tell them. They then took him and put him on a firing line and threatened to execute him unless he turned over the treasures.

"Por favor, do not shoot. I'll give you the vessels."

This was the voice of Father Ocampo, the pastor who interceded to save Damaso's life. But it was a ruse; he only turned over a few of the least valuable sacred vessels. Not knowing better, the soldiers were satisfied and released Damaso. He thanked Father Ocampo profusely.[6]

But Damaso knew that things would only get worse. He packed up his family and fled. They crossed the border little more than the clothes on their backs and after a short stay in the American border town of Eagle Pass, Texas, went to San Antonio, where they had relatives. Tío Nacho or Uncle Nacho, a brother of Inez Olivares, lived in San Antonio and he helped them cross the border and to relocate. Besides Damaso and Inez, the family included Damaso Jr. (Luis Olivares's father), who was the oldest child and who was anywhere between twelve and eighteen at the time of the family's immigration to Texas, depending on which Olivares sibling one talks to. Luis Olivares notes that his father was only twelve.[7] Then there was José, Eduardo, Concha, and Marina, who later died at age fifteen or sixteen. Nacho had a Motel T with a rumble seat and, somehow, he packed in all of Damaso's family and drove them to San Antonio. According to Luis Olivares, Nacho transported immigrants, apparently with or without documents, from the border to San Antonio. This was his business and he represented an early version of a *coyote* or labor smuggler.[8]

A hard worker all of his life, Damaso had little formal education, but could read and write. Inez, by contrast, had received more education in Mexico and in fact had been a teacher on the Madero ranch. She also had the honor of tutoring Madero's children. She somehow managed to bring with her to San Antonio some of her school books, which she used to tutor her own children and grandchildren in Spanish.[9]

Deeply religious, the first thing the Olivares family did on arriving in the city was to thank God.

"We have arrived safely and we have to thank the Lord," Inez said.

"Damaso, you and José walk and look for a Catholic church so we may thank God that we arrived safely," their father ordered them.

After some walking, the boys found the Immaculate Heart of Mary Church in the west-side Mexican district. This would become the family church. The Claretian order staffed the parish, the very order that Luis Olivares would later join. Some of these priests were those whom the Olivares family had assisted in Mexico. They were a missionary order, and their zeal for their faith and to convert others would have an important impact on the Olivares family, especially on Henry and Luis.[10] The order was founded by St. Anthony Claret (Antonio María Claret y Clará) in 1849 in Barcelona, Catalonia, Spain. Its formal name is the Congregation of Missionaries, Sons of the Immaculate Heart of the Blessed Virgin Mary (CMF).[11]

Luis Olivares's maternal family members were victims of the Mexican Revolution. His grandparents originated in Miquijuana, a small town close to San Luis Potosi in north central Mexico. They later moved to Ciudad Victoria, in the state of Tamaulipas along the border with Texas.[12] His grandfather, José Aguiar, owned a store that apparently prospered until the revolution. José was in his forties when he married his wife, Leondise Equia, who was only fifteen or sixteen. He had already been married once and had a son from this prior marriage. Luis Olivares observes that on this side of the family his great-grandmother was an Indian while other family members on both sides were mostly mestizos (Spanish and Indian).[13] José was likewise a supporter of Díaz. That proved to be his doom. Villistas, followers of the revolutionary Pancho Villa, went to his store and asked if he sold bullets.

"Yes, what gauge do you want?"

When they told him, he turned around to get the ammunition, and the Villistas shot him in the back. "¡Viva Villa!" they shouted as they looted his store.

José Aguiar left behind his wife and three children, two sons and a daughter. A Villista colonel wanted to take his daughter, Victoriana, at

age fifteen, with him. The practice of stealing young women to be concu-
bines was common among the revolutionaries. To prevent this, Leonidas
gathered her children, including Victoriana, and fled into the mountains.
To avoid detection, they traveled by night. Fortunately, they found their
way to the border and crossed into Texas. This was also around 1917. Like
the Olivares family, they had relatives in San Antonio who welcomed them
and aided them. Hence, both families fled the Mexican Revolution and
became political refugees in the United States. Much later, Father Luis Olivares reminded his sister Socorro of this history when, on a visit to La Placita Church in Los Angeles, she teased her brother by saying, "Louie, why
do you help these Salvadorans? They don't even pay taxes!"

"Socorro," Father Luis responded. "You need to understand that these
people are coming just like our grandparents and parents."[14]

In San Antonio, Olivares's paternal grandfather started working in construction but became incapacitated when he fell at work. His accident left
him paralyzed from the waist down. Consequently, his young sons were
forced to find work to help the family. This also meant that they did not
attend school in San Antonio as teenagers. José, for example, got a job at
the Mexican Manhattan Restaurant where he washed dishes. He encouraged his brother, Damaso, to also apply for a job there. Instead of being put
to wash dishes, he was hired as a bus boy, which paid a higher salary. Both
brothers soon realized that the difference in their employment had to do
with race or racism. José was dark-skinned, while Damaso was more light-
skinned. Their boss preferred light-skinned Mexicans to serve as bus boys,
busing the tables of his white customers, and preferred to keep darker-
skinned Mexicans such as José out of sight in the kitchen.[15]

While unskilled jobs were plentiful in San Antonio in the 1920s, they became scarcer as the Great Depression loomed. Perhaps understanding this
or just wanting to get a better job with a higher salary, Damaso enrolled in a
correspondence course to learn how to become an electrician. He received
his classes by mail and after successfully passing them obtained a certificate as an electrician that allowed him to secure some jobs even during the
depression. He worked at the Travis Building as the building engineer. If
the elevator failed, he fixed it, among other tasks. "He could do anything,"
his son Damaso Jr. said of his father's skills. Damaso and his brothers thus
became the main breadwinners for their family, including their disabled
father who died not many years after the family arrived in San Antonio.[16]

On Luis Olivares's mother's side, that family also suffered through hard
times. Her Tía or Aunt Martina married the owner of a funeral home on the
west side, Domingo Rodríguez. The Rodríguez Funeral Home prospered

and later became the main funeral home in the Mexican barrio. However, that prosperity at first had little to do with funerals and more to do with the fact that Domingo was also a bootlegger in the 1920s, during Prohibition. He put contraband liquor inside empty caskets and transferred the hidden liquor to other bootleggers for a price. In time, authorities discovered the ploy and took Rodríguez's funeral license away. Nevertheless, the funeral home continued, but this time as a legitimate business when Martina obtained a new license under her name. The business allowed her to help care for her extended family including her niece, Victoriana, even after her husband died.[17]

To help support the family, the adult Aguiar children had to find employment. There was no time for their education beyond what they had received in Mexico. Victoriana, Luis Olivares's mother, for example, worked at one of the city's large *nuecerias* or pecan-shelling plants. Pecan shelling represented a major industry in San Antonio; pecans grown in the surrounding area were transported to the city, where the *nuecerias* workers— almost all Mexican women—sat in long tables and shelled the pecans. They put the pecans in one can and the shells in another. While not a high-paying job, it still allowed Victoriana to contribute to the family income.[18]

II

Religion, the Catholic faith, is what brought these two exiled families together. Both lived on the west side, and both attended Immaculate Heart of Mary Church. Both families were extremely religious, including Damaso and Victoriana. Damaso became active in the Society of San Luis Gonzaga and the St. Vincent de Paul Society. Victoriana enthusiastically participated in the Hijas de María. Besides being spiritual fraternities and sodalities, these groups assisted the poor and the needy. But religion and romance coincided. Damaso first noticed Victoriana at one of the daily Masses and became attracted to her. In order to see her more and to meet her, he then started attending daily Mass as well. Brought together by their faith and their religious activities, Damaso and Victoriana fell in love, courted, and with the permission of both parents married on August 13, 1928. Of his parents' courtship, Damaso Jr. observed:

> She [mother] was the president of the Hijas de María, but my Dad was the president of San Luis Gonzaga. So they met through a group of people that used to put on little plays in the church for the benefit of the church. They went to play practice. It was not a question where you sneak off and go date somebody. It was very formal, very deli-

cate. And grandma [Inez], of course, was elated that he [her son] was choosing a girl that was a good Catholic woman.[19]

Henry Olivares adds that both his father and mother were good actors in the *comedias* or comedies and dramas put on by the church. "My father was quite a performer especially doing dramatic parts," he noted. "My mother was the same way. She also loved to do dramatic parts and sing and all that. As a result of that we got a little hint of the performers in all of us. We all like to perform. We've never been bashful."[20]

Despite the depression, the newlyweds rented their own home in the barrio, although it appears that only Damaso continued to work. They rented different homes, all on the west side, including for a time moving into an apartment adjacent to the Rodríguez funeral home owned by Tía Martina. They lived in a Mexican and Mexican American world in which Spanish was the dominant language and Mexican customs and traditions prevailed. San Antonio, in fact, was a highly segregated city. Mexicans could only rent or own homes in the west side. Informal real estate covenants did not allow Mexicans to live in other sections of the city, especially in the Anglo north side. Blacks were restricted to the east side. Segregation also prevailed in citywide swimming pools and movie theatres as well as in the public school system, in which Mexican American students had to attend the infamous "Mexican schools" that operated throughout the Southwest and southern California. Even Catholic churches were segregated. Those on the west side attended "Mexican churches," including the San Fernando Cathedral that bordered the barrio. Anglo Catholics, including clergy, frowned upon Mexicans attending "Anglo churches."[21]

Not only was it not traditional for married Mexican women to work outside the home, but Victoriana was very busy raising a family. She gave birth to seven children: three sons and four daughters. One of them was Luis Olivares, born February 13, 1934. His siblings included María Teresa (Sept. 23, 1929); Damaso Jr. (May 10, 1931); Enrique (Henry, Oct. 9, 1932); María del Rosario (June 17, 1935); Socorro (December 9, 1936); and Josefina (April 3, 1938). All were born at home, either with the aid of a Dr. Lozano or by midwives.[22]

The Olivares family was loving and close-knit, and part of an extended family that included Damaso's and Victoriana's families. The parents impressed upon their children a deep devotion to their Catholic faith and to the Church. The family always attended Sunday Mass and the older children often accompanied Abuelita Inez to daily Mass. Damaso and Victoriana also socialized their children, by their own example, to help the less privileged and to be charitable. Henry Olivares remembers his father as being inwardly religious. "He was a very gentle, very kind man." He recalls his mother as also being very religious and very social through her work in the parish.[23] Damaso Jr. adds that his mother was very high-strung and very protective of her children. "One thing that would upset her the most would be if anybody touched us," he notes. "In any manner or shape. 'These are my children.'" He further observes that his brother Luis would also be very high-strung, a characteristic he inherited from their mother.[24]

Teresa, the oldest sibling, recalls her mother as always being beautifully dressed. "She would make her clothes and she was always very feminine in her ways," she points out. She wore bright clothes favoring blue and coral colors. She had a light complexion with a dimple on her chin that Teresa says her brother Henry inherited. Of her father, Teresa observes that he was always a very caring person and very devoted to her mother. He was not a macho type. He would help with the children at home. He was fair in complexion and, according to his daughter, had beautiful eyes. "He was such a loving, giving person," Teresa adds. "Even after mother passed away, he couldn't bring himself to spank us." She recalls one incident after she and her older brothers had misbehaved and her father told them how hard it was for him to spank them, but he had to do it. "When he took his belt off," Teresa says with fondness, "I was laughing because my dad was gonna spank us, because he never did."[25]

Part of the tradition that was passed on to the Olivares children and that would impact Luis Olivares many years later was providing sanctuary to those being religiously persecuted. Their parents did not call this sanctuary but it was the same practice. This tradition began with their grandparents on both sides, who aided and protected Mexican priests fleeing the persecution of Catholic clergy into the 1920s as a result of the Cristero War (1926–29), when many Catholics, led by their clergy, rose up in revolt against the strict anticlerical laws and restrictions on the Catholic Church imposed by the new revolutionary government. Many Catholics, including clergy, were killed in this civil war.[26] Some fled Mexico and sought refuge in San Antonio and other places in the United States. The Olivares family and the Eguia family assisted them. Some of these priests later visited Damaso and Victoriana into the 1930s. "From them we developed a desire to be priests," Henry Olivares says about himself and Luis.[27]

Luis Olivares also recalled that his parents often talked about how they helped these Mexican priests: "One of the things that they did both in Mexico and here in the U.S. was during the so-called persecution under [President] Calles in Mexico. They were like an underground railroad for the priests who would come from Mexico to San Antonio. My dad used to hide priests behind the walls, so he was involved in a kind of sanctuary movement as a young adult. This was around 1925, '26, '27."[28]

Religion, helping others, and maintaining a close family unit represented the core values of the Olivares family. They struggled economically but kept their dignity. "We never thought we were poor," one of Luis's sisters emphasizes.[29] They would never be poor as long as they stayed together. *La familia*—the family—was a concept deeply ingrained in them. Yet it was also a concept that went beyond the nuclear or extended family and embraced the community through the good social work of their parents.[30]

Tragically, this sense of *la familia* faced a major blow when Victoriana died a few weeks after giving birth to her daughter Josefina. She died on May 15, 1938, aged 37. Two days later her oldest son, Damaso Jr., made his first Holy Communion. "We had a tremendous change when my mother died," one of the sisters observes. Luis Olivares was only three and a half years old when this happened. He had no memories of her. What he came to know about his mother was what his father, his grandparents, and his older siblings passed on to him. Teresa, who was eight at the time, has the strongest memories of her mother. She recalls her mother as loving but also very strict and very religious. "She took us to church all the time," Teresa notes. Victoriana was also a very meticulous person. She bathed her children every afternoon and then warned them not to get dirty. Needless to say, Teresa observes, her mother was very protective of her children. She was especially concerned about Luis when the family lived adjacent to the Rodriguez Funeral home. The workers would tease Luis by calling him "blackie" or "mosca en leche" [a fly in milk] because of his darker complexion, compared to his other siblings and his parents. Her mother would not allow Luis or any of the children to get close to the workers.[31] Henry, who was five years old at the time, retains faint memories of his mother and recalls her as a very nurturing and affectionate parent.[32]

For Luis, at least as a symbol, Victoriana was a loving and giving mother. Needless to say, her husband was devastated. Perhaps sensing her own mortality and at a time when incidents of infant mortality were high in the Mexican immigrant and Mexican American communities, Victoriana told her husband that, if anything were to happen to her, she wanted her children to be cared for by Inez, Damaso's mother. Apparently, she repeated this every time she went into childbirth, and it would prove to be prophetic the last time.[33]

She gave birth to Josefina but died three to six weeks later. (Some of the Olivares siblings say three weeks; Teresa says six weeks.[34]) Apparently, she developed an infection and there were no antibiotics to help her. Damaso Jr. believes that her death can be blamed on the midwife who did not use certain precautions in the birth process. Before she died, her husband promised to fulfill her wish. Both understood the importance of keeping the family together. One can only imagine what it took for Damaso to explain to his children that their mother had died. Teresa notes that her father sat them down and told them that their mother was not returning home, but she does not remember crying. Her mother was buried at San Fernando Cemetery on the west side, where her father would also be laid to rest next to her, many years later. Victoriana's insistence that her husband's family step in for her was even more prophetic, as her mother died two weeks after Victoriana's death. Consequently, the Olivares children became closer to their paternal side of the family.[35]

The pressure on Damaso as a single parent must have been incredible, especially with a newborn baby. They had to move out of their apartment, which had become too congested with so many children, and start looking for a new home. Putting all the children into his *troque* or truck, Damaso drove throughout the west side looking for a place to rent, with the intent that Abuelita Inez and Tía Concha, his unmarried sister who lived with her mother, would move in with them, fulfilling Victoriana's wish. However, no one would rent to him with such a large family.[36]

Fortunately, Damaso's brother José or Joe, who had a steady job, intervened and told Damaso: "Look, I'll provide the funds for a house. That way you can bring our mother, Concha, and the children together in one place."[37]

Uncle Joe's generous offer was fortuitous because Martina Rodríguez had already planned to take the children herself. She would keep a couple of them in her home, but the others she would distribute among relatives or send to friends in Mexico where a family she knew was willing to adopt them.[38] Only Luis and Socorro would remain with Damaso and his family.[39] Joe's offer circumvented all this and the Olivares family stayed together. This is when Damaso fully revealed his love for his children. He was not a father who openly told his children that he loved them, but when presented with the proposal that his children would be dispersed, he stood up to Martina and said, "No, I don't want my family divided. My family is going to stay together." According to Henry, "that's the image of love that I have of my father."[40] Because they could not adopt the children, Victoriana's family became estranged from Damaso and his family, although the children occasionally visited their mother's family.[41]

Damaso and the children moved into the new house with Abuelita Inez and Tía Concha at 1210 South Laredo in the west side. The house still stands. Like most other homes in the barrio, it was built of wood and stucco, including wooden floors. It had a garden where Inez grew fruits and vegetables, and raised chickens that were the source of eggs and meat.[42] In fact, Inez taught the boys how to behead a chicken. She would first cut the head off with a knife and then make a cross in the dirt and placed the dying chicken on top of it. Apparently, this was to thank God for this food. The boys would sometime forget to make the cross and lay the chicken on it, and so the headless chicken would run all over the yard spilling its blood.[43] People took pride in their homes, kept them clean, and exchanged fruit and vegetables with neighbors. People were poor in the barrio. Gil Villanueva, who also grew up in the west side and went to the seminary with Luis, recalls that since they all were relatively poor they did not necessarily identify as poor.[44]

III

But the new house also represented a new family structure. Both Abuelita Inez and Tía Concha would become major influences on the Olivares children. Abuelita (which the children pronounced *wellita*) represented the matriarch grandmother, while Concha would become the surrogate mother and, in fact more than surrogate. She became "mami" or "Ya Ya," as the children also called her. She was the only mother the younger ones, including Luis, knew. Luis already possessed strong bonds with both of them, since even before his mother's death he was Inez and Tía Concha's favorite among his siblings. They spoiled him even when Victoriana lived. In fact, because of this relationship, Luis wanted to live with his grandmother and aunt even before his mother died.[45]

Even before they went to live with Abuelita and Tía, the Olivares children were already very close to them. Every day their father and mother dressed them up and they visited Inez and Concha. Damaso would arrive home from work, bathe, change into nicer clothes, and by then his children and wife were ready for the *visita* or visit. Victoriana dressed them in order of their age, beginning with the oldest. Luis, already somewhat spoiled, could not understand why he had to wait his turn to be dressed as the fourth child, since at Abuelita's he was always treated as the number-one child. Consequently, according to Damaso Jr., "Luis always wanted to spend the day with them. Wanted to go live with them."[46]

In fact, Luis already was living with his grandmother and aunt before his mother died. This occurred because his mother needed some help with the other children as she gave birth to new children. At such a young age,

Luis told his parents that he needed to stay with his grandmother and aunt because they did not have a "honey" to take care of them. As part of this differential treatment, for example, Abuelita fixed Luis special foods just the way he liked his *platitos* or dishes. She strained his *caldo* or soup because he preferred only the liquid of the soup and not the vegetables. Luis always disliked his food mixed together in one plate as his mother typically served food. At Abuelita's, he was served the different portions in separate little bowls.[47]

Despite having to care for her other children, Victoriana missed not having Luis at home all of the time and told him as much. Of course, he did spend time at home with his parents, but often complained about not receiving the preferential treatment that he did with Abuelita Inez and Tía Concha. He also was not fond of a weekly laxative his mother gave the children in the form of castor oil. Luis would say, "Abuelita doesn't give me a laxative. Why do I need one here?"

"Because when you're over here," Victoriana sternly told him, "you have to do like the rest."[48]

Although they were all together, the new Olivares home was quite congested. In addition to the Olivares children, their cousin, Fernando, recently born to Tía Concha, became part of the family. Sleeping arrangements proved to be a real art. The boys slept together; the girls, including baby Josefina, slept with Tía Concha; Damaso, the father, had his own room and built a separate room for Inez. Each of the older children, in addition, took turns sleeping in their grandmother's bed. There was only one bathroom, which must have posed quite a problem for eleven people.[49]

Despite their tight living conditions, the Olivares family maintained a sense of *la familia*—the family. This is what Victoriana had wanted and appealed for even as she was dying. Everyone supported each other through their tragic loss. "We stuck together," Sister Victoria Olivares (María del Rosario, now a nun) notes. "Regardless of the differences that we had, we always came out together. It's going to be all right. Everything was going to be all right." This strong family bond was a characteristic that was deeply imbued in all family members. It motivated them at the time and later in life to help other families, especially those in need. Luis Olivares expressed this characteristic in his own later work with refugees and immigrants. His sister Socorro recalls that her brother in his ministry stressed the concept of *la familia*: "I saw that coming from our home to the work he was doing and all of this was to help the people."[50]

To reinforce family solidarity, their father once told them never to do anything that would bring disgrace to the family name, because their name was in the Bible and if it was in the Bible the name was sacred. He said that if you go to Genesis in the Old Testament and read the Garden of Eden story that there is mention of olive groves and that in Spanish this is translated as "olivares." "So don't do anything to ruin your name," he admonished his children.[51]

IV

But there is no question that the pillar of the Olivares family was Abuelita Inez. As the matriarch, she set the tone and the value system, especially for the children. Their father, Damaso, was of course an important parental figure, but he had to work hard to provide for the family and therefore turned over much of his children's upbringing to his mother and sister. Moreover, he remained for many years distraught over the death of his wife. Consequently, Abuelita dominated the home. Tía Concha became the loving mother figure and cared for many of the children's needs, but clearly the household leadership remained in the hands of Inez.

Abuelita centered her leadership on her deep Catholic faith. It touched every aspect of her life and was the barometer for all of her actions. She and her faith were one. She not only socialized her grandchildren, but introduced them to the faith. Catholicism—Mexican Catholicism—permeated the Olivares household. "My grandmother Inez Olivares was the backbone of the family," Henry points out, "because she is the one that participated very actively in the church. She believed that the church was not only the center of our faith but also the social center of the community."[52]

Sunday Mass, daily Mass, evening rosaries both in the church and at home, evening prayers, all of this was a constant in the Olivares home led by Inez. Her faith and example to the children extended to her charity work. She believed that to be a Catholic was to help the needy and the poor, and there certainly were many in the barrio, especially during the depression. People begged for food by knocking on doors. Abuelita never turned them away. One of Luis's sisters links this charity to his later acts of charity. "I think that the seed that Louie got was that my grandmother was always helping people," she states. "Anybody that would knock at the door would not leave without eating. If they didn't have a place to sleep, they would find a place at the house. Our house was always packed."[53]

After feeding her family, Abuelita never threw any leftovers away and instead gave them to the poor. She baked goodies not only for her family, but for her neighbors. When her son José asked her if she could make tamales as part of a fundraiser for one of his religious organizations, she made as many as 600 tamales to sell.[54] She also gave away used clothing, shoes, and any other household items no longer needed to those who could use them. After Mass, if she saw anyone who looked hungry, she invited them to her home and fed them tortillas and coffee. She would also invite homeless people at church to stay with the family for a short while, even though they were total strangers.[55]

Inez's good works extended to healing and comforting people. She was a *curandera* or faith healer. She healed through praying over people that God release them of their physical or emotional troubles and she added her knowledge of herbs to fix teas and other potions for those who came to her. Sometimes she made the equivalent of doctor's house calls by going to minister to the sick in their homes. On these visits, she always took the older children with her, including Luis. "Whenever there was somebody sick, they would call her to do a healing," Henry remembers. "She would go over there and we would go with her."[56] Luis also recalls his grandmother as a healer: "She wasn't exactly a *curandera*, but a lot of people came to the house to be prayed over . . . it just happened that she had a reputation for holiness and people would come to her and she would pray."[57] According to Teresa Olivares, her grandmother also always dressed in black.[58] One of the ailments that she treated was *susto*—a type of shock or scare that a person experienced that became lodged as a pain in a certain part of their body, usually the abdomen, chest, or back. Even a baby could suffer *susto*, that might lead to developmental handicaps. Anyone at any age could suffer from this affliction. Abuelita's remedy, as Luis remembers, was to perform a counter-shock that would drive the original *susto* away. She would drink some whiskey but not swallow it and when the patient least expected it, she blew the whiskey on their face and then covered the person with a towel and dried them off. More than likely, the effect of this counter-shock was more psychological than physical, but it appears to have worked.[59] "I don't know how to account for it working," Luis stated. "She claimed it was her faith, of course."[60] As part of her healing practices, Inez would invite a *sobadora* who healed through massages. Inez invited the priests over for massages. "We always had priests at the house," Teresa notes.[61]

Abuelita applied these rituals and healing to the children as well. They never went to doctors because Inez treated them for any physical problems they had. If they had a stomach ache, for example, she would take a raw egg and break it over their stomach and wherever the egg landed that was where she believed the *empacho* or pain was. She then rubbed that area with oil and whoever was sick had to sleep with the raw egg.[62]

Abuelita, Tía Concha, and Damaso also stressed good behavior, good manners, respect for others, and always being presentable. Being clean and wearing clean and ironed clothes with shined shoes were part of the household culture. Abuelita sewed most of the children's clothes and stressed personal hygiene. She often told her grandchildren: "Somos pobres pero no somos sucios" (we may be poor but we're not dirty). Early in his ministry when he became the treasurer for the Claretian order, Luis was sometimes criticized, usually behind his back, by fellow clerics for wearing expensive clothes and some suggested at the time that this expressed a certain conservatism and lack of community involvement on his part. His siblings strongly disagree with this view. They instead link their brother's taste for being well dressed and presentable with his upbringing. Damaso Jr. notes, for example, that their Uncle Joe "was an immaculate dresser" and that he had an influence on Luis. "We were always very, very personally clean," one of Luis's sisters stresses. "Even if you had a little hole in your clothes, they were still always 'bien planchaditos' [well pressed]."[63]

Leadership was part of what the children learned. Damaso continued to be a leader in his religious organizations as did the uncles on their mother's side. Damaso was an usher at the church, and about his work with the St. Vincent de Paul Society, he told his children: "We help people. People that need money. We collect the money and then we just pass it around."[64] This impressed Luis: "The thing I remember is that even though we were poor . . . yet the thing that I remember is that my grandmother and my dad and my uncles exercised a leadership role, not only in the church, but also in the barrio. People looked up to them for advice on community and personal matters, on church activities, and so forth."[65]

Abuelita further expressed pride in her Mexican origins and culture including the Spanish language. She, Concha, and their father only addressed the children in Spanish. Prior to the older children attending English-language schools, Abuelita commenced a type of preschool each Saturday, in which she taught them how to read and write in Spanish. According to Henry, knowing the structure of Spanish prior to going to school made it easier for him and his siblings to master English faster. "So our roots are really bilingual," he stresses.[66] These Spanish classes at home continued throughout their elementary-school years. Inez used Spanish-language books that she had brought from Mexico as part of her lessons.[67]

While Abuelita Inez certainly dominated the home, the role of Tía Concha, or Ya Ya, in the formation of Luis Olivares and his siblings should not be overlooked. This was especially true for the younger children including Luis. Besides raising her own son, Fernando, Concha, who was in her late thirties when Victoriana died, served as the other children's mother. While Inez cooked the meals and sewed clothes, Concha took the children to school and when needed met with the nuns, even though she could not speak English. However, she did understand enough English that she was able to speak in Spanish and the nuns would respond in English. There were two Cuban nuns who spoke Spanish and Concha could more easily converse with them.[68] She also arranged for the children to have swimming lessons. She dressed them and when needed bought them shoes. Tía Concha likewise influenced them socially. "She always told us to stand up for ourselves," one of the sisters recalls. That and staying together and not going in different directions. This would involve going to church together, going to school together, and wherever else they went. "If any one of you gets hit by a bus," she said, "I want all of you to get hit by a bus." This was not meant to frighten the children, but to stress always staying together.[69]

Concha in particular emphasized the importance of education and of studying hard. Discipline and education complemented each other. "Even if you're barefoot," she told her children, "if you put all the effort in school, learn what they teach you, you can get anywhere. With an education, you cannot miss anything." Another sibling concludes of Concha: "She was a very strong woman in that sense." Three of the Olivares siblings observe that Concha had to be strong because as a single, unmarried woman with a child, she faced criticism from others in the barrio, a kind of "scarlet letter," Mexican style. "But she never went into her room and hid herself," one sister notes. "We learned to go swimming, dance, piano lessons, cooking lessons. She took us everywhere, and everywhere she took us, she took us on the bus." She would not be shamed and fulfilled her responsibilities not caring what others thought of her.[70]

All of the Olivares children, but especially Luis and the younger ones, became very close to Ya Ya. Having no memories of their real mother, they embraced Tia Concha as their mother. Teresa remembers her aunt as a very happy person, always singing along with the Mexican music on the radio and telling the children stories. She took them to school and picked them up. She helped them with school projects such as participating in school plays. On weekends she took them to the Mexican theater to see Spanish-language movies. "She was a very, very protective, very loving person," Teresa concludes. "I keep telling my brothers and sisters that we lost our mother, but we were blessed with a very caring grandmother and tía to take care of us."[71]

V

Of course, despite the expense, there was never any question but that the children would receive a Catholic education. Not only did their parents believe—and probably correctly so—that the Catholic schools provided a better education, but they taught the faith as well. All of the children, despite their age range, attended either Immaculate Heart of Mary elementary school, which was their parish school, or other Catholic schools. By contrast, in the 1930s and 1940s the public schools on the west side—the "Mexican schools"—were overcrowded, lacked desks, books, and other facilities such as cafeterias and playgrounds, and were staffed by too many teachers who possessed low expectations of their Mexican American students. The schools were segregated and inferior.[72]

The religious training that the children received at Immaculate Heart was reinforced daily at home, especially by Abuelita. Home, school, and church were all intertwined in a Catholic environment. This culture commenced bright and early each morning when Inez took the older children with her to daily Mass. "My grandmother raised us," Luis observed. "She was very religious—daily mass, the whole bit. She would take us, my older brothers and me, we would go with her at six fifteen in the morning every single day to Immaculate Heart. That's the origin of my vocation and my brother's [Henry], too. We spent a lot of time in church."[73] His sister, Teresa, notes that she also had to attend these early-morning Masses with Abuelita; this meant that when they later were in school they had to attend two Masses each day since the school had an 8 A.M. Mass. Olivares also linked his future mission to the priests at the church: "We practically lived at the church, and you got to know the priests, their work and what moves them. The kindness and dedication of Father John Arans and the other priests was very inspiring. They became my heroes."[74]

Besides daily Mass and Sunday Mass, Luis and his siblings also had to pray the rosary each night with their grandmother. As they prayed the rosary in Spanish, Abuelita would take turns cuddling each of the children in her arms and wrap her shawl around the child. "A lot of times," Henry observes, "Luis was the one that was being held under the shawl." Their religious training would be intensified during feast days such as *Semana Santa*, or Holy Week, before Easter. Following a Mexican tradition, during Holy Week Abuelita visited several Mexican churches on the west side, with the kids in tow. The children joined their grandmother in the additional tradition of doing penance by processing up the main aisle toward the altar *en rodillas* or on their knees. If they toppled over, they had to start all over again, but from the back of the church. Like most Mexican women and Mexicans in general, Abuelita had a devotion to Our Lady of Guadalupe, the patron saint of Mexico, although her devotion to Guadalupe seems to not have been as intense as other Mexicans in the barrio.

She also honored the more European Virgin Mary and had an image of the Blessed Mother in a *cajita* or empty small box. She had some of the children take it from home to home in the neighborhood. In fact, the children were put in charge of this ritual. At each home, they said the rosary. The *cajita* remained in each home for eight days before being picked up and taken to another home.[75]

Needless to say, as part of their Catholic education, all of the boys served as altar boys.[76] Henry and Luis started as altar boys in their early grades at Immaculate Heart. They would often serve Mass together and sometimes each or both served the early morning Mass attended by Abuelita or the Sunday Mass attended by the whole family.[77] They would sometimes be allowed to leave school to serve a wedding or a funeral. As altar boys, on occasion they ate lunch with the priests in the rectory and even slept there before Midnight Christmas Mass so that they would not be late for the service.[78] Henry remembers that once in a while an old lady, besides putting in a few coins into the collection cup, would slip a dollar bill into Luis's hands. This was intended for him and not the church. Apparently, this occurred more than once because Henry notes that his brother had a "little arrangement going on."[79]

As altar boys, they served the Claretian priests. Hence, at least for Henry and Luis, the Claretians became role models and inspired them to become Claretians themselves. Most of the priests were Spaniards but some had earlier served in Mexico. Besides Immaculate Heart, the Claretians also staffed some of the other west-side parishes. The priests, including those whom the family had aided in Mexico, often visited the Olivares home. These included Fathers Castillion, Arans, and Sunye. Henry Olivares remembers these visits:

> These priests would always in a way inspire us because they were such a happy bunch of guys and they would just get into our family, sit down and eat with us and be part of the give and take of the rapport that existed in our family. Everyone would talk back and forth. Many times we had three, four, five priests at home. They would play with us and we would have a great time. From there we [Henry and Luis] developed a desire to be priests.[80]

Henry further recalls that the priests always came dressed as priests. They never wore casual clothes in public.[81]

The priests reciprocated by always including the family in church activities. When Immaculate Heart of Mary was reconstructed, the Claretians included the name of the Olivares family in the corner stone as a family who had assisted in the reconstruction by contributing funds for the purchase of new statues. This acknowledgement included mentioning the family in a special prayer that was installed in the statue of the Blessed Virgin Mary. Where the heart of Mary was displayed on the statue, there was also a compartment that could be opened, which is where the prayer was inserted. This story became part of the family lore passed down to the children—the fact that the Olivareses had helped built the new church.[82]

Religion at school, religion at church, and religion at home. This pervasive Catholicism enveloped the Olivares family. It was part of who they were and what helped to hold them together. "The Church was the center for us," one of Luis's sisters comments. "Some other families would go to picnics. We would go to church."[83]

VI

As a child and an adolescent, Luis displayed some of the character traits which would carry over to his later life. First and foremost, he was the preferred child; some might call him a spoiled child. All of his siblings agree that Luis was *el preferido*. Both Abuelita Inez and Tía Concha made him feel special. Because he was quite thin and seemed more delicate than the others, especially his brothers, he was nicknamed Flaco (Skinny) by the others, and his grandmother would fix him special meals.[84] It was not, it seems, because they loved him more than the others, which would have been cruel, and none of the siblings recall feeling any resentments toward their brother. It appears that Inez and Concha (it is not clear about his father) saw in Luis some special qualities and they prophetically saw in him someone who would in fact turn out to be special. "In my grandmother's and my aunt's eyes, he [Luis] would always shine out," Damaso Jr. states. "He was it."[85] They told the other children to protect and look after Luis. How this treatment personally affected Luis is hard to say, although as a child and as an adolescent it seems as if it gave him a sense of privilege and leadership among his siblings. It was as if he were the chosen one whose mission was to lead others.

Henry recounts an interesting story that speaks to the preferential treatment that Luis received at home. When it came time for Luis to start first grade, he refused to go. He put his foot down and said, "No, I don't want to go to school; I want to stay with Abuelita." His parents tried to force him to go, but he literally would not budge even though his tuition at Immaculate Heart school had already been paid. To further complicate the matter, Luis was recovering from an intestinal flu. In the end, he was allowed to stay home one more year and in his place his younger sister Rosario was enrolled in school even though she was a year younger. But she was next in line and the tuition could not be returned. Rosario agreed to go in Luis's place. After he did start school, he advanced to the age-appropriate grade.[86]

Henry does not admit that Luis was "spoiled," but in a more diplomatic way says that his brother "was given a little more attention."[87] By contrast, his older sister, Teresa, more bluntly says that her grandmother and aunt spoiled Luis.[88]

One character trait that would continue in Luis's life was how organized he was. Even as a child, he had a sense of order. There was school work and there were chores at home and he had to abide by this schedule. There was no room for being scatterbrained or fooling around. "Everything he did, he had already planned it," one of his sisters says. This included telling his siblings what their duties or responsibilities were—not necessarily in a bossy way, she explains, but just as part of his leadership skills. "By the time he came to you and told you, he had already assigned people to what he wanted them to do. It was not like he would sit down and say, 'Can you do this, can you do that?' No, it was already laid out."[89]

When his little sisters started school, Luis organized how they would walk back to school with him, and he insisted that they follow his orders even using a brotherly threat. "He would tell us, 'you all wait for me here,'" a sister remembers. "'When I get out of school, I want you all three . . . to wait for me here and if you're not here, I'm gonna leave without you.'"[90]

While it seems that Luis could be stern on some occasions with his siblings, they also fondly remember his sense of humor. This humor would remain with him even to his dying days. He liked to joke and especially tease his sisters, but not in a cruel way. In fact, he could even be a little *travieso* or naughty. "He had that little streak of doing things underhanded," one of his sisters notes.[91] But Luis could also have his quiet moments, Teresa recalls.[92]

At the same time, the other children sometimes reacted by teasing or making fun of Luis. Unfortunately—and this speaks to the internal issue of race and the ideology of "whiteness" among Mexicans and Mexican Americans—they would make fun of the fact that Luis was darker or more olive-skinned than the rest of his siblings. In Mexico, despite the fact that most Mexicans are *mestizos* (Spanish and Indian), there remained a Spanish colonial residue of preference for European culture, including favoring those with lighter complexions. Luis's siblings would say to him, "tu eres prieto [you're dark]." Sensitive to this, Luis cried when taunted this way. He went to his Tía Concha and Inez and told on his brothers and sisters.

"Mama [Concha], tell them that 'yo soy blanco de nieve' [I'm as white as snow]."

Apparently assured of this by his aunt and grandmother, the next time he was teased about his complexion, Luis would respond, "Yo soy blanco de nieve dice mama [I'm as white as snow, mama says]".[93]

Luis was also smart and bright and exhibited an early intellectualism in school. His favorite subject became history.[94] This bookish quality might have been used against him by other classmates by teasing him or scorning him; however, according to Henry, to the contrary, his brother's intelligence not only made him a good student but also very popular with others, despite the fact that as a boy he did not participate in sports like his older brothers, due to his thinness and more delicate nature. He rarely played outside with his brothers or participated in sports such as baseball with neighborhood boys. Instead, he stayed inside and played games with his sisters. "For a while we thought he was sickly," Henry notes, "but he was just different." Despite his lack of traditionally masculine qualities, his brother observes, "Luis had a winning personality. People really liked him. He had a way of having people be nice to him. Ever since I can remember, his personality was very attractive to other people." Luis reciprocated by being very outgoing and gracious to others. He built friendships, a trait that he would carry on in his seminary years.[95]

Although Luis was for the most part well-liked by other students, there were a few who did pick on him; this even included some of the bigger altar boys. They bullied him for being skinny and less boyish. This bullying included hitting Luis. Henry recalls more than once having to rescue his brother because he would not fight back:

> This one time this guy was beating up Luis and I went over and I beat this guy up. I defended my brother. . . . Another time some guy threw a rock that hit Luis, so I went over and kicked this guy and he turned on me and we got into a fight. I am not a fighting man but if I have to fight, I will fight. . . . Luis didn't fight back. To this day, my image of Luis is one that would just cry and tell the nuns that such and such a person was picking on him.[96]

Nevertheless, Luis was still popular and his popularity extended to some of the Benedictine nuns who, like his parents, favored Luis. He was the classic teacher's pet. This was especially true of Sister Mary Mildred, who in particular signaled him out among her exclusively Mexican American students, both boys and girls. "This was her boy," Luis's sister observes. "Luis could do no wrong." In fact, there was an interesting rivalry between Sister Mary Mildred and Sister Scholastica, who favored Henry Olivares in her classes. Both nuns tried to outdo each other in promoting their favorites. "If Sister Scholastica would brag about Henry," Damaso Jr. recalls, "[Sister Mary Mildred] would brag about Luis."[97] All of the nuns were second-generation Anglos of German descent, with the exception of two Cuban ones.[98] Luis fondly recalls the nuns as being very compassionate and understanding. "They may not have had all that experience in dealing with Mexican American kids," he noted, "but they sure didn't make them feel inferior."[99] Luis believed that he received a good education at Immaculate Heart, although in retrospect he recognized certain deficiencies, such as not teaching math proficiently, in the school's curriculum. He recognized this gap in his education when he entered the seminary and had to be tutored in math. Still, as he put it, "I have nothing but high regards for my teachers in grammar school."[100]

The nuns themselves were quite the disciplinarians. They did not tolerate any bad behavior in class or outside of class. Part of the discipline involved the use of uniforms. The boys wore khaki shirts with a black tie and khaki pants. The girls wore blouses and skirts.[101]

Although a favorite at school, Luis did not let it get to his head. He always did his school work and was courteous and helpful to his teachers. One of his sisters remembers that helpfulness along with her brother's leadership qualities when she relates the story of how, at Luis's eighth-grade graduation, it appeared that some of the other students, especially the other boys, had not had their graduation gowns pressed. Somehow, he found an old stove-top iron and told the boys that he expected them to use it that very morning, before the graduation ceremony, to press their wrinkled gowns. Apparently, they followed his orders.[102]

A sign of Luis's developing leadership among his siblings and sense of himself as a leader included his playing the role of priest and saying the Mass at home. As an altar boy, Luis closely studied how the priest said Mass, listening to the prayers and observing his body language. He seemed to love the ritual and the drama of the service. He learned not only his responses in Latin, but the entire Latin liturgy of the Mass, since Latin then was the language of the Mass and not the vernacular. What is remarkable is that, according to Henry, his brother started playing priest at home as early as six or seven years of age.[103] He arranged a home altar in a back room, with a big table that he used for the altar, and directed his brothers and sisters to participate as altar boys and the girls as the congregation. For his vestment, he used a little blanket that he wrapped around his shoulders. On occasion, he allowed Damaso Jr. and Henry to play the role of priests and concelebrate the Mass with him, directing them as to what to do. When his siblings sometimes teased him about all of this, he would get mad and call out, "Abuelita, they're making fun of me." Undoubtedly, his grandmother scolded the children and instructed them to play along with Luis.[104]

Luis's Masses, however, were no ordinary Masses. He always said a High Mass with more prayers and more ritual and, of course, all of this in Latin. "Dominus Vobiscum," he would recite and his altar boy brothers would respond "Et cum spiritu tuo." He delivered his own homilies or sermons, usually about proper church etiquette such as kneeling down and making the sign of the cross.[105] Luis was the high priest and this even extended to some occasions when a family friend, Father Correa, visited the Olivares home and Luis would include him in his Mass, not as a fellow priest or concelebrant, but as an additional altar boy. For the "blessed wine" in the Mass, he used the wine that his father drank at home. Luis even officiated at "funeral Masses." Besides saying Mass, Luis also baptized his sister's dolls. To complement his role as a boy-priest and thanks to the piano lessons he received at school and his practice on the home piano, Luis also learned to play the organ at church. On one occasion his grandmother returned from Mass at Immaculate Heart especially happy. "There was someone playing the organ," she said, "and it sounded like angels." It turned out this was Luis playing the organ. Ironically, he was playing "Solamente una vez," a very popular romantic song. All of these priestly acts by the young Luis impressed upon one of his sisters that her brother always wanted and intended to become a priest.[106]

Besides playing priest, Luis and his brothers also played doctor. They used their sisters' dolls as their patients and sometimes opened them up to see what was inside.[107]

Although Luis was the *consentido*, he still had to perform his home chores like his other siblings, as directed by Abuelita Inez or Tía Concha. This included doing the laundry and ironing, and cleaning the yard. The boys were also responsible to take care of the family dog.[108] As the boys got older, Inez encouraged them to find work outside the home. She got Damaso Jr. a job at a neighborhood clinic cleaning the facility each weekend. He received three dollars a week. "That was a lot of money then," he notes. On the other hand, it does not appear that Luis worked outside of the home. However, as part of his household chores, he learned to sew by observing his grandmother. After Inez died in 1947 and before Luis left for the seminary, he finished sewing some clothes for his sisters that their abuelita had not completed.[109]

A strong sense of ethnic identity also formed an important part of Luis's character. He recalls that at school this was challenged when the nuns changed his name from Luis to Louis. "You shouldn't use Luis," one of the nuns told him. "You should use Louis."[110] This practice was not unique to him: most other Mexican American students, whether at public or parochial schools, had their first names changed from Spanish to English. The Anglo teachers could not pronounce their Spanish names; moreover, this was part of the "Americanization" programs initiated in the 1920s to acculturate Mexican American children and to wean them from their Mexican cultural background, which was seen as an impediment to their becoming "Americans."[111] The change in first names, in fact, represented one of the first signs or symbols of the acculturation or transculturation of Mexican American children. While such changes might have been traumatic and dislocating for some, for others this does not appear to have been the case. Mexican American children—the Mexican American generation of the 1930s through the 1950s—did not want to be treated as different and the Americanizing of their first names was accepted as part of their going to school and of being Americans.[112] It was seen as "cool" to have a new English first name. Once one got their new name, their peers also wanted one. Luis and his siblings experienced this process. But name acculturation was complicated, because some of the kids would still have Spanish nicknames, such as Luis, who at home was called "Flaco." "And over the years I bought into that," Olivares observed of his name change, "I accepted it in grammar school, I went with Louis to the seminary, I was Louis through those first seventeen years of my priesthood. But I was always Luis, I just used a different name for a while!"[113]

"But I was always Luis." Henry Olivares, whose name was changed from Enrique by the nuns, asserts that his brother always recognized himself as a Mexican or Mexican American growing up in San Antonio. You could not avoid this ethnic recognition. They lived among other Mexicans on the west side, where Spanish was dominant. They spoke Spanish at home to their parents. Their father, grandmother, and aunt did not speak English, although Luis recalls that his father knew some English but spoke with a very heavy accent.[114] Even with each other and even while attending school, it appears that the children spoke Spanish, the exception being when they studied together. When they ventured outside of the barrio, they encountered racial segregation and discrimination. They could not attend certain public swimming pools outside of the Mexican district, even though Henry on occasion was allowed into one of those pools because his lighter skin allowed him to be mistaken for an Anglo.[115] If they went to the downtown movie theatres, they could not use the front entrances that were reserved for whites; they had to buy their tickets at the back entrance, enter there, and sit in the balcony with blacks, apart from Anglos. Anglo restaurants also would not serve Mexicans. They could patronize the downtown department stores, but they could not sit at the lunch counters. Even on buses, Gil Villanueva recalls, Mexicans had to sit in the back.[116]

As a result, despite their acculturation, which included learning and speaking English without accents, Mexican American children recognized their Mexicanness or "lo Mexicano." Henry notes that Luis always said, "I am Mexican" and asserted his Mexican culture. "He always knew who he was."[117] This included maintaining his ability to speak Spanish—even though due to the English-only policies of the schools, both Catholic and public, English became Luis's dominant language. He had entered school knowing very little English.[118] At Immaculate Heart, Spanish was prohibited; while the students were not punished as they would be in the public schools for speaking Spanish, Luis recalls that they were corrected. Still, whenever possible some of the Mexican American students spoke Spanish among themselves.[119] At the same time, Henry further observes that he and his brothers were not immune to the influence of the *pachucos* and zoot-suiters in the barrio. The *pachucos* especially represented young Mexican Americans throughout the Southwest during the 1940s, but especially during World War II, who as a result of their alienation from both Anglo and Mexican culture, created their own oppositional counterculture that in some cases led to gangs and conflict with the police. On social occasions, some sported the infamous zoot suit, with its exaggerated features.[120] Many in the barrios did not embrace the *pachucos* and saw them as both a threat and an embarrassment. The Olivares brothers were too young to wear the zoot suit—which their parents would have never allowed anyway—but they still had some familiarity with other aspects of this counterculture such as *caló*, the street language of the *pachucos*. Henry notes that at least he and perhaps Luis used this slang. "We used it but not at home," he says. "My dad would tell us you don't talk that way."[121]

VII

Despite their strong family cohesion, the Olivares family suffered still another major blow and change when Abuelita Inez died in December 1947. According to Teresa Olivares, her grandmother died around midnight. "She just woke up and passed away," she remembers.[122] Luis was thirteen and in the seventh grade. All of the children, from the oldest to the youngest, would now be without the bedrock of *la familia*. For Luis, it meant the loss of perhaps the biggest influence in his life. However, they still had their mother, Tía Concha or Ya Ya, who now assumed the matriarchal role and who, for the next several years as the children grew up, would be not only their loving mother, but their spiritual and moral inspiration.[123] Nevertheless, the passing of Inez signaled the beginning of a new chapter in the family's history. That same year, Henry decided to pursue his own vocation to the priesthood. According to him, before her death his mother had designated him, not Luis, to be the priest among her boys. "I was always told 'you're going to be a priest,'" Henry recalls. This included his teachers, who told him that he did not have to master math since he was going to be a priest and reading was more important. Because he was the designated priest, as a young teenager Henry was not allowed to attend dances. It appear that Luis himself did not go to dances either. Inspired by the Claretian priests at Immaculate Heart of Mary Church and counseled by them, Henry decided to enter the Claretian seminary in Compton, California. One year later, Luis, already convinced of his own vocation, followed suit and joined his older brother in California. Henry does not remember if his younger brother had expressed an interest in becoming a priest while in school.[124] Both left with their family's blessings, even though both would be dearly missed. It was seen as a great honor and blessing, and as a testimony to the family's strong Catholic faith, that not just one son but two were to become priests. It seemed like a natural extension of the family's Catholic heritage.

TWO

Seminary

In Compton, California, in an area that is part urban and part rural, there sits the remains of what used to be Del Amo Seminary and Dominguez Seminary. This first was the minor seminary and the second was the major seminary. Del Amo was high school and Dominguez was college. Both were operated by the Claretian order. For eight years, including one year at the novitiate in Los Angeles, these buildings separated by railroad tracks would be home for Luis Olivares. If he were alive today and visited these sites, he would be saddened that Del Amo was razed, and only the refectory and kitchen remain. It is now surrounded by a trailer park. The more elaborate and baroque Dominguez building still stands, protected as a state landmark and the resting place for deceased donors of the land. These sites contain many memories and even legends of students and teachers. Above all, this is where Luis Olivares began his journey to becoming a priest. All he knew at the start of that journey was that he wanted to become a priest; this was the location where it all started, at least officially.

I

Of course, Luis's older brother, Henry, was the first to see these buildings when he arrived in the fall of 1947, one year before Luis, to start his own journey toward the priesthood. He was the first to produce both joy and sadness in the Olivares family. His father and Tía Concha were very happy at his decision, but at the same time, *triste* or sad.[1] Since there was no Claretian seminary in Texas, Henry was assigned to Del Amo in California. His family took him to the train station and put him on the train. "I came [to California] all by myself," Henry remembers. A Claretian priest, Fr. Luis Vásquez, picked him up at Union Station in Los Angeles, and drove him to the seminary in Compton, some forty miles to the southeast.[2] At Del Amo, Henry would open up the way for Luis to follow.

In his eighth-grade year at Immaculate Heart, Luis concluded that he

56

also wanted to become a priest. He had his own vocation and he wanted to join his big brother.[3] Like Henry, he chose the Claretians because he had no other role models. The Claretians were his priests at Immaculate Heart. "As you live as a priest," he later said, "you get to learn more about what it is to be a Claretian."[4] Of course, the young Luis did not understand this profound statement at the time. He probably believed that one went to the seminary and there you became a Claretian, all nicely packaged for the rest of your life. But this was not how it really was or would be. No doubt it took Luis many years to realize that becoming a priest was a lifelong matter; it was a process, and one changed along the way. Being a priest was always a process of becoming. But at age thirteen, when he decided that he had a vocation, what could Luis possibly know about this life-long journey and the twists and turns involved? All he knew was that he wanted to become a priest. There is a certain problem in all of this. At that time, in the late 1940s and even before, the Catholic Church focused on encouraging "vocations" for the priesthood at a very early age. Nuns and priests encouraged this in Catholic elementary schools. They wanted to select the "best and the brightest" among the young boys for the priesthood. They impressed upon young and inexperienced minds that they had something called a "vocation," whereby God called them to become his ministers on earth as priests. This was the custom then, certainly before Vatican II, after which seminaries began to change and no longer recruited potential priests as early as thirteen and fourteen. Call it socialization. Call it a "calling" from God. Whatever was involved, it affected Luis, and he intended to pursue this goal.

Henry informed Luis that he had to follow the same steps he had taken, by first talking to the Claretians at Immaculate Heart; they would take it from there. But Henry also added, "but it would be good for you now to learn more Latin, but don't worry too much about this because you will get plenty of Latin here."[5]

Following his brother's advice, Luis met with Father Bossi at Immaculate Heart, who initiated the contacts for Luis to go to Del Amo and who also took him under his wing and taught him more Latin. This tutoring seemed to have worked, and Henry notes that when his brother arrived at the seminary that "he was already somewhat proficient in Latin."[6]

But in hindsight, Luis's decision to become a priest seems to have been the result not just of his own spirituality and faith, but something more earthy—at least his later recollections suggested this. He later admitted that he chose to become a priest because it was a status symbol. After all, hadn't the young Luis already had the honor of being the "high priest" at home when he played at saying Mass? "Going into the seminary was moving up in the world," he told an interviewer as he prepared to die, which may have made him reveal more of his inner memories and intentions.[7] Who is to say? But in his later confession, he also linked this sense of mobility to the poor conditions that he grew up with. "For those of us who were in the poor class," he said, "there was a certain prestige even about being a seminarian. I think I would be dishonest if I would not admit that that had something to do with it."[8] Of course, this was nothing unusual in the history of the priesthood, both in the United States and elsewhere, and is probably still the case especially in Third World countries that continue to supply many priests to the United States. Historically, becoming a priest was in fact a step up socially and economically. It gave you, as Luis noted, status, a sense of importance, but also lifted you up economically. This did not mean that becoming a priest would make you wealthy—hardly! But it did mean that the Church would provide all of your material needs. You would never be out of a job or homeless. It is amazing to even think that in one way or another all of these thoughts might have been circulating in Luis's thirteen-year-old mind.

Because he was already at Del Amo, Henry, who undoubtedly also went through the same thought process, was not privy to Luis telling his parents about his decision.[9] Had he been there, he would have witnessed that his parents, not surprisingly given their deep faith, supported Luis's choice. As Luis was preparing to graduate from Immaculate Heart, his father announced to the rest of the family Luis's decision. Joy and sadness were again the reaction. Happy for Luis but sad that he would be leaving. But at least, they consoled themselves, he would be with Henry. "Henry and Luis were very, very close," Teresa emphasizes.[10]

When that day came in early September 1948, Luis was ready. The trip on the train from San Antonio to Los Angeles, some 1200 miles in distance, on the Southern Pacific rail line had been coordinated between his pastor at Immaculate Heart Church and the Claretians at Del Amo. His father had bought his ticket and Tía Concha had packed his bag. He would not need many clothes since the seminary students wore uniforms, still another expense that Luis's father had to incur so that his son's uniform would be ready when he arrived. All of these preparations were made easier in Luis's case since the same preparations had been done for Henry one year earlier. No doubt Luis was apprehensive. He had never been on a train and he had to think of leaving his parents and his siblings. Only Abuelita Inez would not be there to see him off and give him her blessing. But anxiety must have been accompanied by eagerness to start what he strongly believed was his destiny.

When morning broke on that day, which promised to be a hot day in San Antonio as most September days are, everything was ready. Luis dressed nicely for the trip, but informally, like most young teenagers. After breakfast and some final play time with his sisters, Luis got into Uncle Joe's car, along with the rest of the family, for the trip to the downtown train station. Sister Teresa recalls Luis's happy feeling about his new adventure. "To him it was a joyous occasion," she notes.[11]

At the train station, they were among many other Mexican American families sending off loved ones to destinations near and far. Still, irrespective of the distance of travel, it was a Mexican American cultural tradition for the entire family to escort the family member leaving to *despedir*. "It was a big send-off," Teresa stresses.[12] It still is, although today this tradition takes place more at airports. Last minute conversations, cautions, and well-wishes filled the large train station. His suitcase checked in, it was time for Luis to get on the train. But before he did, Luis and his family encountered two other Mexican American families whose sons were also going to Del Amo. Luis knew one of them, Juan García, since both had been altar boys at Immaculate Heart, but he did not know the other, Gil Villanueva, who would become a good friend of Luis. Gil recalls that his entire family was there, including four aunts.[13] The train whistle blew—perhaps a fateful sign—and it was time for last hugs and kisses before the boys got on the train. As was part of the tradition in Catholic Mexican families, the boys kneeled and their parents gave them the *bendición*—their blessing that they be safe on their trip and in their new lives. This was not embarrassing because it was expected and because there were hundreds of *bendiciónes* taking place simultaneously at the train station, which had temporarily become converted into an informal chapel or church.[14]

The boys entered their car, found seats together, and went to the windows to wave to their families. The train slowly pulled out of the station but the boys undoubtedly remained waving until they could no longer see their loved ones. Now they were alone.

As the train headed west—first into the still-green rolling hills of south central Texas before it reached the large desert terrain in west Texas that would continue through New Mexico and Arizona, and accompany them all of the way into California, the Promised Land, and into the city of angels—the boys had a chance to get to know each other and exchange personal histories. All were Mexican Americans and were from the west side of San Antonio. They talked in both English and Spanish depending on the conversation. They began to bond because of their shared experiences and shared expectations. "We huddled together," Villanueva recalls. "We became friends by fear."[15] He also remembers Luis as being very friendly and an intellectual type. He felt a symbiotic tie with Luis. Each of their parents had packed bag lunches for the boys, and they soon got hungry and reached into them. Perhaps they had some money to buy a soda or candy on the train, but they relied mostly on their bag lunches, which contained familiar home foods. Gil Villanueva, for example, had taquitos made by his mother and more than likely Luis and Juan García also had good home Mexican food easily eaten on a train, such as tacos and burritos. The boys sat wherever they wanted to since there was no seating segregation for Mexicans on the train like there was for blacks. During the long hours of the trip and perhaps when they tried to sleep, homesickness and other feelings must have surfaced. Villanueva remembers feeling scared because this was his first trip away from home as it was for Luis. They had lived, as Villanueva correctly puts it, in isolation in the barrio. They had not dealt with many non-Mexicans, especially Anglos or "whites." "We didn't know what the world was like outside our own barrios," Gil notes. Luis perhaps shared some of these feeling, but at least he knew that he had his big brother waiting for him and that no doubt allayed some of his fears and feelings of loneliness.[16]

After what seemed like many hours for the boys, the train conductor finally called out as he passed by their car: "Next station, Los Angeles; next station, Los Angeles. This is the final stop for this train."

The boys exited and went to get their baggage. They found themselves in what seemed to them a huge underground tunnel, and as they entered the main sitting room they saw the name "Union Station." They had arrived.

Somehow, they connected with the people who would escort them to Del Amo. Villanueva believes that they were either people from one of the Claretian parishes in Los Angeles such as La Placita Church (Our Lady Queen of Angeles), or they may have been from the Claretian main headquarters in the city, or from Del Amo itself. He just remembers that after they got their luggage, they were taken outside into a station wagon and driven to Compton and Del Amo, their home for the next four years.[17]

II

Having arrived in midday, the boys were able to see the downtown buildings and even then-heavy traffic of Los Angeles. There was no freeway yet, so they were driven south on the main highway toward Compton. The ride did not take long, and in half an hour they arrived. They bypassed Compton, since the seminary was about five miles from the town itself. They were struck by the fact that they drove into a more rural area. They first sighted Dominguez Seminary, built on a hill, and were awed by the magnificent façade of the main building. It was awesome. They continued and crossed the railroad tracks and then sighted Del Amo on another hill. With its more functional architecture, it was not anywhere as impressive as Dominguez. Del Amo was a more simple concrete and steel building and had only been built five years earlier in 1943. They later learned that the building and grounds had belonged to the Del Amo family, which married into the Dominguez family, an older nineteenth-century ranchero family going back into both the Spanish and Mexican periods of California. The rancho land had originated from a land grant given to the Dominguez family by the King of Spain. Both seminaries together consisted of eighty-six acres of grounds.[18]

As they got out from the vehicle, the boys were struck by the rural setting with rolling hills and nearby cow pastures, which they later learned belonged to the seminary and provided both milk and beef. They also sighted and smelled pig pens that likewise served as a source of food for the seminarians and their teachers. They later were told or learned that the surrounding orchards belonged to Japanese farmers who grew flowers. No doubt they had been victims of the Japanese internment after Pearl Harbor when people of Japanese descent, including those born in the United States, were sent to internment (concentration) camps in California and elsewhere in the West. Many lost their farms and properties during their confinement, but those who were able to lease their lands for the duration were able to come back to them. Apparently, this was the case with those who tended their farms in the vicinity of the seminary.[19]

The boys would also come to distinguish Del Amo, which was one large building, by the resemblance of its construction to the letter *H*. In the middle of the two-storied H were the dorms on the second floor, and washrooms including showers. On the bottom floor were the classrooms. On one side of the H on the bottom floor was the chapel and on the other side the kitchen and refectory, or dining hall. Surrounding the building were a football field, basketball courts, and a swimming pool.

Overall, the boys were struck by the beauty and serenity of the location and the imposing structures. They had never seen anything like it before. This was their new home and it must have been impressive and probably intimidating. They would come to know Del Amo very well over the next four years.[20]

Luis and the other incoming first-year students would come to recognize Del Amo as their high school. This was the nature of the minor seminary. It was the first step in becoming a Claretian priest, but only the first of many steps that would take a total of thirteen long years. Del Amo provided the equivalent of a high school education but, of course, with a strong religious and spiritual component. Needless to say, it was an all-boys school. Olivares was excited on that hot September day (although not as hot as San Antonio) to be starting at Del Amo, but many years later learned he was told that the seminary was not accredited by the state. This fact, if true, was not something that a young and impressionable young boy such as Luis would have even understood, much less cared about.[21]

The initial adjustment to seminary life was difficult and a shock for most. Some have equated it to entering the military and that comparison has some merit since seminary culture possessed an almost military character. Changing into uniforms was one of the first changes that Luis and his classmates underwent. They put aside and stored the clothes they brought with them, and on the first morning of their Del Amo experience, they put on their uniforms. Carrying out the military analogy, their uniforms consisted of military-style khaki shirts, khaki pants, a blue tie, and black socks and shoes. They had at least three sets of uniforms. In addition, their parents also had to purchase a black suit and a white shirt to be worn on special occasions. The boys all knew how to dress themselves except, perhaps, for how to put on their ties. They had seen their fathers do so especially for Sunday Mass and some probably knew how to tie one by having observed their fathers. But some of the boys did not and so they relied and learned from those who did or how the priests in charge instructed them to do so.[22]

Part of the initial adjustment was just plain homesickness. It might not have affected Luis as much as his classmates because at least Luis had his big brother there. But it was different for Henry when he arrived and knew no one. "I remember," he notes, "going to sleep the first night I got there and just crying. I don't remember Luis crying. He never told me."[23]

Getting used to one's new classmates, of course, was part of Luis's adjustment. He knew only Henry and the two other boys who came with him on the train, but that was it. He soon realized that there were boys from other parts of the Southwest, California, and even a few from other parts of the West. At the same time, what helped in his adjustment, at least from an ethnic perspective, was that many of the students, especially in his class, were Mexican Americans like himself. It wasn't that Luis had a profound ethnic consciousness yet, but growing up in a predominantly Mexican barrio in San Antonio, he was aware of being Mexican. This number of Mexican American students had to do with the history of the Claretians in the Southwest, where they ministered in Mexican American parishes and recruited seminarians. In Luis's class about three-fourths, according to Villanueva, were Mexican Americans. But Luis also adjusted to new classmates. Since his entering class was relatively small, it didn't take long for him to recognize these boys. Villanueva remembers from ten to twelve students, while Pete Gómez, from the same class, puts it at eighteen. Either way, it was a small class that also reflected the small overall enrollment in the seminary. Henry's sophomore-year class only consisted of three students. Even though in the post–World War II era the Catholic Church grew and prospered, especially in parochial education and in seminaries, this seems not to have been the case at Del Amo. This may also reflect the fact that the Claretian order itself was small, and hence this affected its seminary recruitment efforts. Overall enrollment at Del Amo, from freshmen to seniors, was only about fifty students. This meant that Luis soon recognized by sight if not by name all of the students in the seminary. These limited numbers were likewise connected to attrition rates. The dropout rate was high. It was not unusual 50 percent or less of the students in one's class who remained all four years to graduate from Del Amo. In Luis's class, it appears that only eight to ten graduated.[24]

Luis and his classmates also had to adjust to a rigorous daily routine that began almost immediately after they arrived. With the exception of the weekend, the students would be woken up at 6 A.M., again like in the military. One of the priests would go down the row of single beds in the large dormitory and get the boys up. If there were some sleepyheads, he would hit their feet, saying, "Let's go!" They had thirty minutes to throw water on their faces, brush their teeth, comb their hair, and get into their uniforms. They were only allowed to shower twice a week, on Wednesdays and Saturdays. They showered in individual showers, covered so that they could not see each other. Modesty was emphasized. You wore the same underwear and socks in between showers. Since all the seminarians wore the same clothes for three days, none was aware of any odor. Jesse Flories, who was two years ahead of Luis, notes that these body odors were referred to as the "odor of sanctity."[25] Everyone had a separate dressing compartment so that no one could see you naked. After dressing in the morning, the seminarians then walked silently and in line down to the chapel where they prayed and meditated before Mass and taking Communion. "Half of the guys were always asleep during meditation," seminarian Pete Gómez acknowledges.[26] Without any breakfast, the students then attended a thirty-minute study hall. Breakfast followed. Classes began at 8 A.M. and went until noon, at which time lunch was served but preceded by a noon prayer. The students could then either return to their rooms and nap or go outside for recreation. Classes resumed from 2 to 5:30 P.M. This was followed by a snack, usually a peanut butter and jelly sandwich, and an hour of recreation on the football field or basketball courts. Before dinner, everyone had to go to chapel for more prayers and then retire to the refectory for dinner until 7 P.M. For the next hour, students would study at their individual desks in the study hall adjacent to the small library. At 8 P.M., they once again returned to the chapel for daily praying of the rosary for about thirty minutes. Then it was back to their dorms to brush their teeth and get ready for bed. Lights out were at 9 P.M. and one of the priests walked around the dorm to make sure everyone was in bed and that there was no talking or any other violations. You could go to the bathroom at night as long as you didn't disturb others. This was a routine that never changed in four years. Although there were no classes on the weekends, this regimented schedule carried over into these days. According to Henry, Luis adjusted well to this schedule, as did most of the other boys. No doubt there was a certain security in knowing that your whole day was planned for you. The routine, of course, was meant to teach discipline, obedience to one's superiors, and dedication to one's faith.[27]

III

Once settled in their new environment, the students began their classes. Although a seminary with the goal of producing new members of the Claretian order, Del Amo was still a high school and offered the normal range of classes at any high school. This included history, English, math, and the sciences. A different teacher would teach each class, although not all the priests had the appropriate backgrounds to teach these classes. At the beginning of each school year, the teachers were told by the Superior of the major seminary which classes they would teach. The assignments came from the Provincial Office which assigned all the priests. Some of the priests had taken specialization classes to teach a particular subject, while others were haphazard appointments. Hence, the quality of the instruction was uneven.[28]

The two main differences in the curriculum from normal high schools were that the students had to take religion courses and Latin courses during all four years. The most challenging course was Latin. Some students, such as Luis, already had some familiarity with it, but others did not and each year the Latin course became more difficult. The students had to read in Latin, write in Latin, and speak in Latin, although English could sometimes also be used. Gómez recalls that if one had a good memory, you could do well in Latin, but if you didn't then you could have problems, as he did. His memory of Luis tells him that even someone like Luis struggled with Latin.[29] The emphasis on Latin, of course, reflected the fact that, prior to the Second Vatican Council (1962–65), Latin was not only the official language of the Church, but the language of the Mass. All church services, with the exception of the Sunday homily, were said in Latin and so aspiring priests had to know the language. Vatican II changed this; beginning in the mid-1960s Masses could be said in the vernacular of a given region.

Memorization and learning by rote was characteristic of the educational model at Del Amo, as it was in both parochial and public education in American schools at that time. Schools, and even more so a Catholic seminary, failed to promote any form of critical thinking that went beyond the textbooks and materials used by the teachers. Of this practice, Arthur Zozaya remembers an amusing anecdote. "We had guys with a photographic memory," he recalls. "They knew classes by heart. In study hall instead of studying, they would read novels or other books that they placed in between their textbooks. They would do the same in classes. The teacher would ask one of them a question and he would stand up and give the correct answer. He then sat down and continued reading his novel."[30] It is doubtful that Luis was one of these boys. He was too obedient and respectful of his teachers to engage in a deceit like this.

In their religion classes, the students also learned about the history of the Claretian order and its founder, St. Anthony Claret. Since the Claretians were a missionary order, the boys were taught about Catholic social doctrine, such as aiding the poor and the oppressed, as well as the missionary goals of the Claretians. "We were missionary sons of the Immaculate Heart of Mary," Rudy Maldonado, another former Del Amo student observes. "We were studying and training to save souls anywhere in the world. That was a theme that ran through us all the time." This included learning about Claretian missionaries in places such as the Philippines, Africa, and Latin America. Maldonado later saw the impact of this training reflected in Luis Olivares's social justice work. He saw Luis as a missionary "dealing with the poor, disenfranchised, politically exiled, and outcast."[31] One can only imagine how the young Luis was impressed with the missionary goals and ideals of the Claretians. This would become part of his spiritual convictions.

In addition to instilling discipline, living arrangements were also intended to create a sense of community among the students. All students lived in two large dorms on the second floor of Del Amo.[32] "It was like military barracks," Gil Villanueva asserts.[33] As they arrived, they were given an identification number that they would keep for the entire four years. That number, among other things, corresponded to the dorm bed and locker assigned to the student. The number was particularly important for Brother Cruz, who did all of the laundry including bedding and students' clothes (one of the few perks in the seminary was having one's laundry done), to know which clothes went with which locker. Students had to put their numbers on their uniforms and other clothes, including socks and underwear. Even their ties had to have their numbers.[34]

The two dorm rooms were separated by the bathrooms, showers, and the laundry room.[35] Each student slept on metal-frame single beds; there were no bunk beds. They stored their clothes and other belongings in metal lockers that were located along the walls. The lockers had no locks, so that they could be inspected by the priests. "So you stuffed everything that you could in these including your illicit candy stash," Gómez recalls. While all of the beds and lockers were the same, the students did compete for beds when possible, such as when a student who had a bed next to the windows that partially surrounded the dorm rooms left the seminary; these beds allowed one to have fresh air. The larger and more muscular students usually won out in claiming these beds. Each morning the students had to make their beds, and in the late afternoon they had to turn their beds down to get them ready for the night.[36]

All four grades lived in the dorms, and students were not separated by grade. The bathrooms were communal. While the dorms were Spartan, for some students, such as Gil Villanueva, they were an improvement over home conditions. Some of the priests lived on the same floor as the students, while others had rooms on the first floor. Two of the priests had rooms adjacent to the dorms so that they could monitor the students.[37] These two priests were responsible for any student needs or emergencies. They also served as counselors, spiritual advisors, and disciplinarians, as needed. Each further acted as a "go between" in any activities the students were involved in or if they had academic issues with the teachers. If they were athletic, they became coaches to special baseball, football, and basketball teams that occasionally engaged neighboring schools.[38]

Despite the military-style conditions of the dorms, some of the students still played pranks on other students. One favorite prank was referred to as "short sheeting." After the beds were made up in the morning, some students would sneak back into the dorms and pick out a bed and redo it, pulling the sheets halfway down the bed. When the student attempted to get into bed at night, he couldn't, because the sheets were tucked tightly down the bed. As he struggled to get into bed, he might put a foot or feet through the sheets, causing a burst of laughter from the other students. Still another prank was to put the mattress on the edge of the frame so that when you sat down on it the whole bed would collapse. "You could get hurt but if you did all the funnier," Gómez notes. According to him, Luis was not spared from being "short sheeted."[39]

V

Mealtime was equally structured. Students went downstairs to the refectory for each meal. The students sat according to their ID numbers. This was referred to as "community order." Gómez, for example, was number 44 and his twin brother, Richard, was number 43, and so they sat together. Gómez believes that Luis's number was either 47 or 48, and he sat at the same table. The priests ate in the refectory, but at their own tables.[40]

The food was cooked in large vats that took most of the flavor away, although this did not affect the big appetites that most students had. Students looked forward to meals as a break in the daily routine. For the Mexican American students like Luis, the food was a big departure from the Mexican food they were used to. No Mexican food was cooked by the Anglo cook, who cooked "American." This adjustment included basics. "In my world," Villanueva states, "we never saw bread. I didn't know what bread was; the cook didn't know anything about tortillas." Still, he fondly remembers the wonderful smell of baking bread coming from the refectory kitchen. Students ate whatever was given to them and ate as much as they wanted, including seconds.[41] One common staple served almost every day was beans, which, Jessie Flores recalls, led to much passing of gas at night.[42]

Each week one table took turns serving the rest of the students, as well as the priests, who got served first. Another table was in charge of clearing tables after the meal, and another table had to wash the plates—big plates made out of melamine, an unbreakable material, to insure that the students did not deplete the plate supply. Some students also assisted the cook in the kitchen.[43]

While eating in the dining hall, students could not talk. You ate in silence; that was part of the discipline. Once every three weeks, the Prefect rang a little bell to signal that he was absolving the students from silence, and they could converse quietly. Such absolution would also take place on special feast days.[44]

Henry Olivares describes the daily meal routine in this way:

You ate in silence while the students took turns reading from a selected spiritual book. In the morning the book was *The Imitation of Christ* by Thomas à Kempis. This practice was voice training for future preaching. Other religious books included the lives of the saints, and each evening we read a short blurb about a Claretian who had passed away that day. The reading was closely monitored. If you made a mistake, a bell was rung and the error corrected. The goal was to read without being corrected, so you were expected to prepare beforehand.[45]

VI

"You didn't have time to be bad," Gil Villanueva observes, although that was not always the case for some boys.[46] What he really means is that the priests tried to insure that there was no idle time, and so they kept the students busy all of the time. This included a rotation of chores to everyone. These chores would be on Wednesday afternoons, when they were exempt from classes, and on Saturdays. Inside the building, they had to do housekeeping work, such as cleaning the toilets, bathrooms, hallways, stairs, windows, study hall, and chapel. They cleaned the marble floors with sawdust in order not to damage the floors. They also helped Brother Cruz with the laundry and took out garbage.[47] In addition, Wednesday afternoon was referred to as "gardening time," and the students had to perform two to three hours of work tending the gardens and grounds. They also worked on the adjacent farm operated by the Claretians, where they produced some of their own food in the attempt to be self-sufficient.[48] To some, gardening was a familiar activity. For example, Arthur Zozaya had learned from his father how to trim bushes and hedges and this came handy for him at Del Amo.[49] For others, gardening and farm work were totally unfamiliar. This was true for Villanueva, who had to learn how to tend to the horses and gather hay. Of these farm chores, he says, "I got into that; it was fun."[50] Gómez and some of the other boys were also assigned another duty with which they had no experience: they had to be barbers and cut other students' hair. They had to cut the hair short, giving crewcuts if the students asked for them. Gómez remembers cutting Henry's and Luis's hair.[51] Luis was particular about his haircut. "He didn't want it too close or too short, but not too long, and it had to be just so." Villanueva adds: "That part was pretty much Luis. He was a man of details."[52]

Luis's particularity may have reflected his own assigned chores. While he had to do some of the work that the other students did, in time as the priests recognized that he was not as strong and athletic as the other students, including his brother Henry, they increasingly gave him less strenuous or nonphysical chores. Instead, he worked in the library and in the chapel where he cleaned the organ and the priests' vestments. Villanueva believes, and perhaps the other students saw it this way as well, that this was not favoritism toward Luis, but the priests' only assigning students to do chores they seemed physically capable of performing. "You would tend to do more of things that were of your nature and personality," he says.[53] Because he was seen as strong, Villanueva had to help slaughter a cow on the farm. "You can't imagine what it's like for a city boy to do this," he observes and adds, "Luis was not that type."[54]

VII

Outside of the classroom, sports and recreation were a big deal at Del Amo. The priests wanted to keep the boys occupied, release their energies, and keep other growing feelings contained. Athletic activity was one way to do this. Many years later, Gómez realized this connection. "We are in our adolescence and we are feeling all our oats and our hormones," he says. "And there's no women; there's no girls. And so you take it out on eating a lot and you take it out very aggressively with sports. That's your outlet." On issues of sexuality, Gómez comments, "We were never talked to about being an adolescent and development, especially the sexual points. It was like repressed. Completely."[55]

Every student had to participate in sports based on the seasons. They played on intramural teams for team sports. This included touch football, basketball, and baseball. Other activities included swimming and volleyball. Nonathletic recreation involved supervised walks once a month into the surrounding countryside and walks to Redondo Beach, about ten miles from the campus. Gómez recalls that he and the Mexican American boys, including Luis, walked together as a group. These walks were usually headed by an upperclassman. On these outings, the students were given a quarter to buy candy or a soft drink but not much more. "You felt so cheap with a quarter in your pocket," Gómez observes. At the beach, the boys swam and enjoyed the sun. For lunch, a truck from the seminary brought sandwiches.[56]

Luis had to participate along with the others in sports, but he was not very good at any of them. He was tall, lanky, and slow, and just not athletic. He was also very nearsighted and wore glasses, and playing sports with his glasses was problematic. By contrast, Henry was bigger and stronger—a natural athlete—and participated in all of the sports. "I was always part of the action," Henry affirms, "but Luis was always kind of like in the background."[57] "He [Luis] was sort of mushy," Gómez observes. "He was not a strong kid at all." Still, despite his own dislike of sports, Luis had to be part of the teams, at least initially, and tried his best. Gómez notes that in football, Luis was not the guy who was going to block anyone because he was too frail. Gómez was the captain of one of the football teams that Luis was on, and notes that Luis was always one of the last to be picked to play. "He wasn't the first to be chosen," Gómez says. "You always took the studs first." Once when Luis was on his football team, Gómez used him as a decoy. He told him in the huddle: "Luis, as everybody goes by, you turn around and I'm gonna pass it to you." Nobody expected a pass to Luis.[58]

Sometimes when chosen, and if there were enough players on the team, Luis was relegated to the sidelines and became more of a cheerleader.[59] In time, Luis just became a spectator to rougher sports like football. Even though it was touch football, sometimes the players resorted to tackling and roughing each other up, especially if it was raining and the field was muddy and soft. This sporadically led to fights on the field.[60] Luis was not part of any of this. In later years, the priests allowed him just to keep score and to serve almost like a mascot, according to Henry.[61] Just what affect this had on Luis, it is hard to gauge, since he later never commented on this part of seminary life. From most accounts, he took it in stride and was not picked upon or harassed by the other boys for his lack of athletic ability. Luis did not identify like other boys with sports; he knew that his talents lay elsewhere. He seemed to have no concerns about being a macho. He had not come to Del Amo for sports.

VIII

He had gone to the seminary to study for the priesthood. He took this responsibility seriously. While it appears that he struggled somewhat in Latin and math, he seems to have done well in his classes, though school records providing his specific grades are no longer available. Some of his classmates remember him as a hardworking and serious student who was respectful of his teachers. He did not fool around in classes, nor was he among the students who enjoyed breaking rules and playing pranks. In an interview many years later, he admitted that he was a serious student and young person.[62] Villanueva remembers him as intelligent and studious.[63]

He was also a quiet student by comparison with more talkative classmates. Gómez calls him a *santucho,* or someone who was not outspoken. He was not someone, Gómez adds, who you would choose to help you play a prank on someone else. He also seemed more devout than others. "A lot of us broke many rules," Gómez admits, "but Luis was very respectful." At the same time, Gómez's memory is that Luis was not one of the best students, but was a "plugger," or did the best he could. Luis was probably somewhere in between being one of the best students and a "plugger." If he was not one of the very best students, he certainly was one of the most respected students by his teachers, and that respect was exactly what Luis desired—as he thought it bode well for his becoming an excellent priest. When asked to list some of Luis's qualities, his classmate Gómez cited the following: empathetic, loyal, reliable, respectful, dependable, well-behaved, sincere, and disciplined. These traits would serve him well throughout his seminary years and beyond. "He had all of that," Gómez concludes.[64]

IX

Despite his lack of ability in sports—a contrast to most of the other students—Luis still developed a very good relationship with most of them. As he matured through Del Amo, he developed self-confidence and translated that into working well with his fellow classmates. Many personal characteristics that he would exhibit later as a priest, especially in his leadership of the sanctuary movement in Los Angeles where he had to work and cooperate with many different people of diverse backgrounds, he was already demonstrating in the seminary. This is not to say that everything was rosy for Luis. Gil Villanueva remembers that a few guys picked on Luis because he was not physical; on those occasions Gil went to his defense.[65] Still, Luis generally developed a strong bond with the other students. This bonding was important, because the students came to realize that they were all in the seminary experience together and that they needed each other to go through the rigors of seminary life. "It was like we knew we were part of this thing," Henry Olivares says of the seminary experience. "We were all together."[66] Henry notes that very quickly Luis's classmates admired him because he was nice to everyone and tried to help others.[67] Luis was liked, older seminarian Ed Quevedo adds, because he was very open, had a warm personality, was gregarious, and just fun to be with.[68] The fact was that, despite his serious side, Luis had a good sense of humor. Many later at his death often mentioned that characteristic. He laughed a lot, Gómez notes and observes: "Luis was not the life of the party. He was not a performer. He was just a nice guy to have around and he was respected by most of us."[69]

But this respect also came from the fact that, as Gómez observes, Luis was more mature than others. He didn't fool around much, but others still appreciated him. "He was more proper," Gómez compares Luis with himself and some of the other Mexican American students. "We were *vagos* [goof-offs]. Luis was not a *vago*. He was not one of the hommies [street guys]."[70] But not being a *vago* or a hommie did not alienate Gómez and the other students from Luis. They accepted him for what he was and liked him.

Some of the boys even seemed to appreciate Luis because of his impeccable appearance, whether or not he was wearing a uniform. This attention to appearance and style would carry over into his later years. Gómez recalls thinking that perhaps Luis's family had money, because he was always well-dressed (when they could wear regular clothes) and -groomed. "He always smelled so good," Gómez remembers, and suspects that this was probably the result of either cologne or just good soap. "Luis was always well coiffed. His hair was always in place. His shoes were always well-shined. I wasn't surprised later on that he was so devoted to looking good."[71]

X

Of course, the most important relationship that Luis had at Del Amo was with Henry. He and Henry had always had a strong relationship as children, and this continued at the seminary. Strong brotherly bonds and yet they were so different. Not only was Henry a year older but, as noted, he was physically bigger and stronger and quite an athlete—everything that Luis was not. On the other hand, Luis was more studious, more personable, and perhaps more focused on his vocation than Henry. In a sense, they complemented each other. But it was not an equal relationship, since one was the older sibling. But this was okay, because Henry watched over Luis and taught him the ropes at Del Amo.

"Henry, what do I do next?" Luis would ask Henry, especially during that first year. Henry would help him out but notes that Luis very soon picked up the routine.[72]

For Luis, the most important thing was just knowing that Henry was there and that he could always consult with him. However, since they were in different grades, they didn't have classes together and in general did not hang out with each other much, since Luis soon made his own friends and Henry already had his.[73]

However, this brotherly relationship changed when, during his junior year, Henry was reassigned along with his class to another Claretian seminary in the Midwest. "There were only three of us," Henry explains, "so we were sent to St. Jude Seminary in Momence, Illinois, for our junior and senior years."[74] Both brothers lamented this change but there was nothing they could do about it. You followed orders. They exchanged letters (of which there are no remains), but these contained nothing profound, just asking how each was doing.[75] Luis was on his own now, but he was ready for that.

XI

While being together at the seminary at least allowed Luis and Henry to retain a sense of family, they missed their parents and siblings and just being at home. Despite being told that they now had a new family—the Claretian order—it wasn't the same. Family was family and always would be. So they adjusted and created a new sense of family, but from a distance. Distance was an operative word. San Antonio was far away, and this geographic fact meant that, with the exception of summer visits, the Olivares brothers could not see their family for months. For example, when Abuelita Inez died during Henry's first year at Del Amo, he could not return for the funeral as it was too expensive for his father to pay for a round-trip train fare. Luis would later tell him about the service.[76] Distance and family finances also meant that the boys could not go home for Christmas—that wonderful time for family. The students who lived closer to Del Amo or whose parents could afford to bring them home, by comparison, could share the joy of Christmas with parents and family at home. Others, including many of the Mexican Americans like Luis and Henry, could not. With no classes for a couple weeks and with fewer students around and less activity, this was the loneliest time in the seminary. Homesickness prevailed, although at least Luis and Henry had each other. The priests tried to fill in the gap by having Christmas events for the boys who remained. On Christmas Day, the students there were allowed to open presents sent from home. If their parents were too poor to send presents, the priests gave presents to those students. Luis and Henry always received some presents from their family.[77]

Luis and Henry adjusted and compensated for being so far away from their family by writing letters and, in return, receiving letters from home. The priests encouraged the students to write letters to their parents, but restricted letter-writing to once a week. The letters had to be put in unsealed envelopes, so that the priests could read them and censor them if need be. The priests also read all incoming mail for the students first, before distributing it to the boys.[78]

Teresa remembers keeping in touch with her brothers by writing to them. Her brothers reciprocated by writing back. She recalls that when her

SEMINARY

father and Tía Concha wrote to the boys that the younger siblings always wanted them to put in something from them.

"Ya Ya, tell Luis and Henry that I got A's in my report card," one of the siblings might say. They missed their brothers and regretted not growing up with them.

Teresa received a letter each month from her brothers, but laments that these letters were lost or thrown away later. She read the letters sent to Tía Concha written in English (which Teresa probably translated) and about how they were doing in school.[79]

Perhaps because of their separation from their family, both Luis and Henry often worried about them. Luis was especially concerned about his mother—Tía Concha—and how she was doing. "That was his main fondness for her," Teresa relates. "That was his mother and he was going to take care of her."[80]

On visitors day, the first Sunday of each month, when parents could visit their sons at the seminary, Luis and Henry had no parents to visit them. However, they were invited by other classmates to spend time with their parents who shared home-cooked food that they brought with them.[81] The exception to this lack of family visits came later, in the major seminary, when Damaso Jr., their older brother, visited them on more than one occasion when he was stationed as a marine in southern California. It was a wonderful surprise and a source of happiness for the boys to see their big brother in his snappy marine uniform. "Instead of going to town on leave and having a ball," Damaso said, "I would go to the seminary to visit my brothers." Of course, Luis and Henry proudly introduced Damaso to their teachers and friends. Damaso was a marine! Probably because of his military status, the priests allowed, at Luis's initiative, to have Damaso stay for lunch. But it was not the ordinary lunch in the refectory. It was a special lunch that Luis, always a stickler for detail, personally arranged with the blessing of the Prefect. Damaso was served his meal in a separate room with a menu specially prepared for him by the cook. Luis, who loved to decorate things and with his eye on style, made sure that his brother dined in splendor. "Luis would set the table with china, goblets, and give me a choice of what I wanted to drink, wine or soda or tea. Very elegant," Damaso fondly recalled.[82]

As a way of keeping his family in his thoughts, Luis sometimes told his friends about his mother, Victoriana, and about how she died early in his life and how he was raised by his grandmother and aunt. This sharing of memories was particularly poignant on one occasion. Each Mother's Day, the priests had each student stand up during the noon meal and say something about his mother. Most said the usual, general comments:

Luis Olivares with father, Damaso Olivares,
San Antonio, summer 1951.
(Courtesy of Henry Olivares)

"My mother is the greatest."

"My mom is the best mother in the world."

"My mother is the best cook in the world."

However, in his junior year, a maturing Luis got up and gave a moving and very personal testimony to his mother—probably referring to Tía Concha, though he may have conflated both his mother-figures in his short but remarkable speech. To this day, Gómez still recalls that moment: "It was Luis's turn, and he got up there and within fifteen seconds he had our attention. . . . He spoke eloquently about his mother. He was absolutely distinguished from the entire student body in the way that he spoke about his mother and how he expressed his feelings and what she meant to him. It was absolutely eloquent. This was the first time when I noticed Luis's ability to speak and to sway people. He was heads above the rest of us. I told him that when he was dying."

"You remember that?" Luis had asked Gómez.

"Yes, Louie. That's when you really showed me who you were."[83]

XII

After several long months, finally Luis and Henry could return home during the summer. The students were allowed to go home for a month and a half. Their father saved during the year so he could pay for their round-trip tickets to San Antonio. He would send the money for them to buy their tickets in Los Angeles.[84] For the rest of the summer, the students had to return for summer classes that were fifty percent less class time than the regular year.[85] Before they left, the priests cautioned them about temptations during their summer break—which meant the opposite sex. The priests were aware that young adolescents were certainly cognizant of girls, but they discouraged dating when they returned home. "If you are going to return to the seminary because you feel you still want to be a priest," they lectured them, "then dating is not appropriate for a priest."[86] Gil Villanueva believes that this was a contradiction. The priests seemed to acknowledge that the boys would be attracted to girls, yet they didn't want them to associate with them.[87] But in fact this was not necessarily a contradiction. The priests themselves had taken a vow of celibacy, and they wanted to begin socializing the seminarians into the life of a priest—they would have to sacrifice sexual relationships with women and could never marry. In many ways, celibacy would be the ultimate test for the students as they continued their seminary training. Of course, all of these rules assumed heteronormative behavior, which over the years may not have applied to all of the seminarians.

With these warnings in their ears, Luis, Henry, and the other students went home. They welcomed this respite. They reconnected with their parents and siblings and caught up with all of the family news and gossip. They saw their siblings growing up and noted how much they looked up to their big brothers and respected them, almost as if they were priests already. For his part, Luis just wanted to relax and do very little. "I've been working all year," he told his family. "Now it's time for a vacation so that's what I want to do."[88] He was falling back on the special and pampered treatment he had always been given at home. He liked being taken care of and fawned over. He never quite gave that up, even in his more politically active life many years later: his downtime resembled how he was treated at home in San Antonio, but the pampering came from his good friends in the Los Angeles area.

Besides relaxing, Luis and Henry visited their extended family of cousins, aunts, and uncles. Everyone wanted to see them—the "little priests." Since their family was predominantly Spanish-speaking, the boys mostly spoke in Spanish on these summer visits. But they also resumed playing and having fun with their siblings. Of course, given the strong faith of their family, they spend much time at church and even served Mass as altar boys at Immaculate Heart. Luis and Henry told their parents and siblings about the seminary and about their new friends and visiting some of their homes. Teresa notes that each year she saw how Luis and Henry were maturing. They were becoming young men. She noticed in particular how much more serious Luis was becoming, though he still retained his sense of humor and still laughed and joked. She witnessed how Luis never changed with his siblings and never considered himself better than them because he was receiving a Claretian education in California. But he also expressed concern about any family problems and during these visits tried to help resolve them. He saw himself as a peacemaker. He was especially concerned about Tía Concha and her wellbeing and how she would be taken care of as she got older. He never lost that concern. She was his dear mother.[89]

Summer vacation was special, but like all special things, it ended too soon. Before they knew it, Luis and Henry had to board that train back to Los Angeles.

XIII

On each return to Del Amo, Luis Olivares exhibited more of the maturity that his sister Teresa observed during his summer visits. By their junior and senior years, it was expected that all students begin to assert leadership. Most did so through sports and being captains or co-captains of their teams, or being responsible for certain extracurricular activities such as leading lower-division students on hikes or beach trips. Luis was not interested in any of those activities and certainly not in sports. But he loved music and had so even as a young boy. He especially liked the organ since he had played it a bit back at Immaculate Heart. So Luis jumped at the chance not only to be in the choir, which every student was required to be in for some time, but to lead the choir and be the choir director, which was something else—it was special! Since he had exhibited musical talent and knowledge, all of it self-taught or what he had learned in elementary school, the Prefect appointed him director in his junior year. Luis thrived in this role. He selected the music, mostly familiar church music, and directed the choir members at their practices and performances. Luis was also the organist, so on some occasions rather than directing, he played the organ for church services or other events in the chapel. For Sunday Mass, he led the choir in singing various church songs. Christmas was, of course, a special time and he chose particular Christmas carols for the choir to sing at Christmas services, before many of the students left to be with their families. The Easter season was a second special time and again he led in the singing of appropriate songs for Holy Week services and for Easter Sunday. One special day for the choir was when they sang, directed by Luis, for the feast day of St. Anthony Claret, the founder of the order. Other events that required his musical leadership were concerts for families and for the nearby Compton community. Luis had leadership ability and he found in music at Del Amo a way to express it.[90]

XIV

Catholicism and ethnicity in the United States were always two sides of the same coin. There had never been a totally neutral, nonethnic, melting-pot American Catholicism, and that is still the case today. Catholics have always identified as *Irish* Catholics, *Italian* Catholics, *Polish* Catholics, *Mexican American* Catholics, and so on. European Catholics, to be sure, because of their greater acculturation, assimilation, and acceptance of being "white" by older-stock English and northern European Americans in the post–World War II period, had a less "accented" Catholicism, but still retained remnants of their ethnic based Catholic background (St. Patrick's Day, Columbus Day, etc.). Ethnicity and American Catholicism also had to do with the racialization of certain Catholic groups, in particular those of Latin American background such as Mexican Americans and Puerto Ricans. Perceived as racially different, inferior, and nonwhite, Mexicans, for example, whether U.S.-born or immigrants from Mexico, faced racial discrimination in jobs, education, housing, health facilities, public accommodations, and numerous other forms of prejudice. The Catholic Church in the Southwest, where it ministered to people of Mexican descent, was not immune to racist practices. In some areas of Texas, Mexican Americans had to attend separate Masses or had to sit in the backs of churches. Although this discrimination was not the norm, patronization and dismissive attitudes toward Mexican popular forms of religiosity were more nuanced expressions of an ethnic/racial divide.

Del Amo and the Claretian order were not by any stretch a racist institution or organization. The Claretians after all had a history of working in Mexican American communities and this included Spanish-speaking Claretians, especially from Spain. Still, ethnic differences manifested themselves at the seminary despite a general "melting-pot" approach at the school. As in the public schools, for example, teachers, in this case the priests, changed the Spanish first names of the Mexican American students so Enrique became Henry; Luis became Louis; Gilberto became Gil and so on. Some of this name changes or Anglicizations had already occurred in the elementary schools, but they continued at Del Amo. Mexican American students such as Luis and Henry recognized that they were being perceived as different and that the prevailing norm was "white" students, who were primarily of Irish, German, or other European family backgrounds. English names and the English language were the norm. It wasn't that the Mexican Americans were segregated at Del Amo, but that they still felt that the pressure was on them to prove that they were "real Americans." It was an elusive feeling, but one that Luis perceived. "I noticed a little bit more in what it meant to be a minority," he later admitted. By "minority" he didn't mean that Mexican Americans were only a small number of the student body; in his class, there were more Mexican Americans than Anglos. "Minority" meant that he was made to feel, perhaps subtly, that he was different from the Anglo-American boys. It was a feeling, not an overtly structural manifestation. "I guess it's just a feeling that maybe they didn't expect as much from you 'cause of where you came from," he added.[91] Holding low expectations for Mexican American students was a prevailing attitude certainly in the public school systems in the Southwest and California where Mexican Americans students attended the notoriously segregated and inferior "Mexican schools." Low expectations at Del Amo were not as pronounced as in the "Mexican schools" but present enough to make a students like Luis and other Mexican Americans feel that the teachers may not have expected as much from them. It was an intangible factor, but one that egged Luis on to prove that he could be an excellent Claretian priest. Rather than allowing this feeling to get the better of him, he got the better of it and overcame it.

This sense of difference showed itself sometimes in episodic fashion. Pete Gómez noticed that the Anglo students on occasion were given certain favors. He recalls that a couple of the older Anglo guys at Del Amo who had driver licenses were allowed use of school cars to go into town to get certain items for the school. He called them "kiss-ass guys." None of the older Mexican Americans, as far as Gómez knew, were ever extended this privilege.[92] Rudy Maldonado does not remember any particular forms of discrimination, but does note that sometimes in sports there were fights between Mexican Americans and Anglos.[93] This sense of difference, as noted earlier, extended to the Spanish Claretians who, in their Hispanophile way, made their Mexican American students feel that people of their background were not as developed as those from Spain.[94] When he returned home in summer, Luis would sometimes tell his siblings that there was lots of discrimination, not just in the seminary but in the L.A. area as well.[95]

One particular form of discrimination at the seminary that the Mexican Americans experienced was the prohibition against speaking Spanish.

The school was an English-only institution. Ironically, even the Spanish Claretians adhered to this language policy. Though one can imagine that among themselves these proud Spaniards—who in classes asserted their lineage from Catalonia, the Basque country, Asturias, and other provinces of Spain—spoke Spanish.[96] Of course, the use of Latin in the Mass and other church services likewise pointed out the irony of the English-only policy. Clearly, this language policy was directed at the Mexican American students, and they knew it. This only further made them feel different and that somehow their bilingualism was un-American. Gil Villanueva doesn't recall that there was an actual prohibition against speaking Spanish as much as an implied sense that it was wrong to do so. "It wasn't prohibited so much as we just didn't do it."[97] If the Mexican Americans did speak Spanish and it was overheard the Anglo students reacted with hostility—not physical but verbal.[98]

Although these conditions and attitudes were not particularly pronounced, they still elicited an ethnic reaction by the Mexican American students. They tended to bond more with each other, not for self-protection per se, but to make themselves feel good about being of Mexican background. In their not-yet-politicized way they were saying, "We can be both Americans *and* Mexicans." They expressed a pluralist view of America and of their school. What is interesting is that this pluralism was very much part of the ideology of the Mexican American civil rights movement of that era, before the Chicano Movement of the 1960s. The Mexican American Generation, of which Luis and Henry and the other Mexican American students were a part, through its leadership rejected the melting pot that was intended to produce a generic American. Instead, they promoted a pluralistic view of American society where you could be a good and proud American citizen while maintaining pride in your ethnic heritage. Unconsciously or not, these young boys were saying the same thing. Perhaps they had heard it from their parents or kept in mind that they came from predominantly Mexican American barrios, where beginning with their parents they were taught to be proud of being Mexican and of speaking Spanish. It was almost a natural reaction for them to bond with each other—especially in a situation where, for the first time, they were mixing with non-Mexican people and in which their ethnic integrity was somehow being challenged and questioned. And so they bonded.[99] Of the "melting-pot" ideology, Luis later remarked, "It was imposed. You felt it was imposed and you put up a resistance to it. Part of it being you hung around with your own in some instances."[100]

Part of this ethnic bonding was the coming together of the Mexican

American students from Texas such as Luis, Henry, Gil Villanueva, and Pete Gómez. According to Gómez, they became the "Texas contingent." They felt that the California students, though primarily the Anglos, looked down upon them and made fun of them because they were from Texas, and that the California kids felt themselves to be better and smarter. "We formed a little bit of a clique because it was self-survival," Gómez says.[101] Ethnic bonding extended into sports where, curiously and contradictory, the school allowed the intramural teams to be formed around ethnic identity. And so there was an Irish team and a Polish team. Consequently, the Mexican Americans formed a Mexican team, and its players came to be referred to, perhaps negatively, as the "Mexican clique."[102]

Part of this ethnic consciousness on the part of the Mexican American students involved using the term "Chicano" among themselves. The term originated from Mexican working-class immigrants in the 1920s, but by World War II it had been appropriated by rebellious young Mexican Americans especially the *pachucos* and zoot-suiters of that period. They self-identified as "Chicanos," and the term became countercultural. Gómez notes that it was not widely used at the seminary, but sometimes one would say in a joking way, "Hey, Chicano guy."[103]

Ethnic awareness among the Mexican Americans at Del Amo also led them to defy the English-only policy and speak Spanish among themselves. They didn't always do so, but when they felt the need especially on the school grounds where they would be less detected, they spoke Spanish; it was their mother tongue. This included Luis and Henry. "We would joke in Spanish," Henry notes. When they talked about home and shared their memories of their family, they reverted to Spanish. "Whenever we wanted to relate something personal, something that happened in the past, we would always use Spanish," he concludes.[104]

So ethnicity was not absent in the isolated atmosphere of Del Amo. Ethnic Catholicism asserted itself in that setting and Luis Olivares and the other Mexican American students were part of this process. Ethnic consciousness would always be a part of Luis Olivares. He was Mexican American, and through his later work with Central American refugees, he also became Latino. He was not ashamed of his ethnic roots. How could he be ashamed of his parents, of Abuelita Inez, of Tía Concha, and of his brothers and sisters? To do so would be to be ashamed of himself. This is not to say that, he didn't feel at times some ambivalence about his identity; how could one not be at times ambivalent when others are telling you that you're an American, not a Mexican. Still, Luis had a strong foundation of ethnic identity and that served him well as he matured and developed a confidence about being a Mexican American or an American of Mexican ancestry. Henry makes an additional, telling point when he notes that race or skin color was part of this ethnic equation. He notes that, because he was much more light-skinned than Luis, if he wanted to he could have "passed" as white although he was just as proud as Luis was about his Mexican background. But his point is that because Luis was darker-skinned, he had less choice, even if he had wanted, to pose as "white." "So," Henry stresses, "Luis would make the point to say, 'I am Mexican.' He kept his identity always. He always knew who he was."[105]

XV

There is no question but that the aspect of Del Amo that made the biggest impression on Luis and the other students was the strict discipline that the priests administered and the different ways that they imposed it. Discipline had little to do with student behavior. Students were generally well-behaved, although Pete Gómez points out that his and Luis's class, with the exception of Luis, could on occasion be rather disorderly and oppositional. Gil Villanueva calls his classmates "mavericks."[106] Of course, students were punished when they did something wrong but the whole point of discipline went beyond that. All future priests had to learn discipline, including self-discipline, and obedience to one's superiors. The hierarchical Church could not function otherwise. But for the Claretians, discipline went one step further. They were missionaries, and missionaries had to be disciplined in order to travel to difficult locations to convert people. "You were going to go out and conquer the world for Christ," Arthur Zozaya observes about learning about missionary discipline.[107] As soon as the students arrived on campus, they were given a rule book called *The Mirror of the Postulant*. It was a little brown book that contained all of the rules of conduct to be followed at Del Amo. The students had to learn these rules and strictly obey them. There were no exceptions and woe to those who broke the rules. "You violated any of those things and there were consequences," Gómez recalls. "The consequences ran from the sublime to the ridiculous."[108]

Not only did the freshmen receive the rule book as soon as they arrived, but shortly thereafter the upperclassmen put them through the rigors of what Maldonado compares to an army boot camp. Discipline was not only mental but physical. You had to discipline your body. The students had to traverse a series of physical obstacles, such as jumping through tires and rope climbs. The whole point was to see if you could take it without either quitting or rebelling. If you quit or rebelled that was a sign that perhaps you didn't really have a vocation.[109] The students also soon learned that being at Del Amo was like being almost in a prison. You could not leave the grounds without permission, and you were confined to the campus. The seminary had its own infirmary, and so basic illnesses could be taken care of without going elsewhere. Only on a rare occasion would you be allowed to go see a doctor in Los Angeles, for example.[110] Of course, wearing uniforms was part of the discipline. The students were literally soldiers of Christ and looked the part.[111] Everything was structured at Del Amo. The ringing of bells was very symbolic of discipline. For every activity, the priests ranged bells. The bells told you when you had to be somewhere, and signaled when this was finished and you had to go to another activity. Bells, bells, bells. Maldonado equated the bells with the Almighty, and so, he thought, you better obey those sounds. "It was very regimented," he says of the seminary. "We were governed by the sound of the bell which was the voice of God. The minute that bell rang, you just better be where you're supposed to be."[112]

Discipline also involved interpersonal relations. If the priests believed that two students were getting too friendly with each other, they separated them in order to avoid any problems, such as those of a sexual nature, although they didn't use the word "sexual." "The unwritten law," Henry Olivares points out, "was 'seldom one, never two, better three or more.'" This prevented what were called "particular friendships."[113] Touching one another was frowned upon. You could touch another student during sports but not otherwise. "You couldn't touch another student," Pete Gómez remembers, "because that might lead to feelings of, they called it, impurity."[114] Jessie Flores, who as a senior was a monitor at night in the dorms, notes that he was never aware of any improprieties among the students in his years at Del Amo.[115]

Silence was to be observed constantly. You could talk almost nowhere: not in the dorms, the refectory, the halls, study hall, while doing your chores, or the classrooms except when you were called upon and, of course, no talking while in chapel and during prayers except to recite the prayers and rosary. Only during sports and recreation could you talk. Otherwise you observed the rule of silence. "You couldn't talk, which is a very unusual thing," Gómez notes. "It's rather an abnormal atmosphere. The whole environment was very abnormal."[116]

But the most memorable form of discipline that seminarians remember were the public confessions and public penance associated with this form of discipline. Students were encouraged to go to confession daily or at least weekly; however, once a month there were public confessions. In the evening, the students assembled in the study hall, where the Prefect would call on some students to engage in public confession. The main difference between a private confession and a public one was that instead of the student confessing on his own certain sins, he was accused by the Prefect of certain wrongdoings. It was not a baring one's soul but of confronting specific, alleged wrongdoings. On top of this, these accusations came from fellow students who were encouraged to report on other students and to charge them with certain improprieties. The Prefect would then have the student stand up and in front of the entire student body he would be accused of various faults or "what they called your shortcomings. Your bad deeds," Zozoya mentions.[117] "It was like a cleansing of the soul," Gómez admits. "Actually, it was more like the Inquisition."[118] These shortcomings could involve falling asleep in chapel; looking around during study hall; talking during silent period; being late for class or for another activity; or not doing your chores well. You then had to admit or deny the accusations. Most felt no choice but to admit. At one public confession, Gómez was accused of keeping pictures of movie stars Rosemary Clooney and Doris Day in his wallet. He did so because he liked their singing and thought "they were cute." The accusation came from Jim Higgins, another student who had looked into Pete's wallet and found the pictures. Gómez had no choice but to admit guilt. He then had to kneel down for twenty minutes in front of the other students. "I didn't mind kneeling down," he notes, "but they took my pictures away." At the same time, he admits that the next day, he and his friends "beat the shit out of Jim Higgins."[119]

The priest called these public confessions "conferences."[120] Every student had to undergo a public confession. "You couldn't escape it," Gómez mentions. Even Luis had to experience this, although he was never accused of many shortcomings. Of this, Gómez, with tongue in cheek, says: "Luis would probably have accused himself of not being pious enough."[121]

Besides kneeling down as a form of immediate punishment at these public confessions, the Prefect meted out other forms of penance. After several admissions of guilt, a student received demerits that would lead to being denied a recreation period or having to do extra chores such as cleaning the toilets.[122] However, the most severe punishment and certainly the most public form of penance involved being sentenced to prostrate yourself at the beginning of one of the meals at the entrance to the refectory. The students were supposed to walk around you, but many took the occasions to instead step on you or even kick you. "Of course, that was the time to get even with somebody so you stepped on him hard," Gómez recalls.[123] Arthur Zozoya adds of this practice: "But you know how kids are. Kind of kick you and say 'oops!'"[124]

During Lent the accusations increased, as did the punishments. One such punishment would be to kneel in front of the chapel altar for a long time. Still another involved the priests making students beg for their food at meal time. You had to walk around the refectory on your knees with your plate begging for others to feed you. "It was an act of humiliation, they called it," Gómez says of this and other punishments. "You must be humiliated, like purged."[125]

Public confessions and public penance were indeed intended to teach not only discipline but humility. What damages these punishments might have done both physically and psychologically is another matter. By contemporary standards such practices might fall into the category of child abuse, but there was a different mindset in seminaries in those years. Undoubtedly, the priests believed that they were not cruelly hurting or abusing the boys, but only impressing upon them the importance of obedience and penance. Luis Olivares, perhaps he was one of the better behaved students who did not receive many punishments, remained curiously silent about these practices for the rest of his life.

XVI

Graduation finally came after four long years, though perhaps for Luis Olivares they did not feel like long years. Graduation at Del Amo did not involve a big celebration. The faculty handed out diplomas, but the student did not wear caps and gowns. Some parents who lived nearby came, but those who farther away, like the Olivares family, could not attend. They had not also been able to attend Henry's graduation in the Midwest seminary the year before. Graduation from Del Amo was only the preliminary phase to becoming a priest. Nine more years still remained, beginning with the novitiate. Luis Olivares looked forward to the next step.[126]

THREE

Priesthood

"I'm leaving and I'm never coming back," Luis Olivares told his younger siblings in the summer of 1952.

"Luis, please come back; don't leave us forever," his sisters anxiously responded.

"Don't be *tontas* [fools]," Luis jokingly said, "of course I'm only leaving for a while."[1]

Luis did return, but never for long, over the next nine years. Studying for the priesthood would now be accelerated, and there would be much less time for family.

I

The next step was the novitiate (the training of the new learners), located in Los Angeles in the Westchester district, where the Claretians had their Western Province headquarters at 1119 Westchester Place. The headquarters was a former three-story mansion donated to the Claretians by a wealthy family in one of the older, elegant neighborhoods not far from downtown. The novitiate was an abandoned Red Cross Service Center utilized during World War II for army recruits and returning service men. A building on the southwest corner of this city block was used as a dormitory. This would be Luis's home for one year. Henry had already been there the year before, but had now gone on to the four-year college at Dominguez Seminary back in Compton. It was a year during which Luis and Henry saw little of each other and had little contact. "They didn't want the novices to become familiar with what was going on in the major seminary [Dominguez Seminary]," Henry notes.[2]

As a novice (new learner), Luis was one of twelve young men, including those who had finished with him at Del Amo plus some new additions from the Eastern Province of the Claretians.[3] They were at the novitiate to enter into a cloistered year of prayer, meditation, and spiritual study. It was

86

almost like a monastery. There was no academic work. They were to learn about the Claretian order and about Claretian spirituality. As Henry put it, "to learn in general what it means to have a spiritual life. To develop your prayer life and meditation." The novices were to prepare to take their first religious vows at the end of the year. It was an intense and focused period.[4] There would be much discipline, silence, and seclusion. They would not be permitted to leave the grounds unless they needed medical attention. Contacts with families were limited. They couldn't read newspapers or listen to the radio or watch television. They had little idea of what was going on in the world, such as the U.S. military intervention in the Korean War or the election of general Dwight D. Eisenhower as President of the United States. They picked up some of this news, but only here and there. Their whole mission was to grow spiritually to confirm their vocation. "It's a year of very intense spiritual life," Henry observes.[5] Gil Villanueva adds of this year, "You were basically going from a secular world and deeply into a religious world."[6] For him, the novitiate represented a weeding-out experience to determine who would go on for the priesthood. He likens it to a marine-style boot camp.[7]

Communication and conversation were limited in part because they had to learn to converse in Latin. Luis and other novices had to participate in a conversation class to become fluent in Latin. They certainly learned more Latin, but there were loopholes, and where possible the novices spoke in English. Some did not learn as much Latin as expected. In his year at Westchester (as the novitiate was referred to), Henry felt that the Latin class was not very effective. "So most of the time we just fooled around," he says.[8]

One of the changes from Del Amo that Luis and the other novices experienced was exchanging their uniforms for cassocks. A cassock was an ankle-length garment with a close-fitting waist and long sleeves that one wore over one's clothes. Black in color, the cassock symbolized that the novices were becoming priests, and so they had to start to look the part. To impress this on the novices, the priests initially had them participate in an investiture ceremony. They were invested with the cassocks that their families had bought for them at the end of the minor seminary. Having being invested, they now wore their cassocks all day long. They wore them even during recreation periods, but not when playing basketball or tennis.[9]

Daily routine at the novitiate was even more structured than at Del Amo. You got up and went to the chapel for an hour of meditation and Mass. Then breakfast, and you cleaned up afterward. You returned to the chapel to say "office," which involved the reciting of psalms as a group. This was followed by a morning session on the history of the Claretians, as well as a class on assigned religious reading including the Bible. Lunch and then back to the chapel for midday prayers. You could then either go to the library or study hall to read, or to the chapel to pray. According to Villanueva, you could also take a siesta. For reading, the priests recommended different books on spirituality. This was followed by classes on spiritual theology. As Villanueva puts it, "religion, religion, religion." You then had an hour for recreation that involved either gardening, playing basketball or tennis, or walking around the grounds. During recreation you were told not to make much noise. Villanueva observes that having fun was discouraged. Recreation was followed by more classes on spiritual theology and later one on spiritual counseling with the Novice Master, followed by more prayer. Dinner and later reciting the rosary and more prayers. Bedtime.[10] You followed this routine through Saturdays. Sundays were more relaxed, with a big Mass that included not only the novices and priests, but also wealthy contributors to the Claretians, including movie stars. Pete Gómez remembers seeing actress and TV star Loretta Young at these Masses. After Mass, the Claretians treated the laypeople to a big breakfast, from which the novices were excluded. The rest of Sunday was involved with chores and recreation.[11]

One of the differences from Del Amo was that Luis and the other novices slept in the dormitory, but each one had their own very small and very sparse room—although they did have more privacy. They had to stay on their side of the novitiate and were not allowed to enter what was referred to as Provincial House, the administrative headquarters of the order and the sleeping quarters for the priests.[12]

The novices were assigned to a Novice Master: a priests who directed the novices in their daily routines and represented the chief authority figure for them. "He was like our guru," Villanueva emphasizes. The novices dealt directly with him on all matters, especially those of a spiritual nature. The Novice Master for Luis's class was Father Aloysius Ellacuria, a Spaniard who had a condescending attitude toward all of the novices, including the Mexican Americans. According to Villanueva and Gómez, Father Ellacuria had a reputation as a very spiritual person, almost holy, considered a mystic by some, and was known for counseling not only the novices, but several movie stars who came to him. But his English was not very good, which only discouraged the novices from actually conferring with him. He looked down on the Mexican American novices and seemed to believe that they were inferior to the Spaniards. "I think it is something that carried over from the conquistadores," Villanueva adds, noting that this was a sentiment that bothered all of the Mexican Americans, including Luis.[13] But they had no choice but to deal with him.

With Father Ellacuria's strict guidance, the novices focused on their spiritual training and exercises. While the novitiate was hierarchical like Del Amo, the novices were encouraged to share their thoughts and reflections on their spiritual readings. Many of these texts were in Latin, but fortunately in their classes they could speak in English. The priest would lead the discussions but prompted the novices to participate. A maturing Luis Olivares began to shine in these discussions. He had already given signs that he had a speaking talent at Del Amo, but he improved even more at Westchester. He was good at verbalizing, according to Villanueva. "He had the knack for it," his fellow novice says. "He expressed himself very well." By contrast, Gil felt that he was not as good. "Luis came into his own at that point," he concludes, "and would become as a later priest, especially at La Placita Church, an extraordinary preacher."[14] Besides their spirituality classes and learning the history of the Claretians, the novices conferred with the priests about their classes, or anything else on their minds, at least once a day. It was very intense.[15]

Whether speaking in English or Latin, speaking in general outside of classes was strictly limited. The rule of silence that defined life at Del Amo also prevailed at Westchester. For most of the day, including at meals, the novices had to be silent. But silence did not impede the novices from bonding together in this one-year seclusion. They were small in number, and they were all one another had. Plus some, like Luis and his classmates from Del Amo, were already friends. The new environment only created stronger ties among the young men. As Villanueva puts it, "When you go into this spiritual boot camp, it brings you closer together."[16]

Cloistered for the year, the novices had no contacts with their families. Occasionally, a family might visit from out of state, but for the most part little physical contact with family members occurred. This extended into the following summer, and Luis could not return to San Antonio then. In addition, they could not phone their parents, and receiving letters was discouraged, though a few letters would be distributed each week. On the other hand, they were encouraged to write the occasional letter home. "They were trying to break us off from the outside world all together," Villanueva notes. At Christmas they could receive presents from their families.[17] The novitiate attempted to impress on the novices that, as future priests, they had a new family—the Claretian order—and so they had to wean themselves from their real families. This was partially done at the minor seminary, but it was still tough for eighteen- and nineteen-year-olds at the novitiate. "You left your past life . . . and from that period on you would not be encouraged to hang on to your mother and father, brothers and sisters," Villanueva observes. "Now, the order was your family."[18]

Steeped in their religious and spiritual activities, the novices also had to undergo penance and public confessions. Penance involved physical suffering. The priests encouraged them to kneel on the concrete floor of the chapel, rather than in the pews, for spiritual reasons. They also encouraged the novices to put a little pebble in one or both of their shoes to deliberately feel uncomfortable but to offer this up to God. You did this for a day, but not so much as to cause bleeding or bruising. The novices didn't see this as a cruel punishment, but as penance. They also fasted each Friday, when no meat was allowed anyway under the then-current Catholic Friday restrictions, but their meals were more limited. Fasting increased during the forty days of Lent. "You fasted in the old fashioned traditional way of the olden days," Villanueva points out. "It meant a meager amount of breakfast and the same thing for lunch. The evening meal was sparse and most of the time it was devoid of meat. We lost weight, let me tell you."[19]

Within this strict and limited structure of the novitiate, Luis Olivares, by all accounts, thrived. He adjusted well to the routine and the demands on the novices much better than some others. As he had at Del Amo, he got along well with his fellow students. "He really enjoyed that year," Henry says of his brother, "being together with his classmates."[20] He embraced the challenge of becoming more spiritual. This seems to have come easy for him given his earlier disposition to become not just a priest but an exemplary one. Villanueva noticed that Luis developed his spirituality faster than the rest of the novices. "He had a strong, unequivocal vocation," he stresses. "There was no doubt in his mind." By contrast, "most of us had a harder time in the novitiate because that is a tough year."[21] As at Del Amo, the priests seemed to favor Olivares and allowed him more leeway, for example, in doing chores. Instead of gardening, cleaning bathrooms, and the other work assigned to the novices, Luis volunteered to decorate the chapel as one of his main chores, and he was allowed to do this. For his decorations, he got the Novice Master to obtain for him the materials he needed. Gómez recalls that Luis was even allowed to leave the novitiate to get these materials.[22] For recreation, Luis walked around the grounds, but the Novice Master also allowed him as part of his recreation and chores to direct the choir and prepare the music for church services, just as he had done at Del Amo. These less physical chores and forms of recreation may have also been due to Luis's still-frail appearance. Villanueva recalls that, while Luis was not sickly at Westchester, he was not very robust.[23]

At the same time, Luis once again demonstrated his leadership and growing maturity, both emotional and spiritual, by his active role as director of the choir. He selected the music and hymns, both in Latin and English, and led the practice sessions with the other novices, all of whom participated in the choir. But Luis was their leader. They looked to him for directions, which he provided with his body language at the front of the choir.[24] He also played the organ and accompanied the choir in some of the musical selections with it. With Luis as its musical director, the choir performed at Sunday Masses and on feast days, including Christmas and Easter. The other novices respected his leadership and saw him coming into his own during the novitiate year.[25] Part of his leadership, Gómez believes, came from his looking the part despite his thin physique. As Gómez had observed at Del Amo, Luis always looked impeccable. He could make a cassock look like an Armani suit. "His pants and his cassock and everything else looked terrific," Gómez admiringly notes.[26]

Finally, in July 1953, Luis and the other novices concluded their novitiate year. It had been a rough and demanding one for all of them, although Olivares seems to have taken it in stride. This was not the case for others. It was, in fact, a weeding-out experience, and at the end of it, one-fourth of the novices did not go on. Either they decided on their own that they did not have a vocation, or they were not recommended to continue in their training. To go on to the next phase of the major seminary, you had to be recommended to do so by the Novice Master, who reported this to the Claretian provincial government.[27] Gómez's brother Richard was one of these casualties who was not recommended to continue.[28] Those who did advance, including Luis, formally concluded their novitiate by participating in an elaborate ceremony on July 16, the feast of Our Lady of Mount Carmel, in the chapel, with some families in attendance, though not the Olivares family, who could not afford the trip.[29] The highlight of the ceremony came when the novices took their initial vows of poverty, chastity, and obedience. These were not their final or perpetual vows, which would come at the end of the major seminary, but it did mean that they were now part of the Claretian order. They were Claretians.[30] From Westchester, the new Claretians immediately moved to begin the major seminary at Dominguez Seminary back in Compton. Luis Olivares was ready for the next challenge. He was now a step closer to becoming a priest.

Dominguez Seminary was the equivalent of college. The main emphasis was studying philosophy, although other liberal arts courses were also taught. You studied philosophy for all four years. The seminary, however, on its own was not accredited by the state of California, largely owing to the absence of advanced degrees such as doctorates among most of the faculty. To compensate for this, the seminary linked itself to Loyola University in Los Angeles, a Jesuit college, and the students officially received their degree in philosophy from Loyola. The seminary was small in numbers, and when Luis and his class arrived the total enrollment was no more than forty students. Not all were graduates of Del Amo. When he began, Luis's class had eight or nine students, and by his senior year it had dwindled to three students. Dominguez was a two-story building, with the student dorms upstairs and with the classrooms, study hall, chapel, and refectory downstairs. In this setting, Luis and the others now were college men.[31]

Although Dominguez was structured around the teaching of philosophy that would be useful to future priests in their ministry, as much as possible within limited resources, it also provided a liberal arts education. The college or major seminary referred to its curriculum as an "in-house program."[32] A typical freshman class schedule might consist of the following courses: Philosophy, Latin, Greek, American History, History of Philosophy, Algebra, and English. In your second year, you would take classes in the History of Philosophy, Cosmology, Psychology, English Literature, Latin, Sociology, and Speech. A third-year curriculum consisted of the History of Philosophy, Metaphysics, Epistemology, English Literature, French, Biology, and Speech. Finally, in your senior year you took Theodicy, Ethics, Criticism, American Literature, Government, Geology, and Speech. Courses in Philosophy and Latin were mandatory, but other liberal arts courses were electives so that, for example, instead of French, you could take Spanish.[33] Philosophy courses were longer than the other classes and averaged four to five hours a week. In keeping with most American college curriculums, Dominguez offered one history course centered on Europe and the United States, with nothing on Latin America or other parts of the Third World. This limited range of classes seems contradictory since the Claretians, as noted, are a missionary order, and so some of their students might become missionaries in the Third World.

Given the limited enrollment at Dominguez, students studied in small classes on a semester system. It was not unusual for a class to be composed of no more than eight students, and sometimes fewer, such as when Luis became a senior and only two other students remained with him in his class group.[34] If one of the three got sick, there would only be two students in the class. Arnie Hasselwander, one of Luis's classmates, noted that this happened once. "Louis had a couple of teeth pulled and has been sick," he recorded in his diary, "that left only 'Dopey' (Adolph Ortega) and me in class."[35] Sometimes, however, classes were "cycled," meaning Luis, for example, could take a class with students one year ahead of him.[36] However, in philosophy classes you were restricted to only the students in your class. Such small classes were almost like a private tutorial.[37] Despite the smallness of the college, Luis and Henry never took a class together, although they were reunited for three years. They did not, according to Villanueva, have as strong a relationship as in the past—although this might have had more to do with the tradition at Dominguez that upperclassmen did not "buddy" with lowerclassmen.[38]

The philosophy courses were the most significant for the students and were more intense. The readings were all in Latin or Greek with some exceptions for more modern philosophers. The students resented this; although they had studied Latin both at Del Amo and at the novitiate and could pronounce Latin, many, if not all, still had problems reading Latin, including Luis. "I never did master Latin so I was lost," Arthur Zozaya notes.[39] He and the other students found Greek even more difficult. They read or tried to read Aristotle and Plato in both Latin and Greek. In these classes, to the students' relief, they could discuss in English sometimes, although the professor mostly lectured in Latin and expected his students to respond likewise.[40] Aristotle and Plato were two of the major philosophers that they focused on more, although they did study others such as Hegel and Kant.[41]

But the main philosopher that the professors introduced the students to was St. Thomas Aquinas, who is recognized as the key founder of Catholic philosophy, and hence Aquinas was the centerpiece of the philosophy curriculum at Dominguez. This was considered scholasticism.[42] The students learned about other Catholic philosophers, especially in their History of Philosophy classes, but they always came back to Aquinas. The Church accepted him as the basic foundation for understanding the Catholic faith. Living in the thirteenth century, Aquinas put together an integral system of philosophy based largely on Aristotle. "He took Artistotle and baptized him, so to speak," Father Ralph Berg explains. As Berg further notes, Aquinas bridged Aristotle with Catholic teachings. Berg also recalls that the professors did critique Aquinas and pointed out where he went wrong, but that these mistakes did not invalidate his whole approach, which still fit together. He adds that even Vatican II, a few years later, did not change the basic philosophy of the Church, which was still based on Aquinas. While Aquinas was integrated in all of the philosophy classes, each year the students concentrated on certain aspects of philosophy, such as logic, cosmology, psychology, epistemology, ethics, and metaphysics.[43]

While there was clearly a Catholic orthodoxy to the learning of philosophy, according to Berg, the classes nevertheless encouraged a critical perspective, a departure from Del Amo. "We were constantly being challenged to be critical," he stresses. As were most other classes, the philosophy classes were lectures by the professors, but they allowed for a good deal of discussion, in which the students expressed their own opinions and much dialogue resulted.[44] Arnie Hasselwander recalled that during a philosophy class in which they discussed art, "we came to the conclusion that art is amoral and that the morality of art is on the part of man."[45] Berg further notes that students were graded by midterms, final exam, and class participation. In addition, they had to write a philosophy term paper of five to six pages. The papers were short, Berg notes, because the professors stressed quality over quantity. The teachers encouraged their students to type their papers, but because the school had few typewriters, most papers were handwritten.[46]

Philosophy absorbed a good deal of the students' time, but they also took classes in other fields both in the humanities and sciences. Arnie Hasselwander, who would become a very good friend of Luis's recalls that in their Spanish class the professor, Father Ambrosi, tried to teach the subject, but his own Spanish was not very good. "Louis would talk Spanish to him," Arnie recalls with humor, "and poor Frank [Ambrosi] couldn't understand or translate."[47] In another Spanish class taught by Father Urrutia, a Spaniard who spoke with a distinct Spanish accent, Arnie got Luis and Pete Gómez to argue with the priest about his pronunciation, giving Arnie a chance to finish his homework for the class. He explains that sometimes these arguments would take up the entire class period.[48] Father Urrutia also taught French, and, to the students' dismay, he insisted that they memorize their prayers in French.[49]

The students further studied classical literary texts in their European literature course. In Luis's senior year, he and the other two classmates who remained, Arnie and Adolph, took a literature course in which they read and studied Dante's *Divine Comedy* with Father Gielow. This led to a funny episode that involved Arnie, who was more willing to break the rules than other students. "I forgot about a test which was on the first ten people in hell and their punishment," Arnie says about Dante. "I didn't remember a single name from Dante so I created my own list—only to find out later [that] Gielow lacked my sense of humor." In his list, Arnie included Pope Pius XII, who was Pope during World War II and the postwar era. "I put him in hell," Arnie went on, "because he failed to write an encyclical (papal letter) condemning the actions of some Germans who were killing Jews. In short, I called the Pope an anti-Semite. I can still hear him [Gielow] screaming at me, declaiming Pius XII was a saint, and how could I condemn so many of my fellow Claretians to hell." Needless to say, Arnie got an F on the test. "Every time Louis brought this up," Arnie notes of his future conversations with his friend, "we would laugh until tears came to our eyes."[50]

Father Al Vásquez recalls teaching Olivares in an Introduction to Sociology course explaining the "do's and don'ts for Christians in a secular society." Olivares, according to Vásquez, was an inquisitive student with a very analytical mind. "He always wanted to challenge you," he observes, "wanted to know the 'why' of things, which is good." Olivares raised questions in class and organized discussion groups. Vásquez notes that Luis did very well in the class.[51]

The routine at Dominguez was much more relaxed than it had been at Del Amo or Westchester. Students still lived in the dorms and had to get up early for Mass, but the rest of the day largely consisted of taking their classes and studying. There were fewer bells compared to Del Amo and, to the delight of the students, the rule of silence was not as pervasive in college. After lunch, they had time for a siesta, as well as an hour of recreation such as football and basketball, since Dominguez had fields and courts for these sports. Most classes were in the mornings, and so afternoons gave the students more time to study. However, prior to going to bed, they did have to go to the chapel and pray the rosary. But in general, the students had more time to themselves.[52]

Within this context of college life, Luis seems to have done well in his classes, although he labored a bit in some, which led even someone as diligent as Luis to temptations of cutting corners. As at Del Amo, the records of grades and student assessments no longer exist or cannot be located. According to Henry, Luis was a good student at Dominguez. Fellow student Gil Villanueva corroborates this and also recognized that Luis was continuing to mature, especially as he now was interacting and competing with more motivated students like himself. Gil particularly noticed how much more Luis spoke out in classes when they included discussions, and how he was developing as an orator, an ability that seemed to come naturally to him. Villanueva recalls that in these class discussions Luis had a lot to say and often engaged in dialogues with the professors.[53]

Despite Berg's assessment of Dominguez, the students still had more opportunities to enjoy themselves and occupy their minds. Although now young men between ages eighteen and twenty-two, they still missed their families and had less and less contact with them. In their four years at Dominguez, Luis and Henry did not go back for summers. Family visits during the summer were not allowed, and the students instead had to stay on campus and take summer classes. Indeed, as at the novitiate, the priests generally discouraged them from reconnecting to their families, although limited correspondence was permitted.[54] Consequently, family life became more and more focused on memories and speculation of how loved ones were doing. Luis and Henry on occasion talked about how they missed seeing their siblings grow up and participating in family events. They were fortunate that they had each other, but this could never be enough, even as they were coming to accept the Claretians as their new family. "Eventually we would say, it's really not our life," Henry notes about their real family. "It's their life and what can we do? There was nothing we could do."[55]

One of the major changes that Luis Olivares encountered at Dominguez was meeting Arnie Hasselwander. They would become lifelong friends, but they were very different. Arnie, who came from the Midwest, was a happy-go-lucky guy who wanted to become a priest, but not at the sake of having fun and pushing the envelope. He was smart, funny, courageous, daring, and loyal to his friends. Luis was attracted to Arnie, as were many of the other students, for his being so *travieso* or naughty, but in a charming way. Luis was different in that he was very focused on his vocation, but at the same time he was not a prude. He had a wonderful sense of humor, as did Arnie. That drew them together. For the first time in his seminary years, Luis became also a bit daring and challenged the rules up to a point. "He had opened up a lot," Pete Gómez says about Luis at Dominguez.[56] This aspect of Luis's personality, which Arnie brought out, is important, because in his later ministry and in particular in the sanctuary movement, Father Luis would challenge authority both secular and religious. Luis did not participate in all of Arnie's antics at Dominguez, but in enough to show that he was not the total "choir boy" that the priests had typed him as. Evidence of Luis and Arnie's relationship, which would continue beyond Dominguez as they both advanced in their education for the priesthood, comes from a remarkable document. Beginning at Dominguez, Arnie kept a diary, in which he recorded daily events, including some of his rule-breaking activities and his efforts to engage others with him in this, including Luis. He would later add explanations to the diary entries, and in the 1990s corresponded with Henry about his memories at Dominguez. Arnie also gave Henry a copy of some of his diary, especially parts where he mentioned Luis. Arnie's diary goes from 1956 to 1960 and covers part of his and Luis's years at Dominguez and their theology education at Claretville Seminary in Calabasas, California, and Washington, D.C.

Arnie pushed against the rules at Dominguez in many ways. Some of this involved activities within the confines of the seminary. For example, he and some other students kept an illicit television in the basement of the building, which they connected to the antenna on the roof without the priests' knowledge. Arnie does not mention in his diary where they got the set.[57] In the basement, he and others watched more TV than they were allowed upstairs. They called the secret TV the "prized machine."[58] In a diary entry, he explained how they hid the TV. "When we finished watching TV," Arnie wrote, "we lowered the box into the hole, put the false shelve back, replaced the boxes on the top shelf onto the bottom, and it looked like a normal storage place."[59] In a later entry, Arnie notes that Luis was not involved in the TV "deal." In this entry, Arnie also assesses Luis's partial participation in his antics. Luis was willing to challenge authority, but only within certain limits. The reason, as Arnie explains it, "was simple. He had a genuine vocation to the priesthood and wasn't going to jeopardize his reputation on our high risk schemes. Louie, like most seminarians, took highly calculated risks with very low-consequences."[60]

Besides keeping the hidden TV in the basement, Arnie also kept a secret refrigerator. He, Gil Villanueva, and Adam Rivers converted an old freezer into a small refrigerator where they kept sodas, beer, and "altar wine."[61] Not only were they breaking the rules by hiding the refrigerator, but also the rules against drinking.

Despite the rules against drinking, it occurred among some of the students, led by Arnie. They also produced moonshine liquor that they called "white lightning." Somehow, they put together a still and brewing apparatus that actually went undetected well after Arnie and his classmates had left the campus. In fact, the apparatus was not detected until that part of the building was torn down. "Amateur drinkers like us," Arnie told Henry in 1999, "experienced ridiculous consequences. In retrospect some were humorous." However, for one student, John Hudak, it was not humorous. He stored two bottles of "white lightning" in his locker; they were discovered by the priests and Hudak was expelled from the seminary. Arnie notes that Luis did not drink the moonshine because he had better sense.[62] At the same time, Luis did drink some of the altar wine that Arnie snatched from the chapel but, according to Arnie, everyone did that, just to find out how it tasted. With his characteristic sense of humor, Luis, in turn, used the altar wine to play a trick on Arnie. One evening, he and fellow seminarian Kenny went over to Arnie's bed and gave him a bottle of wine that Luis probably told Arnie that he had taken from the chapel. Since Luis spent much time there with the choir, it was a believable story.

"Hey, Arnie. Look we brought you some altar wine," Luis told his gullible friend.

But the trick was on Arnie. "I drank as much as I could in one big gulp," Arnie explained, "before I realized it was colored water and not wine! Louie and Kenny had set me up!"[63]

Arnie was all for breaking rules that made no sense to him, while Luis was impressed with Arnie's gutsy attitude and was willing to play along with some of his actions. Luis was all for having a good time and for skirting some of the rules, but not anywhere as blatantly as Arnie. In turn, Arnie loved and respected Luis; however, their friendship was not going to deter him from having fun at the seminary.

One area in which Arnie and Luis collaborated was playing pranks on other students. One particular prank that Luis loved to recount later in his life involved a prank in the chapel and the "apparition" of St. Anthony Claret, the founder of the order. One day Luis and Arnie were decorating the chapel altar with flowers. Another student, John Senerius, showed up tired and sleepy. Arnie told him that under the altar was a big open space where he could take a nap. Luis picked up on this and told John that he, Luis, often slept there during siesta time because it was the coolest place in the building, especially on warm days. According to Arnie, Senerius was very gullible and took a nap under the altar while Arnie and Luis left to do some gardening chores. Senerius was still sleeping when the students came into the chapel for the evening rosary. One of the other students spotted him there, but, not recognizing Senerius, shouted out, "Oh my God, it's St. Anthony Claret!" Another student also screamed out, believing that they were witnessing an apparition. "What really happened," Arnie later explained, "was Senerius woke up, didn't know where he was, and looked at us. All you could see was his head. He wasn't wearing his glasses and even frighten [sic] the hell out of me. He then walked toward the sacristy and everyone realized it was John and not Claret. Louis and I pointed our fingers at each other as if to say 'that was your fault.' We then laughed through the rest of the rosary."[64]

Arnie and others, including Luis, sometimes cheated on their work or were not as attentive as they should have been. One such transgression involved taking class notes from another student without his permission. Arnie notes that Jere Holmes took great class notes, which he typed up but refused to share with other students. Consequently, one day when Holmes was out playing tennis, Arnie, Gil, and Luis somehow got access to his notes and took pictures of them. One of them had a camera and took pictures of the notes and later had the photos developed in the dark room kept at the seminary and then copied the notes by hand. Holmes never found out.[65] Cheating also involved finding out the questions prior to an exam. This happened on one occasion when Arnie was trying to finish his senior dissertation, but also had to take an American literature final exam, along with Luis and Adolph. Prior to the exam, Arnie was asked by another professor to run off his test in the staff office. While doing this, he noticed in the waste basket a copy of the American literature exam. Arnie took it and wrote out the answers using his books before the exam was given. Having done this, he used the three hours for the exam to finish one of the chapters to his dissertation, unnoticed by his professor. "Louie noticed I completed my test and answered all the questions," Arnie recalled. "He quickly slipped me a note saying he needed help because he had trouble remembering some of the authors. Since cooperation leads to graduation, I let him and Adolph look at my test. They knew I didn't study for the exam because I was working on my dissertation. I [later] told them they underestimated my brilliance!"[66] How all this went on without the professor noticing is quite interesting since there were only the three students taking the exam. Arnie finally finished his dissertation by engaging in another offense. He plagiarized the rest of his thesis from the dissertation that Henry had completed the year before, which may have been available in the library, and from that of another former student named O'Malley. The plagiarism seems not to have been detected.[67]

In another class on Dogma, Arnie put cheat notes in his textbook, and when called upon, simply read from these notes. When Luis was called upon, they somehow switched books and Luis responded with the cheat notes. "This method helped us fake our way through Dogma," Arnie remembers. Apparently bored in one of his philosophy classes, Arnie also took his textbook apart and inserted sections of the *National Geographic*. "When things got boring in class," he later related to Henry, "I turned to the section [in the magazine] which had pictures of naked native women!"[68]

If students were caught breaking rules, they were "clipped," meaning they received demerits for disobedience that could lead to being punished or even being asked to leave the seminary. You could also be clipped by not being allowed to take your perpetual or permanent vows as a Claretian at the end of college.[69] "I remember being 'clipped' over the years," Arnie noted, "and then receiving the letter from my Provincial [head of the Claretians] stating the reasons why. They generally were the silliest and most petty reasons. I could have given a hundred better reasons."[70] Being clipped prior to graduating and taking perpetual vows could be very serious and could mean not being allowed to graduate or not being allowed to go on to the last phase of seminary life before being ordained a priest. Clipping might also result from being confronted with wrongdoings at public confessions that also were part of seminary life at Dominguez. Already Arnie had been accused at public confessions of losing his temper in sports, breaking silence on certain occasions, not getting up on time, and a lack of humility.[71]

Arnie and Luis graduated and went their separate ways, but they had forged a strong friendship at Dominguez. Arnie had touched that part of Luis Olivares that was rooted perhaps in his sense of humor, but also a part of him that, by his time at Dominguez, wanted to express itself in terms of a more liberated seminary experience. This, of course, is a contradiction in terms. Seminaries by their very definition are not liberated environments. But something in Luis was beginning to rebel against the stifling and confining nature of the seminary. He was undergoing, in his own way, a youthful rebellion and youthful alienation from authority figures. He wanted more of himself and perhaps of his desires to be expressed. There was something of the *travieso* in Luis that had been repressed, and now as a young man coming into his early twenties, some of this was beginning to emerge. Luis was not Arnie, but there was something in Arnie that he admired and wished to emulate. That other part of Luis was still there—the part that accepted discipline and authority. Dominguez began to expose contradictory aspects of Luis's personality and to reveal a very complex individual—a complexity that would only continue to evolve into his later years. In a way, he was beginning to struggle with his vocation and his humanity. Dominguez brought out that humanity; the transgressions he participated in humanized him. Of the internal struggle within Luis that became more evident at Dominguez, Arnie wrote in 1997: "Louie was a highly complex person who definitely wanted to be a priest; however, 'people' placed many obstacles in his way. Both of us were 'clipped' . . . so after that, I began looking for a way out, but Louie insisted on 'fighting the good fight' until the end."[72]

Arnie may have brought out a certain fun-loving and even transgressive side of Luis Olivares, but Arnie did not dominate or unduly influence him.

PRIESTHOOD

Luis was still his own man, and he had his own leadership skills. He continued to exhibit this leadership and his charisma—a charisma recognized by many in later years—at Dominguez. "I remember that he blossomed as a seminarian," Henry says of his brother at the major seminary. Luis showcased his leadership by again being named choir director at Dominguez by his junior year. He loved music and relished this opportunity to direct the other choir members. This is where he thrived. "Luis was wonderful with music and liturgy," Henry adds.[73] Arnie agreed in his diary: "Luis had a marvelous talent for music."[74] Luis's skills and leadership as the choir director were enhanced and expanded because he directed not only the college students, but the high schools students at Del Amo. While at Dominguez, the choirs of both schools were combined for certain occasions, but Luis now had to direct thirty choir members. He rose to the occasion and made the combined choir into a functioning and inspirational musical group. When they performed, the Del Amo students wore their uniforms and the Dominguez students wore their cassocks. They not only performed together but had to rehearse together under Luis's direction. Rudy Maldonado, who was in Del Amo, at the time recalls that directing the high school kids and keeping order was quite a challenge for Luis. The students, according to Maldonado, were a "bunch of ruffians," but he notes that Luis was able to keep them under control. "You knew when he wanted your undivided attention," he says.

Besides directing the choir, Luis also displayed his leadership at Dominguez by being the president of the Mission Academia. This was a student organization whose aim was to raise funds to purchase medicines for the Claretian missions in the Third World, but especially in the Philippines, where the Claretians had a long history of service. His fellow students elected him president in his junior year. Luis personally visited hospitals in the Los Angeles area and got them to donate medicines for this project. However, the biggest fundraiser involved Luis, on his own, designing Mother's Day and Father's Day greeting cards that not only the students at both the major and minor seminaries purchased, but were sold in many Catholic schools and, according to Henry, sold all over the world. Luis in this enterprise supervised the other members of the club in the packaging and mailing of the cards. He also went into Los Angeles to make the arrangements with a company that printed the cards. The sale of the cards resulted in much revenue, which Luis turned over to the Provincial at Westchester. Henry notes that Luis's involvement in Mission Academia added to his popularity among the other students.[75] In one of his diary entries, Arnie, tongue in cheek, wrote of Luis's leadership in the club: "In its day that was quite an organization—a big money maker. Luis was the right man for the job. The first wise move he decided on was to make sure Adolph [fellow student] and me couldn't be made members: He didn't need guilt by association."[76]

If directing the choir and heading up Mission Academia were not enough, Luis also edited the college's newsletter published each month. He served as editor for three years beginning in his sophomore year. He wrote articles for it as well. Adding to his business acumen, he managed the expenses for the publication and negotiated with the printer in Los Angeles.[77]

Olivares further displayed leadership by beginning to question some aspects of seminary life, such as what seemed to be the continued discriminatory treatment of Mexican Americans. Spanish was still outlawed at Dominguez, and some of the Spanish Claretians in the administration devalued the Mexican American experience or seemed to imply that the Mexican American students were not as smart as the Anglo ones. Gil Villanueva recalls this persistent bias, and notes that Luis, too, began to see that something was not right about this attitude and treatment of the Mexican American students. Gil spoke out against it, as did Luis but in a more subtle way. He recalls that he and Luis did not directly speak about these conditions, but that each sensed that they were on the same page. While Gil emphasizes that Luis was not a "rebel," he recalls that in his own way Luis questioned these practices, and among his Mexican American fellow students, referred to the Spaniards as "*gachupines*," a derogatory term for Spaniards. To Villanueva, this questioning of and opposition to discrimination represented part of the roots of Luis's social-justice consciousness, which would manifest itself much more explicitly in the 1970s and 1980s.[78]

As evident by these various leadership roles, Luis Olivares seems to have become even more confident of his abilities and of his vocation at the same time that his identity as a person and as a future priest evolved. He was beginning to confront his multiple selves. Of this maturity and evolution, Henry concludes of his brother's college years, "I think he began to formulate already his ideal of what he wanted to do as a priest. He already began to envision himself being in administration, being in control, and he already began to sense that sense of power in himself over the running of things and the operation of whatever programs were available. . . . He didn't wait around for somebody to say we should do this. He would say, 'No, I'm going to do this.'"[79]

Having finished his last final exams in the late spring of 1957, Luis Olivares looked forward to his graduation on June 16, when he would receive his BA in Philosophy from Loyola University. Perhaps more importantly, he would take his perpetual or permanent vows as a Claretian the following month. He would still not be an ordained priest, and four years of theology study lay ahead, but taking one's perpetual vows was nevertheless a milestone. But first graduation. Without any of their families present, Luis, Arnie, and Adolph received their degrees; they would be the last such cohort to get degrees from the Dominguez-Loyola connection, as the Jesuit school then dropped its affiliation with Dominguez, due to the seminary's library being deemed inadequate for a college education. That evening, one of the priests, Father Resendez, took Luis and Arnie (perhaps Adolph had other plans) out to a steak dinner.[80]

Unfortunately, Luis and the other two taking their perpetual vows hit a snag. Luis was caught up in an effort by the college administration to punish students like Arnie and Adolph who had been "clipped" several times—as had Luis although not to the same extent. They were informed that their taking of perpetual vows would be delayed and might not even be approved. Apparently they were not told on what specific grounds this serious delay or denial was based, other than their participation in "extracurricular activities" not approved by the seminary. "These were tough days for Louis," Arnie noted in his diary. According to Arnie, Luis spoke to Father Joachim De Prada, a former Provincial and a friend of his family when he served in San Antonio. It seems that De Prada intervened on behalf of a troubled Luis, who believed that someone was "trying to make a mountain out of a mole hill." Arnie and Adolph, on the other hand, seem to have taken all this in stride, and Arnie believed that this might have been a fortuitous lesson for Luis. As Arnie put it, "it was a good lesson in discernment." At the same time, he admitted that it caused Luis grief.[81]

Not knowing their final fate, Arnie, Adolph, and Luis were given permission to take a short vacation together in the mountains. During the trip, they discussed their "possible pending doom—what would happen to us if we were not approved for vows." As Arnie later explained their discussion, "Adolph and I felt it would be a sign from God we didn't have a real vocation. Luis insisted he had a calling, and any rejection would only mean God didn't want him to become a Claretian but eventually he would be ordained a priest."

However, Luis's spirits were lifted later that day when they each received letters from Dominguez. "Louis was the first to open his," Arnie observed. "The joy and relief on his face was something to see." The administration informed all three of them that they had been approved to take their perpetual vows on July 16, 1957.[82]

Luis Olivares, first year of theology at Claretville Seminary, 1957.
(Courtesy of Henry Olivares)

Returning to Dominguez, Luis, Arnie, and Adolph got ready for the big day. With none of their families present, the three first took their yearly vows, and, most importantly, their perpetual vows, for the first time. They now moved on to four years of theology. They had dodged a bullet and priesthood was now in sight.

III

In late August, Luis prepared to move to Claretville to begin his last four years of seminary training, focused on theology, before he could be ordained a priest. He looked forward to this last phase, which would involve two years at Claretville and two years at Catholic University in Washington, D.C. Luis was now twenty-three years old and very different from the young thirteen-year-old who had begun the journey at Del Amo. He was now a young man who had survived nine rigorous years of seminary training. He never doubted that he would. There is no evidence that he ever wavered in his goal of becoming a Claretian priest. He embraced his vows of poverty, chastity, and obedience. While he had known poverty in the San Antonio barrio—even though his family was better off than others— he had never really seen himself as poor. In his seminary training, poverty was a theoretical issue, since he and his fellow seminarians' needs were provided for. To Luis, poverty meant an embrace of the poor, and this belief would manifest itself more as he continued in his priesthood. He had learned that the Claretians as a missionary order worked among the poor and that this was a priority for them. He accepted that concept, though poverty as poverty did not affect him personally. Chastity did not seem to be an issue per se for Luis. He understood and accepted that he would never be married and have children. He seemed accepting of this; for him, he was "married" to the Church and his order, and his "children" would be his future parishioners. Sexual feelings were supposed to be repressed and struggled against; one can assume that to one degree or another this affected Olivares as it did all of the other young men. Some eventually concluded that they could not live with this repression and left the seminary. Others, like Luis went on and continued to wrestle with it. Obedience was, of course, drummed into Luis and other seminarians from the very beginning. While, at Dominguez Luis challenged some authority, in general he accepted obedience to authority and to the hierarchical Church. Comfortable with all of this, he and the other seminarians who had graduated from Dominguez and received their perpetual vows arrived at Claretville on September 3, 1957.[83]

Claretville was located in Calabasas, just a few miles northwest of Los Angeles in beautiful, rolling-hill country. If Del Amo and Dominguez were semirural and pastoral, Claretville represented a significant location change. Here is how Henry Olivares describes the change: "The physical transition was more jarring as the students moved from the inner-city park like oasis of Dominguez Seminary to the spectacular and serene landscape surrounded by the Santa Monica mountains, known as Claretville."[84] It resembled a gentleman's estate or a country club. In fact, it was the former mansion of razor-blade magnate King Gillette and later the home of movie director Clarence Brown.[85] It was idyllic. It was different, but Luis and his cohort immediately liked the setting.[86] He and the others drove up and settled in on a quite warm day. While they had worn their civilian clothes on the drive, they quickly exchanged them for their now-familiar black cassocks. On arriving, Luis was greeted by Henry, who had already spent his first year at Claretville.

After settling into their accommodations, they very quickly began their studies. Having studied philosophy at Dominguez, theology, or the study of religion and God, seemed just one more step up in abstract thought. Theology was fundamental for future priests, since their entire role as priests lay in their understanding of God and their faith, as taught by the Catholic Church. Theology would guide them not only in their priestly duties, but in their personal lives. The seminary wasted no time in loading up the students with an array of theology courses that first year. Initially, they had to study Dogma, Canon Law, Church History, Moral Theology, Scriptures, Greek, and Homiletics, or how to write and deliver a homily or sermon. They didn't take all of these classes at once; they were spread out in a two-semester style system. Most classes met twice a week. As at Dominguez, the students were required to read and translate in Latin, and took their exams in Latin. Professors, all Claretians, delivered their lectures in Latin. Discussion occurred both in Latin and English. However, the use of Latin began to be modified toward the end of the first year, and some professors began to lecture in English and to administer their exams in English. This change foresaw similar changes that would be introduced more widely, as a result of Vatican II.[87] Latin seemingly became less of a problem for Luis and the other students; however, Greek remained quite a challenge. "I know as much Greek as I do Hebrew," Arnie complained in his diary, "and I don't know any Hebrew."[88]

A new challenge involved their first classes in Homiletics. This was a crucial lesson, since as future priests they would have to deliver sermons at Sunday Masses. They learned from their priest-professors the techniques of writing and delivering what was considered to be a good sermon, one that would teach a scriptural lesson and, at the same time, keep people's attention. This was harder than it appeared. One exercise was to write practice homilies and present them to their class for critique. There is no remaining evidence of Luis's practice homilies; however, based on his already-developing ability to articulate his ideas well in his classes, one can assume that his performance in his homiletic class was more than satisfactory. But the class consisted of more than simply learning techniques. Their professor, Father Bonano, also lectured on scriptural issues such as the Commandments and showed the students how to apply them to a homily.[89] More than likely, Father Bonano focused on sermons that aimed to teach people how to get closer to God, rather than applying the social and even political lessons that one could take from the scriptures—lessons of the kind that the future Father Luis Olivares would become known for at La Placita Church.

While at Dominguez some of the students, led by Arnie, created more freedom for themselves, Claretville seems to have allowed them more freedoms appropriate for young men now into their early and mid-twenties. As such, students like Arnie didn't sneak around as much or leave the campus without permission. Arnie notes that he and other students, including Luis, went to see the Dodgers play a double-header at the Los Angeles Coliseum (after the team had moved to Los Angeles from Brooklyn); during this period, Mexican American residents were being removed by city officials from their homes in Chávez Ravine to make room for the construction of Dodger Stadium.[90] According to Henry Olivares, the students got tickets to Dodger games from Mrs. Casey Stengel the wife of the legendary manager of the New York Yankees. The Stengels had a home near Claretville, and she welcomed students to it, especially during the summer when Casey was away managing the Yankees. She treated the students to apple pie and ice cream and regaled them with stories about Casey and the Yankees. Occasionally, she gave them tickets to Dodger games, which the students would raffle back at the seminary.[91] Students played football and baseball on the campus fields and had access to a recreation room where they could play pool and listen to music.[92]

Birthdays could also be celebrated, such as Luis's twenty-fourth birthday, on February 13, 1958. "Luis's birthday is today," Arnie jotted in his diary. "He's 24 now. My! We're getting old. Always living in the present and forget there was a past."[93] Arnie's reflection is important and alludes to the fact that he, Luis, and the other seminarians were still being counseled that their new lives, family, and future were as Claretians, and not what they had been before they chose seminary life. Their non-seminary past had, in a very strict and some might even say cruel way, to be expunged or severely marginalized. How successful this was is questionable. Memory is very strong and powerful, and Luis, for one, never forgot his earlier family life and the socialization he received then, which would help guide him in his later struggles.

Claretville also had a choir and Luis quickly became its director in his first year. Besides singing at their own Masses and services, the choir also performed at other nearby churches.[94]

Although expected to study at Claretville for two years before going to Washington, D.C., and Catholic University, Luis and his classmates were informed at the end of their first year that the theologate, or school of theology, would now be completely transferred to Washington, to take advantage of the more expansive faculty from different orders at Catholic University and to allow time to build new facilities at Claretville. This would be a temporary change. It meant that first-year students such as Luis would do their remaining three years of theology back east. For Luis, this involved not only experiencing Washington, which excited him, but also meant that he and Henry would remain together again, since Henry would finish his last two years in Washington. Luis looked forward to this. However, before they left they received their Minor Orders, which represented further steps toward ordination. There were four such orders, and each symbolized some aspect of monastic discipline. As Henry Olivares describes them: "Tonsure, for example, involved the cutting of a strand of hair to symbolize separation from worldly attractions. Porter was the order to symbolize the opening of the door to strangers and guests making them welcome in the Church. Lector was the order designated to read the scripture readings for worship at Mass; the Lector could read all except the Gospel. Finally, Acolyte was the server at Mass and indicated the closest a layperson could get to the celebration of Mass."[95] That summer, he, Luis, and the other seminarians renewed their perpetual vows and got ready to move.[96]

From all appearances, Luis Olivares experienced a good year at Claretville and continued to impress his teachers and fellow students with his friendliness, sense of humor, and his leadership qualities. Of the latter, Ralph Berg recalls, "He was a very talented person. He had leadership qualities. He was an intelligent man."[97] Henry also observes that at Claretville Luis was already looking beyond Washington and even his ordination. He was beginning to map out his future as a Claretian priest. He talked to Henry about this, and Henry came away from this discussion with an observation that became a prophesy, at least in the initial years of Luis's priesthood. "In a way," Henry notes, "Luis wanted power. He began to see himself as a person of authority, in the position of power to be able to guide the order and the congregation. He already had ideas like that."[98]

With aspirations of becoming a major player in the Claretian order, Luis took a short vacation with Henry to visit their family in San Antonio before going on to Washington and the last lap of a long race to become a priest.[99] Henry recalls that he and Luis very much appreciated being allowed to see their family. It had been six long years since they had visited San Antonio. As Henry observes:

> It was a precious time to renew relations with family members that had become somewhat distant. Brothers and sisters were now fully grown. One older brother and older sister had married and had started their own families, the others were employed and numerous uncles and aunts and cousins made it a point to invite the future priests to their homes for dinner and laughter and good family fun. It was a whirlwind vacation that was most beneficial personally and socially.[100]

IV

Taking the plane to Washington from San Antonio in late summer 1958 must have been an exhilarating adventure for both Luis and Henry, the start of a new adventure in the nation's capital. Upon arriving, they went to the Claretian House of Study, recently built and located a block away from Catholic University.[101] Seeing the sights and monuments on the way from the airport was impressive, even inspiring. Many other Catholic orders, such as the Jesuits, Franciscans, and Dominicans, also had houses in the same vicinity. The Claretian House provided the accommodations for the Claretian seminarians, as well as for clergy either studying there or assigned to the house. Some students, of course, were already studying there and welcomed the new arrivals. Arnie, Adolph, and the others from Claretville arrived at about the same time.

Luis and Henry welcomed each seminarian's having his own room, bathroom, and shower. They appreciated the individual privacy that this provided. Their rooms were sparse, with a bed, desk, chair, and closets, but this was fine for them. They put away their civilian clothes and toiletries, donned the cassocks they would wear whenever in the house and attending classes on campus. Their rooms were on the second floor of the two-story building. Downstairs were the dining room, living room, and recreational room, with a TV that they could watch with few restrictions. On the

Luis Olivares (left) and Henry Olivares, Washington, D.C., late 1958.
(Courtesy of Henry Olivares)

other hand, the house had few newspapers or magazines. Such items were not particularly welcomed in the house, although the students could read the sports pages. They could listen to the radio in the living room, but were not allowed radios in their rooms.[102]

Catholic University was an imposing campus that included the recently constructed National Cathedral of the Immaculate Conception. Catholic University, or CU as it was referred to by faculty and students, was a pontifical college, which meant that it had been founded by the Vatican to train clergy primarily for administrative and hierarchical ministry, as opposed to pastoral or parish ministry, although some seminarians after their ordination did one or the other or both.[103] While mostly seminarians and priests studied at CU some lay students, both male and female, also attended in other liberal arts fields that the university provided. Predominantly clergy, with PhDs and from different orders, taught at CU, though some non-clergy faculty taught in the non-theological areas. CU's theological studies were considered some of the best, if not the best, in the United States.[104]

Coming to CU to finish their theology studies, Luis and his Claretian cohort took courses in such areas as Dogma, Canon Law, Moral Theology, Scriptures, Archeology of Religion, Hebrew, Music, Church History, Liturgy, Mysteries, Sacraments, Pastoral Theology, Homiletics, Ascetical Theology, Practical Administration of Penance, and Missiology. Some of these courses, such as Canon Law and Moral Theology, were taken all three years. At the end of three years, Luis and the others would receive a licentiate in sacred theology that represented an advanced degree, almost the equivalent of a PhD. In their first year in Washington, the students took most of their courses, except for Scripture, with the Claretian faculty in the Claretian house; however, with fewer new students, by the second year they took all of their courses at CU.[105]

In their classes, they still had to use Latin, though less and less frequently. By the end of their tenure, Luis and the other students had their classes taught only in English. Moreover, they were allowed to take classes other than theology, if they so wished. Arnie, for example, took some biology courses.[106]

An important influence on the curriculum at CU during the late 1950s and early 1960s were the winds of change within the Catholic Church that would be more evident during the Second Vatican Council. However, prior to the meeting of the Council in 1962, some of the calls for a more open and relevant Church, initiated by Pope John XXIII when he assumed the papacy in 1960, were already being felt in Catholic universities such as CU.

This became reflected in a new attitude expressed by the faculty. Arnie noticed this and later expressed it this way:

> In our 3rd and 4th years we practically had all Catholic University professors. . . . They threw out most of the things we previously learned from our own people. It was at this time we were influenced by the ideas of supremacy of conscience, literary criticism of Scripture, liberation theology [working for justice with special care of the poor], and Vatican II. In our ranks we were considered a different breed of priests—liberals![107]

You could literally feel these winds of change, Ralph Berg recalls, that were leading to Vatican II; they were exciting and full of expectations.[108]

Despite the fact that Luis and the others were well into their twenties, they still had to observe the rule of silence at mealtime, which ironically included a Mexican supper at the house as a Mardi Gras celebration. As in earlier seminary experiences, the students could only talk if the ranking clergy permitted it, such as on the Rector's or Prefect's birthday. Moreover, students had to continue to wear their cassocks most of the time, including when they attended classes. One change in the dress code was that for the first time, they were allowed to wear the white collar worn by priests with their cassocks or black suits. Undoubtedly, Luis and the others wore their collars with pride, and despite their commitment to humility, they must have admired how they looked with them. On the other hand, when allowed to go out of the house to sightsee in Washington, they could wear their "civvies," or street clothes. However, they could not venture out on their own and instead had to always be part of a group. No drinking was allowed, and going to bars was absolutely forbidden.[109]

A very welcome opportunity involved being allowed to sightsee in the nation's capital. They could participate in what were called "monument hunts." On certain weekends, Luis and his classmates visited such sights as the While House, the Capitol building, the Lincoln and Jefferson Memorials, the Library of Congress, and various museums. For young men who had been quite sheltered for many years in the seminaries, or who came from more provincial locations such as San Antonio, these excursions must have spun their heads and expanded their horizons. They knew about these sights, but to now see them was incredible. One can only imagine that for Luis it provided a cosmopolitan, sophisticated perspective and approach that he would further cultivate later as treasurer of the order. The only downside to their sightseeing was that they had no money—the vow of poverty—to spend on souvenirs, or even a decent lunch. However, sometimes the Prefect gave them some spending money to at least buy a soda or hamburger.[110] Moreover, the students also received five dollars a week to teach them budgeting techniques. They used this to pay for entry to museums, exhibits and, at times, for lunch.

Going to and from the CU campus also provided certain opportunities that may not have been permissible according to the seminarians' set of rules. For example, Arnie on occasion walked Sister Gerald, a student at CU, back to her order's house.[111] Moreover, the fact that CU was somewhat coed allowed some of the male seminarians the liberty to "sightsee" members of the opposite sex. Manuel De Santos, who was three years ahead of Luis, notes that while he did not get involved with any of the female students, "every once in a while, I looked at a girl going by."[112] Since nuns, in general, were diligent in their studies, it was not uncommon to join study groups consisting of nuns and seminarians or an occasional layperson who needed help in a class.[113]

Birthdays could also be a respite from the rules and restrictions. Arnie observed that, beginning as a seminarian, he always helped celebrate his friend Luis's birthday. More than likely, birthdays were acknowledged at the evening meal.[114] Christmas was unfortunately not a time for family since most of the seminarians lived too far away to go home for the holidays. Even then, the Claretians in Washington did not encourage home visits and may even have prohibited them. They again wanted to stress that the students now had a new family and community and needed to celebrate Christmas and other holidays with this adopted community. "We lived a community life," De Santos observes. "That was our family." They could, however, receive Christmas presents and cards from family and friends.[115] Olivares family members never visited Luis and Henry because of the expense involved, and so for an additional three years the Olivares brothers had only sporadic personal contact with their family, missing many birthdays and other family celebrations.

On one occasion, Arnie stole some gin and Tom Collins mix that the resident priests had left out while they went to vespers or evening prayers at the Shrine of the Immaculate Conception on campus. Ironically and contradictorily, the priests could drink but forbade the seminarians from doing so. Arnie took the gin and mix to his room and invited Luis and Adolph to join him. Luis may have drunk some of the gin, although not much. As Arnie explained to Henry years later, Luis proved to be their guardian angel:

The next day, Louie told me I passed out and Adolph was so drunk he had a hard time getting him back to his room. He then returned to my room, cleaned up the mess, put me to bed, and poured the rest of the Tom Collins mix into the gin bottle. He took the bottle to his room where it exploded during the night. I guess the gas in the mix didn't have room to expand. Thus ended our first Vespers and of what I can remember—a good time was had by all![116]

Perhaps because Luis and the other Mexican American seminarians were so far away from the more familiar Mexican American settings of San Antonio or Los Angeles, their ethnic identity seems to have been somewhat more defined in Washington. According to De Santos, about 50 percent of the Claretian students at CU were Mexican Americans. They especially craved Mexican food. "We can't be devoid of any Mexican food; that's a mortal sin," De Santos recalls one of the Mexican American students proclaiming. The lay brother at the Claretian House only cooked "American," or occasionally an unsatisfying version of Mexican food. Consequently on some of their permitted outings, some of them searched for Mexican restaurants, of which there seemed to be few or none in the city. However, Luis came back after a solo venture and told the others, "I found one; I found one!"

"Found what?" the other Mexican Americans inquired.

"A Mexican restaurant!" Luis exclaimed.

They visited the restaurant, located on Connecticut Avenue, and were pleased with it. Luis, especially, went out of his way to meet the Mexican owners of the place and impressed upon them that he was one of several Mexican Americans at CU. "Luis was very social," De Santos stresses. "He wasn't afraid to talk to people." Impressed with Luis, the owner sometimes gave him food, such as enchiladas and tacos, to take with him back to the house. Luis got the Rector to approve the serving of the food for supper which the cook warmed up for them, and which they shared with everyone else, including the priests. It was a delicious departure from the more bland food they usually had every night.[117]

In Washington, Luis continued to stand out among his fellow seminarians. As always, he befriended everyone and was, as a result, very popular. He expressed his leadership once more by directing the Claretian House choir, which performed for Masses in the chapel and for holidays. De Santos remembers Luis as strict in his direction, knowing how to control the different types of voices and where to position singers with high voices and those with low voices. Although he was three years ahead of Luis, De

Santos couldn't help but be impressed with Luis's leadership abilities and growing charisma. He observes that the other students considered Luis to be a "wheeler dealer" but in a positive sense—that is, someone who could get things done and who had influence with the Rector, the Prefect, and other priests. He had a presence among the other students. "Everybody listened when he talked," De Santos says of Luis. "He was not a shrinking violet. There was an aura about him that he would be able to get into administration or something like that."[118]

A further expression of Luis's leadership, and his devotion to his older brother, came when Henry finished his theology studies one year ahead of Luis and decided to be ordained back in Los Angeles. Luis obtained permission from his superiors to not only attend Henry's ordination, but to help organize it, especially with respect to family arrangements. "Luis makes it a point," Henry observes, "if it's an important event, he's gonna be there."[119] Before Luis left for California, he received the first of the Major Orders, which meant becoming a Sub Deacon, one more symbolic step toward his own ordination.[120]

One of the qualities Luis had already exhibited was his meticulousness to details. He was a stickler for organization, something his siblings recognized ever since he was a young boy. Prior to leaving for California, Luis arranged for the ordination invitations to be printed and sent out. When he arrived in Los Angeles, he arranged the logistics for his family to travel there for the ceremony. He booked the train tickets for the entire family including his father, Tía Concha, and all the siblings except for Damaso, who could not make it. He arranged for the hotel and for transportation to Blessed Sacrament Church in Hollywood, where Henry was ordained on June 16, 1960, as well as for the banquet that followed. He had even worked out the seating arrangements at the church. "Henry didn't have to lift a finger," Luis's siblings recall, still in awe of their brother's management of the ordination.[121]

While Luis seemed to be happy in Washington, he still had concerns and even anxieties typical of young men his age and in his situation as a seminarian. This was exhibited one night when Arnie heard Luis and entered his room, where he found Luis having trouble breathing. Or at least that is what he wrote in his diary. Years later, Arnie explained what he really found:

I couldn't write the real problem Louis had because he didn't want [Father] Granier or others to find out. Louis began to suffer anxiety attacks during the night. He felt he couldn't breathe. I would put a paper bag over his head and eventually he would breathe normally. It was a psychological condition brought on by nerves. One night I decided to check on him and found him in bed reading the Bible. When I asked him why he was reading the Bible, he told me he was going to die. I thought that was so funny and laughed because he wasn't suffering from any physiological condition. Louis was serious and couldn't understand why I was laughing. He eventually outgrew that condition![122]

Another four years had passed and it was time for the major final exams in late spring of 1961. Each seminarian would be tested on all four years of theology. The exams were in four fields: dogmatic theology; moral theology; scriptures; and canon law. The exams were divided into two parts, written and oral. The orals would be before a tribunal of professors. If you passed, you received your licentiate of theology. The next step would be your ordination as a priest. If you failed the exams, however, you could still be ordained. Everyone, of course, was anxious to pass and began preparing for the exams months in advance. Some professors organized study groups that met each week, or more frequently in some cases, and reviewed what the students had learned in classes over the past three years. Luis, himself, was anxious but determined to pass, as his brother had the year before. He knew the material and was confident as the date of the exam approached.[123]

That day arrived. The written exams in all four fields were given in one day. The exam lasted over four hours, with one hour per field. Luis and the others were relieved that the exams were in English and not Latin, or even worse in Hebrew or Greek. They assembled at Trinity College, just across the street from CU, where the exam was administered. After four hours, Luis and the others finished but would have to wait a week for the results. If they passed, they then took their orals. Luis passed and now prepared to face his tribunal.[124]

The oral exam also lasted four hours, with one hour devoted to each written exam. The tribunal of professors asked questions about the written exams. They inquired why the student had responded the way he did or asked the student to expand on a certain point. In both the written and oral exams, it was not acceptable for the student to provide his interpretation of the question. They were to show that they knew the doctrines in question. No interpretation, just the facts. The orals could be grueling. Luis no doubt was relieved when he finished his.[125]

"Louis, will you please leave the room and wait in the lobby while we discuss your exam. We'll call you back in when we're finished," one of the professors told him.

Luis waited for what must have seemed an eternity. He waited by himself since the orals were staggered for each student. Finally, the door to the exam room opened, and one of his professors came out and walked toward him.

"Louis, congratulations! You did very well and passed."

A look of relief came over Luis. He had done it! The priest then escorted him back to the room where his other inquisitors likewise congratulated him.

Back at the Claretian House, Luis received more congratulations from his fellow students, and over the next few days, congratulations went around as others such as Arnie reported that they had also passed.[126]

Luis must have reflected on how far he had come from that day in 1948, when his family drove him to the San Antonio train station. The little boy of thirteen who got on the train had no idea how long the trip to become a Claretian priest would take. So many years at Del Amo, the novitiate at Westchester, Dominguez, Claretville, and then Washington, D.C. Thirteen years! He was no longer a little boy but a young man in his mid-twenties, who had survived not a personal ordeal, but a long process of spiritual education and preparation for literally the final step—ordination. He felt good about himself and with even more confidence looked forward to his future as Father Luis Olivares.

V

Luis wanted to be ordained in San Antonio. He wanted to spare his family the expense of traveling again to California, as they had done the previous year for Henry's ordination. Besides he wanted to be ordained in his hometown. To be ordained in a particular archdiocese, you had to get the permission of the local bishop. In San Antonio this would mean the permission of Archbishop Robert E. Lucey, who had been the head of the Church in San Antonio for a number of years and had championed the cause of Mexican Americans. This would make Luis's ordination even more appropriate there. Archbishop Lucey approved his request and that of the Claretians, and the date was set for May 27, 1961. The service would be held at San Fernando Cathedral, with the archbishop ordaining Luis and a few others.[127] Olivares would only be one of the seven Mexican American priests ordained in the San Antonio archdiocese over a period of 250 years.[128]

Needless to say, Luis's family was overjoyed. Luis would join Henry as the second priest to be ordained from the Olivares family. His family was very proud of this. Arriving a few days early, Luis was "wined and dined" by family and relatives. He was back to being the "high priest" that he had pretended to be as a child. It was good to be back home. His siblings had grown up even more, and he enjoyed the time catching up with them as well as time with his father and Tía Concha. No doubt his thoughts also turned to his mother and Abuelita Inez, and how proud they would have been. They would be with him in spirit on that special day.

The day, a Saturday, dawned with lots of sun and growing heat and humidity, typical of summer days in San Antonio. It would get even hotter and more humid at noon, the time of the ordination.[129] The whole family was excited as, of course, Luis was. Dressed in their best clothes and Luis in his cassock, they all drove to the cathedral. Henry, who had arrived a week later than his brother, was staying at the rectory at Immaculate Heart of Mary Church; he joined the family at the cathedral. Luis's parents and family took their reserved pews in the front of the imposing altar while Luis went to the sacristy with the other seminarians to prepare themselves for their ordination. "I remember the church was packed and the crowd was buzzing with anticipation, waiting for the arrival of Archbishop Lucey," Henry recalls. "Finally, the organ resounded with the traditional 'Tu es Sacerdos in aeterinum'" (You are a priest forever). The Mass began with Archbishop Lucey officiating along with other priests. Luis and the other seminarians positioned themselves in the front of the sanctuary or altar. The ceremony was beautiful, Damaso Jr. remembered. Sitting just behind Luis, Damaso saw his brother's back moving. He was crying. "You could see his back moving," he noted. "We were right there in the front pew. Dad was very proud of the fact that his son was being ordained. He was overwhelmed."[130]

Luis dedicated his ordination to his parents. Because of their love and support, he had become a priest. "He wanted all the glory for his parents," Damaso stressed, "and that's what he got." Besides prostrating themselves in front of the altar as part of their ordination, Luis and the others had their hands tied—"ata manos"—to symbolize their commitment to the Church. The thumb and index finger of both hands were anointed with the oil of chrism and then wrapped with linen bands to signify the consecration of hands for holy purpose. The hands remained wrapped until the imposition of the Bishop's hands on the candidates to be ordained. Henry notes that the linens used to tie Luis's hands had been made by their Tía Luz. When they were untied, Luis went over to his Tía Concha and in her honor presented the linen bands to her.[131]

PRIESTHOOD

Ordination of Fr. Luis Olivares, C.M.F. (receiving blessing),
San Fernando Cathedral, San Antonio, May 27, 1961.
(Courtesy of Henry Olivares)

Luis's big sister, Teresa, remembered how beautiful the ceremony was and how packed the cathedral was, including many parishioners from their home parish of Immaculate Heart. "We were all there and it was a very meaningful occasion because it was taking part in San Antonio where he [Luis] had grown up." She likewise recalls how excited and happy Luis was that day. "That's all he could think about," she states. "He had gotten to what he always wanted to be."[132]

At the end of the Mass, Archbishop Lucey called upon each seminarian to approach, and he individually placed his hands on their heads to ordain them. No doubt many thoughts filled Luis mind as he waited for the archbishop to call his name.

"Luis Olivares!" the Archbishop called.

"Adsum" (I am present), Luis answered firmly and convincingly.[133]

As he approached the Archbishop, his family looked at him with love and pride. Archbishop Lucey then laid his hands on the head of Luis as the essential act of the Sacrament of Ordination. He blessed him and before the entire congregation pronounced Luis Olivares to be a follower of Jesus Christ and now one of his ministers—Father Luis Olivares![134]

The whole church responded with joyous applause. Next, all of the priests present proceeded to lay their hands on Luis and the other newly ordained priests to welcome them into ministry. Henry laid his hands on Luis.[135]

Luis had reached his goal. He was a priest forever, according to the order of Melchizedek, as the Roman rite of ordination dictates.[136]

Joy and happiness filled the cathedral. The service was over, and Luis joined his family in celebration, but not before each member of the family and the assembly approached to receive the new priest's blessing. Many of the old parishioners, as well as Luis's former elementary school classmates, approached to offer congratulations and ask for a blessing.[137]

The news of his ordination became a news items in the local newspaper. "Local Boy Ordained as Catholic Priest." "Everybody was proud of him," Henry observes.[138]

Henry poignantly recounts the rest of this memorable day, referring to himself in the third person:

The ordination ceremony was followed with a luncheon hosted by Tía Martina, who owned the Rodríguez Mortuary. The luncheon was held in the large dining room which had been the scene of memorable family meetings. The most memorable was the meeting in which my father announced that the family would be kept together after my mother's death and arrangements had been made for our Grandmother Inez and Tía Concha, his sister, to help in raising the orphaned children. As in family gatherings, the talk after the ordination was about family and the road traveled to reach this day. One of the highlights was the presentation of ordination gifts from various family members. Among these gifts was a golden chalice designed very simply by an artist in Mexico in which the words "Pray for me each time you use this cup" were engraved inside the base. This was the gift the newly ordained priest treasured all his life and travelled with him wherever he went. It had to be consecrated to be used the following day for Father Luis's first Mass.

After this luncheon, Luis wanted to go to the San Fernando Cemetery where his mother, Victoriana, and Grandmother Inez were buried. This was arranged and I do not recall a more emotional occurrence. When we arrived, Louie was quite composed and relaxed from the morning ceremonies, but he broke down into an outburst of tears that seemed uncontrollable when he began the funeral rite of burial. He insisted that he wanted to sing the parts of the ceremony. No doubt overwhelmed by all the excitement of the previous events, he began to cry. His brother Henry took over the ritual until Luis let him know that he was under control and resumed the ceremony for the other deceased members of the family. No doubt, this emotional outburst was the catharsis he needed to be himself once more.

Regarding the deceased members of our family, Louie felt that our family was so fortunate not to be afflicted by frequent deaths in the immediate family as other families had been. I had to remind him that we had lost our mother early on in life and our dear Grandmother. He agreed with me and added, "but we never lacked for love or not being wanted." This remained his one cornerstone of his personality that nothing could destroy.[139]

The next day was just as exciting and happy. Father Luis Olivares was scheduled to say his first Mass at his home church, Immaculate Heart, where he had been an altar boy. Henry concelebrated at his brother's Mass but this was Luis's day—his first Mass. The church was packed with his family, relatives, friends, and parishioners, many of whom remembered Luis as a young boy and, of course, remembered Abuelita Inez and her devotion and charity. Dressed for the first time in his priestly robes and using the chalice given to him by his uncles and aunts, Luis officiated in a Solemn High Mass, accompanied by Henry and the priests whose Masses he had served as an altar boy. Facing that alter as an ordained priest filled him with an overwhelming joy that he expressed with a big smile as he processed down the familiar aisle, followed by an entourage of clergy and ministers.[140]

At first facing the altar, with his back to the congregation in the pre–Vatican II style, he then turned to the people and said in Latin, again with a big smile, *"Dominus Vobiscum"* (God be with you). And with these words, Father Luis commenced his first Mass.

As part of the Mass, although not usually allowed at a first Mass since the High Priest serves as the homilist, Olivares also gave his first homily or sermon and he did it in Spanish, in tribute to his family and to the Mexican character of the parish. All those courses in homiletics may have helped. He paid tribute to all the women of the Olivares family who had a part in raising and nurturing him throughout his early life. He further included the nuns from the Benedictine Order who had educated him, furthered his faith, and given him courage for the future. He did not fail to mention the *viejtas* (little old ladies) that came to Mass every day and prayed for him. These women had now brought him to this special day. Articulate even in Spanish, Luis no doubt previewed his future self—a strong, inspiring, relevant, and charismatic preacher.[141]

Teresa remembers the church filled with flowers and music performed by the church choir, which Luis no doubt appreciated. She notes that Luis was not nervous about saying his first Mass, but excited and happy. "Everybody was just so excited," she says. "They couldn't believe that one of their own was saying his first Mass there."[142]

At communion time, Luis's father and Tía Concha came up to the altar rail to receive the first Holy Communion that Father Luis had ever administered. The rest of the family followed, as did the other members of the congregation.

Luis gave the final blessing, and the first of many Masses that he would say was over. Luis was ecstatic. This was no longer playing Mass; this was the real thing.

A reception followed in the church hall, attended by all.[143] It had been quite a weekend. It had been quite a journey to this day. Not all of his cohort had made it with him, and that same year, Father Luis officiated at the marriage of his friend Gil Villanueva, who had traveled with him thirteen years earlier to Del Amo.[144] Olivares's first Mass ended with a large family and friends gathering in a restaurant on Bandera Road in San Antonio. "The memory of that event has faded from memory," Henry Olivares laments, "just as the memory of that restaurant has faded when it burned down."[145]

"I remember that Luis was so happy, very, very happy that he had reached what he wanted to do," Damaso Jr. asserted. "He reached his goal and he said, 'This is not the end; I will continue working.'"[146]

VI

In looking back at Luis Olivares's seminary years, one can ask what he learned in those years that would manifest itself later on, especially in his work with faith-based movements such as the sanctuary movement. In addition to his socialization at home to care for others, especially the poor, which Abuelita Inez taught through her example, Luis learned discipline, commitment, compassion, self-sacrifice, social justice, leadership, and the importance of organization and community. He also learned that he indeed had a strong vocation for the priesthood. At the same time, as he began to display, especially at Dominguez, he was a complicated and multidimensional individual who needed to express his sense of humor and his love of life, and he was not afraid to challenge authority even within the Church. These were qualities that began to reveal themselves, but as he himself later acknowledged, his life as a priest evolved, and therefore these qualities evolved and became more evident with time. In a sense, despite his confidence in his vocation, when he was ordained Luis Olivares was still very much in search of the "real Luis Olivares" and a work in progress. Each subsequent stage of his life as a priest would reveal more of this reality and evolution, accompanied by internal struggles like anyone else. Father Luis Olivares may have been elevated to the priesthood, but he was still a human being.

FOUR

Company Man

Luis Olivares walked on cloud nine after his ordination. He was finally a real priest. This was no longer playacting, as a child, at being a priest. It was a long process, and it seemed light years ago since he first entered the seminary at age thirteen. Unlike some of his fellow seminarians who had dropped out, he displayed the commitment and tenacity to achieve his goal. He might not have been competitive in sports, but he had excelled academically and overcome all hurdles to his ordination. With that, he was now ready to embark on what he was certain would be a proud and productive career as a Claretian.

I

It was Camelot in Washington. Americans, especially younger ones, expressed excitement about the election to the presidency of the youthful John F. Kennedy in 1960. This seemed to have also affected Luis Olivares. Not that he was political—he was not. But American Catholics, including Mexican American Catholics, enthusiastically welcomed the election of the first Catholic president. Mexican Americans for the first time organized in a national presidential election through Viva Kennedy clubs throughout the Southwest and Midwest, where most Mexican Americans lived, in support of Kennedy. They identified with his seeming underdog status in a country that was still predominantly Protestant, in which Catholics were an often-persecuted minority. In that election, Mexican Americans voted overwhelmingly for Kennedy. It is not known if Olivares voted, but as a Mexican American Catholic he very likely identified with Kennedy and supported his election.

Moreover, Olivares was part of the sixties generation, and he also welcomed the new decade and the spirit of renewal and change that President Kennedy called for in his inaugural address: "Ask not what your country can do for you, but what you can do for your country." But this new spirit

Fr. Luis Olivares, 1961.
(Courtesy of Henry Olivares)

also had Catholic overtones. One year after Olivares's ordination, Pope John XXIII commenced the Second Vatican Council, which would meet for the next three years in Rome and initiate major reforms within the Church to make it more relevant to the modern world. Olivares saw himself as part of these changes. It was a good time to begin his priesthood. He welcomed the opportunity to be part of a new generation of clergy who would inject new energy and leadership into the Church, and specifically into his own order.

But little did he know that the sixties would also turn out to be such a tumultuous decade. In 1962, the United States and the Soviet Union seemed on the brink of nuclear war over Soviet missiles in Cuba. Both sides blinked and resolved the crisis. One year later, President Kennedy was assassinated. The nation mourned, and many Mexican Americans added the picture of Kennedy to their home altars alongside that of the Virgin of Guadalupe. In spite of racist attacks, the black civil rights movement led to major civil rights legislation in 1964 and 1965. President Lyndon Johnson escalated U.S. involvement in Vietnam by sending in thousands of combat troops, and America was once again at war—a tragic war of choice that included thousands of young Mexican Americans and other Latinos being killed. The war, in turn, led to the largest antiwar movement in the nation's history. This movement included Chicanos who, on August 29, 1970, in East Los Angeles, organized the largest anti–Vietnam War protest by any minority group in the country. Two years earlier, Dr. Martin Luther King Jr. was shot and killed in Memphis. Two month after King's assassination, the country mourned another Kennedy when Senator Robert Kennedy met the same fate as his older brother. Race riots enveloped many inner city neighborhoods, including Watts in Los Angeles in 1965. Richard Nixon was elected President in 1968 and escalated the war in Southeast Asia. Closer to home for Olivares, a new generation of Mexican Americans, proudly and defiantly calling themselves Chicanos, initiated the Chicano Movement and called for Chicano Power.

The sixties proved to be more challenging than Olivares could have foreseen. His own Church had to relate to the reforms that emanated out of Rome and the Second Vatican Council. It caused tensions and uncertainty, and many clergy found it difficult to adjust.

Within this context, Olivares began his priesthood. He saw himself as part of a new and vibrant generation, though curiously not in a political sense. He refused to be caught up in all of the turmoil. He remained aloof from these historical changes as he focused only on his own career and duties as a Claretian. His decade of change and "conversion" would come later.

He didn't have to think about where he would go after his ordination. The order mandated a one-year practicum following ordination. A practicum involved doing parish work in a Claretian parish. Henry, for example, was assigned to a parish in Perth Amboy, New Jersey, while also working on an MA in Classical Studies at CU. Luis was assigned to a parish in the Washington, D.C., area where he said Mass, heard confessions, and was of any further assistance needed by the pastor. During their practicum, the newly ordained priests also had to attend classes at CU concerning confessions, how to counsel, and how to assist in rectifying marriages. Olivares appears to have enjoyed this parish experience although it is not certain that he wished to do this for any extensive time as a priest. Luis already had a sense that he would rise up in the order and become a major player in it, although the outline of his trajectory toward this goal was as yet unclear. What seemed to be clear was that he did not wish to return to Texas, including San Antonio. He had been spoiled, living as a seminarian all those years in southern California, and that is where he hoped to return. Moreover, this is where the administration of the western province of the order was located, and Luis wanted to be close to the seat of power and authority.[1] "He said 'I'll never come to Texas,'" brother Damaso recalls. One sister adds: "He said if he was sent here he would come gladly, but he wanted to work in California. He enjoyed working there."[2]

Luis got his wish when, after his practicum, the order or at least his superiors in the western province assigned him to return to where it all had started for him: the minor seminary in Compton. He was going to come full circle. This was fine for him as long as he returned to southern California. He was assigned to be a faculty member and a so-called "disciplinarian" at Del Amo. However, around the time that Luis returned or soon thereafter, Del Amo, which had been the minor seminary, and Dominguez Seminary, which had been the major seminary, were combined into the minor seminary and simply referred to as Dominguez Seminary. The two campuses still existed although Luis primarily taught at the old Del Amo grounds, where the freshman and sophomores studied. To make matters more interesting and to keep all this a family affair, Henry later joined Luis at Dominguez, also to teach, but primarily at what used to be the major seminary, now housing the high school juniors and seniors.[3] At Dominguez from 1962 to 1965, Luis taught religion, English, Spanish, History, and Latin. As he reflected on this many years later, he said: "Like right after ordination I went to the seminary as a member of the faculty and disciplinarian for the minor seminary, administrator for the seminary. I taught religion, history, and, well they assigned things regardless of your expertise. I even taught English for two years. It's a good thing I didn't teach math!"[4] However, despite Luis's reluctance to teach math, former student Glen Peterson notes that he studied algebra with Father Luis as well as English, Spanish, and Latin.[5]

Peterson also observes that Olivares's return to Dominguez was likewise a time of continued retrenchment, especially with respect to student dropouts, as it had been in Luis's student days. Peterson entered as a freshman in a class of sixty in a total high school enrollment of 130; however, only fourteen, including himself, graduated. None went on to become priests. He left after his senior year in college.[6]

Peterson further remembers with fondness Olivares's role as a teacher. The students referred to him as Father Luis, and Peterson adds that he always wore his cassock. He also observes that Olivares was very kind and erudite. Peterson was especially impressed with Father Luis's oratory. "He had that great sense of being able to speak." Peterson admired his intelligence. In class Olivares shared his boyhood stories about growing up in San Antonio. The students appreciated his sense of humor. Peterson especially remembers a joke that Father Luis told in class. "It was a dumb joke but for some reason it stuck."

"What happened to the Indian who drank 5,000 gallons of tea?

"What?" the students asked.

"He died in his tee-pee."

According to Peterson, Father Luis always had a sense of humor.[7]

The students enjoyed Olivares as a teacher and had fun in his classes. This did not mean, though, that they didn't learn from him; they did, and Olivares could also be strict with them. "He was demanding," Peterson says, "but he wasn't the toughest teacher." There were other priests who were much tougher and administered more discipline. "There were two or three that were the tough guys," he says of the other teachers. "Luis wasn't one of them. . . . He was a good guy."[8]

Of course, Luis functioned not only as a teacher but as a priest. He said Mass each day along with the other priest-teachers, sharing the three altars in the chapel. He heard confessions and, as he had in his own seminary years, he led the choir in singing at church services. Peterson served as one of his altar boys and recalls being impressed by Olivares's homilies, which came across as very humane. He would talk in his sermons about his own youth, which made his sermons very relatable. When Olivares returned to Dominguez, the Mass was still said in Latin; however, by 1965 due to the reforms of the Second Vatican Council, he now said the Mass in English, with the altar now facing the congregation rather than the other way. This was to indicate that the Church was composed not only of the clergy but lay Catholics as well. The use of the vernacular, in this case English, was to facilitate greater communication and involvement by the laity in the Mass.[9] Although trained in Latin and in the more formal pre–Vatican II liturgy, Olivares accepted the new changes and applied them. He admired Pope John XXIII. Olivares saw himself as part of the changes in the Church, although he was not certain exactly what role he would play.

Remembering his own seminary years and how parents were not very involved in the education of their children, Olivares initiated a parents' club for those parents who lived nearby. Such an organization had never been done before, but Olivares felt that new traditions—in the spirit of Vatican II—were needed for teenagers who missed their parents as he had. The club allowed parents to come to Dominguez and participate in a number of activities such as keeping the playing fields in shape by sodding new grass, and helping out during games as coaches, referees, and even cheerleaders. This brought the parents closer to their children and to their teachers and the seminary. Through the parents' club, Luis became very close to some families.[10] He remembered that he had become close to some families when he was in the minor seminary, due to his friends inviting him and Henry to their homes. In a way, Olivares was always in search of family, since his own, other than Henry, was far away. It would become a familiar pattern for him to adopt surrogate families during his life. "He wanted to have the seminarians to be in contact with their parents and have the parents involved on projects," Henry says of his brother's initiative and of his leadership. "Luis was responsible for a lot of that which we never heard of before. So that's the kind of guy that he was. He saw something that needed to be done so he would do it."[11]

But besides his teaching and priestly duties, Olivares also received an opportunity to become an administrator, which he welcomed. Father Eduardo Quevedo, the Prefect, appointed Luis as Vice or Assistant Prefect, to assist him in the administration of the minor seminary. Olivares enjoyed wearing this other hat, and he did his job loyally and well. By working closely with the young Claretian, Quevedo had an opportunity to judge him, and he was impressed. He found him to be very obedient. "He was just a good priest," the former Prefect says of Olivares. "He was very dedicated to his religious obligation." Quevedo particularly remembers that when he began to argue with the order that Dominguez Seminary should provide a good, solid Catholic education for the students first and foremost, and not pressure the boys to go on to the priesthood, he got in trouble with his superiors. However, Luis shared this belief and supported him. Quevedo, who left the priesthood in 1968 and became a Chicano Movement activist and Chicano Studies professor, notes that in the early 1960s Olivares was not socially engaged in that he didn't seem to share concerns about social and political issues, but instead focused on his Claretian duties. He was not politically conservative, according to Quevedo, but simply reflected how most priests at the time were generally apolitical. This, of course, was prior to the new changes and accompanying consciousness that followed the Second Vatican Council and its call for the Church to become more socially engaged. This would affect many clergy later in the 1960s. Of Luis in the early 1960s, Quevedo adds: "His goal was to fulfill his duties as a priest and go as high up in the chain of command of the order as possible, which he did."[12]

The early 1960s were, of course, also the era of the civil rights movement and struggles led by black Americans and leaders such as Dr. Martin Luther King Jr. But these movements also seemed not to have affected Olivares. It wasn't that he didn't support them, but they did not motivate him to become involved in such struggles or stimulate his own ethnic awareness. Olivares recognized himself as Mexican American and had shown signs of a fledgling ethnic awareness during his seminary years; however, this did not go much beyond a simple acknowledgment of his ethnic background. As he himself later admitted, he was trained as a priest in the 1950s, a time when the Church in the United States was deemphasizing ethnicity and forging its own consensus ideology of Americanism. This reflected the Church's successful efforts to become an accepted American institution in the post–World War II period, characterized by the growth of the American Catholic population and its greater mobility into middle-class status, and the prosperity of the Church through its extensive parishes and schools throughout the country. To the American bishops, such acceptance and integration called for a new American Catholicism that downplayed ethnicity, especially since many of its predominant European ethnic groups had now also become more accepted, integrated, and acknowledged as "white" Americans.[13]

Despite the social changes happening in the country, Olivares remained focused on his role within the order. That role was further advanced when he became the bursar or treasurer for Dominguez Seminary. Although he was not a math person and teaching algebra was certainly not his favorite subject, Luis still rose to the occasion and learned how to administer the seminary's finances. This would serve him well in the future, and some believe that his superiors in the western province had already recognized him as a future high administrator for the order. He did this for three years and seems to have done an exemplary job.[14] Of this service, Luis later reflected on its importance for him and what it said about him at the time. "I was bursar for the seminary for a while," he said. "It was a position of some authority and a policy-making position within the seminary administration. At that time being Claretian to me meant being a company man. Your identity is almost exclusively Claretian."[15] Henry observed at close range his brother's initial administrative career, his growing ambitions, and what he was learning in this position; he notes: "There he began his career where he began to put his fingers into the ins and outs and whatever is happening in the order. Whoever controls the money controls what's happening."[16]

After three years at Dominguez—crucial ones for Olivares in beginning to define his role within the Claretian order, especially as a young administrator—he was temporarily reassigned to Immaculate Heart Church in Phoenix for about a year, though it is not clear how long he was there, what he did other than being a parish priest, and why the order sent him there in the first place. It may have had to do with Del Amo closing and all the students being transferred to Dominguez. According to Henry, Luis enjoyed working in this Mexican American parish and struck up a good working relationship with the pastor, Fr. Pete Farrell. Still, given his growing ambitions to become a prominent leader within his order, it's conceivable that he was not satisfied just doing parish work.[17] He undoubtedly also did not appreciate being sent out of southern California. This "exile" proved to be temporary, especially since the order still saw him as a potentially valuable administrative asset. In 1966 the order brought him back to the Los Angeles area and assigned him to be the Rector and Superior (interchangeable terms) at Claretville, which by then administered the novitiate and housed the seminarians studying for their college degrees, now at Loyola University. Moreover, by 1967 due to his proven administrative skills and potential, the order elected him treasurer for the entire western province. He was thirty-three years old. This was like being named Secretary of the Treasurer of the United States. Next to the Provincial, the head of the order, treasurer was the second most powerful position. Olivares jumped at this opportunity. It was recognition that he had made it in a sense in the order. He was now not only a major player, but one of the most important players. But to help him move into this new position, Olivares convinced the order to pay for him to work on an MBA at Notre Dame University, in a special program called Financial Administration for Religious Communities. The order could not afford to release him for a long stretch of time for this but did agree that he could spend summers at Notre Dame studying, which he did for several summers, gaining his degree in 1972. Not much is known about his experience at Notre Dame, but he seems to have worked hard and learned much that would assist him in his role as treasurer.[18]

III

When Luis and Henry found themselves back in California in the early 1960s, their return was augmented by their sister Teresa also moving to southern California shortly thereafter. In 1961 or 1962, Teresa Garza and her husband, Robert Garza, moved with their four children from Texas to the Los Angeles area. Robert had gotten a job with a pharmaceutical company as a salesman. They first lived in Chatsworth, in the San Fernando Valley, and later moved a bit north to Thousand Oaks. However, during their move, the moving van with all of their furniture and belongings burned, and they lost everything. Luis and Henry, delighted in having their sister living close to them, immediately helped out. "We were in a motel for six weeks," Teresa explains, "and he [Luis] and Henry would come and babysit so we could start building, setting up a house."[19]

Once the Garzas settled in, Luis and Henry frequently visited. Every Sunday, Teresa invited them to a family dinner with her, Robert, and their children. The Olivares brothers looked forward to these visits, for which they wore their civilian or street clothes. They no longer had to limit themselves to their surrogate family of Claretians; they now had real family—*la familia*. Teresa cooked their favorite dishes that Abuelita Inez and Tía Concha had cooked for them as kids. This included enchiladas, picadillo, and rice and beans. She didn't do this every Sunday; Robert would sometimes go out and get prime rib or steaks and barbeque them, or make lasagna. Luis and Henry would arrive around four or five in the afternoon and stay late, until the Garza children were put to bed. At dinner, the brothers talked about their work and their everyday experiences. Luis told them about the parents' club he had organized at Dominguez, about his choir, his teaching, and his role as Vice Rector and as bursar. In fact, he invited the Garza family to attend some of his events on campus, and they did. At dinner the conversation would be in both English and Spanish. In fact, the three siblings teased each other about their Spanish becoming less fluent. These weekly Sunday dinners brought much fun and joy to all and allowed Luis and Henry to become very close to their nephews. They took part in the eldest nephew's confirmation and in two of their other nephews' First Communions. "The children were very attracted to them when they were little," Teresa says of this relationship. Luis as bursar at the seminary had contacts with various business people in Los Angeles and on one occasion obtained free tickets to the Ice Capades (a traveling ice-skating show, now defunct) for Teresa and her family. These were wonderful times for both Luis and Henry, because it was family and they had now reconstituted some of it with Teresa being in Los Angeles.[20]

In fact, Luis and Henry's visits became even more frequent when Teresa told them that she was having marital problems with Robert. That's when Teresa noticed that both Luis and Henry began to talk more to her husband, with whom they got along well, at least until they became aware of the tensions. According to Teresa, Henry was more diplomatic in these discussions, trying to see both sides. Luis was much more direct in trying to find out from Robert what the sources of the problems were. Of course, both assumed that Robert was responsible, not their sister, and they may have been right. Teresa observes of Luis's inquisitorial approach to Robert: "He pulled no punches. He would ask questions, very intimate questions, of my husband. He would be very abrupt with him. . . . Luis was just concerned about his sister. If we had always been close, that's when we became very, very close."[21]

When the problems continued and Teresa and Robert began to consider a divorce, Luis, in particular, attempted to discourage it. This in part had to do with the Church's prohibition of divorce, but it also seems that his main concern was protecting his sister, who now had five children. He wanted the marriage to still work.

"Terry, you've got to keep up, keep fighting. It's your life," he told his sister.

But despite Olivares's best efforts, the marriage failed, and Teresa and Robert divorced in 1973 after several years of separation. Luis at first did not accept the separation and later divorce (Henry seems to have been more accepting of it). "Why do men all of a sudden not want to stay with their wives?" he asked Teresa. Out of concern for his sister, who was on the verge of a nervous breakdown, Luis spent even more time with her and her children and also arranged for Teresa to get counseling from priests and lawyers. "Luis came to my assistance when my marriage broke up," Teresa says. "I used to tell him that I would hear bells at night and I was crying a lot. He saw to it that I got psychiatric help and counseling. He would take care of my little girl. He would change her diapers, give her formula. Then he would take me to the counselor and would wait in the waiting room while I was going with my session and take care of my little girl."[22]

In the end, Olivares seems to have accepted the divorce and was very compassionate to his sister. His attitude toward his former brother-in-law was probably less accommodating. When Teresa later in 1969 decided to return to Texas, Luis kept in close touch with her, calling every week, counseling her, and asking about her children. "It was a very personal relationship," Teresa concludes, "and to me it was something that cannot be measured." Luis reacted to his sister's divorce first and foremost as a brother, but part of him also reacted as a priest. He wanted to know, for example, if Teresa had any resentments toward the Church as a result of her divorce. He seemed relieved when she told him that she didn't. But Luis may have asked this question only out of a sense of obligation. Whatever religious issues were involved, Teresa was still his sister. "He was being my brother first," Teresa says of Luis.[23]

The anxiety that Olivares faced as a result of his sister's divorce was only compounded when Henry, also around the mid to late 1960s, decided to leave the priesthood. After the Second Vatican Council, he became disillusioned with his order. He accepted Vatican II's decisions about the Church's reforming itself, but found opposition to this within the Claretians. At Dominguez, Henry was in charge of administering the training of the young seminarians. Influenced by the winds of change initiated by Vatican II, Henry wanted to now prioritize educating the students to first become good Christians before becoming good priests. His superiors, however, felt the reverse, and opposed Henry's proposed changes, removed him from his position, and sent him to teach high school at San Gabriel Mission High School. Henry liked teaching but remained disillusioned with the order. "So I said," he recounts, "'well if that's the way it goes, I'll go my way.'"[24] He remained at San Gabriel until 1969, when he left the priesthood. According to Luis, Henry received a dispensation from his vows.[25]

These two family crises tested Luis's status as both a brother and a priest. Henry first told his brother about his doubts about remaining in the order, and Luis took it hard. He never imagined that this would happen. It was in part because of Henry that Luis had gone to the seminary and become a priest. Henry was his role model, and he always believed that they both would remain priests. He tried to dissuade Henry. They went out to dinner to discuss this.

"You made a promise; you took a vow; you have a responsibility," Luis lectured Henry. "That's the bottom line."

"No, that isn't the bottom line," Henry forcibly responded. "There's another side to it. If you're not in love with something any more then you can't support it. It doesn't fire you up like it used to. When you fall out of love that's the worst thing that can happen."

"You have the feelings of a man who is about to execute someone," Luis countered, perhaps too harshly, but he was determined to convince Henry not to leave. "You're totally lacking emotional expression. You don't have any feelings. You've lost them."

Despite Luis's almost desperate efforts, Henry did not change his mind although, he consulted a psychologist and sought counseling.[26]

Luis didn't resent his brother's decision, but he worried what would happen to him. Because Teresa was going through her own problems with her marriage, Luis did not tell her right away. In fact, he first told Robert.

"You better be prepared, Robert," he told his brother-in-law, "because Teresa is going to get another shock."[27]

It was Robert who told Teresa about Henry's decision. Perhaps Luis didn't want to be the one to break what he considered to be bad news to his sister, or perhaps he felt embarrassed to do so. Teresa was taken aback by the news. When she finally talked to Luis on the phone about it, she couldn't help but ask, "Are you also going to leave?"[28]

Teresa recalls that Luis in fact took Henry's decision very hard. "He broke down with me just that one time over the phone," she says.[29]

Teresa and Luis agreed that he should be the one to break this news to their parents. This was not easy to do, and Luis agonized over it but finally called them. As one can imagine, they, too, took it very hard. This was not only unexpected, it was unacceptable. A priest did not leave his vocation and his vows, and certainly not one of their sons. They had sacrificed for their sons to become priests and were elated and felt blessed when the two were ordained. They were proud beyond belief. And now this? What would the rest of their family, relatives, and friends think? Not only did they see what Henry was doing as a breach of faith, but at a personal and family level, it was an embarrassment—*un escándalo*.

But there was nothing anyone, including Luis, could do.

Luis still kept in touch with Henry and knew that he had decided to marry and try to become a teacher in the public schools. How much of this he related to Teresa is hard to know, but she eventually found out. In fact, one year later, she received a letter from Henry informing her that he had been looking for a job. She believes that he was then living in the San Francisco Bay area. She further believes that Luis knew where he was. Later she received a second letter from Henry telling her that he had gotten married and would be in touch. Teresa might have known already, but this was now confirmed by Henry's letter. Soon after, Henry called her. He asked her if he could visit her while she still lived in Thousand Oaks and bring a "special person." "Of course," Teresa replied, knowing full well that this was Lillian, Henry's wife. On the day of the visit, she decided to make an Italian meal not knowing that Lillian was of Italian ancestry. When they arrived, Teresa found this out. "I thought we were going to eat Mexican food," Lillian kidded her. But Teresa was gracious and glad to see how happy Henry was; Henry had embraced Lillian's two young children, whom she met on this visit. Teresa came to accept the marriage and to love Lillian and her children. "I had made up my mind that no matter what he [Henry] did," she recalls thinking. "First of all, he was my brother, and if this is what made him happy, that was fine with me."[30]

Although he found it hard at first to accept what Henry had done, in the end, Luis also adapted to the situation. Henry was his brother, too, and blood was thicker than even his belief in the priesthood. He also came to love Lillian and thought the world of her and her children. "There was time to be serious and a time to laugh and a time to tease and joke, and a time to take things very seriously," Teresa observes about Luis's reconciliation. "But there was always that kindness and that thoughtful feeling toward his family."[31]

IV

Despite these family issues, Luis Olivares had plenty else on his plate. By 1967 he wore two hats: Rector/Superior at Claretville and treasurer of the western province. Of the two, the latter occupied the bulk of his time and gave him the most fulfillment.[32] As treasurer, Olivares was in charge of fundraising and investments for the order. In fact, the order had considerable investments, including a portfolio in the stock market worth $25 million. He also administered the vast properties owned by the order.[33] As treasurer, Olivares primarily made sure that the western province of the Claretians had the financial resources it needed to maintain its ministries, including parishes that it administered, residencies, as well as support for its foreign missions in the Third World and other countries. This also involved future financial planning for the province. All this translated into a large operating budget. In effect, Olivares served as the CEO of the province.[34] He served as treasurer for ten years, until 1977. "He was a talented man," Father Bernie O'Connor, one of Olivares's colleagues, says of his work as treasurer. "He was a bright fellow."[35] Henry Olivares put it more succinctly about his brother's role as treasurer: "It gave him power and Luis enjoyed power."[36]

Olivares operated out of the former novitiate in Westchester, in central Los Angeles. The Claretians transformed the seminary into its administrative offices. There, Olivares had his office and did his considerable business. It also served as the headquarters of the Provincial, the head of the order. Westchester was also referred to as Provincial House. Olivares at first resided there but soon moved back to Claretville, where he also served as Rector.[37]

As treasurer, Olivares had a seat on the Provincial Council of the western province, the major policy-making body of the order, a position which made him into one of the most powerful and influential Claretians. Five members composed the council, which officially advised the Provincial and, with him, determined the direction of the order.[38] As treasurer, Olivares wielded much influence on the council and was more the Provincial's equal than the other four council members. One issue that Olivares disliked about his work on the council was that it got bogged down with issues such as personnel cases and finances (his area), instead of providing new directions and vision for the order. It should have provided the latter, but it didn't; Luis no doubt thought he shared the blame for that. He believed in institutions such as the order, but he learned, especially in his role on the council, that institutions could also be ineffective in working toward higher goals, instead just attending to more mundane duties and day-to-day administration.

Still, Olivares enjoyed being part of the power structure. He had no intention of just being an ordinary priest; he had a more ambitious view of himself. He also had always been pampered both by his family and, in a way, by his order. He was seen as a model seminarian and early on was perceived to possess leadership qualities. Becoming treasurer, with its many perks, was just a continuation of this pattern. Olivares thrived in this setting.

As treasurer, one of Olivares's main responsibilities was to invest the assets of the order in a way that would provide additional revenues for its needs. These investments represented millions of dollars. The funds that Olivares invested came from different sources. One source involved the salaries of the order's clergy assigned to parishes throughout the western United States. Local diocesan bishops owned and controlled the parishes, but paid either diocesan priests or those of religious orders, such as the Claretians, to administer these parishes. Parish priests, whether secular (diocesan) or religious (members of an order) received a salary. However, religious priests, unlike secular ones, took a vow of poverty and hence turned over their salaries to the order. This became part of the investment funds available to Olivares. To meet their daily needs, Claretian priests, whether in a parish or not, received $25 a month. Of course, most of their needs, such as housing and food, were taken care of by the order. Donations to the order represented another source of investment funds. Sometimes a layperson would leave in his or her will the transfer of their home ownership to the Claretians.[39] Other benefactors might leave cash donations sometimes in the thousands of dollars for the order.[40] Private endowments provided additional revenue. The most notable case involved the Dominguez family, who had donated part of their endowment, including the properties for Dominguez seminary, to the Claretians.[41] Fundraising likewise added some additional funds. Olivares, for example, contracted with both Hallmark and American Greetings to provide Christmas cards and other greeting cards designed by the seminarians, as he had done himself as a seminarian, for reproduction and sale by these corporations. In return, the order received a percentage of the profits.[42] Still another funding source was the sale of properties owned by the order and the investment of the sales revenue into the stock market. This occurred, for example, when Olivares sold the Claretville seminary, due to the declining number of seminarians. By 1975 its enrollment was down to ten students.[43] These different types of revenue formed the basis whereby Olivares, in turn, invested these funds in the stock market in order to gain more revenue.

Olivares invested the Claretians' money in order to meet the various needs and expenditures of the order. This included the upkeep and support of its members, including a variety of bills, such as utilities, that needed to be paid.[44] The order also had to pay health insurance for its clergy and liability insurance for its properties. In addition, it had to fund its seminaries. Moreover, the Rome worldwide headquarters of the Claretians collected a quota from each of its provinces in order to finance its foreign missions.[45] "We're certainly not what you call wealthy," Father Frank Ferrante, a colleague of Olivares, observes, "but we have to budget ourselves. The treasurer is the one that has to be on top of things and make sure we don't go kaput."[46]

During his tenure as treasurer, Olivares was able to accumulate a multi-million dollar stock market portfolio for the order.[47] He also invested in some properties.[48] What stocks he bought had, in theory, to be approved by the Provincial Council. In fact, he made the decisions, and they were simply accepted by the council and the Provincial. "Of course as the treasurer he had tremendous influence," Msgr. O'Connor says of Olivares, "but still things had to be approved by the board [council]."[49] Rolando Lozano, a seminary student at Claretville when Olivares served as treasurer, notes that Olivares was very savvy about finances.[50] At the same time, Olivares did not make investments all by himself. He hired brokers and other investment consultants to advise him on what stocks to buy and when to sell them.[51] He did this, according to Ferrante, in order to make sure he invested wisely and responsibly. "We don't have zillions of dollars," Ferrante further reiterates. "But still what we do invest for our particular needs, have to be done in responsible ways without subsidizing companies that are unjust." How Olivares applied a kind of moral test to which stocks to buy, Ferrante does not elaborate on.[52] Even if he did use a moral litmus test, the fact is that Olivares proved to be very successful in investments that produced millions of dollars in dividends for the order. This was his job, and as with everything he undertook, Olivares applied himself fully and displayed an incredible work ethic. At the same time, he liked to impress others with his success and enjoyed being complemented and acknowledged for it. He had an ego. Taking the vow of humility was one thing; living by it was a more complex and human task.

But as an institutional man, or as treasurer, Olivares also had to be a "hatchet man."[53] He sometimes had to cut funding or check the books of certain pastors. Brother Modesto León recalls of his parish work that "Luis was tough on us and he was a budget man. He was a hard core administrator. He would come in and harass us for spending too much money on this or driving a car from here to there."[54] Rosendo Urrabazo recalls that, as a seminarian at Claretville in the early 1970s, he became aware of this side of Olivares's work, but also observes that Olivares paid a price for this. "You had to call people to account," he says of Olivares. "And Luis was strict on those things. He was very strict with money, especially the money of the order, and money in terms of accountability of money. And he developed enemies because of that. Not enemies. In religious life you don't have enemies, but people just didn't like him because he had to call them to account. And people don't forget those things."[55]

As treasurer, Olivares traveled a lot. He visited Claretian-run parishes throughout the western province, in Texas, Colorado, Nevada, Oregon, and Washington.[56] But he also traveled to New York to meet with potential investors. Desiring the order's money, Wall Street bankers and investment firms paid for his travel, put him up in fine hotels, and wined and dined him. "They would have a limo pick him up," Henry Olivares says, "and treat him with all the sophistication and luxury of a CEO."[57] Olivares enjoyed this treatment and liked "hobnobbying with corporate executives and being in the clerical fast track."[58] He sometimes flew to Europe to meet with European financiers. All this made Olivares feel important and gave him a sense of power. He accepted his role as "CEO" and even likened the leaders of the order to corporate heads. "The Provincial Council is the board of directors for the corporation," he reflected later, "and I managed the financial and business side of the operation. As the treasurer, I was put up in the best hotels, limousined [*sic*] to Broadway shows and shown the nightly in cities all over Europe by people who were basically interested in getting our accounts. It was a cushy lifestyle."[59] In Europe, he also met with his counterparts from other Claretian provinces throughout the world, since the order had missions in over sixty countries.[60] Teresa mentions that her brother enjoyed traveling and would always bring her gifts from his travels, especially when he visited New York and Europe.[61]

Olivares's time as treasurer allowed him to indulge in wearing elegant clothes, as much as a priest could have elegant clothes. Of course, he had always been conscious of his appearance and, as noted earlier, in the seminary always kept his cassock nicely pressed. But now as treasurer and as a major player in the order, he stepped up his apparel by several notches. He bought tailor-made suits—some made of black silk that, according to one source, cost up to $500, which in the late 1960s was quite a bit of money.[62] "He always looked great," one seminarian at Claretville observed. "He took on this high-powered very elegant financier look. We thought it was really cool."[63] With his suit, and underneath his collar, he wore nice shirts with French cuffs and expensive cufflinks.[64] One of his sisters remembers that he also wore a black velvet coat.[65] Brother Modesto León believed that it was important for Olivares to look professional and business-like, given his position as treasurer. "Luis . . . was working with bankers," he stresses. "So when you go to a bank, you're not gonna walk in with a serape on."[66] In his early thirties, tall and thin, and with an almost aristocratic look, Olivares not only fit well into his clothes, but looked very much like a member of an elite class. Only his thick glasses, for his nearsightedness, disrupted this look—but the glasses also made him look professorial.

Others, both fellow priests and seminarians, sometimes commented on his clothes; however, what brought the most attention to Olivares's appearance were his Gucci shoes, although one of his sisters says that he also had Armani shoes.[67] Much later, one Catholic newspaper referred to him as "the priest with the Gucci shoes."[68] Father Juan Romero recalls that some teased Olivares about his shoes. "I don't know if he actually did," he admits. "I didn't even know what Gucci shoes were."[69] One who teased him was Father Manuel De Santos, who was pastor at Our Lady of Soledad and a fellow seminarian in Washington with Olivares. "Luis, you're a crook," he told him because of his wearing Gucci shoes, kidding that Olivares bought the shoes from the funds he was collecting as treasurer.[70] "He had special shoes," seminarian Urrabazo observed. "They were not the shoes from Thom McCann or from Sears, what I wore. They must have been Italian or something."[71] The fact is that Olivares did wear Gucci shoes, as his sister

Teresa acknowledges. "He always had such nice clothes," she admits, adding that this included civilian clothes, such as nice sports jackets, that he wore on his days off. "I don't think that I ever saw him in jeans."[72]

Teresa and Olivares's other siblings defend their brother's nice clothes, observing that this was part of family tradition. Their father dressed very well and he passed this on to his children. "He was very classy," Damaso Jr. said of his father. One of Olivares's sisters, Rosario (Sister Victoria Anne), who became a nun, adds about this socialization: "I feel that even myself as a nun, I'm very classy. I got this from my father. I think the teaching moments were when he said, 'When you go out dress properly. I don't want to see you with curlers in your hair. You take time to put your makeup on, get up early.'" She notes that her father passed on this sense of proper appearance to her brothers. Damaso Jr. further observed that Luis was also influenced in his clothes by their Uncle Joe. "He was an immaculate dresser," he said of his uncle. "Different suits every day. Hat to match; shoes to match; the whole thing. Luis was very close to him. He [Uncle Joe] would go and visit my brother in California. Uncle Joe was able to portray that image of dressy." Luis took after his father and uncle in his dress style, according to the family. "I don't want to look cheap," Damaso remembers Luis telling him. "People look up to me. I represent the Claretians."[73]

But it wasn't just nice clothes that characterized Olivares's role as treasurer; it was also a lifestyle that reflected other fine tastes and luxuries. "I can tell you that Luis enjoyed luxury," Henry Olivares observes. "He enjoyed living luxuriously. If he had not been a priest, he would have probably been a corporate executive because he found this very satisfying. It gave him power and Luis enjoyed power. Very much so."[74] He adds of his brother's lifestyle: "He enjoyed the atmosphere."[75] Father Frank Ferrante adds: "Luis's personally was one of elegance. He liked fine things."[76] Urrabazo was struck by Olivares's lifestyle, which was unlike any other Claretian. "Luis lived a lifestyle that really was not normal for a priest," he says, "especially for a religious person." Still Urrabazo somewhat admiringly admits, "Any time he did anything or bought anything, he did it with a certain flair and style that was just above everybody else."[77]

Expensive cars were another luxury Luis allowed himself. It appears that during his tenure as treasurer, Olivares had the order purchase a Lincoln Continental and a Cadillac for his personal use. Urrabazo learned that Olivares purchased a new car at least every other year.[78] Glen Peterson recalls that Luis gave him rides from Claretville to downtown Los Angeles, where he had summer employment, in his black Lincoln Continental. Once, he let Peterson drive the car on his own back to the seminary, because Olivares was going to spend the night at Provincial House.[79] Olivares rationalized such a perk to Henry. "I need to have an air conditioned car because what if I'm called to a meeting and I'm there and I'm all sweaty," he said. "I wouldn't make a good presentation. The Claretians would not get a good return on their money."[80]

Olivares also developed a taste for fine dining at expensive restaurants, both when he traveled and in Los Angeles. He took potential contributors to the order to dinner. On occasion, he would also treat his fellow priests and seminarians at nice restaurants. Luis often took Henry out to dinner. "The bill would come to a hundred dollars and he would pay for it." Henry enjoyed this.[81]

Olivares, who like all Claretians received $25 a month for his personal expenses, could not afford his high lifestyle on this meager amount. He was able to have nice clothes and dine in style because, as treasurer, he had an expense account and a credit card. No other Claretian had those resources.[82]

V

Besides his role as treasurer, Olivares was also the Rector/Superior of the Claretville major seminary and novitiate in Calabasas, near Malibu. The seminarians lived in Claretville, but as college students, they studied at Loyola University in Los Angeles, while others fulfilled their one-year novitiate there. Claretville had been the former location of the theology school before it moved to Washington, D.C. Since Dominguez Seminary ceased to serve as the major seminary, Claretville assumed its role, though no academic teaching took place there. Olivares served as Rector for approximately ten years, several of those years overlapping with tenure as treasurer. Claretville had an interesting history. As noted, prior to being owned by the Claretians, it had been the home of King Gillette, the razor blade tycoon. It's most distinctive feature was a swimming pool resembling a razor blade. The grounds contained several buildings including the original mansion where the Gillettes had resided going back to the 1920s.[83] As Rector, Olivares lived at Claretville.

Olivares acted as the main administrator of the seminary. He insured that everything functioned well. Former seminarian Rolando Lozano described Olivares's job as being "in charge of making sure that we had the proper direction and guidance and formation." While no formal classes took place at Claretville, there were weekly spiritual conferences on vows of religious life, on prayer, and on the sacraments.[84] Olivares was in charge of as many as twenty-five seminarians in 1967, for example, but the numbers fluctuated, and overall they decreased.[85] He seemed comfortable being both Rector and treasurer, although, as Brother Modesto León points out, Olivares was more of a figurehead as Rector. Two other priests, including the resident Prefect, basically ran the seminary, due to Olivares's main responsibility as treasurer, and the fact that he had to commute each day from Claretville to Provincial House in Los Angeles, a commute of an hour or more each way, with heavy traffic.[86] "It was a nasty drive even back then," Lozano notes.[87] Because of Olivares's schedule as treasurer, the seminarians only had limited access to him. "We'd seem him mainly at [morning] Mass and meals because we were at school during the day and he was working during the day."[88] One aspect of the seminary that Olivares had to deal with involved some students who for various reasons needed to be expelled. The Prefect recommended the expulsion, and Olivares signed off on it.[89]

At Claretville, Olivares, now accustomed to a nice lifestyle, did not live with the other resident priests in buildings closer to the seminarians quarters. Instead, he moved into the Gillette mansion; only his black German shepherd Nowall lived with him.[90] His bedroom alone was 500 square feet. King Gillette had decorated his bedroom all in black and his wife's all in pink. Olivares's bathroom was also all black: black tiles, black sink, black toilet, black everything. The mansion also had a huge ballroom, with an organ. Peterson, who as a seminarian occasionally visited Olivares in the mansion with other seminarians, describes it as "really elegant."[91] He also observes that Olivares's moving in to the mansion seemed consistent with his new lifestyle as treasurer. "It kind of fit his persona of the day which was high roller financier," he says.[92] When he moved in, Olivares refurbished much of the mansion with new and comfortable furniture. "He kept everything very clean," Lozano recalls.[93] Frank Ferrante was not surprised that his friend Luis lived in the mansion. "Luis just enjoyed the good things in life," he stresses.[94]

Despite the fact that Olivares spent most of his working day at Provincial House attending to his duties as treasurer, he did spend some time in the evenings and on weekends with the seminarians, performing his role as Rector. But his dual roles sometimes meshed together, as when he had the students assist him in mailing out Christmas cards and other holiday cards to potential benefactors who might donate to the Claretians.[95] According to Father Carlos Castillo, who was one of the seminarians, he and the others did not mind assisting Olivares, because he was very friendly with them and quite popular with the students. "So that was like a social event for us," he says about mailing out the cards.[96] Lozano recalls that Olivares was "always very, very friendly, very supportive."[97] The seminarians also appreciated Olivares's sense of humor. At dinner time, even though he sometimes ate with the priests, he also dined with the students sometimes, and mingled with them at other times.[98] Castillo observes that Olivares spoke in English to the students, although sometimes he spoke in Spanish to Castillo who as an immigrant from Cuba, had retained much of his Spanish. Castillo admired that Olivares's Spanish was impeccable, and on occasion he heard Olivares deliver homilies in Spanish that were very impressive.[99] "He had a very projecting voice," Castillo says of Olivares's preaching. "He was tall; he had a very nice personality. . . . I heard a lot of compliments on his Spanish."[100] When Castillo was ordained in 1973, Olivares gave the homily in Spanish and another priest, Tom Loftin, said a homily in English.[101]

During the time he spend with the students, Olivares talked with them about their studies and how they were doing. He would sometimes meet with smaller groups of eleven or twelve, and sometimes in the evening after dinner. He would also arrange for individual sessions if a student requested one.[102] "He was an easy person to talk with," Father Al López, another former seminarian, recalls.[103] "Luis was very good at human conversation," Lozano adds. "It was a very friendly conversation." Sometimes Olivares would share thoughts with the students about his responsibilities and experiences as both Rector and treasurer.[104] Perhaps he did this with the expectation that one or more of these seminarians might rise to these positions later. Despite the pressures on his own time, he still saw himself as a mentor and role model for the students. But the fact was that he genuinely seemed to enjoy spending time with them. It was a refreshing break from his daily administrative work, and his "power" lunches and dinners with bankers and Wall Street executives. He had fun with the students, and at the time this filled an important gap in his life. He liked hearing them call him "Father Luis," as opposed to the more formal "Father Olivares."[105]

On occasion, Olivares gave rides to the seminarians in his car. Glen Peterson especially appreciated this at the time that he had decided to leave the seminary, and the long ride from Claretville to downtown Los Angeles where Peterson worked gave him an opportunity to discuss this decision with his Rector. Olivares expressed understanding and did not attempt to convince Peterson otherwise. "His brother had left the priesthood and I think he understood," Peterson remembers this experience.[106] Olivares would also allow some students to use his car if they needed to go to the doctor or had some other important appointment.[107] This effort extended, at least once, to those in the minor seminary. Rosendo Urrabazo tells the story of how, after his first year at Dominguez and in preparing to spend the summer back in San Antonio with his family, Olivares offered to give him a ride all the way, since he was going to be driving there with his sister, his aunt, and his uncle who had been visiting him. Urrabazo gratefully accepted the offer. On the day of departure, Olivares picked him up at the seminary in his black Ford LTD and introduced him to his family members. Sitting in the back seat with the two women, Urrabazo, who was only fourteen, said almost nothing on the three-day trip with overnight stops in Phoenix and El Paso, and with Olivares doing all of the driving. "I don't think I said a word the whole trip," he admits, due to his being intimidated by being with the adults, his shyness, and his lack of facility in Spanish. Olivares and the others spoke mostly in Spanish and mostly about family members. Despite his silence, Urrabazo was not only appreciative of Olivares's generosity, but was in awe of him and of spending this time with his superior. "So here I was just a young kid," he fondly says, "the end of my fourteenth year, going home with the provincial treasurer. This was a big thing for me. I just couldn't believe it."[108]

Conceivably, anyone of Urrabazo's age and position would have been awed by Olivares, but this was not necessarily the case for some of the older seminarians at Claretville. Of course, they admired and liked Olivares very much; however, they also had the courage to tease him in a friendly way about his lifestyle. Perhaps this attitude had to do with the Second Vatican Council and the result that seminaries reevaluated themselves and attempted to create a relationship between clergy and seminarians that allowed for a more collegial atmosphere. Moreover, since the seminarians studied and discussed the documents of the Council calling for reforms within the Church, some were inspired to assert themselves more in the seminary and to even challenge the clergy. Within this context, friendly banter between some of the seminarians and Olivares took place. It was bantering, and yet it was also a form of criticism of Olivares's penchant for luxury and high living. "There was some friendly bantering at times about a car that he purchased," Lozano recalls. "He purchased a new, black LTD, Ford LTD. Of course, back then tape decks were almost unheard of in the late sixties. He got it with one of those eight-track tape players. Some of the students would in a friendly way joke with him about this: 'Wow, because you're the treasurer, you can buy these really nice cars with a tape deck!' they said."

According to Lozano, Olivares took this in stride and just laughed. But he kept the car.[109]

The seminarians also joked about Olivares's clothes, although this may have been only among themselves. "I can remember," Lozano adds, "people would joke about the fact that his clothes were probably better than that of the average gum-chewing priest." Yet Lozano further added: "He knew how to dress. When he would wear a black suit, it would be a nice black suit. Or when he would wear a cassock, it would be impeccably pressed. It would look good. He was just good at clothing."[110]

When he later moved from Dominguez to Claretville, Urrabazo apparently lost some of his shyness and timidity around Olivares when he learned that the treasurer of the order did not know how to type.

"Father Luis, how could you go to school and never learn how to type?"

"That's what secretaries are for," Olivares responded good-naturedly.[111]

As part of his relationship with the seminarians at Claretville, Olivares performed liturgical services for them. He said daily Mass, heard confessions in the evening, and said Sunday Mass. At Sunday Masses, attended both by seminarians and laypeople who lived close to the seminary, Olivares often delivered the homily.[112] He liked to preach and was good at it.[113] In his sermons, he linked scripture to people's personal lives. "It was colloquial," Urrabazo notes. "In the early years it was more related to morality. The moral side of the teaching of the Church." He did not connect it with social justice issues. Although his sermons did not comment on social issues, he made an exception in the early 1970s when he spoke out against abortion and the Supreme Court decision in *Roe v. Wade* sanctioning the constitutionality of abortion. The Catholic Church vehemently opposed this ruling and openly articulated its opposition. Olivares followed suit and minced no words. "It was the legacy of the *Roe v. Wade* kind of stuff, all the abortion stuff," Urrabazo states of Olivares's homilies on the subject. "And he was very staunch against abortion. And he would preach very graphic homilies. His argument was if people knew what an abortion was, they would never do it. So he would give homilies giving very graphic descriptions of what happens during an abortion. And it shocked people."[114]

Though conservative on abortion, Olivares supported the liberal reforms of Vatican II on the liturgy, such as the use of the vernacular; the altar now facing the congregation; the use of secular music such as guitar and folk Masses; and the general effort to involve the laity more in the liturgy.[115]

His support of Vatican II further extended to the training of the seminarians. The spirit of the Council inspired a revitalization of the emphasis on social justice and on the needs of the poor and the oppressed. Loyola University, where the seminarians studied, was a progressive Jesuit campus that stressed classes on social justice and on Catholic social doctrine that likewise stressed the human rights of working people. It is also possible that by the late 1960s and early 1970s, liberation theology from Latin America was taught or at least referred to by theology professors at Loyola. Liberation theology represented the response of more liberal bishops and clergy in Latin America to the the Second Vatican Council's call for the Catholic Church to be more responsive to the needs of the modern world. Given the poverty and lack of democracy in Latin America at the time, liberation theology prioritized the needs of the poor and oppressed. It called for a "preferential option for the poor."[116] At the same time that the students were studying such concepts at Loyola, these influences were further reinforced by the resident clergy at Claretville. This was not a major departure for the Claretians, since their original mission had always been to administer to the poor; Vatican II only served to reinforce this mission. "We primarily were with the poor, the Latinos, Spanish-speaking immigrants, undocumented," Lozano declares of this mission. "We knew that at the time that that was what we were preparing to do. And those are the people we were preparing to serve someday."[117] Fellow seminarian Carlos Castillo echoed this view when he observes that their training at Claretville was centered on social justice. "You cannot deal with the poor," he stresses, "if you don't deal with justice."[118] The Council further reminded the Claretians about their origins as a missionary order. "We're sent to those who are the poorest of the poor economically," Lozano says of this objective, "and our mission is to bring the Gospel to them, to evangelize them to work for justice, to work for transformation and against unjust social structures."[119]

In addition to the Council's effect on theological studies at seminaries such as Claretville, it also introduced a more relaxed, if not fully equalitarian, relationship between seminarians and clergy. Among other changes, seminarians did not have to wear their cassocks all the time. Moreover, they had more freedom to choose their classes and their academic majors.[120] Of course, not all of the clergy eagerly accepted some of these changes, especially older priests in all orders and some diocesan priest; however, younger ones, including Olivares, did. Despite his own contradictory lifestyle, which he justified as part of his efforts to raise revenue for the order, Olivares as Rector accepted Vatican II and the changes it brought. He was not yet a liberationist himself, but he endorsed the renewal of the Church's ministry to the poor and oppressed. This backdrop, of course, is important to consider later, when Olivares would undergo his "conversion." "Luis read a lot and kept up to date with what was going on in the Church in terms of theological thinking," Urrabazo observes. "He was always an avid reader. He would talk about books he was reading."[121]

The years that Olivares served as Rector were also the years of the development of the Chicano Movement of the late 1960s and into the 1970s. The movement was the largest civil rights and community empowerment movement by Mexican Americans up to that time. It was led by a new generation who now defiantly called themselves "Chicanos," an older barrio and counter-cultural term of working class Mexican Americans. The movement elevated the term from an ethnic marker to a more politicized one. To be a Chicano during the movement was to be engaged in the movement, to be an activist in the struggle—*la lucha*. It was in part an effort by Chicanos to regain their ethnic-racial identity by rediscovering their history and cultural heritage, which had been denied them in the schools, for example. It was an effort by Chicanos to know themselves and use that recognition to not only challenge assimilationist efforts to deny them this history and heritage, but also to have the power to name themselves and be themselves—Chicanos.

Beginning with the farmworkers movement led by César Chávez and Dolores Huerta, by the late 1960s the movement had spread into the urban areas where the majority of Chicanos lived, including Los Angeles. The movement further manifested itself in school protests such as the 1968 East L.A. "blowouts," when thousands of Chicano high school and junior high school students walked out of their schools demanding a better education. University Chicano students struggled to get more Chicanos admitted and to establish Chicano Studies. Chicanos also protested in large numbers against the war in Vietnam, where many drafted Chicanos were being sent. The movement also spawned an independent Chicano political party, La Raza Unida Party, to achieve more effective political representation for the communities. These and many other manifestations, involving both men and women, composed the Chicano Movement—*El Movimiento*—that awakened the country to the history of Chicanos and their growing numbers. It provided the foundation for today's rise of Latino political power.[122]

Living in Los Angeles where many of these movement manifestations occurred, Olivares was no doubt aware of the movement, but there is no evidence that he related to it or that it affected his sense of identity. Olivares recognized himself as Mexican American, but he was not a "Chicano" even though, being from San Antonio, he knew that term. But he did not wear his ethnicity on his sleeve. This was not the case for the younger Mexican American seminarians at Claretville, who began to identify with the Chicano Movement and to be inspired by it. The movement made them rediscover their ethnicity and to link the movement with the cause of social justice, which they were studying in their classes. They became Chicanos. Urrabazo declares that when he first went to Claretville, no one, including

Olivares, stressed his ethnicity. However, Urrabazo encountered the movement through the lay Chicano student movement at Loyola. He and other Chicano seminarians began to relate to it and its ideology of Chicanismo, or cultural nationalism. Soon he and other Chicano seminarians, not only at Claretville but other Los Angeles seminaries, began to meet and organize as Chicano seminarians. They made contact with still other seminarians in California. They also attended meetings and conferences sponsored by PADRES, a new organization of Chicano Catholic priests in Los Angeles and throughout the Southwest that called for the Church to be more sensitive to the needs of Chicano priests, including the naming of Chicano bishops, of which there were still none in 1970.[123] Olivares was not part of all this; his own Chicano identity was still latent, yet he did not oppose the movement or the efforts of seminarians such as Urrabazo to participate in it. In fact, Father Juan Romero, a diocesan priest and one of the founders of PADRES, recalls that in the early 1970s and while still at Claretville, Olivares helped to spread the word about the new organization.[124]

Although as treasurer and Rector, Olivares had a very busy schedule, he still made time to socialize with some of his fellow Claretians. One such friend was Father Frank Ferrante, who was only a few years younger than Olivares. He and Ferrante often had dinner together in Westwood, adjacent to UCLA, where Olivares liked to go. Afterward they might see a movie. Both liked adventure movies, dramas, and romantic comedies. They did not like violent films. Ferrante saw Olivares as a confidante. "He was a good friend and if I wanted to share something with someone I could trust, Luis would be the one I would go to," Ferrante says. Olivares listened and that impressed Ferrante, but he also opened up to Ferrante and shared some of his feelings. This was a good release for Olivares, given the pressures of his work especially as treasurer. "He would share with me in terms of his own personal life, in terms of his work life," Ferrante recalls with fondness. "I would say it was kind of a mutual friendship. . . . He was a fun person to be with."[125]

VI

In his role as treasurer and Rector, Olivares was not immune to criticism of a more serious sort than the seminarian bantering. This came both from seminarians and some fellow Claretians. As one of the seminarians who was strongly influenced by Vatican II and by liberation theology, Rosendo Urrabazo openly voiced his criticisms of Olivares's lifestyle directly to him. This was not personal. Urrabazo admired Olivares in many ways, but believed that his preference for nice clothes and nice cars seemed to be in direct contradiction to what the seminarians were learning. He notes that because of this he began to distance himself from Olivares. "I would criticize him because I'm eighteen and I'm very idealistic about what it meant to be religious . . . and what a priest should be doing or not doing." He further describes his reasons for this criticism:

> This is the impact of Vatican II. This is all the books that we're reading about religious life and the changes in the Church and how the Church has to be one with the poor. It's the beginning of liberation theology. It's the beginning of the United Farm Workers movement. All this was having an influence on us in terms of how we saw what should be the role of the Church. And the Church would be on the side of the poor and the Church would be poor. And here our superior was just living another kind of lifestyle.[126]

Urrabazo was not alone in criticizing Olivares and doing something about it, as he and other seminarians moved from an earlier friendly kidding with him to more overt criticism and direct action. On one occasion, Urrabazo and another seminarian covered Olivares's car with toilet paper. "And then the dew came in that night and it ruined it," Urrabazo explains. "The car was a mess in the morning because the water made a mess of all the paper. . . . It was a criticism. I thought it was wrong for him to have a car like that." Other seminarians, according to Urrabazo, agreed with him and supported the action taken. "What is this guy?" the seminarians asked. "He's a priest and he drives around like a Cardinal?"

When he discovered what had happened to his car, Olivares, in what may have been a rare loss of temper, demanded to know who had done it. The students including Urrabazo told him that they did it.

"Clean it up," Olivares instructed them.

They did so, but had made their point.[127]

Urrabazo also admits that in general Olivares was willing to hear these criticisms, even if he might not accept them. "He would listen. He would smile. And he would disagree," Urrabazo states. Instead, Olivares told the students that he needed a certain lifestyle due to his position as treasurer and to impress the people he dealt with. Urrabazo thought that this was "a bunch of BS."[128]

Urrabazo concludes that the problem at that point in Olivares's life was that he had a pre–Vatican II mindset about being a priest: "It was the idea that a priest is a professional like other professionals and therefore should also have the same level of education and should be able to live a lifestyle where he can talk to other people that are professionals." Urrabazo and some of the other seminarians rejected this and saw themselves as future priests of the Vatican II era.[129]

But this criticism of Olivares did not just come from the students. Some Claretians also did not care for his lifestyle and even questioned his role as treasurer. One such criticism came from Brother Modesto León, who in the early 1970s was a member of the Social Justice Committee of the Claretian western province. He and other members of the committee "were young and in those days we were questioning the system." This questioning included their own order. One area of disagreement with Olivares had to do with the wages and benefits that the order provided its lay employees, and they confronted Olivares over the need to increase these compensations. According to León, Olivares resented this because it was an impingement on his "territory." León saw Olivares as much more a manager for the order rather than an advocate for social justice. "So we had some big old fights," he admits. It is not clear whether Olivares raised wages and benefits for those employees. At the same time, León recalls that an even bigger fight between the committee and Olivares occurred over whether Olivares as treasurer was investing in banks and Wall Street firms who were supporting the apartheid system in South Africa. It is remarkable that young Claretian clergy were already promoting disinvestment in South Africa in the early 1970s, years before this became a national and international movement in the 1980s. No doubt its missions in Africa made the order sensitive to this issue. "That was the biggest fight with Luis," León says, "because in those days Luis was kind of black and white as an administrator. He wasn't too worried about social justice and that kind of stuff."

"Are we investing in places that are affecting what's happening in [South] Africa?" León confronted Olivares.

The committee's position was that if the order had thousands of dollars invested in a bank that in turn invested in South Africa, then the order was complicit in supporting apartheid.

"I can't answer this because I don't know," Olivares responded.

Olivares did not admit to such investments, but did agree to investigate the order's possible connection to financial firms that invested in South Africa, and agreed that if this was the case that he would begin to disinvest in such firms. Though León and his committee pushed Olivares on such issues, León also realizes that Olivares was not a supporter of apartheid, but was simply looking out for the financial interests of the order and was not aware of the possible apartheid connection.[130]

At the same time, most Claretians seemed to have respect and admiration for Olivares and were grateful for his work as treasurer.[131] "He was a fair man," Ferrante states, "but at the same time, he liked to let you know that he was in charge of finances; Luis was a take-charge person." However, Olivares could be dialogic as treasurer, especially within the Provincial Council. On the whole, Ferrante believes that Olivares did an excellent job and that he never took himself too seriously. "He didn't feel that he was a god or something." Yet the criticisms affected Olivares. Ferrante asserts that, as a man, his friend Luis was a very sensitive person and was attuned to what people thought and said of him.[132]

In his own analysis of his role as treasurer, years later Olivares concluded that he had done a good job; at the same time, he admitted in retrospect that he had some deficiencies. But as far as his record and his role at this time, he had no feelings of guilt. "I don't regret those years," he told an interviewer in the early 1990s. "It would be very dishonest of me to say I didn't enjoy all that, because I did. I enjoyed the power, being treated royally, being picked up at the airport in a limousine. Definitely my family felt a great pride that I was making it."[133] He prided himself in being able to raise a great deal of money for the province to keep up the work of his fellow Claretians. Moreover, in response to the claim that as treasurer he did not treat lay employees well, he observed that he initiated a fair pay and benefits program for them that included medical insurance and retirement plans. While he did this not strictly on social justice principles, he noted, "These were all good innovations . . . that were bound to come, but the fact remains that I did it."[134] Olivares openly admitted that as treasurer he could be considered a "conservative," especially in financial matters and the fact that he was not doing parish work, but he asserted that one had to view his role as treasurer and a high official of the order in the context of the time. "I certainly did not have a reformist vision at that time," he stated. "I was kind of a conservative cliché, as a finance man, a Claretian, and as a member of the council. You're in the middle of decision-making, so your whole life revolves around what it means to be a Claretian. That's why being a Claretian had such a clear meaning for me during those years."[135] Olivares admits to being a good company man, and he had no qualms about this. He strongly believed in the institution of the Claretian order and worked to maintain and improve it. He did not believe in working outside of his system even after he underwent his "conversion." "I'm a very strong institutional person," he asserted.[136]

While Olivares had no regrets about his record as treasurer or his lifestyle, he did react with some sensitivity to a comment that his own father made about his being treasurer. While his father and whole family were extremely proud of Luis for his accomplishments and for the respect he'd earned, his father still had one nagging concern; he felt that Henry, not Luis, should have been treasurer first and risen in the ranks of the order. Olivares explains his father's view in this way:

I remember a comment that my dad made that has stuck in my mind because it puts a little different color on the whole situation of how my family looked at what I was doing. My dad said of my brother, "Of course he left [the priesthood], I don't blame him for leaving. He should've been the treasurer. He was older." It was that kind of reaction. It struck me; it kind of hurt. But it reveals very traditional Hispanic family beliefs about the older brother being responsible for everyone else.[137]

Olivares hastened to add that Henry did not feel the same way and that his brother's reason for leaving the priesthood had nothing to do with Luis being treasurer.[138]

VII

Despite his own defense of his work as treasurer and Rector, by 1975 Olivares seems to have reacted to some of his critics who felt that he was out of step with the reform spirit of Vatican II and the social movements of change during the sixties. "Reform-minded priests and seminarians saw Olivares as a representative of a leadership that had completely lost touch with the working-class and poor people who remained the lifeblood of the Church," the LA Weekly observed years later.[139] In part because of this challenge but also because, by Olivares's own admission, he thought doing parish work would look good on his record, he requested and was approved to be the pastor of Our Lady of Solitude Church or Soledad Church in East Los Angeles. At the same time, he was not yet willing to give up power, and so he remained as treasurer while stepping down as Rector of Claretville. Olivares saw the writing on the wall with respect to the seminary. Fewer students were enrolling, and even fewer were remaining.[140] While he was not aware of it at this time, opting for parish work represented a personal crossroads for Olivares. The decision would start a new history for Luis Olivares.

FIVE

Conversion

Although it is not clear what motivated Luis Olivares to decide to change course in the mid-1970s and return to parish work, the fact is that around 1974 he requested to be assigned to Our Lady of Solitude—La Soledad—in East Los Angeles. This was a Claretian-run parish, and it was a Mexican-American parish. "He could have chosen wherever he wanted," Rosendo Urrabazo observes.[1] But he didn't. He chose Soledad. A part of him, probably reacting to some of the criticisms he had received for his lifestyle as treasurer, went in this direction not only to counter these criticisms but, as he noted later, he felt that it would look good on his résumé. This revealed the still-ambitious Olivares who not only stayed on as treasurer, but hoped to rise further in the Claretian ranks, which meant becoming Provincial of the order.[2] At another level, a part of him seemed to want to get closer to the grassroots, and especially to working more directly with Mexican Americans. Olivares might have been ambitious, but he was not an opportunist, and he never lost his sense of duty in helping others, including the poor. East Los Angeles was as close as he could get to West San Antonio. "I had a wonderful experience with being involved in the parish," he would observe later. "It's different from being ensconced in a fancy office. You're dealing with people day-in, day-out."[3] Complex and with many feelings, Olivares did what he felt he had to do at that moment, and probably no single, specific motive can explain this.

Provincial Bernie O'Connor and the Provincial Council approved his request without any apparent concerns. As long as Olivares remained treasurer and continued to bring in revenue for the order, it didn't seem to matter whether he lived at Claretville as Rector or at Soledad. Probably to make sure that he would still have time to carry out his role as treasurer, O'Connor and the Council appointed Olivares as part of an experimental team ministry, in which two Claretian priests would be co-pastors of the parish. By sharing pastoral duties, Olivares would still have time for his work as

treasurer. Team ministry seemed to represent an engagement with the out-
comes of Vatican II by moving away from the more hierarchical structure
of one pastor being the main overseer of a parish and establishing a more
cooperative leadership.[4] Although used to making his own decisions, Olivares agreed to this arrangement. Claretian Brother Modesto León, who
had been at Soledad in the early 1970s, sensed that Olivares welcomed the
change as a possible way of easing out of being an administrator. "I think
he had kind of gotten tired of doing administration," he says. "He wanted
to do something different."[5]

Located in Boyle Heights on Brooklyn Avenue (now César Chávez Avenue), Soledad became Olivares's new home by mid-1974.[6] It was situated
in the largest Mexican barrio in the nation. It was not just one barrio, but a
series of barrios east of the Los Angeles River that in popular parlance was
referred to as East L.A. It was composed of both Mexican immigrants and
second-generation Mexican Americans. Like all barrios, it contained poor
housing, but for its residents, it was home. Commercial areas contained
restaurants, barbershops, *panaderias* (bakeries), five-and-dime stores,
botanicas (stores selling a variety of herbal medicines), and various other
businesses. And, of course, it had churches, mostly Catholic, but also some
Protestant and Pentecostal. Spanish was the dominant language although
second- and third-generation Chicanos spoke mostly English with a smat-
tering of Spanish, or *caló*, the street language of the pachucos and zoot-
suiters of the 1940s.[7]

All this was a significant change, for Olivares, from the King Gillette
mansion in Claretville, and no doubt a humbling one. Olivares adjusted
and seems to have combined parish work with his duties as treasurer while
working out of the parish office rather than at Provincial House although
he still did some business at the latter. What didn't work so well was the
team ministry. Although a noble concept of shared authority, Olivares soon
quickly discovered, as did the Provincial, that in practice you still needed
one person accountable for finalizing decisions. It was difficult and clumsy
to do so with co-pastors who might differ on certain issues. Moreover, Olivares was a take-charge and charismatic leader, and it was difficult for him
to not assert himself. In less than a year, Olivares was named the sole pastor at Soledad. "We found out that you still need somebody who can make
the final decision if there's a disagreement," O'Connor admits.[8]

By 1975, Olivares reoriented himself to running a parish. He, of course,
said daily and Sunday Mass, heard confessions, married couples, baptized
babies, confirmed teenagers, did *quinceañeras* (fifteenth-birthday celebrations of young Mexican American girls), attended to the sick, and buried

the dead. Soledad also had a parochial school, and so Olivares had to administer the school and work with the nuns who taught there. "It was a whole different world than what he had been living and working up to then," Fr. Ralph Berg, who was at Mission San Gabriel at the same time, points out.[9] Olivares was comfortably easing into this new world as a parish pastor, when history caught up to him.

I

That history had to do with the conditions of farmworkers in California, many of them of Mexican descent. Since the early twentieth century, Mexican immigrants and their offspring picked the fruits and vegetables of the expanding agribusiness empires in the Golden State. As immigrant workers, they were part of the first major mass-immigration wave from Mexico to the United States. Between 1900 and 1930, over a million Mexican immigrants crossed the border to labor not only in the fields, but on the railroads, mines, ranches, and urban industries and services throughout the Southwest, and even in other regions, such as the Midwest. Many also arrived, as did Olivares's family, fleeing the ravages of the Mexican Revolution of 1910. Coveted by white Americans for their cheap labor and viewed as members of an inferior race, Mexican immigrant workers contributed to the wealth of the nation despite not reaping the full fruits of their labor. In spite of the Great Depression of the 1930s, when John Steinbeck's Okies and Arkies competed for these "Mexican jobs" in order to get "Mexican wages," and during which the U.S. government approved the deportation of half a million people of Mexican descent (including U.S. citizens) for allegedly causing the depression and spreading diseases, Mexican farmworkers continued a legacy of farm labor that extended into the post–World War II era. During the war, growers augmented their labor supply by the importation of *braceros*, part of a wartime emergency-labor contract program between the United States and Mexico that brought in five million workers, adding to the cheap labor market in the fields. The program continued well past the end of the war, until 1964, at the behest of California agribusiness. Over the years, agricultural owners amassed billions of dollars of profit by exploiting the labor of both domestic workers and the braceros.[10]

Into the 1960s, poverty characterized the lives of many domestic farmworkers. Their annual income averaged only $1600 and sometimes less, due to seasonal employment. Moreover, they endured oppressive labor conditions. Labor contractors and foremen cheated them out of wages. They had no Social Security or other benefits. Their working conditions in some of the fields included the use of the short-handle hoe that made them work with hunched backs for hours leading to various physical problems, for which they had no health insurance coverage. Their dignity, especially that of women workers, was offended by the lack of bathroom facilities in the fields. Management sprayed them with pesticides as they worked. Child labor was rampant, and children of migrant workers had little access to education. Up to 1964, domestic farmworkers had to compete against the braceros, who were paid even less. Moreover, unionization in the fields was outlawed by farm owners and opposed if attempted.[11]

Despite these conditions, in 1962 a former farmworker with few if any resources believed that farmworkers could be organized and unionized. *Si se puede* (It can be done), he said; and this phrase became the motto of a movement. This was César Chávez. Three years later, he had organized enough Mexican and Filipino workers to strike against the major grape growers in the San Joaquin Valley. This became the largest farm-labor strike in American history. In this five-year struggle, Chávez displayed his brilliance as an organizer and a quiet but powerful charisma based on non-violence. A devout Catholic, he did not organize marches but *peregrina-ciónes*, pilgrimages of farmworkers and supporters, to call attention to the strike and to spiritually prepare the workers for the long struggle. To hit the growers where it hurt—in the pocketbook—he organized a national and international boycott of table grapes. When some of his members began to decry the benefits of nonviolence, Chávez engaged in a twenty-five-day fast in 1968, the first of many in his life. After five long years and with a un-yielding confidence that history was on their side, Chavez and the United Farm Workers (UFW), like David fighting Goliath, overcame the growers, and for the first time in American history, farmworkers obtained union-ization and contracts with higher wages and benefits. This victory, de-spite later defeats and internal problems, secured César Chávez's place in American history.[12]

But this was not just a bread-and-butter victory. It was a victory for the human dignity of the workers. They had been denied their humanity and social justice for years by growers, and a major part of the struggle was to secure their human rights. This was driven very much by the religiosity and spirituality of the workers, and certainly by that of Chávez. One can-not understand Chávez without understanding his spirituality. Many years later and after continued struggles to carry on *La Causa* as growers re-scinded contracts or signed with the more conservative Teamsters Union, Chávez was asked what kept him going, what kept him struggling? He tellingly replied: "Today I don't think I could base my will to struggle on cold economics or on some political doctrine. I don't think there would be enough to sustain me. For me the base must be faith."[13] That said it all.

César Chávez and the farmworkers made history, and that history would come to envelop Luis Olivares and lead to his "conversion."

II

"I would like to work with the farmworkers grape boycott campaign," seminarian Richard Estrada proposed to his faculty in the spring of 1974.[14]

Over the summer, each seminarian had to do some kind of student ministry or pastoral work. It could be in a parish or a mission. Rosendo Urrabazo, for example, taught at Our Lady Queen of Angeles school besides being a part-time chaplain at County General Hospital in Los Angeles. But Richard, who was from East Los Angeles, wanted to do something different. He wanted to work at a parish preferably in East L.A., but also to be part of the UFW boycott efforts. This was the renewal of the earlier boycott that had led to the initial victories and contracts. However, after the expiration of the contracts, the growers refused to re-sign, and so the union reignited the boycott, which had also been extended to lettuce when lettuce growers in the Salinas Valley refused to negotiate with the UFW. Estrada's faculty recommended this proposal to the Provincial Council in Los Angeles, who approved it, but with the proviso that he had to have a priest supervisor. It is not clear whether they asked Olivares to be that supervisor, whether Olivares volunteered, or whether Estrada asked Olivares to supervise him, since he was now going to be at Soledad parish, which would be perfect for Estrada's proposed work.[15] In any event, the two came together and this marked the beginning of Olivares's "conversion." "This was the beginning of a journey, a wonderful journey," Estrada notes.[16]

Estrada recalls that he first met Olivares at the University of San Francisco (USF) when Richard was a Claretian seminary student there. His first impression was not particularly favorable. Olivares seemed like a conservative priest. Estrada then encountered Olivares at Claretville at a retreat, and this impression did not change. "He was real stern like he was an español." He noticed that Olivares drove a big black LTD, wore shiny black silk suits, and had a big German shepherd. As a seminarian at USF, Richard on one occasion was actually assigned to pick up Olivares at the airport for a meeting on the campus. He remembers being afraid of the treasurer of the order. Still, now that Olivares would be at Soledad, this would be the ideal location for Estrada to work on the boycott.[17]

Olivares's recollection of meeting Estrada is a bit different. "It's all by accident that I got involved with the Farmworkers," he later related. "I was on the [Provincial] Council at the time and one of the seminarians asked if he could work with César. The Council said on the condition that you have a priest supervisor and I was in Soledad at the time, that's where the [boycott] organizing was going on very strong in East Los Angeles, so it would be easy for me to do that. But I thought it would be just checking in with me once in a while, but it didn't turn out that way."[18] According to Olivares, he volunteered to supervise Estrada.[19] Little did Olivares know that this decision would change his life.

No sooner had Estrada started at Soledad, which included living there, than he pulled Olivares into the boycott efforts. Olivares supported the farmworkers and their cause in theory and admired César Chávez from afar, but this type of political and community engagement had been foreign to him. However, as pastor at Soledad he thought that the boycott efforts would be one way for him to better know his parish and the people in it.[20]

"Father Luis, the union would like to know if it could use the parish basement for organizing sessions," Estrada asked Olivares.

"Well, Richard, I think that would be alright," Olivares responded.

"There's just one thing," Estrada further said. "It would be great if you could attend the meetings as a way of showing parish support."

"Now, Richard, is this your way of getting me involved in the boycott?"

"I think you would like the organizers and they would appreciate your support and whatever time you can spare in helping with the boycott."

"Okay, but I can't promise that I will be very much involved," Olivares concluded.[21]

Olivares gave his blessings to having the parish become involved. Estrada got him to agree to allow the union to hold meetings in the church basement and use it as a staging area for the volunteers, who would go picket at various supermarkets, such as Safeway, in the barrio. At 7 A.M. each morning, the boycott organizers and volunteers gathered in the basement. Both Estrada and Olivares attended. Olivares, according to Henry, soon began to realize that instead of him supervising and teaching the seminarian, the opposite was happening.[22] Usually about thirty people met there, who, according to Estrada, represented a future all-star cast of Chicano community leaders, as well as future politicians. Olivares became part of this stellar group. The meetings were also to train volunteers how to become boycott organizers themselves.[23] Estrada convinced Olivares to participate in this, as a way of showing further support for the union. He agreed, not fully knowing what this would entail. "The Farmworker organizer made a very strong pitch to involve me more directly," Olivares observed. "I became one of the organizers of that boycott in that year."[24] This involved more extensive training sessions with key organizers such as Fred Ross, who had taught César Chávez how to become an organizer back in the 1950s, when both belonged to the Community Service Organization (CSO), an early Mexican American civil rights group in California.[25] One of the organizing techniques that they learned was arranging for house meetings. They would get a community person to host a gathering of a few friends or neighbors at his or her home. At these meetings, one of the organizers would engage in a dialogue with them about the boycott and its importance. The intent was to not only spread the word about the boycott, but to recruit new volunteers for it. Soon Olivares was hosting at the church and participating in house meetings in East L.A.[26] As he became more involved, the people he worked with inspired him, and he began to reorient his priorities.[27] "We became friends," Estrada adds of his growing relationship with his pastor, who in turn befriended the organizers and volunteers, with whom he shared his great sense of humor.[28] "So that's where it starts," Henry concludes about his brother's transformation from a Claretian administrator with a rich lifestyle to pastor who worked with the poor and oppressed.[29] Meeting César Chávez himself would further this conversion.

How does one explain this change in Olivares even before he met Chávez? Based on his own Claretian support for social justice issues and the order's tradition of working with the poor and specifically Mexican Americans, Olivares already had an affinity with the cause of the farmworkers. This would only grow as he became more engaged. Moreover, by his own admission, working with the union intrigued him and sparked his curiosity about it. "It's a developmental thing that you start by curiosity," he later admitted about his initial involvement, "wondering what's going on at the meetings, and they tell you to come on in. They give you a bucket 'go and get a collection' and then the involvement with them, little by little."[30] But I also think that Luis Olivares, as a hands-on person and a proven administrator, was not someone who sat on the sidelines. If he became involved in an issue or cause, he did so completely. He was a natural leader, and he was aware that his clerical position already marked him as a leader. He wasn't going to sit back and follow. He was going to lead in the boycott effort. That was just his personality. As Henry said of him, if Luis saw a problem he took it on fully. This was who Luis Olivares was.[31]

III

César Chávez had always reached out to religious communities for support for the farmworkers struggle. Early on in the strike, he had such support from liberal Protestant congregations and groups, including the Migrant Ministry, a Protestant group that had been working in the California fields since at least the early 1960s to help farmworkers in any way they could. Jewish rabbis and organizations also rallied to his support. Ironically, the Catholic Church, as an institution, initially did not endorse the strike or boycott. Individual priests and nuns did, and participated in the union's marches and demonstrations, but not the Church hierarchy especially in the Central Valley. The fact was that the Church found itself caught in the middle of the dispute between the workers and the growers. Mexican and Filipino farmworkers, for the most part, were Catholic. On the other hand, so, too, were the growers, many of them of Eastern European or Italian ancestry. But it was the growers who substantially contributed financially to the Church. It would not be until almost the end of the strike in 1970 that the Church as a body supported the workers and helped to mediate the end of the initial conflict. With the commencement of the succeeding strikes and boycotts, the Church and Catholic clergy more openly sided with the union.

Sometime in 1975, Chávez visited the Provincial House in Los Angeles to see about securing funds from the Claretian order to help sustain the boycott. Here, he and Olivares met for the first time. The Claretians had tentatively agreed to provide some funds but wanted Olivares as treasurer to first meet with Chávez. The affinity between Chávez and Olivares was almost instantaneous. Not only did Olivares approve the funding, but he found himself drawn into Chávez's aura.[32] It was not that the UFW leader had a charismatic appearance. He was a dark-skinned Mexican American man, into his 40s, a bit paunchy, wearing a Pendleton shirt probably bought at Sears with rolled up blue jeans, who spoke softly. By contrast, Olivares was tall, thin, lighter in complexion, and elegant in his nicely-tailored clerical suit, and who spoke with authority. And yet, it was Olivares who was drawn to Chávez. It wasn't quite like St. Paul being struck by lightning, but meeting and talking with the farm labor leader seems to have profoundly affected Olivares. If beginning to work with the boycott was already converting him to social action, his encounter with Chávez was, by his own admission, a transformative moment.

Whatever questions Olivares had or what they specifically talked about is less important than the emotional effect that Chávez had on him. All we know is that, in later years, Olivares attributed what he himself called his "conversion" to meeting César Chávez and becoming more involved with the farmworkers. This was his baptism of social activism, and would later lead to his involvement with other faith-based movements including the

Fr. Luis Olivares and César Chávez, late 1970s.
(Courtesy of Henry Olivares)

sanctuary movement. Of this change, one of his sisters along, with Henry, states that there is no doubt but that Chávez played an important part in their brother's life.[33] The Rev. Chris Hartmire of the Migrant Ministry, who came to know Olivares well, opines: "I believe that meeting with César and getting involved in the farmworker movement made a huge difference in Luis's life."[34]

There was a power of attraction that Olivares felt about Chávez. It was like a centripetal force pulling him in to César's orbit. He had never experienced this with anyone else. Luis knew instantly that here was not only an important historical figure, but a real person with human attributes that Olivares wished to emulate.[35] "Never did I dream that I would be meeting César personally," he reflected later. "Something clicked between César and me. I was very attracted to him because of everything that he stood for."[36] Olivares seemed rejuvenated in meeting the farm-labor leader. It was exciting to be with César because he reminded Olivares that life had to have a meaning and that one had to have a cause rooted in helping others. After meeting Chávez, Olivares could no longer go back to being just an administrator or even just a parish priest; he had to become involved in *La Causa*. "It was exciting for me," he said, "it was like there was a purpose to what I was about."[37] He was attracted to César's integrity. "This is a man who had no political ambition, no economic ambition," Urrabazo says of Chávez's attractiveness to Olivares. "He [Chávez] just wanted to help his people. And that came across."[38] Olivares could not help but respect Chávez. He believed that he was a great man doing great work.[39] Moreover, Olivares was attracted to Chávez's passion and his sense of mission, observations that would be made of Olivares himself after his conversion. Arturo Rodríguez, who worked closely with Chávez in the UFW and would replace him as head of the union after César's death in 1993, has this to say about this connection between Olivares and Chávez:

> He [Olivares] was very business like . . . and very straight forward in terms of his work. And it was in the meeting with César and talking with him and beginning to learn about those experiences that farmworkers were going through that he [Olivares] really realized that there was something more that he could be doing. He could make a bigger contribution. His mission and his passion really changed at that point in time. And he really became dedicated and committed and passionate about social justice. . . . He mushroomed into a social activist after meeting with César. . . . And it was a real conversion.[40]

Finally, Olivares was attracted to what he saw as Chávez's holiness. One theologian, in fact, has called Chávez a mystic.[41] There was something saint-like about him, and this drew in Olivares. Of Chávez's holiness, Urrabazo notes: "And he was holy. He was a holy man. Some people say he is a saint."[42]

But this attraction was mutual. Chávez was also attracted to Olivares and what he saw in this Claretian priest. This attraction was not immediate, unlike Olivares's, but evolved over time, as Olivares worked with the union. César came to respect Olivares because, like Chávez himself, he made a decision to forego other possibilities for career mobility in order to dedicate their lives to the poor and oppressed. Chávez had been a key leader of CSO and could have remained as such. He was even considered for a position in the Kennedy administration in the early 1960s. But César turned his back on these possibilities, including a good salary with benefits that would have better taken care of his family, and instead chose to organize farmworkers and act as director of the union, getting paid only $5 a week like other union workers. Olivares, after his conversion, left his position as treasurer of his order in 1977 and focused his efforts not only in participating in the UFW's strikes and boycotts, but also in helping to organize his parish and other Catholic parishes in what came to be called the United Neighborhoods Organization (UNO), which took on discriminatory conditions in East L.A. Like César and like St. Francis, he also walked away from a position of privilege and opted to work with the disadvantaged. This similar background brought Chávez and Olivares together and was one of the attractions between them.[43]

Chávez also found Olivares attractive due to his ability to preach and speak well in public. Olivares was a natural and articulate orator with a powerful voice. Chávez lacked this speaking ability and admired it in Olivares. César recognized that Olivares could become literally an important voice for the farmworkers cause. Fr. Juan Romero, who also worked with the UFW, came to recognize this appeal that Olivares held for Chávez. He notes that he himself was close to César, but that Olivares was a notch or two closer, "because Luis had the gift of gab, the charisma of speech. He was a wonderful, powerful speaker and César didn't have that speech. He was pretty good [at speaking], and everything he ever did in his heart is what reached people, but Luis was a big orator. He did it really well, and I think that just speaking in some main events of the farmworkers brought them close."[44]

Above all, Chávez saw in Olivares a type of priest that became not only fully committed to the union but to the struggle for social justice. He could rely on him and be always confident of his support and leadership. He was a model priest for César. Rev. Chris Hartmire observed: "I think they were much closer than the time together would seem to indicate. I think there was a kind of a human connection there. And I think it was partly that Luis was both a traditional Catholic and a committed Catholic. That appealed to César a lot. He was very leery of the avant-garde priests. He sensed the instability that would underlie that, and with Luis there was none of that. This was a solid person who was clear in his faith and on his convictions."[45]

They also connected spiritually. Chávez's patron saint was St. Francis, who had given up family riches to minister to the poor and founded the Franciscan Order. César likened Olivares to St. Francis; this resemblance especially appealed to Chávez and made Olivares an exceptional person. "He [Chávez] just felt that Father Olivares was a special man," Paul Chávez adds. "I know that my father's patron saint was St. Francis, and I know that one of the reasons that St. Francis meant so much to him was because of the opportunities that St. Francis had during his lifetime and he chose the road of being of service and of volunteering poverty to serve people as opposed to enjoying the benefits his parents could give him. And I gotta believe that he felt some of that in Father Olivares."[46] According to his son, Chávez believed in "constant conversions" and that he applied this theory to Olivares. He saw over time that Olivares continued to evolve or convert to a deeper experience in working with the poor and oppressed. "Who we are when we die isn't who we began life as," César said.[47] Because Chávez had also gone through his own conversions, he could bond with Olivares on this.

Part of this spiritual bonding came to include Olivares's serving almost as a personal chaplain to Chávez. He began to travel to the Central Valley and not only say Masses for the farmworkers, but for César at the family compound at La Paz in the Tehachapi Mountains, where the union head-quarters had been transferred from Delano in the 1970s.[48] Soon Olivares was performing weddings and baptisms for the Chávez family. "César would call me and ask me if I would say the Mass," Olivares noted.[49] This only brought Olivares closer to Chávez.[50] As a personal chaplain to Chávez, Olivares seems to have also become his personal confessor. Paul Chávez observes that he wouldn't be surprised if this wasn't the case. "I know that they spent a lot of time together and I know that my father was a daily cele-brant [of Holy Communion]," he says. "I know that he and Father Olivares had long talks. So that doesn't surprise me at all. I just know that they were that close. I think their affinity went beyond their daily work and I think it went to something much more deep in our souls than talk about the re-sponsibilities that we have while we're here on earth."[51] Chávez worked with many other clergy, both Catholic and non-Catholic, but his relation-ship, both personal and spiritual, with Olivares stands out.[52]

Henry Olivares likewise testifies to this spiritual bonding between his brother and Chávez. He refers to them as "spiritual children." "They com-municated with this type of intimacy about their life," Henry notes. "He [Luis] told me that 'César tells me about his struggles and I tell him about my struggles. We compare. He's bucking the political authorities and I'm bucking spiritual authorities.'"[53]

The unique tie between Olivares and Chávez extended to social rela-tionships involving the Chávez family. Frequently, César invited Olivares to La Paz for dinner, Olivares often spend the night there. This included Chávez's wife, Helen, and their several children, most of whom were young adults. Almost all of the offspring worked for the union. Helen Chávez also loved and respected Olivares and saw it as an honor to host a Catholic priest for dinner, especially someone like Father Luis. She made special dishes for these visits, which Olivares relished. Helen liked to feed him be-cause she thought he was too thin. "I remember my Dad saying that the best way to show your love for somebody is to give them a plate of food," Paul Chávez states in connection with Olivares coming to dinner, "and I know that she [Helen] did that on more than one occasion."[54] At dinner, Chávez and Olivares shared stories and the rest joined in. Afterward, both retired to the living room where they talked about their work and sought guidance from each other. It would be quite late when Olivares finally retired to his guest bedroom.[55]

Olivares's social relations with the Chávez family also included marrying two of César's sons, Anthony and Paul. Both weddings were in La Paz with Olivares officiating at Anthony's and concelebrating at Paul's. These were outdoor ceremonies, since there was no church at the compound. "He was with us not just for the hard work," Paul stresses. "He was also with us on real important changes in our personal lives, ours and our families."[56] Next to family weddings, César's birthday on March 31 represented a particularly special occasion, and the family always invited Olivares to attend and give a blessing.[57] These invitations to special family events only served to highlight how close Chávez and Olivares became. Few others in Chávez's circle held such a special relationship. "I knew that my Dad worked with many people during his life," Paul concludes. "I know that there were just a handful of people that I know my father really considered a true friend. Not that he didn't appreciate relationships with other people, he did. However, there was a special bond with just a few and I know that one of those persons was Father Olivares."[58] Olivares welcomed his inclusion into Chávez's extended family, which provided once again that surrogate family he always seemed to seek.

Chávez and Olivares's friendship was not all limited to heavy discussions about their work. Both shared a love of life; they enjoyed laughing and joking and savoring life—*sobrevivir la vida*. Both had wonderful smiles and ways of laughing, and they laughed a lot together. They loved to tell jokes. Both had a wonderful sense of humor.[59] They worked hard, but they also socialized hard. Paul Chávez puts this part of their relationship very well:

> My father was a very serious man, just like Father Olivares. But I also know that they had a way of living life in a manner that the burdens of their work didn't take over the essence of who they were as human beings. They saw injustice, and they fought very hard to right it, but they also knew how to love life and live it to its fullest. So I gotta believe that that was a big part of their relationship. . . . They worked like there was no tomorrow, but they lived like there was no tomorrow as well.[60]

From that initial meeting in 1975 all the way to their deaths (both in 1993), Olivares and Chávez developed a rich and lasting friendship based on their politics and their personal affinity for each other. People saw this and admired their special relationship. Dolores Huerta, who became vice president of the union, notes that Chávez and Olivares saw themselves as brothers or *hermanos de espiritu de la causa* [spiritual brothers of La Causa].[61] UFW organizer Oscar Mondragon witnessed firsthand this attraction. "They believed in each other," he noticed. "They were open people. They were humble people with great respect for each other."[62] Mondragon also observed that both of them quickly came to talk like old friends.[63] Chávez reciprocated Olivares's visits to La Paz by visiting his friend at Soledad and later at La Placita. [64] They also talked to each other on the phone.[65] When in Los Angeles during the 1980s, Chávez would attend Mass at La Placita. He loved to hear Olivares preach. After Mass, Olivares would arrange for a breakfast for César and his entourage in the church hall. Olivares always had to be cognizant that Chávez was a vegetarian, and so he had the cook make a special breakfast for him while making *huevos con chorizo* for the others.[66] "When César came," Lydia López, who worked with Olivares, observes of the farmworker leader's visits, "it was like having the most important person in the world."[67] The friendship between Olivares and Chávez transcended their work. "It was a really profound personal relationship," Paul emphasizes.[68]

At the same time, Olivares's embrace of Chávez and the farmworkers, and his deep friendship with César, had consequences. It meant that he had chosen to no longer chart his career by being an administrator but instead to become an activist priest in the community. Not all in his order supported this change, and some would hold it against him.[69]

IV

While there is no question that meeting and engaging with César Chávez proved to be an epiphany and the key source of Olivares's conversion, still one might suggest that there were also other influences in this transformation. For one, as Richard Estrada points out, it was also meeting and engaging with the farmworkers themselves that converted Olivares to a new life of social activism. He met farmworkers on the picket lines in Los Angeles promoting the boycott of grapes and lettuce, and also in the Central Valley on his trips to Delano and other farm-working camps. He was moved by their poverty, but also by their spirit to change their conditions. He vowed to help them. They inspired him to be part of their struggle for human dignity and social justice.[70] He ministered to them by saying Masses in the fields and in their churches. He married them, baptized their children, and buried them. He was especially moved by the funeral of one worker, Porfino Contreras, who was killed by one of the growers in the Calexico area. On hearing of this tragedy, Olivares immediately drove there to try and comfort the family. He arrived at midnight and participated at the *velorio* or wake; he prayed in Spanish for the soul of Contreras. His presence helped lift up the family and other workers. The next day, he marched with others on the main street of Calexico, calling for justice for Contreras. He felt as one with the farmworkers.[71] This was only one of several protest marches, rallies, and UFW conventions where he joined hands with the workers. This touched him immensely. "Working with the farmworkers, being in touch with people out in the fields, going out to the funerals and their victory marches and to their rallies and to their protest marches," he said later, "I got the sense that that was where I belonged rather than in a fancy office juggling figures and managing portfolios and selling stock and buying properties."[72]

This part of Olivares's "conversion" reminded Rev. Hartmire of Archbishop Oscar Romero in El Salvador, whom the Vatican appointed as the chief prelate in that country under the assumption that he was not a liberationist priest, but a conservative follower of Pope John Paul II. However, Romero underwent his own conversion by his ministry to the poor and suffering people in the midst of a brutal civil war. Romero became a martyr to his people when assassinated in 1980. Hartmire likened Olivares to Romero, who would become one of Olivares's inspirations. Of this comparison, Hartmire reflects on Olivares: "Essentially middle of the road, respected clergyman, ambitious, and never known for taking risky stands. Suddenly encounters the farmworkers and becomes this entirely new person. Something lurking there in his spirit that got unleashed."[73]

Richard Estrada, who traveled with Olivares to be with the farmworkers, witnessed the profound affect that they had on his mentor. He was moved by their hospitality as they invited him into their humble homes. "Venga, Padre, venga," (Come inside, Father]), they called out to him. He, in turn, admired their warm hospitality and their resilience. Despite their poverty, they were a people of much personal and collective dignity. "It was really beautiful," Estrada says of this contact between Olivares and the workers. Estrada is of the opinion that while meeting Chávez was of great importance for Olivares, it was really the farmworkers—the people—that converted him.[74] "They transformed him and he blossomed," Estrada asserts. "Luis was like he needed to be loved and nurtured and this is what the workers and their families offered him—a new family."[75]

Olivares acknowledged that he learned many lessons from the farmworkers, in particular that you are converted by the people you serve. "You may initially get involved in a cause for altruistic reasons, because you want to help those 'poor people,'" he testified. "But pretty soon you are fighting with them and they are doing more to convert your way of thinking than what you are doing for them. After a while, the enthusiasm comes out of that rather than out of your own conviction."[76]

But it was not just the farmworkers who helped convert Olivares. While living at Soledad, Estrada also witnessed that the poor and humble parishioners likewise affected Olivares's views. He not only worked with them on the boycott, but very soon also became engaged in community organizing to address the needs of this urban flock (see chapters 6 and 7). Barrio people and their needs, Estrada contends, were also responsible for the new Olivares.[77]

This new Olivares, however, was not only converted into a social activist, but to a reawakening of his Mexican American or Chicano identity. The farmworkers movement was both a labor movement and an ethnic one. Most of the workers were of Mexican descent. Some were immigrants while some were U.S.-born. Chávez brilliantly tapped into this ethnic background by using Mexican symbols and iconography in the movement. He put a modified version of the Mexican eagle of the Mexican flag on the banner of the union, or at least this is how people interpreted it. He had a special devotion to Our Lady of Guadalupe, the patron saint of Mexico, as did most other Mexican Americans, and hence he used the image of La Virgen in the marches and rallies. He used terms such as *huelga*, the Spanish term for strike, and *La Causa* to mobilize the workers. By using familiar historical and cultural markers, Chávez wanted to convey to the workers that the UFW was not an outside union, but in fact a homegrown, Mexican American one. This was their union. His use of ethnic and cultural symbols, in turn, inspired a new generation of urban Chicanos—the Chicano Generation—who began to explore their Mexican roots and cultural heritage, leading to the cultural nationalism of the Chicano Movement.

This same process also affected Olivares. César and the farmworkers' version of cultural nationalism restored Olivares's ethnic identity. It was okay to be a Mexican. He had put this identity aside as he moved from being a seminarian to being a Claretian priest, and then a top administrator of the order. "I credit [César Chávez] with his reintroducing me to my roots and my background and my ethnicity," he reflected, "because being an administrator you have a different perspective on life, your profit motive is very strong."[78] This experience put him back in touch, as he put it, with his Mexican American roots and the Spanish language, the primary language of the farmworkers.[79] "My getting to know César and working with the farmworkers was a wonderful experience which had a great impact upon my relating to myself as a Mexican American," he concluded.[80] Olivares noted that this ethnic resurgence further involved regaining his Spanish first name—Luis—that had lain dormant until his conversion. Some of his colleagues in the order kidded him that they had known him as Louis, but now that he had become involved with the farmworkers he had changed his name to Luis. This suggested some kind of opportunism, and Olivares rejected this implication. "My original name is Luis on my birth certificate and my baptismal certificate," he said. "It's just that . . . in school they tell you that's your Spanish name, your *real* name is Louis. And over the years I bought into that. I accepted it in grammar school, I went with Louis to the seminary, I was Louis through those first seventeen years of my priesthood. But I was always Luis, I just used a different name for a while!"[81]

Olivares's conversion can also be said to contain still other influences that his involvement with the farmworker and the East L.A. community revealed. For one, caring for the poor is what Abuelita Inez had taught him and his siblings by her acts of mercy and compassion for the poor in the barrio. The same was true of his father and Tía Concha, who also helped the downtrodden. So this liberationist tendency was in his social DNA; it was part of his cultural background, which he had set aside in his ambitions to go up the Claretian administrative ladder. In a sense, he was just coming back home to a family who cared for the poor and did not look down on them, but saw them as children of God. "The roots were there," Urrabazo observes, and continues:

> Luis came from a poor family. . . . I think he probably, like many of us, hated poverty. We didn't join the religious order to be poor. We joined [a] religious order to change the world because we didn't like what we saw in our own families and our own upbringing. I think Luis had some of that. He grew up in that kind of environment. His family was working class. . . . This concern for the poor, I think, was always there. I think his initial formation did not foster that side of him. It developed the more administrative, leadership side of him. But leadership for the Church. It wasn't so much leadership to be among the poor, but for the Church. He was groomed to be a leader in the Church.

Urrabazo believes that the transformed Olivares would have become a terrific bishop, but a controversial one.[82]

If family socialization established a type of preferential option for the poor, as liberation theology stressed, then Olivares's Claretian training can also be said to be part of the explanation for his conversion. He was of course well aware of the Claretian emphasis on ministering to the poor; this had been part of his seminary education, even if he had not put it to work in the early years. Still, it was there and his moving to work with the poor in part is a reaction to this training or to a resurfacing of this influence. This sentiment was there, as Fr. Al López, who worked with Olivares at Soledad, notes in relation to Olivares: "'Do all you can do, be on fire with God's love' was a Claretian mantra with respect to working with those less fortunate. It was there but not quite as radical as Mother Teresa, but I think it was an awakening for Luis."[83] The Claretians' stress on the poor was buttressed by the fact that they were a missionary order. They had been founded to be missionaries to the poor in Third World countries and also in developed ones. Olivares inherited this missionary mandate even though he was removed from it early on in his career. Rudy Maldonado, who had been a seminarian with Olivares, observes: "We were missionaries sons, of the Immaculate Heart of Mary. That was a theme that ran through us all the time."[84]

Finally, one can also attribute the influence of the Second Vatican Council to further explain the new direction that Olivares took in the 1970s and after. By calling for the Church to be more open and involved in the modern world, it put greater emphasis on parish work, among other things. But this was to be a new parish work beyond the confines of the church, rectory, and parochial school. Priests were to become engaged in their communities, to become community priests in working on more secular issues. Olivares, himself, later confirmed that Vatican II allowed him to go beyond his more strictly priestly duties and go out into the community instead.[85] In theological terms, it meant, Maldonado suggests, a warmer God more sensitive to parishioners' needs, and not just spiritual needs but material ones as well.[86] Vatican II further stressed the Church as being the people, not just the clergy, and so the Church had to be involved in this world and not just the one after death. Such social action called for or indicated by Vatican II, Fr. Ferrante believes, put flesh on the concept that the people are the Church.[87] Henry Olivares seconds this and notes that Vatican II impacted him and his brother, though not right away. What Vatican II meant, Henry contends, was that it was okay for priests to go out of the sacristy of the church and to go into the world and get involved with people. Vatican II gave Luis permission to become involved when he was ready to do so.[88] As Henry puts it, it "allowed Luis to fly." As part of his epiphany, Olivares recognized that what he had been doing was not what Vatican II wanted of the clergy. "He realized that what he was doing then was not really what he should have been doing," Henry concludes. "The greatest influence in his life, his later years, was César Chávez. That's when he becomes aware of 'the Church' meaning the people, rather than just the hierarchy or the well-to-do."[89] Olivares went from an intellectual support of the poor and oppressed to an actual encounter with "*los de abajo*" (the underdogs). "Yeah, the Church has to help the poor," Juan Romero says of Olivares's initial position and his change. "It was up here [points to head], but it wasn't in his gut or as much. It wasn't a lived experience, and then you experience the farmworkers and getting close to César, he [Olivares] saw that it was more than just a general thing, up in the air, that it had names and faces and people and their struggle that he identified with and became a part of."[90]

Meeting Chávez was the catalyst but all of these other influences, in turn—his own family socialization, his training as a Claretian missionary, and the impact of Vatican II—were reawakened within Olivares and played a role in his new life. All of us change and all of us can point to certain points in our lives where we go in new directions. Sometimes it involves one major and unforgettable moment and encounter, but sometimes it involves a series of influences on us. Olivares was no different. He believed that his life was going in the right direction even though as he looked back on it, this involved mostly his individual ambitions. Meeting Chávez and then becoming part of the farmworkers' struggle made him realize that his priorities were misplaced and that one can more fully satisfy individual desires within a collective struggle. Yes, Luis Olivares still had an ego—he still wore his nice suits, for instance—but now he was placing this ego at the service of others.

V

Luis Olivares's engagement with César Chávez and the UFW was not just philosophical and ideological, but it was a practice as well. He had a praxis that he followed. He observed the conditions of the workers, reflected on them, and then acted. In this praxis he became involved in a number of union activities and as a leader. As noted, at Soledad he hosted boycott training sessions where he himself learned to be an organizer. He invited parishioners to house meetings at the parish and helped organize house meetings in the barrio.[91] As a UFW organizer, Olivares headed up boycott activities in the Boyle Heights section of East L.A.[92] Soledad became the main organizing center for the boycott. "That was our local parish contribution," Fr. Al López stresses.[93] The church, according to Dolores Huerta, was the official campaign office for the boycott, and Olivares housed some of the farmworkers who went to Los Angeles to picket the stores.[94] On certain occasions, Olivares hosted Chávez at Soledad where the farm-labor leader encouraged the boycott organizers and volunteers to continue their work.[95] As an organizer, Olivares would also travel to La Paz, or other places in the Central Valley, to attend strategy sessions.[96] In addition, he picketed in the fields with the workers.[97] He also used his position as both pastor and as treasurer of the Claretians to provide housing for farmworkers who came in to Los Angeles to be part of the boycott activities. Rev. Hartmire recalls that he once approached Olivares at Provincial House about being able to house some of the workers and volunteers from outside the city. Olivares arranged for this and did so on various other occasions.[98] He also fed the workers and volunteers both at Soledad and when he moved to La Placita. Mondragon remembers that he did this even at a time when Olivares was becoming more involved in the sanctuary movement. He still had time for the UFW.[99]

In effect, Olivares became one of the key contacts for the union in Los Angeles. Whenever the union needed something in the city, they called on him. "From 1975, my contact was very close and whenever anything happened in L.A., I was involved," Olivares observed. "César would call me personally to say 'you know we're gonna do this, we're gonna do that.'"[100] As he usually did in any pursuit, Olivares plunged in fully. "Whatever the campaign was, Luis was always there," Hartmire notes.[101] Due to his union activities, many in the UFW believed that he was a full-time organizer for the union at the same time that he was a full-time pastor.[102] This all put a lot of pressure on Olivares, yet somehow he kept up. "He chose to take the path that was a lot more difficult, was nowhere near as easy, required a lot more of his personal time and his work and his energy," Art Rodríguez admiringly recalls Olivares's involvement with the union.[103]

One of Olivares's main activities, and one that took much of his time, was picketing the supermarkets with other volunteers and farmworkers. They picketed against non-union grapes, non-union lettuce, and against Gallo wine, which was owned by one of the companies that refused to negotiate with the union. Gallo wine was not exactly a premium wine, but it was popular among working people, including Mexican Americans, because of its low price.

"Huelga! Don't buy non-union grapes!" he called out as he and many others would circle the entrances to the Safeway and other stores in East L.A.

His boycott activities even extended to his family in Texas.

Fr. Luis Olivares (left), Dolores Huerta, César Chávez, and Fr. Juan Romero,
East Los Angeles, picketing in support of farmworkers, late 1970s.
(Courtesy of Fr. Juan Romero)

"Teresa," he would tell his sister, "don't eat non-union grapes because
they're grown by companies that don't want to recognize the union. Tell
others in the family to also not eat those grapes, and tell your friends."[104]

Olivares also encouraged other Catholic clergy to join the picket lines. It
was impressive to see priests in their clerical clothes on the picket line, and
Chávez and the union encouraged this because of the Catholic background
of most Mexican Americans. Their presence showed that the Church ap-

proved of the boycott and so the faithful should observe it.[105] Hartmire recalls one particular picketing event that impressed him: "There was a big picket line in East L.A. and we were trying to get some religious people out in the picket line. Luis would come. He would wear his clerical collar. Sometimes César would come down, part of a publicized picket line. He and Luis would walk together around the picket line."[106]

On such occasions, Olivares would not only wear his nice suits with a collar, but also his Gucci shoes. Some of the other organizers would good-naturedly kid him that those were the only shoes he had.[107] But on other occasions, Olivares changed his picketing attire. Richard Estrada recalls seeing him on a picket line on Soto and Olympic wearing Levi's jeans, a jacket, boots, but with his collar on and carrying a picket sign.[108] He also proudly wore a button on his coat or suit that read "Boycott Grapes," or when he and others picketed a Vons grocery store, his button would say "Boycott Vons." At one Vons store, Olivares joined Chávez and others in protesting a court order that prohibited picketing too close to the store. The union challenged this and still picketed close to the store. Apparently, no arrests resulted and the picketing continued.[109] In fact, Olivares carried his own UFW flag, which he kept with him at his rectory. On these picket lines, Olivares was vocal and always leading the line. "He was up front," Mondragon states. "He wasn't in the background. He was a brother and a supporter."[110]

Besides picketing the supermarkets, Olivares joined other union organizers, volunteers, and farmworkers in picketing the downtown Los Angeles produce market, where the non-union grapes and lettuce were delivered from the fields. Their purpose was to convince the workers who unloaded this produce not to do so and instead to support the boycott. In most cases, they were unsuccessful, but they made their point, especially if the media covered these demonstrations. The produce market workers were huge guys, many of them Mexican Americans or African Americans, and not very friendly toward the UFW. "This was hostile territory," Paul Chávez says. But he always remembers how cool and collected Olivares was in the face of this hostility:

> When we went there, you had to have pretty thick skin, because many times we were berated or yelled at or cursed by some of the workers at the produce terminals. I can remember a couple of times where Father Olivares led the delegation only to be met with pretty harsh words, and I remember his composure and continuing to try to explain to those guys why they should stop doing what they were doing.

He was always a very determined man, but he did it in a way that impressed us. He had this quiet elegance about him that really complemented that determination.[111]

But Paul Chávez also recalls that at the end of this confrontation, Olivares would make all of the UFW supporters feel easier through his sense of humor, and making them laugh by cracking jokes about what had transpired. It was not that he was making fun or light of the activity. He wanted to defuse any tendency toward violence and to lift their spirits. "I remember he had a way of meeting the uneasy situation with a good laugh."[112]

Olivares further supported the union cause by speaking at news conferences held by the UFW. With his strong and eloquent voice, he reached out to others, both in public and through the media, to tell of the plight of the farmworkers and their right to a union that would improve their lives and those of their families. Even into the 1980s, when Olivares became the voice of the sanctuary movement, he remained a voice for the farmworkers.[113] "He spoke when we needed him to speak," Hartmire says.[114]

Marches and rallies also formed part of the UFW's tactics, and Olivares participated in many of these.[115] Olivares spoke at many of these events. "Those were the days when we could mobilize 10, 15, 20,000 people for a rally," he described the mid-1970s. "They were exciting times. And the people's response to you was infectious; you couldn't help but get sucked into it."[116] Such mass political activities empowered union members and their supporters. It taught Olivares a lesson about how to use public demonstrations as a tool for community empowerment, a lesson he would employ in his barrio community work and in the sanctuary movement.

As he became more involved with Chávez and the union, Olivares attended the annual UFW conventions, usually held in Fresno. He often gave the invocation, and on several occasions, was asked to address the convention. Olivares considered this a great honor. He spoke in Spanish and English. In his speeches, he rallied the workers to continue their struggle and assured them that God was with them.[117] "Luis would be present," Art Rodriguez notes of Olivares's attendance at the conventions, "and would always be there to help us understand and put into context what it is that we were doing within the social teaching of the Church."[118] With his voice, Olivares touched the emotions of the union members. "What I remember most of all was his tone of voice," Paul Chávez observes. "His conviction in speaking."[119]

As treasurer of his order up to 1977, Olivares also managed to get the Provincial Council to provide funds for the UFW.[120] Moreover, he participated in fundraising activities for the union, lending his name to these events and speaking at them well into the 1980s. Oscar Mondragon recalls one particular fundraiser in the 1980s, when Olivares delivered the keynote address at the event, held at the downtown Hilton in Los Angeles. Luis Valdez, the founder of the Teatro Campesino (Theatre of the Farmworkers) served as the master of ceremonies and additional speakers included Jane Fonda, Peter Fonda, Linda Ronstadt, and Martin Sheen.[121]

Finally, part of Olivares's praxis was to minister to the farmworkers in his role as a Catholic priest. He never divorced his social activism from his priestly responsibilities. He was an activist priest and now saw no contradictions in this. He did earlier, when he was just focused on being an administrator. His spiritual outreach to the workers in the fields was part of his role within the union. Hence, he said field Masses, performed weddings, baptized the babies of the workers, blessed their homes and cars, and, at times, buried the dead. At the UFW conventions, he concelebrated the Mass with other fellow priests. All this was just as important to him as speaking at a rally or picketing at the stores. He was now a converted priest.[122]

VI

Finally, Olivares's conversion is linked to a new way of doing ministry. Ferrante, in particular, emphasizes this aspect of the change. In this interpretation, Olivares represented a vanguard of Claretians who became community priests and applied their teachings to social action. Olivares led the way by going beyond the more conventional parish work of most Claretians. To Ferrante, Olivares was on the cutting edge of a new form of ministry that Ferrante applauded.[123] Fr. López agrees and defines this new ministry in the following way: "I just knew that Luis was very charismatic. Strong personality. . . . He could see beyond the structure. He could see that this is where the call was to be a Christian, to support people, to become actively involved."[124]

If the Claretians had particular reactions to Olivares's conversion, so, too, did his family and friends, who were taken aback by this change in him. Henry Olivares subscribes to the notion that it was meeting César Chávez that led to his brother becoming political.[125] Some of his other siblings have a slightly different view. They believe that their brother was political all along and wanted to become an activist, but that he didn't at first out of respect for his parents, who did not believe that priests should be political. So he waited until the death of his father and Tía Concha before becoming an activist. They point out that their father disliked the Chicano Movement. "My father was very, very adamant against activism," Damaso Jr. says. "He did not think that it was right to go out into the streets. My aunt was the same way, as was my grandmother." However, when his parents died, Damaso suggests, that allowed Luis to move in another direction. "Now I can be myself," Damaso conjectures that his brother said to himself. "Now I can be one of them."[126] The problem, however, with this theory is that their father did not die until 1980 and Tía Concha lived until 1982, whereas Olivares had already been an activist since 1975.[127] Henry Olivares disagrees with his siblings on this. "I personally believe that whether my father was alive or dead," he says, "Luis still knew what he had to do and did it no matter who might oppose him." He hastens to add that his family would accept anything his brother did, because of family bonds.[128] The contradiction between the chronological facts and the other siblings' account may be resolved in considering that Olivares never told his family, especially his parents, about his activism and was not open about it until after their deaths. This is corroborated by Teresa Garza, who says that she initially did not know that her brother was involved with the farmworkers or in community politics in the 1970s. When Luis would call her, he never mentioned these activities. All they talked about were personal and family issues, although he did tell her not to buy non-union grapes. "I didn't know of his turnaround," as she puts it. "I didn't know what was going on."[129] At the same time, Teresa connects this activism with the influence of Abuelita Inez, who always told them as children to help the poor. Teresa sees continuity between this family influence and Luis's political involvements. She notes that her brother had no reservations about his activism and was not afraid to challenge the higher-ups. "I saw him as—his primary goal was that he was a priest first of all," she adds. "But he became more aware of the poor people, of what they needed, and what the Church needed to do. Some priests would agree with him and others wouldn't. Luis believed or came to believe that everybody should get involved to help the unfortunate people."[130]

Arnie Hasselwander, who kept in contact with Olivares throughout this period, was not so surprised at his change. It may be that, going back to their seminary years, Arnie saw a spark in Luis that suggested he would not accept the status quo. Perhaps it was the *travieso* in Luis, which Arnie seemed to bring out in him. Arnie seems to believe that all along Olivares was a rebel like he was, but was just waiting for the right moment to "come out." "Louis understood the difference in education from the priests in his Province," Arnie later told Henry. "He laid low for a while and would bloom later on."[131]

And then there are Olivares's own views about his conversion. Like César Chávez, he agreed that one goes through a series of conversions in life. He understood that one of his conversions was meeting Chávez and beginning to work with the farmworkers. These conversions, however, don't just happen, he believed, but are interventions by God. "I actually think we go through a series of conversions," he reflected, "and that we are given opportunities along the way to get closer to Christ by the challenge we are presented."[132] He referred to these as "conversion opportunities."[133] Without qualification, he affirmed that the "farmworker experience changed my life."[134] He said of this experience: "It was very liberating. Seminary molds you in a uniform way, which makes you lose your sense of where you're from. Suddenly I was back to my Mexican-American roots, and meeting social activists and union leaders who were making a difference in people's lives. I met César Chávez early (into my transformation), and he has been a strong influence on me as an activist. But notice, this was not until well into my life."[135] To Olivares, "roots" meant not only his Mexican American background, but helping the poor. "It made me realize that *that* [his emphasis] was more my roots than where I had been the past 15 years. I recognized that was where I really should be working."[136] According to Olivares, his conversion gave him a "purpose to what I was about."[137] He believed that by his new ministry he was living the Gospel message of sacrificing for others in order to be saved. This was the Jesus story, and Olivares was following it. "I think that through all of this activism I was given the opportunity to live the Gospel more fully," he concluded. "As a treasurer, I gave vent to my enjoying the good things of life. I had the opportunity to travel all over the world, to be wined and dined as the treasurer of my religious order. And I enjoyed all that. But that's not as important to me in my life now. I don't really need it, because my activism gave the Gospel a totally different perspective. If I'm going to be saved, I think it's because of my association with the poor."[138]

VII

All of us change in one way or another throughout our lives. We are never quite the same, as we go through the lifecycle. No one is born with a particular worldview or conscience. We grow into that and even then continue to change. No one stands still. So, too, Luis Olivares. Certainly during those long years as a seminarian, he developed a focused view of becoming a priest and of the meaning of Christianity. Consequently, he felt perfectly at ease in becoming a top administrator as treasurer of the Claretians. He was loyal to his order, and he worked to raise the funds it needed to operate. At the same time, Luis had been brought up with the sense that he was special and that he deserved to be treated specially. His embrace of a high lifestyle was a reflection of this. Everyone admits that Olivares had a big ego. This is not to say that he wasn't kind and gracious to others, but he had a certain sense of entitlement. And yet, I believe that there was something in him that was predisposed to changing his life to help the poor and oppressed. His family socialization, especially the influence of "Abuelita Theology"—the spiritual and moral influence of grandparents and parents—through Abuelita Inez and her outreach to those less fortunate was, I believe, very much in his social DNA. I think, too, that Olivares was an intellectual and read widely, and at an intellectual level accepted Catholic social doctrine, the Claretian sense of mission, the opening up to the world called for by Vatican II, and the stirrings of liberation theology out of Latin America. All of these, and perhaps more, made him susceptible to change and made him open to accepting César Chávez's call to join him to work for the farmworkers and the poor in general. Olivares did undergo a conversion, but it was the result of many influences, triggered by his meeting Chávez. This changed his world, and Olivares set out to change the world himself. During the 1980s, he continued his support of the UFW, but as a parish priest in East Los Angeles, he also came to recognize that there were many urban problems facing Mexican Americans. And so he also addressed those issues and became a "community priest."

SIX

Organizing the Barrio

Luis Olivares went to Soledad parish in East Los Angeles because he not only wanted parish experience, but he wanted to reconnect with Mexican Americans. His parish was composed almost completely of Mexican Americans, including immigrants from Mexico. There was something that still stirred in him about working with the poor and disadvantaged just as his Abuelita Inez and his family in San Antonio had done. His "conversion" back to these roots commenced with meeting César Chávez and his involvement with the farmworkers. This work was fulfilling, but Olivares did not come from a farmworker background, and though he sympathized and loved the workers, they were not really "his people." He came from an urban Mexican American background established in the west side barrio of San Antonio. He felt the need to work with similar people in his Soledad parish. East L.A. was not the west side of San Antonio, but it was as close as he would come without returning to his hometown. Perhaps Olivares might have requested a transfer back to San Antonio; however, it was hard to go back home after having been in southern California for so many years. Los Angeles was now his home and East L.A. was his new barrio. Here is where he would continue his Abuelita's work, in ministering to the poor and oppressed. "I was with people day in and day out, with Mexicans, and it certainly brought me back in touch with my past," he later recalled. He got his chance to become even more involved in the community and to become a "community priest" with a new and dynamic community organization called UNO (United Neighborhoods Organization).[1] As in every aspect of his life, Olivares not only participated in UNO, but he would become one of its major leaders, and its most important public voice. Before learning how Olivares became a key activist in UNO, it is first important to know about the origins of the organization, how it was formed, and its mission. Olivares significantly advanced his organizing skills and his leadership development through his participation in UNO. Hence, it is important to understand the nature of this faith-based organization that would inspire Olivares's later work in the sanctuary movement. With this as a backdrop, the subsequent chapter will examine Olivares's specific role as a community priest within UNO.

I

The origins of UNO lie in a visit that Auxiliary Bishop Juan Arzube took to Olivares's home town of San Antonio. Arzube, who was originally from Ecuador, had been named the first Latino bishop of the expansive Los Angeles Archdiocese in the wake of the conflict between the Chicano Movement in Los Angeles and the archdiocese. In 1969 a movement group called Católicos Por La Raza led by Richard Cruz challenged the Church to do more for its Mexican American parishioners, especially in East Los Angeles. Católicos displayed the militancy and oppositional politics of the Chicano Movement. It likewise seemed to be influenced by liberation theology out of Latin America. Católicos issued a variety of demands on Cardinal James Frances McIntyre, the head of the archdiocese. These demands called on the Church to increase its social and educational programs in East L.A. as well as to increase the role of Mexican American clergy and laypeople in the governance of the Church, especially as it applied to the barrios. It called on the Church to return to its roots as a Church of and for the poor. Católicos was not only a representative of the Chicano Movement and of liberation theology, but also of the influences of the Second Vatican Council and its call for a more open Church, one that elevated the role of the laity. Cardinal McIntyre, however, would have none of this. He disdained the Chicano Movement which he considered to be filled with Communists. He also had no love for liberation theology, which he regarded as Marxist-inspired. To add insult to injury, he opposed the reforms of Vatican II. McIntyre, a former Wall Street banker before he became a priest, built churches and ruled over a multi-million dollar archdiocese that spanned from Santa Barbara to Orange County with an iron fist. He refused to listen to Richard Cruz and Católicos.[2]

Rebuffed by McIntyre, Católicos raised the pressure through a dramatic act of resistance when it organized a demonstration outside of St. Basil's Catholic Church on trendy Wilshire Boulevard at the same time as the Cardinal's annual Christmas midnight Mass in 1969. St. Basil's was a recent three-million-dollar church that McIntyre had completed at the same time that he closed a Catholic school for Mexican Americans. Católicos considered this an example of the Cardinal's priorities. At the end of their demonstration, Católicos members and supporters entered the church and disrupted the Cardinal's Mass. Being alerted to a possible action by the Chicanos, McIntyre had positioned undercover sheriff's deputies as "ushers," who confronted the Católicos and literally fought them in the vestibule of the church. Hearing the noise of the fisticuffs plus the shouting of "Let the poor people in" by other Chicanos outside of the church, McIntyre stepped up to deliver his homily, but first condemned Católicos as being similar to the rabble that had crucified Jesus. Police arrested twenty-one demonstrators, including Cruz, who became the "Católicos 21" and faced various misdemeanor charges. A trial jury convicted Cruz and several other Católicos, who served several months in jail.[3]

At the same time, Católicos considered their actions a victory, when the Vatican forced or strongly encouraged the elderly McIntyre to retire within a month of the demonstrations. It appeared that the Vatican considered the Cardinal to have lost control of his archdiocese. In his place, it appointed Bishop Timothy Manning as the new Archbishop of the archdiocese. To his credit, Manning engaged in a dialogue with Cruz and the other Católicos and began to implement new initiatives in East L.A., to suggest that the Church was not insensitive to the needs and conditions of Mexican American Catholics. One such initiative was the selection and appointment of diocesan priest Father Juan Arzube in 1972 as the first Latino Bishop in Los Angeles, albeit only an Auxiliary Bishop, or advisor to Manning.[4]

Arzube was selected not only because he was Latino (although Mexican American Catholics did not look with favor on the naming of someone of Ecuadoran background and not of Mexican American background, since Catholics of Mexican descent represented a sizeable percentage of Catholic parishioners in the archdiocese), but also because he was considered to be a good company man like Olivares was prior to his conversion. Yet Arzube proved to be more than just a yes-man. He genuinely sympathized with Mexican American Catholics and hoped to do what he could when he had the chance. That opportunity came in early 1975.

Arzube went to San Antonio for a festival at the Mexican American Cultural Center. The center was associated with PADRES (Padres Asociados para Derechos Religiosos, Educativos, y Sociales, or Priests Associated for Religious, Educational, and Social Rights), which had been formed by various Chicano/Mexican American priests in 1969 as a reaction to the Chicano Movement, as well as to Vatican II. PADRES represented a lobbying or pressure group within the Church to advocate, as had Católicos (indeed they took up the mantle of Católicos) for greater involvement and influence by Mexican American Catholics in the affairs of the Church, especially as they pertained to Mexican Americans. They likewise advanced the enculturation of Mexican American Catholic traditions and practices within the Church.[5] The Mexican American Cultural Center was a PADRES creation intended to further such enculturation. At the center, Arzube, who was affiliated with PADRES, met with certain members of the group who in turn introduced him to the work of COPS (Communities Organized for Public Service), which had been formed in 1974 and had quickly become the leading grassroots community organization in the barrios. Organized around the Catholic parishes in the Mexican American neighborhoods, COPS was in turn affiliated with the Industrial Areas Foundation (IAF) out of Chicago, which had been founded by legendary organizer Saul Alinsky in 1940. Alinsky/IAF groups had been formed in many urban areas of the country, especially in working-class and minority communities. Such groups aimed to develop strong grassroots leadership that would in turn organize the communities to struggle for their rights and to bring about needed reforms in their neighborhoods.[6] COPS was the latest Alinsky/IAF creation and had, in a short period of time, not only successfully organized new Mexican American community leaders, but also spearheaded various reform efforts and made local politicians responsive to the Mexican American community.[7] These reforms included street repairs, new drainage channels, new neighborhood parks, regulating junkyards, and various other needed improvements.[8] While building on the original Alinsky model of organizing temporary interest groups, COPS instead organized around institutional churches to provide more continuity and utilize religion and faith beliefs as guiding principles for social action. It was a revised Alinsky method.[9]

Arzube was amazed at what he witnessed. He met with his counterpart, Auxiliary Bishop Patricio Flores of San Antonio, who in turn introduced him to Ernie Cortes, the hardnosed and committed IAF organizer who had helped put COPS together. Cortes took Arzube to an "action," or protest, by COPS members before the city council. The bishop could not help but be impressed by this collection not of Chicano Movement "radicals," but of senior citizens, family people, working people, and those active in their Catholic parishes. "He was very impressed by that, and he saw them holding the public officials accountable. And he was particularly impressed by some of the older people who were there, the fact that they were articulate [in English] and prepared," Cortes recalls.[10] "What impressed me the most," Arzube told reporter Frank Del Olmo of the *Los Angeles Times* two years later, "was the type of people I saw. The faces I saw were not those of zealots, but average people—the elderly, some middleaged [sic] and some young."[11] He was particularly taken by an elderly woman at the city council meeting who pinned down a council member and insisted that he respond by simply saying yes or no to her question. "I became enthusiastic," Arzube further added. "There was no violence. It was well organized. . . . I thought it would be wonderful if we could do this in East Los Angeles."[12]

Arzube further learned that COPS actions had helped secure street lights in the barrio where they had not existed before, good drainage, and street cleaning, things that the city had ignored in the past. Moreover, COPS took on supermarkets in the Mexican American areas that provided a low level of service to the public, such as staffing too few cashiers, which created unduly long checkout lines. These and other grassroots issues the San Antonio activists successfully accomplished.[13] It was an expression of participatory democracy and making democracy work.[14]

Arzube returned to Los Angeles very excited about the possibilities of establishing an organization like COPS in East L.A. He informally called a meeting of some of the pastors in the barrio and informed them of his visit and how impressed he was with COPS. These were pastors concerned about the role of the archdiocese in the Mexican American community, which represented 71 percent of all Catholics in the archdiocese.[15] Arzube transferred his excitement on to them. One of them was Father Al Vásquez, the pastor of La Placita Church (Our Lady Queen of Angeles) in downtown Los Angeles, adjacent to the tourist-oriented Olvera Street, but also the historic founding church of Los Angeles under Spanish rule. After meeting with Arzube, Vásquez and four other pastors continued to meet and soon came up with some seed money from their congregations to start an organization that would further explore establishing a COPS-like group in East L.A. Olivares was not a part of this initial meeting or initial organizing group, since he was just transferring to Soledad.[16]

The committee soon expanded to include other pastors in East L.A., among them Olivares. Forty-one people constituted the committee, with most being priests.[17] Fr. Vásquez observes that while Olivares was not part of the initial group, "he came in with a lot of energy and charisma which some of us did not have."[18] "That's when I got in on the ground floor of this project," Olivares recalled later.[19] The group deliberately did not formally affiliate itself with the archdiocese in order to have a degree of independence similar to COPS. Bishop Arzube was not part of this initiative, but served as the point person with the archdiocese. On its own, the group soon moved to see whether the IAF would be interested in working with it on an organizing drive in East L.A. similar to what the Alinsky organization had done in San Antonio. Father Raul Luna, a member of the Salesian order, remembers that, upon returning to East L.A. in August of 1975 after several years away from his hometown, he was invited to a meeting in November of various eastside pastors at the Doheny Center to meet with IAF representatives. Luna would soon become one of the key leaders of the new group. He had left Los Angeles in the early 1970s to study liberation theology in Quito, Ecuador, before going to work at the Mexican American Cultural Center in San Antonio and then PADRES for two years, doing community leadership development. He returned to East L.A. to become pastor of St. Mary's parish.[20] At the meeting attended by just a few people, including both clergy and laypeople, Ernie Cortes along with Ed Chambers, the executive director of the IAF, discussed the possibility of organizing in East L.A.[21] In a letter to Olivares at that time, Mike Clements, affiliated with the IAF in Orange County, wrote: "Some of us have observed the Industrial Areas Foundation–built organization in San Antonio, Texas, Communities Organized for Public Service, and realize the impact that a citizen organization will have as an instrument through which poor, low and middle class constituents can convert their powerlessness."[22] Olivares was present at that meeting and recalls that the word up to then was that it was impossible to organize the Mexican American community. Others had tried and failed. "And here comes 'an outsider' saying we would like to try," Olivares said of Cortes.[23] At the end of the meeting, Cortes and Chambers, no doubt knowing about Luna's earlier work, approached him to see if he would be willing to take the lead in seeing about the establishment of an IAF affiliate. Luna agreed and was put in touch with Peter Martínez in Chicago, who suggested other people whom Luna could contact. As Luna talked to other pastors, including non-Catholic ones in East L.A., he and the initial group more formally organized into what they called the Interreligious Sponsoring Committee (IRSC). It listed itself as an educational and community-development nonprofit organization and drafted a set of by-laws.[24] In a position paper, the organization noted the problem that it would address: "The Mexican American population of Los Angeles is the largest single minority in the city and county of Los Angeles. Yet it does not have even one single elected official in city or county government. The Mexican American population of this area finds itself without a voice in the political and economic arena and is in a state of apathy and hopelessness. It needs desperately to come together and get organized."[25]

They further noted that people of Mexican descent composed 83 percent of East Los Angeles, but that it was a disempowered population with much poverty and a lack of opportunities. Mexican Americans born in the United States represented the majority of the community, but a third of its inhabitants were born in Mexico, and many had no documents. Only one-fourth of residents owned their own homes. Most had only an eight-grade education with high school drop-out rates at about 50 percent. "Is it any wonder," the committee noted, "that East Los Angeles has the worst gang problem of any metropolitan area in the United States?" Added to this was the reality that some 22 percent of the area's population lived in poverty, with most residents being blue-collar workers, and the area's unemployment rate exceeded the statewide rate of 10 percent. "East Los Angeles," the committee concluded, "has been described like a foreign country within the city of Los Angeles." The committee noted that it represented "sisters, ministers, priests and laypeople, who live and work in East Los Angeles and who are keenly concerned about improving this community."[26]

The IRSC stressed being an interreligious or ecumenical organization, at the suggestion of the IAF, in order to expand its reach to non-Catholic churches on the east side, but also to maintain its independence from the archdiocese. Luna contacted all twenty-two Catholic parishes in East L.A., along with some Protestant ones such as the Church of the Epiphany, an Episcopalian church in Lincoln Heights, whose pastor, Father Roger Wood, was very supportive. As Luna expanded his work, the main task was to raise funds from the different churches to allow the IRSC to function and more importantly to raise the funds to contract the IAF. This would take thousands of dollars.[27] To assist him, Luna organized a board consisting of a few other pastors. It's not clear whether Olivares was part of this board, but his involvement in time became quite noticeable.[28] With indirect IAF assistance, including providing how much money would be needed to contract the Alinsky organization, Luna and the others did a great deal of legwork in the effort to secure funds. Their goal was to get each parish and each religious order operating in East L.A. to contribute $5000. To reach this goal, Luna wrote to each pastor and to each Provincial of the different orders, or got the pastors affiliated with an order to mediate the fundraising. They also attempted to get a total of $10,000 from the different female religious orders operating in the eastside. "The core group that started UNO was religious," Olivares later reflected, "and it was obvious at that time that the reason they had selected these priests and nuns was because that's where the money was for the organizing."[29]

With a lot of energy and hard work, the committee was able to obtain contributions. The biggest ones came from the religious orders. Olivares, as treasurer, for one, got the Claretians to contribute the $5,000.[30]

While this initial fundraising was no doubt beyond the expectations of Luna and the others, the IAF also advised them to attempt to secure funding from the Campaign for Human Development (CHD), the community funding source for the archdiocese. It requested $60,000.[31] Bishop Arzube was the key to acquiring this endorsement, and he moved to arrange meetings between representatives of the group with Archbishop Manning and his advisors. As Arzube negotiated these connections, the IRSC, at the behest of the IAF, drew up a mission statement to introduce itself not only to the archdiocese, but to others as well, including the Mexican American community. "An ecumenical group of religious men and women and laypersons, calling itself [the] 'Interreligious Sponsoring Committee,' has been formed in Los Angeles to raise funds to begin an organizing drive in the barrios of Los Angeles," the statement read. To this end, it proposed "to establish a large-scale, metropolitan multi-issue Mexican American (predominantly) citizens' organization in the Los Angeles area."[32]

The statement further recognized the success of COPS in San Antonio and that such an organization was needed in East L.A. To do this, however, it necessitated contracting with the IAF. "To begin an organizing drive to establish a COPS type of citizens' organization," the statement emphasized, "a full-time professional staff is required. It cannot be done by part-time volunteers. A two-year organizational effort will cost around $100,000 per year for staff, office space, equipment and materials."[33] While the IRSC was raising some of that money from churches, religious orders, and even a private foundation, it hoped to acquire the bulk of the necessary funds from the CHD, hence the need to meet with Church officials including Archbishop Manning.

The key to meeting with Manning and other archdiocesan officials was Bishop Arzube. In time, the persistence of Arzube and the IRSC paid off. At a meeting on September 24, 1976, of representatives of the IRSC and Manning's staff, the Cardinal agreed to support funding from the CHD for $120,000 for two years, but with certain stipulations. He insisted that whatever additional funds were secured for the IAF project from the parishes should not come from the regular collections, nor should this project receive priority from other parish commitments, such as contributions to Catholic Charities. The parishes could contribute through special collections or specific fundraising efforts.[34] Moreover, he asked that every effort be made to exclude radical elements from participation. Luna and the others (it is not clear whether Olivares was present) agreed. Manning further noted that while he would not formally endorse the proposal, he would not veto it or stand in its way, which for all practical effects meant endorsing it. He observed that the IRSC had already raised $60,000 on its own and had aligned itself with the IAF, and so, as he put it, "the affair has gone beyond the point of no return."[35] It appears that while Manning and his key advisors did not particularly care for the IAF type of organizing, they recognized that the IAF was not a "radical" or leftist group, and one that did not take on issues such as abortion, women's ordination, or other issues sensitive to the Church.[36]

While the IRSC had attempted to get funding from the CHD over the course of several months, its other work did not stop. Since early 1976, it had already developed a close working relationship with the IAF, although it had not yet raised sufficient funds to contract an IAF organizer. Much of this work had to do with groundwork in East L.A. to determine whether there would be support for what Chambers referred to as a mass-based, multi-issue organization. One of the first initiatives by the IAF to determine this was assigning Peter Martínez to go to Los Angeles and conduct a number of interviews with clergy and laity to assess leadership potential—what the IAF called "natural leaders"—and to get an idea of what kind of issues seemed of community importance.[37] These interviews would also lead to suggestions of others whom Martínez could contact. He interviewed, for example, seminarian Richard Estrada at Soledad. Of Estrada, Martínez wrote: "Very sharp kid, very interested in the project . . . I think we ought to pay some close attention to this guy. Could probably be very helpful in the organizing effort."[38] He was also impressed with Fr. Al Vásquez at La Placita Church. Although he did not interview Luna or Olivares, since both were already active in the effort to recruit the IAF to East L.A., Martínez did express some concern about Luna, who he felt did not have a strong relationship with the other eastside pastors. His interviews included both men and women and even some Chicano Movement activists, such as Rosalio Muñoz and Gil Cano. In these interviews, some of the issues raised as possible actions included conditions in the public schools, high dropout rates, gangs, jobs, housing, welfare, police harassment, lack of public transportation, urban renewal, and drainage problems. Father Atwell at Our Lady of Guadalupe Church raised the issue of abortion, but Martínez assured him that this was not an issue for an IAF organization.[39]

With the pledges already in hand, and even without the funding requested from the CHD, the IRSC went ahead and in July contracted with the IAF for an organizer to begin the work in East L.A. Both the IRSC and the IAF agreed that Ernie Cortes, who had already been involved in the initial phases, should become the lead organizer and establish a staff of other IAF organizers and set up office space.[40] Cortes, according to his wife, liked big challenges and recognized that going to Los Angeles was a big challenge.[41] Under the contract, Cortes and the other IAF staffers would be hired and paid by the IRSC.[42] The contract also made the IAF organization in East

L.A. part of a network of IAF affiliates.[43] The IRSC was elated but also recognized that the hard work was still to be done. On hiring Cortes, Fr. Pedro Villarroya later noted that they were getting a dynamic and experienced organizer who had previously worked in Chicago, Milwaukee, Denver, and, of course, in San Antonio. "We wanted an objective observer," Villarroya stressed. "Someone who could come in and analyze things without prejudice, take them apart, and start building something completely new."[44]

II

From the very beginning, the IAF had decided to emulate the organizing strategy that had worked with COPS in San Antonio and apply it in East L.A. That strategy was based on organizing around the churches and parishes in the barrio. This would be a faith-based organization. The IAF's concept of a church network was centered on the notion that, as Richard Estrada put it, "the churches were a base for people," or as Fr. Al López says, "that's where the people are."[45] Ernie Cortes added: "The churches are logical units because you cannot find another institution that touches everyone in the community and which they trust."[46] In addition to Catholic churches, the IAF hoped to also organize around Mexican American Protestant ones as well.[47] This concept found much favor among many, if not most, of the pastors and clergy. The IAF had historically not organized around churches, but rather around issues, and was more movement-oriented than institutionally based. In organizing drives in other parts of the country, it focused on a single issue and built a movement around it, as it did in Chicago to oppose the expansion of the University of Illinois, Chicago Circle into minority neighborhoods. However, in San Antonio, Cortes as the lead organizer shifted that strategy and utilized the churches, believing that if COPS was going to have staying power and focus on multiple issues, it needed an institutional base such as the churches. "These organizations," an IAF report stressed about groups such as COPS and UNO, "recognize that, in our country, one of the largest reservoirs of untapped power is the institution of the parish and congregations. Religious institutions form the center of the organization."[48] In this strategy, membership was not based on individuals but rather on supporting institutions. The denomination of churches depended on the location of the organizing. In San Antonio it was exclusively Catholic parishes. Cortes hoped to apply the same strategy that had succeeded in San Antonio to Los Angeles, but to have a more ecumenical approach and include Protestant churches that operated in East L.A.[49]

From the very beginning, this IAF strategy found much support. Sister

Maribeth Larkin, a professional social worker with the Sisters of Social Service who became involved in the organizing at Dolores Mission Church, observed that people were more willing to participate because of the connection with the churches:

The Church is a very important institution that people have confidence in, and, people find, where their values are shared. People who wouldn't otherwise be out there in some kind of a movement or activist agenda see themselves now as that part of our life and work as people through our particular faith tradition. The Church embraces the need to help people understand the social gospel, the tradition of justice within their denominations and a lot of the training was about that exactly. What are we supposing to be doing as Catholics, as Christians, as Jews, as religious people in the face of what clearly is injustice in our communities?[50]

While Cortes and supporters such as Larkin hoped to duplicate the COPS model, they recognized that the communities were different. What helped the IAF in San Antonio was that the Mexican American community was more stable and permanent, composed largely of U.S.-born Mexican Americans. East L.A. was different. It was more in a state of flux. While many Mexican Americans lived there, many tended to move from one barrio to another in search of better housing. In addition, Mexican immigrants also settled in the older barrios, such as Boyle Heights. This affected the nature of the parishes, which contained a mix of people, and would be one of the challenges for the IAF.[51] Luis Negrete observes that when his parish attempted to organize some people you never knew if they would still be around a month later.[52] Still, in time, all of the Catholic parishes became affiliated with the IAF drive, although the ecumenical goal never fully took hold and only the Episcopal Church of the Epiphany participated, although other Protestant churches contributed funds.[53]

Parish support was not immediate in all cases. Fr. Luna, who was the assistant pastor at St. Mary's, recalls that some of the pastors, especially those who were Spaniards and not Mexicans, were more conservative, and it took time to sell them on the idea of the IAF organizing. "They were afraid we were maybe too radical or we were going to be political rabble-rousers or something," Luna states.[54] Despite this, Luna's pastor, Fr. Rafael Sánchez, a Spaniard, eventually supported the effort and allowed Luna to discuss this with the parishioners and to pledge support to the IAF. As Luna puts it: "My pastor was afraid of me. He gave me free reign. I more or less could do whatever I pleased."[55] Support came quicker at parishes headed by Mexican American pastors, such as Soledad, where Olivares served as pastor.[56] But it was not just Mexican American pastors who championed the IAF. Fr. Walter D'Heedene, a member of the Mission Heart Order from Belgium, as pastor of Dolores Mission Church in Boyle Heights, also endorsed it. For him, activity to improve the lives of people in the barrios was a logical extension of the reforms of Vatican II. "We became very sensitive to the needs of the poor," he notes.[57] Support at Dolores Mission, for example, came in the form of the parish committing from 1.5 to 2 percent of its operating budget to the IAF, including a $3,000 contribution out of the parish's budget for adult education. In addition, the church defied Cardinal Manning's insistence that support for the IAF not come from weekly collections by allocating some of these funds, plus special collections, to the IAF.[58] Many of the other parishes followed suit. "It just seemed to me for a way for people to have their parishes respond to their needs," Sister Jo'Ann DeQuattro, who taught at St. Mary's parish, observed.[59] In a few months, twenty-three parishes and congregations became involved with the IAF.[60]

With all of this early legwork in spreading the word about the need for an IAF organization in East L.A., obtaining parish support including financial contributions, and in negotiating the CHD grant, plus, indirectly, the consent of Cardinal Manning, the IRSC was ready by the fall of 1976 to formally establish an IAF organization. At a convention in October of some one thousand people, clergy and laity, the UNO was established. Ernie Cortes admits that he came up with the name and catchy acronym while driving on the freeway.[61] Having guided the formation of UNO and having arranged the contract with the IAF, the work of the IRSC had successfully concluded; however, it continued to function primarily to raise yearly funds for the operation of UNO.[62] But UNO was now the focus.[63] It started with a budget of $124, 000 for the first year.[64] "The community organization which we are seeking to establish will be an organization of organizations," UNO proclaimed in a statement. "It will be a federation of community groups or organizations, which are well established. It will be as strong or as ineffective as the organizations which form it. Since the Catholic and Protestant churches are the most stable and viable institutions in the barrio, it is essential that they take a very active role in the organizing process."[65]

III

Having been established as a community organization, UNO moved to have a presence in East Los Angeles. At first, Cortes set up headquarters in some of the parishes, such as at St. Mary's in the church hall, where he hired a secretary. He later moved to Our Lady of Lourdes before renting space in a commercial building near Atlantic and Whittier.[66] By 1980, UNO moved to a more permanent location at 5331 East Olympic Boulevard.[67] As an interparish entity, UNO's work included the parishes located in Boyle Heights, Lincoln Heights, El Sereno, and unincorporated East Los Angeles. Together, these districts were all considered to be "greater East L.A." Hiring a part-time secretary, renting office space, and other office expenses, along with Cortes's salary and that of other IAF staffers, proved to be one of the biggest budget items for UNO.[68]

Of course, the key to getting UNO off the ground was Ernie Cortes, the organizer. Besides putting together an office, Cortes had already immersed himself in the project even before he was officially hired. The first thing he did was to meet with the pastors and other clergy on the east side to determine the level of support and to identify potential leadership among the clergy. As noted earlier, Cortes and Peter Martínez also asked in these interviews what they thought were key issues for UNO to address. "What are you going to do about it?" he challenged them. Fr. Al López recalls the charisma of the IAF organizer. "This guy could convince a plant not to sprout. He would get under your skin and into your heart like nothing else."[69] Getting clergy support would be critical to getting the laity to become involved. One of the first pastors he interviewed was Luis Olivares. He immediately recognized in the Claretian priest not only leadership qualities, but experience in leadership, due to his role as treasurer of his order and his growing involvement with César Chávez and the farmworkers. The meetings with the clergy were also a way to identify key lay leaders in their parishes who might become involved with UNO. Besides himself, Cortes hired other organizers from some of the religious orders, such as Sister Maribeth Larkin, and Sister Georgiana, who also served as the Director of Catholic Community Services.[70] Cortes paid these assistants.[71] He assigned some of them to different parishes.[72] There is no question that Cortes was the major figure within the UNO staff. Smart, articulate, committed, aggressive, and even abrasive, with a take no prisoners attitude, Cortes stood head and shoulders above everyone else, with the possible exception of Olivares, with whom he would develop a close relationship. Of Cortes, Fr. Luna said: "Without him, you can just about forget UNO or COPS. I mean that guy is in many ways a genius. He's very sharp, very perceptive; he can recognize leadership qualities in people."[73] Despite his own leadership, Luna left the priesthood in 1977 and did not continue his work with UNO.[74]

To begin to identify potential leaders as well as issues that UNO might take on, Cortes and his staff, aided by other IAF organizers such as Martínez, first focused on one-on-one or face-to-face individual meetings with both clergy and laypeople.[75] Cortes notes that this whole exercise was intended to find leadership talent by interviewing people involved in parishes, congregations, schools, and labor unions. They needed those "who seem the most aggressive and interested," Peter Martínez observed.[76] With these types of laypeople, Cortes conducted, by his own count, several hundred one-on-one meetings, along with Martínez and Sister Lucille Martínez, a member of Our Lady of Victory order, who along with Cortes set up as many as eight individual interviews per day.[77]

Although many of the laypeople interviewed enumerated many of the same issues in the barrio that the clergy had told the IAF, many of the laity had become frustrated that earlier efforts to deal with these issues had come to nothing. Cortes and the other organizers sympathized with this frustration, but pointed out that the difference now would be that UNO would organize hundreds if not thousands of people and that this would have an effect.[78] This frustration seemed to be gendered, in that many of the men apparently seemed more frustrated than the women. Many of those interviewed who expressed a strong interest in becoming involved with UNO were women, and they already were active in their parishes and community. They exuded much confidence. "We had a lot of strong women," Fr. Al López says of the women at Soledad. Many of them developed as UNO leaders in the parish.[79] At the same time, some women interviewed had not been as active, but UNO brought out their activist side. "If you had told me a year ago that I would be doing this I would have said you're crazy," Christina Saenz told the *Los Angeles Times* about her UNO involvement, "that's not me. I don't think I was capable of it."[80]

In addition to face-to-face meetings, Cortes also organized house meetings. These occurred after the individual interviews had identified laypeople who seemed to have the requisite leadership qualities, and who volunteered to host meetings in their homes, where they would invite several others who had not been interviewed. At these meetings, the goal would be the same as in the one-on-one interviews: to identify other possible leaders and to ascertain additional issues to work on. However, these meetings also laid the basis for larger parish groups as part of UNO. As UNO put it, "Every house meeting generally is organized by two persons that are doing interviews. Each one is responsible to recruit from five to eight persons for that meeting. The main focus of the house meeting is the establishment of the parish organization. Each one is asked to take an active part in bringing it about."[81] These house meetings were very much a part of the IAF organizing strategy, and César Chávez, as a former IAF organizer in CSO in the 1950s, had employed them and continued to do so in organizing farm-workers.[82] On average, about eight to ten people—but sometimes as many as twenty—participated in such meetings, which usually took place in the evenings,[83] both on weekdays and weekends, which ever was most convenient.[84] Each meeting, which lasted about an hour, started with a prayer and a reflection.[85] In time, some gatherings were organized by those who received IAF training on organizing and leadership.[86] Moreover, as more people from the parishes, including the clergy, participated in UNO, additional house meetings for further recruitment and conversations on issues were organized by the parishes; in some cases, these groups met weekly. Fr. Al Vásquez recalls, "We had a meeting to prepare a meeting."[87]

Besides being a means of recruiting new leadership, house meetings were also crucial in ascertaining possible action issues that UNO could take on, either at a parish level or across the organization, involving all parishes. A bevy of issues were raised.

"I'm concerned about the quality and price of food and housing."

"I'm worried about the quality of education."

"We need more and better street lighting and more traffic lights set that allow you to cross the street safely."

"The police respond too slowly when a crime is reported."

"One of the grocery stores doesn't let us use their restrooms and keep them locked."

"Our car insurance rates are too high."

Parishioners raised many other issues, and Cortes and other UNO leaders recognized that they could not take them all on; nevertheless, it was important that it was the people who were expressing their concerns, and not the organizers or leaders imposing issues on them. It was easier to get people involved if they felt that the organization took their views seriously. This is what the IAF referred to as "relational organizing"—organizing around people's needs.[88] "It wasn't us bringing the issues out," Brother Modesto León observed. "That's why you do house meetings."[89]

IV

The face-to-face interviews and house meetings identified potential UNO leaders and activists. The next step involved training them to be organizers and public citizens.[90] This, in fact, was part of the contract between the IROC and the IAF, with the understanding that the former would be responsible for funding such training.[91] Initially, the IAF and UNO focused on training the clergy. It was important that both priests and sisters take the lead as organizers in order to show their parishioners that UNO possessed the institutional support of their churches and that their priests were committed to UNO. UNO, like COPS, was a faith-based organization, and thus it was critical that the priests, at least at first, take the lead.[92]

Hence, the IAF first trained the clergy, in particular the pastors. As pastor of Soledad, Olivares was among the first trainees. Fr. Al López notes that Olivares was part of the core of those trained.[93] In time, however, and within the first year or so of UNO, this training was extended to include laity. These would be the laypersons identified with leadership potentials by the interviews and house meetings some of which the priests conducted themselves after receiving their training.[94] At first, some twenty to thirty laypersons a year received training, and within the first five years of UNO hundreds would follow.[95] These included both men and women. Martha Rocha de Zozaya recalls her IAF training in San Antonio, and Gloria Chávez, who in 1979 became the first official President of UNO, credits her IAF training with developing her leadership skills.[96]

Once accepted into the training program, you attended sessions either in Chicago (the IAF headquarters), New York, or San Antonio.[97] Among the first to be selected, Olivares actually received training in all three cities. "So, now I was into community organizing," he noted. "It was very exciting because I was in on the ground floor, and we received wonderful training in every possible detail of a campaign."[98] Other clergy from East L.A. followed, such as Brother Modesto León and Fr. Al Vásquez, both who trained in New York.[99] A standard IAF training session was usually a ten-day commitment, although its length could vary.[100] Olivares first attended a ten-day session.[101] Some UNO laity participated in two-week sessions.[102] But some were shorter. Fr. Luna went to one in Chicago for three or four days.[103]

At the training session, IAF personnel instructed Olivares, the other clergy, and laypeople about various organizing techniques and strategies and the rationales behind these. This training was referred to as the Alinsky Method, based on the various organizing theories developed by Saul Alinsky. Some also called it the IAF Method. Instruction followed a tutorial style. The instructors lectured and led discussion based on a selection of readings from books, articles, or newspapers. The reading would be used to illustrate the various organizing skills and methods that the training institute fostered.[104] This reading also included the writings of Alinsky.[105] Cortes's wife notes that her husband was a master teacher who challenged others rather than entertaining them. Ironically, although Cortes employed the Alinsky Method, he personally did not like Alinsky and what he considered to be his abrasive personality, even though the two had only met a couple times before Alinsky's death in 1972.[106]

Utilizing Alinsky guidelines for organizing disempowered communities, the IAF taught UNO members the golden rule of Alinsky-style organizing. The rule was a simple one: listen to the people that you are trying to organize. Don't go with your own agenda, but attempt to understand what people are concerned about. "Organize people at the level they're at," Cortes told them, "and on issues central to people being organized."[107] Fr. Al Vásquez remembers very well the Alinsky golden rule: "The first thing you would do is ask them [the people], 'What is your main concern in the community. Is it drugs, liquor, jobs, housing, health insurance? What is your main concern?'" If you followed this rule, you would be a successful organizer, or at least that is what the IAF hoped. The key to successful organizing was how many people you organized. "You're only as good as how many followers you have," Vásquez recalls learning. "This is important. If you don't have any followers, you're not doing your job."[108]

A very crucial part of the training had to do with distinguishing between problems, on the one hand, and issues, on the other. The IAF and its affiliates only concentrated on issues and not problems. What was the distinction? Problems, according to the Alinsky Method, were larger and more abstract conditions that would be very difficult to organize around. For example, it might involve the growing disparity of wealth as a major problem, but this would be difficult to organize most people around. By contrast, the effort to reduce discriminatory auto insurance rates in East L.A. represented an issue that UNO could use to organize many Mexican Americans, as indeed it would. Moreover, the IAF considered "winnable" issues to be concrete and specific issues that people were concerned about, and UNO members were taught that they should only engage in winnable issues. The job of the organizer was to elicit from community people what they were concerned about and then define them as issues. "Most people don't have issues at their fingertips," Ernie Cortes observes.[109] He continues:

They have concerns; they have problems and difficulties. You make this distinction between problems and difficulties and concerns and issues. Issues are things that are very specific and concrete that you can very well define, where you can identify a target and go after it. It's very specific, very winnable, and affects a lot of people. There's kind of an analysis we go through of breaking down problems into issues. Analysis we go through of taking people's inarticulate, not-very-well-formed concerns and then figuring out what do you do about them. People start off concerned about their children or concerned about their children's future, but they don't know how to articulate it. So part of our organizing process is getting people to learn how to articulate.[110]

At his training sessions, Fr. Luna appreciated this distinction between a problem and an issue. He observes that one can be concerned about the schools in general, which constitutes a problem, but you can better organize by focusing on the lack of books in the schools, which is an issue. "What you need to do," he learned, "was not concentrate on a generic problem but break it down to something that people can really put their teeth into." Taking on larger and more involved problems that might not be resolved ran the risk of wasting time and energy and could lead to frustration among activists.[111]

The IAF's focus on finding "winnable" issues was pragmatic. Winning served to raise morale among members and a sense of empowerment. "We'd say we only go after issues we can win," UNO leader Lydia López states. "We don't want to lose and have people defeated."[112] The challenge for UNO would be to discern from their interviews with community people which of their concerns could be transferred into such issues. Mike Clements knew very well the importance of selecting winnable issues. People who had only known defeats didn't need more defeats by taking on unwinnable problems. He puts it more graphically: "People who have been beaten up a lot of times already don't need to take another blow to the chops."[113]

People needed to know that they could win, and this is what the IAF taught them.[114] The IAF succinctly defined what it meant by an issue in a training document that listed key points for what constituted an issue:

(a) specific and concrete
(b) immediate
(c) feel strongly about it
(d) controversial
(e) affects many persons
(f) possibility of winning[115]

Part of identifying issues also was part of understanding the system and how power operates. Sister Maribeth Larkin recalls that she learned at her training session the difference between organized money and organized people and how to maximize people power. Money power had to be checked, but it could only be done by the countervailing power of the people; that was what the IAF did and what UNO needed to do. "It's really a reflection on public life," she says of her training, "and how to effectively develop strategies for change."[116] Martha Rocha de Zozaya also understood the importance of knowing how the political system in one's community operated. "So understanding the system," she observes, "was a way of operating in such a way as to use that system in order to get what we needed for a better community."[117] Cortes adds: "Power comes in two forms. Organized people and organized money. The other side, the big guys, they've got lots of money. Our power is mainly with people."[118]

But change could only be achieved if there was collective action. "Action is to organization what oxygen is to our bodies," the IAF stressed.[119] The IAF emphasized that only by people joining together would social reform take place. Individuals were not the focus; the collective of individuals was. The IAF taught not only organizing skills, but the "capacity to act together over the long term."[120] Olivares appreciated the stress on collective grassroots organizing. "That's the crucial point," he reflected, "that's the whole difference of the community organizing process is that you involve everyone."[121]

Collective action, the IAF stressed, went hand in hand with confrontational politics. In order to achieve any reforms, the power structure had to be confronted, whether it involved city hall, county government, or a big business. This was not always easy since most people did not think in this way about taking on the system. They deferred to authority. The IAF challenged this way of thinking and instructed UNO members to impress upon their constituents that power had be confronted by a countervailing power of the people. Diplomacy or compromise was to be shunned. Direct action in the form of confrontation was the only viable strategy. Such direct action resembled the strategy of the Chicano Movement. "The thing was to try to help people understand that you don't get anything unless you are somewhat confrontational," Martha Rocha de Zozaya recalls learning at her IAF training in San Antonio. When she began organizing for UNO, some people felt that they did not have the right to demand certain changes. Based on her IAF training, Rocha de Zozaya responded: "You have every right to do so. You pay taxes; you live here; you're the people that know what is really going on. You need to understand that a lot of the politicians are there not out of the goodness of their hearts, but out of money, out of deals they make."[122]

Olivares learned this type of strategy from the IAF, and it would serve him well both in his work with UNO and later in the sanctuary movement. "So I got trained in confrontation," he recalled. "Our confrontation tactic today," he said of his sanctuary years, "comes right out of the UNO experience. It became my style."[123]

In the end, the objective and value of IAF training was to empower the trainees in this case UNO members who were referred to as "leaders" by the IAF.[124] Empowerment meant that individually they felt secure and confident to become organizers in their parishes and communities. What they learned at these sessions provided this sense of empowerment. Collectively it meant that UNO members could go back to East L.A. as an organization, feeling that they possessed group power—people power—to take on the system and establishment. They learned how to empower the community by sharing with others the concepts and tactics that they had learned.[125] They were to be community builders.[126] "It was always constantly reminded that power was not for power's sake," Rocha de Zozaya notes, "but that power was to try to create change."[127] To Ernie Cortes, a sense of empowerment was crucial in organizing, because people would not get involved unless they had a sense of their own power. "Part of the difficulty," he notes, "is that people are not going to spend the time and energy needed to find out what the issues are unless they've got some power. First you build power, then you build the program."[128] "Power" meant people power, but you had to organize it. Lydia López understood this from her training. "What is power?" she observes. "Who has it? How do you organize it? How do you work with people? How do you organize a community?"[129] Cortes answered these questions by responding that the elements of power already resided within the community. All they needed was awareness that what they already had could be used to empower them. Teaching them to recognize this was engaging in what Cortes called "adult basic education." "We are teaching political literacy," he stated. "We are not really organizing a community, but reorganizing what is already there. We teach people how to use the networks they already have and how to build new ones."[130] For Cortes, what Mexican Americans in East L.A. had was their churches and their religious organizations; these would be the basis for organizing a new effort through UNO to achieve basic reforms in the barrio. Cortes understood that, initially in this empowerment movement, the clergy would be the catalyst; however, he also envisioned that in a short time lay leaders would also surface and even supersede the clergy. Richard Estrada specifically remembers that laypeople at his session were taught to have a sense of independence, including from priests.[131]

The focus on the empowerment of Mexican Americans through UNO meant that members learned they needed to build UNO rather than forming coalitions with other groups who might be stronger or weaker than

UNO. UNO had first and foremost to empower itself.[132] For Olivares, how he interpreted empowerment meant a new way for people—both clergy and laity—to see themselves as possessing power, which began in every individual's mind. "The value of UNO is what it does for the person," he concluded. "Our whole objective is the empowerment of people. You ought not be subjected to any kind of domination—whether from the Church or political system or economic structures."[133]

V

UNO was structured as a faith-based organization, and as such its ideology, such as it was, related to the Christian, and more specifically the Catholic, nature of that faith. Christian and Catholic ideological influences represented a very significant part of how UNO organized and presented itself. Although not officially a part of the Church structure, in that it was not affiliated with the Los Angeles archdiocese, UNO nevertheless possessed a strong Catholic posture. This was certainly because the parishes formed the basic core units of the organization and the key role that clergy such as Olivares played in UNO. Hence, there were various faith and theological influences that can be ascertained in the ideological superstructure of UNO. It represented a theology of organizing.[134] Some of this, according to Sister Maribeth Larkin, was built into IAF training. She notes that the training sessions had religious and theological connections that were useful in organizing. "It helps people reflect on their [religious] traditions," she stresses, "and then decide what does this compel us to do in terms of action and change."[135] Brother Modesto León makes the point that it was more UNO, rather than the IAF, that integrated theology into organizing, but that the IAF did not oppose it, since the IAF had a history of linking Catholic churches to labor union organizing. What UNO did, according to León, was to bring together IAF organizing with theology; they were not separate.[136] One way that theology connected with organizing was the example of Christian-based communities influenced by liberation theology. UNO represented such a community. León notes that this construct was used in house meetings where biblical and faith references were utilized by organizers to impress upon laity the faith-based nature of UNO. "It was very scriptural," he notes, "because we would go to house meetings and talk about the Old Testament. You talk about how the basic Christian community lived, how the apostles got together in common, how the faithful—when they were getting persecuted—how they came together and were able to give their love for their faith because they had community in faith that loved them."[137]

Part of linking faith and theology to organizing UNO involved stressing that in such work UNO members were simply putting their faith into action and living it out. It was not just talking or believing in their faith; it was practicing their faith. It was going back to basic Christian principles about being your brother's keeper and trying to make life better for others. Social justice could inspire social action.[138] "UNO has given me the vehicle to do the Christian things the Church and Christ wants me to do," one UNO member, a Mrs. Christina Saenz, told the *Los Angeles Times*.[139] Organizing UNO encompassed the Christian call to make the world a better place for everyone. "That's our mission," Martha Rocha de Zozaya emphasizes, "and it was a call to participate in making our community a better place to live."[140]

While the theological influences in UNO came from basic Christian beliefs in Jesus's mission of assisting the poor and oppressed, it also in part seemed to have been at some level affected by liberation theology, emanating from Latin America at that time, that prioritized working with the poor and oppressed. Liberation theology was nothing more than returning to the Jesus story. What particular influences liberation theology had on UNO members in East L.A. is hard to determine. It appears that as part of his conversion and working with both the farmworkers and with UNO, Olivares was becoming more familiar with liberation theology and beginning to read some of its founding texts, such as those written by Father Gustavo Gutiérrez from Peru, considered to be the leading theologian of liberationist thought. Fr. Al Vásquez believes that Olivares and UNO activists were influenced by liberation theology. "It's a belief in God," he says. "A belief which goes directly to the people. It's based on the Bible. It's just simply to put into practice the teaching of Jesus." He was aware of Gutiérrez and other liberationist writings and believed that so, too, was Olivares.[141] León suggests that whether or not liberation theology had an influence on UNO, the fact was that it fit in well with its goal of empowering people to liberate themselves by "cutting the chains that bound them." Liberationists in Latin America and UNO members in East L.A. were applying the same principles based on the New Testament and the life and practice of Jesus. As León put it in East L.A. terms: "UNO worked to get people to say, hey, you can put a street light up there; you can get a gang program that's needed; you can look at car insurance redlining; you can get a ban on assault rifles; you can fight against the immigration deportations; because you've got power. They have power too, but you have power, too, even though you don't have all the money they have. We have the people."[142]

While Catholic theological influences clearly affected UNO and marked it as a faith-based organization, it was not devoid of more secular ideological influences. There is also a strong pragmatic aspect to the ideology shared by UNO and the IAF. This pragmatic ideology is strongly seen in the views of Ernie Cortes and the important role he played in organizing UNO. Cortes had no issues with a faith-based organization and, in fact, he created UNO as he had COPS. He also read widely in moral theology and Catholic social doctrine. In his training sessions, for example, he would use the Exodus story and likened it to the Mexican American struggle.[143] At the same time, he recognized that UNO had to possess a pragmatic side to complement the more spiritual and theological one. He based his pragmatism around what he called "relational power." He distinguished this from "unilateral power," which emanated from the top—the moneyed and political power brokers. Relational power, he says, "is when you organize using our model, which means that you try to develop collaboration and solidarity; and the way you develop relational power is by listening to people, listening to their stories, to their pain." Taking this pain and translating it into the basis for public action, relational power was based on life experiences and how you could connect them to issues of power—people power. Part of this was to link your own self-interests with that of others and in so doing create relationships that bring people together to change their lives. In doing so, people had to confront their lived experiences and their desires to go beyond those experiences to achieve a better life. "We have a world as it is," Cortes observes, "and the world as it should be and the tension between the two." But that tension, in turn, created the relational power to transform the world. Relational power was also what he called a trust relationship, whereby people established relationships based on trust, a trust that each individual had the others' interests in mind. Solidarity comes from trust. But such relational trust or relational power was based not on idealistic ideologies, but from life experiences and from what people read and talked about. Cortes's pragmatism was centered on employing the practical strategy of organizing around where people were and not where they should or wanted to be.[144]

UNO was structured to win, and this meant taking on practical issues that could be won. As such, priorities needed to be set as to which issues were considered winnable. "Can we do something about it or is it going to drag out for three years," Cortes notes. "So we had to be fairly instrumental or pragmatic." UNO could not take on every issue and didn't have the power to do anything about some; therefore, the challenge was to take on those issues that would empower its members. Once this occurred, then they could take on even larger issues. Pragmatism was based on strategies that gave people a sense of their power. That is what UNO was about. It was not based on righting wrongs, but of changing people's perspectives of their ability to create change. "The difficulty is when organizers forget what their purpose is," Cortes concluded. "It's not to right every wrong or solve every problem, but rather to build an organization so that the leaders themselves can take on these issues. But sometimes we get myopic and forget that we're supposed to teach them how to build power, not to solve their problems."[145]

VI

Structurally, UNO was composed of two levels of organization. The first was at the individual parish level and the second at the interparish level or the federation of all of the participating parishes. In this manner, individual parish participation was encouraged including specific parish actions on issues. At the same time, cooperation and joint actions on issues affecting all of the parishes in East L.A. could be achieved through the federation. Governing bodies for both were worked out in a way that provided some level of parish autonomy while establishing an overall authority through the federation.

Above the local parishes or "units" was the interparish UNO federation. When reference was made to UNO, it usually meant the federation which represented the highest authority for the organization. The governing structure at this level went through various evolutions. At the commencement of UNO, the main policy-making body was the Temporary Organizing Committee, or TOC, composed of representatives from each parish unit of about twenty parishes. From these twenty, five co-chairs were elected.[146] Stressing the development of lay leadership, only one out of these five was a member of the clergy. Fr. Wood from the Church of the Epiphany served in this capacity.[147] By 1978 as UNO became incorporated as a nonprofit, the TOC was replaced by an interparish strategy committee composed of both laity and clergy and representing all units. Olivares served on this committee. In 1979, twenty-three representatives composed the committee. Membership seems to have varied, but the emphasis concerned having representation of all parishes and encouraging lay participation in it. The strategy committee focused on developing issues and actions that pertained to all of the parishes. The committee was headed by a president, such as Fr. Pedro Villarroya, the pastor of Our Lady of the Rosary of Talpa in Boyle Heights. Membership involved both men and women. Once the committee arrived at such issues and actions, interparish assemblies ratified them. These assemblies could include several hundred people from all of the parishes. Once issues were endorsed, the strategy committee carried out subsequent actions by forming subcommittees pertaining to the actions to be undertaken. Throughout this rather involved governing process, collective leadership was stressed.[148] Of course, all decisions had to also be sanctioned by IAF organizers who worked very closely with the federation through the strategy committee. In 1979, UNO claimed that through its twenty church affiliates it represented 93,000 families.[149]

The federation was furthered solidified at UNO's first formal convention in October 1979. Held at the Shrine Auditorium close to downtown Los Angeles, some 5,000 delegates attended, representing all of UNO's member units or parishes.[150] Olivares represented Soledad, along with many of his parishioners. The atmosphere was electric with much enthusiasm and a sense of accomplishment. "Today we are putting everyone on notice that things have changed in East Los Angeles," Lydia López stated, "that we are going to take charge of our neighborhoods!" Gloria Chávez, another delegate, seconded this sentiment by proclaiming: "We have proven [that] the people of East Los Angeles are prepared to fight for the survival of their families and their values."[151] At the convention, delegates voted and approved a constitution for the federation. Olivares along with other UNO activists took turns presenting the different parts of the document.[152] Adopted by the delegates, the constitution created a set of officers as well as new governing bodies. This included a new executive committee of twenty to twenty-four people that in practice became evenly divided between men and women.[153] In addition, a strategy committee composed of one hundred members was likewise created. Olivares came to serve on it. Finally, monthly UNO assemblies would ratify proposals by both the executive and strategy committees. These assemblies could be as large as four hundred people.[154] The constitution likewise called for the election of officers to lead the federation. The key positions included president, vice president, and secretary-treasurer, and only laity could run for these offices. Hence Olivares, played a major role in UNO, yet never served as an officer, though at the convention he was elected as an honorary vice president.[155] Delegates nominated candidates who campaigned for the positions by giving speeches at the convention, which were delivered in English. Delegates then voted by secret ballot for their selections with one person one vote. Thousands cast ballots and elected women to the top positions. They endorsed Gloria Chávez for president, Lydia López for vice president, and Sister Jo'Ann DeQuattro as secretary-treasurer.[156]

The election of these women not only emphasized the emergence of lay leaders within UNO to complement the leadership of clergy, but it also underlines the key roles that women played in UNO, as they also did in COPS in San Antonio.[157] Both at the parish level and in the federation, women, mostly housewives and working women, proved to be in many ways the backbone of the organization.[158] UNO created the opportunities for women to emerge as leaders. Many had already been involved as leaders in religious confraternities and church support groups, so that it became only natural for them to evolve with UNO as community and civil rights leaders. "It [UNO] created the space for women who may have not ever thought of themselves as activists or particularly involved in public life to suddenly discover that sense of themselves," Sister Maribeth Larkin comments.[159] Martha Rocha de Zozaya echoes this view. At her parish, Assumption, two-thirds of UNO activists represented women. She notes that the organization allowed the women to hone their skills as leaders. She further comments that the men did not resent this strong female participation.[160] At Soledad, Fr. Al López recalls that at least half of UNO members were women. "They knew how to ask for something; they knew how to get it," he emphasizes.[161] The same was true at La Placita. "The women were just as fantastic as the men," Fr. Al Vásquez observes. "The women can talk. At the beginning the women would be more timid and more cautious. But then once they got going, they're very articulate."[162] At the same time, it was not a question of rivalry between women and men. "Leadership in UNO transcends the female-male thing," Lydia López told a reporter. "The issue is who can best serve the organization."[163] With this leadership, both women and men and both laity and clergy, UNO continued to pursue various issues and actions as the new voice of East Los Angeles. Olivares would be a key part of this.

SEVEN

Community Priest

Fr. Luis Olivares entered the home of potential UNO members, as well as some who already had made a commitment to UNO. This was one of many house meetings that the Claretian priest participated in, including some he himself hosted. Everyone welcomed him warmly, for they knew him already as the charismatic pastor of Our Lady of Solitude (Nuestra Señora de la Soledad). The meeting was to discuss issues that UNO might take on, especially at the federation level. This would involve all parish units of the new organization and would have to be one that they could all rally around. It also had to be a winnable issue. But what issue?

"How about the conditions in the schools?" someone contributed.

"We need assistance to upgrade our homes and the banks are reluctant to help us," another chimed in.

"But I think an issue that we all face is the high car insurance rates that we're paying here in East L.A.," still another added.

"Insurance rates?" "Yeah, we're being screwed on this," others called out as their level of anger rose. "We're paying way too much. We can't afford it which is why some of us don't have insurance."

Olivares realized they'd found their first issue. He reported this back to Ernie Cortes, who told the pastor that he and other UNO members were getting the same reaction in their meetings. High car-insurance rates seemed to be a major concern for many East L.A. residents. But was it a winnable issue?[1]

Whether it was or not, the important thing was that it was coming from the people. This was how it was supposed to work. UNO leaders were not supposed to propose what they believed to be the key community issues. This was neither authentic nor organic. It had to come from the people themselves. Only in this way would they support it and work for it. "What are the pressures on your family?" Cortes asked at a house meeting.[2] High auto insurance, or so-called redlining, a practice in which insurance companies redlined East Los Angeles as an area that they felt people drove more carelessly and with more accidents. This was not true, but the insurance companies used the beliefs to justify higher rates than other locations in the greater Los Angeles area.[3]

Olivares later reflected on this community input into the selection of redlining as the first major action undertaken by UNO: "We picked the insurance red-lining because, well, the way the issues were picked at that time . . . what was very impressive was that the issue was determined through personal interviews. We went from house to house to house talking to people, asking, 'What are the things that are bothering you? What are the things that you've got to solve in your community?' Well, this insurance thing kept coming up, that it cost more to insure the car than the car was worth. They were paying twelve and thirteen hundred dollars in insurance on an old jalopy. It had to come from the people. We couldn't go in there and tell them what we thought should be the issue. That is the main difference in successful organizing."[4]

Cortes notes that it didn't take long after UNO was organized to discover that redlining seemed to be an issue to all parishioners from different parishes. "We would talk and ask them about auto insurance and they would just jump out of their chairs about how expensive it was."[5] Cortes and UNO needed an issue that transcended individual parishes, and auto insurance seemed to be it. Other issues, such as problems with schools or housing, while no less important, seemed too complicated, with no assurance of success, and UNO needed a major success at the start to help built the organization.[6] Fr. Raul Luna believed that redlining could be an issue that would unify and bring people together.[7] Smaller actions in some of the individual parishes were already taking place, regarding traffic lights and street crossings, but these actions would not put UNO on the map. Auto insurance might.[8]

I

Before UNO decided to focus on redlining as its first big action, it researched the conditions on auto-insurance rates in East L.A. This research would have direct application to UNO's goals of empowering people through confrontation with the powers that be. The first thing that Olivares, Cortes, and other UNO activists discovered was that the various auto-insurance companies divided Los Angeles into different statistical insurance-rates districts. In this division, every company lumped East L.A. with West L.A., which included Beverly Hills. This automatically raised the rates in the barrio, since working-class drivers had to pay the same premiums as the well-to-do on the west side. In researching this district, UNO discovered that the same number of car accidents occurred on the west side as the east side. However, higher rates in this district in part were driven by the fact that in West L.A. most accidents involved higher repair costs, as well as expensive litigation. Consequently, the companies compensated for this with high premium rates. At the same time, on the east side many fewer accidents involved litigation.[9] Despite the differences in income between the two sections of the city, the insurance companies charged even more in the barrios, because they believed that East L.A. drivers there were less responsible. "We found out," Ernie Cortes observed, "that people in East L.A. were paying three and four times the amount of insurance that people in West L.A. were paying for the exact coverage on cars that were not nearly as expensive."[10]

Further research revealed other interesting comparisons that exposed the discriminatory insurance rates in East L.A. Mike Clements, who worked for the IAF in Orange County, reported that residents there paid less for auto insurance than in East L.A.[11] Moreover, Olivares recalled that the rates in the east side were double what they were in Santa Monica and San Diego.[12] Modesto León notes that it was not unheard of for barrio residents to pay $1,200 for car insurance, yet in Long Beach the average premium was about $400. "How did they go from $400 to $1,200 over here?" he questioned.[13]

Such disparities were based on racist stereotypes, as Olivares was aware: "For example, East LA had double the rates of Santa Monica and all because of the stereotype that these are Mexicans and they don't care about their cars, they drink too much, they don't have garages because they rent them out to other people, and so they leave their cars on the street." He concluded that because of these falsehoods or convenient rationales, the companies charged more.[14] Additional UNO research showed that these companies unfairly and unscientifically assumed low-income areas were high-risk ones concerning auto accidents.[15] Moreover, they further argued that because East L.A. was split apart due to the various freeways that passed through, it posed a higher risk for accidents. "Hey, that's not our fault that you guys tore the community apart," León recalls thinking about the six freeways that went through the east side. "We called it redlining," he adds, "and started seeing where the poor areas and where the freeways were; it was a trend."[16]

UNO did not have paid or volunteer researchers to examine the facts and figures on redlining; the activists and organizers did it themselves. Cortes, for example, bought an insurance book on redlining.[17] Olivares also did some of his own research. Henry Olivares observes that his brother saw the injustice in the discriminatory auto insurance practices and so he read up on it and "he says something has got to be done."[18] One of the things that Fr. Luis discovered was that there was little difference in accident rates between the east side and the west side, and also little difference in claims rates between East L.A. and other parts of Los Angeles.[19] In her research, Sister Maribeth Larkin interviewed a University of Southern California expert on the issue about how rates were set and the role of the state insurance commissioner on seeing that rates did not discriminate either against companies or consumers. She also read technical books on the subject. She found out that it would be actually cheaper to insure people on the east side than in wealthier areas if companies used zip codes to determine their rates rather than arbitrarily throwing together geographically distinct districts; these companies would discover that their settlement losses in East L.A. were much less than on the west side. She learned that while people in high-income areas litigated accidents about 90 percent of the time, eastside residents only did so about 15 to 20 percent and so that insurance costs to the companies were much lower in East L.A.[20] This and other research would form part of the basis for the decision by UNO to prioritize redlining for its first major action.

II

Having researched redlining, the UNO executive committee of which Olivares was a member discussed whether this was the inaugural action that the new organization preferred to take on. Olivares supported this, but others were not sure.[21] Cortes believed that this was a winnable issue, but held his opinion back so that the members of the committee could arrive at their own conclusion. Only by discussing differences could a strong decision be made and implemented. Those who seemed doubtful of the issue wondered if in fact this was a winnable issue, since it meant taking on the big insurance companies with no guarantee of success. But these debates were exactly what Cortes desired. He was not going to impose his views as organizer on the others. "There are always tensions," he notes about the process. "In fact, I would hate to think that there was never tension. Because if there is no tension and conflict, then you're not dealing with diverse people or you are putting it underneath the rug. So the whole point is how do we get people to articulate their differences, but also teach them how to negotiate their differences. You welcome the tension. If there's no tension then something's wrong. . . . When everybody's thinking alike, no one is thinking."[22] Out of this thinking, the committee finally came to a consensus that UNO would take on redlining as the federation's first major action.

It did not take them long to further decide that Olivares would be the chair of the established action committee on auto insurance to spearhead the issue. While UNO, at least rhetorically, hoped to develop lay leadership so that the clergy would not dominate the organization, for this first major action the view was that they needed an experienced and articulate leader such as Olivares. He had negotiated with bankers and other executives in his capacity as treasurer of his order, and this experience would serve him well in confronting the corporate heads of the insurance companies. Moreover, everyone recognized his wonderful speaking abilities, which would be useful at mass meetings and with the media.[23] Of these attributes, Fr. Luna notes: "Olivares had a gift of eloquence when he spoke. He had the gift of speech and liked to speak. He liked to be in front of people."[24] Brother Modesto León seconded this but also noted Olivares's background. "He had the skill of a business manager, a business person," he says. "He was able to do the research. Why is there redlining? He really got into that because of his experience with finances. . . . He would be able to question whoever it was he had to deal with, the attorney general, the county supervisors, or the insurance companies."[25]

Very early, Cortes targeted Olivares as one of the keys to UNO's success and felt completely comfortable and secure with Olivares being the lead person and voice of UNO on this first action. "He was a very, very active, thoughtful, insightful, and aggressive leader," Cortes says of Olivares. He felt that he had what he called an "embarrassment of riches" with other key leaders, especially among the clergy, but that Olivares stood out amongst all others. Besides Olivares's experiences, Cortes also appreciated his charisma and speaking abilities. Cortes recognized that the battle against the insurance companies would not only be played out by mass action, but in the media, and he had in Olivares someone who was attractive to the media and whom the media would be attracted to. "He [Olivares] was able to capture the imagination and attention of the media," Cortes concluded.[26]

Already immersed in the research on redlining and as a member of the executive committee, Olivares had no hesitations about agreeing to chair the insurance committee. He knew it would be a hard struggle and a long one, but he also recognized the injustice at work and the importance of UNO winning this first major action. He quickly immersed himself in planning and implementing the strategy on what would prove to be UNO's signature issue.

Having committed to work on redlining, UNO first planned on implementing its strategy. Ernie Cortes as organizer was the key here in putting together a strategy based on mass mobilization and pressure on both the County Board of Supervisors, state officials, and on the insurance companies. Cortes drew on what had been successful for him with COPS in San Antonio. Pressure on the Board of Supervisors and state officials was important to get them in turn to put pressure on the companies to revise their premium rates in East Los Angeles. But in the end, Cortes knew that the most critical pressure would be applied to the companies themselves. This is where the power was, and the IAF stressed going right at the power source and not relying on secondary players such as the Board of Supervisors to achieve UNO's goals. The only way the companies were going to change would be the countervailing power of the people. Cortes knew that success would not occur overnight, but would take several months or perhaps a year. In fact, it took about two years. "We had action after action," Sister Maribeth notes, "and Father Luis was at the center of all that."[27]

To apply this pressure, Cortes along with the other UNO leaders, planned on mass meetings with both county and state officials, and the insurance companies. But such meetings had to first be pre-planned and rehearsed. UNO at the federation level met each Tuesday, and so if a mass meeting was scheduled, Cortes and other UNO members met prior to the public meetings to plot out the action. Rehearsal meetings for an action sometimes occurred several times before the actual meeting.[28] The first thing was to plan an agenda and set the goals for the mass meeting. Nothing was left to chance. Everything was planned down to the smallest detail. UNO entered into an action already sure of the outcome, due to its preparation. "It didn't just happen," Fr. Roger Wood of the Episcopalian Church of the Epiphany observes.[29] The planning included what UNO expected from the invited guests, either government officials or corporate players. Rehearsals included acting out the confrontation so that everyone involved knew their roles. It was like preparing for a play. "The meetings are usually very planned out," Fr. Al López recalls. "We talked about what was the goal of the meetings. What was the minimum amount you wanted from the other group and how are you going to get it. If you wanted them to say 'we'll investigate' then that was your goal. You already planned for this. You almost act it out. And that was strategized way ahead of time. And then you take it to the next step. 'Could you get us a meeting with your superior or ranking officer?'"[30]

As part of setting agendas and goals for the meetings, UNO also prepared questions for the officials whom they would confront at these settings. These questions were not general ones or asked to solicit a monologue. Quite the contrary, the questions were aimed at putting them on the spot, in the hot seat. The questions were structured to obtain a simple yes or no response. "Are you willing to work for lower insurance rates? Yes or No?" If the response was a yes, then the official was allotted two minutes to explain. If they said no, they were given no time. "If we didn't hear the yes," Modesto León explains, "we were going to make him look bad."[31] In case an invited official failed to show up, UNO was already prepared for that. If they knew the official was not attending, UNO activists simply placed an empty chair with the official's name on it. Then they would call the press to let them know that the person in question would not be there and ask the media to cover the meeting. The next day UNO members would go to the official's office and protest the no-show.[32]

Planning also included who would speak for UNO at these mass meetings, where thousands of UNO members were expected to attend, mobilized by the individual parishes. These meetings would be held either at the auditorium of East Los Angeles College or in the larger parish halls of some of the eastside churches.[33] Of course, not everyone could speak, and so there had to be limits. The more people who spoke the more likelihood there was of people repeating themselves and muddling the message. UNO needed to speak with one voice, and its message had to be clear and strong.[34] Olivares, as chair of the insurance committee, would be in charge of the meeting. He would introduce the meeting and would address the invitees as to what UNO expected of them. He had been selected, in part, for his great speaking abilities, as exemplified by his passionate homilies at Sunday Masses. In addition, he orchestrated the event. He did this by signaling when the audience should sit down, when to stand, and when to clap. Of course, every meeting began with a prayer. Besides Olivares, a few other individuals, preferably laypeople, were selected from different parish units to speak or give witness. These were mostly testimonies about the hardships of having to pay such high auto-insurance rates. Those selected to speak would have to rehearse their short speeches prior to the meeting. All testimonies, including Olivares's statements, would be done in English, although these were translated into Spanish to accommodate the members more proficient in Spanish.[35] "It was very well-rehearsed," León recalls of the preparations, "and we would have seven or eight people that would tell their stories."[36]

Part of the strategy was to demystify UNO's opponents. People were used to being intimidated by Anglo authority figures, and UNO wanted to change this by stressing that these officials, whether in government or the private sector, were just people like UNO members. Pointing this out would empower the people not to be intimidated or scared of confronting people in power. At the Church of the Epiphany, for example, parishioner Lydia López remembers that this demystification took the form of her having done research on the officials who would be interrogated at the large meetings. At the planning meetings at her parish, she showed the photos of these individuals. She also found out whether they were married or divorced, the clubs they belonged to, where they had gone to school, and what had been written about them. She did all this to humanize these people and to familiarize UNO members with their opponents, or what she called their "targets."[37]

At these planning sessions, Ernie Cortes was very much involved. It was his experience and political savvy that influenced the nature of the planning. He would not play a public role at the meetings themselves, since he needed to have members take the lead and would remain in the background at these forums. But that was not the case at the planning sessions. Here he served as the director of the drama that UNO would perform. He coached members on where to position themselves, how long the presentations should be, how Olivares would signal to others about sitting or standing or applauding, and how to conduct themselves with the officials. Cortes was the consummate professional, and he passed on his expertise as an organizer to the members. "He was the key to what we did," Fr. Luna says. "He would make sure that we knew exactly how to handle something."[38]

Cortes also understood the importance of the media in UNO's actions. It was important to get the organization's message out to the media and to shape it in UNO's favor. Consequently, part of the mobilization strategy was to inform the media, such as the *Los Angeles Times*, other area newspapers, television news, and radio stations, about the mass meetings so that they would cover them. These meetings would take place in venues such as the auditorium of East Los Angeles College, where UNO would pack the place with as many as 3,000 people.[39] This outreach included the Spanish-language media, such as *La Opinión*, the oldest and leading Latino newspaper in Los Angeles, in addition to Spanish-language television and radio outlets. In this media outreach, Olivares played a major, if not the leading, role. As a chair of the insurance committee, the media naturally gravitated to him on the issue. Moreover, Cortes was aware that Olivares would do well with the media, due to his articulateness both in English and Spanish and his knowledge of the issue and other issues that UNO would take on.[40] Getting the word out to the media involved holding press conferences in which Olivares explained the nature of the action; sending press releases to the media; meeting with newspaper editorial boards; contacting editors and reporters to follow up and make sure they covered the meetings; impressing the media with the research information UNO had on redlining; and honing down their message to make it clear what the issues were while being aware that the media needed short sound-bites. The message was: the insurance companies are discriminating against drivers in East Los Angeles. UNO did all of this with Olivares as the point person with the media. Olivares and UNO recognized that they had to win the hearts and minds of the media. They had to paint themselves as the good guys and the insurance industry as the bad guys. Olivares explained the process in this way:

> We had two distinct approaches to the media. One was in preparing a press conference to make sure that all the information is delivered by hand to the different radio and TV stations, to make sure that they get it, to take a personal interest in making sure that they have all the information. Then you follow up by phone to make sure that a reporter is assigned. It's a tremendous amount of work. You can't just send out a press release and expect the media to respond; they don't. You have to coddle them into it. But aside from that, we had many meetings with editorial boards. We'd go in and explain the issue to the editorial board. The issues were clean and sharply defined. The key to successful community organization is the honing down of the issue to where it makes it exciting for them to want to deal with it. We had very high level editorial board meetings with the *Los Angeles Times*, *The Herald-Examiner* [sic], *La Opinión*, the top radio stations, and TV also. We would take . . . five or six people, and each one had an aspect of the issue to present. We were well-versed in it, so *they* found it exciting to meet with *us* because of all the information we had. Then, because of that relationship, we were also able to garner some editorials from these major media institutions. The insurance people were lobbying back, too, but . . . they were so obnoxious, the whole business community was so sure that nobody could shake them, that the media didn't like them, so they favored us.[41]

Olivares soon became a media star, due to his charisma and speaking abilities. The fact that he met with the press dressed in his clerical garb made him even more attractive to the TV cameras. His collar and tailored black suit with Gucci shoes became almost like a prop. "Luis had this charm, this public presence and ability to talk in front of the press," Lydia López comments. She adds that some in UNO joked that "there's never been a television camera Luis didn't like."[42]

Olivares's growing media presence did not come without criticism, as the above joke indicates. Some began to believe, if not complain, that the media was too focused on Olivares as the key leader of UNO. Of course, Olivares did in fact emerge, especially due to the insurance issue, as one of the key figures of UNO; however, based on its ideology, the organization attempted to discourage any semblance of a top-down structure with indispensable leaders. But what UNO desired was not what the media desired. They wanted, indeed demanded, a key spokesperson for the group that they could go to for commentary not just about UNO, but Latinos in general. "He became so known by the press that they actually wanted him to be like a spokesperson for the Hispanic community," Fr. Walter D'Heedene explains. "They wanted to make him like a Jesse Jackson for the community."[43] But not everyone in UNO was sympathetic to this, not because they did not appreciate Olivares, but because they did not feel it appropriate that only one individual should speak for the whole organization. They were also concerned that UNO members, including clergy, not speak out on their own.[44]

Because of these concerns, UNO adopted certain rules of operation with respect to relations with the media. If one received a call from a reporter, you could not take a position on behalf of UNO until consulting with other members and Cortes. These additional members would then decide who would speak to the reporter, and it would not just be one person but several. Sister Maribeth Larkin recalls that Olivares and some of the other clergy did not particularly like this rule since they were used to openly speaking to the media. They found it difficult to adjust. "Just operating like this was so contrary to how this group worked," Larkin says about the clergy. At the same time, she admits that this rule was not always enforced or adhered to, especially by the clergy, including Olivares. The fact was that as head of the insurance committee, Olivares was the logical person to address the media on this issue and so he continued to do so. Moreover, Cortes wanted Olivares as the key spokesperson on redlining because of his personality and experience. He could trust the Claretian to stay on target.[45]

Having prepared its strategy, UNO first focused on getting the County Board of Supervisors to agree to hold a hearing on insurance rates and redlining. It did not expect a resolution of the issue from the board since only the insurance companies could change the rates; however, the strategy was to use the board to at least hold hearings that would not only call attention to the issue but would put pressure on the companies.[46] Olivares and his committee first held several meetings with the staff of County Supervisor Ed Edelman who in part represented East Los Angeles. Through UNO's persistence, Edelman agreed to get the Board to hold a public hearing.[47] Once a date was set, Olivares and the committee organized further rehearsals for the meeting. These preparations consisted of house meetings at the different parishes and larger training sessions. Turnout for the meeting would be crucial, and Olivares encouraged competition between the parish units as to which could turn out the most. In this competition, Olivares did not neglect his own parish. At Sunday Mass, he brought attention to the meeting and the importance of a sizeable Soledad turnout. The meeting with the supervisors was scheduled to take place at the board's auditorium in downtown Los Angeles; however, the board met on Tuesday mornings, and this only increased the importance of getting UNO members there during the day. All of the parish units worked on this, recognizing the importance of the meeting. Both men and women made whatever arrangements were needed at work and at home to go to the meeting. With such detailed organizing, Olivares and UNO knew almost exactly how many people would attend in order to overwhelm the supervisors by this expression of people power. "Each single parish had a disciplined organized turnout," Larkin recalls.[48]

The day of the meeting dawned. It was scheduled for 9 A.M. Prior to that time, as Olivares and his committee arrived and settled in, other UNO members began arriving. Olivares was not worried; he knew there would be a large turnout. "Buenos días," he welcomed UNO members. As he greeted those who first showed up, more entered the chambers as the supervisors took their seats in front of the audience. Then more people showed up. The auditorium accommodated 500 people, but around 700 UNO members attended.[49] The fire marshal had to be called in to deal with the overflow. Some who could not be seated moved outside, where other UNO members staged a rally in front of the county building, calling on the supervisors to investigate redlining. Inside the meeting commenced. The board members seemed amazed and astonished at the huge turnout. "They'd never seen so many people there," Larkin observes. "They just kept on coming."[50] After preliminaries, Olivares along with a few others were invited to speak. Speaking in perfect English and with his usual eloquence, Olivares summarized for the board the concerns of UNO about the discriminatory auto-insurance rates in East L.A. He drew attention to the discrepancies in rates between the eastside and other areas of the city and county, as well as other findings from UNO's research on the issue. A few other UNO members gave testimony to the financial hardships posed by having to pay several hundreds of dollars each year for auto insurance. All of the presentations went exactly according to the rehearsals. The board listened and asked some questions and then ended this part of the meeting. Olivares and the others left the chamber elated at their presentation and resolved to maintain the pressure on the board. Cortes had sat in the back of the auditorium and was equally pleased with this first public action by UNO.[51] One reporter wrote that something "revolutionary" seemed to be happening and especially noted the leadership of Olivares and other clergy.[52] The "revolution" seemed even more real when, shortly thereafter, the board passed a resolution calling for the state legislature to hold hearings on auto-insurance rates. Olivares and UNO knew that the county board could only do so much about the issue, but they also knew that any attention to it by public officials at any level played in UNO's favor and strategy of publicizing redlining and putting public pressure on the insurance companies. They viewed the board's action as a victory.[53]

Besides putting pressure on the Board of Supervisors, UNO also pressured the state government in Sacramento. In an impressive mass mobilization of 2,000 people from all of the parishes that received much media attention, UNO members met on May 6, 1977, with members of the State Assembly Subcommittee on Auto Insurance headed by Democratic assemblyman Art Torres, who represented East Los Angeles, and who supported UNO. Olivares again delivered the main arguments concerning redlining. The Democratic-controlled subcommittee expressed empathy and promised to further examine the issue.[54] UNO welcomed this because it first desired to make the discriminatory rates into the key issue, but its real strategy was to force the state insurance commissioner and more importantly the insurance companies to agree to negotiate with UNO.[55]

Cortes tells a funny story about this meeting. UNO followed a practice that when one of their key speakers stood to address the assembly, in this case Olivares, that all members also stood up. Assemblyman Torres did not understand this and asked the audience to sit down. But they didn't. "Please sit down," Torres asked again. "Por favor sientense," he pleaded in Spanish. "Please take your seats." But the audience remained standing. After these unsuccessful tries, one of the other members of the assembly committee remarked: "I think you better ask Father Olivares to get them to sit down." Cortes signaled to Olivares to tell the members to sit down, and so he did and they sat down. All of this was part of UNO's strategy to show solidarity and discipline, and it worked. After they sat down, Cortes overheard one of the politicians say, "That priest has too much power!"[56]

However, the main target at the state level for UNO was Wes Kinder, the state insurance commissioner. Kinder was a former executive with the Prudential Insurance Company, although he had been appointed to the position by liberal governor Jerry Brown, a Democrat.[57] The main objective in confronting Kinder was to not only force him to put pressure on the insurance companies to change their rates in East L.A., but to also collect data that would show the prejudicial policies and attitudes of the companies toward Mexican Americans.[58] But UNO did not want to meet with Kinder in Sacramento, on his own turf; it wanted him to come to East L.A., just as the subcommittee had done. Olivares and the others wanted to make it uncomfortable for Kinder in having to find his way into the barrio. Lydia López notes that they wanted Kinder, as well as other officials invited to the east side, to feel ill at ease as a way of exerting more pressure on them and disarming them.[59] UNO acquired the use of the auditorium at East Los Angeles College, the same venue used for the subcommittee, and requested that Kinder appear there on June 1, 1977. Kinder initially agreed; however, when he heard that 2,000 people or more might attend, he pulled out and apparently called Olivares to inform him that he would not be there because he did not want to meet with an "angry mob." This was not the first time that Kinder had refused to meet with UNO. Incensed at Kinder's arrogance, Olivares and Fr. Al López called Governor Brown's office to complain about Kinder's refusal to attend the meeting. Brown responded to this pressure by ordering Kinder to attend. Brown's action further played into UNO's strategy of getting the Governor involved with the issue.[60] Kinder, according to Larkin, was "mad as a hornet" when he arrived and had to face not 2,000 but 3,000 people.[61] Larkin reflects on her own transformation by this display of mass mobilization: "I never imagined myself as an activist involved in this kind of stuff. But here we all were."[62]

The meeting had been heavily rehearsed by Olivares, Cortes, and the insurance committee. They physically arranged the setting to put even more pressure on Kinder by isolating him. He was forced to sit by himself behind a table but in front of him at a higher level sat Olivares and the selected speakers from the different parishes who would provide testimony— what Larkin called "horror stories"—about the hardships of redlining that forced many people to drive without insurance.[63] Behind Kinder sat the thousands of UNO members who responded to Olivares's signals about when to sit, stand, and when to applaud. Faced with this arrangement,

Kinder, according to Fr. Luna, was "sweating bullets."[64] Olivares opened the meeting with a blessing and then led the presentations and the questioning of Kinder.[65] Kinder had little choice but to promise that he would put pressure on the companies to lower their rates in East L.A., perhaps by as much as 50 percent.[66] In February 1978, Kinder ordered the companies to reassess their territorial ratings to see if excessive rates were being charged, especially on the east side. Kinder further noted that if any company defied this order they would be subject to severe penalties.[67] Kinder had in fact rejected in 1977 a 31 percent rate increase requested by the companies.[68] UNO considered Kinder's order to the companies to be a major victory.[69] Regarding Olivares's strong role in the meeting with Kinder, Sister Maribeth observed that his sense of injustice in working with farmworkers had clearly been transferred to his involvement with UNO, especially on the insurance issue. "It's kind of the same inspiration that got his dander up when he was dealing with somebody like Wesley Kinder," she states, "someone who was clearly not of the mind to take people seriously and to give people the dignity that they deserved."[70]

In addition to putting pressure on Kinder, UNO pushed the state legislature to do more. This resulted in UNO members led by Olivares going several times between 1977 and 1979 to Sacramento to lobby and to testify before various legislative committees on the need to eliminate redlining and to impose on the insurance companies a different and less discriminatory way to establish rates.[71] In Sacramento, Olivares worked very closely with Art Torres, who authored a bill that would force insurance companies to calculate their rates by zip codes, which would more closely take into account the rates of accidents and resulting litigation in specific areas such as East L.A.[72] Assembly Bill 3596, supported by UNO, passed the legislature and Governor Brown signed it into law on September 21, 1978. This officially required auto-insurance rates to be determined by zip codes. Olivares and other UNO members attended the signing ceremony and hailed the new law. At the same time, they recognized that this did not mean that the insurance companies would comply, or that, even if they did, they would reduce rates. UNO still aimed to force the companies to negotiate; however, they claimed a further victory not only in the new law, but more importantly in getting Brown even more involved on the issue, with the hope that he would exert additional pressure on the companies.[73]

Besides making redlining into a local and state issue, UNO also made it into a federal one when, in July 1978, the Federal Trade Commission (FTC) extended an invitation to the eastside organization to testify about its concerns in Washington. The Commission had never before held such hearings on redlining. As chair of the insurance committee, Olivares was selected to represent UNO at the hearing. He invited Sister Maribeth and Lydia López to accompany him. Although Olivares had traveled east as treasurer of his order, he felt more pressure and even anxiety on this particular trip. He felt that he had to do particularly well in this setting. At a convent in Maryland, where they stayed in guest quarters, Olivares had his own room while Larkin and López shared another one. None of them could sleep that night due to nervousness. "Are you awake?" Olivares said as he knocked on their door. They let him in. Olivares, according to López, also threw up that night. The public Olivares always seemed calm and collected; however, the private Olivares was quite different, especially before a big public presentation. "It wasn't always easy for Luis to gear up and get ready for these public statements," López observes. "It took a lot out of him but when he did it, he was committed."[74] López and Larkin were equally anxious. "We were in the big leagues now," López recalls thinking. Olivares spent most of the night walking the corridors and had to have the other two help him get ready in the morning to go to the capitol. He felt that his testimony in some ways might assist working families and the poor, and hence felt that there was a lot on his shoulders. "It was big time," López comments.[75] Despite his lack of sleep and his apprehensions, Olivares seems to have made a strong and impressive presentation. Among other things, he criticized Governor Brown in California for not doing more and hoped that the Carter administration would do more.[76] While the FTC did not rule on redlining, Olivares's appearance before the federal agency put additional pressure on the insurance companies back in Los Angeles. This is exactly what UNO's strategy had been from the beginning: to publicize the issue of redlining, make it into a social-justice issue, and, through public pressure, force the companies to voluntarily reduce their rates. Olivares returned to Los Angeles believing that perhaps full victory was near.

IV

Meetings with public officials, although part of UNO's strategy, could not replace dealing directly with the insurance companies. UNO understood that this was where the power resided and that it had to confront them. UNO members learned that organizing on the redlining meant meeting power with power.[77] UNO did not wish to win this action solely as a result of government intervention; it wanted to win directly over the companies that represented corporate power. A victory over them would empower UNO members and the Mexican American community in the most profound way. Reduction of insurance rates was the pretext, but the real objective was empowering the people and giving them a sense that they could control their own community. "It was the analysis of power structures and strategies," Sister Jo'Ann DeQuattro concluded as to why it was better to put the ultimate pressure on the companies. "If you can embarrass somebody into doing something, that was always a greater way than to go through traditional channels."[78]

UNO carried out this power-to-power strategy with the companies in two ways. It invited insurance representatives to meet at different parish assemblies, such as at Soledad with Olivares. Other meetings also occurred at Our Lady of Lourdes and at Our Lady of Guadalupe. "We would divide them up," Modesto León notes.[79] Prior to these large public meetings in the parish halls, Olivares and the insurance committee, along with parish representatives, had pre-meetings with the executives. This was done to warn them that they were there for a simple reason: to ask when they were going to reduce rates. This strategy was to preemptively put them in the hot seat and force them to consider how they were going to respond. "We didn't surprise anybody," León further observes about UNO's well-planned agenda for the public meeting. At these pre-meetings, Olivares as chair of the committee, put it to the executives:

> We are going to ask you two questions and we're not going to ask you to speak until you answer them. The first question is, "Are you will-ing to reconsider changing your rate zones in conformity with zip codes?" And the second questions is, "Are you willing to reduce rates in East Los Angeles?" And we're not going to let you speak until we hear a "yes, yes." You can then speak for two minutes. However, if we get a "no, no" you won't be allowed to speak at all and that's it.[80]

The representatives did not have to respond at these pre-meetings, but would have to do so before UNO members at the parish assemblies. At the one scheduled for Soledad some 500 people attended and made them promise to change the rates. "Of course, Luis was right in the middle of it," Fr. Al Vásquez stresses. "He was energetic, great charisma for speaking. Both languages. He was perfectly bilingual."[81]

Secondly, UNO met individually with some of the insurance executives in their offices. Meetings were held with All State, State Farm, GEICO, and several others.[82] Olivares and his insurance committee represented UNO. Such meetings were perfectly comfortable for Olivares. Although there to confront the companies, Olivares did so with style, eloquence, and humor. It was just like his meetings with Wall Street types as Claretian treasurer.[83]

Meetings such as these, in addition to the ones with public officials, began to pay off, as Cortes, Olivares, and UNO members had believed they would. The first big break came in November 1977, when the smaller Mercury Casualty Company agreed to adopt a zip-code system to setting rates and promised that it would immediately lower rates. Although responding to UNO's pressure, Mercury also hoped to undermine its larger competitors not only by attracting new policy holders, but drawing away those who had policies with the bigger companies.[84] George Joseph, the CEO at Mercury, announced at a packed UNO meeting at East Los Angeles College that Mercury would now pursue what he called "greenlining" by insuring anyone who was not already insured or who wanted to switch policies. "Our studies have shown this area deserved a lower rate," he said. "We felt it should be lower than Beverly Hills, Central Los Angeles, and Hollywood where the losses are greater."[85] He offered a premium of $400 to a family who had previously been assessed at $1800.[86] Families would now save $200 to $1400 a year and the average premium would be $330 compared to All State's average in East L.A. of $660.[87] Joseph signed a letter of agreement with UNO on November 4, 1977. The company further agreed to reduce rates in East Los Angeles by the beginning of 1978. This would include bodily injury liability and property damage liability reduced by 8 percent and other provisions such as medical, collision, and comprehensive coverage would go down 50 percent. In turn, UNO agreed to conduct a public education program among its members concerning the morality of safe driving and the immorality of insurance fraud and unjustified lawsuits. Both sides also agreed that future rate changes would be determined by the state commissioner of insurance or by a consulting agency of UNO's choice. This agreement would be valid until January 1, 1981, but could be extended by mutual consent.[88] Sign-ups for Mercury auto insurance would be conducted on a parish-by-parish enrollment.[89] Of this breakthrough agreement by UNO, the *Los Angeles Herald Examiner* said: "Just last week a relatively new citizen group managed to pull off a coup most of us can only dream about: it got some of its members reduced automobile insurance rates. Imagine."[90] It further noted that UNO represented some 700,000 Mexican Americans although this number clearly referred to the number of residents in East LA and not members of UNO. The *Herald Examiner* added: "This will make it [UNO] a staggeringly huge and potentially consequential pressure group in an area of our city as noted for its poor representation in our city, county, and state organs of government as anything else. That UNO appears to have already attracted such an enormous following is itself a significant measure of how inadequate traditional government appears to have been for them."[91]

The following year, in reaction to Olivares's testimony before the Federal Trade Commission the previous summer, State Farm, the largest insurance company in the United States, announced that it would lower its rates for its policyholders in East L.A. by an estimated 13 percent to 15 percent. It had concluded that residents of this area represented lower insurance risks than the company previously had thought. It did not, however, provide any evidence as to how it had come to this conclusion or explain why it had not done so before. Clearly, it was reacting to UNO's pressure. The *Los Angeles Times* called this "A Grass-Roots Victory in East LA."[92] State Farm admitted as such. "The State Farm spokesman acknowledged that the chief reason for the reduction was the long campaign by the United Neighborhoods Organization of East Los Angeles to lower auto insurance rates in the area," the *Los Angeles Times* reported. "It was in response to Father Olivares," the spokesman told the paper. Moreover, the company noted that it was shifting East L.A. to a different rating territory in part based on zip codes. The new premiums would go into operation immediately. "All this shows is that it can be done," Olivares told the *Times* about the rate reductions. "But where are the other insurance companies? What are they going to do?"[93] The *Wall Street Journal* also reported the State Farm announcement and observed that the actual cut in rates would be closer to 37 percent and would represent an annual average reduction of $314 to insurance holders. The *Journal* likewise noted that the change was the result of UNO pressure.[94] In an editorial, the *Los Angeles Times* further credited UNO for the major transformation: "Most of the pressure for these actions came from the United Neighborhoods Organization, a vocal and highly organized neighborhood lobby with ties to the Roman Catholic Church and a growing ability to push political bodies for attention and action."[95] In another, later statement to the *Times*, Olivares reiterated UNO's position on its priority to empower people. As the paper reported: "While Father Olivares says UNO is not an altruistic organization, he will concede that 'we're not just out for ourselves. We're endeavoring to change the insurance companies thinking to benefit everyone. Our whole objective is the empowerment of people. You ought not be subjected to any kind of domination—whether from the church or political systems or economic structures.'"[96]

Following State Farm's concession, a few other companies followed and reduced their rates in the barrios. These included GEICO and All State.[97] It was just a matter of time now before all of the companies succumbed. This occurred after Olivares and his committee met with Governor Brown and reminded him that in his 1976 gubernatorial campaign, he had promised that he would bring together the companies to get them to reconsider their rates.[98] Mexican Americans, Olivares no doubt reminded Brown, had voted overwhelmingly for him, especially because of his support of César Chávez and the farmworkers; now Mexican Americans in Los Angeles expected him to reciprocate their support. To his credit, Brown did so. In early January 1979, he strongly encouraged the key insurance companies, even those that had had already reduced their rates, to meet with him in his Los Angeles office, along with UNO, represented by its insurance committee, to discuss and arrive at a formal agreement between the companies and UNO on a mutually satisfactory process of reducing insurance rates and removing redlining. At what Frank Del Olmo of the *Los Angeles Times* called a "summit meeting," executives of ten major insurance companies met with UNO representatives, headed by Olivares. Brown hosted the meeting and insurance commissioner Kinder attended. The executives agreed to adopt or had already adopted a new insurance rating system based on zip codes rather than larger geographic territories, with the intent of lowering rates in East L.A. They promised to reduce premiums an average of 30 percent in the east side. They further agreed to consult with UNO about any future rate changes and explain why they felt they were necessary; they would even open their books to the organization. The companies included the Auto Club of Southern California, Aetna, All State, California Casualty, Fireman's Fund, GEICO, Ohio Casualty, Prudential, Safeco, and State Farm. Del Olmo observed that these ten companies constituted 60 percent of the auto-insurance market in California.[99] "The action sets UNO . . . as the community watchdog over the insurance industry," exclaimed the *Herald Examiner*.[100]

Needless to say, UNO members were delighted. It had taken two years, and many actions and mass mobilizations, but UNO had won its first large victory, which decisively put it on the political map. In this process, members led by Olivares and the insurance committee and coached by Cortes had shown commitment, patience, and new organizing skills that they had learned from the IAF. The victory justified UNO's establishment, and in the process its Mexican American members had empowered themselves. They now knew the meaning of people power. Olivares, while no doubt proud of his performance in the struggle, downplayed this to correctly stress that it was not just his work but the collective leadership of UNO that had succeeded. In responding to reporters, Olivares noted that UNO would continue to monitor the insurance companies as a result of the agreement. "The insurance companies that met here with us today are willing to continue cooperating with the community of East Los Angeles," he stated. "The significant aspects of insurance companies' willingness to justify their rates to the community by virtue of continuing meetings that we're going to have is that whenever there are rate changes we will have an opportunity to justify these changes." He went on to suggest that UNO's victory would not just be restricted to the Los Angeles area, but would resonate nationwide, "particularly for lower income and urban areas." He also observed that UNO expected that Brown would also continue to monitor the agreement. "The governor has committed himself to make sure that whatever role he can exercise in leadership," Olivares noted, "he will . . . so that those meetings take place." For his part, Brown downplayed his role and avoided discussions of "arm-twisting" of the executives. "This is the kind of meeting that comes together," he told the press, "when a citizen's group can organize, bring their message to the politicians, and then, industry respond."[101]

As far as the public and the media were concerned, there was no question who had won. UNO was David, and it had slain the giant. For some outside of East L.A., UNO's success was not just limited to the barrios, but was a victory for all consumers. KNXT, Channel 2 (CBS) editorialized in "Score One for UNO": "If your auto insurance rates are lowered in the next three months, you can thank UNO. . . . While we haven't gained full victory in the auto insurance war, UNO has certainly won a first major battle for consumers."[102]

For his part, Olivares, reflecting on the redlining action years later, stressed the importance of a collective movement, but at the same time acknowledged his own personal role, in it that brought him much attention. Olivares was a team player, but he still had his ego:

> The most significant project that I have been involved in with UNO was insurance redlining. We had a long, very exciting campaign to change the stereotypes that insurance companies were operating under in determining the rates for different areas. . . . Well, we blew [those stereotypes] out of the water. . . . We actually reduced the rates for East LA by about 42 percent. That process took a couple of years, and the community was involved with us. That's the crucial point, that's the whole difference of the community organizing process, is that you involve everyone. We used to have very, very impressive meetings on the issue, with three thousand people in attendance, and confront top insurance officials. We met in different auditoriums. During the whole insurance issue, I was the lead man in it, and that's where I got a lot of media exposure.[103]

There is no question that as a result of the redlining action, Luis Olivares emerged as the public face of UNO. His leadership abilities, honed first as a high official of the Claretians and, second, with his work alongside César Chávez and the farmworkers, well prepared him for his leadership role within UNO. It also introduced him to the Los Angeles media, who turned to him as the voice of UNO. Olivares's relations with the media would later serve him well in the sanctuary movement. Perhaps Olivares was a born leader, but in many ways, he also became a leader. He rose to the occasion, and the fact that he enjoyed being in the limelight only led him in that direction. It is also important to note that since UNO served as a faith-based group and organized around parishes, the role of clergy would be critical to its success. Clergy, by their very position were perceived as leaders, and serving as pastors of their congregations certainly bestowed leadership. Hence, because of institutional factors, Olivares was further positioned to be a leader of UNO. However, because of his own personal qualities, Olivares became an exceptional leader.

Beginning with the insurance issue, Olivares began to take on a larger role in UNO. The fact that he was selected and supported by Cortes to be the chair of UNO's auto-insurance committee only moved him further in this direction. People in or near UNO very quickly recognized this emergence. Mike Clements saw him taking an increasingly larger role and becoming the preeminent leader in the insurance fight.[104] Lydia López, observes that Olivares could get nervous before an action, as he had in Washington, D.C., but that when he went into action he thrived. "He loved having the spotlight," she says, "but it also came with a cost. But once he was ready, he was ready. It was a strong determination to go after the target . . . but he was wonderful about, to use UNO jargon, polarizing."[105] Richard Estrada remembers Olivares at various confrontations with public officials on redlining when "mobs of people going to supervisors and city hall, and this is when I saw Luis really loving people."[106] The more Olivares emerged as UNO's point person on auto insurance, the more he was seen by the industry and public officials as the person to contend with. Larkin observes that in the eyes of Commissioner Kinder and insurance executives, Olivares "was the man to be feared."[107] Olivares himself came to recognize the larger role he played in UNO. "That's when I became more public," he told a reporter in 1991, "because I became a chief spokesperson for the organization. The press or anyone interested in UNO would want to have my perspective on the organizing from the advantage of an insider."[108]

Olivares's leadership was evident in his running of the mass meetings that UNO organized on redlining with both public officials and insurance representatives. At these gatherings, it was clear who was in charge: Olivares. This is where his experience as a priest, as the treasurer, of leading his parishioners in his saying of the Mass, and his ability to reach people with his strong homilies all came together and helped him become, in a sense, a secular leader as well, or a religious secular leader, a combination in which he did not see as a contradiction. For Olivares, faith and politics intersected. Just as he had a commanding stature at Mass, so, too, did he have this in the mass meetings. "He called the shots," as Fr. Roger Wood recalls of Olivares's handling of these gatherings.[109] Others observed that in this setting, he had a good grasp of the issues, knew the details, and had a "good sense of himself."[110] Part of chairing the meetings was that he, as Wood further observed, possessed a variety of leadership qualities. He was very sharp; could sense what was happening; his timing was good; he could respond well spontaneously; he had good instincts; and he never lost control or got carried away; he was disciplined. "There were times when you could call him fiery," Wood adds, "but it was never shouting, never irresponsible."[111] Henry Olivares adds that his brother would tell him how proud he was of himself about being able to not only help organize these actions, but being able to effectively run the meetings. "All I know," he told Henry, "is that if I say stand, I give them the sign, they'll stand up. If I say walk out, we all walk out."[112]

Everyone who knew Olivares attests to his great and mesmerizing speaking style. In his Sunday homilies, for example, he would link the gospel message to UNO's actions. He motivated his parishioners into action. He got them passionate about participating, as Modesto León recalls his exhortations: "Are we really going to make a difference or are we just going to talk about it? If we don't have 500 people here when the supervisor comes then it's going to show our lack of commitment to our cause." León notes that 700 people showed up for the action. "Luis was a master at preaching," he concludes.[113] Like Archbishop Oscar Romero in El Salvador, who would become a role model for Olivares, the Claretian pastor provided a "voice for the voiceless."[114] Oralia Garza de Cortes, Ernie Cortes's wife, recalls witnessing Olivares preach and observing that he had what she describes as a sort of trembling voice but a mesmerizing one. But she also notes that Olivares further communicated with his eyes, which showed much expression.[115] Moreover, he did not use jargon or fancy words; he spoke directly in Spanish and in a way that connected with people. "Up in front of a whole group of people, he was masterful," Fr. Wood, still in awe, explains.[116]

People further observed Olivares's speaking abilities in UNO's actions. He could articulate his arguments well, was to the point, and spoke with great passion. Fr. Al López noticed that Olivares conveyed the same passion in his public speaking that he did in his homilies. "He was very dramatic," López admiringly says. "He knew how to speak."[117] At the same time, as so many others recall, Olivares had a wonderful sense of humor, and he used humor to lead. Larkin observes that Olivares used humor to cool down people when things got heated in the confrontations. He was able to bring out the humor in others who were more reluctant. His jokes and playfulness, she notes, helped "relieve the heaviness and the feeling of risk." At the same time, he poked fun at himself. Humor was also a way for Olivares to relieve himself of his own nervousness before an action. Larkin observes that Olivares couldn't eat before a mass meeting. "Don't get me near food because I'm going to get sick," he would say before having to chair one of the assemblies. But he would get over this once the meeting started and then afterward be his playful self again. "He was just fun to be around," Larkin says.[118]

Finally, central to his leadership was his charisma. He was not a particularly handsome man, but he was a striking figure in his fine priestly suit, coupled with his committed and passionate persona. He was also relatively tall and elegantly slim. Not all leaders have charisma, or they have it in different ways such as César Chávez. Olivares had charisma and that only bolstered his leadership. "He had a leadership that just drew people to him," his former student Rolando Urrabazo notes. "People from all walks of life. Because he could talk to people from any category."[119] He drew even his opponents to him. Lydia López noticed that after confronting public officials or insurance executives, Olivares was a master of "depolarizing," meaning he could disarm his opponents by his charm and humor and by his stature as a priest. But this depolarization was part of the strategy. As López describes it:

> Luis was very good at depolarizing because he had that kind of charm about him. He could go up to an insurance commissioner or whoever the target was and shake their hand and slap them on the back and say all the nice things. And he would just be disarming. "Oh, Father Luis, well, yes, yes." Because he's got the little collar, everybody said "Oh yes, Father." The rest of us were the SOBs in the room. We had been so naughty to them, but Father Luis, "Oh, yes." Then they would say "my dear friend, Father Luis," never knowing that he was leading the pack but also being the leader to disarm them, to depolarize them. That was part of the plan.[120]

Olivares thrived as a leader and very quickly became identified with UNO. He became Mr. or Fr. UNO.[121] At the same time, Olivares was thankful for this opportunity to lead and to evolve his leadership. He learned how to be a leader within the Claretian order; he learned about leadership from engaging with the farmworkers; and he learned from Cortes and UNO how to organize. All this he would carry on to his later work on the sanctuary movement. "So I got trained in confrontation," he admitted. "Our confrontation tactics today," he said in 1991, "comes right out of the UNO experience. It became my style."[122] Olivares enjoyed being a leader because he enjoyed power. He appreciated power. Not personal power, but the good that he could do with power. Of course, there is often a thin line between personal and public power, and power in general can be seductive. Olivares liked the attention that the possession of power brought him, but at the same time, he kept this under some control so that the major thrust of whatever power he had was aimed at doing good for others. He seemed to know how to do a tightrope walk with power so that it did not consume him. His brother, Henry, saw this aspect of Luis. "There was a lot of injustice going on in East L.A.," he says, "and Luis enjoyed power. He knew what power was; he knew how to use it; and he knew he was using it properly for the sake of the people."[123] Olivares would later observe that power was sinful if it was used only to rule, but it was not sinful if it was used to serve. Olivares used power to serve.[124]

VI

While Olivares emerged as the image and voice of UNO, behind him and the mass actions was Ernie Cortes. He had his own ego, but it was subsumed as the IAF organizer. He represented the coach, if you will, of team UNO, but like a coach, he was restricted to the sidelines. However, at practices such as the planning sessions before actions and in the discussions after the actions, it was Cortes who dominated. He plotted out what would take place at the action and afterward, again like a good coach, analyzed the outcome of the actions and how they could be improved next time. During the mass meetings, he usually stood at the back, observing and only occasionally, perhaps, quietly passing on some instructions. This nonpublic stance was not just Cortes's style; it was mandated by IAF guidelines for organizers. They were not to participate in the actions themselves, in order to allow grassroots leadership to emerge, and so that UNO would not be accused of being led by outsiders. Cortes knew his place, but UNO members, including Olivares, depended on his experience and judgment. This was enough personal satisfaction for him. He played this role and played it well for the two years that he served as organizer before being replaced, since IAF policy did not favor keeping organizers too long in any one location, lest they lose perspective and that community become too attached to them.

At the same time, UNO members acknowledged Cortes's contributions in the redlining action and the key role that he played behind the scenes. One of those contributions was in the reflection sessions after an action. He met with Olivares and the insurance committee, for example, along with representatives of the parishes to go over their performances. "There is where we would talk about what we learned from our experience," he explains. "How did you deal with the corporate community; how did you deal with the governmental community. So we would talk about these different experiences and evaluate them. We'd think about what we learned differently connected to what we read in the newspapers or about what we read in articles and magazines or in different books."[125]

Brother Modesto León best summarizes Cortes's role in not only the redlining action but in others as well. "He was there in the background," León states. "Organizers never speak out. That's not their job. Their job is to empower the leadership. . . . His job was to say this is the way we do it and you bought into this so don't go over this and change it because you're going to do this and that. So Ernie was in the background. He'd be all nervous and he wouldn't get you until after when we had the debriefing. After the politicians go home, we had the fifty leaders and got a meeting and fought it out. What went right, what didn't go right. That's part of training. If we don't do that—hey, you know what, you went too long; you let him speak five minutes. We told you two minutes."[126]

As the two major figures in UNO, Cortes and Olivares developed a close working relationship. They always consulted with one another. Sister Maribeth, who worked closely with each of them, admired both men. She notes that each was equally strong in different ways. Cortes was a brilliant strategist, and Olivares was a brilliant practitioner. She saw each learning from the other. Both men liked and respected each other and became friends. Both needed each other. Lydia López observed Olivares and Cortes as being very direct and honest with each other. "Almost like brothers," she comments, "because they'd joke with each other. It was a good relationship."[127]

Becoming friends and collaborators, Cortes and Olivares also shared some social time together. Sometimes they would go out to dinner with other UNO staffers such as Larkin, but Cortes and his wife, Oralia, likewise on occasion invited Olivares to their place for dinner. Before and after dinner they talked and joked. Both loved books, and Cortes had a large library, which he shared with Olivares. Oralia felt that Olivares was intrigued by her husband's brilliant mind although, of course, she was biased on this. She remembers the priest's great sense of humor on these occasions. For one dinner, Oralia made turkey, but not the whole turkey, only three turkey legs, one for each.

"Do you like turkey?" she asked Olivares.

"Yes, I do," he replied.

However, when Oralia came out with the three legs, Olivares with a twinkle in his eye said: "Oh my god, a three-legged turkey!"

The combination of Cortes's leadership as organizer and Olivares's public leadership, along with the active and spirited participation of other UNO leaders and activists, represented a powerful coalition that led to UNO's first major victory and the empowerment of its adherents. But this was only one action, and many other followed.

VII

Redlining and the auto-insurance action represented UNO's signature triumph; however, both during the two years that the struggle over this issue ensued and after, the organization conducted successful actions on a number of other problems facing the East L.A. community. Olivares participated in many of these, but not necessarily as the key leader or spokesperson, due to the prolonged insurance battle. Still, he supported them and was still seen by many, certainly the press, as the key voice of UNO. Fr. Luna recalls that Olivares was the main speaker at many of these other actions.[128] At the same time, Cortes and the executive committee organized various other subcommittees to deal with a variety of issues. Indeed, it is remarkable how many issues UNO took on from its founding to the early 1980s, the heyday of the group. At its 1979 convention, for example, a UNO "Statement of Problems" pointed out the extent of the conditions that East L.A. suffered that it believed was the result of the disinvestment or lack of funding from both public and private sectors to upgrade conditions in the barrios. These problems included:

- Deteriorating housing
- Deteriorating and underdeveloped commercial strips
- Lack of retail served by major chains
- Poorly maintained structures and service from the few major retailers in the area

- Insufficient funds at affordable interest rates for rehabilitation of existing structures for low- and moderate-income families
- Poor public transportation
- Lack of street repairs
- Inadequate schools
- Insufficient public libraries
- Inadequate health services, including for undocumented immigrants
- Inadequate police protection, especially with respect to gang problems
- Inadequate funds for citizenship programs[129]

These issues were just some of the many for which UNO successfully led and participated in actions, from its inception in 1976 to 1981, when Olivares left the east side and his pastorship at Soledad to become pastor of La Placita Church in downtown Los Angeles. UNO, led by men and women but in many cases by women, would continue for several more years as an example of a faith-based movement and a major player in local politics. It would later expand to include other minority communities, such as African Americans, in a coalition effort. Some of the additional actions concerned voter registration, though UNO did not endorse candidates; increasing the state minimum wage; restricting liquor stores on the east side; and providing citizenship classes. All of these actions led to various improvements for eastside residents, but more importantly, as planned and anticipated, it led to the empowerment of UNO members and of the Mexican American community. Some on the political Left, including activists in the Chicano Movement, criticized UNO for being too reformist and willing to work within the system and for not addressing the root causes of poverty and oppression as the result of capitalist exploitation and racism. While UNO did not address such root causes, it nevertheless helped to improve conditions in the barrios and, more importantly, helped to empower many to believe that they alone could change their conditions (self-determination). It also accomplished what the movement failed to do in Los Angeles. UNO created a community base in the barrios for political action. The Chicano Movement, as movement activist Rosalio Muñoz admits, did not.[130] This might not have satisfied the political Left and perhaps even some left-wing intellectuals today, but it certainly satisfied many in East L.A. In this process, Olivares played a major role, including his very visible leadership on auto-insurance redlining but also through participation in his own parish actions and other interparish ones. Other clergy and, more importantly, UNO rank-and-file members recognized Olivares as their most inspiring figure.

VIII

Toward the end of the 1970s and before transferring to La Placita Church in 1981, where he would engage with the sanctuary movement, Luis Olivares rounded out his new activist life as a community priest by participating in PADRES (Padres Asociados para Derechos Religiosos, Educativos, y Sociales). This was a social movement of Chicano Catholic priests, formed in 1969 in San Antonio, that aimed to pressure and lobby the Church, especially in the Southwest, to be more conscious of and attentive to the needs of its large and growing Mexican American contingent, who represented 25 percent of all Catholics in the United States. Indeed, some even saw the Anglo Catholic Church as part of the historical oppression of Chicanos. It represented a colonial Church. Clearly influenced by the Chicano Movement, the founding priests became "Chicanos" and underwent their own conversions from parish priests to political activists. They saw themselves as part of the movement.[131] "We were all heavily involved in the Chicano Movement," one Chicano priest, Fr. Alberto Carrillo, recalls about the founding of PADRES, "and the purpose of PADRES was to bring the Chicano movement to the church."[132] PADRES aimed to push for greater representation in the Church hierarchy and at its founding pointed out that there were no Mexican American bishops in the Church and a lack of Chicano priests. It called on the Church to make the recruitment of Mexican American priests a priority. Only 200 Mexican American priests, for example, existed in a Catholic Mexican American population of between 8 and 10 million. It further promoted the enculturation of Mexican American popular religious traditions in the Church, such as more Spanish-language Masses, Mexican American music, and regional feast days such as the celebration of Our Lady of Guadalupe. It also called for support for the farmworker struggle and the grape boycott; the protection of undocumented Mexican immigrants; more parochial schools for Mexican Americans; the establishment of national parishes to minister to the Spanish-speaking; and the investment of Church funds to develop minority businesses.[133] Although PADRES reached out to Chicano priests, Olivares at first was not involved or particularly interested. He had not been affected or involved in the Chicano Movement and more than likely saw PADRES as too radical and militant for his tastes as a high official of his order. He saw it as too controversial a voice. He acknowledged that he knew little about the group and that at its establishment he had not yet gone through his own conversion. "Well, I wasn't involved in that either," he recalled about PADRES. "It's amazing, all that was completely outside of the realm of my consciousness! You know, I was sitting in a fancy office, and I was very comfortable."[134]

However, his first contact with PADRES came in 1970 when his superior, Fr. O'Connor, invited him to accompany him to San Antonio to attend the ordination of Fr. Patricio Flores as the Auxiliary Bishop of San Antonio on May 5 (Cinco de Mayo), 1970. Flores became the first Mexican American and Latino to be appointed as a bishop of the American Catholic Church. It was a historic event. As Provincial of the Claretian order, which had a long history of working with Mexican Americans, O'Connor was invited to the celebration. PADRES had pushed for Flores's selection. O'Connor not doubt felt that it would be good for Olivares to attend, since he was Mexican American and from San Antonio. Olivares agreed to attend. He met some of the Chicano priests involved in PADRES, such as Fr. Juan Romero from Los Angeles and one of the founders of the group. César Chávez attended the ceremony and participated in the Mass by reading some of the scripture. However, it is not clear if Olivares was introduced to him and Olivares does not mention it in later interviews.[135] For his part, Romero invited Olivares to attend a PADRES meeting, also in San Antonio, later in 1970, and again Olivares agreed to attend. Romero remembers Olivares at that meeting. "So he was there, very much in his French cuff state, being groomed to be an ecclesiastical bureaucrat." Olivares told Romero that it was a good meeting and said, "You've got some heady people here."[136] But Olivares still did not join the group. Henry Olivares notes that at first his brother was put off by PADRES, but that after he became "converted," he realized its importance.[137]

Despite Olivares's aloofness, Romero still invited him to other PADRES meetings. Slowly but surely, Olivares began to realize that the group was not as radical as he might have first perceived and that he agreed with its stress on the greater integration of Mexican Americans into the Church, including the appointment of additional bishops. It is conceivable that, given his own ambitions, Olivares came to recognize that he personally could benefit from PADRES's advocacy. In any event, he became more involved and, in 1974 (before his conversion), agreed to serve on its board of directors, representing the western region and becoming the regional director for PADRES. At one of the first board meetings in Yakima, Washington, Fr. Robert Peña, another PADRES founder, was very impressed with Olivares and mentioned to Romero that he believed the Claretian was "presidential timber," meaning capable of becoming a future president of the organization.[138]

As western regional director from 1974 to 1978, Olivares witnessed certain reforms within the Church that affected Mexican Americans and other Latino Catholics, as promoted by PADRES. By 1975, for example, the number of Latino bishops grew to five, and Latino Catholics now also had representation within the National Conference of Catholic Bishops, which established a Secretariat for Hispanic Affairs. In a report, Olivares noted the importance of having more Mexican American representation in the western Church within his region and especially in the Los Angeles area. Latino Catholics constituted 66 percent of all Catholics in the West. He called for the Church to establish regional, pastoral, cultural, educational, and leadership training centers for Latinos in the western region. He emphasized the importance of the Spanish language with respect to the Church's ministry to Latino Catholics by calling for 50 percent of all clergy to possess an adequate knowledge of Spanish by 1982, and for this to increase to 99 percent of clergy by 1986. Moreover, he advocated the greater participation of Latino clergy and laity in leadership and decision-making roles at all levels of the Church. "The Church in this region has a Hispanic face," he stressed, and hence the structures and the leadership of the Church had to reflect this. This applied to pastoral councils, diocesan boards, chanceries, and local parish structures. Olivares further called for a greater sensitizing of priests, seminarians, and religious orders to the culture and needs of Latinos. "We do not seek a separate Church," he wrote, "on the contrary, we only seek to be more that Church whose faith we share without a proportionate share in determining its destiny." Finally, he called for the Church to issue a clear and public statement of support for Latino Catholic issues and in support of priests and other religious groups working with farmworkers, undocumented immigrants, and on auto insurance redlining. "We all need an effective sign that the Church is really with us," he concluded.[139]

But the most important issue that Olivares dealt with as regional director, and a foretaste of his later involvement with Central American refugees and Mexican undocumented immigrants, had to do with growing concerns and even hysteria about the increase of Mexican "illegal aliens" into the United States, especially in California. The elimination of the Bracero Program in 1964 and the cap on legal Mexican immigration imposed by the 1965 Immigration Act, plus continued Mexican economic underdevelopment and the desire of many U.S. employers for cheap immigrant labor, all contributed to a significant increase in Mexican undocumented immigration in the late 1960s and into the 1970s. Reaction to this movement resulted in increased apprehensions and deportations of undocumented immigrants and new proposed immigration legislation to deal with the perceived threat. As this reaction intensified in the mid-1970s, when Olivares underwent his conversion and the beginning of his involvement with UNO, his emerging political consciousness led him to support the undocumented. Curiously, this support clashed with the view of César Chávez and the UFW, who called for immigration officials to remove the undocumented from the fields where they were being used to replace UFW strikers. Chávez minced no words in calling the undocumented workers "scabs," or strike breakers, and a threat to his union. There is no record that suggests that Olivares and Chávez discussed this issue, but despite Olivares's growing relationship with the farm-labor leader, he still chose to differ with him in this one area.

PADRES opposed congressional legislation aimed at stemming undocumented immigration by imposing penalties on employers who knowingly hired these immigrants. This involved the Rodino Bill in the House of Representatives and the Eilberg Bill in the Senate. Both contained the so-called employer sanctions provisions. PADRES also helped influence the U.S. Catholic Bishops to oppose this legislation. The opposition centered on the employer sanctions provision, which PADRES and the U.S. Bishops believed would lead to widespread discrimination against the hiring of documented Mexican immigrants as well as U.S.-born Mexican Americans by employers who did not want to take a chance that they might be hiring the undocumented and so to be safe would not hire any person of Mexican or Latino descent. Instead, PADRES advocated a comprehensive immigration bill that would provide amnesty for many of the undocumented who had been in the United States for several years and had their families with them, including U.S.-born children, in order for them to legalize their status and for a preferential system of immigration favoring Mexico and other Latin American countries that would increase the number of documented immigrants and reduce the rate of the undocumented. As regional director, Olivares endorsed this position and publicized it among Mexican American Catholics in California.[140] In response to an article by Frank Del Olmo of the *Los Angeles Times* critical of the proposed immigration bills in Congress, Olivares agreed with Del Olmo that any proposed legislation had to be carefully and rationally discussed, which had not been the case with either bill. "We especially protest the attempt to make the Spanish-speaking community bear the burden of carrying proof of citizenship at all times," he wrote in his letter to the editor, which the *Times* published.[141]

Becoming more involved with PADRES, especially as a board member and as western regional director, Olivares became better-known and appreciated among other members. Moreover, they became aware of his leadership in UNO and the success that he was having with this group. It reinforced the impression of Olivares as a strong leader, one who could also lead PADRES. Hence, in 1978 members elected him as First Vice President. At the time of his election, PADRES counted over 900 members, although the great majority were not active. However, the group was still not clear on its identity. Was it a service organization or a social movement? There was a felt need to reorganize it.[142] One year later at a meeting in San Bernardino, members elected Olivares as president after the resignation of Fr. Roberto Peña. Peña had alienated the Latino bishops as well as the more moderate and conservative members of PADRES. According to former priest Anthony Stevens-Arroyo, who was elected First Vice President, board members believed that Olivares was more diplomatic and that he could have better relations with the bishops.[143] Olivares accepted the position and was pleased that his good friend and ally César Chávez spoke at the convention. Chávez warmly congratulated his friend.[144]

Olivares believed that as president he could revitalize PADRES and make it into a more powerful organization within the Church. To do so, however, he wished to broaden the group's base by opening it up to non-Latino clergy and laity. Prior to Olivares's election, PADRES had already agreed to allow non–Mexican American Latino clergy, such as Puerto Ricans and Cubans, to become members. "Olivares spoke about the need to carefully build a bigger 'power base' for Padres," the *National Catholic Reporter* stated, "so that someday the Church will think more than twice before appointing an Anglo bishop in a predominantly Hispanic diocese which it had recently done in San Bernardino."[145] At a news conference, Olivares laid out his vision of broadening PADRES's base to make it into a major player within the Church. "I'm committed to the reorganizing of this body into a visible strategy group for the Hispanic agenda," he proclaimed, "that no longer chases after trains that have left the station and no longer is involved in crying sessions whether in Washington or San Bernardino."[146] He stated that he hoped to make the group open to all clergy and laity, men and women, Hispanic and non-Hispanic, Catholic and non-Catholic. "Our goal is a national organization," he said, "truly ecclesiastical, that has power and influence."[147] He observed that PADRES had provided a support group for Mexican American clergy and had been responsible for the selection of the first Mexican American bishop in the United States. "The question now," he stressed, "is whether as a movement we have the power and influence to be taken seriously as we move into the '80s." He added that for PADRES it was now a matter of survival. His mission was to achieve certain goals. These included maintaining a prophetic stance on issues, especially in relation to Latinos in the Church; to build for power by strengthening relationships from within but also broadening the base; to serve as a strategy group for Latino bishops; to form necessary alliances with those who understood Latino issues and were willing to work with PADRES; and the need for the group to be proactive rather than reactive to issues.[148]

As president of PADRES, Olivares first strongly encouraged the appointment of a Mexican American to become the Archbishop of San Antonio. He understood the symbolism that this would convey. PADRES had successfully lobbied within the U.S. Church to get several Mexican Americans and Latinos to be appointed bishops, but to get one of them possibly appointed Archbishop, the position in the Church hierarchy next to being a Cardinal would be a great coup. On learning that Archbishop Francis Furey of San Antonio had died, Olivares minced no words and went straight to the top to advocate for Furey's replacement to be a Mexican American in a city with a Mexican American majority. He wrote directly to Pope John Paul II in Rome in April 1979. "All throughout this great city [San Antonio] and in other parts of the Archdiocese," he stressed, "the Mexican and Mexican-American Catholics are talking about their hopes and desire for a shepherd that will identify ethnically and/or respond to the predominant cultural identity of his flock." Such an appointment would immediately become a role model, especially in the recruitment of young Mexican Americans to the priesthood. "PADRES has been concerned with the issue of native leadership since its beginning," Olivares concluded, "and so it is that we are asking our Holiness to appoint a Mexican/American to the See of San Antonio, Texas."[149] In addition to the Pope, Olivares also wrote to the Apostolic Delegate in Washington, the Vatican's representative to the U.S. Catholic Church, strongly calling for a Mexican American appointment to the San Antonio vacancy.[150]

PADRES's lobbying had an effect, and the Pope selected Bishop Patricio Flores from San Antonio, who was serving as Bishop of El Paso, to be the new Archbishop of San Antonio. Olivares and his colleagues were elated at the news and felt that their efforts at greater Mexican American and Latino representation in the Church's hierarchy were being fulfilled. By 1980, ten Latinos had been appointed as bishops. That year Olivares hailed the naming of Fr. Raymundo Peña as Bishop of El Paso to replace Flores. "The more visible the Church's concern for Hispanics in the country becomes," he wrote to the Apostolic Delegate, "the more truly Catholic the American Church becomes."[151] The biggest celebration was the installation of Flores in San Antonio on October 13, 1979, at San Fernando Cathedral. Olivares attended along with many dignitaries, including César Chávez. Olivares no doubt reflected on his own ordination two decades earlier in the cathedral and the road that he had traveled. Perhaps he himself harbored thoughts that one day he might become a bishop or an archbishop and, of course, he was committed to the cause of the appointment of additional Latino bishops. However, he must have also been aware that his conversion to political activism would be more than likely to make him too controversial for such an appointment. The Church shied away from appointing anyone it considered "controversial" to high offices. Flores had been active in PADRES, but not in a confrontational way, and he certainly was not involved in political struggles such as Olivares had been in with UNO.[152]

As he had as regional director of PADRES, Olivares as president continued to advocate for the rights and protection of undocumented Mexican immigrants. During his tenure in office, PADRES issued a number of positions with respect to this issue. These included the following: opposition to a national I.D. card, which it considered to be discriminatory "internal passports" for Latinos and other non-white people; opposition to the militarization of the U.S.-Mexico border and the building of more border fences; opposition to long prison terms for merely entering the United States without documents or inspection; opposition to continued reduction of immigrant quotas for Mexico and the Western Hemisphere and obstacles toward family reunification of immigrants; freedom from deportation and separation of family members; support for full educational opportunities for the children of the undocumented; the right to unemployment insurance, social security, disability insurance, Medicare, and labor law enforcement as it applied to the undocumented; and opposition to the stereotyping of the undocumented.[153] These were far-reaching and controversial positions; however, Olivares and PADRES believed that they were essential for the protection of the undocumented, and that morally as well as politically, these were the right things to do.

Besides his initiatives, Olivares also represented PADRES at different Catholic events, meetings, and conferences. His most significant representation came with Pope John Paul II's fall 1979 visit to the United States. President Jimmy Carter hosted a reception for the Pope at the White House and invited Olivares, along with many other religious officials, to attend. Olivares, in turn, invited Fr. Juan Romero and Lydia López to join him. López remembers hundreds of people at the reception and that all of the Catholic clergy including Olivares were star-struck by the charismatic Pope and, according to her, they were all like putty in his hands. Olivares loved the occasion.[154] He was also flattered when *Time* magazine interviewed him along with other religious figures such as Billy Graham, Fr. Theodore Hesburgh, the president of Notre Dame University, Fr. Daniel Berrigan, S.J., and many others. It appears that the magazine requested that Olivares and the others write up their reaction to the Pope's visit from an American perspective. In his response, Olivares displayed both his liberal pastoral or community views along with his more conservative or traditional theological ones, especially on the role of women in the Church, birth control, and celibacy for priests. He wrote:

> The Hispano-Catholic relates to the family, not affluence. Ordaining women is trivia. Birth control or married priests are non-issues. By his presence the Pope can give tangible evidence of the concern expressed in his message about the poor, the alienated, the consumer society. The Pope can also directly appoint more Hispanic bishops in this country. The American hierarchy as a whole fails to recognize the Hispano-Catholic and his values. You cannot alienate people for too long. The Hispanic is a patient and long-suffering soul. John Paul II gives us cause for hope.[155]

It is possible that Olivares's comments, especially on ordaining women and on married priests, may have been taken out of context; if they were, there is a question as to whether Olivares was saying that the Pope's visit would do nothing about these two controversial issues, given the pontiff's conservative theological views, or whether Olivares himself was also opposed to female priests and to married priests. Olivares was becoming or was already a liberationist in 1979; that is, a believer and practitioner of liberation theology. He applied liberation theology to his work with UNO and PADRES with respect to the Mexican American community. However, like other—but certainly not all—liberationist priests, Olivares still possessed his own, more traditional Church socialization that would not permit him to extend liberation to include the ordination of women and the right of priests to marry. There was a duality to his theology. Women were considered second-class citizens of the Church as long as they were not allowed to be priests, and priests, because of celibacy, were repressed with respect to their sexuality. Olivares, a political liberationist, could not expand this to gender and sexual liberation, or at least not publicly.

Overlaying Olivares's presidency was the increased influence of liberation theology on PADRES and on Olivares himself. It appears that following his "conversion," Olivares began to read some of the writings on liberation theology coming out of Latin America, beginning with the Medellín conference in Colombia in 1968, where representatives of some of the Latin

American bishops gave voice to this new theology in response to the Second Vatican Council's call for the Church to be more responsive and relevant to the modern world. In the Latin American context, characterized by much poverty and oppression, the clergy at the conference called for the Latin American Church to have a "preferential option" for the poor.[156] In 1979, a follow-up liberationist conference was held in Puebla, Mexico. During the period between the Medellín and Puebla conferences, Chicano and Latino clergy in the United States began to become more aware of liberation theology and to adapt it to the struggles of Mexican Americans and other Latinos for their rights. Olivares began to see the connection between liberation theology and his own growing political involvements as a community priest with the farmworkers and UNO. For Olivares and for many in PADRES, civil rights was theology and in particular liberation theology.[157] This liberationist influence on Olivares only increased as he became a member of PADRES, and during his presidency. In his personal files, evidence of his familiarity with liberation theology can be found. For example, there is an unpublished text with no author listed, but dated August 1975, entitled, "The Chicano Struggle: Viewing it [from] Latin America's Theology of Liberation." The essay's author focuses on the need of Latino Catholics in the United States to assert themselves within the Church and to apply liberation theology in the barrios:

> La iglesia [the Church] for the Chicano is still madre [mother], but one who was confronted out of love, especially at the beginning of our struggle for liberation. Lately, however, an attitude of indifference has occurred amongst a significant number of Chicanos because they do not see the institutional church as one that is relevant to them or they do not see el padre [the priest], la monjita [the nun], being present with them en la lucha [in the struggle]. Others Chicanos see the church as contradicting in its expression of poverty [in] its alliance with the powerful upper and middle classes. There is, however, amongst the Chicanos, some that do recognize the church as being involved, as in the farmworker struggle for justice and the latest concern with nuestros hermanos [our brothers] without documents"[158]

PADRES positioned itself, under Olivares's direction, as endorsing liberation theology. In *Entre Nosotros*, the newsletter of the group, Fr. Gilbert Romero (Fr. Juan Romero's brother) wrote an essay titled "Liberation Theology and the Hispanic Church," in which he stated: "There is now a greater awareness among Hispanics of the need for a theology of the Hispanic Church in the U.S. due in some measure to the influence of Latin

American liberation theology. The major input of this influence can be felt in the area of 'praxis,' i.e., the lived experience as basis for theologizing. The lived experience in the pastoral and political, must be rooted in the theological."[159] Romero suggested that this lived experience connected to theology for Latinos in the United States could be found in the culture and history of the people themselves, especially their *religiosidad popular* or popular piety. Popular religiosity—the way that Latino Catholics practiced their religion at the grassroots level in their homes and in their communities often with little or no connection to the institutionalized Church and an Anglo Church in the Southwest that had historically demeaned their popular devotions—was the way in which Mexican American Catholics, for example, had preserved both their religious and ethnic identity. Latino Catholics had been oppressed not only economically and politically, but also culturally. Liberation theology for them had to extend to the cultural realm. Cultural liberation, according to theologian Fr. Virgilio Elizondo, represented the U.S. Latino's most significant contribution to liberation theology, which in Latin America focused more on economic and political liberation. In this sense, U.S. Latinos were influenced by liberation theology coming out of Latin America, but they also contributed to it.[160]

While Olivares hoped to further expand the political agenda for PADRES, his efforts caused tensions with the Latino bishops. The bishops' main efforts within the Church were to institutionalize Latino, or what they called Hispanic Catholic, issues through the National Secretariat for Hispanic Affairs established by the U.S. Catholic Bishops.[161] While the American bishops had acquiesced to PADRES demands that they support the appointments of Latinos as bishops, they recommended to the Vatican the selection of more moderate or conservative Latinos who saw PADRES as too militant and confrontational and too independent from their influence.[162] This reflected the conservative theological and political influence of Pope John Paul II, who was skeptical, for example, of liberation theology in Latin America, and forbade priests from engaging in political activities. Hence, the Latino bishops were prepared to work with PADRES, but only if it became more "respectable." Olivares and others within PADRES were not willing to do this. "Respectable" for them meant lessening their pressure on the Church to implement more changes that would recognize the importance of Latino Catholics, and it also meant losing their role as an independent pressure group. As Fr. Romero, who had served as the first executive director of PADRES, put it: "It seems they [Latino bishops] wanted PADRES to become respectable and sophisticated but this was not in the nature of . . . Louie."[163] Romero agreed with Olivares that PADRES should remain independent, for only in this way could it continue to pressure the Church. The secretariat, because it was part of the Church structure, could not do this and thus was not an oppositional body.

Olivares's last major effort to advance PADRES came when he proposed that membership be opened up not only to clergy but to laypeople as well. This would be one way to expand membership and bring in new ideas and energy. What Olivares wanted to do was to further modify the membership to now include the Catholic laity. This was not inconsistent with earlier PADRES support for lay leadership.[164] But he wanted more than this. Obviously recognizing the success that UNO had become because of its relationship with the IAF, Olivares wanted the same thing to happen to PADRES. He wanted to transform PADRES into an IAF affiliate. This was not a farfetched idea, since some of the early members of the group, such as Romero, had connections with the IAF in the early 1970s, and some like Romero had undergone IAF training. In fact, Romero had been one of the leaders of UNO.[165] Olivares discussed this first with Ed Chambers, the director of the IAF, who seemed willing, but only if PADRES opened up membership to laity. PADRES had to become more of a mass-based organization and more grassroots in order for the IAF to enter into an agreement. Under such an accord, the IAF would train both the clergy and laity.[166] To accomplish this, Olivares invited Chambers to speak at a PADRES board of directors meeting in Oak Park, Illinois, in April 1979. In his presentation, the head of the IAF called for PADRES to move from being a reactionary movement type of organization to an organization of power. It should not just react to issues; it had to lead in issues. However, to accomplish this, he agreed with Olivares—and no doubt had indicated as such to him—that the base had to be increased to include laity, which was a way to keep the organization close to the people. Chambers also called for PADRES to develop a message and agenda that would provide a clear purpose to the group. Moreover, accountability within PADRES had to be part of the change. Leaders and members had to be accountable to the group as a whole. Finally, Chambers concluded by stressing that "power is not something given. It is something we take. No one confers it on you."[167]

One year later, at a joint meeting of the Latino bishops and representatives of PADRES in Chicago, Olivares reiterated what Chambers had said. Olivares proposed to the bishops that his top agenda item as head of PADRES was "a broadening of the organization's base so that it could be truly representative of the views of Hispanics in the country." PADRES needed a much larger constituency. Although it had 800 members, only 200 were full members. However, an increase in membership could not be legislated by new bylaws; it had to be part of a process. This process was linked to PADRES's reorganization as a grassroots organization similar to UNO. Olivares knew the power of the IAF affiliates, and he wanted PADRES to be similar. This might be considered by some as a radical change, but Olivares called on the bishops and members of PADRES to trust him; he knew what he was doing. "I was elected president in San Bernardino in February of 1979," he reminded his audience, "because a majority of those present put their trust in the organizing skills I can offer P.A.D.R.E.S. That's my mandate, my mission." Olivares concluded that he was "committed to organizing for power" so that PADRES could make a difference for Latino Catholics within and outside the Church.[168]

However, many PADRES members did not want power by becoming attached to the IAF, nor did they want to expand to include laity, both men and women. They rejected Olivares's proposal. A disappointed Olivares interpreted this decision as a vote of no-confidence in him and in his hope to expand the role of PADRES to make it into a true power player within the Church. Clearly, other members did not want to go this far and probably were fearful of the IAF affiliation, which might tag the group as radical and militant and perhaps as Communists. Moreover, they had seen that some PADRES members had suffered personal consequences for their political engagements and were not allowed to move up the clerical hierarchy.[169] They did not want to be associated with liberationists such as Olivares and instead increasingly reverted to being pastoralists or parish priests dealing primarily with the spiritual needs of their congregations.[170] Rejected, Olivares resigned and only served as president for two years. "I gave my reason," Olivares said about his resignation, "being that as long as PADRES was going to focus itself . . . on being a support type organization for clergy then I didn't think that was the kind of thing I wanted to be involved in. And as a leader, I wanted to see a much broader-based process."[171] Romero notes that after Olivares's departure the organization became more conservative, more influenced by the Church bureaucracy, and began to decline and ceased to exist in 1989.[172] Some of the early founders of PADRES believe that by the 1980s the Church had successfully co-opted the group.[173] To his credit, Pablo Sedillo, the director of the Secretariat for Hispanic Affairs, and PADRES's rival, took the occasion of Olivares's resignation to thank him for his services as president of PADRES. Writing to Olivares in Spanish (translated here), Sedillo wrote: "These last two years have been difficult ones for our community and especially for our leaders. I know, in my heart, that you have always had our community in your heart and in your thoughts and that you did everything you could for our community in these two years. . . . I know that you will continue to fight for the rights of our people and especially the poor and that you will continue to encourage us to do likewise."[174]

IX

The year that Olivares resigned from PADRES is also the year that he transferred from Soledad to La Placita Church, the popular name for Our Lady Queen of Angeles Church in downtown Los Angeles, across the street from the touristy Olvera Street, but in the heart of the original Spanish settlement of what came to be Los Angeles. He had come a long way from San Antonio, from the seminary, from his ordination, from his rise in the Claretian hierarchy, and from his "conversion." Since his encounter with César Chávez and the farmworkers, he had become a community priest, one who embraced a new form of ministry steeped in the involvement with the Mexican American community and for its empowerment. His association with UNO was the highlight of this new ministry and he emerged as no doubt its most important public figure and leader. He had always had leadership abilities and the personal charisma to go with it, but the years from 1975 to 1981 were still formative ones for him, for the type of new priest that he wanted to be, and that was with the people and their struggles. He had learned much from UNO, the IAF, and from Ernie Cortes, but he was ready to move on and allow others to lead. He remained a member of UNO into the 1980s, and he and his new parish participated in some of its actions in the new decade. These included successful efforts to raise the state minimum wage in California and to have some gun control to deny gangs additional firepower.[175] But just as Olivares had changed, so, too, had UNO. It would continue for several more years until it merged with a more expansive effort by the IAF to go beyond East L.A. to organize other areas of metropolitan Los Angeles, as it continues to the current day. The name UNO was dropped and replaced by LA Metro, and the group came to include, besides the east side, the San Fernando Valley, South Central L.A., the Pico Union district in the downtown area, and the San Gabriel Valley. Moreover, although still heavily Latino, it became more multiethnic.[176] UNO had won many victories and Olivares was very much a part of this. However, its greatest victory, as noted by union leader Jimmy Rodríguez, was "that the people in that generation learned about power in unity, power in organization. I think that was the biggest victory of UNO."[177] The *Los Angeles Times* concurred as early as 1977 when it wrote: "[T]he group's most important achievement is to have created a large cadre of disciplined, trained volunteers to attend hearings and meetings, grill poli-

ticians and speak loudly and firmly for their communities' interests. Whatever becomes of the United Neighborhoods Organization itself, that newly
evident strength is unlikely to disappear."[178]

UNO and to some degree PADRES, like the Chicano Movement, initiated the long march to contemporary Latino political power in the United
States, clearly manifest in the new millennium. As for Luis Olivares, he
would not disappear, nor would his commitment to being a community
priest; he wanted to still be very much a part of the action. Moving to La
Placita, administered by the Claretians, marked a step up, in that this parish
was seen as the center of Mexican American Catholicism in the city. That's
where Olivares desired to be, not just for his own aggrandizement, but for
the continuation of his political activism. It may be that he had a personal
prophetic vision that La Placita would in fact become the focus of the biggest challenge of his ministry and of his life—the sanctuary movement.

EIGHT

Preparing Sanctuary

La Placita Church (Our Lady Queen of Angels Church) is located in the heart of downtown Los Angeles. It is one of the smallest churches in the city, yet it is perhaps the most significant. It is, or has been, a Mexican church, and today it is also a Latino church, though most parishioners are still of Mexican descent composed of both U.S.-born and immigrants. It is a parish, yet it has no real parish boundaries, and what can be considered to be parish borders are very limited. To the west and north, the church is bordered by Chinatown, housing projects, and commercial businesses; to the east, there is Union Station and the railroad and commuter trains; and to the south is the Hollywood Freeway and the downtown skyline, including City Hall.[1] Adjacent to the church is Olvera Street, which, beginning in the 1920s and 1930s, became transformed by Anglo boosters into a fantasy Mexican village aimed at attracting tourists to its Mexican restaurants and shops and providing them a little bit of "Old Mexico." La Placita is a parish, but it draws its parishioners from many other parishes in the Los Angeles Archdiocese. Mexicans and other Latinos historically have come from miles to attend a church that represents a comfort and safe zone for them, providing services in Spanish and nurturing Mexican and Latino Catholicism. Today it lies in the shadow of the nearby and recently constructed Cathedral of the Queen of Angeles, a massive, postmodern church in comparison to the simple and functional architecture of La Placita. The cathedral is the cathedral, but to many Mexican Americans, Mexican immigrants, Central Americans, and other Latinos, La Placita is the real cathedral, or *their* cathedral. As Father Juan Romero observes of this little church: "It's the very center, historically and certainly anthropologically and sociologically. It's the heartbeat of Los Angeles. It's the crossroads. It's the real cathedral."[2]

La Placita is also located in the historical origins of Los Angeles, where the initial Spanish settlement or pueblo was founded in 1781. It came to be called La Iglesia de Nuestra Señora la Reina de los Angeles (The Church of Our Lady Queen of the Angels), and its original construction was commenced in 1784 and completed in 1790.[3] This structure was later modified, and the founding date for the renovated church is August 18, 1814. Although age and earthquakes affected the original structures and what exists today are relatively newer buildings, still La Placita or Old Plaza Church, as Anglos called it, maintains its legacy as the heart of Mexican and Latino Catholicism in Los Angeles. In 1981, when Olivares became pastor, its key physical features consisted of the older and more baroque chapel where people, especially older women, could and still can be seen reciting the rosary out loud all day long. Next to the chapel is the more modern but simpler larger church where all of the Sunday Masses take place. It seats about a thousand people. Across from the main church is the rectory and living quarters of the clergy, and connected to it on the eastern side are various administrative offices. All of these structures surround a modest-sized plaza where parishioners and others congregate at different times of the day, and especially after Sunday Mass. Finally, at the eastern entrance of the property, across the street from the Old Plaza and Olvera Street, is a gift shop. The church is at 535 North Main Street.[4] First administered by different orders, the Claretians took over the parish in 1908 and have administered it until 2015, when Archbishop José Gómez replaced them with diocesan clergy. This became Luis Olivares's church and the center of the sanctuary movement in Los Angeles. He was 47 years old when he became its pastor.

I

Olivares inherited a church with a rich history and varied traditions. For one, it involved many more parishioners than he had at Soledad. The *Los Angeles Times* in 1986 reported that about 100,000 families were constituents of La Placita.[5] On average, 10,000 to 12,000 people attended Sunday Masses. To accommodate such a number, La Placita offered eleven Masses all day long on Sundays, as well as many confessions and baptisms. According to Fr. Al Vásquez, who served as pastor of La Placita from 1973 to 1981 and who had been one of Olivares's teachers at Dominguez Hills in the major seminary, 99 percent of parishioners were of Mexican origins. Under Vásquez, a Centro Pastoral was built in the courtyard of the church to administer not just the religious programs but the social ones as well. This included providing meals for the homeless twice a day, housing some of them at night, and also providing baskets of food and clothing for the needy. As in most if not all Claretian parishes, the clergy ministered to the

Fr. Luis Olivares, La Placita Church, Los Angeles, 1980s. (Courtesy of Dept. of Special Collections, Charles E. Young Research Library, UCLA)

poor and powerless. Olivares would add to this tradition as he already had at Soledad.[6]

Olivares not only inherited all of this pastoral and social activity, but the tradition and spirit of its people, who worshipped at La Placita because it related to them ethnically and culturally. This was an ethnic or national parish in the best sense of the term. "Placita was like your hometown," Juanita Espinosa, a long-time parishioner who worked at the church as a part-time receptionist in 1964 while in high school, says, "a parish that spoke your language where others didn't."[7]

While Olivares welcomed going to La Placita, the transfer also had to do with Claretian rules of not allowing pastors to stay too long at any one parish. The usual tenure was an initial three years that was renewable for another three years. Olivares had already been at Soledad six years, and Fr. Vásquez had likewise been at La Placita six years, so the changes coincided with the order's tenure regulations. These limits had to do with a sense that pastors should not become ingrained in anyone parish or feel that they were indispensable. But it was also a way to create new leadership and new energy by these shifts.[8]

Olivares expressed enthusiasm about the change. He had thrived at

Soledad as a community priest, especially with UNO, but he was ready to take up new challenges. It is not clear whether he personally requested to go to La Placita or the order made that decision. Fr. O'Connor, the Provincial at the time, says that Olivares's being named pastor at La Placita probably was a combination of his wanting to go and the order's need to replace Vásquez after his six years there.[9] Olivares accepted the position without hesitation. He wanted Placita because it was the flagship parish of the order in Los Angeles, because it was a step up for him as a pastor, and because it would give him a larger venue, not only personally, but for his community work. Henry Olivares acknowledges these motivations. "Luis wanted a bigger, wider audience," he says. "He saw a need."[10] Rolando Lozano seconds this by observing that Olivares wanted to be pastor at Placita because the church was much more in the public eye than other Claretian parishes. "It was like it gave him an opportunity to have a soapbox because the press was always there," he notes. According to Lozano, regarding anything related to the Catholic Church in Los Angeles, the media would always go to the pastor of La Placita for comments. He adds that Olivares liked this. It was like being in the big leagues.[11] Yes, his ego was involved, but there was also that part of him, as a result of his "conversions," that sincerely wanted to continue to help the poor and the voiceless, as he had done with UNO and at Soledad.[12] He also seemed to be aware by 1981 that something was happening at Placita that he could work on, and this was the arrival of Central American refugees, especially from El Salvador, who were fleeing their countries' civil wars. Perhaps he could assist them in some way.[13] He did not go with the intention of declaring La Placita a sanctuary church and had not even thought about it yet. But he did in his first few years prepare the way for sanctuary.

II

Imbued with new energy and spirit, Olivares took up his new duties at La Placita in 1981. Besides the greater pastoral duties he would have to deal with, he also expected to continue his work with UNO and engage in community politics. La Placita was a member of UNO and, under Fr. Vásquez, had participated in many of the organization's activities. As he settled in to the rectory and assembled his staff, he did not expect to engage in any significant new directions, but to build on what he had already been doing. But this was not to be. Thousands of miles away in El Salvador, a civil war and political repression would lead to thousands of political refugees fleeing their country and looking for refuge. They believed that they would find it in the United States. They crossed into Guatemala, then Mexico, and then without documents into the United States, largely through southern California. They especially hoped to find help in Los Angeles. This civil war and this human migration would come to transform Olivares's ministry at La Placita, and transform him personally.

Characterized by dictatorships and military juntas for years, and supported unfortunately by the United States because of Cold War politics that led to American endorsements of right-wing repressive governments in Latin America and, indeed, throughout the world, as long as they professed being anti-Communist, El Salvador was a tragic, underdeveloped small country of 5 million with no freedom or democracy for its people. A powerful clique of fourteen families—*los catorce*—controlled most or all of the wealth including most of the productive land, largely used for exports such as coffee to the United States, and in cooperation with American companies. The Salvadoran people, by contrast, lived in poverty, especially in the countryside where they attempted to survive on small plots of land or by working on the large plantations. In the cities such as San Salvador, many more lived in poverty in the barrios. The average per-capita income was below $900.[14] Still, there existed a history of resistance and rebellion by many that brought on military attacks, killings, arrests, rapes, and tortures. Despite this counter-resistance, many in the labor movement, university students, and others continued to protest and call for change. The resistance, including armed resistance, came to be represented by the FMLN (Farabundo Martí National Liberation Front). Among the voices for change were many Catholic clergy, who called on the military regimes in the late 1970s to end the killings and repression of the people. In 1979, the government troops killed on average 1,000 people a month.[15] For their courageous stand, some priests and other clergy were murdered as the Salvadoran government declared war on the Church.[16] This included Fr. Rutilio Grande in 1977, a Jesuit and the first priest in El Salvador killed by a death squad, who would become a symbol of those Catholic clergy who sided with their flocks; he was seen as a martyr.[17]

The accounts of the plight of the Salvadoran people became increasingly known to the outside world, as the civil war continued into the 1980s. This unfortunately included even stronger U.S. support, under President Ronald Reagan's administration, for the military that included infamous death squads, para-military groups that indiscriminately slaughtered innocent civilians, all in the name of anti-Communism, by falsely claiming as did the U.S. Right, that the opposition was a Communist movement supported by Cuba and the Soviet Union.[18]

Personal testimonies by refugees who successfully made it to the United

States further substantiated the level of persecution in El Salvador. Mario Rivas, who later worked with Olivares, stated: "In 1980 I left my country, a couple of years [earlier] I was jailed and tortured by the police. In April of 1981, Mauricio, 25, and Carlos Alberto, 20, two cousins of mine, were brutally killed by government death squads. Another cousin Rolando, 24, was disappeared by the Army in June of the same year. In November 1986, my own brother Miguel Angel, was disappeared by the Army. My family has not heard from him since."[19] Rivas was eighteen years old when he arrived in Los Angeles with no documents.[20] By the mid-1980s, some 50,000 people had been killed in El Salvador.[21] Fr. Dick Howard, a Jesuit who worked in El Salvador, also recalls the horrors he personally witnessed: "I saw how the Salvadorans lived and what they went through. You have no idea of the courage of the people who risk their lives every day. Everywhere there were bodies in the streets."[22]

The civil war in El Salvador, and the repressive tactics of the government and military, were tragically brought to the attention of the world by two horrific political murders. On March 24, 1980, Archbishop Oscar Romero of San Salvador was assassinated as he said Mass. A lone gunman directed by the military shot and killed the beloved priest, the highest-ranking Church official in the country. Although appointed in 1977 by Pope John Paul II as a conservative, after his ascendancy Romero began to sympathize with the suffering of the people and was scandalized by the use of force by the military and government. He was especially alarmed at the killing of Catholic clergy. He became a liberationist and supported liberation theology spawned by progressive Catholic clergy in Latin America that, among other things, called for the Church to cease its historic alliance with the rich and powerful and instead possess a "preferential option for the poor." He began to speak out against the murders and the tortures and to support community-based groups, though not directly the rebel factions. His outspoken positions only angered the Right, and Romero began to receive death threats.[23] Of this, he courageously said: "I am prepared to offer my blood for the redemption and resurrection of El Salvador."[24] Prior to his death, Romero had sent a letter in February 1980 to U.S. president Jimmy Carter asking him not to supply military aid to the Salvadoran military. He wrote: "It disturbs me deeply that the U.S. government is leaning toward an arms race in sending military equipment and advisors 'to train three Salvadoran battalions'. . . . Your government, instead of favoring greater peace and justice in El Salvador will undoubtedly aggravate the repression and injustice against the organized people who have been struggling because of their fundamental respect for human rights."[25] One month later,

Romero was dead; he became an instant martyr to his people and to many Catholics around the world, including the United States. Olivares admired Romero and saw him as one of his heroes.[26]

The level of brutality by the Salvadoran military, which shocked people in the United States and throughout the world, was further magnified by the killing and rape of four American female missionaries in El Salvador, three of them nuns and one a layperson. Sister Ita Ford and Sister Maura Clarke both belonged to the Maryknoll order; Sister Dorothy Kazel belonged to the Ursuline order; and Jean Donovan was a Catholic lay volunteer. On December 2, 1980, as the four of them drove from the San Salvador airport to the rural communities where they worked with the villagers, soldiers stopped their car. They raped two of the women and shot and killed all of them. Peasants discovered their bodies the next day. U.S. ambassador Robert White, who knew the women, expressed shock and blamed the military for the murders. President Carter temporarily suspended military aid to El Salvador, although it would be restored under the Reagan administration.[27]

Especially after the assassination of Archbishop Romero, many innocent Salvadorans began to flee their country. Most hoped to get to the United States, either because some had relatives already there or, more importantly, because of a sense that they could find refuge there, even though they did not have immigration papers. Most who left did not favor one side or another in the civil war; they just wanted to leave before they lost their lives. Some had already seen family members arrested, tortured, and even killed.[28] Over 80 percent of the refugees had lost family members in El Salvador.[29] They left with very little other than the clothes on their backs and whatever else they could carry.[30] One year later, by the time Olivares became pastor of La Placita, the number of Salvadoran refugees significantly increased, as it would throughout the decade as the civil war intensified. Moreover, much of Central America became a war zone when the Reagan administration, for all practical purposes, declared war on the Sandinistas in Nicaragua, who had successfully overthrown the forty-three-year Somoza dictatorship in 1979. Reagan considered the Sandinistas to be Communists and organized a counter-revolutionary group called the Contras. The United States, rather than sending troops to Central America, instead engaged in low intensity warfare or indirect ways to overthrow the Sandinistas and reinforce client states in El Salvador, Guatemala, and Honduras. War raged in Nicaragua in the 1980s, as did civil war and repression in neighboring Guatemala, whose governments and military had historically repressed indigenous communities as well as any opposition. Many

Guatemalans also began to leave their country and find their way to the United States.[31]

Those who arrived at the U.S. border then crossed without documents by themselves or those who could afford it paid a *coyote* or Mexican smuggler to get them across. Some made it and others did not, having been captured by the U.S. Border Patrol and deported back across the border, where they tried again.[32] Some in Tijuana were assisted by Catholic groups, including one former Jesuit who provided a safe house for refugees until he could get them across to San Diego, where they were given sanctuary at Christ the King Church, whose pastor, Fr. Mike Kennedy, a Jesuit, would shelter them until he could transport them to Los Angeles and other cities.[33] Gloria Kinsler, who assisted the refugees in Los Angeles, recalls that some were put on planes in San Diego and flown to the Burbank Airport, where she met them after being told what clothes they were wearing, in order for her to identify them. She then provided a new set of clothes for them to put on at the airport so they would not look so conspicuously like refugees.[34] Many of these early refugees were young men still in their teens or early twenties, who were escaping forced recruitment into the Salvadoran military. In the early 1980s, Fr. Richard Estrada, who worked in juvenile detention centers, began to notice young Salvadoran men there.[35] Some families also arrived through a form of chain migration: after one relative crossed the border, others would follow.[36] By 1987, some 350,000 Salvadorans and 79,000 Guatemalans were in the United States, many of them in Los Angeles. By the end of the decade, about a million Salvadorans had sought refuge in the United States, with between 300,000 to half a million Salvadorans in the Los Angeles area.[37]

Although they sought protection across the border, they did not find it. Despite an 1980 U.S. Refugee Act, passed by Congress and signed by President Carter, that aligned the country with United Nations resolutions on political refugees to be defined as anyone who would be persecuted, tortured, or even killed if they were returned to their home countries, the Reagan administration refused to recognize the Salvadoran and Guatemalan refugees as legitimate political refugees. Instead, Reagan claimed that they were simply "illegal aliens" attempting to take jobs from American citizens, the same position it took on Mexican undocumented immigrants. Hence, very few Central American refugees, with the exception of Nicaraguan refugees who left their country protesting the Sandinista revolution, received favorable treatment. Clearly, Cold War politics played a decisive role in these unjust treatments, including the fact the Reagan, Carter, and previous administrations supported repressive governments and military forces in Central America as long as they proclaimed that they were anti-Communist and protected American economic interests in their countries. The Reagan administration was not going to embarrass or challenge these client states by endorsing the refugees as legitimate refugees since this would have been seen as a criticism of these countries and of U.S. policies in the region. By 1986 no more than 2.5 percent of all Central Americans and only 3 percent of Salvadorans were granted refugee status.[38] Three years later, out of 26, 791 Salvadoran requests for refugee status only 211 were granted, with over 10,000 rejected and the rest pending.[39] Ernie Gustafson, former official in the Los Angeles office of the Immigration and Naturalization Service (INS), observes that many Salvadorans and other Central Americans did not even bother to apply, believing that their requests would be rejected.[40] To his credit, he recognized that, despite the insistence of the Reagan administration and the INS that the Central Americans were only illegal economic refugees, he could see this was not the case for many of them fleeing civil war. "There were valid reasons for some of these people. No question about it," he asserts.[41] "How am I an economic refugee when I'm here to save my own skin—to save my life," Mario Rivas stresses.[42]

III

No doubt moved by the assassination of Archbishop Romero, the killing of the female missionaries, and the general persecution of Catholic clergy who spoke out in defense of the poor and against military violence, the Church in the United States condemned the violence in El Salvador, protested against the Reagan administration's arming of the Salvadoran and Guatemalan militaries, and called for the recognition of the Salvadorans arriving in the United States as legitimate refugees who should not be deported.[43]

Many of the refugees not only went to Los Angeles, but specifically to churches such as St. Vibianas, the cathedral adjacent to skid row, in search of assistance.[44] They did not find it in some, but did in others, and not all Catholic. Philip Zwerling, at the First Unitarian Church in South Central Los Angeles, witnessed by 1980 the arrival of Salvadoran and some Nicaraguan refugees. His church provided some assistance to them.[45] However, many of the Salvadoran refugees went to La Placita. Some had heard that it was a Catholic church and that it would help them. Lydia López, who worked with the refugees there, recalls that some arrived with the church's phone number or address, or both, written on little pieces of paper that others had provided them either in El Salvador, on their journey, or when they crossed the border.[46] Fr. Brian Cully, who served at La Placita at this time, noted that as early as 1982 refugees started arriving and that Olivares attempted to assist them as best he could, though not yet in an organized fashion.[47] Not only Salvadoran refugees arrived but also Mexican undocumented immigrants.[48] In time, as more efforts to assist the refugees were organized at La Placita, many later refugees arrived already knowing the name of Fr. Olivares and of La Placita, where they could get at least a meal and some lodging.[49]

Based on his own faith and his commitment to assist the poor and powerless as he had in working with the farmworkers and with UNO, Olivares almost instinctively reached out to the refugees and attempted to do what he could to help them. Olivares supported the American bishops' position on Central America and on the refugees and he was informed of the situation there. Mike Clements, who had visited El Salvador and Nicaragua in the early 1980s, remembers discussing the situation in those countries with Olivares, who expressed interest in doing something with the refugees and raised this with Claretian authorities. Clements adds that he could tell that Fr. Luis seemed inspired by the Sandinista revolution in Nicaragua and with the opposition in El Salvador. "He seemed to have a really strong attraction to what was happening," Clements notes.[50] Recognizing the plight of the refugees, Olivares welcomed them to La Placita, even though some of his Mexican parishioners seemed to dislike this. But this did not bother him and he believed that he was following Jesus's example of preaching salvation to all ethnic groups despite the opposition of some fellow Jews to this. "So when someone advocates for the downtrodden, the immigrants, you make yourself unpopular," Olivares later told Juan Romero, "but you become popular with the poor."[51] Olivares wanted to make the refugees welcomed at Placita. As he did, he also started to listen to their stories. They talked to him about their families and mothers disappearing in El Salvador. "I think it weighed on him enormously," attorney Peter Schey, who assisted some of the refugees, says of Olivares. "He was privy to so many stories about human rights violations that refugees suffered in Central America, topped off only by maltreatment at the hands of the United States government once they got here, that he was probably the most sensitized person in the country to the contradictions of U.S. policy because these policies were talking to him on a daily basis." Schey believes that Olivares was hearing things from the refugees that no one else was and therefore was in a unique position with respect to the exiles. These people, according to Schey, went to Olivares because, as a priest, they believed he could help them.[52] Although he knew he would be up against the whole federal government and this to some degree frustrated him, still he vowed to do what he could to assist these people. "I know that it's not enough to just listen to their stories and pray for them," he said, "I have to do more. I can't just say there's a need and then just pray about it."[53] One way was to include, for example, stories about Archbishop Romero, using quotations from his writings, in the parish bulletin, as well as hosting programs on Central America, so that his parishioners would also learn about what was happening in Central America and assist him in his outreach efforts to the refugees.[54]

IV

But in order to do what he could for the refugees, Olivares first had to organize a program and assemble a staff. He inherited a fairly large staff, including six resident priests. La Placita, with its large congregation, provided many religious and social services, hence the large number of employees. The priests, of course, were the main members. Olivares knew all of them as fellow Claretians and, in his earlier role as treasurer of the order, had interacted with them, as well as at retreats and other Claretian assemblies. He considered them friends, although not close ones. They were Claretians, but not really his kind of Claretians. They focused mostly on spiritual and pastoral issues and activities rather than political ones. They had not been involved with UNO, for example. One of these priests was Fr. Tobias Romero, the father of Fr. Juan Romero, who shared Olivares's views. However, his father, who became a priest after his wife died and joined the Claretian order, did not. The elder Romero believed that a priest's main duty was to be within the church, say Mass, hear confessions, baptize babies, marry couples, and in general serve the spiritual needs of the people, but not their temporal ones. This was not Olivares's orientation. He had become a liberationist and he wanted his parish to reflect this. He knew that he needed other priests to join him, not because they would be younger than the resident priests, but because they would share his commitment to being community priests.[55]

To assist him in his social ministry, as Henry Olivares refers to his brother's work, Luis recruited more activism-oriented priests, who also happened to be younger. For one, he brought Richard Estrada with him from Soledad. His former student, Rosendo Urrabazo, joined him after studying at the Graduate Theological School at Berkeley. Other new additions included Ken Gregorio and Brian Cully, still a seminarian. It wasn't that all of them were steeped in sociopolitical activism, but they nevertheless supported Olivares's direction and countered or contrasted with the older, more conservative clergy. "Luis had a way of attracting fellow workers. . . . He had a way of presenting what he needed: 'You help me and I'll help you,'" as Henry puts it.[56] By 1985 the clergy at La Placita had been almost completely transformed, and only two of the priests that Olivares had inherited remained. To be sure, some who replaced the others were not community-type priests, but they did not predominate. Nevertheless, there always was during Olivares's years at La Placita some tension between those clergy who favored more pastoral or religious services and those, led by Olivares, who believed that being a priest also meant politically serving the community, including refugees and immigrants.[57]

Assembling, as much as possible, a new team, Olivares also wanted to develop a team ministry. He had attempted this at Soledad but with a much smaller staff there, he had reverted to a more top-down authority structure, where he as pastor pretty much made the decisions. But La Placita was different. It had a much larger staff composed of clergy and administrative workers. He thought the concept of a team ministry, in which he as pastor could delegate much more authority, was feasible. Under a team ministry, the members do work previously done by the pastor.[58] There were simply too many activities for one pastor to be in charge of. Moreover, as he moved to accommodate the Central American refugees and undocumented Mexican immigrants this would entail even more work, and he could not do this all by himself or even with the help of a small group. Team ministry, of course, came out of the changes from the Second Vatican Council that stressed a more grassroots approach by the Church, as well as the development of lay leadership. Certainly in his work with UNO, Olivares had worked to develop community-based lay leadership. His new challenge at Placita would be an expansion of this earlier practice.[59] This would not mean that his leadership would be diminished, only that he would be more of a quarterback, not the whole team. He would direct others and help them develop their leadership, but he would still be the ultimate authority as pastor. It was indeed a challenge for someone of Olivares's charisma, but he hoped to successfully implement it. At the same time, Olivares's persona still remained very dominant. "Luis's natural leadership abilities always came forward very strong," Urrabazo says. "We looked to him not just for concrete things but for the thrust, the spirit."[60]

This new system at Placita replaced the more traditional one that Fr. Vásquez had administered. Olivares placed certain people in charge of certain projects, whether of a religious nature or of a more secular one, and trusted them to do the work.[61] Virginia Mejia, whom Olivares hired to work with the refugees, observes that Olivares trusted her and expected her to tell him what she needed to accomplish her job. She adds that the team-oriented approach was "really nice to meet in that atmosphere." This involved team meetings at least once a week, sharing meals together, and doing at least three retreats each year, usually in the nearby mountains. Meetings were held in Spanish, English, or both, depending on which language people were comfortable with. Olivares was seen as part of the team. "He would let us do our job," she says, although he wanted to be kept informed of their doings.[62]

To fully implement the team ministry, Olivares also moved to bring on additional staff, such as Mejia, especially as work with the refugees increased.[63] Lydia López, who was a close colleague and friend of Olivares from the UNO years, later joined the staff at La Placita even though she was Episcopalian, and observes that this mirrored Luis's ecumenical commitment. She served as a fundraiser and media liaison for the parish. Olivares paid her, she recalls, but it was only part-time, although paid staff did receive a bonus at year's end. She also observed many volunteers and others coming to assist at Placita, and notes that everyone seemed to covet Olivares's attention. "We were very jealous of the time we could get with Luis because he was so important to us." She hints that it was not just jealousy over time with the pastor, but over who spent more time with him.[64] Twenty-four-year-old Lisa Martínez joined to help shelter the refugees. She was on salary, but some of this was her own room and board. She notes her excitement in working at La Placita and how, being young, she was not afraid of anything.[65] Chicana writer and university professor Graciela Limón volunteered to interview some of the refugees as they sought assistance at the parish.[66] Some staff and volunteers were themselves refugees, such as Mejia and Martínez, and they soon were joined by other key staffers, such as Mario Rivas and Arturo López, also refugees who had faced persecution in El Salvador.[67]

Of all the new staff and volunteers, there is no question that the most important, especially in promoting Olivares's and La Placita's work with the refugees, was Fr. Mike Kennedy. Age thirty-six when he first met Olivares, Kennedy was described by one reporter in San Diego three years earlier as "a tall, thin man—with blue eyes, a high, suntanned forehead and a neatly cropped brown beard."[68] He was born in San Jose in 1948, the second of three children and the second son. His father worked for the National Labor Relations Board in San Francisco. He attended Catholic schools, including a Jesuit boys prep school in San Jose. He concluded that he had a vocation when he graduated in 1966 and entered the Jesuit novitiate in Los Gatos. These and later years as a seminarian coincided with the changes associated with Vatican II and profoundly affected Kennedy. "I entered the novitiate at a real good time," he stated, observing that the Church was moving from an emphasis on personal salvation to, as he put it, "What does it mean to serve people in the world?" With this new outlook, Kennedy spent his seminarian summers tutoring black children in St. Louis, protesting against the Vietnam War in Chicago, and attending the trial of activist priest and antiwar protestor Fr. Daniel Berrigan in Harrisburg, Pennsylvania. He also went to Appalachia and ran a camp for poor children in that area. After taking his preliminary vows, Kennedy taught back at his prep school, Bellarmine, in San Jose. During his summers, he continued working in poor communities in the Oakland area, as well as supporting César Chávez and the farmworkers. In Oakland, he helped establish a Summer Institute of Community Organizing that utilized the Alinsky method of organizing to improve poorer neighborhoods and to empower community people. In 1974, the order sent him to the Dominican Republic as a missionary, where he witnessed incredible poverty, injustice, neglect, and oppression. He later also served in Mexico City and traveled to Central America including Guatemala and other parts of Latin America. In 1977, he was formally ordained a Jesuit priest and assigned as pastor to Christ the King Church in southeast San Diego, an impoverished black and Latino community.[69]

Besides working with blacks and Latinos, Catholics and non-Catholics, on community issues generally having to do with neglect of this area by the city administration, Kennedy also encountered by 1980 the early influx of Salvadoran refugees, some of whom came to his church. He heard their stories of oppression and hardship and provided what help he and his staff could in the form of food and arranging shelter. However, faced with a continuation of this migration, he proposed to Bishop Mahan, the head of the archdiocese, that he be allowed to declare Christ the King a sanctuary to publicly demonstrate the support of his church and encourage other churches to do likewise. Sanctuary would also put Border Patrol officials on notice that refugees staying at the church would be safe from arrest and deportation. Unfortunately, the Bishop refused his request, and Kennedy chose not to challenge him, but to continue to support the refugees. Shortly thereafter, he left to go to Peru and Bolivia to complete his "churchmanship" by serving as a missionary. He later visited El Salvador.[70]

In his travels to Latin America and his work with Latinos in San Diego, Kennedy learned Spanish, but apparently a halting or very accented Spanish that did not improve over the years. Ken Gregorio observes that Kennedy's Spanish was not very good, but that this did not deter his work with the Spanish-speaking, including the refugees. "Mike's been speaking Spanish for twenty-five years," Gregorio says, "and it's as awful as ever."[71] At the same time, Gregorio points out Kennedy's unique personality, attested to by others who worked with him. For one, he was passionate about his work with the poor and oppressed. He had become an adherent of liberation theology. He was not a theologian, but someone who put into practice the tenets of having a preferential option for the poor. He was an idealist and a poet, a product of the sixties oppositional generation, who challenged authority and believed that the world and people could be changed and that the poor would indeed inherit the earth. Gregorio categorizes this intense and countercultural young priest when he says about Kennedy: "He'd go sit under a tree and do yoga and paint some sort of abstract. Mike was hardly an intellectual. Not at all. Mike was in some respect the bumbling anti-Jesuit. He was not articulate, not intellectual. He was not an academician. He was a prophet, a man of passion. He was an artist."[72]

After returning from Latin America, Kennedy found himself in Milwaukee, visiting a friend at a time when one of the Catholic churches in that city declared itself a sanctuary for Central American refugees. This apparently was either in 1983 or 1984, a time when, led by liberal Protestant churches in Arizona, sanctuary as a movement was catching on throughout the country, including some Catholic ones and even some Jewish communities. His friend also hosted a Salvadoran family who shared stories about conditions in El Salvador with Kennedy that corroborated what he himself had witnessed there. Kennedy left Milwaukee determined to find a place where he could best work with such refugees. He went to Washington, D.C., but that did not work out. He returned to California, first to San Francisco, where he did not feel encouraged that this was the best place. He then visited Los Angeles in 1984 and went to Catholic Charities to see if they would sponsor a program for the refugees. According to Kennedy, they did not seem interested. Somehow, someone put him in touch with Sister Jo'Ann DeQuattro, who was already working on the refugee issues, but more on policy issues, to advocate that they been given temporary legalization. She advised Kennedy to go to La Placita and to see Fr. Olivares. She told Kennedy: "La Placita would be the perfect place to work with the refugees. It has the central location and potential. Olivares is charismatic with proven leadership in his work with UNO. He also has name recognition and a platform as pastor of La Placita that is already well known in Central America and among the refugees whom he is assisting. I think this is where you can best do your work."[73]

Kennedy did his homework and researched Olivares, discovering that he was indeed very progressive and that La Placita was in fact the logical place for Central American refugees, as well as already attracting many Mexican immigrants. Kennedy tried to get an appointment to see Olivares, but Luis was always busy. However, he met with Sister Modesta, who worked at La Placita and who expressed support after hearing him out.

"Sister Modesta, it's impossible to ever see him," Kennedy told her.

"No, don't worry. I'll get you an appointment. Come tomorrow."[74]

True to her word, Sister Modesta arranged for the meeting. The two priests had never met before, but they had an initial and instinctive favorable impression of one another and a shared conviction to help the refugees. Kennedy explained his intent and why he believed that La Placita was the logical place to organize a specific program aimed at the Central Americans and that he would be willing to help put this together. Kennedy was not too specific as to what this proposed program would consist of, but his enthusiasm and passion came through and affected Olivares. On the spot, Olivares agreed to have Kennedy join his staff and put the program together. He told Kennedy: "This church used to be all Mexican; it's no longer all Mexican. It has at least a fourth Central Americans. I like what you have to say. Okay, come tomorrow; we'll find you an office."

"That was it," Kennedy says. He left the meeting with a very positive view of Olivares. He appreciated that the Claretian was a good listener and that they both connected very well. "We were on the same page, and we didn't have to do a lot of explaining about a lot of things. There was so much understood." As someone who always balanced his own seriousness with his humor and enjoyment of a good time, Kennedy detected a similar personality in Luis. He came to observe that Olivares was fun to be with and never took himself too seriously, even in the hardest situations. "He had a perspective that was really unique and knew how to let go. Some people drive you crazy and he was never like that. He really had a good perspective and he could have fun." Kennedy left the meeting believing that being at La Placita was the right fit for him. "That kind of changed my life."[75]

But there was more, and Kennedy notes the profound decision that Olivares made in agreeing to organize a systematic program for the refugees: in so doing, Olivares was ahead of his time in recognizing the changing nature of not only La Placita but of Los Angeles. Of this, Kennedy says about Olivares: "So from the very beginning, as someone who was obviously from Mexican origin, I think he was at that particular time unique in the sense that he understood that L.A. was no longer just one culture. I mean L.A.

will always be predominantly Mexican but there's a church [La Placita] that's different. And he got it and a lot of people really didn't. I think a lot of people still had a problem with it."[76]

Kennedy returned the next morning and moved into a small office that Olivares found for him.[77] His first job was to begin to plot out what the new refugee program would look like and what it would entail. In the meantime, he secured permission from the Jesuit Provincial to work at a Claretian parish. The Provincial had no problem with this because Kennedy had earlier worked with refugees in San Diego.[78] Nor did Olivares request permission from the Claretians for a Jesuit to work at La Placita. Olivares just did it. Frank Ferrante, who was the Claretian Provincial at the time, notes that he did not have a problem with Kennedy being at La Placita.[79] Although Kennedy would work at the parish, he did not live there, but at Dolores Mission in East Los Angeles, a Jesuit parish close to La Placita. Brian Cully recalls that Kennedy's living and working arrangements caused one particular difficulty. Kennedy left his laundry to be washed by Cristina, who was in charge of laundry at La Placita, and who resented doing so since he didn't live there. She serviced the resident priests, not outsiders. It's not clear whether Kennedy continued to leave his wash there.[80] Kennedy's arrangement at La Placita also raised eyebrows because, though officially he was part of the clergy at the parish, he did not or was not assigned to do as many pastoral duties. While he said some Masses, including at least one Sunday Mass, he did not hold regular office hours for parishioners and only did a few baptisms, weddings, quinceañeras, funerals, or other such services. According to Kennedy, he told Olivares that he couldn't work with the refugees and still do the same amount of pastoral work as other resident priests. "I can't do this," he told the pastor. "Let your other priests do this."[81] Olivares agreed. Because there was a sense that Kennedy was not pulling his oar, some of the more traditional priests seemed to resent him. Cully recalls that these priests and some of the staff saw Kennedy as a "foreigner" and, while generally welcoming, still did not know quite what he was doing there.[82]

There is no question but that Mike Kennedy represented a strong stimulus for Luis Olivares to become even more involved with the Central American refugees and to establish the basis for the sanctuary movement at La Placita. Others who witnessed the relationship between the two testify to Kennedy's influence on Olivares with respect to the refugee outreach as well as his growing involvement in protesting U.S. policy toward both the refugees and in support of the right-wing government in El Salvador and American policies in Central America in general. Dick Howard believes that it was Kennedy who convinced Olivares to focus on the refugees because it was natural for La Placita as the center of Latino Catholic culture in Los Angeles.[83] Staff members Mejia and María Valdivia saw Kennedy as having the same effect on the pastor, and Valdivia adds that it was Kennedy's influence that allowed Olivares to put scripture into practice.[84] Juan Romero also agrees on this theological and praxis effect that Kennedy had on Olivares. "Father Kennedy's arrival [at La Placita]," Romero wrote, "enabled Fr. Luis to fulfill some of his vision of the Gospel in light of this new reality of Central American immigration."[85] And attorney Cynthia Anderson-Barker, who worked with both of them on refugee issues, observes that Olivares came to heavily rely on Kennedy's opinion concerning the refugees and became his alter ego. "Mike was his emotional side," she says. "Luis was much more intellectual in the way he expressed himself. 'What does Mike think?' he would say. 'Does Mike agree with this?' They were so close."[86]

While these opinions about Kennedy's influence on Olivares are no doubt accurate, there is evidence that Olivares did not need to be convinced about working with the refugees or to develop a commitment on this matter. The fact is that, as noted, he was already assisting the Salvadorans and others from Central America, as well as undocumented Mexican immigrants, before meeting Kennedy. Both his political and his religious views led him down this path. He didn't need Kennedy's guidance. It's possible that, absent Kennedy, what developed as the sanctuary movement at La Placita might have taken a different direction; it's hard to say, but there is no doubt that Olivares in his own mind had already made the commitment at least to aid the refugees. But one has to acknowledge that Kennedy's presence and influence allowed this movement to accelerate and to become institutionalized at La Placita. Olivares and Kennedy were two sides of the same coin, and their relationship was fundamental in many ways.

That relationship involved various connections. For one, there was an age difference. Olivares was fourteen years older than Kennedy. However, that difference did not seem to matter and, in fact, was part of the attraction. Olivares was attracted to Kennedy's youth and exuberance. Kennedy, in turn, was attracted to Olivares's charisma, proven leadership, and experience. It was a symbiotic relationship.[87] As staffer Lisa Martínez puts it: "Kennedy was the wind beneath Fr. Olivares's wing."[88] The relationship also involved Olivares's caring support and defense of Kennedy, especially against some who saw the Jesuit as an interloper. Lydia López attests to this. "He [Kennedy] was a Jesuit in a Claretian community," she remembers some saying and thinking. Olivares just dismissed such thoughts and would say, "Oh, that's just jealousy, that's just nonsense. Mike's doing good work. I support him."[89] At the same time, there is no question that their personalities were different. Ken Gregorio especially noticed this. "Mike was the pied piper," he observed.

> He was an artist, poet, and a painter, and a hippy. Modest to the max. And yet had this quirkiness about him. By contrast, Luis was much more strategic and pragmatic. Mike was just all about passion—the whole spirit of what Christianity and social justice is about. This ran through Mike's veins twenty-four hours a day, seven days a week. And that was enough for him. Luis understood at the same time the need to be strategic about how to move the issue from point A to point B to point C. Yet Luis was also turned on by Mike's passion, vision, and spirit. The one thing they did have in common was that both were extremely playful.

Gregorio concludes his pop psychological analysis of the Olivares-Kennedy relationship by noting one additional difference. Kennedy had zero ego, while "Luis had a good old ego."[90]

Despite these differences, not only did they work well together, but they had fun together. Olivares, with his own special humor, kidded Kennedy. "Mike," he would say about Kennedy's casual civilian appearance, "you look like you came out of Goodwill!" Or he would kid him about his halting Spanish. "Mike, your Spanish is terrible and so is your accent!" But this was all done in playfulness, and Kennedy took it this way.[91]

In all, they had a special relationship, which some saw as a father-son or uncle-nephew relationship. Virginia Mejia notes that this tie was "como un papa con un hijo."[92] But above all it was a relationship of two men, two priests, loving each other as fellow human beings both devoted to caring for the poor and oppressed, both liberationists, and both coming together to change and make history.

Mike Kennedy, along with other key staffers such as Richard Estrada, represented what labor leader Jimmy Rodríguez jokingly referred to as Olivares's *pistoleros*—his hired hands or guards. "I used to tease Father Luis," he notes, and say, "hey man, we saw you with your pistoleros the other day."[93]

V

Mike Kennedy did not initiate La Placita's outreach to the Central American refugees, but he expanded it. Prior to both Kennedy's and Olivares's arrivals at the parish, Fr. Vásquez had established a Centro Pastoral where varied social programs, such as providing free meals, helping immigrants and some of the refugees with their particular problems, and even housing for the homeless, were administered by parish staff.[94] However, to expand the work of the Centro Pastoral especially with the refugees, Olivares and Kennedy inaugurated in June 1984 a new refugee center, Centro Pastoral Rutilio Grande, named after the first Jesuit and the first priest killed in El Salvador by the infamous death squads. In the new Centro, Kennedy, or Fr. Miguel as he came to be called, as director, organized a refugee support program with a staff of five.[95] Olivares delegated Kennedy to be in charge of this program because, as pastor, he needed to attend to many other parish activities, even though he consulted daily with Kennedy over the refugee issues.[96] In an announcement in Spanish placed in the parish bulletin, Kennedy noted the inauguration of the new Centro that, as he put it, "would be located in La Placita to serve the needs of our Central American brothers and sisters arriving in Los Angeles." The notice contained five objectives of the Centro: (1) to promote the cultural identity of the Central Americans; (2) to form "comunidades de base" or base communities and other pastoral programs to assist the refugees; (3) to provide counseling to the refugees to assist with their particular problems in this country; (4) to be a support center for the many human problems faced by the refugees; and (5) to be a center of welcoming and support to the refugees.[97]

Olivares renamed the expanded Centro the Rutilio Grande Pastoral Center ("El Centro" for short) on his own jurisdiction and did not feel the need to get approval from his order. He had the administrative authority as pastor to do this.[98] He was also aided in doing this because, even though La Placita was predominantly a Mexican American parish, there were no entrenched parish groups, since the parish actually drew its parishioners from many other parishes. This, according to writer Rubén Martínez, gave Olivares space to do the outreach to the refugees without needing parish approval or consultation.[99] To promote the work of the Centro, Kennedy and his staff published a newsletter called *Centro Pastoral Rutilio Grande*.[100]

From the very beginning, El Centro provided a variety of services to the refugees, in some cases building on what La Placita had already been doing under Fr. Vásquez and during the first three years of Olivares's pastorship. What Kennedy did was to centralize these services and new ones under one roof to better administer the assistance. Shelter was a basic need and would also become a controversial part of the services. Feeding the refugees was essential as well. Many arrived hungry from their long and perilous journeys. "There were not many *gorditos* or fat refugees," Jimmy

Rodríguez observed.[101] Each evening, the staff provided meals for two hundred. Some parishioners, some of whom were themselves poor, donated some of the food, such as beans and rice.[102] Rodríguez, who worked with the butchers' union, provided sausage, bologna, and pressed ham at reduced prices for La Placita.[103] It was also a lot of work to prepare, cook, and serve the meals. Fortunately, some parishioners again volunteered to help, especially those who participated in the base communities that Olivares organized to further assist the refugees. These were mostly Mexican Americans, but also included a few refugees who had arrived earlier.[104] Aracely Domínguez recalls one occasion when she saw some 500 cakes being prepared and served to the refugees.[105] The volunteers cooked the food in the church basement but served it in the large outdoor patio, unless it rained, and then the basement also served as a dining area.[106] Meals could sometimes be as simple as bologna and cheese sandwiches. Some refugees also participated in cooking meals such as chicken with rice and beans. They would also help to clean up after meals including washing dishes.[107] Later, Olivares and Kennedy developed a system of providing meal tickets to the refugees that could be used in nearby restaurants. Olivares, in particular, gave these tickets to families so they could eat together in more private settings where, according to Fr. Cully, they "could sit down and get a basic meal with some dignity." Cully notes that Olivares was especially concerned for families.[108]

El Centro also arranged to provide refugees who needed it with new clothes or at least better used clothes. Olivares and Kennedy organized drives to encourage parishioners to donate clothing for the refugees.[109] Many did and these were accumulated in the church basement where staff and volunteers dispensed them to the needy refugees and also to the homeless. Providing decent clothing, Cully adds, was important in enabling the refugees, especially the men, to be able to go look for work and not look too shabby.[110] On some occasions, parishioners donated the clothes they were wearing at one of the Masses officiated by Kennedy where instead of a regular homily, he had people do role playing where they acted out the plight of the refugees. Some of the people, for example, gave to the refugees in attendance the jackets or other outer garments they were wearing.[111] One way or another, Kennedy and his staff clothed the refugees.

Refugees likewise needed various forms of medical assistance. Some had been tortured or wounded in El Salvador, including children maimed as a result of aerial bombardments on their villages or towns. "We had people whose bodies were covered with scars," Kennedy observed about some of the refugees.[112] In addition, some also arrived bearing emotional and psychological trauma and needed psychological counseling.[113] Refugee Mario Rivas, who worked at La Placita interviewing fellow refugees, recalls that many had been tortured or had family members who had been tortured or killed.[114] Some women had been raped either in El Salvador or on their journey to the United States through Mexico and, in some cases, by their *coyotes* or smugglers.[115]

To determine these and other needs, Kennedy, with Olivares's approval, arranged for those refugees seeking help at La Placita to be also interviewed by staff members, including himself and sometimes Olivares as well. These were not formal interviews, but an opportunity for the refugees to tell their stories. "They were traumatized," Kennedy notes, "they had been in the war; they had had somebody in their family killed."[116] Those interviewed were mainly young men and mostly civilians. Gloria Kinsler, a volunteer, interviewed a number of them. She and her husband were Presbyterians who had been missionaries in Guatemala for thirteen years. Back in Los Angeles in the early 1980s, they began to work with some of the ecumenical support groups that sprang up in support of the refugees and in opposition to Reagan's policies in Central America. DeQuattro, also a participant in these groups, suggested that Gloria meet with Olivares and Kennedy and offer her assistance in interviewing the refugees at La Placita because of her background and because she was fluent in Spanish. "Don't tell Mike Kennedy," DeQuattro told her, "but your Spanish is much better than his."[117] Kinsler followed through and joined El Centro's staff. She interviewed the refugees with Kennedy and later with former refugee Mario Rivas. Through these interviews, Kinsler and the others not only determined the needs of the refugees, but also screened them to assess if they were legitimate refugees. "Based on these interviews," Olivares told a reporter in 1986, "we determine if there is sufficient reason to provide refuge. We sometimes have to verify some information with the Church in El Salvador."[118] Besides hearing their stories, Kinsler also attempted to see if they had other family members already in Los Angeles with whom they could find shelter. She did her interviews orally because she did not want to tape them or take notes, in order to protect the refugees, and also because in Arizona some in the sanctuary movement had been indicted for breaking federal law and their notes and tapes with refugees were used against them. "I didn't want to have any record of anybody, who they were, where they were," she stresses.[119] Olivares himself participated in some of these interviews and was moved by the refugees' stories. According to Richard Estrada, Olivares by listening to the refugees in a sense became a refugee himself or at least envisioned himself as one to better appreciate what he was hearing. Estrada explains: "So therefore he was a refugee, in their flight, in their stories, and they told him what he was going to be doing."[120]

Kinsler recalls that in these interviews, the refugees expressed a great deal of anxiety. "They were very anxious to know what was going to happen to them." They were afraid but also realized that their worst fears were over. "Their worst fears were in their own country." Still they felt in limbo. They didn't know anyone in Los Angeles or in the United States and if they did, they didn't know where they lived. They also didn't have any money, and if they had children with them, their anxiety level was even higher. Kinsler interviewed mostly Salvadorans, but also some Guatemalans, who were even more afraid. They were mostly Mayans who had been brutalized for many years in that country. After the interviews, she and Kennedy went over the information they'd learned to determine how best to help the refugees.[121]

Novelist Graciela Limón, a volunteer at La Placita, also interviewed some of the refugees although she sometimes did it as part of a group discussion. She recalls the following:

> My involvement/activities at La Placita were very basic (as they were for all the other volunteers): I went most Saturdays and Sundays, at which time I helped out by serving coffee, interacting, but most especially (as time passed) leading small discussion groups. Almost like comunidades de base. At these times, my function was to listen, make it easy for the *refugiados* to speak, to share their experiences, their pain, their emotions. And emotional it was! Because most times, we all wept at what we were hearing and speaking of. . . . My involvement was mostly one of being present, of listening, of sharing. My recollection is that the general condition of the refugiados was pretty heart-breaking: raggedy clothing, obvious neglect of person, fright, a feeling of inadequacy, of displacement. However, I also remember a high spirit of hope and a lot of compassion and commiseration one for the other. There was a strong feeling of comradeship and understanding.[122]

Later into the 1980s, when Salvadorans and other Central Americans such as Guatemalans still were arriving, El Centro began to more systematically record interviews, including the creation of typed summaries of those interviews. Beginning in 1985, staff wrote up a file for each refugee interviewed.[123] While many of these records are no longer accessible, one such document was available in the Dolores Mission archives, which includes material that Kennedy himself collected. This document reveals specific information on conditions in El Salvador that forced many into exile. The interview was done with José Daniel Castellanos Herrera; the interviewer is not noted. It took place on March 26, 1988, at La Placita. Castellanos Herrera told his story of coming to the United States in January of that year. He left after his mother was killed by the National Guard in El Salvador. One day, his mother went with coworkers from the Social Security office in their town of Zacatecoluca for a day at the beach to celebrate the end of the year and the Christmas holidays. After spending the day there at the Costa del Sol, they drove back in a Social Security van. On the road, a pickup truck from the National Guard intercepted them and opened fire with machine guns. After the van came to a stop, the truck also stopped, and guards exited the vehicle and proceeded to fire more rounds into the van, as well as hurling grenades into it. All were killed, including Castellanos Herrera's mother. A peasant on the side of the road identified the assassins as members of the National Guard, although the media falsely reported that the FMLN was responsible for the attack. After the murder of his mother, Castellanos Herrera and other family members received death threats after they had called on officials to investigate the attack. Castellanos Herrera, an agricultural engineer, decided to flee the country. He had to leave his father, sister, and two brothers, who were all less capable of leaving. "I came to Los Angeles," he said in his interview, "for one simple reason: my life in El Salvador was endangered."[124]

Based on such interviews, the staff determined what kind of medical and/or psychological care some of the Salvadorans needed. Those needing mainly physical care were taken to doctors or the county hospital, where El Centro had made arrangements for the care of the refugees without regard to their immigration status.[125] Emotional problems, on the other hand, were more difficult to determine. One psychologist, Dr. Saul Niedorf, who testified in a federal case in Los Angeles on behalf of some of the refugees who requested temporary asylum, noted that psychological traumas experienced by both children and adults who had fled their country, in this case El Salvador, usually did not manifest themselves until much later. He noted that in his experience, Salvadoran refugees who had an urgent need to escape from their war-torn country felt that crossing into the United States without documents did not constitute a crime. They were trying to survive. Niedorf compared the condition of Salvadoran refugee children to other children who had experienced concentration camps or prisons. "The symptoms don't appear until they have been removed from those conditions," he concluded. Salvadoran refugees in general, he added, felt guilt and shame for having left their country, gone into exile, and for having left behind other family members and loved ones. "It's like a woman who has been violated but is ashamed to talk about it," he said. "The physical and emotional pain does not appear immediately, but it's there."[126] Refugees determined to be in need of psychological assistance were taken to the county hospital or to a professional psychologist such as Dr. Niedorf.[127]

Although El Centro could help the refugees initially, as they came to La Placita, in the long run the refugees had to find work to sustain them while they looked for asylum in the United States. Those who were sheltered at the church or nearby facilities had, as part of being allowed temporary shelter, to go out each morning and look for work. Kennedy and others directed them to particular businesses or industries where they might find employment, even if only temporary or part-time. They were not allowed to just remain at the church during the day; they had to try to help themselves.[128] As part of this encouragement, Kennedy set up a job placement service where potential employers could call in to ask for workers. At La Placita and at Casa Rutilio Grande (Casa Grande), where some of the refugees where housed in the Hollywood area, people called in needing workers. Most requested female workers for house cleaning and babysitting or childcare. Staffer Rosita Enriquez notes that in a few cases, male employers hired young Salvadoran women for house cleaning, but once employed expected sexual favors as well.[129] The women complained and La Placita ended the work relationship with those employers. Some employers called looking for men for moving household furniture and other heavy items or house painting. At both the job placement service and at Casa Grande, the staff assisted the refugees in filling out paperwork for jobs.[130] To attract potential employers, Kennedy also placed ads in the church bulletin calling attention to the availability of the refugees for work. "Necesitamos Trabajo" (We Need Work), the ad would read. "If someone needs workers or knows of jobs, please contact Father Miguel Kennedy who is in charge of assisting the Central Americans who have recently arrived in Los Angeles."[131] When Kennedy was invited to speak at local college campuses or at other churches or synagogues about the refugee issue, he always made it a point to appeal for jobs for the Central Americans. He observes that some employers were very supportive, especially those from the Jewish community and from some of the Protestant churches, such as the Methodists. Organized labor leaders such as Jimmy Rodríguez also pitched in and did what they could to get jobs for the refugees; they also warned refugees about employers or others who might try to cheat them on wages or exploit them in other ways. Looking for work and going to work in a large city such as Los Angeles also meant knowing how to get there. El Centro provided information on transportation, such as how to use the bus system and dispense bus tokens. Some enterprising refugees received permission from Olivares and Kennedy to sell homemade products, including food, at La Placita to earn money.[132]

As a way of further helping the refugees adjust to a new environment, El Centro provided adult English classes for them. It consisted of what Kennedy calls "survival English" or practical English.[133] Classes were held in the evenings and students went once a week. They learned simple phrases such as: "Where is the bus route?" or "I need food." Volunteer teachers taught the classes. These included college students, mostly Anglos, who themselves participated in the Central American solidarity movement.[134] However, some Latino high school students also served as teachers. High-school student Araceli Espinosa, for example, volunteered to teach English at La Placita, along with her brother. Both of them attended Catholic schools, but some students from the public schools also participated. She recalls that there were about ten tutors. They taught the refugees how to read and write and utilized the meetings rooms at the church as classrooms. The students were mostly men and, according to Espinosa, they expressed a positive attitude about learning English.[135] Interestingly, Spanish was also taught by some volunteers. This was not aimed at the Spanish-speaking refugees from El Salvador, but at some of the Mayan Indians from Guatemala who arrived speaking only their indigenous languages, with little or no Spanish. In order for them to communicate with the Spanish-speaking Central Americans, El Centro, for example, offered such Spanish classes at Casa Grande, where they could learn practical sayings such as "How do you turn on the shower?"[136]

Since some refugee families arrived with children of school age, El Centro also assisted in placing the kids into public schools. Staff and volunteers helped enroll the children and negotiated the paperwork for the parents. These students entered not knowing English and so schools placed them in ESL classes.[137] Some children, especially boys, arrived as unaccompanied teenagers, and so La Placita likewise reached out to help them, especially those who unfortunately got into trouble and had to be put into juvenile detention centers. Fr. Estrada, as part of Olivares's team, especially worked with them in his capacity as a youth detention minister. Assigned to Juvenile Hall in downtown Los Angeles, Estrada noted in 1983 the large numbers of Central American youth arriving in the city. He estimated this numbered in the thousands and that at any one time some 200 were being held in Juvenile Hall. It was a growing crisis, as he put it, due to conditions in their home countries and their undocumented status in the United States.[138]

For Fr. Richard, there was no better way to practice the Gospel than to visit and counsel these incarcerated young refugees and other young Latinos in similar situations. He also offered Mass and other religious services in the detention center. "I go to jail to be present to them," he said. "I like to think that this presence represents to them the powerful passage from Luke, 'To give knowledge of salvation to his people in the forgiveness of their sins through the tender mercy of our God'. . . . Scripture becomes alive and powerful when it is lived."[139]

Since the federal government refused to extend refugee status to Salvadorans and Guatemalans fleeing civil war and repression, El Centro attempted to provide what legal assistance it could for the refugees to appeal for asylum, especially if arrested and threatened with deportation. To begin with, Olivares hired a social worker, a nun, who helped refugees and undocumented immigrants to fill out immigration forms.[140] In addition, La Placita arranged for pro bono attorneys to assist the refugees through other Central American support groups such as CARECEN (Centro de Refugiados Centroamericanos), which had two staff attorneys and a number of pro bono ones.[141] Olivares would sometimes personally contact Susan Alva, the director of CHIRLA (Coalition for Humane Immigrant Rights of Los Angeles), an organization that also provided legal assistance to refugees, about defending some of those staying at La Placita. Alva would take the matter up with the INS, especially when she could argue that there existed a compelling health or family issue to warrant temporary legal status. Olivares wrote on behalf of the Central Americans, and sometimes even appeared on their behalf in front of the INS.[142] Kennedy did the same, including one 1987 court case in Los Angeles involving several Salvadorans threatened with deportation, who with legal assistance filed a case against the INS arguing for asylum as well as for more humane treatment of detained refugees at federal detention centers such as the one in El Centro. At the federal court hearing, Kennedy stressed that the refugees were legitimate political refugees due to the severity of the civil war in El Salvador, which he had personally witnessed on his several trips there. "The Salvadoran military, in my experience, treat the civilian population as the enemy," he testified. "They despise the common people especially those who organize in rural cooperatives."[143] Moreover, as a form of legal assistance, Kennedy and his staff arranged logistical support for some refugees who in order to escape deportation utilized the "underground railroad" network throughout the country. This network ferreted refugees from border areas, including Los Angeles, to interior areas of the country where they might find more protection, or to Canada, which recognized the Central Americans as legitimate refugees under international law.[144] Canada did not accept all such refugees, but its acceptance rate of 30 percent was far higher that the 2 percent acceptance rate in the United States. Marita Hernández, a reporter for the *Los Angeles Times*, wrote in 1987 of one Salvadoran couple who had been accepted to enter into Canada:

> The couple—who, like the vast majority of their countrymen in the United States, have been denied political asylum here—have packed their meager belongings into two cardboard boxes and are steeling themselves for the journey to Canada and what Silvia ominously calls "an unknown destiny." But it is preferable, César said, to the danger that awaits him in El Salvador.
>
> César, a government social worker back home, was active in a conciliatory political party that became the target of right-wing death squads. He was twice arrested and tortured by national police who accused him of being a subversive. Cesar said . . . "Thank God for Canada."[145]

Olivares himself personally placed some of the refugees into the underground railroad system. Henry Olivares remembers visiting his brother once at La Placita and witnessing this type of assistance.

"Henry, come with me," Luis, who was in a rush, said.

"I went with him and there was a couple that had come in from El Salvador and they were on their way out of L.A. into the Midwest. Louie gave them money and told them what they needed to do because they were fleeing from El Salvador. That's the kind of thing he was doing. He had this desire to help people."

Henry asked, "Louie, these people are they going to pay you back?"

"I don't care," his brother compassionately responded. "That's not what I'm interested in. I want to help them because they're fleeing persecution."[146]

For all of the services, including sheltering the refugees, La Placita did not lack for funds. With so many parishioners and those attending the eleven Sunday Masses who contributed to the weekly Mass collections, the parish accumulated thousands of dollars each week. Most parishioners were hardworking people, and they gave what they could. Plus, from the many baptisms, weddings, and quinceañeras each week that entailed a charge, La Placita had quite a bit of funds for its many social services.[147] Fr.

Lozano notes that, due to this funding, Olivares never had to ask the Claretians for additional funds for the refugees.[148] In addition to the weekly collections, Olivares and Kennedy also appealed, in the Centro Pastoral Rutilio Grande, newsletter for donations for refugee services that were sent to the extensive parish mailing list. People generously responded and monthly donations amounted to $20,000.[149] Moreover, Kennedy organized fundraisers for El Centro, such as dances at La Placita. One such dance celebrated Día de La Raza on October 11, 1986, and began with a Mass at six in the evening with Olivares officiating, followed by the dance including dinner in the church patio. Donations were $2 to benefit El Centro. Activist Madeline Janis-Aparicio observes that people supported such efforts. "The whole church was opened to the movement," she emphasizes with respect to assisting the refugees.[150]

Despite the fact that some parishioners felt Olivares was paying too much attention to the Central Americans, many others accepted and supported the refugees. They did this not only through their weekly donations at Mass, by attending fundraisers, giving food and clothes, but in other ways as well. The comunidades de base, or base communities, that Olivares and Kennedy organized as expressions of liberation theology, composed of both Mexican Americans and Central Americans, further aided the refugees. There were several comunidades and each met after Sunday Mass to reflect on the homily, including the testimonios that some of the refugees gave as part of the homily. Based on these reflections, the comunidades planned out future liturgies that would involve attention to the plight of the refugees. These might involve additional testimonios or the type of role-playing that Kennedy preferred instead of homilies. One such role play involved acting out the life of Archbishop Oscar Romero at Mass. This innovative liturgy was aimed at making parishioners aware of the needs of the refugees, but also aimed to motivate parishioners to share, such as through donations of food and clothing. They stressed praxis: observe, reflect, and act. Base community members also served as volunteers at El Centro.[151]

But Olivares and Kennedy were not just interested in providing services to the refugees; they also wanted to develop leadership among them so that they could protect themselves. "He wasn't just interested in giving out charity," Fr. Estrada says of Olivares, "but in developing leadership and consciousness among the refugees." He did this not by organizing leadership training classes such as UNO or the IAF did, but by getting some of the refugees actively involved in speaking out about their conditions and the need to be recognized as legitimate refugees. This was largely done by encouraging them to go with Kennedy to speak at different churches or synagogues that invited them, and which didn't have refugees themselves. Some did so and participated in what came to be referred to as "public sanctuary." Kennedy would translate for them. Some also spoke out at press conferences arranged by La Placita to get their stories out. These courageous men and women told Olivares and Kennedy that they felt that they had no other alternative. They believed that telling their stories would better protect them than staying in the shadows. This was risky, but being sent back to El Salvador posed a greater risk. Some refugees had been leaders in the FMLN and therefore already had leadership skills. Olivares, in particular, expressed excitement in developing refugee leadership as he had done with his Soledad parishioners with UNO. "Luis thrived in all this," Estrada emphasizes.[152]

VI

The most important service that La Placita provided for the Central American refugees, and at the same time the most controversial, was shelter. Many had no place to live or sleep at night. While El Centro could not accommodate all of the refugees streaming into Los Angeles, it did what it could with its limited space and resources. This involved allowing refugees to sleep on church property, either in the church itself or in the basement hall. In fact, such sheltering had already been going on even before Kennedy organized El Centro. In the early 1980s, some refugees and homeless, mostly Latinos, were allowed to sleep in the church hall, about fifteen to twenty each night. Fr. Cully recalls that this was low key and done with little fanfare.[153] At first, more homeless were being sheltered than refugees. It was also a time when the archdiocese had already been discussing the construction of a new cathedral to cost between $40 million and $50 million. Urrabazo remembers that Olivares challenged this cost and said: "What about the homeless?" Olivares allowed the homeless who congregated around La Placita to sleep in the church even before he began to do the same with the refugees. Urrabazo observes that the intention was good, but in practice there were some difficulties. "They stank," he says of the homeless. "They stank up the place. In the morning, we had to clean the church." He further makes the point that after Olivares turned his attention to helping the refugees that he never forgot the homeless and continued to welcome them at night.[154]

Into the decade, as more refugees arrived, La Placita provided as many as possible accommodations at the church. They had to undergo screening that was part of El Centro's outreach to the refugees, but for those needing shelter Olivares and Kennedy did not ask them whether they were refugees or not. "They just let people who needed to sleep, sleep there," Gloria Kinsler notes.[155] Olivares and Kennedy did not distinguish between political and economic refugees for housing. "The basement was like a second home [for the refugees]," Janis-Aparicio stresses.[156] At the same time, those who were allowed to sleep in the church or the hall had to undergo some socialization, at least for some of this period. They had to attend a class at St. Francis Center at St. Joseph's Church to see a video about what rights they possessed in the United States even though they did not have documents and, very important, how to react if confronted by the police or immigration officials. To sleep at La Placita, one had to have a card stamped at the St. Francis Center that certified that they had attended the class. This was a way of not just sheltering the refugees, but of helping them adjust to a new country. According to Sister María de los Angeles, who worked at La Placita's social office, some screening had to be done because some men wanting shelter unfortunately were alcoholics.[157] Moreover, those who were allowed to sleep at La Placita had to agree to have their feet washed, for sanitary purposes. The church had no showers, only bathrooms with toilet facilities. Of course, the washing of the feet also had symbolic biblical implications, as Jesus had washed the feet of his disciples before he was arrested and crucified.[158] Juanita Espinosa recalls that she and other volunteers washed the feet of the refugees supervised by the custodian.[159]

It is not clear whether the refugees and homeless, as well as later undocumented Mexican immigrants, were first housed in the church itself or in the basement hall. In these facilities only men were allowed sleeping privileges in order to avoid any trouble if women were also allowed to sleep there. El Centro arranged for other accommodations for women. However, according to Rosita Enriquez, who worked on the staff at La Placita, a few women were allowed to sleep in the chapel.[160] The numbers who slept at La Placita grew incrementally each year, as more and more refugees arrived and after Olivares officially declared La Placita a sanctuary in 1985. Kennedy told Catholic reporter Moises Sandoval that in 1984 only fifteen people slept in the church, but that one year later that had increased to 150. These numbers, however, continued to grow. By 1986, much of the church was filled with sleeping refugees; Olivares and Kennedy decided that a refugee could only stay for three nights, and then they would direct them to other shelters in order to accommodate additional refugees in the church and basement. Estimates of the number of people who slept inside the church vary from 200 to 700 although the higher figure probably is unrealistic.[161]

The most controversial aspect, of course, had to do with Olivares and Kennedy converting the church sanctuary into a dormitory at night. This was especially illustrated by people sleeping in the pews, images some-times published in the newspapers or shown on television. They slept any-where there was room, although they were only allowed to use the back pews and not the ones closer to the altar.[162] Several men slept in each pew and this was one of the reasons for the foot-washing, since they all slept with only their socks on. Each was provided with a sleeping bag and if there were not enough to go around, they were given two blankets and a sheet. If you did not have a sleeping bag, you slept on one blanket and used the sheet and second blanket for covers. In most cases, each person was also provided with a pillow. If the church and hall became full, some were placed in the chapel adjacent to the main church. On rare occasions, some even were allowed to sleep in the patio in the open air. They could use the bathrooms on church grounds, but no food was allowed inside the church. In the mornings, all of the refugees and others had to leave the premises after a small breakfast. They were encouraged and instructed to spend the day looking for jobs and given possible job contacts. After they left, a crew of volunteers cleaned up after them and made the church ready for services and the hall for other parish business. They then returned in the late afternoon for an evening meal and to get ready for bed again.[163] "It was a very poignant moment to watch them leaving and watch them coming back," Lydia López still remembers. "My heart would go out to them." She saw them sleeping on the pews on cold nights and thought: "How many churches do this? How many ministers or priests do this?"[164] Fr. Ferrante, the Claretian Provincial in the 1980s, also observed this ar-rangement and felt it was amazing. "It's an eye opener," he says. "You're used to a church where people go for Mass. But you now saw it as a func-tional place for those [the refugees] that were really hungry for respect and hungry for some kind of outreach." The transformation of the meaning of church made Ferrante proud to be a Claretian.[165] Some priests, such as Fr. Chris Ponnet, occasionally slept with the refugees. He remembers Olivares saying to him and other clergy who did this: "Oh, you're young kids; you can do this!"[166]

The basement hall could accommodate between 200 and 250 people. When Fr. Al Vásquez returned as pastor in 1990, he notes that some 250 people still were sleeping in the basement.[167] With that many there and many more in the church, each night several hundred slept at La Placita. While those in the church slept on the pews, Olivares purchased cots and mattresses for up to 200 people to sleep in the basement. As the issue of men sleeping inside the church continued to be publicized and cause controversy, and with growing difficulties in maintaining such an arrangement, by the end of the 1980s Olivares and Kennedy cut back on the number that could stay there and focused more on using only the basement. Some of the pressure of housing the refugees was somewhat alleviated when Dolores Mission parish in East L.A., under Jesuit pastor Fr. Greg Boyle, began to allow them to sleep in its church.[168] "Their basic essentials were being taken care of," Fr. Ferrante observes of the housing provided. "This was not checking into a five-star hotel. On the other hand, it was certainly better that being out on the streets or running away from the military in their own country."[169] By comparison, in San Francisco, where many other Central Americans relocated, they had to sleep in parks or cars.[170]

Because only men could sleep at La Placita, Kennedy made other arrangements for women and families with children. He got his Jesuit order to allow him to use a large former convent behind Blessed Sacrament Church in Hollywood, a Jesuit parish, as housing for the refugees. He called it Casa Rutilio Grande, and it became popularly referred to as Casa Grande. This was also a Latino area. As many as thirty families could be housed there along with some single men. Volunteers such as Lisa Martínez and Virginia Mejia, herself a refugee, lived and worked there to assist the Central Americans. It is not clear whether volunteers were paid, or instead given free room and board. Families lived in one room, while the single men shared rooms with bunk beds. There were common bathrooms, one for women and one for men, separated on different floors of the building. Refugees also shared a common kitchen and different families took turns cooking and washing dishes. Everyone ate meals together unless during the day they were out looking for jobs or working. Laundry facilities, unlike at La Placita, existed for the refugees. In a recreation room, they could watch television. Although there was more order and supervision at Casa Grande than at La Placita concerning housing arrangements for the refugees, some tensions still occurred. Mejia recalls one incident when a Salvadoran woman started a big argument one day about why she was not allowed to use the dryer for her clothes. Mejia had to explain to her that they had to preserve energy because of the costs of electricity. Also, some of the single men, or *solos*, did not want to help clean up after themselves saying that this was women's work. They were told that if they did not do their share of cleaning they would have to leave.[171]

Those staying at Casa Grande could live there for no more than three months, during which time they had to find jobs or housing with other family members if they could be located. Still others were given vouchers that paid for them to stay in cheap hotels. The volunteers assisted them in job hunting and in locating other housing. Some moved into apartments in a working-class neighborhood of Hollywood. A few went to Canada. Kennedy did not want the residents to become dependent on Casa Grande.[172] Once they found alternative living arrangements, they could use furniture donated to either Casa Grande or La Placita. The refugees also had access to some of the same services provided at La Placita, such as medical assistance including psychological help, with some psychologists making visits to Casa Grande. Mejia notes that one young man had such problems; he had been tortured in El Salvador and had recurrent dreams of soldiers coming after him. As part of their stay at Casa Grande, some of the refugees agreed to go to different churches, especially Anglo Protestant ones, to tell their stories and ask for donations for Casa Grande. Some also gave their testimonios at Catholic Masses, including at La Placita.[173] Olivares, who would often visit Casa Grande, also used the facility to invite wealthy Anglo professionals, including movie stars such as Martin Sheen, for a monthly sponsors meeting aimed at raising money for the facility.[174] Olivares mailed solicitations to other possible donors. In addition, food sales after Sunday Masses helped raise funds for the complex.[175] By the end of the 1980s, Olivares estimated that the annual budget for Casa Grande amounted to $36,000.[176] With different families rotating in, there was a continued need for bedding and bath towels.[177] While Casa Grande could only assist a small number of families over the years, it still made an important contribution. According to Olivares, by the middle of 1986, they had housed 250 families.[178] Clearly, the refugees were thankful not just for a place to sleep, but because Kennedy, Olivares, and the volunteers fostered a sense of family for people torn from their own families in El Salvador.[179]

By allowing the refugees, undocumented immigrants, and the homeless to sleep at La Placita, Olivares and Kennedy challenged authority. What authority? The city of Los Angeles and the archdiocese. What they were doing was also to show that neither the city nor the Church seemed to be concerned about the needs of these poor people. The city was not providing enough shelters and was doing nothing about the needs of the refugees. The archdiocese was just as bad. By contrast, Olivares, as pastor of La Placita, used his authority to do what he could. Urrabazo believes that Olivares accepted, perhaps even welcomed, the resulting tensions with these authorities, because he believed in what he was doing and felt that certainly the Church should be addressing the needs of its own poor and oppressed. Urrabazo asked him how he could do this without alienating Church officials.

"You don't bite the hand that feeds you," the younger Claretian told Olivares. "You can't win against the Church. You don't take on the bishop, the cardinal. You can't win because they don't play by the same rules as politicians do. They can't. Also, is this even a winnable issue?"

But Olivares didn't accept this argument. It didn't matter to him if he alienated these authorities. "It was very conscious of Olivares to allow the refugees and others to sleep in the church even if others didn't like it," Urrabazo adds. "It wasn't just to give them a place to sleep. It was to embarrass the city of Los Angeles and the Church. 'We're not doing enough for these people.'"[180] Was it a winnable issue? Certainly not by UNO/IAF standards, but Olivares was not doctrinaire. Some problems were not winnable issues, but they were moral issues. And he had to address them one way or another.

Some of Olivares's critics, even within his own order, believed that, by sheltering the refugees, Olivares was involved in a power grab to get attention for himself. Urrabazo disagrees with this and notes that Olivares did what he did because he knew it was the right thing to do even if it did alienate others.[181] Kennedy agrees, but adds about allowing the refugees to sleep in the church: "Was it crazy? Of course, it was. Was it logical? No. Was it right? Yes."[182]

Despite all of Olivares and Kennedy's good intentions and their moral response to the refugee crisis, there in fact did exist problems with sheltering the people, problems they chose to ignore. Fr. Cully points out that the church stank due to the men passing gas at night. Fortunately, although the church was cleaned in the morning, the Masses on weekdays were held in the side chapel including funerals. Moreover, despite what limited screening existed to determine who could sleep either in the church or the basement, it was not effective. The night janitor, rather than Olivares or Kennedy, had the authority to let in those who would sleep at La Placita and this proved to be a problem. Some allowed entrance, especially the homeless, had mental problems, or were alcoholics or drug addicts. Not all but some. Some of the men would break into the air-conditioning system to get water to drink. Others wrote dirty words in Spanish and English on the walls inside the church. The janitor was afraid to remove these words, fearing retaliation by those who slept there. Hence, during the day Olivares cleaned it up and ordered the janitor to help him. Cully once heard that one of the residents was stabbed with a knife. Some simply jumped the fence surrounding the church in order to sleep there. He believes that the sheltering might have worked better if Olivares had hired paid guards, but he blames Kennedy more than Olivares for some of these screening failures.[183]

Journalist Rubén Martínez remembers that the basement in particular was total chaos. "The basement at La Placita was not meant to be a homeless shelter," he stresses. Everything was helter-skelter. Some men drank liquor and carried on; some slept on the naked floor. "It was crazy," he observes. "It was one thing to announce sanctuary; it was another thing to run a sanctuary." He believes that Olivares and his staff were simply not prepared to shelter several hundred people; they did not have enough resources. Because of these limitations and problems, Martínez suggests that La Placita functioned better as a symbol than an actual shelter and social agency for the refugees and undocumented immigrants. He does not discount its historical importance, but does stress that what assistance La Placita gave to refugees and others was always limited and by no means affected the large majority of Central Americans in Los Angeles.[184] On one of his visits to La Placita, Fr. George Regas, an Episcopalian priest in Pasadena, also witnessed this mess but points out that it was not easy to shelter people. What difficulty existed in allowing the refugees and undocumented immigrants to sleep inside the church grounds also only exacerbated tense relations between shop owners in nearby Olvera Street catering to tourists. They felt that what Olivares was doing was offending tourists and driving them away, believing that the congregation of poor people across the street was dangerous. Finally, some parishioners did not favor this practice. None of these issues and complaints fazed Olivares and Kennedy, and they just continued to do what they believed was the right thing.[185]

VII

All of this work with the refugees and also with undocumented Mexican immigrants was infused with a deep and abiding faith that what Olivares and La Placita was doing was the work of God and that only a faith-based movement could sustain the vision of organizing the refugees and immigrants. You cannot understand what Olivares attempted to do at La Placita without understanding his faith. Such a movement was oppositional in that it was a new and more challenging way of being Church or, one could say, a return to the original roots of the Church. Olivares believed that the Church, by which he meant the hierarchy, had become too complacent, too comfortable with the rich and powerful, too afraid to speak out on social and political issues, and too distant from the poor. Father Luis moved to make La Placita a different kind of Church. His Church would be just the opposite, and the sanctuary movement would reflect this. He under-stood that the Church was political despite its statements to the contrary, but it was political either in the direction of the power elite or in support of certain public issues such as antiabortion legislation. What he wanted to do was to channel the Church's politics into confronting more directly the issues of poverty and oppression. If the Church did not stand up for the poor and the oppressed, then the Church might as well not exist. He declared, "If it is expected for the Church's survival to align itself with the rich and the powerful, I'd go so far as to say that the Church should not survive."[186]

He scolded the Church hierarchy, as had Católicos Por La Raza years earlier, for believing that the position of accommodation was the best. If the Church was of the opinion that it could do more for its people by align-ing itself with the ruling elite, it was sadly mistaken. This would only lead to more oppression of poor working people. Instead, Olivares called for what Juan Romero terms a "new evangelization" based on the Gospel and its priority being the poor, the oppressed, and the marginalized. "Through a new method of *concientización*, new ideas of faith will be announced and social injustice denounced," Romero wrote.[187] *La Opinión*, the major Spanish-language newspaper in Los Angeles, referred to this new evange-lization practiced at La Placita as "Evangelio en la calle" (evangelization in the streets).[188] Kennedy added that the work they were doing at La Placita represented an "evangelical commitment."[189] Through this evangelization for the poor, based not just on words, but on action, Fr. Luis wanted to make what came to be the sanctuary movement a way not just of assisting the refugees, but of creating what he called an exaggerated symbol of hope.[190] He very much believed in symbolism and thought the movement should stand as a symbol that the Church in the face of great suffering truly cared.[191]

It was faith in a new kind of Church that inspired and motivated Fr. Luis and his apostles. It was faith in the teachings of Jesus and in the incarna-tional (the Word became flesh) and salvational meaning of the Gospel. The Gospel was the basis of his faith. It was the Gospel, both Old and New Testaments, that revealed a God who cared for His people and protected them against oppression. It was the passage from Leviticus (19:33–34) that reads, "When aliens reside with you in your land, do not molest them. You shall treat the aliens who reside with you no different than the natives born among you; have the same love for them as for yourself; for you too were once aliens in the land of Egypt." And it was Matthew 25:35–36: "For I was hungry and you gave Me food; I was thirsty and you gave Me drink; I was a stranger and you took Me in. I was naked and you clothed Me; I was sick and you visited Me; I was in prison and you came to Me." In this respect, the sanctuary movement at La Placita was not just a social movement; it was a practice of faith. It was both. It was faith politics.

Much of Olivares's revisionist views of the meaning of Church and of the Gospel message had to do with his evolving embrace of liberation theology, which began with his work with the farmworkers and UNO, and which intensified with his work with the refugees and immigrants. Urrabazo observes that if Olivares had specialized in theology he would have become a liberation theologian.[192] This affinity especially involved the concept that the Church should have a "preferential option for the poor." Fr. Luis personally identified with this, what in Christian theology is also referred to as the "holiness of the poor," and he spoke of it as if it disturbed others, including his superiors.[193] He once remarked to his brother, Damaso, that God had made the world and its resources not just for some, but for all of God's children. "If there is so much food here," he said, "it should be taken and given to the ones that are less fortunate because it's all God's things."[194] Olivares believed that faithfulness to the Gospel meant identifying with the poor, and not just the economic poor, but the refugees, the undocumented, and others less fortunate.[195] "One of the greatest joys in association with the poor and the marginalized," he said, "is that you have a very keen sense of the presence of God."[196] One of his favorite sayings, which Henry Olivares calls his brother's mantra, went thus: "When I come to my final judgment the Lord is not going to ask how many times I went to Mass. He won't care if I gave at Sunday collection. I know that I will be asked: When I was homeless, did you give me shelter? When I was hungry, did you feed me? When I was naked, did you clothe me? When I was a foreigner in your midst, did you take me in?"[197] This he took from Matthew 25, which also became the biblical source and inspiration for those in the country, Catholic and Protestant alike, who aided and gave sanctuary to the refugees. He viewed the Gospel, according to Lydia López, from the perspective of the poor.[198] He believed, like other liberationists, that to mistreat the poor was to mistreat Christ.[199] Richard Estrada points out that what linked Olivares to liberation theology was his compassion that compelled him to do what he did at La Placita. It helped him articulate his compassion. Liberation theology did not give Olivares his compassion for the poor and oppressed; according to Estrada, it was already inside of him.[200]

Of his embrace of the liberationist call for the Church to possess a preferential option for the poor, Olivares said in one of his homilies:

This community of La Placita has distinguished itself by its preferential option for the poor. And the *migra* [border patrol] doesn't like it, and the FBI doesn't like it, and many civic authorities don't like it, and many times our very own ecclesiastical authorities don't like what this community proclaims: the defense of the poor, of the rejected, of the undocumented. But it is because of this—precisely because of this—that this Christian community deserves respect. They can kill us, they can reject us . . . but this community will continue faithful in its commitments to the poor.[201]

If Olivares believed that the Church should be overtly political in its option for the poor, then he further accepted the concept that priests needed to be politically and socially involved in their defense and support of the poor and oppressed. They should practice "revolutionary spirituality."[202] Jesus was his role model. He came into the world not only to baptize, but also to practice a new life and not only in philosophical terms, because how then would one explain the crucifixion? Fr. Luis rejected the idea that priests should stay in their churches and administer the sacraments. "Our ministry," he proclaimed, "has converted us as agents of social transformation. This, in turn, has a political resonance that is inevitable. But we accept this with all of its consequences."[203] Along these lines, he inserted in the church bulletin a quote made by Pope John Paul II: "Christians are called upon by God to transform the world in accordance with the Gospel."[204] Episcopalian Fr. Regas refers to this socially conscious ministry as a "radical ministry" in that, as he puts it,

Olivares didn't disrespect his obedience to his bishop, but, at the same time, he gave his ultimate loyalty to taking care of the poorest, the most vulnerable people on his doorstep. And if that caused the power structure to be rattled, then he was willing to do that because the claim of the God of justice had a much higher priority upon his life. And he was willing to live out that obedience to the lowly ones, the hurting ones, the outcast, the strangers, the prisoners. Those are the ones that claimed his life and if that caused trouble with the power structures, then he was willing to do that. That was the radical understanding that I would have as I looked in on his ministry.[205]

For Olivares, preaching the Gospel went hand in hand with social action. The Church, including priests, could not remain neutral on what liberationists call "social sin" or organized sin: slavery, oppression, injustice, racism, class exploitation. Olivares said: "You cannot be witness to human suffering and not be convinced of the existence of social sin. We are all responsible unless we take a stand and speak against it."[206] Fr. Luis recognized that, unfortunately, there was a divide within the Church on the proper role of priests and that this reflected the tension between what he called "iglesia-institución" and "iglesia-pueblo." He identified with the latter and believed that the institutional Church in fact needed those whom he referred to as the "locos," such as himself, Kennedy, and other activist priests, like Fr. Greg Boyle, the pastor of Dolores Mission, who spoke out against injustice and who were politically involved. "I cannot remain independent of my people's suffering," Olivares said.[207] Those who opposed his work, according to Henry Olivares, used to tell Fr. Luis, "Go back to your rectory, stay in there. The Church belongs in the church. The priest belongs in the sacristy." But he would respond, "I don't belong there."[208] But if he belonged there, it was to open the doors to the refugees and immigrants. He could not in good conscience reject them. As he told reporter Marita Hernández, "What if that person is Jesus and I turn Him away? How can I do that?"[209]

In redefining the role of the Church and of priests, Olivares clearly connected traditional Catholic social doctrine based on social justice with movements for social reform and even revolutionary changes. Of course, Olivares knew and read many of the major liberation theologians. These included Gustavo Gutiérrez, Jon Sobrino, and especially Pedro Casaldáliga of Brazil, his favorite. Among his writings, Olivares no doubt agreed and was influenced by some of the following reflections by Casaldáliga:

> If we re-examine our image of God we will also have to revise this idea of religion as apart from history (the single history), apart from human beings, peoples, processes in history, politics. . . . If we really believe in the God of Jesus (I have no other God in mind) we cannot avoid getting into politics.
>
> "Outside salvation there is no church." Outside liberation, in this sense, there cannot be church. The church is either liberating or it is not the church of Jesus Christ the Liberator.[210]

Gustavo Gutiérrez, considered to be the founder of liberation theology, also wrote about what he called "A Theology of Hunger," which Olivares read and integrated into his own thinking. He agreed, for example, with the following quotes from Gutiérrez:

> Hunger, poverty, and social injustice are certainly not the end or the fulfillment of my own theological principles. Rather, hunger, poverty and social injustice are the starting points of my faith.

> In the poor today we encounter God.
> To know God is to do justice.[211]

He was also inspired by Archbishop Romero and Bishop Samuel Ruiz of Chiapas, the so-called Red Bishop, as well as other liberationists in Latin America. Of Romero, Olivares later said: "I love his writings, and his message is very strong. He becomes, rather than a hero, a model for me as to how far to go in loyalty to the Gospel versus loyalty to the Church."[212]

Olivares was familiar with liberation theology, but, as Kennedy astutely points out, what he practiced at La Placita was not textbook liberation theology. In fact, Kennedy prefers the term "liberation from the base." By this he means that the people themselves, the refugees and those who aided them, were the real theologians or "spiritual guides," rather than the intellectuals. As one sanctuary Protestant minister in Tucson observed, it was reading the Gospel from the perspective of the Central Americans and the refugees.[213] The people did not expound on this theology; they practiced it. Archbishop Romero talked about the people being the agents of their own liberation.[214] But this was nothing new; it was just going back to the Gospel and what Kennedy calls "gospel theology." As he explains it,

> It's like, do you serve the poor? Do you visit the people in prison? Do you believe that God's spirit is working in the whole community? And that it is sinful that a few have so much and the majority don't? *Punto.* Now does that have consequence in politics? Yes. Does it make [some] people feel uncomfortable? Yes. So don't call it liberation theology. . . . It's theology from the base and that means all of us.[215]

As such, Olivares's application of liberation theology, based on his reading of the Gospel message, was not an exercise in abstraction but in practical application. It was an applied or practical theology. Maryknoll priest Blase Bonpane, who was part of the Central American support network in Los Angeles and who had served in Central America, recalls that his discussions with Olivares were always about concrete issues rather than theological abstractions. He agreed with Bonpane that the worst sin of all is to take that which is concrete and make it abstract. For Olivares, any theology had to have a practical application, in this case to help the refugees and immigrants. He agreed with Bonpane that: "We're going to do the work that Jesus spoke of, being peacemakers and of seeing the presence of Jesus in the people."[216]

Catholic journalist Moises Sandoval observes that, even if Olivares had never heard of or read about liberation theology, he would still have struggled for the liberation of Latinos in the United States. Olivares was not a theologian himself and he was not an academic. He knew liberation theology but was not as steeped in it as, for example, Kennedy, who had studied with Gustavo Gutiérrez in Peru and also personally knew other key theologians, such as Jon Sobrino in El Salvador.[217]

As part of this faith-based process that Olivares unleashed at La Placita, he also stressed the priority of God's law over human law. He believed that if civil society contributes to injustice, then it is the responsibility, if not the duty, of those who believe in a merciful God to first obey His laws even if it means violating Caesar's laws. God is not neutral on injustice. Fr. Luis believed that neither should he or others be.

Olivares was unquestionably political, but his politics were based on his faith. His belief in God, in a just and merciful Savior, in the Jesus who came to save, in the sanctity of all of God's creatures, and in salvation in this world as well as in the next—all of this oriented Fr. Luis's politics and that of his ministry at La Placita. The church symbolized the New Jerusalem and the New Church. It was both reality and symbol. If the reality has its historical moment, the symbol continued. As Fr. Boyle said: "Olivares stood as a countersign to the kingdom of power, greed and violence. He pronounced what the kingdom of God should look like, a place in which people share and live in equality."[218]

And in representing a countersign, Olivares also functioned as a prophet who, like John the Baptist, pioneers the way for the Lord and announces the Kingdom of God on earth. He did not refer to himself as a prophet although he believed that it was important to be prophetic, and so without saying so he in fact saw himself as a prophet. Referencing John the Baptist, Olivares said: "Like John the Baptist was called . . . so each of us, upon being baptized, is called to be a prophet . . . of love and justice."[219] Others clearly saw Olivares as a prophet. Fr. Lozano considers his mentor to have been a modern-day prophet: "Someone who took risks for the sake of God's people, especially the poor."[220] Fr. O'Connor, his former provincial, notes that Olivares was very prophetic.[221] Like a prophet crying in the desert, Fr. Luis cried out for the refugees and immigrants, and like Archbishop Romero, he gave a voice to the voiceless. "He fashioned himself over the years to be a key spokesman for low-income immigrant workers in the United State," the late labor leader Miguel Contreras said of Olivares.[222] Refugee Mario Rivas considers Olivares a modern-day prophet because like a true prophet he not only announced God's word, but he also denounced injustice.[223] Fr. Regas, who became friends with Olivares by supporting the cause of the Central American refugees, from time to time had lunch with Fr. Luis and discussed religion "in the sense that both of us interpreted religion as God's urgent call to us to be prophets of justice and be willing to see God's claim in us as a higher claim than the laws of the state which were judged to be unjust." Regas goes further and asserts that Olivares indeed saw himself as a prophet and that he accepted this role. "He saw that's what his life was called to be," he says, "to be faithful to what he saw as God's claim on him to be an instrument of justice and peace and to challenge the structures of power, to speak truth to power as he understood it. Unquestionably, he saw himself as a prophet."[224]

But it was not just Olivares's persona that made him prophetic or a prophet; it was also the circumstances of his position as pastor of La Placita and the need to embrace the refugees and immigrants. There was a structural or communal prophesy to the church. Kennedy recognizes this and observes that La Placita became a focal point for the refugees, for example, because (1) it had hands-on experience with the refugees; and (2) it had a "prophetic religious element."[225] The combination of these two insured that the movement to aid the refugees and undocumented immigrants would be a faith-based movement. It could not be otherwise.

VIII

Luis Olivares flourished at La Placita, but he also believed that he could move the Claretian order in a more liberationist direction, including working with the refugees and immigrants, if he could become Provincial or the head of the order's Western Province. He had his chance in 1983. Provincial Bernard O'Connor had completed his required six years, and it was time for a changing of the guard and the election of not only a new Provincial but a new Provincial Council. Although Olivares was no longer treasurer, he had remained on the Council as Prefect of Ministries. Customarily, one went from treasurer to Provincial and even though he had stepped down from being treasurer, Olivares and many others as well believed that he would succeed O'Connor. Olivares seems to have welcomed this prospect not only because he would be in a position to wield even more influence in the order, but it would represent a personal achievement. From a young Mexican American seminarian some three decades earlier, he would become the first Mexican American Provincial. He would make history, but it would also be a crowning personal honor, which he did not shy away from. He seems to have believed that the order owed him this due to his faithful loyalty and hard work.[226]

The election for Provincial involved two steps. The first constituted a nominating process called a *sondeo*, or straw vote.[227] Every ordained Claretian, whether priest or brother, was eligible to nominate one person on ballots sent out to them throughout the western province.[228] The sondeo was held about a month before the actual election.[229] These nominations were tabulated and reported on March 4, 1983. The sondeo resulted in forty-nine nominations for Olivares and forty-two for Frank Ferrante, by far the two leading candidates.[230] It is not clear if by tradition there was only one sondeo, but in this case, there was a second one. Fr. Ralph Berg believes that there was supposed to be only one sondeo, but that for some reason the Provincial Council called for a second one.[231] In this case, Claretians were asked to put down their first and second choices for Provincial. Again, Olivares came out ahead, by an even larger margin, in the results announced on April 7. He received forty-four first-place votes and twenty-two second-place ones. Ferrante received twenty-one first-place votes and twenty-two second-place votes.[232] "I never really campaigned," Olivares stated, perhaps fudging a bit, "but the numbers were so strong. Province-wide I was coming out way, way ahead of everybody else." Olivares's memories of these votes suggest that he was not just a passive observer to this nominating and election process, but that he really wanted to be elected for both political and personal reasons.[233]

With the nominations completed, composed of thirteen names, the actual formal election, or what the order called the "chapter" or assembly, met on April 11 at Provincial House in Los Angeles.[234] However, in the chapter, instead of all Claretians voting, only certain members voted. These included the superiors of local communities; elected delegates selected by all clergy; and members of the Provincial Council.[235] In all, forty-five delegates including Olivares and Ferrante elected the Provincial.[236] To be elected, one needed to get 50 percent plus one of the vote.[237] They met in the basement of the house.[238] Steve Niskanen, only a novice then, recalls that novices were allowed to sit in on the discussion and vote, and how exciting all this was. He notes that some of the voting clergy were in Olivares's camp while other favored Ferrante.[239] Those voting could only write one name on their ballots. The votes were collected and put in a cardboard box, not a gold chalice, as Lozano, somewhat tongue in cheek, observes. A member of the council then drew out each ballot one by one and announced the name on it. This way others could keep a running count on the voting results. "Olivares; Ferrante," the council member enunciated. By the time of the last announcement everyone knew the results: Ferrante had upset Olivares! Many, including Olivares, were stunned. How could Olivares have lost when he had come into the election with many more nominations than Ferrante? But there was no appeal or re-vote allowed. The

Provincial Council confirmed the results. Ferrante had received twenty-three votes and Olivares, nineteen, with three votes for other nominees. Frank Ferrante would be the next Provincial, to serve for six years until 1989.[240]

By all accounts, Fr. Luis took the results very hard. "I just saw the look on his face," Lozano observed after the votes were announced. "He was just devastated. It's like he couldn't believe that had happened."[241] Lozano further notes that Olivares had gone to the chapter in his best silk suit, expecting to be elected and for the media to cover it. He later told Lozano that if he had been elected, all the TV stations would have been there as well as the *Los Angeles Times*. But nobody came because Ferrante won. Olivares wondered why more hadn't voted for him. Lozano believes that Olivares really wanted to win, but he puts it in good perspective that merges the spiritual and political Olivares with the personal Olivares, and no doubt Olivares's true feelings were somewhere between the two. Lozano says,

> He wanted to be elected Provincial, not so much for himself but for what he felt he could have done, the changes he could have made. Part of this was his ego, but we're all human. We all have egos that get damaged. It's just part of human nature, human psychology. But it was also his faith and strong desire to bring about social justice. He felt he could advance this even more as Provincial by influencing other Claretian ministries throughout the province. I think that's something that any prophet feels throughout his or her lifetime. But we don't always achieve everything that God wants us to do. I'm sure that he felt as any prophet would that we're not where we're supposed to be yet. There's still a long way to go.[242]

Olivares never complained about not being elected Provincial; however, Lozano feels that he never completely got over this and probably felt that his order did not fully support him and his ministry.[243]

Why wasn't Olivares elected Provincial? He had seniority, experience, and, obviously, leadership quality. Different reasons are given and more than likely it's a combination of all of them that explain his defeat. One is that, as treasurer for many years, he had built up resentment among other Claretians. As Urrabazo explains it, Olivares had the baggage of doing the dirty work of the Provincial, in cutting funds for certain parishes and calling in pastors to account for certain shortcomings under their jurisdiction. "You're the hatchet man," as Urrabazo puts it.[244] Olivares's more open political involvements, such as with UNO, may have also played a role in some clergy being uncomfortable with him as Provincial.[245] The fact that his involvement with UNO had made Olivares a public figure and media celebrity of sorts may have not played well with his fellow Claretians, at least those who voted against him.[246]

For his part, Olivares does not seem to have discussed his feelings about why he was not elected Provincial with other clergy, but he did so with Henry. According to Henry, his brother told him that he believed that race had something to do with it. He didn't say race, but he did say that his being Mexican might have had something to do with it, especially among the Spaniards in the order who did not want a "Mexican Provincial" over them. Luis told Henry: "Instead of the Spaniards dominating the Mexican, now the Mexican is dominating the Spaniards," and that some Spanish clergy were very adamant about this. Olivares couldn't believe that some would go this far and in effect play a race card. "I don't see what Mexican has to do with it," he told Henry, "if you have the ability."[247] Six years later when the next Provincial election came up in 1989, Olivares's name was mentioned but by then he was in no position to think about being Provincial due to his health problems. Moreover, he had become even more politically controversial.[248]

IX

Despite his disappointment at not being elected Provincial, Olivares did not dwell on this; he had too many other things to do as pastor of La Placita, plus his increasing engagement with the Central American refugees as more and more entered Los Angeles during the 1980s. As part of this engagement, Olivares began to travel to El Salvador and Central America by the middle of the decade. He needed to see for himself the conditions faced by the people there and how the repression by the government and military were forcing them to flee. Using his IAF training, he wanted to listen to the people talk about their problems.[249] But these visits were also to show solidarity with the refugees by attempting to do his part to help the Salvadorans in their own country as best as he could. Finally, by traveling to Central American, including as part of U.S. delegations, he could raise American awareness of the conditions there and the culpability of the Reagan administration in creating the refugee crisis by its support, especially in military aid, to the Salvadoran government. As Fr. Dick Howard noted, "It is important to see the connection between the situation of the displaced in El Salvador and refugees from El Salvador and Guatemala in the U.S. They are the same people. They are people who have suffered bombings, who have been forced to flee their places of origin."[250]

Kennedy, who had already been to El Salvador, encouraged Olivares to go there, and they sometimes traveled together.[251] Olivares went to El Salvador about once a year beginning in 1984, the first of what Kennedy recalls were six visits in all, including one to Nicaragua.[252] On these visits, for the most part, Olivares and Kennedy did not wear their collars and priestly attire in order to move more freely among the people.[253] Still, they were not always welcomed by the Salvadoran government, which did not want American clergy or other Americans making negative reports about the government when they returned home. This reservation included the U.S. Embassy in San Salvador, the capital. On one visit, an embassy official told Fr. Luis: "We would just rather you people not come down here."[254] Although acquiring visas to El Salvador and Nicaragua was not easy, Olivares never encountered a problem entering these countries.[255]

On these trips and with the aid of Kennedy's fellow Jesuits such as Dick Howard, Olivares particularly focused on the poor barrios in San Salvador, as well as refugee camps, within the city or on the outskirts, that housed internal refugees from the countryside. They fled the civil war, but in particular they were trying to escape Salvadoran military bombardments and attacks on villages on the unproven grounds that they sheltered FMLN combatants or that the villagers supported the insurgents.[256] Despite the dangers, Olivares ventured into the rural areas to visit some of these villages. With his facility in Spanish, he could easily relate to the people and converse with them.[257] On one such visit, Olivares called media in Los Angeles to report a critical condition in Aguacayo. In his telephone call he said, "The people here are really worried by what might happen to them. The military would not allow anyone to leave nor enter the town. They have completely 'sealed off' the area. The Salvadoran authorities have to be pressured to allow international relief agencies to enter the zone and assist the many elderly, women and children presently in the town."[258]

On some of his visits, Olivares likewise met with Catholic Church officials in San Salvador, such as Archbishop Arturo Rivera y Damas, who had replaced the martyred Archbishop Romero. He also met with government officials and the U.S. ambassador.[259] On one trip, he visited the church where Romero is buried and said Mass there.[260]

But danger did lurk on some of these visits, especially in the villages. The danger did not come from the villagers, who embraced Olivares especially after they discovered that he was a priest and a Latino priest at that. According to Henry Olivares, his brother was shot at a couple of times. "We would worry about him," Henry says about these trips, "but that's what he wanted to do." He further notes that the Salvadoran government knew who Luis was, and on some occasions as he visited the villages, the military had orders to detain him. "They were looking for him," Henry explains, "but they never found him. The villagers would hide him." Olivares, in turn, was grateful to the people for protecting him and he linked this to his own family history of sheltering Mexican refugee priests in San Antonio. "I just trust the people," he told Henry. "The people are the best people and they hide me. I feel like Abuelita when she was hiding the priests. I feel these people are like my abuelita, hiding me."[261]

Not only was the army looking for him, but Henry adds, so, too, were the infamous Salvadoran death squads. Olivares told Henry, "I'm ready to give my life for these people."

"Luis, how can you?" Henry replied. "They're not even your people. You're Mexican."

"Oh, no. We're in this together," Olivares responded. "We're in this together. They're as Latino as I am. We're all Hispanics. We're all people of God. If they were Anglos, I'd do the same thing."[262]

In spite of these dangers, Olivares continued to return to El Salvador when he could. One of the reasons he did so, and perhaps his most important work there, was to take money to the poor and the needy, both in San Salvador and in the villages. He literally took cash, thousands of dollars with him and never was questioned about this by either American or Salvadoran officials. No doubt he took it on him or in his briefcase that apparently was never searched. These were American dollars since he did not trust the banks in El Salvador to exchange the money there.[263] A secretary at La Placita once told Henry that Fr. Luis had given her a signed check for $20,000 to take to the bank and cash it for tens and twenties.

"What is this for, Father?" the secretary asked.

"I'm taking it to El Salvador with me," he said.

According to the secretary the money came from an UNO account, as well as donations that parishioners gave to help the people in El Salvador and fundraisers. It appears that UNO approved the use of its funds for this purpose.

When Henry found out about this money, he asked Luis: "Why are you doing this?"

Luis: "Henry, I'm the only hope that these people have. I'm the only hope that these people can safely get out of El Salvador and go to Honduras. If they don't have money, they can't do it. They're totally helpless. People know what they have to do. All I'm providing is just a little help for them."[264]

Olivares, according to Henry, gave the money to the needy, to heads of villages to distribute to the *campesinos*, and to Salvadoran church groups

aiding the displaced people including setting up co-ops for them.[265] Mario
Rivas recalls that on occasion, Fr. Luis and sometimes Kennedy took
cashier checks. Rivas himself says that he was given money by Olivares to
take to El Salvador.[266] Attorney Cynthia Anderson-Barker observes that she
often visited El Salvador to do a needs assessment for Fr. Luis and others
who contributed money about which communities could best use the
funds. She concluded that most of the money should go to villages composed primarily of women and children, since the men were either fighting
for the guerrillas or had been forcibly drafted into the Salvadoran military.
Anderson-Barker herself took money that she raised in Los Angeles and
distributed it to such communities, or to orphanages. She never encountered a problem transporting this cash.[267] Rubén Martínez, on the other
hand, asserts that if Olivares did take money to El Salvador, it probably was
used to purchase weapons for the FMLN on the international black market.
"That money didn't go to babies," he surmises, "it went into the war."[268] It
is possible that Martínez may be partly correct, but undoubtedly Olivares
insured that most of the funds went to needy people.

On at least two of his trips, Olivares also visited Salvadoran refugee
camps in neighboring Honduras. As part of its counterinsurgency strategy,
the Salvadoran army destroyed numerous villages claiming they sheltered
FMLN rebels. Those villagers whom they did not kill were rounded up and
forced out of the country. This strategy of forced depopulation emanated
from U.S. tactics in Vietnam, which were taught to the Salvadoran military
through their training in the United States. Many of these people fled to
refugee camps in Honduras operated by the United Nations or religious
organizations. The Honduran military surrounded these camps and often
harassed the refugees and did not allow them to leave.[269] Olivares, accompanied by Kennedy, first visited these camps in November 1984. At an ecumenical Mass at La Placita attended by representatives of other Catholic and Protestant churches, along with UNO officials that sponsored the
trip, Olivares explained that their intent was to observe conditions in the
camps to better determine how La Placita and other concerned groups in
Los Angeles could best support the refugees confined in Honduras. "One
of the other reasons for our trip," Olivares added, "is to establish a bridge
of communications between Latinos in East Los Angeles and the Central
American refugees whose problems as pointed out by the American bishops cannot be ignored. The Central Americans are our brothers and sisters and they need to be informed of conditions in El Salvador and among
the displaced in Honduras."[270] In this transnational outreach, he and Kennedy would be taking letters from refugees at La Placita to family mem-

bers in both countries.[271] One of the largest camps that they visited was Mesa Grande, just across the border from El Salvador. They stayed there and listened to the people tell about their conditions and their wishes to repatriate themselves back to their home villages. Both were moved by the plight of the Salvadorans who had to live in deplorable conditions in the camps with minimum shelter and lack of food. Kennedy recalls that they froze at night at the camp. Already having a bad back, Olivares in particular suffered as his back went out on him. "He was really suffering," Kennedy notes. However, whatever inconveniences they both experienced paled in comparison to the lot of the refugees.[272]

While Olivares either traveled on his own or with Kennedy, he also joined group delegations from the United States to El Salvador. These were either sponsored by church groups, usually Protestant, but also by Central American support groups.[273] Jewish rabbis from Los Angeles sometime participated in these trips.[274] They met with Church officials working with the internal refugees and even traveled into FMLN zones of control.[275] On one of these delegation visits, Olivares and the group met with President Napoleon Duarte in his presidential office in San Salvador. They delivered to him somewhere between 10,000 and 20,000 letters from people in the United States, including Salvadoran refugees, calling for an end to the civil war and encouraging a negotiated settlement. "We literally handed them to him on his lap," Kennedy, who was part of the delegation, recalls. "I mean literally."[276]

"Mr. President," Olivares addressed Duarte, "here are these letters from American citizens and Salvadoran refugees in Los Angeles that wanted to send them to you. They are asking you to stop bombing civilians in El Salvador."[277]

On the trip including the meeting with Duarte, Anderson-Barker could not help but be impressed with Olivares. "When we were in El Salvador," she notes, "I really saw him in action as a very quick mind. He could grasp concepts, translate what was happening to the group in a very successful way." She observed that Olivares seemed fearless and that he included everyone in the delegation on an equal basis, never spoke down to anyone, and included everyone in the group discussions. "He was very empowering to me," she adds. Regarding the meeting with Duarte, she further recalls that Olivares spoke for the group and did not mince words with the President: "Mr. President, our delegation opposes U.S. military aid to your government and we believe that you should no longer accept this aid that is being used to kill your people and drive them out of their own country."

Duarte, according to Anderson-Barker, remained very formal and diplomatic and never got agitated. The group left their meeting, led by Olivares, who for this meeting wore his clerical suit, quite pleased and feeling they had achieved their mission.[278]

Although Olivares during the 1980s visited primarily El Salvador, he did make at least one trip to Nicaragua that was also embattled. Following the overthrow of the Somoza dictatorship in that country, the revolution-aries—the Sandinistas—came to power and attempted to institute various reforms including agrarian reform to take the land from the powerful land-owners and redistribute them to the peasants. Viewing them as Commu-nists from a Cold War perspective, the Reagan administration organized a counterrevolutionary group—the Contras—to overthrow the Sandinistas. In this effort, the administration also imposed strict economic sanctions against Nicaragua. Moreover, unlike the administration's refusal to accept Salvadoran refugees, it embraced right-wing Nicaraguans leaving their country and provided them refugee status. Although very few poor Nica-raguans went to La Placita, Olivares expressed interest in the Sandinista revolution and contrasted it to the repressive government in El Salvador. However, to get a more firsthand account of what was happening in Nica-ragua, he joined a delegation organized by Alice McGrath, a longtime po-litical activist from Ventura, California, to that country. During their week in Nicaragua, they visited not only the capital, Managua, but also the countryside, and talked to people. Activist attorney Linda Wong, who was part of the delegation, notes that Olivares and the rest of them discovered how slanted American media reports on Nicaragua were, which focused on how the Sandinistas were betraying the revolution and not favoring democratic rule. The delegation found otherwise and especially was im-pressed by the reforms in education and the distribution of land to *campe-sinos*. She recalls Olivares telling her that what he had observed was more than he had imagined with respect to social improvement in Nicaragua despite its still prevalent poverty. He became more cognizant of how re-pressive and unjust the Somoza dictatorship had been. "I thought that kind of injustice was confined to El Salvador," he told Wong. People still lacked basic household goods that were difficult to import due to the U.S. em-bargo. They asked the delegation if they could send them toilet paper and other such products. Besides meeting with ordinary people, Olivares and the delegation also met with government officials who briefed them on their reforms as well as their fight against the Contras. She notes that Oli-vares asked many questions about conditions and what the Sandinistas were doing about them and what Americans could do.[279] Olivares's visit to Nicaragua only broadened his views on the Central American wars and the role of the United States in them and led to his own involvement in attempting to stop this American intervention.

These trips to Central American, although not that frequent, were taxing on Olivares, who had earlier been diagnosed as a diabetic and had to take medication for this. Modesto León remembers that Luis returned from these travels drained.[280] Still, returning home revitalized him. He was elated once when Fr. Cully hired a mariachi group to go to the airport with him to welcome Olivares and Kennedy back. Cully notes that he had to use the altar server fund to pay for the musicians. Fr. Luis loved this greeting and, according to Cully, hammed it up with the mariachis.[281] But he also cried when he returned and told others of the horrible conditions he had witnessed in El Salvador. "I actually once saw him crying," refugee Arturo López remembers. "He was crying because he had seen the situation of the refugees in Honduras and of the displaced within El Salvador. He told us 'how is it possible that these people are suffering in the camps, children dying of hunger, children dying due to health issues, and having to drink contaminated water? People are eating the herbs from the ground because they have nothing to eat. And this country, the United States, is sending $400 million annually to cause destruction.'"[282]

Upon returning from these trips and despite his exhaustion, Olivares made it a point to report on his visits to Central America. He organized press conferences and invited both the English- and Spanish-language media to attend. It appears that the latter covered them more often. He would also meet with the Central American support groups to discuss the conditions he found in El Salvador, for example.[283] He would also discuss the situation there with other individuals involved in supporting the refugees and protesting U.S. policy in Central America.[284] At one news conference in 1986, he reported on his recent trip made in part to investigate why an American religious delegation accompanying displaced Salvadorans in San Salvador who were attempting to return to their villages were deported out of the country.[285] They were told by officials that they had entered a conflict zone without permission. Fr. Dick Howard, one of those deported, spoke at the press conference with Olivares. He stated that he and the other clergy had never been told that they needed a special permission to accompany the villagers. Olivares criticized U.S. embassy officials for facilitating the deportations rather than representing the interests of the American citizens.[286] He also consistently brought attention to the atrocities being committed by the Salvadoran military against its own people. "How does this affect us?" he said to the media. "It affects us by the augmentation of more refugees entering into the United States. We at

La Placita as a Christian church are doing what we can by providing safe haven for them."[287]

Olivares's trips to Central America and his opposition to U.S. policies in the region further politicized him and made him align himself with the insurgent movements. "I certainly make no bones about my bias toward a revolution in Latin America that brings about more of a socialist democratic approach to government," he later told Rubén Martínez. "I have seen what our capitalist agenda . . . is doing to Latin America."[288]

Jo'Ann DeQuattro believes that Fr. Luis's trips to Central America represented another form of conversion for him.[289]

X

To further prepare for sanctuary, Olivares had to foster a sense of pan-Latino identity among his parishioners at La Placita. Although over 90 percent of them were either U.S.-born Mexican Americans or Mexican immigrants, the increasing growth of the Central American population not only at La Placita, but in Los Angeles meant, at least for Olivares, that in accepting the refugees, his parishioners had to go beyond their Mexican-based identity to a larger concept of themselves as Latinos. The same would be true for the Central Americans; however, the larger challenge for Olivares was to affect the consciousness of his Mexican parishioners. He began with his own vision of bringing people together into a new form of community based on faith principles. "I think the role that we have as leaders in the community," he later told Juan Romero,

> is to foster the growth of relationships that can exist amongst us as human beings despite our differences. Well, this work with Mike Kennedy gave me the forum to influence a predominantly Mexican-oriented pastoral ministry toward attracting Central Americans. As so we had many Salvadorans and Guatemalans, other people from Central and South America. And that to me is the Gospel. That love that Christ calls for all of us is exemplified when we are able to express it amongst people who are different than we are.[290]

Fr. Cully observes that Olivares's embrace of Kennedy's initiative with the Central Americans laid the foundation for this pan-Latino identity. Kennedy inspired this move but, as Cully further notes, it was Olivares's sense of vision that carried it out. "Luis had a vision that could incorporate lots of changes and lots of people," he says. "Not all the rest of us would be so catholic with a small c."[291] Even before meeting Kennedy, Olivares referenced the concept of "la Iglesia mestiza Hispano-Americana."[292] Olivares in many ways personified this new identity, as he merged his own Mexican-American identity by identifying with the Central American refugees. He became Latino, and this is what he hoped he could accomplish with his parishioners in order to prepare for sanctuary. Moises Escalante witnessed, for example, that the Salvadorans did not see Fr. Luis as Mexican or Salvadoran, but instead as someone who believed in a just cause and who spoke the truth.[293]

But changing people's sense of themselves was not easy. Some Mexicans expressed discomfort in the demographic changes at La Placita, which led to tensions between Olivares's pastoral team and parishioners. They believed that Olivares was paying too much attention to Central American issues and not enough to Mexican American ones. "I think more and more people wanted a bigger share of Luis's time and energy and just of Luis," Cully says, "but that became a little harder."[294] Others felt that their church was being taken over by the Central Americans. "They felt that the way Olivares was talking seemed to imply that most parishioners were from El Salvador," Cully adds. "I think they were a little bit hurt." At the same time, the Mexicans liked and admired their pastor, but felt that they were losing him to the refugees. Their feelings did not turn into overt opposition to Olivares; they simply felt that they were not getting as much of him as they wanted. "I think they felt like their hero was being taken from them a little bit," Cully concludes.[295] Still others blamed Kennedy for this new orientation and believed that he had come in and changed Olivares's agenda. Kennedy refutes this and observes that Olivares was too secure in his values and his work to be swayed by someone else. The fact was, Kennedy states, that Olivares was already moving in the direction that would ultimately lead to sanctuary and would not allow petty complaints to dissuade him. He had that vision. "He was a dreamer," Kennedy asserts. "He didn't get tied down in all this pettiness. He couldn't stand it. . . . He called it like it is. He was bigger than all that."[296]

Henry Olivares endorses Kennedy's notion that Olivares was already leaning toward institutionally integrating the Central Americans. He notes that upon arriving at La Placita at the same time as the Salvadorans began arriving, Luis very quickly understood that he had to help them. "He already knew what his focus was," Henry says. "He told me that 'there is a need for these people. . . . All they need is a little guidance and that's what I want to provide.'"[297] Besides the different forms of assistance provided to the refugees by La Placita, Olivares likewise integrated them into the religious practices of the church. He held Masses dedicated to the refugees and to the people of El Salvador including those who had given up their lives to assist others being oppressed. Olivares considered them to be contemporary martyrs. In their homilies, Olivares and Kennedy called upon some of the refugees to tell their stories to the largely Mexican congregation. To make the church familiar to the refugees and to help develop a pan-Latino consciousness, Olivares also integrated Salvadoran iconography into the church, such as a colorful Salvadoran cross and a side altar in memory of Archbishop Romero with an image depicting his assassination. In his own office, besides pictures of Mexican historical figures such as Emiliano Zapata, Olivares also put up an image of and quotation from Nicaraguan revolutionary Augusto Sandino, as well as a Christmas card from Nicaraguan President Daniel Ortega. Of course, he also had a picture of the ever-present Our Lady of Guadalupe.[298] Finally, by speaking out in defense of the Central Americans in his homilies, for example, Olivares, as a Mexican American, helped to bridge Mexicans and Central Americans together.[299] La Placita became a transnational church.

These efforts at encouraging pan-Latino solidarity helped in socializing the Mexican-origin parishioners about supporting the refugees. However, some, perhaps many, found this support not too difficult to accept because it was part of La Placita's legacy. It was a parish that had historically helped everyone: the homeless, the poor, the unemployed, and those suffering from alcoholism—the *borrachitos*. Hence, assisting the Central American refugees was simply an extension of this history.[300]

Olivares further promoted a pan-Latino awareness by hosting key Central American dignitaries at La Placita. In fall of 1984, for example, he organized a breakfast in the church basement hall for President Daniel Ortega during the Sandinista leader's official visit to Los Angeles, sponsored by the Office of the Americas, after his speech at the United Nations, in which he accused the United States of planning to invade Nicaragua that October. He was accompanied by an entourage of former revolutionaries who were now part of the new government. Olivares, in turn, invited other Angelino religious and political leaders, the heads of both Protestant and Jewish congregations, as well as Hollywood figures who supported what he was doing at La Placita, such as Martin Sheen. Of course, always mindful of the importance of the media, he made sure that press releases announcing the breakfast reached TV, radio, and print outlets, many of which covered the gathering. In fact, Mike Clements, who attended the breakfast, saw it as a media event and thought that there might have been more reporters than actual guests. Blase Bonpane served as Master of Ceremonies, and certain speakers, including Ortega and Olivares, gave short speeches, mostly giving updates on conditions in Nicaragua.[301] Olivares presented

Fr. Luis Olivares with Nicaraguan president Daniel Ortega,
La Placita Church, fall 1984. (Courtesy of Henry Olivares)

the President a plaque welcoming him to La Placita.[302] A press conference
at La Placita followed the breakfast. Cully, who was not in town at the time,
later heard from the cook at the rectory that she had to put up with U.S.
Secret Service agents accompanying Ortega going through her kitchen on
the second floor of the rectory overlooking the plaza as they checked out
the building. "Luis loved the drama of those things," Cully observes with
respect to Ortega's visit.[303] Olivares, of course, knew that by hosting Ortega,
he was thumbing his nose at the Reagan administration, but he didn't care.
"Olivares loved playing the countercultural voice during the Reagan years,"
Rubén Martínez, who attended the event, asserts. "It was a necessary voice
to have. He was the countervailing force in Los Angeles in the 1980s. I can't
think of anyone else in Southern California."[304]

Perhaps the most important Central American guest who visited La Placita was Archbishop Arturo Rivas y Damas of El Salvador, in 1986. He went
to Los Angeles at the invitation of Archbishop Roger Mahony. The very
fact of Damas y Rivas's visit to a mostly Mexican parish, but one providing sanctuary for Salvadoran refugees, significantly advanced the coming
together of the two ethnic groups. The archbishop accepted Olivares request to help celebrate the second anniversary of La Placita declaring itself
a sanctuary (see Chapter 10) and to help concelebrate the annual Mass
on the feast day of Our Lady of Guadalupe on December 12. Through the

archbishop's visit on the most Mexican of religious celebrations, in effect Guadalupe was transformed into a pan-Latino icon. The image of the archbishop at the altar, with Olivares and Kennedy saying Mass, was a major symbol of both spiritual and ethnic unity. These were Latino clergy (Kennedy being seen as an honorary Latino) and it sent out the message to a jam-packed church composed of both Mexicans and Salvadorans that their clergy were united and so, too, should they be, as Latino brothers and sisters. "We take this opportunity to express in person our solidarity with the Salvadoran people," Olivares said, "and our support to the efforts of Archbishop Rivas y Damas to achieve peace in Central America through dialogue and not war."[305] In his homily, the Archbishop said that he had come to Los Angeles and to La Placita to visit his Salvadoran compatriots in exile in the area, some 300,000, and to thank La Placita for its generous support for those seeking refuge and assistance. He also thanked the parishioners for their generous contribution to the victims of the major earthquake that had struck San Salvador on October 10. He further noted the contradiction of U.S. officials deporting the victims of persecution back to the very source of their persecution and remarked that this was "an act of injustice in the eyes of Christian love."[306] The Archbishop's visit revealed the transnational religious ties between the Salvadoran refugees and their home country.[307] A dramatic moment of the Mass occurred when one of the Salvadoran refugees gave testimony about her rape and torture in El Salvador. Her account was very graphic; Gloria Kinsler, who translated it into English, had no choice but to use the most accurate, if graphic, words to describe, for example, the woman's being anally raped with a broomstick. Both Olivares and Kennedy expressed embarrassment at Kinsler's translation, but she felt a literal translation would do the most justice to the account.[308]

Still another way that Olivares promoted a pan-Latino identity at La Placita was by working with other Central American support groups in Los Angeles who likewise provided refuge and support to the Salvadorans, Guatemalans, and other refugee groups and by announcing their activities to his parishioners. Central Americans alongside Mexican Americans or Chicanos spearheaded some of these organizations, such as CARECEN and El Rescate along with several others. CARECEN, for example, was organized in 1982 formed by refugees to stop the deportation of Salvadorans, to achieve refugee status for them, and to organize and empower them. Olivares not only participated in them, but became the titular head of several of them (see chapter 11).[309]

Through these efforts, both before and after declaring sanctuary, Olivares helped to motivate a feeling of oneness or a new "cultural citizen-ship" among his parishioners, mostly Mexicans, and the Central Ameri-can refugees.[310] While some of the Mexicans might still have had concerns about the changes, most seem to have accepted them or reconciled them-selves to them. As early as 1983, Olivares observed, "The congregation now reflects the local Latino population more accurately. It is heavily com-posed of Central Americans. And the commemoration itself has taken on [a] more American aspect."[311] According to Kennedy, they came together due to common issues such as survival and justice. He believes that in this sense La Placita represented a great experiment and that unlike other parts of Los Angeles, where there continued to be tensions between Mexi-cans and Salvadorans, this was not the case at La Placita. "We could have never done our work without the Mexican community," he concludes.[312] Fr. Gregorio observes that, while the integration of Central Americans was not perfect at La Placita, due to the efforts of Olivares, Kennedy, and their staff, the Mexican parishioners came to accept them as part of the parish com-munity. "So they were really welcomed and integrated into the absolute life blood of the parish," he concludes.[313] Such integration led Olivares to call La Placita "la cuña del hispanismo" in Los Angeles or the cradle of His-panismo (Latinismo), saying that it resembled almost a cathedral of His-panismo or Latinismo that transcended individual ethnic allegiances.[314] In part because his parishioners loved him and believed in him, Olivares created a more hospitable environment that brought Mexicans and Cen-tral Americans together in both a spiritual and political alliance.[315] Of this, Olivares fondly recalled years later:

> There certainly was a chasm in the efforts to make the Central Ameri-cans welcome. To the best of my ability that I can judge, there was a difference from the way people thought at the beginning of that mis-sion from the time I left. Many people even thought I was Salvadoran because of my involvement with Salvadoran refugees. They were OK with it. There are always some who object, but on the whole, at the end, I felt great acceptance of what we were trying to do.[316]

XI

Like a good prophet, Luis Olivares prepared his people not just for the coming of the Lord but, in his case, for declaring La Placita as a sanctuary for Central American refugees. In effect, prior to 1985, Olivares was already providing a de facto sanctuary for them. He did this not only by allowing them to sleep in the church, the basement hall, and Casa Grande, but also in the many services that he, Kennedy, and their staff at Rutilio Grande Pastoral Center provided. This included food, medical assistance, legal assistance, transportation including the underground railroad to other sanctuaries such as Canada, practical English, and sundry other help. Olivares likewise embraced the refugees by integrating them, as much as possible, into the religious and spiritual life of La Placita. La Placita became a sanctuary, but Olivares, as a strong believer in symbolism and in media attention to publicize a just cause, wanted to go one step further. He wanted to officially declare his church a sanctuary and to do so publicly. La Placita would become the first Catholic church in the Los Angeles archdiocese, which had the largest Salvadoran community next to San Salvador, to do so. This fact was not lost on Olivares. In effect, La Placita would become the leader of the sanctuary movement in the City of Angeles. By the end of 1985 Olivares, his staff, and his parishioners were ready for this next stage.

NINE

Declaring Sanctuary

Having prepared the way for declaring sanctuary at La Placita for the Central American refugees, by 1985 Luis Olivares was ready to go public on it by embracing "public sanctuary." This meant that officially La Placita would be declared a safe space for refugees and challenge the position of the Reagan administration on the Central American diaspora. In effect, Olivares was saying to federal immigration officials: "You may consider the Salvadorans and Guatemalans 'illegal aliens,' but we at La Placita consider them to be legitimate political refugees based not only on American and international laws on refugees, but also on moral grounds, and we are going to provide them sanctuary." Of course, Olivares and Mike Kennedy were already sheltering and providing for the refugees; however, going public was a way of elevating the issue to try to win the hearts and minds not only of Angelinos, but of the American public, and to attempt to counter the Reagan administration's support for the oppressive regimes in Central America.

It was also a way of joining the American sanctuary movement, which had commenced as early as 1982 in Arizona, when Quakers such as Jim Corbett began an "underground railroad" to transport refugees across the border and send them to other, safer locations in the country or on to Canada. The Quakers, of course, had a long tradition of assisting oppressed people, such as slaves fleeing the South prior to the Civil War. Needing to house these refugees soon after crossing the border, Corbett appealed to several Tucson churches. The first to positively respond was the Rev. John Fife, the pastor of the Southside Presbyterian Church. On March 24, 1982, the second anniversary of the assassination of Archbishop Romero, the church became the first in the country to declare itself a sanctuary for Central American refugees.[1] It posted a sign outside the church in Spanish that read: "This is a sanctuary of God for the oppressed from Central America." Another sign said: "La Migra [INS], don't profane the sanctuary."[2] In addition, the congregation submitted a letter to attorney general William French Smith that forcefully asserted its stand:

> We are writing to inform you that the Southside Presbyterian church will publicly violate the Immigration and Nationality Act Section 274 (a). We have declared our church as a 'sanctuary' for undocumented refugees from Central America. . . . We believe that justice and mercy require that people of conscience actively assert our God-given right to aid anyone fleeing from persecution and murder. The current administration of U.S. law prohibits us from sheltering these refugees from Central America. Therefore we believe the administration of the law to be immoral as well as illegal.[3]

Although centered on this Presbyterian church, the sanctuary movement in Arizona and elsewhere was an ecumenical effort composed of both Protestants and Catholics. As more Central Americans entered, many more churches, both Protestant and Catholic, along with some Jewish congregations, pronounced sanctuary. They drew their inspiration from biblical Old Testament passages concerning the sheltering of the persecuted. In the Book of Numbers, for example, God commanded Moses to establish "cities of refuge" for the Israelites and for the stranger and sojourner among them. Later historic examples of sanctuary, especially in the Christian tradition where churches became safe haven for the persecuted, added to the appeal of applying sanctuary to the Central American refugees.[4] Rev. Philip Zwerling of the First Unitarian Church in Los Angeles informed a reporter in 1983 that the concept of sanctuary "has a long tradition, dating back to Exodus and to medieval canon law. If you offended the king and were in fear of your life, you could seek refuge in the church."[5] La Placita trailed in this effort, at least with respect to public sanctuary, yet it would come to represent one of the most important centers and symbols of public sanctuary in the country.

I

Within a short period of time, the sanctuary movement in the United States significantly expanded and became a political movement. By 1985, some 300 religious groups had joined the movement. This involved churches and synagogues in various regions of the country. Religion-based sanctuary movements sprang up in Chicago, Berkeley, Milwaukee, Washington, D.C., Boston, Colorado Springs, Madison, Wisconsin, San Francisco, Seattle, and various other cities.[6] The movement involved Catholics, Unitarians, Lutherans, Methodists, the Church of Christ, Episcopalians, and conservative and reform Jewish groups.[7] These included not only individual churches, but in the case of Protestant denominations also national organizations such as the National Council of Churches, the United Presbyterian Church in the U.S.A., the American Baptist Churches in the U.S.A., the United Methodist Church, the Unitarian Universalist Association, and the American Lutheran Church. In addition, the Rabbinical Assembly passed a resolution supporting sanctuary.[8] By 1987, up to 400 churches, cities, and other jurisdictions had declared sanctuary.[9] In Southern California, thirty-five to forty Protestant, Jewish, and Unitarian congregations, including the Unitarian Church of Orange County, openly aided Central American refugees and endorsed sanctuary.[10] In Los Angeles, the first church to declare sanctuary was the First Unitarian Church at the University of Southern California. Its 300 members voted in 1983 to extend protection in any way feasible to the refugees. Its pastor, Rev. Zwerling, believed that this might save some lives and also be a political commentary on U.S. intervention in Central America "because it would bring a human face of what the costs were for the kind of U.S. intervention in El Salvador, Guatemala, and Nicaragua." A Lutheran church in Los Angeles likewise declared sanctuary at about the same time.[11] Other Protestant denominations in the area that supported the movement included the Methodists, Unitarian Universalists, the Presbyterians, and several others. In Pico Rivera, the Rev. Fernando Santillana, pastor of the Pico Rivera United Methodist Church, had protected twenty-eight Salvadoran and Guatemalan refugees since 1982.[12] According to Zwerling, between twenty and thirty churches, predominantly Protestant, in the Los Angeles area declared sanctuary, although this was mostly politically symbolical since few of them actually housed refugees.

The position of the Catholic Church nationally and locally was more complicated. Individual Catholic churches, although not the U.S. Catholic Bishops as an organization, promoted sanctuary. This included individual archbishops, such as Fr. Raymond Hunthausen of Seattle and Fr. Rembert Weakland of Milwaukee.[13] In Los Angeles, some individual clergy, both priests and sisters, along with laity became involved; however, no specific Catholic church adopted sanctuary until La Placita did. Sister Jo'Ann De Quattro notes that Catholic pastors were scared of declaring sanctuary.[14] She concedes that some of the churches worked with the refugees, but not as sanctuary churches.[15] One pastor, Msgr. Burke at Our Lady of Assumption in East L.A., had a friendly bet with Olivares as to which of their churches would be the first to declare sanctuary. They kidded with each other about this; however, Burke had a caveat. He would declare sanctuary if 50 percent of his parishioners approved. They never did.[16] A major factor in inhibiting other Catholic churches from publicly adopting sanctuary had to do with the fact that the U.S. Catholic Bishops, themselves, shied away from approving of sanctuary as an official body. The Bishops did not want to openly defy the Reagan administration. While they might support individual churches and clergy, including bishops in participating in the movement, they did not want to publicly endorse these actions as the official representatives of the Catholic Church in the United States. Hence, at the grassroots level, this probably influenced individual churches not to declare sanctuary. Olivares believed that sanctuary was too political an issue for the U.S. Catholic Bishops although he lamented that they seemed to be intimidated by this.[17] At the same time, to the credit of the Bishops through the U.S. Catholic Conference, they did critique the Reagan administration for not recognizing the Central Americans as legitimate refugees and called for it to at least provide "extended voluntary departure" status that would allow asylum until the wars ended in El Salvador and Guatemala.[18]

In addition to churches, various city governments throughout the country supported the sanctuary movement by declaring that they would not inquire about the legal status of any person in providing city services, nor would they allow their police to report the legal status of any immigrant arrested by the INS unless it involved a major crime. Some went further, such as Berkeley and St. Paul, and declared themselves "sanctuary cities" where Central American refugees would be welcomed and protected.[19]

The response of the INS and the Reagan administration, as noted, was to reiterate that the Central Americans were not covered by the 1980 Refugee Act concerning political refugees. Instead, according to immigration officials, they were coming into the United States without documents solely for economic reasons—to get jobs—and hence were "illegal aliens." The INS further emphasized that anyone assisting the Central Americans or any others without documents to cross the border and to shelter them were themselves breaking the law as human smugglers and subject to being prosecuted. Such actions were considered felonies and carried a maximum sentence of five years in prison and a $10,000 fine.[20] At the same time, immigration officials often stated that it was not their policy to raid churches in search of "illegal aliens." However, as the sanctuary movement grew in defiance of the INS, the Reagan administration decided to make a case of those in Tucson who openly aided refugees. They brought charges against them, and in January 1985 a federal grand jury in Arizona indicted sixteen persons, including Jim Corbett and Rev. Fife, three nuns, two priests, and others on smuggling charges. The major charges involved conspiracy, bringing aliens into the country illegally, transporting "illegal aliens," concealing, harboring, or shielding them, and encouraging or attempting to encourage the entry of "illegal aliens." Each of the charges carried a maximum punishment of five years imprisonment and fines ranging from $200 to $10,000. Lasting several months, the trial in Tucson led to the conviction of eight of the defendants although curiously Corbett the founder of the movement was not found guilty of any count.[21] Moreover, the presiding judge did not allow any testimony or evidence as to the religious and moral reasons for the defendants' action and instead focused only on their involvements in transporting the refugees across the border. This unfortunately took away a key element of the defense and reduced the case to one of smuggling "illegal aliens." Although found guilty by the federal government, the sanctuary workers vowed to continue their work because it was the right and Christian thing to do. "No, I have no regrets," Sister Darlene Nicgorski, one of the defendants, told the press. "There have been other cases in history where people had to stand up to be a Christian. If I am guilty of anything, I am guilty of living the Gospel." The defendants appealed their cases and eventually settled on only being put on probation. Still, the Reagan administration and the INS had put on notice others in the sanctuary movement that they, too, could be prosecuted.[22]

II

"Louie, I think the time has come to publicly declare sanctuary at La Placita. People are putting themselves on the line like the ones in Tucson. We have to be part of this by declaring sanctuary. Don't you agree?"

"Mike, I think you're right. It's time to go to the next level. Let's start preparing for this."

With this conversation, Kennedy recalls the initial steps to La Placita's becoming a public sanctuary for the refugees. He may have suggested the idea, but he knew that Olivares was already predisposed to this, especially after what had occurred in Tucson. No Catholic church in the Los Angeles area seemed willing to go public on sanctuary, and no one was already doing what La Placita was doing with the refugees. It was a no-brainer. They had to do it.[23] The prosecution of the sanctuary workers in Tucson proved to be the catalyst for La Placita proclaiming itself a sanctuary church. Olivares and Kennedy felt that they had to do so in solidarity with not just Tucson, but with the national movement. They could not be credible if they did not move in this direction.

Olivares also had to go in this direction for a number of other reasons which reveal his own makeup and complexity. First, he believed that it was the moral responsibility of the Church as an institution to support public sanctuary. "The Church is above political issues," he told his brother Henry. "The Church needs to help the people and the only way to do this is to tell government officials, including the President of the United States, that providing sanctuary has nothing to do with politics, but that it's the right thing to do. The refugees need a sanctuary where no one can affect them."[24] It wasn't that he was going to go public on sanctuary because it would bring attention to him. "I'm doing it because Jesus would do it."[25] It was also because he loved the refugees as he loved all others. He had a great propensity to love, as Lydia López observed: "There was this man [Olivares] that cared about them [the refugees] so much and he loved them so much that he was willing to put himself out to work for them."[26] But it also had to do with who he was—Luis Olivares—the son and grandson of a family in San Antonio who had provided sanctuary for the oppressed and for the poor. Sanctuary was part of his family tradition. Abuelita Inez and Tía Concha were telling him to do this. "I saw this coming from our home to the work that Louie was doing and all this was to help those people," his sister Socorro says. Once Socorro told him, "Louie, those people don't even pay taxes."

"Socorro," Olivares responded, "you need to understand that these people are coming just like our family came from Mexico—remember how Abuelita and how they came."[27]

Henry Olivares adds that if their father were still alive when Luis declared sanctuary at La Placita, he would have approved. But even if he didn't, his brother would have still done it no matter who opposed him.[28] His passion for justice, as others noted, would leave no other option.[29]

Olivares had no choice but to declare sanctuary. "I don't know if it will succeed and I don't know if what I do will continue even after I'm no longer pastor," he told Catholic journalist Moises Sandoval, "but I have to do it; it's worth doing."[30]

La Placita had already been functioning as a kind of non-public sanctuary, and so the logical next step was to go public. Kennedy calls this an organic evolution. "And we did it," he stresses. "It was an organic thing. It was a natural consequence of our work. It wasn't like it dropped down from heaven. So not to have done it would have been pretty inorganic. It wouldn't have been consistent with what we were doing and it did bring us into a different forum. It did change the equation. We never knew really what was going to happen."[31]

Olivares and Kennedy might not have known what would happen by declaring public sanctuary, but they welcomed this next step. Going public was entering into a new forum, but one that they could utilize to promote the rights and interests of the refugees. By becoming part of the public sanctuary movement, La Placita joined the debate about the status of the refugees and about U.S. policy toward Central America. It became, according to Kennedy, a player in this drama. But neither Olivares nor Kennedy had any illusions about what they wanted to do. They knew they were entering into rough seas with much controversy. "We were upping the ante in a sense from what we had been doing but in a quiet way," Kennedy says. "Declaring sanctuary, the purpose of it is to have a platform in what you say to the INS, really to the federal government, that we're breaking the law because we feel that what you're doing in El Salvador is evil by sending in military aid, is wrong, sinful. And so that did have a consequence." Both understood, however, that by declaring sanctuary, they could voice their concerns in a more public way. They were not under any illusions about how much they and La Placita could do in these matters that were not only national, but also international. However, Olivares and Kennedy believed in the power of symbols, and they saw La Placita as a sanctuary church as representing a very powerful symbol for the refugees and for those who struggled to change U.S. policies in Central America. La Placita could be a beacon for others. "Sanctuary was a symbol," Kennedy observes. "Like any good symbol, it is more than just what it is. La Placita became a symbol of hope and light internationally. People throughout the world and specifically in El Salvador knew there was a place in L.A. where the Church stood for people, helped them, and was working to end the war." This was part of Olivares's legacy, Kennedy concludes: "He was willing to let what he was responsible for become more."[32]

Others saw it this way also and applauded the move to make La Placita a public sanctuary. They agreed with Olivares and Kennedy that this small church could only do so much with over 300,000 Salvadorans already in Los Angeles by 1985. But it was the symbol that mattered and the influence it could assert to others. Moreover, it was a small church, but it was a Catholic church and the large majority of refugees were Catholics; it was critical that at least one Catholic church in Los Angeles stand up and declare sanctuary. "So it was like the mother church welcoming them," Gloria Kinsler asserts.[33] Moreover, La Placita was not just any church; it was La Placita, the most historic and recognized Catholic church in Los Angeles and Southern California. "Certainly getting La Placita aboard as a sanctuary church was a big deal," Unitarian minister Phil Zwerling recognized, "because La Placita had the profile, a very high profile in the city.

Everybody knew where the church was. To have it as a sanctuary church certainly magnified interest in the whole movement."[34] But it was more than La Placita standing out as a symbol. There was also the symbol of Fr. Olivares. Zwerling observes that the sanctuary movement in Los Angeles would not have been as effective without La Placita and without Olivares. "He was probably the most prominent clergy person in L.A. because of where he was and how he was known," Zwerling adds.[35]

Going public on sanctuary, moreover, would create a more public Luis Olivares. Both were two sides of the same coin. "Luis was a big ham," Richard Estrada says, but with much love and admiration for his mentor. "He had to be in the center and he was very articulate."[36] But having an ego, even for a priest, was not altogether that bad. "I think you have to have a huge healthy ego to be involved in public life," Lydia López notes affectionately of Olivares.[37] "Olivares was a remarkable person," UNO organizer Clements observes, "someone who had a strong ego but was not arrogant."[38] Above all, Olivares was a leader and he knew it, but he wanted to place his leadership, despite or because of what personal recognition and accolades it brought to him, at the service of people. "Luis was a leader," Fr. Gregorio concludes, "When Luis spoke, people listened. When Luis led, thousands of people followed."[39]

III

Having decided on announcing public sanctuary at La Placita, Olivares began a process of informing and consulting with various groups and individuals about what he was going to do. He wasn't asking permission; he didn't need it, nor did he necessarily want it. He knew what he wanted to do, what he needed to do, and he would do it. He did not need the permission of the Claretians, for example. As pastor, he had the authority, or so he believed, to do this.[40] Fr. Ferrante, the Provincial, recalls Olivares raising the issue before the Provincial Council, but that it was more informing it what he intended to do. Ferrante does not remember any questions raised about it from other council members. He agrees that Olivares did not need the council's approval, and he did not ask for it. "My guess," Ferrante says, "is it was more like our dialoguing about it and acquiescing to the fact that this was a natural flow of the events of La Placita given the nature of the people that were there. So we supported it."[41] Although Ferrante notes the council's support, this was not fully the case with other clergy. Some supported it; some opposed; and most were in the middle and took a wait-and-see approach to what would happen.[42] Although Olivares did not seek approval from his order, Ferrante's support was still crucial in aligning the order with him. Ferrante considered Olivares as the avant-garde of the order and he had no problems with this.[43] At the same time, some of the older and more traditional priests had trouble understanding what Olivares proposed to do.[44] Former Provincial O'Connor recalls this re-action by the old-timers, but still acknowledges the historical importance of public sanctuary.[45] Others remember that most Claretians supported Olivares.[46] Fr. Lozano expressed admiration for what his former teacher was going to do and for challenging unjust immigration laws.[47] Fr. Al Vás-quez, moreover, believes that it was in the spirit of the Claretian Order to support sanctuary. "Luis was the man of the hour," he observes and the order supported him.[48] Olivares was respectful of authority; after all he had been and still was part of the Provincial Council. However, he was not sub-servient to authority, whether of a religious or secular nature. His authority, as he said, came from God, and that is what he adhered to.

The planning and preparation for the declaration of public sanctuary did not occur overnight. It had to be perfectly done and with as much fan-fare and media exposure as possible. This was part of the politics of the action, and Olivares had learned from UNO that any action first had to be carefully planned and organized and that it was important to have as much media coverage as possible. This preparation occurred over several months in 1985. Olivares and Kennedy first began with their staff and pas-toral team. The older priests such as Fr. Tobias didn't really seem to grasp the importance of going public on sanctuary, but, according to Cully, they went along with it.[49] "They didn't have a vision like Louie had," Kennedy says. "They were more focused on sacramental life. Well, that's not what Louie was about."[50] The rest of the clergy, El Centro staff, and the admin-istrative staff supported the issue after Olivares and Kennedy explained it to them. "I think there was some sense of we have to help the refugees," Cully notes. "We have to show our support. There was at least some pride in that we were doing it, but not necessarily realizing that it would bring in another level of actions and consequences."[51] Having the staff behind them, Olivares and Kennedy then began, over at least a couple of months, to inform parishioners. They did this largely at Sunday Masses where they discussed the importance of what they planned to do. "Do we want to be a sanctuary?" was a rhetorical question that Olivares raised with the people knowing full well that he was going to do it. He believed that he knew his parishioners well enough to know that they would support him. Perhaps this support was more for him than for the Central Americans or for the concept of sanctuary, but regardless they would support him. He had al-ready laid the groundwork for this in promoting a pan-Latino consciousness within the parish that paid dividends when his parishioners, for the most part, endorsed his action.[52]

To get a better idea of the legal and political implications of declaring sanctuary, especially in light of the Tucson show trial of sanctuary activists, Olivares met with activist attorney Peter Schey, the head of the Center for Human Rights, which was providing legal assistance to some of the refugees in Los Angeles. Olivares already knew Schey from their common association with the Central American support groups that sprang up in the city. Olivares visited Schey in his office.

> Peter, I want to declare La Placita as a sanctuary. How do I do this? What will it mean for my employees and the other clergy and what does it mean for the refugees sleeping in the church? I don't want to contribute to a situation where the INS or Border Patrol agents can storm the church and arrest 700 people. I don't want to be a catalyst for that, but how can I provide sanctuary and what are the legal parameters of that and the justification?

Olivares's questions might suggest that perhaps he actually had some doubts about the efficacy of declaring sanctuary; however, this was not the case. Olivares was going to do a public sanctuary whether it was legal or not and irrespective of what happened in the Tucson trial. His meeting with Schey was primarily to inform the attorney and his group of the forthcoming action and to see what legal protection, if needed, he could rely on from him.

Schey notes that Olivares was not worried about himself, but how others might be affected by the action.

> Fr. Luis, let me first say that theoretically you might face liability under federal law. You could become the target of a criminal prosecution for harboring undocumented immigrants and for transporting them even if this only involves taking them to a job interview or to see the doctor. You might be faced with this, but I understand the spiritual justification for what you want to do and why.

Schey did not attempt to dissuade Olivares from his objective. Instead, he told him that he had a fair amount of experience in criminal law and that if Olivares became the target of retaliation by the government in the form of criminal prosecution that the Center would support and represent him. "And if there are mass arrests of the refugees," Schey continued, "and if they are alerted to their rights beforehand, the Center will also protect them. We'll organize a team of pro bono attorneys to represent them."

These would be the possible legal ramifications of declaring sanctuary, but Schey also observed potential political consequences. "You no doubt will be put in an adverse relationship with the INS and you may face issues within your own Church especially from the hierarchy." On the latter, Schey mentioned that the Center had developed good working relations with the archdiocese and with newly appointed archbishop Roger Mahony on immigration issues, and so he and the Center might be of assistance on that front. After Olivares left the meeting, Schey had no doubt that nothing would deter Olivares from what he wanted to do.[53]

In addition to Schey, Olivares likewise informed and consulted with others in the Central American support groups such as Sister Jo'Ann De-Quattro. The Catholic nun and the head of the Southern California Ecumenical Council's Interfaith Task Force on Central America extended her support and that of her group without reservation. She felt that La Placita was the perfect place to declare public sanctuary.[54] Olivares also approached Jimmy Rodríguez to determine how much support he might get from the labor movement. "Jimmy," Olivares said, "I know that I'm going to get a lot of flak even by my own Church officials, but it has to be done. Nobody else is doing it and sometimes we have to step out in front and walk out on the gang plank. If you succeed, you can walk back off of it. If you don't then you just fall into the water. But even if you fall in the water, you're bringing attention to the issue; you're bringing it out into the open."

"You're really sticking your neck out," Rodríguez responded, "but I'll do everything to support you and get others in the labor unions to do the same."

"Thanks, Jimmy, we may need that."[55]

He would need that support, but the next step was to inform the Archdiocese of Los Angeles of the public declaration of sanctuary. The relationship of the archdiocese and the sanctuary movement out of La Placita would be an interesting one, to say the least, over the next few years. Olivares, as he did with his own order, did not believe that he needed permission from the archdiocese to declare sanctuary, and he did not request it.[56] At the same time, he and Kennedy believed that it would help the cause if they could get its blessings, which would help shape public opinion to their side. They felt that this was possible especially due to the changing of the guard at the archdiocese. Cardinal Manning had retired and had been replaced in 1985 by Bishop Roger Mahony of Stockton who would be the new Archbishop of Los Angeles. Mahony, a Los Angeles native, had served a number of years in the Central Valley and had received recognition as a liberal priest due to his work in mediating the crisis between César Chávez, the UFW, and the growers. After the Agricultural Labor Relations Act was adopted in 1975 to handle disputes between the UFW and the growers on conducting union elections and representation, Governor Jerry Brown appointed Mahony as chair of the California Agricultural Relations Board, where he was seen as sympathetic to the farmworkers. He brought that liberal reputation and his work with Mexicans in the fields to his new position. Moreover, unlike the dour Manning, Mahony possessed a stronger personality and was clearly a cleric on the rise and with ambitions. These qualities, similar to those of Olivares, would make for a complicated relationship between the two.[57]

Olivares knew Mahony due to his own association with the farmworkers, and this gave him a sense that the new archbishop would also be sympathetic to the sanctuary movement. Shortly after Mahony arrived in Los Angeles that summer, Olivares and Kennedy scheduled one of the first appointments with him in September. They told him that they planned to declare La Placita as a sanctuary church and briefed him on all of the work with the refugees that they had already been doing. "He was very excited," Olivares later recalled, "he thought it was the greatest thing, and he wanted to be part of the sanctuary movement. He told us that he'd be there with us on the day we would announce our plans which would have been a strong statement of support. We were delighted. We knew he had a progressive reputation, and we thought he would say go ahead, but we didn't think that he would come out and say he wanted to be a part of it."[58]

Olivares and Kennedy left the archbishop's office on a high from the supportive reaction that they had received. With the archbishop's blessing and even involvement in the declaration of sanctuary, they felt that this would widen the support for it and also fend off any INS action against it. It would be one thing for immigration officials to take them on, but it would be another for them to prosecute the Archbishop of Los Angeles. However, this euphoria did not last too long. After Mahony returned to Los Angeles from a meeting of the U.S. Bishops in Washington, D.C., that November, where the Bishops avoided supporting public sanctuary, Olivares received a call from Msgr. William Barry from the Chancery, who was very close to the archbishop. Barry told Olivares that the archbishop was having serious doubts about whether to participate in the public sanctuary, and he suggested that Olivares talk again with Mahony. Barry hinted at what seemed to be the problem. "If you can assure the Archbishop that you are not going to be anti-Reagan, he might be more inclined to continue being part of it. In any case, you talk with him."[59] Olivares and Kennedy followed up on this and arranged a meeting with Mahony. He informed them that he had had a change of mind on publicly supporting their efforts.

"What's the problem?" Olivares asked.

"The problem is that I can't be part of this event."

"But why?"

"Because it's not a diocesan thing; it's just a parish thing. I don't have to be at a parish thing."

Olivares and Kennedy were taken aback. They had been told that their meeting with the archbishop could only last for five minutes, but as they discussed Mahony's change of mind, the meeting went on for forty-five minutes. Olivares felt that Mahony was battling with the issue and that part of him wanted to support them, but that he felt institutional restraints by the U.S. Catholic Bishops. Mahony ended the meeting by at least conceding that he would think more about it. In the meantime, the Los Angeles City Council voted to become a sanctuary city, which seems to have affected Mahony's position. Olivares received a call from him either on December 7 or 8. He told Olivares that the city council vote now made it easier for him to publicly endorse public sanctuary and that he would join them at the official declaration. Needless to say, Olivares and Kennedy were in seventh heaven. The Archbishop of Los Angeles, the highest ranking Catholic official in the Archdiocese, would stand with them at La Placita and announce to the world that the Church was on the side of the Central American refugees and against the immigration policies of the Reagan administration.[60] But this drama with Mahony would continue. In the meantime, Olivares and Kennedy, as they had already been doing, made final preparations for the official declaration.

IV

While the Los Angeles City Council debated about declaring the city a sanctuary, Olivares and Kennedy continued their preparations for their own declaration. The first thing they did was to select the feast day of Our Lady of Guadalupe, December 12, as the day they would proclaim sanctuary. It was the perfect day. The feast day was one of the most important feasts at La Placita, as it was in all parishes with many Mexican-descended parishioners. Our Lady of Guadalupe was the national religious symbol of Mexico and had always symbolized the Virgin Mother's embrace of the poor and oppressed, beginning with the indigenous Juan Diego, to whom she appeared, according to the story, in 1531 as a sign of hope for the conquered Indians of Mexico after the Spanish conquest. Moreover, in the history of Mexico and Mexican Americans, she stood for freedom and liberation, as her image was used in Mexico's war of independence beginning in 1810, in the Mexican Revolution of 1910 against the dictator Porfirio Díaz, and in the farmworker's movement led by César Chávez beginning in the 1960s. Like Chávez, Olivares himself had a special devotion to Guadalupe, a devotion he inherited from his own family. But the choice of December 12 was also a way of extending a sense of pan-Latino consciousness at La Placita by bringing together Mexican Americans and Central Americans. In a press release on November 18, Olivares connected the importance of the feast day to the sanctuary movement. He wrote:

> On December 12, 1985, the feast of Our Lady of Guadalupe "La Placita" (Our Lady Queen of the Angeles Church) will be the first Roman Catholic Church in the city of Los Angeles to offer PUBLIC SANCTUARY to Central American refugees. This is the fulfillment of Mary's mandate to Juan Diego at TEPEYAC: Build a temple "where I can demonstrate and impart all of my love, compassion, aid and defense." Later on she says, "Why is your heart troubled? Why are you afraid? . . . Am I not here who am your mother?"[61]

Olivares also wrote and disseminated a "Pastoral Statement on Public Sanctuary at La Placita." In it he stated that he and his church felt called to respond to the anguished voices of their Salvadoran and Guatemalan brothers and sisters. "We wish to undertake this dramatic step of declaring LA PLACITA a Public Sanctuary," he proclaimed, "because we are compelled to exercise the option of obedience to God by having to say 'no' to civil authorities." While the federal government claimed that those in the sanctuary movement were breaking the law, he and others challenged that because the Central Americans were legitimate refugees. "In this instance," he said, "Thoreau's words gain full meaning: 'They are lovers of the law who uphold it when the government breaks it.'"[62]

To build for a large turnout and to alert the media of the event, Olivares sent out press releases and did additional outreach with reporters. He also contacted other churches and synagogues, as well as Central American support groups. The releases informed that the declaration would occur on December 12, the feast day of Our Lady of Guadalupe. One press release in part read: "SANCTUARY! Illegal? Political? Civil Disobedience? The debate goes on. We at 'LA PLACITA' Church firmly believe that we have a moral imperative: 'The obligation of persons of faith to stand with the persecuted.' We cannot and will not stand idly by and permit our brothers and sisters from Guatemala and El Salvador to be deported to their homeland where their very lives are at risk." Another release noted that various religious, civic, and labor leaders would attend including Jimmy Rodríguez from the AFL-CIO, state senator Art Torres, city councilman Michael Woo, and actor Mike Farrell, all of whom would speak at a press conference following the declaration. Priests from other churches willing to concelebrate the Mass were told to bring their own vestments, such as alb and stole. Moreover, ecumenical and interfaith clergy, Protestant and Jewish, were also welcomed to attend and told to wear appropriate vestments. "La Placita would declare sanctuary," Olivares told a reporter, "not for political reasons but in order to comply with an evangelical mandate to extend a hand to oppressed brothers and sisters. The political and legal aspects should not distract from the moral obligation that we have to defend the persecuted."[63]

At the same time that Olivares alerted the public and media to December 12, he and Kennedy planned the liturgy for that day. The day would commence with mariachis playing the traditional Mexican birthday song, "Las Mañanitas," to Our Lady of Guadalupe as people arrived. This would be followed by the Mass. Participating in the Mass would be two Central American couples, one Salvadoran and one Guatemalan, who would be symbolically extended sanctuary even though many others were already receiving "nonpublic sanctuary," but the couples would be representing the others. Following the Mass, there would be a press conference in the chapel. Everything was planned to the last detail exhibiting Olivares's propensity for detailed organization.[64]

Everything seemed to be in place on the eve of December 12 except the role that Archbishop Mahony would play. As far as Olivares was concerned, the archbishop had approved the declaration of sanctuary at La Placita and had promised to concelebrate the Mass. In a November 18, 1985, news release, Olivares wrote: "Archbishop Roger Mahony will celebrate a Mass in honor of Our Lady of Guadalupe at 9:00 A.M."[65] Olivares repeated this announcement in a subsequent news release, observing that "the Most Reverend Roger M. Mahony, Archbishop of Los Angeles, will be the principal celebrant at a Mass commemorating this historic event."[66] Moreover, the *Los Angeles Herald Examiner* headlined a story prior to the event that read: "L.A. church to join sanctuary movement with Mahony's blessing."[67] However, the confusion as to exactly what Mahony's position on the declaration was, and whether he would attend the ceremony, became muddled when an archdiocesan spokesman, Fr. Joseph Battaglia, on December 6 told reporters that the archbishop "is not taking a stand on approval or disapproval" on the declaration. Battaglia noted that Mahony "wants to distance himself from the sanctuary movement, which is a red flag to some people." He added that the archbishop would not attend the Mass, but that instead his letter to the Los Angeles City Council, in which he supported the need to provide temporary refugee status for the Central Americans, would be read for him.[68] Yet, one day later Olivares was quoted by the Spanish-language newspaper, *Noticias del Mundo*, as saying that Mahony would say the Mass on December 12 and would in his homily declare La Placita a sanctuary church. Despite these countering stories, Olivares maintained that the archbishop approved of the declaration and that he would be there that day. Olivares and Kennedy concluded their preparations and looked forward to December 12.

V

Luis Olivares probably did not sleep very well on the night of December 11. Tomorrow would be a historic day, and his mind must have kept going over all of the details for the ceremony. He had earlier written out the declaration of sanctuary in both English and Spanish. The day would be the culmination of the work he had started with the Central American refugees when he arrived at La Placita in 1981 and which was accelerated with Mike Kennedy. He looked forward to the day. He was always nervous before any major event and public appearance, but he knew that once the day started he would be alright and would rise to the occasion. This day was not just for him, although he knew he would be the center of attention, especially from the media, but it was for the refugees and for his staff that had worked so hard to assist them. He probably somehow finally got some sleep.

He awoke to what looked like it would be a nice but crisp and windy December day, but at least no rain was forecast. The Mass would commence at 9 A.M. according to the flyer that was widely distributed. It read:

SANCTUARY
December 12th celebration
Honoring our Lady of Guadalupe.
LA PLACITA CHURCH WILL DECLARE
ITSELF PUBLIC SANCTUARY
For
CENTRAL AMERICAN REFUGEES

Let's celebrate Mass together with
Archbishop ROGER MAHONY
And REV. LUIS OLIVARES

Although Olivares more than likely felt some trepidation about whether Mahony would show up or not, he had definitely not heard from the archbishop; so as far as he was concerned he would celebrate the Mass as the flyer indicated.[69]

After Olivares dressed and ate a most-likely meager breakfast, he went to the church to get ready along with Kennedy who had arrived from Dolores Mission where he stayed. After they put on their white vestments indicating a new beginning honoring both Our Lady of Guadalupe and the refugees, they joined the arriving crowd that was treated outside the church to the mariachis who played and sang "Las Mañanitas."[70] The mariachis would also supply some of the music along with the church choir for the Mass. Inside the church was decorated and featured the image of Our Lady of Guadalupe above the altar, with a flag of the United States on one side and the flag of Mexico on the other. The people then entered and soon filled the church to its capacity of between 900 and 1,000.[71] Parishioners, including both Mexicans and Central Americans, made up most of the congregation. As they entered the church, ushers handed them the program for the Mass. On the front cover, an artist had illustrated an image of Guadalupe holding hands in a circle with three figures—two men and one woman with a child on her back—depicting the refugees, with La Placita in the background and parishioners looking on. A poem in Spanish (probably written by Mike Kennedy) dedicated to the refugees was part of the program, with no author cited. In one stanza, the poet wrote:

Nuestra Señora de Guadalupe
proteje a estos nuevos
Juan Diegos entre nosotros.
Ayudanos a acabar con la
violencia en
Centro América.
Trae Justicia a estos países
destrosados por la Guerra,
hasta que la paz finalmente
llegue.

Ayudanos a tener amor y
compassion hacia estos
Juan Diegos Refugiados."[72]

("Our Lady of Guadalupe
Protect these new

Juan Diegos among us.
Help us to end
the violence in Central America.
Bring Justice to these countries
torn apart by War,
until peace finally
arrives.

Help us to love
and to pity
these rejected Juan Diegos.")[73]

In addition to parishioners, many local religious leaders attended. Olivares and Kennedy had made a concerted effort to make the ceremony an ecumenical and interfaith one. Olivares believed in ecumenism and interfaith relations, especially with Protestant and Jewish clergy, many of whom he knew and considered friends. Some eighty clergy representing various Catholic, Protestant, and Jewish denominations participated in the Mass, dressed in their own vestments which made for a colorful appearance. One of the Presbyterian pastors carried some of the gifts as part of the Communion liturgy and a Jewish rabbi read from the Torah.[74] A photo in the *Daily News* showed Episcopalian bishop Oliver Garver comforting a refugee child inside the church.[75] Joining the different clergy were various Hollywood celebrities who were politically involved in the Central American support groups and especially to stop the U.S. intervention in Central America. These included Martin Sheen and Mike Farrell.

Everyone appeared to be there at the commencement of the procession of the priests who would concelebrate the Mass, except for one obvious omission—Archbishop Roger Mahony. About thirty or forty minutes before the service, Olivares received a phone call telling him that Mahony would not be attending. It's not clear whether the phone call came from the archbishop himself or from his staff. Grace Davis, deputy mayor of Los Angeles, recalls that she heard from Lydia López that Mahony in a phone call, although perhaps another one, had strongly protested Olivares's declaration of sanctuary.[76] In any event, this was the first time that Olivares had definitively heard that Mahony would not participate.[77] Why didn't Mahony show up? Various reasons were given. Of course, he had already mentioned to Olivares and Kennedy that, as archbishop, he felt the event was a parish one and he could not possibly attend, nor did he have to attend a parish as opposed to a diocesan event (though the historic importance of what was going to transpire at La Placita was not in the same category as a parish picnic or bazaar). Ken Gregorio heard that the problem was that the archbishop had been caught in heavy traffic, although that seems unlikely since the archbishop's residence was quite close to La Placita.[78] Another theory was that Mahony was called away at the last minute, although his office never offered this explanation.[79] Still another explanation was that he did not support public sanctuary and did not want to get involved in it.[80] Finally, there are some, including Olivares, who believed that it was political pressure, not just from the U.S. Catholic Bishops but possibly also from the Los Angeles business donor establishment, who did not believe the Church should be involved in controversial political issues, that affected Mahony's decision not to go to La Placita. Fr. O'Connor is sure that the Archbishop "got a lot of flak" on the issue.[81] This latter explanation would appear to be the most plausible and one that Olivares seemed to agree with. "That's one of the problems that I see with the Church," he said of Mahony's absence. "In terms of its leadership, no matter how well inclined they might be to pursue these perhaps risky decisions, they are somewhat hampered by the finances for the Church, or concern for their own relationship to their peers or superiors."[82]

Needless to say, Olivares was very personally disappointed that the archbishop did not attend and that he was not notified of this until the last minute. "It was a tremendous, tremendous disappointment to Luis," Gregorio says.[83] Olivares had been told, according to Fr. Cully, that Mahony would be there "unless he was run over by a truck." Then he didn't go. "Oops, better watch out for those trucks," Olivares quipped, but no doubt with much frustration and perhaps even resentment.[84] Lydia López suggests that Olivares was heartbroken by Mahony's failure to support sanctuary.[85] But even if there was resentment, Olivares did not give public voice to this feeling. He had too much respect for authority, including that of the archbishop. On his own, Olivares tried to put the best face on the situation. For one, he reiterated to the press that despite the archbishop's failure to show up he favored what La Placita was doing. "In his mind and heart I'm sure he supports us," he stated. "There is no question of his solidarity with us, but he walks a thin line."[86] In responding to the *National Catholic Register*, Olivares nuanced his earlier statement by saying: "The archbishop would probably prefer us not to be so public about being a sanctuary, but he didn't prohibit it. If he did, we would not have done it. I think his main concern is the misuse of sanctuary by some people involved whose motivation are exclusively political. But the idea of sanctuary itself is something a Christian conscience calls for."[87]

Privately, he told some of his staff about Mahony, "Hey, he's gotta do what he's gotta do. He's not putting any obstacles in our way. God bless him. He may have had other issues. But we're going to do what we need to do. Let's focus on that."[88] This statement speaks not only to Olivares's respect for the position of the archbishop, in that he chose not to badmouth him, at least not among others, but it also reveals Fr. Luis's own sense of determination. Although he had told the press that if Mahony had prohibited sanctuary at La Placita that he, Olivares, would not have done it does not ring true. There is little question that he and Kennedy were totally committed to declaring sanctuary, and no one, including the archbishop, was going to get in their way. Clearly, Mahony did not favor public sanctuary, which is why he did not attend the declaration and, in this sense, was trying to prohibit it. Olivares and Kennedy were politically astute enough to know this, but they were not going to be deterred. They knew it was the right thing to do and they did it.

While Olivares publicly was gracious to the archbishop, others were less so. Some saw it as a betrayal on the part of Mahony. "He didn't show and I think many of us would use the word betrayal. He betrayed Luis," Cully declares.[89] Ken Gregorio believes that jealousy was involved—Mahony's jealousy of Olivares due to his leadership among Latino Catholics, a leadership that Mahony hoped to possess himself. "La Placita was like its own little cathedral," Gregorio explains. "Many people thought, and it was probably true, that Mahony really envied the kind of leadership that Luis exercised among the Latino immigrant community through La Placita because it dwarfed the archbishop's leadership as the official bishop, certainly at least to the Latino segment of the Roman Catholic Church in L.A. . . . People had an affection and a loyalty for Luis that the archbishop could only dream of."[90] Parishioners likewise expressed disappointment and even anger about Mahony's absence. "No viño Mahony" (Mahony didn't show), some people said.[91] For Juanita Espinosa, the failure of the archbishop to participate was like a "slap in the face."[92] Years later, some still express resentment toward Mahony for this. For Gregorio, "it still is a very hot-button issue. The archbishop's lack of support, lack of visibility that day in what was really a historical event."[93]

Clearly planning on not attending, despite various excuses expressed, Mahony arranged in advance for Auxiliary Bishop Juan Arzube to represent him as the main celebrant of the Mass. As a result, Arzube, who had worked with Olivares in UNO, arrived in time to inform Fr. Luis that he was substituting for the archbishop and to put on his white vestments for the Mass. Arzube declined to comment after the Mass when asked why Mahony did not attend; however, he did concede that his own presence represented a form of archdiocesan support for public sanctuary at La Placita. When informed of Arzube's comments, Fr. Battaglia, director of communications for the archdiocese, refuted them, thus giving proof that Mahony had never intended to participate. Battagilia denied that Arzube's presence could be inferred as support by the archdioceses much less by the Archbishop. "Any declaration of sanctuary is the pastor's decision," he claimed. "He's on his own. Arzube was there, as Mahony would have been, because it was the feast of Our Lady of Guadalupe. It didn't have anything to do with the declaration." However, it had everything to do with the declaration. All of the promotion for that day linked the feast of Guadalupe with sanctuary; the two were never separate and Mahony knew that. Yet Battaglia went further and, in effect, told the *National Catholic Register* the real reason why the archbishop did not go to La Placita that day. "Archbishop Mahony's stance is the same," he said, "he'd rather not deal with independent churches as sanctuary since all churches should technically be sanctuary. He's distancing himself because sanctuary can take on another meaning, a political one. His response to the plight of the refugees is to urge the government to grant extended voluntary departure to Central American refugees."[94]

For his part, and again trying to put the best face on Mahony's absence, Olivares noted that Arzube's presence was an indication of Mahony's support. Olivares was sharp enough to recognize Mahony's strategic weakness by having another high official of the Church represent him, even though he himself refused to be there. But Olivares wouldn't let him have it both ways. By having Arzube substitute for him and say the Mass and participate in the declaration of sanctuary, in effect Mahony was there and was supporting sanctuary. Olivares was not going to allow Mahony to outfox him.[95]

With the mariachi music filling the church, Olivares, Kennedy, and Arzube, along with the altar servers and the robed religious guests, processed into the main part of the church and to the altar, where the three concelebrants of the Mass ascended, while the others took their seats in the front pews. The bilingual Mass then proceeded as usual with opening prayers both in English and Spanish, singing by the choir, and the two Gospel readings also in both languages. Olivares then went to the pulpit to deliver his homily as pastor of La Placita. It is not certain if he had a prepared text or not, but unlike his usual homilies where he descended into the aisles to be closer to the congregation and make better eye contact, Fr. Luis on this occasion, perhaps because it was a more formal one, spoke at the pulpit in front of the altar and facing the gathered participants. He spoke in both English and Spanish. If he had a text of his remarks, it no longer exists or could not be found; however, news coverage of the Mass provides some of his remarks. He opened by bringing together the feast of Our Lady of Guadalupe with the declaration of sanctuary. "On this day, the feast of Our Lady of Guadalupe," his strong voice exclaimed amplified by the microphone, "who embraced a humble Indian, we too today raise our voices of support for the poor and the oppressed."[96] He continued: "We have become a place of tranquility and security for Central Americans and others who are victims of violence and war, who are victims of unjust discrimination and who are labeled criminals when their only wrong is to take seriously their 'inalienable right to life, liberty and the pursuit of happiness.'"[97] As part of his homily, Olivares criticized U.S. policy in Central America especially the arming of the military and death squads. He told the standing-room-only congregation that their being there and their support was part of "the process of creative escalation in the struggle against repression at home and militarism in Central America."[98] Madeline Janis-Aparicio remembers thinking, at the conclusion of Olivares's homily, that she and others at the church probably felt a little scared about the implications of the church publicly proclaiming sanctuary, but her fears were allayed after hearing Olivares's homily. "Luis was really inspiring," she notes. "He made us all feel confident that it was the right thing to do."[99]

Mike Kennedy followed with a few words about the importance of the day and the meaning of sanctuary.[100]

The Mass continued through the offertory, the offering of gifts, and then the consecration of the bread and wine into the symbols of the body and blood of Jesus Christ. Olivares, Kennedy, Arzube, and some of the other Catholic priests then distributed Holy Communion to the Catholic worshippers. With such a large turn-out, the sharing of the bread and wine took some time. Bishop Arzube said the closing prayers and the Mass came to an end. However, then came the most powerful part of the day's liturgy. Two Central American families, a Salvadoran couple, "José" and "Patricia," and a single Guatemalan mother, "María," with her three young children, ascended to the altar area completely dressed in black from head to toe. These were not their real names. Their entire faces were masked including the top of their heads, and only slits in their masks revealed their eyes. Their faces were hidden in order to protect their identities from the INS, and they asked not to have their pictures taken. Fr. Gregorio observes that their anonymity conveyed that they were "non-people" in the United States who were being hunted down. He connects this to others, including Americans, when he notes that it "also symbolized ways that we have to hide our-

Declaring sanctuary, La Placita Church, December 12, 1985; Fr. Luis Olivares (left), Fr. Mike Kennedy, S.J. (center), and Central American refugees (right). (Courtesy of Dept. of Special Collections, Charles E. Young Research Library, UCLA)

selves in order to make it through society."[101] The refugees had been sitting on one side of the altar during the Mass and made for a striking image as the people entered the church and saw them, no doubt wondering who they were. Although Henry Olivares did not attend the ceremony, he recalls that his brother told him that he planned the appearance of the refugees for dramatic impact. It was almost like a play. Fr. Luis mentioned that the people in the church would see the refugees, feel sorry for them, and support the concept of sanctuary.[102] Recall that Olivares had always been into play acting since childhood, when he staged his own Masses at home.

Olivares explained that the Central Americans had been selected by him and Kennedy as representative of the refugees, to symbolize that they would now receive sanctuary in La Placita. Of course, the church had already been sheltering refugees for four years, but the symbolic presence of the hooded refugees was still telling. As they faced the congregation, the three children held up signs that read in English: "El Salvador, 70,000 Persons Killed, 1980–1985," and "Guatemala, 50,000 Persons Killed, 1980–1985." Each of the refugees also held in one hand a red rose symbolizing the roses that Our Lady of Guadalupe gave to Juan Diego to prove her apparition to Church officials. Kennedy introduced "Patricia," who proceeded to address the audience in Spanish, translated by Gloria Kinsler.[103] "Patricia" gave her testimonio about how her family and that of her husband had been killed and tortured in El Salvador and how she and her husband had been likewise threatened. "For me," she tearfully said, "it is a real pleasure to feel I am under the protection of this church." She told about having to leave behind her four children and gave graphic details about the horrors that she and her husband experienced in El Salvador. She said that two family members had been taken from their home by soldiers earlier that year. "About three days later," she recounted, "we found them dead; their faces disfigured. They were clad only in their underwear." Later, a brother-in-law disappeared and a twenty-year-old nephew was found dead, along with seven fellow students. After she and her husband received a death threat, they felt they had no choice but to flee the country and leave their children with friends. "Mothers, how do you think I feel, having to leave my children behind," she sobbed. "I want you to understand how we Salvadoran mothers feel when we have lost a family member. Yet, the president of this country continues sending arms and bombs to destroy our homes, our families, and our country. It is not just!" She hoped that such public support for refugees would "touch the heart of the President of the United States so he will know how we mothers of El Salvador feel." Addressing directly the INS, perhaps thinking some were inside the church, she concluded: "We have been told that we have come to this country only to make money, but that is not why we have come. I don't like being in the United States; I'm not happy here, but we had to come after they had killed all of my husband's brothers." This was high and powerful drama, and drove the point home of the need for sanctuary, unlike anything anyone else, including Olivares, could have said. The people in the church were stunned, moved, and supportive.[104]

Unitarian minister Zwerling, who was present, also was moved by the testimonios of the refugees; however, he did not like them being hooded and their identities hidden. He knew the threats and dangers that the Central Americans faced even in Los Angeles. "So I certainly understood why people would want to use the masks," he says, "but I felt that it was simply bad PR. It allowed people to say, 'Well maybe they're not really refugees. They could be anybody behind those masks. How do we know who they are?'" He also felt that the masks disguised their humbleness. Still, Zwerling believed that it was a beautiful ceremony.[105]

After the testimonios, Olivares stepped back to a standing microphone, with Kennedy right behind him and Arzube at the altar. Fr. Luis held in his hand the declaration of sanctuary written both in English and Spanish. He asked the congregation to join him in making the declaration by responding "We Do" after each statement. First in English and then in Spanish, the declaration was read to the people. Olivares began with a sense of history for what was about to transpire:

> Brothers and sisters, we are gathered here together today with a long tradition of how our faith has taught us to stand with the poor and the oppressed especially exemplified by this Feast of Our Lady of Guadalupe who chose to protect a simple peasant.
>
> We have just heard a testimony of one of our families from Central America. LET US NOW STAND IN ORDER TO ENTER INTO COVENANT WITH THESE REFUGEES BEFORE US.
>
> Do we as a community of faith commit ourselves to support our brothers and sisters from Central America?
>
> WE DO.
>
> Do we commit ourselves to work together to end the violence, the war and the torture so prevalent in these countries?
>
> WE DO.
>
> Do we commit ourselves to work together to bring about peace with justice in all of Central America?
>
> WE DO.
>
> My brothers and sisters we have just publicly declared and committed ourselves here at Our Lady Queen of Angeles Church to provide Sanctuary for Central American refugees.[106]

The Spanish-language version was then read. Strong applause followed each presentation.[107] Bishop Arzube thanked everyone for attending the ceremony and the event ended. "It was a very joyful day," Kennedy says.[108]

In order to maximize the importance of the day, media-savvy Fr. Luis arranged for a press conference immediately following the Mass. Olivares and Kennedy escorted invited dignitaries and reporters to the chapel, or "old church," for the conference.[109] Still hooded, the refugee families also attended, but did not speak. Olivares opened the press conference by noting the importance of declaring sanctuary and the poor conditions of the refugees as they arrived in Los Angeles. But he also raised the political implications of La Placita's action. "These are the kind of issues we can't be silent about," he said. "We are moved by the conviction that whatever you do—be it nothing, something privately or something publicly—you are taking a political position. And clearly, this is part of the Church's right to attempt to impact the political position of the government. It also forestalls accusations that we are being conspiratorial—any action taken, by us or the government, will not go unnoticed."[110] He stated that the church had decided to go public on sanctuary at this time because "staying quiet about this does not address the root causes of the problem, which is American backing for the death squads waging war in El Salvador and Guatemala."[111] He went on to say that his Mexican parishioners were completely in support of sanctuary.[112] When asked what would happen if the INS attempted to go into La Placita to round up the refugees, Olivares responded that he did not think this would happen since it had not occurred over the last few years. Moreover, any such intervention would result in a public outcry against immigration officials. "There's always the risk there may be consequences to our providing public sanctuary," he conceded, but "any reaction or harassment that the INS might attempt would draw public reaction."[113] Moreover, before the INS could enter the church they would have to show a search warrant. Olivares concluded his part of the press conference by asserting that La Placita would remain a sanctuary until the conditions in Central America that caused the refugee exodus ceased. "We have put no time limit on sanctuary and it will remain as such until the conflicts in Central American come to an end."[114] Kennedy added that the INS had never interfered with El Centro's activities or made any arrests of refugees at La Placita.[115]

The news conference proved to be only one facet of what was a media event around the proclamation of sanctuary. Olivares transferred what he had learned from UNO about using the media to La Placita and the sanctuary movement. He knew that if the media did not cover the event then it might as well not have happened. Olivares was playing to a larger audience in Los Angeles, and he meant to reach it through the media. This meant not only the print media, but especially television, both English- and Spanish-language. He needed English-speaking Angelinos to know what sanctuary entailed and to gain support from them, but he was likewise alerting the Anglo/white-male establishment that he and the sanctuary movement out of La Placita was a player in city politics and that the needs of the refugees and, indirectly, undocumented Mexican immigrants had to be dealt with, and this included his peers in the Catholic Church including Archbishop Mahony. Spanish-language TV, by contrast, connected Olivares to his natural constituency including the thousands of other Central American refugees who lived in different parts of the city and whom he could not accommodate at La Placita, but whom he wanted to reach and inform where they could get assistance and what groups provided this. Latino support only strengthened the cause. The media, especially television, was thus the vehicle to achieve these goals and Olivares became a master in utilizing it. This is why December 12 was very much not just a religious event; it was a media event, as almost every print, radio, and television outlet covered it, and Olivares and his staff especially accommodated them such as allowing early entry into the church for the TV cameras to set up. Moreover, Olivares and Kennedy deliberately timed the Mass and press conference to take place between nine in the morning and twelve noon, to make sure they got TV coverage in the news broadcasts that evening and print coverage that next morning.[116] "It was like a national event," Kennedy said with respect to the media coverage.[117] In fact, media outside Los Angeles, primarily print media, carried stories about the event. Teresa Garza remembers that it appeared in the San Antonio papers as well as on radio and television.[118] The sanctuary story at La Placita even was reported in European countries such as Germany and Italy, as well as in Mexico and Latin America.[119]

Olivares knew the media and its hunger for news, and he used this to insure that December 12, 1985, became a media event as it indeed was.

But it was not just Olivares who played the media; so, too, did the INS, although not as effectively as the pastor of La Placita. In a battle of news conferences, INS regional commissioner Harold Ezell held his conference later that day following the declaration of sanctuary. He called the sanctuary movement "a Trojan horse that held within it persons whose agenda is to change the foreign policy of the United States" and criticized the declaration as "a contrived media event." Ezell's strategy appeared to be to discredit Olivares and the sanctuary movement in Los Angeles at one level by repeating the Reagan administration's line that the refugees were not legitimate political refugees, but "illegal aliens" who entered for economic reasons. However, he also intended to expose that the real motives of Olivares and his supporters had to do with their political intend to attack the Reagan administration. For Ezell, the sanctuary movement was composed more of anti-Reaganites than true supporters of the refugees. He hoped that the media would convey his point that Olivares was a hypocrite. At the same time, Ezell said that the INS had no immediate plans against La Placita unless it became involved in the actual smuggling of the Central Americans. "It is not agency policy to enter churches or residencies looking for illegal aliens," he told the press. What he did not tell the press was that such raids, especially if conducted in a Catholic church, would backfire against the INS and produce much negative reaction. Ezell was not about to do this. He would wage war against Olivares instead, in the media and by applying pressure on Archbishop Mahony to rein in Olivares and Kennedy.[120]

The declaration of sanctuary likewise brought forth both negative and positive reactions among parishioners and others in attendance, though it appears that most parishioners of La Placita supported it.[121] Still, some opposing voices did surface before and after the event. Henry Olivares heard rumors about his brother that he was "blowing his own horn"; that he wanted to be better than the Pope; and that he wanted people to notice him.[122] However, the most controversial opposition to Olivares took the form of a flyer that anonymously circulated before December 12, and perhaps after as well. The anonymous nature of the document makes it impossible to know whether these were parishioners, though the flyer is written to suggest that it represented the feelings of some parishioners. It was controversial in that it essentially threw the feast day of Our Lady of Guadalupe at Olivares's face. It countered his use of her feast day to support sanctuary by alleging that Guadalupe did not support it because it was an attempt to politicize her day. It was a battle of two Guadalupes. In the flyer, which included an image of Guadalupe, the authors appealed to La Virgén to help in the removal of Olivares and his group:

> Help us to get rid of Olivares and his gang of "guerrilleros" who disturb our faith and separate us from you, who destroy our families with envy and conflicts, who foment violence and destruction, and who use your church to achieve their perverse goals. Dear Mother hear our prayers and banish from here Olivares so there can be peace in La Placita church. Please help us in ridding ourselves of those priests and nuns who bring us pain and suffering with their false ideals.

In an innovative narrative, the flyer went on to include Guadalupe's voice as if she were speaking to the readers of the document. "On this my feast day of December 12, 1985, my children," the alleged voice of Guadalupe reads, "who are the images of Juan Diego, I ask you to defend and protect our faith from false priests and nuns who use my name and image as political instruments for perverse causes against our Catholic traditions." The voice of Guadalupe, besides addressing Mexican Catholics, also appeals to the Central Americans by saying that she, too, wants to love and protect them, but that she will not be used as an image of war, hatred, and violence. She goes on to instruct the people to contact Fr. Ferrante, the Claretian Provincial, and to tell him to oppose the actions of "Father Olivares and his gang." However, if Ferrante did not accede to their demands, then she further instructs them to go directly to Archbishop Mahony. She concludes by saying that from Heaven, she blesses her children and that she will continue to protect them, but they in turn cannot allow atrocities to occur in her church, La Placita, which is a house of prayer. The flyer concludes by telling readers to circulate it to others.[123]

Despite the creativity of this flyer, it does not appear that it successfully challenged the strong support that parishioners at La Placita and others gave to Olivares and to the declaration of sanctuary. The proof of this is that there was no major negative reaction at the church calling for an end to the sanctuary work of Olivares and Kennedy. Most seemed to agree with UFW leader, Arturo Rodríguez, who says that Olivares's declaration of sanctuary inspired many, including him, and gave them courage. He adds: "And it made us feel like, wow, all right, Father Luis, you're taking them on; you're stepping up to the plate; you're doing what everybody else should be doing. You're setting the pace here for all of us."[124]

VI

The declaration of sanctuary at La Placita introduced a new phase of the sanctuary movement that spurred on tense relations with Archbishop Mahony, with which Olivares would have to contend with for the rest of the decade. This relationship was complex and even troubling for Olivares because of his belief in the authority of the Church. Despite his "conversion" to becoming an activist priest after meeting César Chávez, he still believed in the hierarchy of the Church. As Urrabazo notes, he was trained prior to the more liberal attitudes released within the Church by the Second Vatican Council. "Luis was not a young radical priest," he observes. Although Olivares accepted many of the new winds of change, at least in the first phase of his priesthood, he was part of the Claretian establishment, a good company man. As a result, Olivares respected and accepted the authority of Archbishop Mahony. However, as part of his conversion, Olivares more and more focused on the nature of that authority. What was the purpose of that authority? Was it being abused to stifle progressive change? Was it being put in support of God's children? Olivares accepted that power and authority lay with the Church hierarchy and with Mahony as the head of the archdioceses. This was a structural authority that he believed in. However, in his own evolution as a liberationist, Olivares drew the line on the context of that authority. What did it authorize, or better still, what did it not authorize? "Luis had tremendous respect for authority," Urrabazo comments, but "because he had that respect he felt it was important to challenge it at times when he felt enough was not being done." He believed that authority should be used at the service of the people. Olivares was not anti-authority. His first allegiance was to the Church. Urrabazo remembers Olivares reflecting on this: "The [Claretian] order made me who I am. I'm nobody. The order is who I am. I am the order." He could not imagine himself as anything other than a priest.[125]

As a priest, Olivares accepted the Church's authority and believed he could work within it.[126] However, he increasingly redefined what authority meant. Was authority just to be a "yes man," as he had been during the first phase of his priesthood including while he was treasurer of his order? This redefinition of authority Olivares clearly asserted when he stated:

> I think there's a general approach to authority on the part of the Church that translates into control. Authority means control. I have a very different approach to authority, and I act accordingly. My approach is from the roots of author, that authority is initiating, encouraging, promoting, supporting, and in a sense being able at times to let go so that things can move. You don't have to be in control. Not every good idea has to come from you. Many times people have found themselves in their relationship to their bishop playing a little game, making them think that this idea is coming from them and that you're just going to play it out. I think that's very prevalent. It stifles creativity, and that's when conflicts develop.[127]

Olivares accepted hierarchical authority, but only if it was used for the good of the Church. He defined Church as Vatican II had redefined it, as the people and not just the clergy. As a liberationist, Olivares knew that too often in the case of the Latin American Church, for example, the Church had used its authority in support of the elite who repressed the people. This was not the kind of authority that Olivares now accepted. If the Church was not using its power and influence to assist the poor and the oppressed, then it was abusing its authority that came from God. For Olivares, God was the ultimate authority and a Church based on the Gospel and the example of Jesus had to pursue the Gospel message of prioritizing its mission to the poor and oppressed. Olivares grappled with this and it defined his relationship with his archbishop. Parishioner Araceli Espinosa recalls Olivares once saying in a homily that it was a fine line between obeying your superior and doing what you feel is right and being true to your convictions.[128]

In assessing his relationship with Mahony, Olivares soon realized that the archbishop was a political animal. One did not rise to become archbishop without being political, both within the Church and outside of it. César Chávez, who had relationships with both priests, sensed that Mahony was a different kind of priest whose ambition superseded everything else. He was not César's kind of priest. The Rev. Chris Hartmire observes that, with Mahony, Chávez "didn't have the same natural click that he did with Luis."[129] Of course, Olivares himself had become a political animal and perhaps he had always been so such as when he served as treasurer. The Catholic Church as an institution was not devoid of politics, nor were its leaders and clergy. Olivares realized that Mahony was going to be a much stronger figure than his predecessor Cardinal Manning and that he would have to deal with the new archbishop much more. He accepted that they would not always be in agreement, but that he had no other choice. He accepted the tensions with the archbishop and continued his work.[130]

Part of the tensions between Olivares and Mahony had to do with a rivalry that came to characterize their relationship. How much of this was real and how much of it was manufactured, especially by the media, is debated. It is probably the case that the rivalry was more of Mahony's doing, but one cannot escape the possibility that, given Olivares's own strong leadership, he also felt some sense of competition with the archbishop. Both had egos and both had strong personalities, although Olivares was much more charismatic than Mahony; charisma is not a word often linked with Mahony. Kennedy observes that what rivalry existed was both personal and political. The two had a professional relationship but not much of a personal one. They were friendly and respectful of each other but not friends.[131] By all accounts, despite what differences he came to have with Mahony, Olivares never publicly criticized or spoke badly about the archbishop. The same was true of Mahony. Moreover, in private conversations with other clergy and sanctuary activists, Olivares seems to never have spoken ill about Mahony. What they might have thought about each other in their own minds, history cannot reveal.

One aspect of the rivalry had to do with tension over perceived dual authorities. Mahony seemed to believe that Olivares represented a challenge to his authority in his actions, but also because of the public attention that the Claretian received. As far as Mahony was concerned, there could not be two leaders of the archdiocese. Fr. Luis Quihuis had the impression that Mahony felt that there could only be one "King" of the Church in Los Angeles.[132] Labor leader Jimmy Rodríguez says that he heard that Mahony was not happy because he felt that Olivares was "shadowing" his image and because Olivares was seen as the champion of workers and immigrants in Southern California, despite the fact that Mahony had championed the farmworkers' struggle. "Roger was a little concerned about all this attention that Father Olivares and La Placita was getting," Rodríguez says of the archbishop.[133] Richard Estrada unequivocally claims that Mahony was jealous of Olivares. "'I'm the leader,'" Estrada says about the archbishop's feelings.[134] After he left La Placita, Olivares told Juan Romero that he had felt that Mahony was jealous of him because he felt that Olivares was acting as if he was the head of the Church. "Whose Church is it anyway?" Olivares believed Mahony said.[135]

The rivalry was not helped by the role of the media. Elements of both the English- and Spanish-language media seemed to relish promoting this rivalry image by contrasting the two priests. The LA Weekly, for example, printed an article with a lead-in that read: "Whose Church will it be: Mahony's or Olivares'?" Despite the fact that Olivares considered this a misguided conclusion, the article did not sit well with the archbishop.[136] Some of the media liked to promote Olivares as a counter-leader to Mahony including one Spanish-language newspaper that referred to Olivares as the true bishop of Los Angeles. This, of course, also was not well received by Mahony.[137] Even the Los Angeles Times played up the rivalry when it once referred to Olivares as the archbishop for Latinos. Olivares, according to Lozano, just laughed this off, but not Mahony.[138] This media coverage made the archbishop believe that he was not getting as much, or as good, media coverage as Olivares. All this only increased tensions that apparently, on one occasion during a meeting between the two, resulted in the archbishop revealing some of his resentment when he asked Olivares, "Luis, do you have to call a press conference or call CBS every time you brush your teeth?"

"No, Your Excellency, not every time," Olivares responded.[139]

These tensions were only exacerbated by the question of the leadership of Latino Catholics in Los Angeles. Mahony had arrived after serving many Latinos in the Central Valley. He returned to Los Angeles, his hometown, prepared to become the leader of Latino Catholics, who were then already becoming the largest percentage of Catholics in the archdiocese. However, upon arrival, he discovered this charismatic Latino pastor, Olivares, who was already perceived by many Latino Catholics as their leader. Susan Alva believes that Mahony saw himself as the "savior of el pueblo" (the savior of the Latino community).[140] Olivares had been championing Latino causes since his work with the UFW and UNO. He was not going to relinquish this leadership role to advance the interests of Latinos to someone else, not even his archbishop.

This rivalry was more covert than overt. They shared a general agreement on supporting Latinos including refugees and immigrants, but differed on the best strategies to do so. This was clearly revealed during the declaration of sanctuary. In part this had to do with both having different constituencies. Olivares catered to his predominantly Latino parishioners including the refugees and immigrants. Mahony also catered to Latino Catholics, but he also had many other Catholics to deal with, many of them white parishioners who did not share his support for refugees and immigrants. Moreover, as archbishop, Mahony was considered part of the elite leadership in the city, and this group asserted much pressure on him to not transform the Church into a "radical" Church, and certainly not one that confronted the law and the Reagan administration. This was not the image of Los Angeles that the elites, both Protestant and Catholic, wished to project. Finally, the archbishop had to deal with the INS and the Reagan administration about what to do about the refugees and sanctuary and the pressure not to allow Olivares to continue to challenge the law and U.S. policies toward the refugees and Central America.

Despite these developing tensions and rivalry, Olivares had to try as best he could to work with Mahony. But it wasn't always easy. It hadn't started this way. Lydia López recalls that, shortly after Mahony became archbishop, he sometimes visited Olivares at La Placita and had coffee. On at least one occasion they went to the movies together.[141] However, the issue of declaring sanctuary negatively impacted the relationship. Mahony not only disagreed with public sanctuary, but he also did not like some of what was happening at La Placita. He especially did not care for Olivares allowing the refugees and others to sleep inside the church. Mahony and his advisors did not want smelly men sleeping in the pews. This also troubled the Olvera Street merchants, who made their feelings known to the archdiocese.[142] However, Mahony's diplomatic style was not to confront Olivares on this, even though it seems to have troubled him. Following their differences over sanctuary at La Placita and Olivares's further efforts to expand sanctuary (see chapter 10), both men came to an informal accord to agree to disagree. Clearly, they did not agree on going public on sanctuary. They disagreed about how best to support the refugees and what might be the best strategy. Moreover, Olivares wanted to go further in not only assisting the Central American refugees, but also to reach out to undocumented Mexican immigrants. Mahony also believed that whatever strategy would be used had to abide by U.S. laws on refugees and undocumented immigrants. By contrast, Olivares believed that sometimes if the law was unjust, he and the Church, for that matter, were bound by a higher moral standard. According to Clements, Olivares did not want to defy his archbishop, but at the same time, he was not going to back off simply because Mahony disagreed with him.[143] Despite these differences, both men did not want to openly have a rupture, and so they in effect agreed to disagree although this was not always possible. "I understand what you're doing," Mahony told Olivares, "and I see that you have to do what you have to do, but don't expect me to be right there on every issue that you get involved in."[144]

For his part, Olivares's approach to working with Mahony and the archdiocese, given the tensions, was to try to circumvent the archbishop. In other words, he would continue to follow his conscience and to do what he felt he had to do on the refugee and immigrant issues as well as on his opposition to Reagan's policies toward Central America. He did not feel that he had to check with Mahony or the archdiocese on these matters. The fact was, as Anderson-Barker observes, that Olivares did not have and would not have a relationship with Mahony where he could just call up and discuss issues with him and ask for support.[145] As long as no one blew the whistle on him, he would follow his own strategy and even if the whistle was blown, he still had to deal with what he believed was the moral thing to do. This was not necessarily an easy situation for him. Olivares was a very sensitive person who respected others and tried to always deal with people in a courteous way. He was not by nature confrontational and an "in-your-face" person. Because of his sensitivity, he wanted to be accepted and even loved by others. It pained him to have tense relations with his archbishop. Lydia López notes that the tensions with Mahony bothered Olivares privately but he would not talk about it publicly.[146] Olivares made it clear to Fr. George Regas that he did not feel that Mahony was really supportive of the kind of ministry (what Regas calls a radical ministry) that he was pursuing. "I remember the distresses that Archbishop Mahony brought to him," Regas says.[147]

In a confessional moment shortly before his death, Olivares told Denis Heyck, during her interview with him, that perhaps his approach and attitude toward Mahony was not the right one. This did not mean that he would not have done what he did at La Placita, but that perhaps he could have been more sensitive and understanding of the other pressures on the archbishop that affected his relations with him. "But maybe I was getting too much publicity, too," he said. "Every time the archbishop turned around, there was Olivares in the news. . . . We had a good relationship on a personal level, but there was on my part a lack of understanding that regardless of what was going on, he's the boss, and he will always be the boss, and there's no getting around that. I can't knock him of his position as the boss. This has to sink in. But, at the same time, I wasn't going to let that stifle what I felt I had to do."[148]

But Mahony sometimes was also not as diplomatic as he might have been. On one occasion when he organized a meeting of business people on immigration issues that included Olivares, Mahony, for whatever reason, started the meeting by saying: "Well, whose meeting is this? Olivares's or Mahony's?"

Olivares responded: "It's your meeting."[149]

Whether both men could have been more diplomatic or not, the fact is that, to his credit, Mahony always left an opening for Olivares to follow through on his programs. Despite the Church bureaucracy, Mahony exhibited some flexibility in dealing with the clergy, including Olivares. He had his reservations about public sanctuary, but he did not forbid Olivares from going through with it. "I'll give Mahony credit," Kennedy opines. "He never tried to stop Luis with respect to declaring sanctuary."[150] Fr. Cully agrees with this and suggests—although this can certainly be debated—that the Church was big enough to allow clergy to be socially active without being punished for it as long as this was within the umbrella of the Church. He believes that Olivares understood this, and it gave him a sense that he could work within the institution. "I think probably that Luis appreciated more than any of us," he says, "that the archbishop sometimes didn't say or do things that were real supportive, but he left a lot of room for things to be done. Luis could joke or tease, but I think he was pretty pleased with Archbishop Mahony's flexibility."[151]

Overall, it may be that the tensions and rivalry between Olivares and Mahony were exaggerated. There is no question that these feelings and conditions existed, but it went with the territory. Any clergy who would engage in activist politics on controversial issues such as sanctuary and undocumented immigrants—which involved not only local politics, but national and even international politics—was going to run into difficulties within the Church. Olivares understood this, but was never daunted or intimidated by it. Would he have preferred a more supportive archbishop? Of course. But, on the other hand, it wasn't like he was dealing with a right-wing reactionary, as Católicos por La Raza did with Cardinal McIntyre. Mahony was not a liberationist like Olivares, but he was a liberal within the Church and on national politics. He supported the refugees and undocumented immigrants, but was not willing to go as far as Olivares in directly challenging the law. He also visited El Salvador and took with him a vast amount of medical supplies.[152] Because he was not a reactionary, he allowed some space for Olivares to pursue his own refugee program. Where Mahony drew the line was on the actual defiance of the law, and this would come into play when Olivares decided to extend sanctuary (see chapter 10). There is no question that the Olivares-Mahony drama is very much a part of Olivares's story in the 1980s; however, it did not consume him. He put it in perspective. Mike Kennedy puts it well when he says he didn't feel sorry about Luis's issues with Mahony and comments about this relationship:

Did he [Olivares] feel sad sometimes? Yes. Did he feel alone some-times? Yes. But then Luis would go with others to La Fonda and hear the mariachis. He didn't dwell on his relationship with Mahony. Could it have been better? Yes. But then there's also good mariachis at La Fonda. Luis's relationship with Mahony doesn't have a lot of weight on Luis's history. We didn't talk about it. He wasn't a negative person. He was too busy in his work to focus on the negative. Luis didn't get bogged down on trivia.[153]

Fr. Lozano agrees with Kennedy and notes that Olivares was going in one direction, and Mahony as the "CEO" of the Church, in another, more cautious direction. Olivares accepted this and went on with his own work. "I think Luis just felt 'I'm going to do what I need to do,'" Lozano suggests. "We'll let the cards fall where they may."[154] Urrabazo remembers Olivares saying: "The Archbishop isn't going to like this but who cares."[155] Richard Estrada puts it even more bluntly about Olivares's relations with the arch-bishop: "It got to the point where he didn't give a damn. He would say what he felt and that made him more loveable with lots of people."[156]

VII

The declaration of sanctuary at La Placita on December 12, 1985, repre-sented perhaps the most important part of Luis Olivares's life. He had been evolving in his role as a priest to the point that for him being a priest had everything to do with a full commitment to working with the poor and oppressed. Working with the farmworkers began this process. His role in UNO advanced it. However, the pinnacle of his ministry was the sanctuary movement. In declaring public sanctuary, he was not only publicly em-bracing the refugees, he was giving his own public testimony about who he was and what he was all about. Declaring sanctuary defined Luis Oli-vares. This was the priest that Abuelita Inez and Tía Concha and his family wanted him to be—a priest who would serve his people and sacrifice for them, as they tried to do for the Mexican American community in west San Antonio. It was also a way to put all of his seminary training to work for the people. December 12, 1985, was a culmination of all of this, but it was not the end. Olivares knew even then that the struggle had to continue, and part of it was to extend sanctuary to undocumented Mexican immigrants. He was ready to move on to this next phase.

TEN

Expanding Sanctuary

In the 1970s and into the 1980s, headlines in newspapers and magazines read "Illegal Invasion." These headlines were not referring to the Central American refugees, but to undocumented Mexican immigrants, whom many referred to as "illegal aliens." While the migration of Central American refugees into Los Angeles and elsewhere in the United States captured media and political attention in the 1980s, the reality also was that an even larger migration was still occurring: undocumented workers from Mexico. This movement had been noticeable and already a contentious issue in the 1970s and would continue to be so into the new decade. Thousands of Mexicans without papers continued to stream across the border, seeking jobs and economic security for their families. Mexicans were pushed out by a Mexican economy affected by globalization that simply did not provide enough good-paying jobs for its people. In addition, the peso devaluation and rising prices in the early 1980s made life even harder. Border industries on the Mexican side—*maquiladoras*—favored only hiring single young women and hence men and those with families were left out of these jobs and had no recourse but to cross the border. The pull on the U.S. side had to do with a continued appetite for cheap Mexican labor that had its roots as far back as the early twentieth century, when large-scale immigration from Mexico commenced. In the 1980s it was no longer the railroads and mines that coveted this source of labor; it was agribusiness looking for farm labor and, increasingly, urban service jobs needed to accommodate the needs of the new postindustrial economy that favored service jobs over industrial ones, many having been transferred to developing Third World countries as part of the new global economy. Immigrant workers, especially from Mexico, were coveted as domestics, nannies, gardeners, car-washers, restaurant and hotel workers, and low-skilled construction workers to build new suburban and high-rise residencies for educated and skilled new high-tech professionals and those in the world of international finance and related industries. As the undocumented arrived into Los Angeles, Fr. Luis Olivares reached out to them, as he had to the Central Americans.

I

Olivares was very much aware of this movement. In fact, at the same time that he began to assist and shelter the Central American refugees shortly after arriving at La Placita, he was doing the same for the undocumented Mexicans. The refugees received the most media attention. Olivares had likewise dealt with the issue of undocumented immigration earlier, in UNO, although it was not an action item for the organization. In PADRES, he had called attention to the plight of the undocumented. Olivares was further aware of the growing nativism against "illegal aliens" and accompanying efforts to pass state and federal legislation to address this growing flow of people across the border. Some of this legislation would punish the undocumented for simply trying to survive. Moreover, immigration officials continued their policies of arresting and deporting thousands of undocumented immigrants.[1] For his part, Olivares saw the undocumented in the same spiritual and moral perspective as the refugees: these were children of God and as such the Gospel called on Christians to embrace and assist them. No one was "illegal" in the eyes of God. The Central American refugee issue took much of Olivares's attention and time, but he was also fully aware that La Placita had to also reach out to the undocumented Mexican immigrants. This became even more the case when, in 1986, the U.S. Congress passed and President Reagan signed a new immigration law aimed at dealing with undocumented immigrants.

Beginning in the 1970s, the U.S. Congress wrestled with legislation that would control undocumented immigration. A bill sponsored by Representative Peter Rodino, a Democrat from New Jersey, and referred to as the Rodino Bill focused on the imposition of penalties or sanctions on employers for knowingly hiring undocumented workers. Rodino failed to pass the bill due to opposition by immigrant rights groups, including Chicano ones such as La Hermandad Mexicana Nacional led by longtime community leader, Bert Corona. He and others argued that such employer sanctions would discriminate against the hiring of all Latinos, even U.S. citizens, by employers who would not hire any Latinos at all to avoid the risk of fines.[2] Instead, these groups called for providing some path toward legalization for the undocumented. In the early 1980s, a bipartisan bill sponsored by Senator Alan Simpson, Republican from Wyoming, and Representative Romano Mazzoli, Democrat from Kentucky, tried to find compromise with both sides of the immigration debate by combining employer sanctions with "amnesty" for those undocumented immigrants who had been living and working in the United States for a continuous period of time. After several years of debate, the U.S. Congress with bipartisan support passed the Simpson-Mazzoli Bill, also known as the Simpson-Rodino Bill, and President Reagan signed into law the Immigration Reform and Control Act (IRCA) on November 6, 1986. The essential core of the bill focused on the compromise between pro-amnesty politicians and the employer sanctions ones.[3] The amnesty provision involved the opportunity for undocumented immigrants who could prove that they had been living and working in the country for several years prior to January 1, 1982, to begin the process of legalizing themselves and obtaining work permits or "green cards." The period to sign up for amnesty went from May 5, 1987, to May 4, 1988. On employer sanctions, the bill provided financial penalties from $250 to $10,000 for each undocumented worker hired by an employer. Moreover, employers would have to certify that they had checked about an employee's legal status by asking for documentation and had to fill out a I-9 form, keep it on file, and make it available to the INS if asked to do so. This would only involve workers hired since the passage of IRCA. Workers seeking jobs since the passage of the law would now have to provide evidence of citizenship or legal residence.[4]

Olivares and immigrant rights groups, while welcoming the amnesty provisions of IRCA, expressed reservations on various grounds. The first had to do with the law's exclusion of millions who did not qualify for amnesty, because many of the 11 million undocumented immigrants had arrived in the United States after the cutoff date of 1982. Not meeting this deadline, they still could be deported.[5] Indeed, some were already being deported even as the law was enacted. "What we are seeing is exactly what we predicted," Olivares said at a news conference in 1987, "and that is the negative implications of this law that further justifies mass deportations. We had warned about this and our worst fears are being realized."[6] The fact was, as *La Opinión* pointed out, that the undocumented were not going anywhere, despite the lack of amnesty. They were in the country working, and they were not going to return to Mexico, despite the threat of deportation. In the meantime, they would remain in a state of limbo wondering if amnesty might still be extended to them. "The immigrants are here," the Spanish-language newspaper stressed, "and what is needed is to help them integrate in a productive manner."[7] Olivares and other Catholic clerics throughout the country called for a change in the law, or at least greater flexibility so that many of those not included under the amnesty provision could also be legalized.[8] In East Los Angeles, according to one news source, many did not greet the law favorably, since many of those without documents feared that they would not be included. "Many feel they won't qualify for amnesty," Fr. Dick Howard pointed out about the barrios.[9] To his credit, Archbishop Mahony expressed concerns about the deadline and thought that many would not be eligible for amnesty. He stated that the archdiocese would stand by the thousands who would not qualify, and he called for an end to deportation sweeps conducted by the Border Patrol.[10]

Olivares in particular objected to the employer sanctions provision of the law. He, like other immigration-rights advocates, believed that employers would refuse to hire undocumented workers and thus negatively impacting their opportunities to help their families. But he also believed, along with others, that a secondary effect of the provision would be to discriminate against U.S.-born Latinos. Olivares had no love for those employers who exploited undocumented workers, but his opposition to employer sanctions had nothing to do with supporting employers. He opposed it for the harm it would do to the workers.[11] Workers had a moral right to work and on this basis, Olivares likewise opposed the provision. "This is why we condemn employer sanctions and the INS's employee-verification protocol as immoral in their intent to deprive so many of their God-given right to work," Olivares wrote in an opinion piece for the *Los Angeles Times*, coauthored with Mike Kennedy and Greg Boyle.[12]

The *Times* substantiated some of this discrimination when it wrote a story concerning Noemi Romo, an undocumented immigrant who qualified for amnesty, but was fired by her boss at a uniform sales firm in the City of Industry because she did not have a work permit or green card. Romo was pregnant with her first child. However, she was fired illegally, the paper noted, because of a provision in the new law that did not penalize employers for undocumented workers hired before the enactment of the law in November 1986. Romo subsequently filed for amnesty and was given her green card. Many others in the same position as Romo probably were also illegally fired.[13] Moreover, Olivares and Kennedy expressed concerns that those undocumented workers who petitioned for amnesty but denied it would also be dismissed by their employers. An additional worry had to do with employers using the law to further exploit and cheat their undocumented workers by paying them even less and threatening to denounce them to the INS if they did not accept such wages.[14]

Olivares further recognized another fault of the law. Some family members might qualify for amnesty while others might not. What would happen then? Family separation was unacceptable, and this major problem with IRCA had to be rectified. No family, even if undocumented, should be torn apart. Other Catholic priests likewise protested this issue. The *Washington Post* reported that a group of Roman Catholic priests and nuns vowed not to comply with the law not only because it discriminated against the hiring of undocumented workers, but also because it would split families "when only one member qualifies for amnesty."[15] *La Opinión* seconded this opposition, especially about the impact the law would have on some families. In an editorial, it noted that at first it had held great hopes for the Simpson-Mazzoli Bill because it would help to legalize many undocumented. However, it had come to realize that, despite its amnesty provision, the law would continue deportations and possibly even increase them. Its greatest fear had to do with the deportation of some family members and not others. "It is possible that within one family the father and one or two of the sons might qualify for legalization, but not the mother and the youngest child. What good will it do for one of the parents to qualify for amnesty if the rest of the family can't?" The paper called for a modification of the bill to allow exemptions for family members who did not qualify to be given provisional permission to remain in the country and to avoid family separations.[16] Such a provision was not included in the law, and Olivares and others called for a Family Unification amendment to IRCA.

Not only would IRCA not cover millions of Mexican undocumented immigrants, but it excluded the large majority of Central American refugees who entered the country after 1982. Between one-half and two-thirds of the nearly one million Salvadorans in the United States, for example, did not qualify for amnesty. Of course, very few, as noted, received political refugee status. Linton Joaquín, an immigration lawyer, observed that the law completely ignored the Central Americans and that 80 percent of both Salvadorans and Guatemalans did not qualify, since they had arrived after 1982. Both Olivares and Kennedy likewise called for the Central Americans to be considered for amnesty not only on political grounds, but on moral ones in that the law violated the human rights of the Central Americans to work in order to survive. At a minimum, the *Los Angeles Times* proposed, the refugees should be given a temporary stay until the Central American civil wars abated, and the newspaper supported legislation in the U.S. Congress to do just this.[17]

For these key reasons, Olivares and other immigrant rights advocates opposed first the Simpson-Mazzoli bill and then the IRCA, when it was enacted. This moral-intellectual opposition, at least on the part of Olivares, had to also be put into practical action, which he did.

II

Olivares, of course, expressed concerns about the rights of the undocumented Mexican immigrants even before IRCA. Besides also sheltering them at La Placita as well as extending some of the other assistance provided to Central American refugees, Olivares alerted the undocumented to their rights. Despite their lack of documents, they still were covered under the U.S. Constitution, which extends protection to people residing in the country and not just citizens. In a 1984 church bulletin, Olivares inserted a section with the heading "Conozcán Sus Derechos" (Know Your Rights).[18]

But it was one thing to inform the undocumented about their rights, it was another thing to take action to confront the new immigration law. Within a few months of IRCA becoming law and being implemented, Olivares, in consultation with his team at La Placita and others, decided to openly defy it, particularly the employer sanctions provision that would harm both the immigrants and the U.S.-born Latinos. On September 11, 1987, Olivares and fifty-two other Catholic priests went right at employer sanctions by calling on all Americans to violate the new law by hiring workers without inquiring about their status. At a news conference at St. Camillus De Lellis Church in Lincoln Heights, the group stated that the law violated basic human rights and that breaking it represented a "just response to the economic suffering and hardship" experienced by those who did not qualify for amnesty. According to the *Los Angeles Times*, this was the first time clergy had advocated violating the new law. At this news conference, Olivares astutely noted that this action was backed by the recent statements by both Pope John Paul II and Archbishop Mahony. He cited the Pope's message from that August, in which he urged authorities to halt "any possible discrimination against immigrants." He then cited Mahony's statement, from April, that the Church had "a moral obligation to respond to those in our midst who do not qualify for [the law's] amnesty provisions." Then, reading from a prepared statement signed by thirty-eight priests, nuns, and laypeople, Olivares added:

> The Lord's command is clear. In the book of Leviticus, God says, "When aliens reside with you in your land . . . you shall treat them no differently than the natives born among you."
> In the light of the Gospel's call to justice, we find ourselves unable

Fr. Luis Olivares with Fr. Mike Kennedy (left) and masked Salvadoran undocumented immigrant at press conference announcing that they and other priests have signed a pledge to hire undocumented immigrants, September 24, 1987. (Courtesy of the Archival Center/TIDINGS Photo Collection, Archdiocese of Los Angeles)

to comply with the current regulations regarding the hiring of un-documented workers.

Today, we stand with these people. . . . Therefore, we commit our-selves: To hire workers regardless of their legal status.

To seek employment for non-qualifying workers by encouraging employers to hire the undocumented.

To feed, clothe and house those rejected by the law.

To call on other congregations and church leaders to respond in similar ways. We challenge the American people to acknowledge that the law, itself, is in violation of human rights, and we encourage them to respond to the needs of the undocumented with justice and com-passion.[19]

To stress his commitment to defying IRCA, Olivares openly admitted that he, himself, along with the other fifty-two priests, had already broken the law by hiring undocumented workers at La Placita and other churches without inquiring about their status. Olivares further stressed that the law had already caused much fear and tension in the Latino community.[20]

Not all agreed with La Placita's pastor. Olivares received a letter from an Ethel Pehrson from Los Angeles who strongly disagreed with assisting the immigrants:

As we see these awful changes largely brought about by the uncontrolled immigration south of our boarders [sic] by the poverty-stricken proliferating Latinos we understand what has resulted as a consequence of a past mistaken policy of the Mexican government aided and abetted by the Catholic Church whose pope on every visit to a third world country tell [sic] these poor, ignorant people to be fruitful and multiply. Apparently the church is desperate for members. . . . Since you are not stupid, you priests, you are either self-deluding, or lacking in integrity by inflicting your policies on an already suffering world. The Catholic Curch [sic] has much to answer for—historically, when she excommunicated and burned at the stake for declaring that the world was round, and now currently as it rigidly holds to its stance on birth control. In the past, overpopulation has been controlled by pestilence, famine, and war. Is this what your church prefers as a way of birth control?[21]

III

It is not clear just when Olivares decided to further oppose IRCA by expanding sanctuary at La Placita to include undocumented Mexican workers. Declaring sanctuary for the Central American refugees was a bold and dramatic move and had helped to publicize the plight of the refugees. He believed that he had to do the same for the undocumented. By 1987 he began to lay the grounds for this unprecedented action. None of the other sanctuary movements in the country had expanded sanctuary for the undocumented Mexicans. La Placita would be the first. Olivares no doubt welcomed being the first to do so. He believed in taking on new and challenging positions and actions. It raised the stakes of confronting authority, especially that of the Reagan administration. It was oppositional enough to defy the administration's position on the refugees, but it would be even more defiant to openly break the law by rejecting IRCA. Olivares raised the stakes by not only providing sanctuary for the undocumented, which would only involve a small number, but by publicly calling for others to defy the employer sanctions provisions and hire the undocumented as he was doing. He apparently hired, at one point, twenty undocumented immigrants for various tasks around the church and paid them cash so there would be no record.[22] This was an act of even greater resistance to a law that he believed was unjust and un-Christian. He knew that this action would bring on even more reaction by the INS, as well as a greater confrontation with Archbishop Mahony. The risks were high, but Olivares had already shown that such reactions would not deter him in carrying out what he believed was the right thing to do.[23]

But first he had to prepare for announcing the expansion of sanctuary. He decided that he would do so on the second anniversary of his declaration of sanctuary for the refugees, and so again chose the feast day of Our Lady of Guadalupe on December 12. He would once again wrap his declaration with the mantle of Our Lady who protected her children, especially the poor and oppressed. The groundwork began by his continuing to speak out against the damages that IRCA would cause and was already causing to the thousands who would not qualify for amnesty and the discrimination employers would exhibit in not hiring Latino workers to avoid the sanctions. He partnered with Democratic congressman Howard Berman of Los Angeles in organizing public hearings on IRCA in the city. He spoke to other church groups and on some campuses. Araceli Espinosa, at that time a freshman at Loyola Marymount University, a Jesuit school that had symbolically declared itself a sanctuary, recalls with great pride that she had been able to get Fr. Luis, her pastor, to speak on her campus about IRCA and the plight of the refugees and the undocumented. "Hey, I know this great person who can speak on sanctuary," she told others on campus. They enthusiastically agreed to sponsor Olivares to speak, and Araceli considers it one of the proudest moments of her life when she introduced Fr. Luis, the priest she had known since she was a young school girl. Olivares apparently also briefed his fellow Claretians on his intentions and, according to Fr. Ferrante, he received nothing but support for expanding sanctuary.[24]

Knowing that he would have to contend with Mahony, Olivares began communicating with the archbishop, at first not about expanding sanctuary, but about his support for Mahony's welcomed statements regarding the Church's concern for those who were not covered by amnesty. In a way, Olivares was attempting to heal some of the tension that had developed between the two over La Placita's declaration of sanctuary for the refugees. It may also have been, and likely was, a political move by Olivares to "soften up" Mahony for the expansion that would be accompanied by breaking the law. Noting that the archbishop would be meeting with INS Commissioner Harold Ezell over IRCA, Olivares wrote a note in June 1987 to

Mahony to try to get him to support Olivares and others who had already declared their opposition to the law. He attempted to do this by referencing again Mahony's statement on IRCA. "I have called to try to talk to you about this but without success," he wrote. "The priests and Religious who are involved in mobilizing around your statement regarding those who will not qualify for amnesty are very anxious to insure that our actions are not seen or interpreted to be in conflict with your plans. To that end I would like to have some time with you to brief you on the strategies we are developing and to look at those instances where our actions can converge."[25] It does not seem that a meeting between Olivares and Mahony occurred, but at least Olivares had made an overture to the archbishop.

Several months later in November as plans for the expansion of sanctuary had continued, Olivares once again wrote a letter to Mahony to praise the archbishop for his work with the National Council of Catholic Bishops in securing a statement in support of the peace process in Central America. At the same time, however, he hinted at his own plans for expanding sanctuary when he wrote about the significance of the upcoming feast of Our Lady of Guadalupe. "The Feast of Our Lady of Guadalupe at La Placita," he observed, "has always been a major event spiritually, culturally and in our context of social justice; in a certain sense, also politically. Since December 12, 1985 when this church was declared [a] Public Sanctuary it has taken on a much broader ecumenical, and social significance."[26] Why Olivares did not inform Mahony of what he planned to do in a few weeks may have to do with the expectation that the archbishop would oppose the move and attempt to pressure others not to participate. This is not clear, but there is no evidence that, prior to that November, Olivares informed Mahony of his intentions, much less invite him to the event. It is, of course, possible that Mahony already knew through others of Olivares's plans, but chose not to openly confront him, at least not then.

Part of Mahony's own strategy was aimed at getting Olivares and the other clergy who had signed the statement on opposing employer sanctions to join him and the other Catholic bishops in an effort not to defy or break the law, as Olivares and the others were already doing, but to try to change the law to accommodate those undocumented who did not qualify for amnesty. Mahony's focus clearly was more on the amnesty provisions of IRCA rather than on employer sanctions. On November 22, Mahony informed Olivares that at the recent meeting of the Catholic Bishops in Washington, D.C., in addition to supporting the peace process in Central America, that he personally had raised the issue of the amnesty default in IRCA. "In addition," he wrote to Olivares,

I brought up on the floor of the Bishops' meeting the tremendous problem of the hundreds of thousands of undocumented people who do not qualify under the new legalization law. I can assure you that the interest and concern of the Bishops is outstanding, thus ensuring us great momentum in being able to move forward on a variety of fronts to help these people.

Very quickly we will be pushing strategy for a "safe haven" provision which we intend to support vigorously with the Administration and Congress.[27]

If Mahony's strategy was to get Olivares not to expand sanctuary to the undocumented, and especially to get him and others to backtrack on defying employer sanctions, it did not work. Olivares proceeded with his own plans, although not as yet declaring the expansion of sanctuary, but calling for others to not cooperate with IRCA. It is possible that he felt that he would obtain greater media attention by not announcing the expansion until the feast day. In an announcement sent to other clergy, including Protestant and Jewish ones, as well as to laypeople one day later after Mahony had written to him, Olivares informed them of the December 12 event and invited them to attend the celebration, ostensibly of the second anniversary of the declaration of sanctuary for the refugees. However, he also noted the concern over IRCA and especially the employer sanctions provision, and he informed others that enclosed with the announcement was a pledge of non-cooperation with that provision, which he encouraged them to sign and return.[28]

Having put out the word about the event at La Placita that would follow with a news conference and having distributed the pledge cards, Olivares finalized the liturgy and other related actions for December 12. In order to reflect wider support for his plans, and knowing that Mahony would once again not attend and yet wanting to have a high official of the Church celebrate the Mass with him and Kennedy, he invited the Auxiliary Bishop of San Diego, Fr. Gilbert Chávez, to participate and informed Mahony of this. Chávez, a Chicano Movement activist, accepted, and without comment Mahony gave his required approval of Olivares's invitation to Chávez.[29] In communication with Bishop Chávez, Olivares sent him material on the opposition to IRCA and also what he might say in his homily. Olivares was a hands-on person and clearly wanted to insure that Chávez would reinforce the intention for that day. At the same time, he did not want to appear to force anything on the bishop and suggested that he did not have to endorse defying the law. "It goes without saying," Olivares informed

Chávez, "that you need not feel obliged to publicly endorse all our activities, that's a choice that each one of us can make in accordance with one's consciousness. If you enunciate the position that the National Conference of Bishops has already taken for Catholic Agencies to increase their already commendable assistance to refugees in need, regardless of their standing before the law, that is already great."[30]

By late November, Olivares revealed that on December 12, in addition to reinforcing his and others' earlier position on opposing employer sanctions and instead encouraging the hiring of undocumented workers, La Placita would also expand sanctuary to these workers. He did not make as big a deal of this expansion as he had done two years earlier. La Placita was already a sanctuary church; it would now simply expand its reach. For Olivares, it is clear that his main emphasis was to defy the new law. He informed Mahony of the expansion of sanctuary on November 26, but in so doing he stressed more the issue of disobeying the employer sanction provision. He did not invite the archbishop to the celebration, but only requested his prayers and whatever counsel he might want to share. To a degree, this seems more like a pro forma note to Mahony, since Olivares, as had been the case two years earlier, was going to do what he wanted to do whether Mahony liked it or not.[31]

Mahony chose not to go. He could not support an open defiance of the law by his clergy, and he would in time respond to Olivares's action. However, many others did attend the feast day of Our Lady of Guadalupe and the historic expansion of sanctuary to now include Mexican undocumented workers.

On a chilly Saturday morning on December 12, Olivares, along with Bishop Chávez and Mike Kennedy, celebrated the annual Mass in honor of the feast day of Our Lady of Guadalupe. Hundreds of people filled La Placita Church. Olivares addressed the congregation and called upon them to adhere to a higher law of "Christ and humanity" and oppose the Immigration Reform and Control Act. As part of this defiance, Olivares formally announced that La Placita would not only continue to be a sanctuary for the refugees, but would now be a sanctuary for the mostly Mexican undocumented immigrants who did not qualify for amnesty. No other sanctuary movement had done this. He received an overwhelming ovation when he stated: "The first law is the one of human dignity." As part of the ceremony, 300 of those in attendance signed the "pledge of non-cooperation" and promised to encourage employers to hire the undocumented and to provide them with food, clothing, and shelter. Bishop Chávez announced that these pledges, along with a statement urging modification of the law to expand amnesty and eliminate employer sanctions, would be sent to legislators in Washington. Following the Mass, Olivares, Bishop Chávez, and Kennedy held a press conference. Chávez took the lead and told the media that the signed petitions represented "a sign of real love and concern. The 300 people who signed are expressing their love for the undocumented who cannot receive amnesty and who are suffering a lot because they have no home and no rights." He concluded by reiterating the moral argument that drove him, Olivares, and Kennedy, as well as others, to challenge the authorities: "Human and Christian laws are superior to any laws in society. It is not our intent to break the law. Our intention is to be human and Christ-like, and through that accidently we violate the law." [32] As he also had done two years earlier by joining La Placita in declaring sanctuary for the refugees, Fr. Greg Boyle announced that his parish, Dolores Mission, would expand sanctuary to the undocumented. [33]

The reaction to this expansion, especially at La Placita, was met for the most part with support by parishioners and others who had supported Olivares's efforts with the refugees. Labor leader Jimmy Rodríguez noted that while sanctuary for the undocumented, as with the refugees, was largely symbolic, it still was of major importance. "It gave the immigrant people kind of an empowerment feeling," he observes, "that somebody's speaking up for them. And that someone speaking up for us is someone in a very, very important position. He's a messenger of God." Susan Alva adds of Olivares's action: "He took that definition of sanctuary beyond its traditional connotation of being a Central American movement. He pushed the envelope." Journalist Rubén Martínez calls Olivares a "visionary" in expanding sanctuary to the undocumented. Yet some had reservations. This included Sister Jo'Ann DeQuattro, who felt that including the undocumented workers would detract from the Central American refugees and possibly affect those, like her, making the argument that they represented legitimate political refugees, not economic refugees like the Mexicans. The coupling of the two groups, in her opinion, would be confusing and complicate the effort to help the refugees. She expressed her concerns to Olivares and Kennedy, but they did not take her advice. In retrospect, DeQuattro believes that expanding sanctuary was the right thing to do. Mary Brent Wehrli, the executive director of the Southern California Ecumenical Council Interfaith Task Force on Central America, also expressed her doubts over expanding sanctuary to the undocumented. "I think we are somewhat divided over this," she told the Los Angeles Times. "Was it realistic to go into congregations and tell people what they had to do? For the vast majority of people, we felt that was overstepping our bounds." Catholic medical facilities, while sympathetic to Olivares's initiative, decided not to endorse it because their tax status might be compromised.[34]

Olivares had no regrets for this expansion and stood his ground, knowing that he would face reaction by both Archbishop Mahony and by the INS, but he was prepared for it. He even had to face his brother Damaso, a policeman in San Antonio, about openly breaking the law. On visiting his brother in Los Angeles after the open defiance at La Placita, Damaso said to his brother, "Luis, you have to remember I'm a police officer. I am sworn to uphold the law."

Olivares gleefully responded to his brother: "Well, you enforce the laws and I'll violate them."[35]

IV

Archbishop Mahony did react, and he was not pleased with Olivares's actions, calling on others to defy the new immigration law and hire undocumented workers. This was going too far. Mahony sympathized with the undocumented and was supportive of helping them, but not by breaking the law. He no doubt heard conservative Catholics complain about Olivares, and he certainly heard from the INS. Attorney Peter Schey notes that Mahony had a monthly breakfast with INS commissioner Ezell and that they developed a positive working relationship. Schey further observes that despite Mahony's liberal pronouncements on immigration and on refugees, he and the archdiocese acted in more institutional and conservative ways, in comparison to a parish such as La Placita ministering to working people, the poor, and the oppressed.[36] Moreover, the U.S. Catholic Bishops demurred on defying the law because it might jeopardize their tax status with the federal government.[37] In fact, Mahony preferred not to use the term "sanctuary."[38] All this left Mahony with little flexibility on the matter. Moreover, his rivalry with Olivares undoubtedly played a role in his reaction. At the same time, Mahony had his own reservations about IRCA including employer sanctions, but the difference with him and Olivares was how to deal with the new law. Olivares noted that he believed that both he and the archbishop understood that the law was unjust, but that the difference was that he believed that the law should therefore be disobeyed, while Mahony believed it should be changed.[39] In this regard, Episcopalian Regas points out the irony of Mahony saying twenty years later that Catholics had an obligation to defy harsh immigration laws.[40] Regas does not believe that Mahony's feelings about Olivares were personal, but that he was dissatisfied with how he was handling La Placita and the "radical" priesthood represented by Olivares and Kennedy.[41] Olivares, for his part, under-

stood and perhaps even appreciated the institutional pressures and con-
straints on the Archbishop and the tightrope Mahony had to walk between
his own concerns for social justice and compliance with the law. Olivares
was not immune from such pressures, but for him social justice and God's
laws were always the priority.[42]

Facing pressures, especially by Ezell, to curtail Olivares's actions,
Mahony talked to Provincial Ferrante about what his order could do, including possibly reassigning Fr. Luis. The INS did not directly complain to
the Claretians about Olivares, but rather pressured Mahony. Ferrante recalls receiving several phone calls from the archbishop. However, on one
occasion, Mahony asked to see not only Ferrante, but the Jesuit provincial due to Kennedy's involvement with Olivares. Mahony wanted to know
what the provincials could do to restrain their priests. He also suggested
or hinted that perhaps the time had come to send them elsewhere. "How
much longer are we going to have the privilege of having Luis at Plaza
Church," he asked Ferrante. Fr. Boyle recalls that he learned that what
Mahony actually said was: "I want these guys removed."[43] To their credit,
both provincials refused to cave in to Mahony's pressure. They knew that
the archbishop could insist on removing the two priests, since La Placita
was owned by the archdiocese, but, for obvious political reasons, Mahony
did not want to be the one to remove them. He wanted their orders to
do his work for him. Neither provincial fell for this ploy. Instead, Ferrante
told Mahony: "Luis and Mike are doing what the Jesuit provincial and I
wish we could do, but have to instead sit behind a desk and do administration. If you're unhappy with them, you remove them."[44] Ferrante notes
that Mahony and Olivares had a more formal relationship. They were not
friends and there were clear tensions between the two. However, he believes that Mahony respected Olivares and was reacting more to the INS
pressures and those of his legal advisors. At the same time, there is no
question in Ferrante's mind that Mahony wanted Olivares out of La Placita. "If Archbishop Mahony had his druthers," he says, "he probably would
have said, 'let's get someone else in there.'"[45] If Olivares were a diocesan
priest, Mahony would have removed him; however, because Fr. Luis belonged to a religious order that had its own administration and control
over its priests, this provided Olivares with some cover. As long as his order
supported him, it would be difficult for Mahony to get rid of him.[46]

One way that Mahony reacted to Olivares's call for disobeying employer
sanctions was to circulate his own petition entitled "The Catholic Church's
Care for Undocumented Persons," which he had written for the U.S. Catholic Bishops, to all clergy in the Los Angeles archdiocese and ask them to

sign an agreement that they would abide by the archdiocese's policy of obeying IRCA while working to change some of its provisions, such as employer sanctions. Olivares and many other clergy refused to sign it and hence forced Mahony's hands.[47] He next called Olivares, Kennedy, and Boyle in to his office.

At Mahony's office, the three could see that the archbishop was not a happy camper. He had his lawyers and key clerical advisors with him, and he did not allow the three priests to talk. One of his staff angrily said to them: "What right do you have to set policy for the archdiocese? You're not the ones who will go to jail if you defy the law!" The three responded: "Great!" An agitated Mahony told them that he had no recourse but to "silence" them, meaning they could not speak out any further on IRCA, especially not to the press. Before they left, the three did get in a comment that they listened to a higher authority. They knew that they would not be silenced. Boyle explains that the archbishop could "silence" them because they were pastors of parishes under his administration. Mahony could have thrown them out of their parishes, but he, according to Boyle, did not want to go to that extreme, understanding that there would be a public reaction in their defense. He couldn't excommunicate them for their actions, as that would also be an extreme measure. After they were dismissed, the three of them left laughing among themselves at the scene they had just witnessed, knowing that they would not abide by the archbishop's silence which he, in fact, later and informally withdrew. At the same time, the three also realized that they were now clearly in hot water with the archbishop and the INS. Sister Patricia Krommer recalls that after the meeting with the archbishop, Olivares and Kennedy were quite upset; while they usually were very discreet in speaking about Mahony, this time they said more.[48] When the press asked him what he might do about the three priests, Mahony responded that he could have them removed from their positions if they did not follow his directives. "But I don't think that's going to happen. What I was really asking for," he said about his discussion with the three priests, "was a way to make themselves mesh with archdiocesan policy. It may be a fault of my own personality and style to find a way to create solutions rather than confrontations." He added that he did not question their moral motives, but feared that they could give the undocumented a false sense that the Church could protect them against the law and, at the same time, that their statements would only flame further anti-immigrant sentiment among some in the city. But in the end, Mahony drew a line on what the priests should or should not do. "While there may be a variety of public policy strategies available to assist the undocumented," he concluded, "I do not and will not sanction any steps which include the direct violation of the law."[49]

V

It was not just Archbishop Mahony who reacted to Olivares and the extension of sanctuary to undocumented Mexicans, but also the INS. The initial response came on the very day of the pronouncement. Ernest Gustafson, the director of the Los Angeles district of the INS, downplayed the extension, calling Olivares's action a disservice to the undocumented themselves. He alleged that La Placita in fact serviced few of the immigrants in the first place and that instead of breaking the law, Olivares and his supporters should instead be helping those who qualified for amnesty. "My question is how many of the illegal alien community have they actually assisted?" Gustafson told the Los Angeles Times. "My guess is that number would be minuscule. In contrast, the 275,000th person filed an application for amnesty today in the district. This group [Olivares and others] should be trying to help the alien community rather than make protests, which do nothing to help the qualified people."[50] For his part, INS Western Commissioner Ezell angrily denounced Olivares, although not by name. He dismissed him and others who supported him as the same small group who had always opposed immigration laws and compared them to the "coyotes" or smugglers of undocumented immigrants. He warned that those who did not obey IRCA could be subject to fines and imprisonment. "This group of religious and activists," he told a press conference, "are the same ones who supported the sanctuary movement and [opposed] the new immigration law even before it became law and they are the ones who are marching and protesting every day to prevent its application." If they were so interested in those who did not qualify for amnesty, he added, why had they not submitted appeals for these people? Ezell defended employer sanctions and announced that, the following week, three employers in the City of Industry would be fined for not complying with the law. Two weeks later, a spokesperson for the INS in Los Angeles called the various priests who had joined Olivares in defying employer sanctions "very irresponsible" and that they were "clearly violating the law of the land."[51]

One year later, however, the INS raised the ante against Olivares, Kennedy, and Boyle when it announced in late September 1988 that it had opened a criminal investigation against all three, including their activities at La Placita and Dolores Mission, following a vandalism attack against the downtown federal building. Police arrested a young Latino man, Wilson Menendez, for smashing in eighteen windows in the first-floor office of the INS. Menendez was identified as a human smuggler of undocumented immigrants. When arrested, he said he did it "to make a statement to the U.S. government." In a bizarre comment, he alleged that the government was making money from his smuggling, and he wanted it back. He also told officers that he slept at La Placita. The connection with the church provided the opening for Gustafson and Ezell to open the investigation against the three priests to determine if their support for the sanctuary movement was linked to the vandalism. Part of the reason for the investigation, according to the two INS officials, also was linked to an opinion piece in the *Los Angeles Times* written by the three and published the day after the assault on the building, and in which they once again called for the defiance of IRCA. This seemed suspicious to Ezell, who told the press that it was ironic that the article appeared the day after the vandalism occurred. "I don't say he (Menendez) was given orders to do that by (the) priests," the commissioner stated, "I say the attitude (the priests) express that there is a higher power, a higher law . . . produces an attitude that fosters the kind of behavior this guy demonstrated." Gustafson added that they were not investigating the sanctuary movement, but "watching" the activities of the priests who, according to Gustafson, "had an attitude of 'come and get me.'" Both INS officials further suggested that this attitude encouraged lawlessness. Ezell fanned the flames by calling it "outrageous" what he considered to be "the audacity of three Catholic priests to say publicly that people ought to disobey the law. . . . That attitude produces this kind of action [the vandalism]." To throw more into the fire, he added that "there is no such thing as sanctuary." Gustafson concluded that, if warranted, the INS would ask the U.S. Attorney's office to file "criminal charges against the priests." Ezell told the press that they would investigate to see if the priests encouraged illegal smuggling of immigrants and if they knowingly harbored "illegal immigrants." These charges represented felonies punishable by two years in prison and a $5000 fine.[52]

When informed by the press about Ezell's investigation and statement, Olivares and Boyle responded that it was irresponsible for Ezell to suggest that they or the sanctuary movement caused the incident. Boyle called it "outrageous." "We called for civil disobedience," he said, "which the spirit of the sanctuary movement has always maintained to be nonviolent and non-destructive. It's outrageous that [immigration officials] would try to connect our statements to the breaking of windows." Olivares added: "We recognize we are not above the law but we must challenge a law that we consider to be immoral because it violates a person's right to survival."[53] They were joined in protesting Ezell's comments by Rev. Tom Smolich, speaking on behalf of the Coalition for Humane Immigrant Rights in Los Angeles (CHIRLA), who at a press conference in front of the federal building, accused the INS of attempting to discredit the work of the three priests in supporting the basic human rights of all immigrants. Peter Schey, representing the three priests, also criticized Ezell's ignorance of the U.S. Constitution and observed that the priests were only providing services to their parishioners that most churches do. "If schools can admit children without regard to their immigration status," he said, "surely a church can provide shelter for the homeless and give them food. To say otherwise displays an abysmal ignorance of the thrust of the First Amendment. People have historically expressed their beliefs through acts of charity and kindness." As part of this ecumenical protest, Protestant leader Rev. James Lawson, a longtime civil-rights activist, compared the INS actions to those of the Nazi Gestapo, and said that the three priests suffered the same kind of persecution as had black leaders in the South at the hands of the FBI and CIA during the 1960s.[54] In reflecting on all this later, Olivares observed that this attempt to link him with terrorist acts was also a way for Ezell to put pressure on Mahony to reel him in and censor him. In fact, after one of his breakfast meetings with Mahony, Ezell referred to Olivares, Kennedy, and Boyle as the three "renegade priests." "We discussed what can be done about those three renegades," Ezell said. Also calling them "rabble-rousers," he charged them with breaking the law by aiding undocumented immigrants. The commissioner especially reacted to a recent comment by Fr. Boyle that he had deliberately hired an undocumented immigrant at Dolores Mission and did not fill out the employer verification form, as required by the IRCA. "It's not just a matter of being kind and helping," Ezell commented. "But when you say 'We're not going to fill our employment verification forms,' you're breaking the law."[55]

Nothing came of the INS investigation and it proved to be more a bluff on the part of Ezell and Gustafson than anything else. Asked if he thought Ezell would still order a raid on his church, Fr. Luis stated: "That's Ezell's decision. He better be sure that he wants to make martyrs out of us."[56] The *Los Angeles Times* agreed and editorialized against any INS action against La Placita: "In plain fact, entering church property and investigating the activities of priests serves no purpose for the INS, and is actually counterproductive."[57] However, tensions between Olivares and the INS would continue as long as Fr. Luis was pastor of La Placita. Attorney Linda Wong observes that Ezell's inflammatory rhetoric affected public opinion even more against the foreign-born in Los Angeles. "It wasn't a surprise to me that tension existed between him and Fr. Luis."[58]

Olivares came to believe that Mahony's close or cordial relationship with Ezell actually helped to fend off the INS effort to prosecute him and the other two priests. The commissioner hoped that the archbishop would be the better way to control the priests, rather than a possibly more controversial and public indictment of them. However, because Mahony only went so far in trying to limit Olivares's action, this created an opening whereby Olivares continued his sanctuary work. Meanwhile, Ezell awaited some kind of archdiocesan censure of Olivares and the other two priests that never came. Mahony was politically astute enough not to do Ezell's dirty work. When asked about the INS investigation of Olivares, Kennedy, and Boyle, Mahony stated that if anyone would have to be jailed for the actions of the Church, he as the head of the Church in Los Angeles should be the one. Moreover, he pledged his assistance to all who came to Catholic churches in need, irrespective of their immigration status. At the same time, he suggested that the three priests tone down their rhetoric and comply with the immigration law until it could be changed. In response for this show of support, La Placita and Dolores Mission parishioners acquired 9,000 statements of gratitude for the archbishop's statement, though they disregarded his comments about the three priests.[59] "In retrospect," Olivares said in 1991, after his retirement, "even though I didn't particularly like it at the time, the archbishop's 'working relationship' [with Ezell] shielded those of us who were more aggressive from outright repressive action by the officials. It confused Ezell, who must have thought, 'How is it possible that the Archbishop, the boss, is saying one thing while this crazy nut over here is doing the opposite?' So we kept right on with our work, and the investigation remained more of a threat."[60]

Moreover, despite Ezell's rhetoric and bravado, he never ordered a raid of La Placita. After the declaration of sanctuary for the undocumented, he did tell Gustafson that something had to be done, including raiding the church. "I don't go into churches," Gustafson, to his credit, replied. "It's against my personal principles and upbringing." He also reminded his superior that the INS had a national policy of not raiding churches. "If we do something like this, we're the ones who will get the bad publicity." Ezell rejected Gustafson's views, but did not order any actions against La Placita. "We would have won the battle, but we would have lost the war," Gustafson says about the fallout out of a raid against the church. Moreover, Gustafson notes that Ezell had his own personal antagonists, which included Olivares, and was also searching for media attention. He never referred to Olivares as Fr. Olivares, instead downgrading him by calling him "Mr. Olivares." While the commissioner called Olivares, Kennedy, and Boyle the "three renegades," Gustafson, by contrast referred to them as "gentlemen." Although no raids occurred, Ezell seems to have kept surveillance on La Placita. Blase Bonpane notes that the INS was often around the church. Gloria Kinsler recalls that when she went to La Placita, she often saw a white man outside the church reading a newspaper and watching what was going on. She figured it was either an INS undercover agent or FBI. "I'd always say good morning to him," she says. "It was so blatant." In addition, it appears that the Los Angeles police likewise had a surveillance of the sanctuary movement in the city that included La Placita.[61] Jimmy Rodrí-guez once drove Olivares to Salinas to say a farmworker Mass; on the trip, they were trailed by four cars that he assumed were either INS or FBI or maybe even CIA agents. In a 1990 news conference, Olivares and Kennedy accused the FBI of unsuccessfully attempting to force a Salvadoran refu-gee under threat of deportation to spy on La Placita. Fr. Luis told the press that he also believed that the church's phones were tapped and that there had probably been earlier efforts to infiltrate FBI agents into the sanctuary movement at La Placita. Lydia López observes that the INS was itching to get into the church, but could not because Olivares would not let them.[62]

As Gustafson acknowledges, Ezell had his own personal vendettas. He was a very religious conservative evangelical Christian who, accord-ing to Rev. Zwerling, sought out publicity by saying outrageous and offen-sive statements. He also had political ambitions. He once said that the INS did not need the National Guard or the military to deal with the undocu-mented and refugees. "We need to catch them, clean them, and cook them without any help," he stated. "What kind of a comment is that?" the more moderate Gustafson comments, "even if you weren't Hispanic, you would take that bad. I took it bad." By contrast Gustafson had more cordial rela-tions with Olivares, and they were on a first-name basis with each other.[63]

But Ezell was not alone in his anti-Latino and anti-immigrant views. Peter Schey stresses that the director of the INS in Washington, Alan Nelson, had similar views and that under him the INS emphasized enforce-ment rather than services. "Both Nelson and Ezell were ferociously anti-immigrant," Schey remarks and adds that Nelson later helped write up the notorious Proposition 187 in 1994 that, in California, would deny state ser-vices to the undocumented. It passed under a cloud of xenophobia until a federal court declared it unconstitutional, since only the federal govern-ment has jurisdiction over immigration.[64]

Clearly, there was no love lost between Ezell and Olivares. They de-bated each other often in the media. At one point, Olivares, perhaps him-self guilty of heated rhetoric, referred to the actions of the INS under Ezell as comparable to those of the Gestapo against the Jews in Nazi Germany.[65] Rubén Martínez notes that Fr. Luis had fun engaging with the INS Commissioner, once even inviting him to speak at one of the Sunday Masses about the amnesty provisions, especially since many undocumented remained scared to sign up for it.

"Harold, come down to La Placita and talk to my people. They're not getting the message. Let's bury the hatchet so come on down."

Ezell did. However, little did he know that Olivares was setting him up. He prepared a very fancy scroll which read: "I, Harold Ezell, will abandon the discriminatory practices of the INS and pledge to work with the people. I promise not to separate families if some members do not qualify for amnesty." At the Mass, Olivares presented this document to Ezell at the altar and asked him to sign it. Ezell refused and, according to Rubén Martínez, ran off in a huff mouthing, "This is a bunch of crap."[66]

To Rubén Martínez, this episode reflected what a good strategist Olivares was and likened the pastor to an expert chess player who carefully and skillfully planned his moves. Of course, Olivares had learned confrontational strategies from Ernie Cortes and UNO. It was right out of the IAF's playbook to make Ezell into a target to personify all of the problems of IRCA and the discriminatory practices of the INS. Mike Clements from UNO saw this influence and how Olivares polarized and personalized the immigration issue by making Ezell into target number one. It put the onus on the commissioner and, according to Clements, drove Ezell crazy. Olivares applied the Alinsky concept of an action resulting in a reaction to his advantage. "Hey, did I get a reaction from Ezell or did I not get a reaction?" he would tell Clements. "He'd have Ezell like a yo-yo," Clements concludes. To Martínez it also suggested how much Olivares was in charge at La Placita. "He was the commandant," Martínez stresses, "and his staff called him that, although sometimes tongue in cheek, but true."[67]

VI

Despite the opposition or resistance by both Archbishop Mahony and the INS, Olivares and his team refused to be intimidated. They continued the sanctuary movement in Los Angeles, which now included undocumented Mexican immigrants as well as continuing opposition to IRCA. One way they did this was by trying to affect public opinion through the media. Besides press conferences and protests designed to reach the media, they also published opinion pieces in the press. In the most controversial one that brought on the INS investigation, Olivares, Kennedy, and Boyle wrote an essay for the *Los Angeles Times* that was published on September 21,

1988. They once again explained their opposition to the new immigration law and called on others to do likewise. They observed that Commissioner Ezell claimed that the priests had stated that they were above the law and that if he found them breaking it, especially by aiding, abetting, and harboring the undocumented, he would prosecute them. The priests responded that they were writing to clarify their position: while they themselves were not above the law, the "struggle of undocumented people to assert their rights as human beings is." They identified with Jesus who would also defend the rights of the undocumented. "What we are doing in our ministry to these people is an attempt to approximate what Jesus would do in the same circumstances," they wrote,

> This is not guesswork on our part, the Gospel is clear and abundantly full of Jesus's concern for the poor, the fearful, the persecuted, those who hunger for peace and justice. It is our strong belief that Jesus would, with ease, find himself aiding, abetting and harboring our sisters and brothers who have come to our community in hope and instead are hunted because they lack the papers that would allow them to stay.
>
> Jesus, of course, would seek to do even more. He would publicly denounce unjust policies and laws so that hearts would change and that such personal conversion would result in the radical transformation of policy and law.
>
> It is our sincere hope to act toward the undocumented as Jesus would. To do otherwise would be to deny a tradition that has been respected ever since the Lord commanded: "When aliens reside with you in your land, do not mistreat them. You shall treat the aliens who reside with you no differently than the natives born among you; have the same love for them as for yourselves." (Leviticus 19:33–34)

It was because of Jesus's example and biblical tradition that they provided for the undocumented. They could do no less. That is why they also opposed the employer sanctions provisions of IRCA: because it would deny the immigrants the human right to work and survive. They called the law "immoral." They called on all people of faith to join them in protecting the undocumented. Any law that designated people as non-persons and subhuman was not worthy of being obeyed. In clear liberation theology language, they noted that Christians had the obligation to have a preferential option for the poor and oppressed. And in an attempt to co-opt Mahony's own words, they quoted his statement that if laws such as IRCA suggested that the undocumented were "people . . . outside the framework of our concern as a society; our Christian tradition tells us the opposite." Then in a straightforward assertion, the three "renegade priests" wrote: "To the extent that we openly aid, abet, and harbor the undocumented, we indeed are breaking the law. The gospel would have us do no other." They concluded by writing:

> We do so fully aware of the consequences of our actions. And yet we cannot help but feel that what little we are able to say and do remains insignificant compared to the depth of suffering and commitment of our sisters and brothers struggling to assert their rights as human beings. Our integrity as ministers of the Word could never be kept whole were we to remain immobile and transfixed by the law's claim and deaf to the cry of the poor.
>
> In seeking to make public again the private and intense pain of the undocumented, we pray that God's grace will break through all hearts of stone so that finally, cold indifference will give way to a compassionate justice for the poor.[68]

To call further attention to the suffering and oppression of the undocumented as a human rights issue, Olivares and Kennedy announced that they would submit a protest to the United Nations Commission on Human Rights in March 1988. They asserted that the human rights of the undocumented who did not qualify under IRCA were being violated not only by the INS, but also by the police and employers. "We are here to raise our voices about the pain and suffering of these people who don't qualify for amnesty and who are forced to live in the shadows," Olivares proclaimed at a news conference at La Placita. As part of assisting them, Fr. Luis stated that his parish would provide food and clothes to both the immigrants and the refugees. "These people don't come to get rich," Olivares added about the undocumented, "they come to work in order to survive [*sobrevivir*]." He called on others to also aid the refugees and immigrants and above all to join in working to change the immigration law. Kennedy pointed out that between 60 and 150 undocumented immigrants each day congregated at La Placita and that when they went out to find work, they were rejected because they could not show employers legal documents. Employers hired some, but paid them a pittance and told them that if they didn't like it, they would call immigration. Olivares further observed that the INS did not have the manpower to enforce employer sanctions and so instead tried to intimidate employers not to hire the undocumented. The police exploited the immigrants by denying them the right to congregate at street corners as day laborers and attempt to find work this way. Some of the undocumented likewise spoke about their conditions, including one who said that at one corner the police ticketed him and others for being there, while at another corner the INS came by. "I think we have the right to work," he stated. "I remember that the Pope [John Paul II] said that all those who seek work have a right to cross frontiers."[69] Kennedy said that the testimonios of some of the immigrants would be sent as part of the protest to the United Nations.[70]

It is not clear if this petition to the United Nations was sent, and if it was nothing seems to have come from it. The important thing was simply the publicity that the abuse of the undocumented had reached an unacceptable level in Los Angeles and that Olivares and Kennedy at La Placita could no longer stand by and witness it. To call further attention to the human rights issues concerning the undocumented, Olivares and Kennedy inaugurated a Center of Human Rights Pastoral Project (Centro de Derechos Humanos-Proyecto Pastoral) at the parish. One of its main projects was to organize protests and news conferences where the undocumented themselves could give testimony to their conditions. At one such protest, over 150 undocumented men, Mexicans and Central Americans, condemned unscrupulous employers who exploited them by hiring them and promising good wages, but at the end of their work reneged on their pay, taking advantage of the fact that the workers would not complain due to their vulnerable immigration status. Some were fired without any pay. "These persons have nowhere to go; they have no choice but to accept abuses and extortions because of the Simpson-Rodino legislation has left them with no dignity," Kennedy stressed. In a form of political theater, some of the immigrants carried signs reading: "Work yes, exploitation no!" Some put on fake handcuffs as a sign of their economic slavery. Then at a certain moment, they tore off the cuffs and shouted out "No mas!" (No more!). Olivares called again on others to assist the undocumented, and Kennedy noted that the Latino parishioners of La Placita had responded to this call by hiring the immigrants after Sunday Masses as gardeners and handymen. The protest ended with Mass, a supper for all, and then Olivares and Kennedy spent the evening sleeping with the undocumented and refugees on the church grounds in order, as they said, "to experience what it meant to be without a home."[71]

As a further expression that they were not going to be silenced or intimidated, Olivares, Kennedy, and Boyle in 1989 called on other churches and synagogues to assist both the undocumented and the refugees by literally opening their doors and providing sanctuary. They did not have to become sanctuary institutions, but they could at least provide overnight shelter for those who were homeless. Using the motto "open your doors" and with an initiative that they called "Puertas Abiertas" or "Open Doors," Olivares and Boyle sent letters to 144 churches and synagogues asking for assistance.[72]

VII

Despite Olivares's opposition to the IRCA, he still recognized the importance of the opportunity for many others to obtain legalization under the new immigration law. As a result, he worked to assist those immigrants or refugees who qualified. He joined other groups that, after the IRCA became law, set up programs to inform and educate those who qualified what they needed to do. One of the most important of these groups was CHIRLA. Actually, CHIRLA as its name indicated represented a coalition of service providers, Catholic, Protestant, and Jewish organizations, immigration attorneys, and immigrant advocacy groups including Central American groups such as CARECEN and the Asian-Pacific American Legal Center, and Catholic Charities, as well as some labor unions. It was established in 1987 although some who joined CHIRLA had already, like Olivares, worked against the passage of the IRCA. It also sponsored several other chapters in southern California and became a part of the United Way at the end of the decade. Volunteers initially composed the staff. However, as it became more active, it needed someone of distinction and credibility to chair it and be its main spokesperson. "Who can we ask?" some said.[73]

It did not take very long for others to respond: "Fr. Olivares." There was really no question about this. "We all felt it was really important for the coalition to have a credible spokesperson," Linda Wong, an attorney for the Mexican American Legal Defense and Education Fund (MALDEF) and who would become a key leader of the group, recalls, "and there was no question that Father Luis was the most appropriate and best person we could possibly find to be the public face of the coalition to advocate on behalf of immigrants in general."[74] He was also chosen because of his work with the Central American refugees. Of this background and proven record, Moises Escalante, who worked with CHIRLA, notes, "This is a man that helped others to get sanctuary in the United States and we have created this organization that will help immigrants. It's common sense, logical that he's the man that we want to call."[75] Olivares, who already had worked with some of CHIRLA's volunteers, readily accepted. He didn't just want to play defense against the IRCA; he wanted to play offense by helping others to get amnesty so that they could begin to have some security and hopefully better opportunities and even citizenship. What further attracted Olivares to CHIRLA was that he had already been bridging the Central American refugee issues with the undocumented Mexican immigrant ones, and the group wanted to be a coalition that addressed both issues and to coordinate with advocacy groups representing the two communities.[76]

As chair, Olivares presided over meetings; however, he did not immerse himself in the day-to-day operations of CHIRLA. Everyone in the group understood and accepted that Fr. Luis already had a full agenda as pastor of La Placita and with his ongoing work with the refugees and undocumented. Olivares also accepted his less active role as chair, but knew that his leadership and name recognition could help. He did what he could, and in fact that was a good deal. He attended almost all the meetings and participated in the discussions. He also helped to recruit other organizations to join CHIRLA and to develop consensus within the group. He served as the public face and voice of the group at press conferences and at rallies. As pastor of La Placita, Olivares allowed CHIRLA to hold some of its meetings in the church basement until the group received more permanent offices at the United Way building.[77] Above all, Olivares brought a commanding presence. "I think people liked him and thought he was really just a good, strong moral leader," CHIRLA activist Ann Kansvaag says, "in the sense that he'd stand up at a press conference and wear his collar and say what needed to be said about the rights of immigrants and refugees. He certainly wasn't a day-in, day-out manager. That wasn't his role in CHIRLA at all. He was the public face which was needed a lot in those days."[78] Niels Frenzen, a key figure in CHIRLA, adds that his impression of Olivares was one of being a conciliator within the group. "He was the one who was able to, although not always, pave over differences. He was the person we would turn to, to settle disputes." According to Frenzen, Olivares possessed the moral authority to do so. By 1990, Olivares shared chairing CHIRLA with Linda Wong as the co-chair.[79]

Some of the CHIRLA activities Olivares endorsed and participated in included first informing qualified immigrants about how to register for amnesty. The window for people applying for amnesty was limited from May 1, 1987, to May 1, 1988, although it was later extended to 1990. The organization applied for funding from both the federal and state governments to publicize the program and in time received thousands of dollars. Frenzen notes that over a couple of years, CHIRLA received over a million dollars for its activities, which allowed it to hire staff. CHIRLA did not itself process the applications, but instead directed applicants to groups such as Catholic Charities (with the support of Archbishop Mahony) and One Stop Immigration that had contracts with the INS to register immigrants. With its large budget, it produced ads on Spanish-language television and radio; it bought signs in Spanish to be placed on the side of city buses and on bus benches. It worked with *La Opinión* to advertise the program. It also purchased a series of 800 numbers through the phone company where people could get information on amnesty in Spanish and other languages. In addition to media ads, CHIRLA volunteers and staff did much legwork to get the word out on amnesty. They spoke at churches, community centers, labor unions, night schools, and parent groups. Frenzen recalls that almost every night of the week staff spoke to groups all over Los Angeles, including Mexican and Central American communities. To reach larger groups, it organized amnesty fairs in MacArthur Park, where many Latinos congregated on weekends and where CHIRLA set up information booths on amnesty. In order to prepare applicants for meeting the language and literacy qualifications of IRCA, it also sponsored English and Spanish classes, as well as citizenship classes for those who qualified already. Olivares himself set up such classes, including amnesty classes at La Placita. Some staff even met with employers to encourage them to provide amnesty information to their employees. In this outreach, CHIRLA stressed to people that they could not be deported if they applied and were not given amnesty. Although many were at first reluctant to apply, eventually over a million did so in the Los Angeles area and eventually some three million immigrants received amnesty nationwide.[80]

VIII

Besides working with CHIRLA, Olivares also worked with many other groups that dealt with the issues of concern to him as part of his refusal to be reined by anybody, including his own Church. Where he got his energy to be so involved in so many projects and still be effective is hard to know. For one, of course, he was totally committed to the cause of social justice. Moreover, no doubt, the discipline he learned in the seminary affected him. It was not that he believed he was indispensable to many of these struggles, although as many strong leaders he might well have felt this, but that he wanted to be involved as much as possible. This was his ministry; this is what it meant to be a community priest; and this was how to extent a faith-based movement. He knew that he was a leader and that others looked to him to lead. He was not afraid to lead.

One of the groups that he participated in was the Southern California Ecumenical Council Interfaith Task Force on Central America (SCITCA). Some in religious ministry such as Sister Jo'Ann DeQuattro organized it following the assassination of Archbishop Romero in El Salvador in 1980 and the brutal murders of the nuns and lay worker in that country later that year.[81] It shocked them to learn not only of these murders, but of the brutal civil wars being waged in Central America; it repulsed them that the United States was supporting the repressive regimes and providing military arms used to kill innocent civilians. At first organized just to know what was happening in Central America, SCITCA evolved to focus on four issues: (1) to protest U.S. military intervention in Central America; (2) to promote a peaceful diplomatic solution to the conflicts there; (3) to support the Central American refugees in the United States; and (4) to give congregations the support and encouragement they needed to offer safe asylum to the refugees.[82] Organized from the already existing Southern California Ecumenical Council, the task force reflected this ecumenism by including Catholic, Protestant, and even Jewish representatives. At least twenty organizations, many of them religious in nature, participated in the group. From these different groups, about fifteen to twenty members actively worked in SCITCA led by Mary Brent Wehrli, its executive director for several years.[83] Olivares and La Placita became members of SCITCA and Fr. Luis served on its advisory council along with other prominent clergy such as Rev. James Lawson of the United Methodist Church.[84]

Finally, SCITCA engaged in public protests against U.S. policies in Central America. These involved marches and rallies in front of the federal building in downtown Los Angeles, and Olivares spoke at many of these events. On one occasion it protested at the Los Angeles International Airport against TACA Airlines, the Salvadoran airline, for cooperating with the INS in deporting refugees. SCITCA also organized ecumenical and interfaith press conferences with representatives of different faiths who called for an end to U.S. military aid to the Salvadoran government and military.[85] At a 1989 press conference, Olivares pointed out that the new president of El Salvador did not have the real power to bring about peace. "Who does have the last word," he said, "are those who fund the military," meaning the U.S. government.[86] Protests likewise involved civil disobedience. At one point, SCITCA members occupied the local offices of both Republican and Democrat congressional representatives and stopped work as a way of stressing the need for these representatives to vote against continued U.S. support for the repressive governments in Central America. In one of the most publicized SCITCA protests, Mary Brent Wehrli, its executive director, interrupted a speech by President George Bush in 1990 at the Century Plaza Hotel by appealing to him as a fellow Episcopalian to end U.S. military aid to El Salvador. As she was escorted out of the ballroom and arrested, she continued to demand that the President stop this policy.[87]

Olivares also worked with many other groups that together represented an informal coalition on Central American issues. Much of this coalition, which included SCITCA, was centered at La Placita. The fact of the matter was that most of those working on Central America and undocumented immigrants went to Olivares for his support and leadership, which he willingly gave. Kennedy notes that La Placita became the center of this coalition against U.S. policies in Central America and that some thirty to forty groups were involved. "We were like the center place," he says because La Placita possessed two important elements that no other church or group had. It had a hands-on relationship with the refugees plus connections to El Salvador and, second, it had the prophetic, the religious spirit and rationale for working on these issues.[88]

Some groups that Olivares related to as part of the broader coalition on Central America and the refugees included the Center for Human Rights (headed by immigration attorney Peter Schey), Proyecto Pastoral, the ACLU, NOW (National Organization of Women), and a loose collection of Hollywood actors and entertainers. Henry Olivares recalls an interesting anecdote about when the ACLU honored his brother for his work on the sanctuary movement. Fr. Luis had some trepidation about the award since he did not agree with the ACLU's pro-choice position on abortion. Henry tried to convince him that despite this, he had to attend.

"The president will be there," Henry said.

"President Reagan?" Luis responded.

"No, the president of the ACLU."

"Oh, because if you had said President Reagan, I would definitely be there to tell him personally my opposition to his policy in Central America."

Olivares agreed to accept the award; however, he insisted that whoever introduced him had to say that Fr. Luis did not agree with the ACLU on all issues. Henry and his wife Lillian accompanied Olivares to the dinner and sat at his table. In his address, Fr. Luis joked about thinking that Reagan might have been invited to the event and his response to Henry.[89]

The Hollywood crowd, who opposed Reagan's policies, gave its support, especially financially, to some of the coalition groups, but many also personally rallied to Olivares himself. As celebrities, they seemed attracted to Olivares's star power and his media presence. They wanted to be identified with him and to be seen with him. This is not to diminish the fact that many were sincerely politically engaged, such as Martin Sheen, Ed Asner, Kris Kristofferson, Norman Lear, and Jackson Browne. Sheen, a devout Catholic, in particular developed a close relationship with Olivares. Journalist Rubén Martínez has a more skeptical view of this Hollywood connection. He suggests that this West L.A. crowd saw Olivares as their "brown priest," and yet he was also very American. "He spoke perfect English so he was safe," Martínez says of the Hollywood stars' reactions to Fr. Luis. Martínez further alleges that these liberals wanted to be close but not too close to the action on Central America, and so Olivares was perfect for them. They could support him without being too directly involved in the sanctuary movement. According to Martínez, they saw Olivares as a romantic figure—a radical. "He was a hit." Martínez further proposes that Olivares astutely worked the Hollywood people and obtained funding from them for his programs.[90] Martínez may be too cynical about this relationship, and may not understand that Olivares undoubtedly was flattered by this attention from the celebrities and enjoyed being with them as well as recognizing their own sincere opposition to what the U.S. was doing in Central America. This was part of coalition politics.[91]

In addition, Olivares supported the efforts of Central American refugees to organize their own groups. The most important of these was CARECEN (Central American Refugee Center). In Spanish, the word *carecen* means "those in need." Founded in 1983 by some of the more educated and professional refugees, CARECEN concentrated on promoting the rights of refugees based on U.S. laws and international law. To this end, it provided representation in deportation cases through its network of volunteers including attorneys from the Legal Aid Foundation of Los Angeles. Moreover, besides legal services, it offered basic English-language instruction, food and clothing, and referral information for emergency housing, employment, and medical care to the refugee community. Many of its volunteers were refugees themselves. Olivares endorsed CARECEN's efforts and helped it in any way it saw fit. He became a founding member of its board and attended many of its meetings, where he participated in the discussions. Member Madeline Janis-Aparicio recalls that he was very outspoken, but respectful of others and never domineering. "He was wise and funny," she notes. In return, CARECEN members loved, admired, and trusted Fr. Luis. "He was a symbol," Janis-Aparicio stresses. "He was hugely meaningful. He was like the U.S. Oscar Romero. He was an extremely powerful figure as a priest, but also he had an amazing sense of humor. He always made people laugh." In 1985, CARECEN honored him and La Placita at its annual dinner banquet "in recognition for their continuous work toward peace in Central America."[92]

The Salvadoran refugees, in fact, accepted Olivares as one of their leaders. This was pan-Latinoism at the grassroots level. Moises Escalante remembers that another Salvadoran-organized group, Casa El Salvador, always looked to Olivares to participate in their educational and cultural events as well as in marches against U.S. policies. "He was in front," Escalante observes of Fr. Luis marching with the refugees, because he had to be there to show support. In turn, the Salvadorans looked to him for leadership and guidance.[93]

Besides being involved in coalition politics with many groups as well as refusing to be silenced by his own Church, Olivares participated in many marches, demonstrations, and rallies especially as a keynote speaker on Central American issues. Many of these protest activities took place at the downtown federal building as a symbol of the U.S. government. In his speeches at these protests, Olivares, like other speakers, focused on bringing peace to Central America by putting an end to U.S. military aid to the repressive governments in the region. Peter Schey observes that the concerns that Olivares expressed in these speeches revolved around certain key issues: (1) concern over the war in El Salvador and U.S. policies there; (2) the effort by the Reagan administration to destabilize and overthrow the Sandinista government in Nicaragua by arming the Contras; (3) the suffering of the people in Central America and the violation of human rights there; and (4) the plight of the refugees and his belief that the U.S. had a moral obligation to receive the diaspora from the Central American crisis with sympathy and in concert with U.S. immigration laws and international laws.[94]

Those who listened to Olivares's speeches at these demonstrations all agreed on how effective and powerful a speaker he was, just as he was in his homilies at Mass. His speeches were effective not because he could shout the loudest or because he was bombastic or used a lot of rhetoric. Quite the opposite. Linda Wong recalls that Fr. Luis on these occasions never raised his voice, although he used the microphone. He always modulated his voice so that people had to quiet down to hear him. "It's an indirect way," she observes, "but a very powerful way to get people to listen to you because you have to come to his terms and not the other way around." She adds that Olivares never expressed things in a political way. "He always framed the issue in terms of human rights and social rights," she says. "This removed the issue of Central American and undocumented immigrant rights away from the political arena." Above all, he could connect with ordinary people whether speaking in English or in Spanish in a way that other activists could not. He spoke in plain language, while others were much too rhetorical and polemical. This made Olivares, according to Wong, more influential especially with politicians. "You knew he didn't have a hidden political agenda," she concludes. "For him it was the question of justice and humane treatment of people." As she witnessed Fr. Luis's speeches, Janis-Aparicio was struck by his confidence and his absolute clarity. Little did they know, as was the case on other occasions when he had to speak, that Olivares often felt sick to his stomach before these public appearances.[95]

Of course, Olivares likewise protested against U.S. policies in Central America via his many media appearances on television and news conferences, his opinion pieces in both the *Los Angeles Times* and Spanish-language newspapers, and his letters to congressional leaders. Moreover, some of the demonstrations that he spoke at were ones organized by La Placita itself. It is fair to say that no voice was so prominent on these issues as that of Luis Olivares.[96]

X

Central American refugees and Mexican undocumented immigrants were also mostly working-class people trying to make ends meet in Los Angeles. Olivares understood this and did what he could to protect their labor rights. Hence, parts of his sanctuary work included joining with progressive labor unions to assist not only refugees and the undocumented, but Mexican American and Latino workers in general. Besides being a community priest, Olivares was also a workers' priest. Of course, he had early on been involved with the farmworkers and the UFW, and he remained close to the union and to César Chávez into the 1980s. Chávez and the UFW supported the sanctuary movement at La Placita. However, just as in the case with UNO, Olivares spent less time with the UFW due to the sanctuary movement. Chris Hartmire acknowledges this, but notes that it also spoke to changes in the union as well. "We didn't need him [Olivares] in the same way," he observes, "and the people fleeing Central American did."[97] Yet Chávez and the farmworkers would always have a warm spot in Olivares's heart, and when he could do something for the union he did. In 1988, when Chávez engaged in his last major fast in support of the renewed and continuing boycott of non-union grapes in California, Olivares and La Placita joined in temporary fasts as a symbol of support. In one of his homilies at a Mass in support of Chávez's fast, Fr. Luis asked those present to pray for the farm-labor leader's health, and for love and peace among people, and for the poor people who entered the country in search of new opportunities.[98]

But if Olivares's engagement with the UFW had abated, it had increased with urban labor in Los Angeles. He championed and involved himself in efforts to unionize undocumented workers in the city. Some labor unions, such as the Packing House Workers, initiated a union drive among packing-house workers in the city's slaughterhouses. Some 60 percent of these workers consisted of undocumented Mexicans and, according to labor leader Jimmy Rodríguez, all joined the union. However, the companies such as Farmer John and the Union Packing Company refused to accept unionization, prompting the workers to go on strike in the mid-1980s. Rodríguez had a close relationship with Olivares and got him to support the strike. Rodríguez astutely observes that Olivares supported the workers because he recognized that the sanctuary movement was not just about sanctuary, but about undocumented workers and the conditions they faced in the United States, where they were vulnerable to exploitation by both employers and merchants. Rodríguez believed that Fr. Luis could be an invaluable asset. He wanted to thoroughly involve him in the union struggles. The labor leader wanted the workers to see that Fr. Olivares and the Church supported unionization. Olivares complied. "So all of this was very demanding on Fr. Luis," Rodríguez says, "and he started to spread himself just everywhere because sanctuary was more than sanctuary; it was about life; it was about people; it was about community and family."[99]

Olivares became part of the effort to empower the workers. Always wearing his collar, he participated in a variety of activities in support of the packing-house strike. He led prayer vigils in front of the plants. This drew much media attention, which is what the union wanted. It was a way of telling the strikers that the Church supported them and that "this hero of immigrant workers was out there supporting them." The media, in turn, helped to publicize the fact that the workers—who were the ones responsible for putting steaks, hamburger, and chicken on people's tables—had problems and needed the public's help. As the strikers assembled at six in the morning to go to the picket line, Olivares joined them. When they ended their strike day at six in the evening, Olivares was there also. Everywhere Olivares went the media followed because, as Rodríguez points out, it was an anomaly to the media to see a Catholic priest as popular as Olivares was to be out with the strikers. Olivares talked with the workers, mostly in Spanish, and gave them pep talks, encouraged them, and gave them strength to keep on struggling. Rodríguez recalls one very cold morning during the strike when the workers warmed themselves by gathering around a fire in an oil drum and passing around a bottle of El Presidente Brandy. It came around to Olivares, who also took a swig, only further endearing him to the strikers. "He's like us," they said. Olivares also loved, according to Rodríguez, to march in the picket lines. He had done so with the farmworkers, and he now did with the packing-house workers. "I'm going to get arrested one of these days on a picket line," he proudly told Rodríguez.[100]

He picketed not only with the packing-house workers, but with the hotel workers, and supported additional unionizing efforts among workers, many of them undocumented, in other industries such as food processing, restaurants, janitorial services, construction, and garment sweatshops. He had, according to Rodríguez, an iconic status in the labor movement in Los Angeles.[101]

As part of his support for labor, Olivares also participated in consumer boycotts. He had done this and continued to do so with the UFW's boycott of grapes and lettuce. In Los Angeles, he joined efforts against the Coors beer corporation for its exploitation of Chicano workers in Colorado. The "boycott Coors" campaign had started in the late 1960s as part of the Chicano Movement, but had continued well into the 1980s, led by some of the unions. On one occasion, Coors retaliated by donating funds to a number of Latino community groups. One such group hosted a large Cinco de Mayo community festival and Coors picked up the entire tab, including the food, music, and advertisements. The unions countered by organizing a protest to be held outside the park where some 25,000 people would enjoy the festival. The idea was to picket the park and call for people to boycott Coors beer. Rodríguez invited Fr. Luis to join the demonstration.

"Okay, count me in," Olivares replied, "but why do we have to protest just in front of the park? Let's go inside the park and march right through all the booths where the people are."

Rodríguez must have said to himself: "Why didn't I think of this?"

The Sunday of the festival, Rodríguez picked up Olivares and drove to the park where they met about 100 union demonstrators. They had their "Boycott Coors" signs ready. When they were all assembled, Olivares said, "This is going to be exciting. Let's go."

Marching in front of the group with a large image of Our Lady of Guadalupe directly behind him and wearing his church vestments, Olivares led the demonstrators into the park. They marched in between booths where surprised Latinos dropped everything to look at them. "This was like the parting of the sea," one union organizer commented, and Olivares was playing the role of Moses. Although they were only a small group, they managed to convince many of the people at the park that they should not be supporting Coors and many left. They abandoned the park as Olivares and the others shouted "Boycott Coors! ¡Abajo con Coors!" (Down with Coors!). Olivares beamed at the success of the demonstration.[102]

Olivares's alliance with labor unions especially focused on those committed to organizing the undocumented immigrants and refugees and those that challenged the AFL-CIO, which remained cool to such organizing. In fact, it had supported the IRCA. To offset this, Latino labor leaders such as Rodríguez and Miguel Contreras organized the Labor Council for Latin American Advancement (LCLAA). Other key labor and future political leaders who joined the new group included María Durazo, Gil Cedillo, and Antonio Villaraigosa. LCLAA supported the sanctuary movement and amnesty. It helped to register immigrants eligible for amnesty. In turn, Olivares supported the group and participated in some of its activities. His involvement, according to Rodríguez, gave the organization legitimacy.[103] By contrast, Archbishop Mahony came in for criticism by union leaders when he opposed the efforts of church gravediggers to form a union. Although he had supported the UFW and, in general, was pro-labor, Mahony did not feel that labor unions had any place in church-related activities. One critic denounced Mahony's actions and compared Olivares to him. "But also in LA," Virginia Reade wrote to the *Los Angeles Herald Examiner*, "we have a Mexican priest who could give us the moral, spiritual, cultural, and political support and leadership our people so desperately need. His name is Father Luis Olivares."[104]

While the progressive labor movement in Los Angeles had, by the last years of the 1980s, moved to organize undocumented workers, other parts of the labor movement in Los Angeles had been under significant duress in the early part of the decade. This had to do with the closure of major industries, most notably the auto plants, in the area. This was part of the deindustrialization of the American economy, as many industries relocated to Third World countries such as Mexico and China to manufacture their products taking advantage of cheaper labor and non-unionized workers. Soon after Olivares became pastor at La Placita, he spoke out against such plant closures, particularly the General Motors plant in Van Nuys. To Olivares such plant closings were not economic issues but moral issues and ones involving people's livelihood and the wellbeing of their families. "I feel this is a very significant moral issue," he told the press, "to which the corporate sector of our economy has not given due notice. They cannot make decisions purely on an economic basis."[105]

One other sector of labor that Olivares supported had to do with day laborers, many of them undocumented and refugees. They concentrated on street corners in the mornings and throughout the day, hoping that some employers would hire them, if only for the day. Merchants and residents began to complain about these congregations and the police stepped in and began to harass and even arrest some of the day laborers. On some occasions, they also called in the INS. Olivares, along with Kennedy and Boyle, denounced such assaults on people who were trying to just make a living. They considered this not only a labor rights issue, but a human rights one. At one protest outside of the main LAPD Parker Center headquarters in downtown Los Angeles, Olivares told the 200 demonstrators, many of them day laborers, "We are here to denounce the violation of human rights. The police action against day laborers is an example of the anti-immigrant attitudes that exists in our city." He reminded the police that the city council had declared Los Angeles a sanctuary city in 1985, and therefore the city had agreed to restrict police asking for people's immigration papers. This no longer seemed to be the case. To offset such harassments and violations, Olivares and Boyle proclaimed that both La Placita and Dolores Mission would offer their grounds as sanctuaries for day laborers, where employers could go to hire them. Olivares told the press that the risk of him and Boyle being arrested for offering a "zone of refuge" to day laborers was one that they were willing to take as part of their "evangelical commitment."[106]

At the same time, Olivares also expanded this zone of refuge to Latino undocumented street vendors who faced harassment by the police, who claimed that they clogged up sidewalks and streets. For many, however, the only way that they could economically survive was by making and selling food in public. While these vendors could be found in many areas of the city where immigrants and refugees lived, many congregated near La Placita, where merchants at the Olvera Street complex of curio shops and restaurants resented their presence, claiming that they discouraged tourists from going there or that they took customers away from the eateries. Showing the same compassion to these vendors as he did to the day laborers and always willing to buck the system, Olivares announced in the summer of 1988 that he was allowing the vendors to sell on the grounds of La Placita. To further protect them, he issued letters to them stating that they had permission to sell inside church property in case the police stopped them outside the property. In exchange, the vendors promised Olivares that they would keep the grounds clean and not impede movement of others to attend church services. Olivares likewise responded to his critics who believed that the vendors represented an unsightly presence. "I am greatly concerned about the beauty and the cleanliness of our great city of Los Angeles," he wrote to the *Los Angeles Times*. "My great concern, however, is that some will attempt to achieve perfect order and beauty at the expense of the most vulnerable in our midst. Perfect order demands that as a society we respond to the poor, the homeless and, yes the undocumented, not by getting rid of them but by creatively seeking ways to aid them in the betterment of their life conditions."[107] He further told a reporter: "Subsistence is a basic human right. We are talking about survival here, I don't want to come across as one who disobeys the law, but this is not a time when we can be so concerned about the beauty of the city."[108] The vendors responded with gratefulness and soon the smell of cooking tamales, tacos, and burritos filled the air of La Placita, and churchgoers enjoyed the food, as did Olivares. Always the advocate of human rights to refugees and the undocumented, Olivares continuously expanded his definition of sanctuary.

XI

But not everyone agreed with Olivares, including some who wished to physically get rid of him. Standing up for human rights and for championing the sanctuary movement at La Placita also carried risks, including death threats. These came from the reestablishment of the notorious death squads in El Salvador, Guatemala, and Honduras in Los Angeles. The death squads in Central America represented paramilitary units composed ostensibly of civilians, but who acted at the behest of the military. Death squads targeted anyone perceived by the military or the repressive regimes of being "Communists" and members of the insurgent revolutionary groups, including Catholic clergy such as Archbishop Rivera y Damas. They killed thousands of innocent people and were responsible for many fleeing their countries. However, the diaspora also brought remnants of the death squads to Los Angeles, as well as conservative Salvadorans and Guatemalans who formed death squads once in the United States. They targeted and threatened those who opposed the governments of their home countries or who spoke out against U.S. military aid to these governments. They were known as *Los Escuadrones de la Muerte* or sometimes as *La Mano Blanca* (The White Hand). At least in the case of Honduras, but likely also in the other two countries, they were trained by the CIA. In Honduras, the paramilitary death squad was known as Battalion 316.[109] *Time* magazine reported in August 1987: "While most of the Central American refugees in Los Angeles are peasants and political exiles, a number of former Salvadoran military men and National Guard members with right-wing connections also live in the area."[110] Their prime target was Fr. Olivares.[111]

The death squad or squads in Los Angeles had already been threatening Central American activists, mostly of Salvadoran background, but their

Fr. Luis Olivares with death threat by Salvadoran death squads, July 1987.
(Courtesy of Dept. of Special Collections, Charles E. Young Research Library, UCLA)

most publicized threat was aimed at Olivares. On July 15, 1987, when he opened his mail, he found a one-page letter that only read E.M. with the number 1 circled below it. So it looked like this:

E.M.

(1)

It was handwritten, postmarked in Los Angeles, and had been mailed the previous afternoon.[112] "E.M." stood for *Escuadrón de la Muerte*, or Death Squad. Olivares first showed it to Fr. Cully in the rectory.

"What do you think about this?" he asked Cully.

"I'm puzzled that anybody could feel this way about someone else," Cully responded in anger.[113]

Olivares then took the letter over to the staff of Centro Pastoral, where those from Central America told him that the death squads in El Salvador usually put these initials on the homes or offices of those they considered to be subversives, and then targeted them for assassination. Moreover, they had seen these initials in Los Angeles used against some of the activists. Olivares called the police and informed them of the threat.[114] Not intimidated, Olivares decided to go public about the death threat in order to inform others about the possible presence of the death squads. He believed the best reaction was to stand up and denounce these threats. Blase Bonpane recalls that Olivares was not happy about the threat, but felt it best to go public.[115]

On July 17, Olivares held a press conference concerning the death threat. "It is ironic that this church, La Placita, which is dedicated to the protection of those who flee violence," he said in his press release, "should itself become the target of a violent threat." He noted that this specific threat had to be placed in the context of other death threats and attacks on Salvadorans in the city by what seemed to be the death squads. "I do not see this threat as a personal attack," he concluded, "but rather an attack on the Church, whose only commitment is to fulfill the Gospel in defending the most rejected and most persecuted in our society."[116] Olivares likewise informed Archbishop Mahony about the threat. He observed that the FBI, which had become involved, believed that there was strong evidence that Salvadoran death squads were operating in Los Angeles. "This is not the first time I am the object of dirty and mean tactics," he wrote to Mahony.

Usually I dismiss all these incidents and discard the letters or disregard the nasty phone calls. Since this particular incident is in the context of a series of violent attacks on Salvadorans and Guatemalans involved in refugee work or are persons who have spoken out against U.S. policy in Central America I am taking necessary prudent steps to avoid undue risks.

As I said in my statement to the press, I do not consider this a personal attack but rather an attack on the Church because of our work among the poor, the refugees and the marginated [*sic*] immigrant in our midst. Whatever may happen, the work of the Church will and must continue. I only ask for your prayers and your support.[117]

One week later, however, Olivares informed the press that his secretary had received a phone call from an anonymous person who said, "Today all of you are going to die." She reported it to Olivares, who called the police again. Fr. Luis expressed satisfaction with the prompt police response. He further noted that this was not the first such phone call that he or his staff had received threatening them. He acknowledged that all this had to do with his and others' criticism of U.S. policies in Central America plus their work in helping the refugees, especially the role of the Church. He also admitted that he and others at La Placita were taking precautions due to the threats. On his day off, Olivares was not letting anyone know where he went.[118]

Olivares was a sensitive person. No doubt, part of him felt some fear and apprehension, but he knew that he had to keep these feelings to himself, or to close confidants. He knew that even if the death squads did not want to kill him, that they wanted to intimidate him and to affect his work. He would not let them have this success. He would take them on and carry on. He was fortified in this by the many expressions of support by others and concerns for his safety.[119]

In a press interview, he added that in fact he felt proud that the threats recognized him as someone who firmly opposed U.S. policies in Central America; the threats actually made him feel much closer to the immigrants who worked hard for years to survive, and to the refugees who came to this country fleeing death and destruction. The threats put him in the same position as the exploited and persecuted.[120]

Besides going public, Olivares also discussed the threats with others. This included Henry, who recalls that his brother took the threats seriously and was concerned. Henry further noted that César Chávez encouraged Luis to have a bodyguard, but his brother refused. "I'm not afraid to die," he told Chávez. Still, the UFW leader counseled his friend to be careful and prudent. "There are people out to get you and you need to protect yourself." But Olivares never got a bodyguard.[121] At the same time, according to Clements, Fr. Luis became more cautious and more careful about his public activities.[122] When he learned about the death threat, Mike Kennedy expressed more fear than Olivares. "I don't think he really cared," was Kennedy's perception, which differs from that of others. He remembers Olivares telling him, "Well, if they want to kill me, I'm not going to move from here. Let them kill me. They know where I live."

Kennedy feared for his friend's life; he was too young to die. He does admit in retrospect that perhaps Olivares did take the threats somewhat seriously.[123]

Lydia López believed that the threats were terrifying and difficult. They were terrifying because you didn't know what might happen. She admits that when she and Olivares went out to the movies or dinner, they were careful. "It was like having to check the back door," she says. "You never know." It concerned Olivares, but López adds, it did not stop him or fundamentally change his life. He would talk about it, but not all of the time, and he certainly did not obsess about it.[124]

As he had on other issues, Olivares consulted with Peter Schey. "I told him that I thought that this somewhat comes with the territory," the attorney said to him, "and that the more reactionary people believe that you are being effective on behalf of oppressed people and minority people, the more they will become vindictive and they will attempt to decrease your effectiveness by instilling fear in you." Schey admitted that he also got death threats, but that these were usually tactics by the lunatic Right; while there was a danger of someone executing a threat, Schey felt the chances of this happening were not high. Still, he cautioned Olivares to be careful and to take some minimal precautions. "He was not looking to become a martyr," Schey confesses.[125]

At the same time, Olivares maintained his sense of humor about the threats. Some, for example, believed that the threats actually came from the FBI or even the CIA. Cully recalls Olivares joking about this.

"Well, if they are listening to our phone calls," he said, "they're spending a lot of time hearing people inquire about baptisms, weddings, and quinceañeras. Their ears must be burning listening to all this stuff."[126]

Of course, Olivares's family in Texas, when they learned of the threats to their brother, became apprehensive and even shocked. Because he lived in the Los Angeles area, Henry knew more about the threats and informed his siblings about the situation. Teresa Garza observes that Luis never discussed the threats with her or other family members, except for Henry. She later learned through Henry that Luis did not want to have much contact with the rest of the family in order to protect them.[127]

For his part, Archbishop Mahony strongly condemned the death squads' threats against Olivares and others. Four days after Olivares's news conference, Mahony issued a statement on the threats. "Our democratic society," he proclaimed,

> our system of laws, and our experience as a country do not allow us to imagine that private, armed, vigilante groups could roam our streets and neighborhoods from other countries and prey upon those living here. As we celebrate the 200th anniversary of our Constitution, we all find such a prospect to be abhorrent and unacceptable.
>
> I condemn without reservation those threats and provocations upon innocent members of our community. . . . Such attacks must be halted with unparalleled swiftness and completeness for they are a deadly cancer upon our society.[128]

Besides the statement, Mahony personally wrote to Olivares, acknowledging his public statement about the threats. "By the time you receive my note," the archbishop wrote, "you will know that I have already issued a formal statement denouncing this particular type of activity here in Southern California and among all of our people."[129]

While the threats against Olivares received much attention, so, too, did other threats in the summer of 1987 against others such as Blase Bonpane, Rev. Zwerling, and Rabbi Freehling.[130] At La Placita, Mike Kennedy and Mario Rivas received a written threat that read as follows:

> Mire, quiero que sepan que ya sabemos que cambiaron la oficina de Padre Miguel & Mario Rivas. Pero siempre van a morir. Viejo bruto. (Look, I want to inform you that we know that the office of Fr. Mike & Mario Rivas has been changed. But they are still going to die. Old asshole.)[131]

Still others received threatening phone calls left on answering machines. These consisted of hoarse voices saying, with Salvadoran accents, "For being a Communist, we will kill you."[132] One person, however, called the rectory at Dolores Mission and, according to Fr. Boyle's secretary, said the following:

> Secretary: Dolores Mission.
> Caller: En Español?
> S: Si, diga.
> C: ¿Con el Padre Gregorio?
> S: ¿De parte de quien?

C: Los escuadrones de muerte—los padres se van a morir por pinchis revoltosos.

S: ¿Usted cree es algo que usted puede decider?

C: El primero va a ser el Padre Miguel.

S: ¿Pero por qué, por qué usted quiere?

C: Estamos muy cerca—los estamos vigilando, por pinchis revoltosos. El sabado, P. Miguel tenía un swéter verde y un pantalón azul. Estamos más cerca de lo que se imaginan. Los estamos vigilando, pinchis revoltosos, pinchi perra, cerda.

(S: Dolores Mission.

C: In Spanish?

S: Go ahead.

C: With Fr. Gregorio.

S: Who may I say is calling?

C: The death squads—the priests are going to die because they are fucking rebels.

S: Do you think that's something you can decide?

C: Fr. Miguel is going to be the first one.

S: But why, why are you doing this?

C: We are very close—we're watching you, fucking rebels. On Saturday, Fr. Miguel had on a green sweater and blue pants. We are closer than you can imagine. We're watching you, fucking rebels, fucking bitch, pig.)[133]

At the same time, the most threatening actions taken by these alleged death squads involved kidnappings of at least two Salvadoran refugee women. The most publicized and heinous involved twenty-four-year-old Yanira Correa, who was kidnapped at night outside the Los Angeles office of the Committee in Solidarity with the People of El Salvador (CISPES), where she had gone to attend a meeting. She told the police and press that two men with Salvadoran accents and a third Central American had forced her at knifepoint into a van, blindfolded her, and questioned her for about two hours about her political activities and those of her colleagues while they drove her around the city. They accused her of being a Communist and a member of the FMLN. They then beat her and tortured her. "At one point they started cutting my hands with a knife," she testified, "and then lit up cigarettes and started touching them to the tips of my fingers." She recalled that one of the men said: "Do you remember that you have a son? We know him. He's three years old. Would you like to see us doing all this to him?" Later, one of the men said to the other, "Just kill her." But the other responded, "No, this way we're going to let them know that we are here." Correa further added that the men said this was just the beginning, that they were first going to target women, and that they knew who was working against the interests of El Salvador. Before they dumped her under a bridge, where she was later found and taken to a hospital, they raped her with a stick. "The pattern of her injuries," said a USC doctor, "is remarkably similar to that of other victims of torture from El Salvador and Guatemala whom I have examined." She also noted that prior to her abduction, she had received threatening phone calls and letters and learned that one had been sent to her father in El Salvador warning him to tell his daughter to stop her political activity in Los Angeles. In addition, a month before she was kidnapped she had been forced off the road while driving by a man who then threatened her and her son. He left, taking her bag, and soon thereafter she received a threatening letter with a photo of her son that had been in her bag.[134]

A few days later, a Guatemalan woman, Ana Marta López, reported being kidnapped at night by two armed men wearing masks, also with Salvadoran accents, on her way to a meeting at the First Unitarian Church, where she worked for the Guatemalan Cultural Center. The men did not physically torture her, but questioned her about her activities and warned her to stop helping Salvadoran groups, or else she would be killed. Before releasing her in Pomona, they forced her to call the church and warn them to evacuate it due to a possible attack. No such attack followed.[135] "It is our belief," Olivares told the press, "that this activity may have its origins and direction in El Salvador."[136] And Rev. Zwerling of the First Unitarian Church commented on the women kidnapped, "I know both these young women. They are not guerrillas. They are people like us who hold jobs and go about their daily business. . . . So far these cowardly death squads have chosen to attack unarmed women."[137]

Alarmed at these kidnappings and other threats against Central American activists, Mayor Tom Bradley requested the city council to authorize a $10,000 reward for any information on who was behind the threats and the kidnappings: "This kind of violence and terrorism, intimidation, murder threats to anyone seeking to espouse as basic a constitutional and human right as to speak in this community will not be tolerated. I will not permit death squads or any other group of terrorists to create a state of confusion and terror in this city. There is no reason why this group of foreign cowards should come to Los Angeles to threaten our people here much less American citizens." The mayor vowed to place all of the resources at his command to eliminate this threat. He concluded by stating about the threats: "If we don't stop it here, San Francisco, Chicago, Miami and Washington, D.C., will be next." The council approved the measure, although no one came forward with any credible information.[138]

The police and FBI investigated these threats, but no arrests were made, and the threats abated later that summer. Some in the Central American support movement expressed skepticism about the credibility of the FBI investigating the death squads, since some evidence existed that it helped to create the death squads in El Salvador. The FBI did, however, investigate Central American support groups such as CISPES.[139] Moreover, unlike Mayor Bradley, Commissioner Ezell of the INS downplayed the threats and questioned the existence of death squads in Los Angeles. He stated that the reports of death squad–style threats in Los Angeles had "no credence" and instead should be seen as an "orchestrated PR campaign" by the sanctuary movement. That campaign had to do with efforts to pass a temporary asylum bill for the refugees in the Congress. He expressed sympathy for the women molested, but he stressed that this happened all the time. "There were 40 murders in Santa Ana last year," he observed, "but do we blame those on death squads?" He questioned the motives of the sanctuary workers because the INS had never heard of any Salvadoran death squads operating in the Los Angeles area. He signaled out Olivares and his followers as part of the PR campaign and their hopes to revitalize their efforts because, as far as Ezell was concerned, "the sanctuary movement is dead." Ezell's comments, in turn, brought on a strong response from others. "I'm truly amazed at Mr. Ezell's lack of discretion," Olivares said. "The FBI and the Los Angeles Police Department have taken a very serious attitude toward the reported incidents. . . . It's absolutely foolish for any person who is as public as I am to almost bait some crazy person to take a pot shot at me." Mary Brent Wehrli from SCITCA added: "I found this the most outrageously insensitive response I could imagine from anyone. It's hard to imagine that this is the man who is directing the affairs for all immigrants here on behalf of Americans. And, as far as his comments on sanctuary being dead go, that's totally inaccurate."[140] Rep. Joe Moakley (D-Mass.) threatened to call a congressional committee to determine whether Ezell could back up his allegations that some individuals or groups were involved in what amounted to criminal activities by conjuring up death threats. When asked in an interview whether he believed the threats had been fabricated, Ezell backed off a bit and said he did not know, but that it was too coincidental that the threats seemed to appear at the same time that Moakley's bill on deferred action was up for debate.

"I'm saying it's an orchestrated PR campaign tied into [a] debate today," he concluded.[141] Finally, the *Los Angeles Herald Examiner* weighed in on this debate by chastising Ezell. The paper editorialized:

> Anyone who's followed Harold Ezell's career as Western regional commissioner of the Immigration and Naturalization Service is no stranger to his shoot-from-the-hip pronouncements. But his comments Monday denying the possibility that Salvadoran death squads are operating in LA were outrageous even for him. It seems his long-running crusade against the religious sanctuary movement has now spurred him to abandon the prudence that all public officials should exercise when remarking on matters of life and death. . . .
>
> What proof does the regional commissioner present for his bold accusations? None. He admits that the INS has no evidence one way or the other about death squads.[142]

XII

The death squad threats abated, but not the controversy over the refugee and undocumented immigrant issue in Los Angeles and other parts of the country. Olivares was at the center of these debates and struggles, not only in having declared sanctuary for the Central Americans in 1985, but in expanding sanctuary to undocumented Mexican immigrants two years later. Despite efforts by his own Church, immigration officials, and death squads to silence him, he continued his involvements and even expanded them during the second half of the 1980s. Olivares seemed like a man not possessed, but so committed and devoted to the cause of justice that he had to almost be everywhere, and he was. Yet, he was not just an activist. He was a pastor and an individual, and he had to both look after his flock at La Placita and attend to his personal needs.

ELEVEN

The Good Pastor

Luis Olivares occupied many roles in his life, but he was first and foremost a priest—a man of God. This was his vocation even as a young boy. He trained for years to become a priest. It was in his very being. He may have redefined being a priest by his political and social actions; however, he never allowed this to detract from his role to administer the sacraments and tend to the religious and spiritual needs of his parishioners. Hence, in the midst of all of the drama and tensions related to the sanctuary movement, Olivares still remained a good pastor tending to his flock by saying Masses, baptizing babies, confessing sinners, marrying couples, officiating at quinceañeras, burying the dead, and the many other duties of a priest. Part of his role as a priest and pastor of La Placita also entailed developing ecumenical and interfaith connections with Protestants and Jews. But being a good pastor also meant that Olivares had to take care of himself personally and have some life beyond his political involvements and his pastoral duties. Even if this only involved his one day off a week, he cherished this time to himself, in addition to his time with Henry and Lillian, and his close friends and surrogate families. Still, the pressure of events loomed over his life and he had to be on call for new political challenges that would arise in the late 1980s. Some of these challenges would strike close to home through efforts to replace him as the pastor at La Placita. Olivares lived a remarkable life and there was never a dull moment.

I

When Olivares became pastor at La Placita in 1981, he immediately faced the pressures of a small parish administering to thousands of people. What he found at La Placita was way more than what he had encountered at Soledad. The demands on him and the other clergy just to administer the sacraments were exceedingly strong, which makes his ability to juggle both his political work and his pastoral work remarkable. Fr. Francisco Gómez, a fellow Claretian, captured this pressure in a report he wrote in early 1982. "I worked at Placita when I was first ordained (1961–67)," he wrote.

> Now I have returned this past year (September 1981). To my surprise, I have discovered that all ministries (except funerals) have since increased in number. There are more Masses, more baptisms, more weddings and Quinceañeras—more confessions, more office hours; many, many more people, in excess of 12,000 every Sunday. The entire weekend would see some 25,000 people attending services or just visiting the church. Countless families from throughout the county of Los Angeles call La Placita their parish and, Sunday after Sunday, worship at this Church.

Gómez further observed long lines at each confessional on weekends, especially on Sundays, many weddings and quinceañeras on Saturdays, and more than 13,000 baptisms in 1981. Moreover, La Placita offered religious or CCD (Congregation of Catholic Doctrine) classes for children, meetings to prepare for quinceañeras, pre-marriage instruction, and twenty-one hours of confessions on Sundays. "All this means a heavy load and dedication required by our people [staff]," he noted, "we try to give the best we can . . . much remains to be done."[1]

What Fr. Gómez describes is what Olivares inherited as pastor. The magnitude of the workload would have been daunting to any pastor; however, as he did most things, Olivares was excited by the challenge. In this spirit, he reacted to an article in the *Los Angeles Times* in 1983, by its religion editor, on the demise of downtown churches. "[I]t seems as though he completely ignored a reality which is in clear contrast to the picture he paints," Olivares wrote to the *Times*.

> I refer to the Old Plaza Church: Our Lady Queen of Angels Church (the Old Plaza Church) has no lack of penitents, we have a combined total of 21 hours of confession with one or two priests in the confessional almost around the clock on Sunday. No absence of new members, 200 baptisms, on the average, every weekend. No empty pews, with 10,000 to 12,000 faithful at Mass every Sunday.[2]

To administer to this large number of parishioners, Olivares also inherited a large staff and added to it during his nine years as pastor. Of course, he had already been a pastor and, more importantly, had been a high-level administrator as treasurer of the Claretians, and so he knew about management. Moreover, he had a graduate degree in Business Administration from Notre Dame. While his work on the sanctuary movement was filled with tensions and problems, he never allowed this side of his work to negatively affect the running of the parish office to deal with the pastoral side of his position. By all accounts, he ran an efficient and tight ship, at the same time encouraging initiative by staff personnel. María Valdivia, who worked for him for six or seven years, recalls that Olivares was very fair with his employees while holding them to high standards. At the same time, he liked that she spoke her mind.[3] Fr. Cully observes that Olivares tried to promote staff from within and that sometimes this worked and sometimes it didn't. Still, he was always willing to try. He also encouraged the staff to make judgments when needed and to use common sense. This was a sharp departure from previous administrations, in which staff, according to Cully, had been forbidden to make decisions on their own.[4]

During Christmas, Olivares would have a party for the staff that would involve a lunch at a restaurant. He also gave staff a Christmas bonus. In turn, the staff respected and loved him.[5] One possible point of tension, however, involved Sister Modesta, who once, according to Cully, snapped at Olivares after a disagreement, saying, "Don't treat me like your Mexican wife." To which Olivares responded: "That's racist." Sister Modesta was a Spaniard.[6]

As part of his administrative style, Olivares delegated authority to the other clergy on his staff. Of course, he did that with Mike Kennedy on sanctuary issues, but he also did it on pastoral issues. One somewhat humorous example of this involved Fr. Cully. After one of his Central American trips, Olivares felt ill and checked himself into Santa Marta Hospital in East Los Angeles. Cully visited him at the hospital only to learn that Olivares was appointing him as acting pastor.

"You're in charge now of the parish," he told Cully, who was shocked that Olivares would do this, since Cully had just been ordained.

Cully was even more shocked when Olivares said: "Also, I want you to anoint me." To anoint someone in the Catholic tradition meant that the person anointed might die.

"I just got kind of flushed," Cully recalls, "and said, 'I'll send Richard Estrada over later. My first anointing is not going to be my pastor!' That was a little intimidating. I didn't quite know how to lead him in prayer just yet."

Olivares relented on both counts, but did appoint Cully co-pastor until he could recover.[7]

II

Pastorally, the greatest challenge for Olivares was the large number of church services that La Placita had to meet. First and foremost were the

Fr. Luis Olivares saying Mass, La Placita Church, 1980s. (Courtesy of Dept. of Special Collections, Charles E. Young Research Library, UCLA)

numbers of Masses, especially on Sundays. Olivares and the other priests said a total of eleven Masses each Sunday, with thousands in attendance in a church that seated around a thousand. Each Mass was standing room only, with some having to stand outside. The overflow spilled over into the smaller chapel, where the Mass could be heard on speakers, though communion ministers distributed Holy Communion.[8] About 99 percent attending were Latinos—mostly Mexicans, but with more Central Americans as the decade progressed. In fact, it was difficult to distinguish who was Mexican and who was Central American. Araceli Espinosa notes that all represented one community of Latino Catholics, and no one cared if you had your papers.[9] Masses started at 6:30 A.M. and concluded at 7 P.M. One Mass finished and another commenced.[10] "It was like a clearing house," journalist Rubén Martínez observed. "It was like Woodstock, a Catholic Woodstock."[11] On Saturdays, there were four Masses and on weekdays the priests said five Masses.[12] On Sundays, each priest, including Olivares, had to say two Masses.[13] Olivares and the other priests said all of the Sunday Masses in Spanish.[14]

Of the Sunday Masses, the most exciting were the two with live mariachi musicians and singers. These were more than standing room only Masses.

Two were held each Sunday, one at 11:30 A.M. and one at 4:30 P.M. Olivares loved to say these Masses. However, he once complained to Cully, who scheduled the Masses, that he was not allowing him to say one of these Masses. Cully got the point and scheduled his pastor to do the afternoon Mass every week or almost every week. "I decided that since he was the pastor and our best speaker," Cully says, "that he was getting the mariachis."[15] In truth, Cully notes that Olivares did not insist on doing the Mass, but he certainly liked to do it. But the mariachis were not just any mariachis; they were Los Camperos de Nati Cano who played at La Fonda, Olivares's favorite restaurant, where he often sang along with the mariachis. This made the Mass special to him. Rubén Martínez recalls attending one of these Masses after having not attended Mass for some time. It was also one of his first encounters with Fr. Luis and it turned out to be more than a Mass, but an experience.

> The mariachis are blasting, the babies are crying, and there's this guy, Olivares, up there. What made him great is that he had the soul of an activist, but he also really knew how to perform the ritual of the Mass. The Eucharist and transubstantiation [the symbolic turning of bread and wine into Christ's body and blood] occurred on the altar when he raised the host up. He was really, really intense about it. And he always had that wonderful voice. He projected really well and he was very theatrical. I just remember really being fully connected to the Eucharist in a way that I hadn't been probably since I was a kid. So my first encounter with Olivares was not a political one; it was a mystical Catholic one.[16]

The Masses including the use of mariachi music reflected the liturgical changes implemented after the Second Vatican Council, aimed at revising the rituals of the Mass to be more inclusive of the laity. This included the priest now facing the congregation in saying the Mass and having laypeople do some of the readings except for the Gospel and, most noticeably, having the Masses said in the vernacular such as Spanish and English rather than the traditional Latin. Olivares incorporated all of these changes both as pastor of Soledad and La Placita. However, he went one step further. He was the first priest in the Los Angeles Archdiocese, for example, to integrate girls as altar servers, or altar girls, where traditionally only boys served in this role. He did this in 1982. Olivares believed that girls should not be denied this opportunity, and besides he needed more servers and the girls could help fill this need. Araceli Espinosa was one of the first altar girls. She felt that it was "really cool" to be one. She notes that Olivares

Fr. Luis Olivares consecrating host at Mass, La Placita Church, 1980s.
(Courtesy of Dept. of Special Collections, Charles E. Young Research Library, UCLA)

encouraged other girls as well. "This was a new ministry," she observes. Araceli was thirteen or fourteen at the time and in the eighth grade at Our Lady Queen of Angeles Middle School, which was not affiliated with the parish, but just a few blocks from La Placita. She served Mass with Olivares, who treated all altar servers equally. At the same time, he made sure that the girls received prominent roles in the Mass. Araceli, for example, became one of his assistants or lead altar servers. For their roles as altar girls, Olivares and the other priests trained them, including teaching them their responses in Spanish and how to prepare incense. "He led us," Espinosa says of Olivares. She felt that Olivares was a great priest. "He really made you feel in the presence of God," she asserts.[17]

Most parishioners at La Placita seem to have accepted the girls as altar servers. One complained directly to the archdiocese. Luz López wrote to Auxiliary Bishop John J. Ward about what Olivares had done. She noted that she was shocked when she went to Mass on Sunday to see two girls as "altar boys." She became very upset. She first complained to the Claretian Provincial House, but was told to contact the pastor. She called La Placita, but told Ward that she was unable to talk to Olivares or any other priest. She then decided to write to him. "It really sickens me," she wrote, "to see such a thing happen in a Catholic Church and I believe that the Pope has forbidden girls to serve the Mass. How can we be expected to obey a disobedient priest? Then again, how many people realize that girls are not supposed to serve the Mass. Is he [Olivares] taking advantage of the people?" López asked Ward to either correct this condition or to assign a new pastor to La Placita "who is obedient and will conduct the Mass as the Pope had directed."[18]

Ward responded with shock at what Olivares had done, and wrote to him to cease and desist. He reminded Olivares that Canon Law forbade the use of girls as altar servers and further noted that it was a mortal sin for women, including nuns, to serve at the altar.[19] It is not clear whether Olivares replied, but apparently he continued the practice, leading Cardinal Manning to become involved and write directly to the pastor. Manning told Olivares that he could not use altar girls, according to Church law. "I recommend, therefore," he insisted, "that you discreetly discontinue the service of girls at the altar liturgies."[20] Olivares wrote back and held his ground. He justified the use of altar girls due to a shortage of altar boys and the large number of Masses at La Placita, including weddings. "In an effort to encourage greater participation," he responded, "we decided to try the approach of including the *entire family* [Olivares's emphasis]; mother and father as readers, ushers or singers, ministers of the Eucharist, etc. and the children as servers." This approach had proved to be very successful and had increased the number of altar servers to thirty, including eight girls. He informed the Cardinal that no one had complained until the one letter.[21] It is not known whether Manning followed up on this, but Olivares continued the practice of using altar girls. He was ahead of his time.

If there was a large number of Masses with many attendees, there were also mass baptisms at La Placita. Each weekend Olivares and his fellow priests baptized as many as 200 babies. So many parents wanted their babies baptized that the sacrament had to be distributed over two days. Each day, two sets of baptisms took place. These were not individual baptisms, but group baptisms. On Sundays, because of the Masses, the baptisms took place in the chapel.[22] When Teresa Garza went to Los Angeles to attend the wedding of Henry Olivares's daughter, she visited La Placita and witnessed Luis and the other priests baptizing as many as 300 babies.[23] The *Los Angeles Times* also noticed this incredible activity. "It is the age of mass transportation, mass media, mass production," its reporter wrote, "and—at the most popular Spanish-language Catholic church in Los Angeles—mass baptisms." The *Times* called La Placita "the baptismal capital of the world." "This parish has more baptisms than any other in the country by far," Olivares told the reporter. "I don't know of any other church that has had this experience in the world. I think we would have heard about it by now if some other church were baptizing more babies that we were." Olivares observed that the large majority of Mexicans in Los Angeles had their babies baptized at La Placita. Out of 300 churches in the archdiocese, La Placita accounted for one-fifth of all baptisms—some 11,800 a year. Because of the demand for baptisms at the church, Olivares only allowed parents and godparents to attend the ceremony, not other relatives and friends. Mexican parents wanted to baptize their babies at La Placita because of its Mexican Catholic traditions, which reminded immigrants of home. Like other immigrants, this represented their transnational religious ties.[24] They appreciated that Olivares and the clergy understood the particular emphasis that Mexican Catholics placed on baptisms. It was more than something that was required of Catholics; it was a deeply spiritual experience for them. They also saw it as a safe place in an otherwise difficult, if not hostile, environment in Los Angeles. "It's more traditional here, more typical of the *bautizos* (baptisms) in Mexico," one parent told the *Los Angeles Times*. While another added: "Here [at La Placita] everyone is Latino, so you just feel more a *gusto* (comfortable). Everybody understands what a *bautizo* means, the festival of it all as well as the religious ceremony."[25]

Olivares loved to do baptisms. He took baptisms seriously because the parents took it seriously. He liked to talk to the parents at the ceremony about the spiritual meaning of baptism and how it signified children entering into the community of the Church. He enjoyed these moments; however, as he became more involved in the sanctuary movement, including his trips to El Salvador, he did fewer baptisms. Cully, who was responsible for making baptismal assignments for the clergy, assigned fewer to Olivares since his being out of town might lead to some baptism cancellations.[26]

Weddings and quinceañeras were happy moments for the clergy. For weddings, couples had to go through three months of marriage instructions involving the responsibilities of marriage and family, and the spiritual connotations. Quinceañeras also required prior instructions. Araceli Espinosa was delighted that Fr. Luis officiated at her quinceañera Mass. Some, if not most, quinceañeras could be very elaborate, resembling mini-marital or pre-marital ceremonies with much expense to parents, who saved for the special coming-of-age celebration of their daughter's fifteenth birthday and her becoming a young woman. Espinosa's parents could not afford such expenses, and so her quinceañera was more modest. At the same time, she was thrilled that, besides Olivares, seven other priests participated in her Mass due to her role as an altar girl. In fact, her court of escorts was composed of other altar servers. Olivares said the homily in both Spanish and English, since Araceli like the other young people was bilingual. Her parents hosted a party at their home, which Olivares attended. Espinosa says of her quinceañera: "The most important thing for me was to give thanks to God."[27]

Araceli considered Fr. Luis her spiritual adviser and would go to him for advice on a number of issues, including her education. She also relates an interesting and amusing story about when she had a date for a Christmas dance as a freshman in high school and her date was from another parish. Olivares insisted that she bring him over so he, according to Espinosa, could "approve" of him.[28]

Besides the weekly Masses and related pastoral activities, La Placita likewise organized for special feast days. Of course, the most important of these was the celebration of Our Lady of Guadalupe on December 12. While Olivares had linked this special day with the proclamation and expansion of sanctuary, the celebration occurred every year, and Olivares, with his own special devotion to Guadalupe, looked forward to it. His devotion first started with his family's celebration of Guadalupe's feast day and his going at age eleven with family members on a *peregrinación* (pilgrimage) to the Basilica of Our Lady of Guadalupe in Mexico City.[29] The celebration at La Placita commenced a week earlier with an eight-day novena to Our Lady. This would consist of Mass with music and special prayers to Guadalupe. Each novena had a particular theme such as "Soy mexicano y Guadalupano" (I am Mexican and a devotee of Guadalupe). On December 12 at five in the morning the celebration began with the singing of "Las Mañanitas" by a mariachi group. Olivares always had his favorite group, Los Camperos de Nati Cano, perform as well as in the Mass. Some people gathered as early as 3 A.M. to get a good seat at what was always a fully packed church. Spanish-language radio station KALI broadcast the ceremonies. In addition, Olivares and his parishioners participated in the annual procession to honor Guadalupe by the largely Mexican parishes. One such procession through the streets of downtown Los Angeles culminated at the Sports Arena where a Mass was held. La Placita provided buses to transport parishioners to the procession.[30]

III

Pastorally, there is no question that the centerpiece of this work consisted of Olivares's weekly homilies at Mass. He came to La Placita with a reputation as a charismatic preacher who linked his Gospel message with a social and political one. At La Placita, he expanded on this especially with respect to the sanctuary movement. Everyone attested to the power of his homilies, whether one agreed with them or not, and most seemed to. The homilies were the highlight of Olivares's week. He enjoyed and found gratification in both his political and pastoral work, but to stand up before a thousand people and open your mind and heart to them was an incredible experience. It was literally a high. It was instant gratification and euphoric in a life that had gratification, but also had its loneliness and separation from the life of most people. Olivares knew he could give a good—no, an excellent—homily and he rarely failed to deliver.

Olivares's homilies had a distinct style. He delivered his homilies, as he had at Soledad, not from the pulpit, but on the ground level in order to be closer to the people. This often meant speaking while kids ran around the church and babies cried, but unlike in other churches, especially Anglo ones, kids were not separated and there was no "cry room" for the babies. It was very Mexican and Latino to have this type of activity in the church. Families stayed together. Occasionally, he might resort to the pulpit but rarely. While he reflected on what he was going to say and how to interpret that Sunday's Gospel, he usually did not write down his sermons. He was prepared and did not ad lib although it might have appeared that way.[31] The style had to do first and foremost with his presence. He had *presencia*.

Fr. Luis Olivares preaching homily, La Placita Church, 1980s. (Courtesy of Dept. of Special Collections, Charles E. Young Research Library, UCLA)

As in his political speeches, he was not bombastic but forceful, persuasive, and charismatic. Kennedy notes that people really liked to listen to him. He was prophetic and passionate. He might be a bit ahead of the people in his thoughts, but he never talked down to them. "He was a great preacher; there's no question about that," Kennedy says. "He wasn't electrifying, but he engaged you."[32]

Fr. Juan Romero captures much of the Olivares style when he observes: "It was rotund. He would look at people and have a nice commanding voice. He was relatively tall for a Mexican American. I would compare him to Martin Luther King. King had an orational style for blacks. Luis had one for Mexican Americans and Latinos. He had a great command of language, both in English and Spanish, a flair in his speaking ability. He was good."[33]

THE GOOD PASTOR

Other adjectives used to describe the Olivares style include forceful, dynamic, strong delivery, sincere, convincing, and self-confident.[34] Cully, who says that Olivares's homiletic ability was better than any other priest he knew, especially brings attention to his cadence. "Some priests deliver homilies in a kind of straight voice," he observes. "He [Olivares] could go up and down. He would build to a high point not just with his words, but with the tone of his voice.[35] Rubén Martínez equates Olivares's homilies in terms of delivery to political speeches. "Brothers and sisters we must do something," Martínez remembers Fr. Luis's words in Spanish addressing his congregation.[36] Another journalist, Moises Sandoval, recalls the Olivares style as not confrontational, but challenging. "He really challenged them in the gut," he says of Fr. Luis's preaching.[37] "You never slept during one of Luis's homilies," Dick Howard observes.[38] His legitimacy as a preacher, however, did not just emanate from his words, but from his deeds. Jimmy Rodríguez believes that Olivares's power with words came also from his praxis in that he was not just a Sunday preacher. During the week he was out with the people, whether the refugees, the undocumented, the street vendors, or the workers. This added to his charisma. "So he was like a Zapata or a Pancho Villa," the labor leader says. "That's the way people looked at him. When he would come into a meeting [or Mass], it would be like on a white horse. Everybody would stop and like, whoa, 'There's Father Olivares.'"[39] Fellow labor organizer, Miguel Contreras agrees, and says of Olivares's homilies: "He touched the souls of his parishioners. You sit in the pew and looking up and hearing him talk, you know you're listening to somebody special and someone who lived what he was talking about. He didn't just read the Bible; he lived the Bible. You could tell that he identified with biblical times. He'd be one of the characters in the Bible."[40]

Olivares embodied all of these qualities; he knew he was a good preacher, and he loved to preach. Sister Jo'Ann DeQuattro, who witnessed many of his homilies, adds of Olivares: "He was a very good speaker. He was quite good. And he knew it."[41]

Part of the Olivares style included his humor, which everyone acknowledged. It was a wry humor but very effective. He like to have fun, and this included having fun in church with his homilies or at least for a portion of his homilies, since he also discussed very serious issues such as the condition of refugees and undocumented immigrants. He usually started his homilies with a little joke or quip to get the attention of the congregation. Sometimes in a light manner he referred to a popular telenovela on Spanish-language TV to get people's attention. Araceli Espinosa notes that he sometimes asked people about these telenovelas as part of his homily even though she believes that he himself didn't watch them. As an altar girl, she saw how he liked to make people laugh.[42] "He was playing," Richard Estrada says of Olivares's preaching.[43] Mike Kennedy would be hearing confessions while Fr. Luis preached and he could hear all of this laughter in the church as people reacted to Olivares's humor. "Why do I mention that?" Kennedy says. "Because he just had the people right with him."[44] Part of his humor, according to Urrabazo, was that Olivares could also laugh at himself. This, the younger priest believes, reflected certain humility on Olivares's part. He knew he had become a kind of political celebrity which he enjoyed, but at the same time, he knew this was transitory and had more to do with circumstances than with him. "I think that's one of the things that endeared him to us a lot," Urrabazo concludes.[45]

As he had done at Soledad, Olivares delivered his homilies in Spanish. While English would always be Fr. Luis's main language, his Spanish had continued to improve over the years to the point that he felt comfortable preaching in the language of his parents. His Spanish was not a formal Spanish, a Spanish learned from textbooks or formal training. It came from his family background, when he had spoken only Spanish at home until he went to school and learned English. It was a Spanish of the working-class people. It was personable and colloquial, utilizing words and phrases that people could identify with. "Every once in a while in his preaching, he would just come out with an expression that people would just roar to hear," Urrabazo observes. "It was a thing that people heard in the streets— sometimes almost irreverent but it had impact."[46] Perhaps it was Olivares's use of colloquialisms that didn't completely convince Ann Kansvaag, who, as a translator of Spanish, felt that Olivares was not truly bilingual and not as effective in Spanish. As a Mexican American, Olivares was not evenly bilingual, but his style, presence, and the context of his message was what was important to those who heard him.[47]

An aspect of his homiletic style included when Olivares didn't preach himself, but instead invited others to do so. First and foremost, he sometimes had some of the Central American refugees tell their stories to the congregation. Technically, these were not homilies and yet they served the same purpose. On these occasions, Graciela Limón remembers: "There was weeping but also laughter; often there was clapping and speaking out. In all, those were extremely positive moments."[48] Under Canon Law of the Church, only priests can deliver homilies, but this did not restrain Olivares. Oscar Mondragon of the UFW has a memory of César Chávez speaking at the church from the pulpit.[49] Other speakers included Catholic journalist Moises Sandoval, who wrote about the sanctuary movement and had interviewed Olivares.

"Moises, how about coming to preach at one of my Masses?" Olivares asked Sandoval on one of his visits to Los Angeles from his office in Maryknoll, New York.

"Hey, I'm not a priest," Sandoval responded. "I can't do it."

"Sure you can, come and tell the people about the refugees. You've written about them."

"Well, okay," Sandoval agreed.

A reluctant Sandoval gave the homily at one of the Masses. "I gave a seat of the pants homily for about ten minutes or so," he recalls. He spoke in Spanish, of course, and Olivares liked what he said. "In La Placita," Sandoval came to understand, "Luis was a guy who was not afraid to innovate."[50] Olivares also invited Blase Bonpane to preach, even though Bonpane, a former priest who had served in Central America, had been removed from the priesthood for his political activities. But as Bonpane says, "Once a priest you're always a priest."[51]

Needless to say, as at Soledad, parishioners reacted very positively to Olivares's homilies and to his pastoral work. People applauded him during his homily, which is almost unheard of in a Catholic Mass. People listen but they don't usually express emotion or applaud.[52] They responded to his preaching, which only energized Olivares more. The people, according to Urrabazo, backed him up.[53] Henry Olivares recalls that they would line up outside of the church to hug his brother after the Mass. After so many embraces, he finally had to excuse himself.[54] Former fellow seminarian Rudy Maldonado observes that after Masses, the people wanted to touch him, almost as if Olivares were a saint.[55]

But the reaction to Olivares's homilies was not just because of his style; it also had to do with the content of what he said. Unlike so many other priests, he did not preach platitudes. Many priests interpret the Gospel in platitudes about loving God, loving your neighbor, and not sinning, but with no social context and all aimed at individual redemption and salvation, and no connection to a sense of community. Olivares was not like that. Of course, he believed in individual salvation, but he did not just want to use his pulpit to sound off generalities that led to little and probably put people to sleep. He would not just say: "Love your neighbor; be good to those who hate you; avoid evil." He would also not simply say: "Don't worry, God will take care of you." Instead, as Fr. Romero notes, Olivares's homilies had a bite to them. "Luis had a much higher perception of things," he says. "But that's the job of a prophet."[56] "God's not going to take care of you," Olivares would preach. "We have to take care of ourselves. That's how God works. God works through us." He didn't mince words when he preached, Dick Howard observes.[57] He spoke from the heart, but intended to motivate people with his social message. Some priests are afraid to alienate parishioners and so avoid controversial topics, but not Olivares. "If he offended them because he preached the Gospel, fine," Fr. Ferrante notes. "That wasn't his purpose. He said what he believed in."[58] Moises Sandoval perceived that Olivares was a low-key person, but with much substance, including when he preached. "He didn't sugarcoat anything that shouldn't be sugarcoated," he observed. "He told it like it was. I think that was his power."[59]

Part of telling it like it was involved linking the Gospel with society. Olivares took the week's scripture either from the Old Testament or the New Testament and interpreted it in light of present-day social and political issues. He believed that the Gospel was a living message that spoke to the present and not just individually, but socially. Ferrante noticed this and understood that Olivares had the particular ability to interpret the Gospel socially, but at the same time make each person listening to it believe that Olivares was speaking to him or her directly. "The people of God in the pews were awestruck," he says of Olivares's ability to do this.[60] To achieve this, he would tell stories about people, perhaps about the refugees or immigrants, but he would connect those stories, as Jesus did to society. For Olivares, scripture was a social text. "Very much in the liberation theology perspective of a Jesus story," Fr. Ponnet says, "and how that would affect people who are marginalized at all different levels."[61]

Bringing together the Gospel and society, Olivares's homilies possessed a political connection, and he made no apologies for that. At the center of his politicized homilies was the issue of social justice. He believed that social justice was at the center of the Gospel and should be the center of the Church. Human sacredness mandated that people in society have justice. No society could adequately function without justice for all people. This is where the Church needed to be, as a champion of social justice. It needed to be where the poor and the suffering were, no matter what the cost.[62] Fr. Vásquez observed that in one sermon Olivares used the word "justice" about twenty times.[63] Henry Olivares recalls that when his brother mentioned justice, the people would interrupt him with applause.[64] Because of Olivares's stress on social justice, Urrabazo observes that his homilies resonated with the poor and working class at La Placita.[65] One aspect of social justice had to do with what liberationists referred to as "social sin." That is, that sin is not just individualized, but also institutionalized in society, such as in racist practices, class exploitation of workers, or the maltreatment by officials of refugees and immigrants. It was not just individuals that sinned; societies also sinned. Olivares addressed such social sin in his preaching. Blase Bonpane observed this in attending one of Olivares's Masses. "He talked about how oppression is a form of sin," Bonpane says. "He based this on the fourth chapter of Luke, when Jesus spoke in the synagogue about the liberation of captives. Olivares would speak frequently of liberation from the oppression of sin and the rights of people to be liberated. He tied all this to the institutional violence of society and the harm it caused. Of course, Olivares got this not only from scripture, but from Archbishop Romero."[66]

Many of Olivares's homilies during the 1980s concerned the plight of the Central American refugees, the sanctuary movement, and U.S. policies in Central America. As he did in declaring sanctuary, he stressed that there was a higher law that superseded that of man-made law and that was God's law. If governmental laws led to the unjust treatment of peoples such as the refugees and undocumented immigrants, he, Olivares, was not going to obey he told his congregation. Instead, he would follow God's law to shelter and care for the stranger and the oppressed.[67] At the same time, much of his preaching focused on the refugees themselves and about their conditions. He wanted them to know that he was there for them and he wanted to inform other parishioners, the Mexican Americans, that they also needed to know about the conditions of the refugee, their fellow parishioners. He accomplished this by relating the scriptures to the conditions of the refugees. According, to Fr. Estrada the people loved this.[68]

Olivares let the refugees know that God loved them in the midst of the terrible upheavals in their lives. He addressed what it meant to be a stranger in a foreign land. According to Cully, Olivares gave the refugees the dignity and respect of including them along with others as the people of God. He did not specifically focus on their refugee status, but more importantly how they themselves needed to adjust to life in the United States and specifically in Los Angeles. Olivares knew that, though the refugees still feared being returned to El Salvador and about their families left behind, they had to think beyond this and deal with their immediate needs on how to survive in Los Angeles, how to make sure that their children had food to eat and a safe place to live. "You have more freedom here," he preached, "and you have to take advantage of it even if you don't have your papers. You have to make sure that your children get an education. You may want to go home eventually, but your children are growing up here.

Help them adapt and not get into gangs and drugs." He did not lecture the refugees as much as tried to impress upon them that La Placita was their home and they could count on its support, because they were all part of "la familia." "We're all immigrants; we're all refugees" he concluded.[69]

But not everyone agreed with his homilies, especially when he first began to preach about the plight of the refugees and conditions in El Salvador. He reflected on this later to Rubén Martínez:

> But I have seen some movement from when I first came when people would walk out and people would get up and shout at me from the pews. Oh, yeah. To where I've come to the point where a lot of people applaud at the service. When I first came . . . I wish I could remember what the topic of the sermon was, but I'm sure it had to do with El Salvador, because I generally use a lot of examples from Romero, you know, as to how he related the Gospel to the people's lives, and this gentleman just stood up—he was about three-quarters back in the church, he just screamed, that "I came here to this church to pray. I don't come here to listen to a political speech!"

Olivares noted that he didn't engage in a shouting match with this person, but just continued his homily and hoped to speak to the individual after Mass and see what particularly disturbed him. This was part of the Olivares style.[70]

Since Olivares did not write out his homilies, few if any survive. However, in the late 1980s journalist Rubén Martínez audio recorded one of his sermons and transcribed it in the Spanish in which it was delivered. Although my English translation does not do justice to the power of Olivares's delivery in Spanish, the reader will still get a sense of his message. In this homily, he interpreted Luke 20:27–38. Fr. Luis's theme was "God is a God not of the dead, but of the living." In part, this is what he said:

> Our faith in the Resurrection is what sustains us and those who are martyrs to their faith. In our time we have the example of Oscar Arnulfo Romero, whose speaking out against injustices in El Salvador was not accepted by the oligarchy and the military. He also spoke out against U.S. imperialism. For this he was assassinated while saying Mass. His blood mixed with that of Christ's. Here we remember his prophetic voice that the authorities might kill him, but he would be resurrected in the voice of the people. Here at La Placita we also live out the Resurrection. We are distinguished by having a preferential option for the poor. The "migra" doesn't like this; the FBI doesn't like

it, and many civil authorities don't like it. They don't like our preaching a radical Gospel that is in defense of the poor, of the refugees, and of the undocumented. But we are not revolutionaries; we are simply following the Gospel. We could also be killed; we could also be rejected; they can take away our parish, but this community will still remain united with the poor.[71]

Parishioners at La Placita not only positively responded to Olivares's homilies, but also to his role as pastor. They not only liked and appreciated him; they loved and admired him. What they especially loved was how he did not have airs about him. He had style but not arrogance. He did not see himself as better than them. He interacted with them as equals, not only at Mass and after Mass, but throughout the entire week. He would talk to people as they came by for services or help from his staff. He talked to the vendors and day laborers who congregated in the church grounds. Of course, he did this with the refugees and immigrants as well. He knew many of their names.[72] He would be talking to a top government official on the phone and then go out to the church plaza and engage with an elderly woman who wanted him to bless her. He talked to her in simple and idiomatic Spanish, not only for her benefit, but because of his own simple way of speaking Spanish. He showed people that they were important to him. His relations with his parishioners included home visits to minister to the sick and those who could not attend Mass.[73] Fr. Cully observed that Olivares had the knack of being comfortable with different classes of people.[74] He was very *cariñoso* or loving.[75] His embrace of people even the most distraught was witnessed by Virginia Mejia at one Mass, when a *borracho* or drunk entered the church while Olivares was saying Mass and proceeded to walk toward the altar. Mejia attempted to stop him, but Olivares saw what was happening and indicated to her to leave the man, who stopped by the altar and caused no problems. "Virginia," Olivares later told Mejia, "we have to know what was in his heart and we have to be sensitive to him."[76] Fr. Luis was not only sensitive to this one man, but to all of his people. He could not have accomplished what he did, including sanctuary, without the support of his parishioners. They loved him and respected him and knew that what he did came from his heart. He was a good pastor.[77]

IV

Part of being a good pastor also involved establishing ecumenical and interfaith relations with other churches and Jewish congregations. The Second Vatican Council had encouraged such relations and Olivares fol-

Fr. Luis Olivares greeting parishioners, La Placita Church, 1980s. (Courtesy of Dept. of Special Collections, Charles E. Young Research Library, UCLA)

lowed through on this. Of course, through the sanctuary movement, he had established ties with non-Catholic religious groups, and so pursuing other ecumenical and interfaith connections only added to these relations. Olivares respected other faiths and, while a devout Catholic, did not believe that his religion was superior to that of others. "He didn't seem to think that his objective was to create new Catholics necessarily," Blase Bonpane suggests of Olivares commitment to ecumenism and interfaith relations. "He was thinking of creating a kingdom of peace and justice—something broader than anything that could be categorized as sectarian."[78]

The base of these ecumenical and interfaith relations involved the sanctuary movement and protests against U.S. policies in Central America. On his trips to El Salvador, for example, Olivares often traveled with Protestant and Jewish religious clergy and leaders. Some Protestant and Jewish congregations also declared sanctuary for the refugees, though rarely housing them, but providing financial and other material support. Of the Protestant churches, the most active in the sanctuary movement in Los Angeles included the Methodists, Lutherans, Universalists, United Church of Christ, and Presbyterians. The sanctuary movement likewise involved Salvadoran Protestant refugees who arrived in Los Angeles. Some who settled in South Central L.A. organized a Christian-based community out of the

United Methodist Church in the Pico-Union district. This group worked with other churches including La Placita.[79] Moises Escalante, who helped organize the Salvadoran Protestants, observes that Olivares was very supportive. "And that made a big difference for us," he says, "because we realized that he was more interested in helping people and not necessarily putting his own Catholic Church in a special place." As part of his support, Olivares purchased airline tickets to fly some of these Protestant refugees out of El Salvador and to Los Angeles.[80]

Olivares's ability to cultivate ecumenical and interfaith relations had to do with not only his sincere embrace of these relations, but also what could be called his ecumenical/interfaith style, or what Kennedy refers to as Olivares's presidential style. This meant that he had a way of making all people, including those of different faiths, feel comfortable, supported, and equal. He embraced everyone and seemed to have a real political and diplomatic style, in the best sense, of doing this. "To be really honest," Fr. Mike asserts, "part of Luis's genius was how he effectively connected with those of different faiths. He was just so good at it. Everybody talks about presidential style and how some of our presidents don't have that and I just think that he did. He could engage people and people felt comfortable with him. He had charisma."[81]

Using that presidential style, Olivares organized ecumenical and interfaith services at La Placita, such as when he declared sanctuary both in 1985 and 1987. But these were not the only such services. The feast day of Our Lady of Guadalupe sometimes involved both Protestant and Jewish clergy. Moreover, the annual commemoration of the assassination of Archbishop Oscar Romero in El Salvador involved representatives from Protestant and Jewish congregations.[82] These joint services not only justified the work on sanctuary, for example, but provided, according to Rabbi Allen Freehling, an added sense of purpose. "There is that phrase in Psalms," Freehling notes, "in which it says, 'My home should be a house of prayer for all people.' This was really being lived out [at La Placita] because not everyone that came to the church was Catholic. Nevertheless, they were being welcomed and embraced. For a brief while they were offered a home with that sacred rite. Therefore, it seems to me that what was being epitomized was really a religious institution at its very best."[83] Fr. Vásquez recalls a Mass at La Placita in which Olivares said the Mass surrounded by Protestant ministers and Jewish rabbis at the altar. "He knew the value of the help from Protestants and Jews," he notes.[84]

Olivares not only organized ecumenical and interfaith services at La Placita, he also participated in some in other churches and synagogues. Rector Regas of All Saints Episcopal Church in Pasadena sometimes invited Olivares to speak to his congregation. Olivares thanked them for their support of sanctuary. He did not concelebrate the Mass, but gave the homily. Olivares reciprocated by inviting Regas to speak at his Masses. "Luis Olivares was grateful to have a good white boy coming down there and saying 'where can I help,'" Regas jokes.[85] Rabbi Freehling also invited Olivares to speak to his congregation, and Olivares also spoke at other synagogues such as with Rabbi Steve Jacobs at Temple Judea. Freehling observes that he never saw Olivares frustrated or despondent, because he was a man of genuine faith. "I think he was very accepting of whatever was going on," the rabbi says. "When in fact it was negative, he would certainly rally himself and then rally us to do whatever we could to turn the tide."[86] Of course, through sanctuary and civil rights issues, Olivares had made connections with black Protestant churches and formed close alliances with black ministers such as Rev. James Lawson.[87]

As noted, Olivares not only supported ecumenical ties but also interfaith ones especially with Jewish communities. Olivares invited Rabbi Freehling to the breakfast at La Placita when Nicaraguan president Daniel Ortega visited the church. Synagogues raised funds for the refugees, arranged for employment, and symbolically proclaimed sanctuary. Refugees would also speak to Jewish congregations. Rabbi Freehling at times translated for the refugees. As a result of these interfaith connections, Freehling came to be impressed with Olivares's courage, compassion, and sense of purpose especially because, as Freehling put it, he "was swimming against the mainstream." "What moved me to tears," he adds, "was his embrace of the refugees and their responding to him as if he was in so many ways their spiritual father or brother."[88]

Through these connections, Olivares made many friendships with Protestants and Jews. Rabbi Freehling, for example, considered his relationship with Olivares as a brotherly one.[89] The Rev. Zwerling points out that Olivares was well-liked and -respected in the ecumenical community, and that in part this was because Fr. Luis did not have any airs of superiority or ego. "I think Luis was probably the friendliest, least stodgy priest that I've ever met," he says. "I don't think you could sit down with him for a few minutes and not feel comfortable. He was very informal. There was no standing on ceremony; there was no sense of hierarchy."[90] And Aracely Domínguez, who knew Olivares well and socialized with him and Lydia López but was a Methodist, notes that Olivares fondly called her "Miss Methodist." "He was a terrific person," she states.[91] Lydia López, an Episcopalian, of course served for many years on Olivares's staff and developed a strong friendship with him, based on what she calls their "shared mission." "For me the connection was the mission," she observes. "It was never this is my pew; this is your pew. I never saw it as Roman Catholic or Protestant. . . . As far as I was concerned, I was helping Luis Olivares do his mission and a mission that I was very much in sync with. It pushed the envelope in a way that nobody else was doing. I loved helping that happen."[92] These friendships even extended to non-believers. Attorney Cynthia Anderson-Barker told Olivares that she was an atheist. It did not faze Olivares at all. He needed her in the sanctuary movement. "Look come along," he told her. "Let's go. We've got work to do." Anderson-Barker felt that his response was "just so great!"[93]

V

Luis Olivares's ministry, both political and pastoral, was exhaustive, and one wonders when he had any time for himself. However, just as he had done as pastor at Soledad and while working with UNO, he managed to carve out some personal time, whether on his day off once a week or in socializing with others after work or after Sunday Mass. Olivares loved to socialize and to have fun. He was not a puritan type of priest. He had his inhibitions like most priests, but he needed time to unwind and just be a person with human needs. He could be shy but, at the same time, he needed to be with people, and not just in the political arena but in just having a good time. He also needed people to want to be with him. He needed to love but he needed others to love him back. It is in these more private moments that part of who Luis Olivares was reveals itself, although never completely.

In writing someone's life, it is an effort to try to understand that person's inner being and the extent of his or her personality. Since I never met Olivares and hence did not personally interview him, I have to try to see his persona not only through the public record, but through my many interviews with family, friends, and colleagues. All of them attest to his complexity, and this is what I hope I can reveal. For one, he seemed to know how to separate his public life from his private life, as much as a priest and especially a community priest like him could. There was a private spiritual side, such as when he prayed the rosary every morning by himself in his room. And then in the evening of the same day, he could go out to drink and have a good time with friends.[94]

Olivares was very emotional, although this could be disguised publicly by a certain "coolness" and dignified appearance that he exhibited, and a steadiness observed by most outside of his inner circle. He contrasted himself with Richard Estrada by saying that while he had "style" Estrada had "pizzazz."[95] However, underneath that determined persona and style was a man who wrestled with his feelings and emotions. He could get frustrated and discouraged over his struggles and the difficulties he had to surmount on sanctuary including his battles with Archbishop Mahony and the Church hierarchy. He would sometimes talk about this with a few confidants, such as Fr. Estrada.[96] "He didn't play games with himself," Regas says of Olivares confronting his emotions.[97] Peter Schey observed that, while publicly Fr. Luis appeared to be certain of his actions, in fact he was not always certain of his decisions and worried over this. "I think in private he was far more circumspect that he appeared to be in public," Schey says.[98]

Perhaps his good friend and coworker Lydia López best captures Olivares's inner feelings. She saw a side to him that many did not. Olivares could laugh, but he could also cry and express deep anxieties both publicly and personally. He expressed a variety of emotions.

> [He was] very human. He would have major upsets, major things that he just wouldn't understand. I saw him weep over concerns that he had. I'd see him get angry. He was a very full-blown human being who felt deeply about things as many of us feel deeply. When we're upset, we cry or if angry we rail. He would do that, too. And that was part of him. There was that part of him that was this gentle pastor to friends and people. There was the other part that was doting—he had his little pets, his little dog, and he used to play with them and spoil them rotten and whether it was a housekeeper that he joked with and dealt with but also was very helpful to her and generous. But also critical. If something didn't happen right, boy, they'd hear about it. As we would.[99]

His sister, Teresa, also attests to her brother's emotional expressions. "That's one thing about Luis," she notes. "He didn't hold his emotions back. If he had to cry, he did. Even in public." She recounts how Luis took the death of his father and Tía Concha very hard and was very emotional about it. This was his family, from which he had been separated due to his vocation, and his emotions must have involved this separation and all of the times he did not see them and could not be with them. He especially took the remarriage of his father very badly. He felt that his father needed to take care of Tía Concha first and foremost. He told Teresa, "Father has an obligation to his sister."

Teresa disagreed: "No, Luis, you're confused. He doesn't have an obligation. He has the right to be happy too."

Olivares attended the remarriage of his father, but did not say the Mass. Later, when Tía Concha died after Olivares's father died, Luis took this even harder since she had served as his real mother. He returned to San Antonio to say her funeral Mass.[100]

Others speak about the range of Olivares's emotions. He could be soft-spoken, Miguel Contreras observed, but when needed, he could use very tough language while still maintaining control of himself.[101] Fr. Gregorio recalls that range when he says that at one moment Olivares could be very serious talking to the press and then go back to his office and play with his cats and dogs and tell funny stories about something that his dogs did the night before. "He had this range about him where he was so incredibly comfortable in whatever situation," Gregorio concludes.[102] Part of that range, of course, was his ever-present humor that all agree was so much a part of Fr. Luis's personality. It also spoke to what Gregorio refers to as his "playfulness." "He was one of the most playful, fun people, I've ever known," he states.[103] Olivares liked to joke, sometimes about himself, but as Rubén Martínez observed, he also possessed a sarcastic sense of irony. "You can't be charismatic," Martínez asserts, "without wit and a sense of irony, and he had it."[104] Olivares loved funny situations. One example occurred when Archbishop Rivas y Damas visited La Placita, and Olivares hosted a dinner for him at the church. He invited Lydia López and her Episcopalian bishop. During cocktail time, Rivas y Damas asked the bishop in Spanish, "How is your relationship with Archbishop Mahony?"

Knowing only a little Spanish, the bishop turned to Lydia and asked, "Lydia, how do you say condoms in Spanish?"

López in turn asked Olivares, who was talking to someone else.

"Luis, how do you say condoms in Spanish?"

"Lydia! Your bishop is here!"

"But he is asking the question!"

"Oh, okay," and so he told her, and she in turn told her bishop, who then responded to Rivas y Damas: "My relationship with Archbishop Mahony is strained because my Church is promoting safe sex and the use of condoms [using the term in Spanish] and, of course, Archbishop Mahony and the Catholic Church do not support this."

On hearing this, Olivares laughed and laughed. He loved such moments. "He found humor in some of the most outrageous and embarrassing things," López says.[105]

Personal life also meant family life. Henry and Lillian and their twin daughters were Fr. Luis's closest family, living in Claremont—east of Los Angeles, but within a reasonable drive. When he could, he would visit them. He loved his nieces and tried to keep up with their lives.[106] Henry would also visit his brother at La Placita.[107] Although it was not possible to visit his siblings in San Antonio or Teresa in Corpus Christi, Olivares still called them and wanted to know everything about their lives and that of their children and grandchildren. "How is Josie? How is Socorro? How is Rosario? How is Damaso?" he asked Teresa. Of course, he always wanted to know how she was, and Teresa confided much to him. Despite the years gone by and so many changes, the Olivares family remained tight-knit.[108] One special reunion, although it did not involve all of the Olivares siblings, occurred when one of Henry's daughters got married in the mid-1980s. Teresa flew out to attend the wedding and Luis picked her up at the airport and took her to show her La Placita and his living quarters. He then took her shopping for a wedding gift before driving her to Henry's home, where she stayed. After the wedding, Luis and Teresa went by train to visit San Diego and Tijuana.[109] Luis loved his siblings and their families, and one of the things he regretted the most about his vocation was how it had removed him from his family since he was a young boy. He didn't blame his vocation for this; it was just the way it was. He needed family and tried to have a semblance of family life.

VI

Olivares loved to socialize, relax, and just to try to have a somewhat normal life. One of his favorite ways of relaxing was going out to nice restaurants with friends, both laypeople and clergy. On Sunday, he would either go out to lunch after the morning Mass, or out to dinner after the late afternoon Mass.[110] Or he would sometimes wait until Richard Estrada finished the last Mass around 8 P.M. "I'd wash up," Estrada says, "and *vamonos* [let's go]." Olivares would tease him: "Where are we going?"

"I don't know," Fr. Richard would respond.

"What do you mean you don't know?" Olivares would shoot back, knowing that they would go to La Fonda.[111]

Sometimes he would go out with Kennedy, Estrada, and Lydia López as a foursome. "We were a little group," López remembers with much fondness. "We had the best times with him."[112] He liked going to Lowry's in Beverly Hills, but his favorite restaurant was La Fonda on Wilshire Boulevard. He not only enjoyed the Mexican food there, but, as mentioned above, he loved the mariachi group Los Camperos de Nati Cano, who performed there, and they loved him. La Fonda was not a barrio restaurant or a mom-and-pop place. It was upscale. Everyone knew Olivares at La Fonda. He sang along with the mariachis at his table and knew all of the songs. Los Camperos would announce to the guests that Fr. Olivares was present and he enjoyed the limelight.[113] "You'd walk in there and they'd give him the best table, right in front of the mariachis," Dick Howard observes.[114]

Besides enjoying good food, Olivares also enjoyed a good drink. Drinking was a way for him to relax. Sometimes he would go out with others just for a drink, but usually drinking accompanied dinners such as at La Fonda. "He loved it," Fr. Estrada says of Olivares enjoying going out to eat and drink. "No one took that away from him."[115] Lydia López stresses that Olivares was a social drinker and especially liked gin—preferably Bombay—and always had a bottle at the rectory, from which he'd take a shot before dinner. However, she also notes that Olivares was a diabetic and had to be careful about drinking; but he did not allow this health problem to prevent his having a good time.[116] At the same time, Urrabazo thinks that Olivares sometimes drank too much, and that when he would sing with Los Camperos at La Fonda, he looked drunk even though perhaps he wasn't. Urrabazo adds that he saw Olivares drinking primarily scotch and also beer.[117] Rubén Martínez once ran into Olivares and his entourage at La Fonda and says that Fr. Luis and Kennedy drank "like good Catholics." "They knew how to unwind," he adds.[118] Richard Estrada seconds all of this, but adds that Olivares also liked to drink tequila and that he was a good drinker. "He was able to put it down," he says of Fr. Luis. "Every Sunday for years after the last Mass at LP [La Placita] we'd go drink, unwind at La Fonda. He loved to be loved. The mariachis (there) loved him, came to the table and drank with us."[119]

Despite an even busier schedule than he had at Soledad, Olivares loved to go to movies on his day off, as he had done for many years. He would go in the evening usually accompanied by Kennedy, Estrada, Ferrante, or Lydia López. They would go to the theaters at the upscale Beverly Center in Beverly Hills, where Olivares also liked to shop and dine. He enjoyed both American and foreign films.[120] He also attended live theater, especially musicals in the downtown theater district. López recalls joining him to see *The Phantom of the Opera*. "He loved music," she notes. "He loved to laugh. He loved to have a good time."[121] At the Beverly Center, Olivares also relaxed by going shopping for clothes, or just window shopping. He still fancied nice civilian clothes and nice shoes, usually Gucci (both dress and casual), that he could purchase at this particular shopping center, which had high-end stores such as Nordstrom's. He had Gucci shoes in black and tan.[122] María Valdivia saw that Olivares was very particular about his shoes and sweaters. She and some staffers referred to him as the "GQ priest."[123] Estrada would sometimes go shopping with him and sometimes, just to please Olivares, would buy a shirt for himself.[124] His friends and colleagues observe that at La Placita, Fr. Luis toned down his fancy clothes, but did not discard them. His closet was full of clothes.[125] Zwerling recalls that Olivares liked to add to his clerical appearance by wearing, for some occasions, his black velvet jacket with his collar.[126] Kennedy observes that Olivares still had several gold watches and gold cuff links. "He simplified his life," Kennedy says, "but he was still a classy dresser."[127] He may have cut down on his shopping and buying nice clothes, but only to an extent. Shopping got his mind off his work, and buying nice things, as for most people, made him feel good about himself. It was one of the few luxuries he had. It's not clear if he had credit cards, but he must have, not only for purchasing his clothes, but also for going out to dine and for movies and the theater. He also loved to shop on his trips such as to Washington, D.C., when on one lobbying trip on Central American issues, he stole away some time and got Cynthia Anderson-Barker to go with him to the nice Georgetown stores to shop.[128] As for the fancy cars he liked to drive, he downscaled a bit at La Placita, but still drove a nice Chevy Malibu.[129]

Part of Olivares's rectory life included his pets. He loved animals and surrounded himself with several pets, upon which he lavished attention. The pets helped keep him company, especially when alone in his room and at night. At one point, he had two Chihuahua dogs, a Siamese cat, two parakeets, and a rare bird. He named one of the dogs Reina (Queen) and the other, darker one Blanca, and one of his cats Salsi from Salsipuedes (Get Out If You Can) in honor of the San Jose barrio where César Chávez had lived in the late 1940s. All of his pets had to be pedigrees, in keeping with his sense of style.[130] On his visits to La Placita, Juan Romero noticed that Olivares had taught the parakeets some songs. "I think he even taught them a couple of cuss words," he says.[131] The rare bird flew all over the room, Urrabazos observed, and defecated all over, which the housekeeper of course had to clean. When Olivares went to watch TV in the downstairs living room, his dogs and cats followed him.[132] One reporter who interviewed him wrote of his dogs: "Two tiny long-haired Chihuahuas, one black, one white and brown, follow close on Olivares's heel as he walks around La Placita. A Siamese cat glowers from its perch in a stairwell as the trio passes on their way into the priest's office. Once inside, the toy-like canines leap across the furniture, tackling one another with playful growls."[133]

Fr. Luis Olivares with his dog Reina, 1980s. (Courtesy of Dept. of
Special Collections, Charles E. Young Research Library, UCLA)

Inviting and entertaining guests for lunches and dinners also relaxed Olivares. The invited guest might be Catholic clergy from other parishes, or Protestant and Jewish clergy, or laypeople. He treated whoever he invited like a guest of honor and made everyone feel at home. Sister Krommer says of this: "Luis was the kind of man who could just meet anybody. He could make a very poor person feel like a prince."[134] Lydia López remembers being invited to have breakfast with Olivares in the rectory following the *mañanitas* (Mexican birthday song) celebrating the feast day of Our Lady of Guadalupe. The breakfast was at 6:30 A.M., and Olivares had *menudo* (tripe stew) for López and others.[135] Of course, he also had suppers with his fellow clergy at the rectory. Not all ate together, but most did and conducted lively discussions about parish work and other issues, including, no doubt, sanctuary. However, Olivares did not always take the lead on this, and sometimes did not even sit at the head of the table. Others such as Estrada and Urrabazo sometimes talked more than the pastor. After supper, Olivares liked to retire to the community room or what served as the living room next to the downstairs dining room and sometimes read sitting in a comfortable chair. He read a lot, including newspapers both in English and Spanish and news magazines, to keep up with the news. He also liked to read books on contemporary politics and the occasional novel. In preparation for his homilies, he read spiritual books, including writing on liberation theology. He also enjoyed listening to classical music either on the radio or on the stereo.[136] When not reading or listening to music, he watched TV usually movies or reruns of older TV shows. "He just needed some downtime," Cully stresses.[137] Special occasions at the rectory included the celebration of his birthday and that of the other priests. For his birthday, the staff would organize a bigger event, with a birthday cake, and hold it in one of the larger staff rooms. The church bulletin also alerted parishioners to Fr. Luis's birthday. In return, Olivares celebrated the birthdays of his staff members.[138]

VII

"He wanted to be loved," as Richard Estrada put it. Part of this involved familial love. Yet he had been removed from his family at an early age. He had grown up with almost no family, at least not in physical proximity, except for Henry. As he grew older, he seems to have still craved a semblance of family life. Obviously, he could not get married and have his own family, but he still wanted a family culture where he could love and be loved and play a family role as a father or uncle figure. At La Placita, he accomplished this by adopting two surrogate families. He knew the Espinosa family because their daughter Araceli had been one of his altar girls at the church, and he knew the Arvizu family because they had been parishioners at Soledad and because their daughter María (Valdivia) worked at La Placita. He became close with both families. The Espinosas invited Fr. Luis to dinner sometimes on Sundays, weekends, or during the week, whenever he could go. "He was part of the family," Araceli stresses. Sometimes they also invited Frs. Estrada and Urrabazo. Olivares would go dressed informally, and chatted with all family members and watched TV before and after dinner. He joked with Araceli and her brother. Araceli observes that Fr. Luis was easy to talk with at the dinner table, and the conversation was wide-ranging. He never preached. "We'd talk about whatever was going on, stuff in our lives, school, et cetera," she says. Of course, Olivares would say prayers before dinner. To Araceli, he always seemed upbeat, despite all his work at La Placita. At the Espinosa home, Olivares spoke mostly English since Araceli and her brother spoke predominantly in English. Her parents also spoke English, but sometimes Olivares spoke Spanish with them.[139]

The Espinosas were very important for Olivares in having a life outside of church; however, even more important were the Arvizus, who represented the ultimate surrogate family for Olivares. He met Arnulfo and María Arvizu as parishioners at Soledad. Both were active in parish work, including UNO. They soon began inviting Fr. Luis to their home in East L.A. for dinner, and he came to also know their children, who attended the parish school. María Valdivia, one of their daughters, recalls a funny incident with Olivares at a Mass at Soledad, when he gave her Holy Communion.

"The Body of Christ," he said before giving her the host.

"Amen," she responded.

"You play very good basketball," he in turn whispered as he placed the host in her hands.

Maria notes that Fr. Luis attended her basketball games.[140]

Beginning at Soledad but continuing after his transfer to La Placita, Olivares visited the Arvizus on a weekly basis. He usually went to their home on Thursdays, his day off. This continued even after the family moved to West Covina, just east of Los Angeles, and bought a home there, consulting Fr. Luis about the value and appearance of the house.[141] Sometimes he would go for lunch, but also for dinner when the whole family was present. For dinner he would arrive at 6 P.M. and stay until 10 P.M. He didn't need an invitation. The family expected him for dinner unless they heard otherwise. "He always knew we were expecting him," Valdivia says. In fact, if he went to lunch or if he arrived early for dinner, Mrs. Arvizu kept a special bed-room for him where he could nap after lunch or before dinner. The Arvizu house became a second home to him.[142]

Part of this home atmosphere was the wonderful and delicious food served up by Mrs. Arvizu especially for Fr. Luis. Olivares loved good food, but he was selective about what he ate, and which in part explains why he was always thin. But he loved Mrs. Arvizu's cooking. "Father was real picky about eating," María Valdivia observes, "but not when he came to our house." He particularly liked Mrs. Arvizu's *carne de rez* or beef dishes, re-fried beans, and home-cooked flour and corn tortillas. On some occasions when he showed up for lunch without alerting the family, Mrs. Arvizu pre-pared tacos and other dishes on the spot.[143]

Feeling very comfortable with the Arvizus, Olivares always went dressed casually, never in his clerical clothes or collar. He liked to wear a Mexi-can *guayabera* shirt in good weather. He also brought one of his dogs with him—usually Reina—who also got served a good meal, since Olivares always insisted that his dogs be served regular food and not dog food. As with the Espinosas, before or after dinner, Olivares joined the family or at least the parents in watching TV, usually Channel 34, the main Spanish-language television station in Los Angeles. They watched the news, includ-ing sometimes the news on the English-language stations. The Arvizus also loved music and shared this love with Fr. Luis. Mr. Arvizu played the guitar, and he and his daughters sang old Mexican songs. Olivares knew and loved these songs and sang along with them after dinner.[144]

At dinner, the conversation was casual. Olivares made it clear that he did not want to talk about work. He wanted to just relax. He enjoyed hearing about what the family was doing and about the kids in the family, such as who was getting baptized, and, if any of the Arvizu married children were expecting children, what names they were considering. In fact, he wanted to name them. "When are you going to name someone Luis?" he asked. Cecilia (Ceci) Arvizu took the more-than-hint and named her first son Luis. In turn, he talked about his own family. In talking to the parents, he used Spanish, but turned to English in talking with the children. Although there was informality to these visits, the Arvizus always referred to him as Fr. Luis. On the other hand, he loved to use nicknames and called María "Chita." In these conversations, Olivares joked a great deal, especially with the Arvizu children. When María Valdivia became pregnant with her sec-ond son, Matthew, Olivares started calling her stomach "Bubbles." "How's Bubbles?" he would ask her.[145]

Fr. Luis Olivares celebrating Christmas at the home of Arnulfo and María Arvizu with children of Cecilia (Ceci) Arvizu, including Alma Leticia (held by Fr. Olivares), Luis, and Andrea, mid-1980s. (Courtesy of María Valdivia)

Olivares came to care very much for his surrogate family and expressed concern over any problems or issues they might have. He showed this concern for Mr. Arvizu, who was in and out of the hospital due to various illnesses. Fr. Luis visited him in the hospital to comfort him. In the late 1980s, Arvizu had kidney surgery and had to be hospitalized for a number of days. Each day Olivares visited him and spent several hours with him, as if Mr. Arvizu were his own father. "Any minute he had he would just go over with my Dad," María explains. "When we would get there in the night, he'd be sitting there on the floor sometimes, just waiting with my Dad like trying to make sure he was okay." He not only cared for the family's physical health, but also for their spiritual health. In effect, Olivares became the family priest. He baptized their children and grandchildren, and he officiated at the Arvizu children's weddings, including María's. He also served as a *padrino* or godfather for some of the Arvizus' grandchildren. When María got married, Olivares paid for part of the reception at the Arvizu home by giving her a check. He loved weddings, and sometimes at Arvizu weddings kidded that he should be allowed to throw the bride's *bollo* or garter to the single men. The one thing that he refused to do was to confess the Arvizus, including the parents and their children. "No quiero saber," (I don't want to know), he told them, meaning he didn't want to know their sins. He was too close to them to deal with this. The one time he did confess María, for example, was at her wedding in 1984. At the altar before Olivares married them, he quietly asked them, "Did you go to confession?" María looked at him and then at her husband-to-be, Rod, and whispered back, "We're at the altar; we can't lie. We didn't go to confession."

Olivares, no doubt with a twinkle in his eye, put his hands on them and softly said: "I just absolved both of you."

He had fun at weddings, including the nuptial Mass. He started María's Mass by saying to the gathered family and friends: "Ahora se casa la Chita con Shorty" (Today Chita is marrying Shorty). "Shorty" was Rod's nickname growing up in East L.A. Olivares's opening line certainly got everyone's attention, including that of the bride and groom, but everyone took it in good spirits knowing Fr. Luis's sense of humor. "It was nice to know somebody like that in your life," María says of Fr. Olivares.[146]

Part of Olivares's relationship with the Arvizuss, and to a lesser extent with the Espinosas, had to do with his wanting to be nurtured, especially by women. Some note that a number of female parishioners competed with each other to care for their pastor and even became jealous of one another if Olivares paid more attention to one and not the other.[147] Being with women seemed to fill a need in his life. Perhaps it had to do with that fact that he had lost his own biological mother shortly after he had been born and never knew her. Tía Concha became his surrogate mother as he grew up, but then in a sense he lost her by leaving for the seminary at such a young age. It was like he needed mothering and found that in other women and certainly with Mrs. Espinosa and even more so with Mrs. Arvizu. One needs to be careful here and not employ pop psychology, yet someone as close to him as Richard Estrada admits that Olivares liked to be nurtured by women and that certain women liked to do so.[148] María notes that Fr. Luis considered her mother to be a "second mother" to him even if he was not that much younger than her.[149] This does not imply any romantic attachments, and there is no evidence of this. Olivares, as part of his personal life and as a way of finding a retreat from La Placita, loved to be with the Arvizus, and they loved to be with him. "They took care of him," his sister Teresa observes. "They loved him."[150]

In 1986, Olivares celebrated the twenty-fifth anniversary of his ordination as a Claretian priest.[151] These twenty-five years had been exhilarating, but also physically and emotionally demanding, and they took their toll in his developing health problems. Despite his thinness, he was a diabetic; it is not clear when exactly he was diagnosed with this illness. Diabetes is also determined by genetics, and it ran in his family. Others of his siblings were either diabetic or borderline diabetics. One of the reasons, no doubt, why Olivares was picky about what he ate had to do with his illness. He avoided sugar, especially at breakfast. Olivares did not help his condition by his feverish schedule. Urrabazo observes that Fr. Luis worked himself ragged. He was always on the go and Urrabazo could see that Olivares was tired. "He wouldn't say no to people," Urrabazo says. He also notes that others knew that Olivares was diabetic, although he didn't talk about it. However, Urrabazo witnessed him talking with others who had the illness about what medicines they were taking. Urrabazo is under the impression that Olivares injected himself for his diabetes, although his sister Teresa says that her brother did not take injections. "We were just concerned," Urrabazo notes about how he and other clerics worried about Olivares's physical conditions and his whirlwind schedule. Not only did Olivares suffer from diabetes, he also had a bad back. Sometimes he couldn't stand up straight. During the 1980s, he had to be hospitalized several times, once for gallstone surgery.[152] In addition, after his trips to Central America he returned physically and emotionally exhausted, which was complicated by his diabetes and his back problems, and so he would put himself into Santa Marta Hospital in East L.A. for several days. He preferred this small hospital because the Mexican nuns and nurses there treated him with

so much care. In return for their kindness, he allowed the sisters to collect donations after Sunday Masses at La Placita. Cully notes that Olivares
never complained about his illness or other physical problems. However,
in retrospect, Cully believes that these physical problems might have been
connected with the AIDS virus that he contracted, probably in the mid-
1980s.[153] In a 1986 letter, Olivares stated that he had returned to work after
"a serious and long illness."[154]

VIII

Despite his health issues, which would only increase, and his need for
some kind of private life, Olivares could not escape, nor did he want to
escape, the politics of his time. The issues of the refugees, the undocumented, and the wars in Central America continued to occupy his time.
One crisis seemed to follow another; there was always one more battle to
take on. This again occurred on November 16, 1989, when the Salvadoran
military brutally murdered six Jesuits, citizens of El Salvador, their female
housekeeper, and her teenage daughter in San Salvador, using U.S. military weapons, on the fabricated pretext that the clerics were Communists
and supporters of the FMLN.[155] Those killed included Ignacio Ellacuria,
S.J., Ignacio Martin-Baró, S.J., Segundo Montes, S.J., Juan Ramón Moreno,
S.J., Joaquin López y López, S.J., Armando López, S.J., Elba Ramos, and her
sixteen-year-old daughter Celina Ramos.[156] They were killed at their residence in the Central American University, a Jesuit school, and the leading university in the country. The news sends shock waves throughout the
world and reemphasized the widespread violence in that country, which
had already resulted in the deaths of some 74,000 people. Pope John Paul II
condemned the "abominable violence" against the Jesuits.[157] "On hearing
the news, most of us," activist Tom Smolick wrote, "especially those who
had met the martyrs or knew of their work, were stunned."[158] Mike Kennedy had been scheduled to fly to El Salvador that day, when the Jesuits
were killed. He knew them. He observes how emotional these killings were:
"It was all very personal. Other friends of ours had been killed. But with
the Jesuits, there was something more. It was kind of like when someone
breaks into your car or into your house; you feel you've been violated. I felt
violated. The war had come to a different level."[159]

   SCITCA, in conjunction with other ecumenical groups including representatives from religious denominations such as the Episcopalian, Presbyterian, Methodist, Jewish, and Catholic churches along with other groups
such as Women of Conscience and with the support of Olivares at La Placita, quickly responded to this tragedy.[160] "We wanted to be the voice of

Fr. Luis Olivares and Fr. Mike Kennedy at news conference,
Wednesday Morning Coalition, November 23, 1989. (Courtesy of Dept.
of Special Collections, Charles E. Young Research Library, UCLA)

conscience when in fact the [U.S.] government was acting with a lack of conscience," Rabbi Freehling states.[161] In less than a week, they organized a mass demonstration to protest the killings and the U.S. role in supporting the Salvadoran military. On November 22, the protestors met at La Placita and followed what would become a familiar route for several months to the nearby downtown Federal Building. There, numerous speakers addressed a large crowd, and volunteers participated in civil disobedience by locking arms and blocking the front entrance to the building. Others picketed around the building.[162] Some, including Catholic sisters, blocked the gates of the building to prevent INS and Border Patrol vans from deporting undocumented immigrants and refugees.[163] Knowing they would be arrested, they nevertheless wanted to stress the urgency of changing U.S. policy in Central America. Sixty-five people, including several religious figures such as Olivares, were arrested. From this reaction to the killing of the Jesuits, a new phase of the ecumenical and interfaith movement was born that came to be known as the Wednesday Morning Coalition for Peace and Justice in El Salvador and the United States.[164] It represented what the initial Tucson sanctuary movement referred to as "covenant ecumenism," a pact between different faiths to protect the refugees and to protest the U.S. role in the oppression of the people of Central America.[165] Olivares and the Rev. Jim

Lawson agreed to serve as co-chairs of the coalition.[166] In other parts of the country, similar protests concerning the killings took place.[167]

Over the next several months, through June of 1990, the coalition sponsored similar demonstrations involving civil disobedience.[168] Each protest took place on a Wednesday, hence the name of the group. On those Wednesdays when mass protests did not occur, vigils formed in front of the federal building. One tactic utilized by the coalition included "Die-Ins," in which masked protestors lay down in front of the building on Los Angeles Street with fake blood on them, under a human-sized skeleton crucified on an M-16 rifle with a sign attached that read "Made in the U.S."[169] At another demonstration, six priests, presumably Jesuits, reenacted the murder of the six Jesuits in San Salvador by lying in front of the federal building under a blood-soaked sheet.[170] Still others including Kennedy, Fr. Chris Ponnet, and Valerie Sklarevsky went on a forty-day Lenten fast, consuming only juice to protest U.S. military aid to El Salvador. Others, including Olivares, joined them in partial fasting. Olivares could only fast for a day, due to his diabetes.[171] Besides its religious base, the coalition grew to include a variety of participants, including lay activists, senior citizens, labor unions, health-care workers, and educators. In addition, the involvement of prominent actors and entertainers such as Martin Sheen, Kris Kristofferson, Ed Asner, Jackson Browne, and others aided in bringing media attention to the demonstrations. Rev. Jesse Jackson also participated in one of the demonstrations and announced at La Placita that he would begin an effort to end U.S. military aid to El Salvador.[172]

The Wednesday protests also came to possess a significant ritualistic character, linking religious symbols and practices with civic ones. The sacred and profane came together. Faithfully on each scheduled Wednesday, participants met at 7:00 or 7:30 A.M. in the basement hall of La Placita for a short prayer or homily service presided over by different ministers, rabbis, or priests, including Olivares who most weeks said a few words.[173] From there they marched, almost as in pilgrimage, to the federal building. Some sang religious songs; others cried out "U.S. out of El Salvador!"[174] Some carried religious signs, such as a Salvadoran cross decorated with religious symbols from that country. "It was a very religious procession by the fact that it was always very ecumenical," Blase Bonpane emphasizes.[175] These rituals created a sense of community and transformed how people saw their lives.[176] At the federal building as people blocked the doors, they employed a litany to help fortify and energize the participants. Those willing to be arrested along with some of the organizers would, for example, call out a statement and the mass audience would respond with a refrain.

Fr. Luis Olivares arrested in front of federal building,
Los Angeles, November 22, 1989. (Courtesy of Dept. of Special
Collections, Charles E. Young Research Library, UCLA)

For example, one statement was: "In March of 1980 Archbishop Oscar Romero is assassinated while saying Mass." And the refrain or response was: "Made in the USA." Several other statements would be made followed by the same response, "Made in the USA."[177]

The protests were, of course, highlighted by civil disobedience, such as the blocking of the front entrance of the federal building, but also included pouring human blood on the entrance sign as a symbolic way of calling attention to the culpability of the U.S. government in the killing of Salvadorans.[178] The use of human blood occurred on May 16, 1990, and involved blood donated by some of the protestors, along with two Salvadoran refugees whose family members had been killed by death squads in El Salvador. Valerie Sklarevsky also poured a baby's bottle filled with her own blood on herself and on the sidewalk and then dropped several U.S. dollars into the pool of blood. "Stop the killing, stop it now," she called out.[179] "The pouring out of *blood* at the Federal Building in Los Angeles [is] to symbolize the passing out of *blood* in El Salvador," stated Sheen, Blase Bonpane, Kieran Prather, and Sklarevsky before being arrested.[180]

Moreover, before each act of civil disobedience, particular individuals, both religious and secular, volunteered to be arrested and they were set apart from the other demonstrators so there would be some order to this

Arrest of Martin Sheen (center) and Blase Bonpane (right) in front of federal building, Wednesday Morning Coalition, early 1990. (Courtesy of Dept. of Special Collections, Charles E. Young Research Library, UCLA)

activity. Different people were arrested each week. At one strategy session, 200 volunteered to be arrested.[181] Lisa Martínez was prepared and had her son with her at one of the demonstrations where she volunteered to be arrested. However, she was told by coalition organizers that she could participate in civil disobedience, but only if she left her son with her husband. "So I did," Martínez says, "and that's when I got arrested."[182] On one of Martin Sheen's first arrests, a reporter called out to him: "Are you a Communist?" Sheen responded, "Oh no, I'm worse than that; I'm a Catholic!"[183]

Some, like Sheen, were arrested more than once. Despite the involvement of clergy and celebrities, the police sometimes used force in these arrests; they handcuffed the protestors including, priests and sisters, and took them inside the federal building, where they were fingerprinted and their photos taken.[184] The high-water mark of these arrests occurred on January 17, 1990, when 234 persons were arrested.[185] "We had to say, not by *our* will; *not* with our consent," activist David Clennon asserted. "But we had to *do* something as well; we had to demonstrate our opposition with our bodies. We had to put our bodies someplace where they would interfere with this United States Federal machine that was grinding up people in El Salvador and here, at home [his emphasis]." [186] Sister Pat Rief added: "I feel privileged and humbled when I risk arrest with people like those in the Wednesday Morning Coalition. They are the 20th century counterpart of the biblical *anawim*, the faithful remnant. They gave me courage and strength to continue the struggle."[187]

Those arrested were taken to holding cells in the basement of the federal building until arraigned. Bonpane refers to the basement as the "bowels of the building" because it resembled a dungeon.[188] Some were kept for ten hours and not fed. Most were released on their own recognizance and paid a minor fine. Some were put on probation. In March of 1990 a judge sentenced Sheen (arraigned under his real name Ramón Estévez) and Olivares to four days of community service. Since both were already involved in community issues, this amounted to no penalty at all. These arrests, according to DeQuattro, drove the LAPD crazy.[189] Moreover, prosecutors did not always get their way. On the occasion of Sheen being arrested for pouring blood on the sign, he, along with Bonpane, appeared before a very elderly judge to be arraigned.

"What did they do?" the judge asked the prosecutor.

"They destroyed federal property. They threw blood on the sign outside of the building."

"What happened to the sign?" the judge asked.

"The blood was washed off.

"That isn't destroying property," the judge concluded. "That's littering. Get out of here!"[190]

The times spent together in the holding tanks, usually for a few hours, proved to be an augmentation of what was already a profound experience. "While waiting to be booked and released," one participant thoughtfully pondered, "we found ourselves sitting on the floor in a basement room and sharing a bit of what had brought us there and what we had felt as we raised our voices to end United States military aid to El Salvador."[191] In the holding tank protesters shared their thoughts including singer Jackson Browne, Episcopal Rector Regas, and, of course, Olivares.[192] Entertainer

Kris Kristofferson, who had been arrested, said "Hi, my name is Kris" as if he were at an AA meeting.[193] Everyone introduced themselves and reflected on what had brought them together. This involved, according to Mary Brent Wehrli, an incredible sharing of stories. She particularly remembers a young Jewish man, Larry Albert, who said that he had strayed from his religion because he didn't hear rabbis speaking to what he felt, but that now he had been arrested with a rabbi and other clergy and this impressed him.[194] Those arrested before Christmas sang holiday carols. All this, Fr. Ponnet suggests, created "a wonderful community of peace people."[195] Sheen, for his part, saw his arrest and that of others as reflecting their willingness to sacrifice in order to save the people of El Salvador. He linked this to the Salvadoran cross that he and others carried during the demonstrations to remind themselves of the sacrifices of the Salvadoran people and, of course, of Jesus's own sacrifice to save humanity. "Christ is crucified again in El Salvador through the deaths of our brothers and sisters," Sheen proclaimed. "The very best among us are murdered and we are reminded how much is demanded of us by the Gospel. . . . The cross is the Way and we are constantly reminded by the Scriptures to take up our Cross and follow Christ."[196] Getting arrested became a status symbol of sorts and some who were not arrested became envious of not being part of the exciting discussions that took place within the holding tank. However, others, such as Lydia López, could not afford to get arrested because they were in charge of raising bail, if needed, for those arrested.[197]

Olivares and his staff, as indicated, actively participated in the coalition. Father Luis had personally known the martyred Jesuits and felt a personal commitment in protesting their deaths.[198] Hence, he played host to the coalition by opening La Placita as the staging area for the demonstrations. Lydia López remembers Sheen, Rabbi Steve Jacobs, and Rev. Lawson arriving at La Placita early each Wednesday morning to first hold strategy sessions with Olivares and others before marching to the federal building. More involved strategy meetings occurred in the evenings at La Placita.[199] "It was all part of keeping the issue alive and in front of people's faces. A very kind of in your face kind of thing."[200] Blase Bonpane appreciated Olivares's hosting the meetings: "Luis was always the host of this whole thing. It was his parish."[201] But his engagement entailed more than just providing support. Olivares's endorsement gave the coalition a particular moral and spiritual legitimacy. Wehrli credits him and the Rev. Lawson with being the "spiritual guides for that amazing period."[202]

At the same time, this activism carried a price, as Olivares exposed himself to further controversy over La Placita's criticism of U.S. foreign policy.

Fr. Luis Olivares speaking at Wednesday Morning Coalition protest, early 1990; Archbishop Roger Mahony is on the right. (Courtesy of Dept. of Special Collections, Charles E. Young Research Library, UCLA)

"Luis was always the heart of this whole thing," Bonpane says of Olivares's relationship to the coalition. "He was the one who was literally sticking his neck out."[203] Indeed, he, Kennedy, Greg Boyle, and Bonpane received death threats for their participation in these protests.[204] One death threat received by Olivares in late November 1989 accused him and the others of being false priests and of supporting the FMLN in El Salvador. The letter warned them that they could easily be assassinated, as the Jesuits in San Salvador had been. At least one other similar threat followed. The tension raised by these death threats was heightened by the police killing of an unarmed young Salvadoran in front of La Placita in early February 1990.[205]

But as with the earlier death threats, Olivares conducted his business. He would not be intimidated or deterred. He continued to march, carrying a picket sign and demonstrated at a number of the coalition's protests.[206] He spoke at some of the rallies. At the January 17, 1990, rally, whose theme was "Send a Message to Congress," Olivares was the featured speaker.[207] According to Kennedy, activists always wanted to have Fr. Luis speak.[208] Moreover, Olivares was arrested several times. When he was arrested, he once again reiterated that there are times when unjust laws must be broken.[209] "It was organic; it just was natural," Kennedy says of Olivares's being arrested. "I mean it was a big deal for him because you don't really picture Luis Olivares getting arrested but it was." Kennedy notes that Olivares being arrested had an inspiring impact on others.[210] Janis-Aparicio witnessed Olivares being arrested. "He loved it," she observes. "He was as happy as could be in getting arrested. He was like as close to Jesus as you could get."[211]

Olivares's involvement with the coalition, however, decreased in 1990, due to his health problems. However, he believed that this last major involvement on the issue of protesting U.S. policies in Central America that had killed so many innocent people, including the Jesuits and causing a massive refugee outflow, was worth it and a highlight of his activist career. "The Wednesday Morning Coalition came together as a response to the brutal murders of six Jesuits, their housekeeper, and her daughter," he said.

> At first, many of us demonstrated to express the anger and outrage in our hearts. This energy was eventually channeled and given the direct purpose of influencing the decisions of our government. A number of people have asked whether we thought we have accomplished anything. Sometimes our actions have seemed futile, but I, for one, am firmly convinced that the Wednesday Morning Coalition is making a strong statement.
>
> As Americans, as religious, and as concerned citizens, we feel it is our duty to question our government's domination over other nations and to put an end to our country's slaughter of innocent people throughout the world. We must continue to protest our government's path of action when the end it seeks to achieve is so immoral.[212]

IX

Even before the murder of the Jesuits and the initiation of the Wednesday Morning Coalition, Olivares carried within him a growing concern that his days at La Placita were numbered. It seemed to be a general feeling he had—although he later told a reporter that he had heard a rumor in the summer of 1989.[213] He couldn't bring himself to talk about this with anyone, but it was a dark cloud over him. He knew that he had served as pastor for some eight years now, two years more than usual. He had been already approved for a third three-year term. It would be unprecedented within the Claretian order, and even among diocesan pastors, for him to be approved for a fourth term. He knew that this probably was not going to happen, but he still hoped it would. He felt that maybe, just maybe, the Claretians would keep him on, based on what he had accomplished and despite the controversies. But he also knew that he had some muted opposition within the order and, of course, there was his tension with Mahony and the archdiocese hierarchy. On his own, Mahony could not transfer him because this was the jurisdiction of the order, but he could encourage, as he had hinted earlier, that perhaps the time had come for another pastor to take over at La Placita. Olivares tried not to think of his having to leave, but the possibility was still there. What to do? Should he take some initiative to try to stay on or just hope this wouldn't happen? It appears that he decided to take initiative and either formally requested another term, or hinted to his Provincial John Martens that he wished to remain.[214]

What he dreaded, however, came to pass in late September 1989, when the order announced that Olivares would be transferred sometime in 1990 and that another pastor would replace him. While Martens no doubt told Olivares of his decision, the public announcement was made by his secretary, who wished to be anonymous. "The only reason is that every six years the pastors are changed to another parish," the secretary told the press. "Fr. Olivares has been re-appointed pastor twice now." The secretary also added that no decision had yet been made on his successor.[215] The *LA Weekly* later reported that opponents of Olivares within the order did not want him to remain at La Placita. The paper observed that at a general Claretian assembly in the spring of 1990, some of his colleagues accused Fr. Luis of being more interested in his personal glory than in the good of the Church. Three months later, the paper further reported, Olivares was called before the Provincial Council and told that he was being transferred and that he had to be out of La Placita by the end of the year.[216] The decision had been made, but what was not known, the press speculated, was whether Olivares would be retained in the Los Angeles area or assigned to another archdiocese.

While the ostensible reason for the removal had to do with Claretian administrative regulations concerning the tenure of pastors, the reality was much more complicated. While the order had consistently supported Olivares's actions, including sanctuary, his defiance of immigration laws, his opposition to U.S. policies in Central America, it still had serious concerns about how Olivares was administering the parish and the impact of his actions. It wasn't that the order did not support his politics, but many within the order or at least the hierarchy did not care for what they believed had become an unruly situation at La Placita especially with the sheltering of refugees, immigrants, and the homeless in the church and the church hall. They believed that all this created unsanitary conditions and unsafe ones with the increase, so the police alleged, of crime in the area. Martens and others felt there was too much noise and congestion, making the church resemble Grand Central Station with people coming and going all day long and into the evening. They expressed concern that priests and others could get mugged and noted that Fr. Tobias Romero had actually been beaten up as he went to his car. Things had deteriorated to such a degree, Martens believed, that he wasn't even sure he could get someone else to replace Olivares. Then, of course, the extent of pressure on Martens by Mahony is not clear, other than the knowledge that the archbishop would welcome a change.[217] Fr. Urrabazo acknowledges that these complaints had much to do with Olivares's transfer. While he notes that the order, at one level, expressed concerns over Fr. Luis's increasing health issues, more to the point was its dislike of "bums" sleeping, urinating, fighting, and passing drugs in the church, so the order alleged. Many within the order felt, so Urrabazo suggests, that Olivares had gone too far in trying to take care of these people and that this needed to come to an end. Of course, Olivares denied these allegations, and Mike Kennedy challenged the idea that increased crime accompanied sanctuary.[218] At the same time, Fr. Estrada notes that things were beginning to deteriorate at La Placita and that the church hall stank after people slept there. He warned Olivares but says, "He didn't want to listen."[219]

The news of his pending removal as pastor of La Placita, of course, upset Olivares. He had given much to the parish and part of him, perhaps a good deal of him, felt this should be acknowledged by his order and the archdiocese, and that he should be kept on. He felt hurt and as if the ground had been taken from under him. He knew that he had no choice but to obey his superiors; at the same time, he felt that they were wrong and that this was more than an administrative change. It was a way of getting back at him. Olivares's initial reaction was that it was his confrontational style of ministry that brought on his transfer.[220]

It was his liberationist politics, he believed, that alienated others and was the root cause of his dismissal. "I make an unqualified statement that we have to have a preferential option for poor people," he told Rubén Martínez. "Some people say, 'well, rich people have souls too.' Of course they do. But they will only be saved if they have a concern for the poor," he concluded. Of course, in his anger, as much as he showed it, Olivares

THE GOOD PASTOR

did not confront the question that, if it were his politics that was involved in the change, why had this change not occurred earlier? His response seemed to be that his removal had to do with the change in provincials. Former provincial Frank Ferrante had always supported him, but with his leaving his position due to term limits, the new provincial, John Martens, did not have the same commitment to Olivares's work at La Placita and, moreover, was more susceptible to pressure from the archdiocese, including from Mahony. Rosendo Urrabazo observes that Martens did not get along well with Olivares. "He respected Luis in terms of what Luis stood for and what kind of work he was doing," he says, "but he [Martens] disagreed with the way that he was doing it."[221] Matters were not helped when Martens informed Olivares in fall 1989, that besides being removed from his parish, he was also not being allowed to stay in Los Angeles, but would be transferred to Fort Worth, Texas, by the summer of 1990. This only added to Olivares's frustration.

He took out his frustration on the order. He understood that it had the right to end his stay at La Placita and to transfer him to another parish even if it was back in Texas. However, what he could not understand was the way it was done. There was no prior consultation with him so that it would not come as a complete surprise. What Olivares was more critical of was the lack of process. That is, there was no effort to obtain from him what the state of the parish was and what he might recommend to his successor. He was likewise disturbed that there was no discussion with him about who his successor might be and how and why his replacement should continue Olivares's work with the refugees and immigrants. He referred to this lack of consultation as a "systemic problem" whereby the order, or at least Martens and the Provincial Council, did not consult not only him, but his staff and the parishioners about its decision. "I was not consulted," he stated. "No one in the provincial council came and made a needs assessment." Olivares told reporter Demetria Martínez of the *National Catholic Reporter* that he might take his complaints to the Claretian Superior General in Rome, Fr. Gustavo Alonso, although there is no evidence that he did. Olivares defended his tenure by noting that what made La Placita unique was its merging of what he called the "popular church"—that is, its work with the people at the grassroots—and the institutional Church, or the more formal side of the Church. "It's a wonderful mosaic," he told Martínez and added that Archbishop Mahony had singled out his parish ministry as exemplary.[222] "I'm not complaining about myself being transferred," he told another reporter, "but the lack of a process regarding what impact the change would have on the parish." As a result, there was insecurity as to the future of the staff and its programs. "I have no idea what is going to happen or what we can do," he told another reporter. He further noted that some were critical of him for making his complaints public and said that he was not being loyal to his order. "The reason I do this in this way," he responded, "is not to defend myself because I have reconciled myself to the transfer. But I do this because this lack of a process and secrecy is not acceptable in this post–Vatican II era where the Church should be more open and this should especially not happen to a church such as La Placita that has a preferential option for the poor."[223] Indirectly, he was criticizing Fr. Martens who, according to Olivares, did not have Ferrante's courage to reappoint him and to stand up to the pressures, even from Mahony, to effectively fire him.[224] Olivares was convinced that if the order had really wanted him to stay at La Placita, they would have found a way to do it. "My only conclusion," he stated, "is that a change was preferable to them."[225]

Then, of course, there was the question of Archbishop Mahony's role. Olivares was much more critical of his order than he was about whatever role Mahony played in getting him out of La Placita. I could find no direct evidence that Archbishop Mahony requested that the Claretians remove Olivares. However, he had, in the past, speculated about when this time would come. Moreover, the tensions between Mahony and Olivares were well-known, even though both tried to put the best face on this. It is very possible that, with Martens becoming Provincial, Mahony or his staff indicated to Martens that perhaps he should make the change concerning Olivares that Ferrante had not wanted to do. For his part, Mahony stated that he had no role in the transfer and that this was the jurisdiction of the order. He likewise praised Fr. Luis for his work now that he was leaving, something he had not done very much while Olivares was pastor. Olivares did not blame Mahony or hold him responsible for his transfer and, in turn, praised the archbishop for his support. Each man was being diplomatic toward the other. It served no political purpose for Mahony to criticize Olivares while he was down. Instead, he sounded gracious and understanding of what Olivares had tried to accomplish at La Placita—and being a complex person himself, he no doubt felt for Fr. Luis. Nor did it serve Olivares to attack Mahony, since Olivares still hoped he could stay in the Los Angeles area, in spite of the order's announcement of his reassignment to Texas. To remain in Los Angeles, he might need the archbishop's support. Hence, both danced around each other.

For his part, Olivares defended Mahony against charges that Mahony had in effect orchestrated his removal. While he believed that the archbishop did support his removal, he seemed not to agree that it was done maliciously. He took exception, for example, to an article in the LA *Weekly* that proposed that the reason for his ousting was because he and La Placita had come to represent a threat to Mahony and constituted an alternative Church. In reality, there is truth to what the newspaper suggested, but Olivares did not want his legacy to be linked to any notion of a schism or to his being involved with any effort to separate himself from the Church. To the contrary, he was working within the Church as a good "company man" to move the Church back to its roots as a Church of and for the poor. If there had been any deviation, it had come from others in the hierarchy who did not prioritize the poor and oppressed and seemed to be more comfortable as bureaucrats who affiliated with the rich and powerful. "I find that I must personally disassociate myself from any attempt to pit me against the Archbishop of Los Angeles, Roger Mahony," he responded in a letter to the *Weekly* that was subsequently published. "I am after all a Pastor in a Diocesan Parish and therefore duty bound to obey the Archbishop and willfully committed to respect and support him. I must also take public exception to the characterization of the ministry at La Placita as an 'alternative' to the established church. Our activist role may differ from the more systematic approach to solutions but there is ample room for both in one same church with a common goal of announcing the GOOD NEWS to the poor." He also dismissed the idea that he had established a "parallel church" at La Placita.[226] Olivares himself was playing politics by not wanting to target Mahony as the cause of his dismissal, but rather attempting to keep the focus on Provincial Martens, who, he seemed to suggest, caved in to perceived pressure from Mahony to get Olivares out. "There is the perception, even by our own superiors that Archbishop (Roger) Mahony would rather I not be here," he told the press. "I don't think that's true." What was more the case, Olivares proposed, was that Martens believed that Mahony wanted him relieved of his position and acted on this notion.[227]

Although clearly upset, Olivares stressed that he was not concerned about himself, but about the future of the ministry he had established at La Placita. He was prepared to accept whatever happened to him. He noted that he was not indispensable and that his work did not necessitate that he be in charge. "I have great concern for the future of the ministry at La Placita," he told the LA *Weekly*. "I do not consider myself indispensable for that ministry."[228] In responding to a question from *La Opinión* as to who would replace him, Olivares stated that he did not know, but that he did not consider himself indispensable to any project. He believed that as long as his successor had the same sympathy for and the interests of the refugees and immigrants in mind, he would succeed. And in a frank statement, he admitted that perhaps his staying on had not been beneficial in creating more parish leadership. It was too easy for others to say, "Oh, Fr. Olivares will take care of this." But with his departure, perhaps, Olivares concluded, others would now say, "Well I guess I have to do it."[229]

Olivares came to reconcile himself to his no longer being pastor at La Placita, but still made a concerted effort to be kept in Los Angeles—perhaps in another capacity in another ministry, but still working with the refugees and immigrants. "The fight is not over," he said. "I don't want to run out on the people whose expectations we have raised."[230] He proposed, for example, to Martens that he be kept on as a staff member at La Placita as head of immigrant ministry. Moreover, when he heard that his possible successor might be Fr. Leo Delgado, Olivares approached him to see if he could become part of his team at La Placita. Delgado told him he would think about it, but in twenty minutes, Olivares received a call from Martens who said that Delgado had decided that he could not retain him. When asked to confirm this by the *National Catholic Reporter*, Delgado denied that he had made his decision based on Olivares's controversial activities. The real reason, Delgado advanced, was that it would be too "awkward" to have Olivares around in case Delgado wanted to change some policies. Olivares then proposed creating an independent center for Central American refugees, sponsored by the Claretians. Martens turned him down. "I am unable to negotiate with my own ministry," a frustrated Olivares told the press.[231] Still another option to keep him in Los Angeles was a proposition that he become the head of a new proposed Mexican American Cultural Center which, in fact, never materialized.[232] Olivares even considered requesting to serve in Central America, which also did not occur.[233] Exhausting these options, Olivares began discussion with his proposed new parish in Fort Worth about continuing his work with refugees and immigrants. He tried to put forth his best face when he stated: "I am very happy about where I'm going, and I've spoken with the Provincial in Fort Worth. He gave me a solid preendorsement [*sic*] of what I stand for."[234] Realizing that he had no recourse but to go to Texas, Olivares in his last remaining months as pastor continued to articulate the need for continuity in his ministry at La Placita and for the services and programs for the poor and oppressed to be maintained. He might be gone, but he wanted his legacy to remain. "If we want to have a significant presence in Los Angeles," he said after his departure, "we have to see La Placita as a symbol of hope. What La Placita has been historically and which must continue is an exaggerated symbol of the love of God for the poor. That is La Placita's calling."[235]

Although Olivares came to accept his future, others did not. Many responded with strong feelings about his removal, including members of his staff. Mike Kennedy, in particular, voiced dissatisfaction with how the decision to replace Olivares was done. He criticized Martens for not consulting with the parish staff as to his decision and how it might affect their work. This seemed unusual to Kennedy. "I've never talked with John Martens," Kennedy told the press. "Usually a Provincial visits a parish during the transitional period, but I've yet to see him here." For Kennedy, it was clear that it was Olivares's liberationist politics bothered others and was at the crux of his removal. "We think the Claretian administration is not happy with high-profile, prophetic ministry," he asserted.[236] Kennedy was clearly saddened and also angry that his good friend and colleague was being transferred, but his concern was also about the future of La Placita and how it would impact the work he, Fr. Luis, and others had done for nine years. "I guess I have some preoccupations and concerns that the person who follows Father Olivares may not be flexible enough for letting [undocumented] people stay at 'La Placita,'" he told the *Los Angeles Times*. "Who knows what the next pastor is going to do?"[237] Fr. Ken Gregorio went even further than Kennedy and directly accused Archbishop Mahony of conspiring to dismiss Olivares because the archbishop thought that Fr. Luis was "too big for his britches."[238]

Other reactions came from parishioners and perhaps some staff who, calling themselves "Friends of Father Luis Olivares," drafted and circulated a bilingual petition to Fr. Martens to rescind his decision about their pastor.

The Pastor of La Placita Church, Father Luis Olivares, will be transferred to Texas in July of 1990.

Under Father Olivares's leadership, La Placita was the first Roman Catholic church in Los Angeles to declare itself a sanctuary for refugees and undocumented immigrants.

The church has provided not only food and shelter but also hope for the thousands of immigrants who have fled their country due to war, repression and poverty.

WE THE UNDERSIGNED, CALL UPON THE VERY REVEREND JOHN MARTENS, CMF TO RESCIND THE DECISION TO TRANSFER FATHER OLIVARES.

WE ALSO REQUEST THAT FATHER OLIVARES BE ALLOWED TO CONTINUE HIS MISSION IN LOS ANGELES.

It is not known how many signed the petition, but it did not persuade Martens to change his mind.[239]

While there was a response and criticism by others to the Claretian order's decision to transfer Olivares, there does not seem to have been an overwhelming reaction by many who worked with Olivares in the sanctuary movement and on opposition to U.S. policies to Central America. This may be because the decision came, as noted, at the same time as the emergence of the Wednesday Morning Coalition that occupied the attention and energy of the activists involved. This was compounded by the fact that Archbishop Mahony endorsed the coalition and participated in some of its demonstrations. No doubt it would have seemed awkward to put pressure on Mahony to reinstate Olivares at the same time that the Archbishop was working with members of the coalition. To his credit, Olivares, although he was critical of his own order for the way they removed him, did not call on others to mount a defense of him. He had his pride and dignity and was not going to make himself a martyr or a cause for others. Blase Bonpane, one of Olivares's strongest supporters, exemplified this cautious reaction. A vocal activist, Bonpane reacted to the issue of Olivares's transfer in a more careful manner, suggesting that there was not a concerted conspiracy to oust Fr. Luis by those who opposed his politics. Rather, he seemed to accept, perhaps conveniently at the time, that the issue was really an administrative one. "I know this much," he told the press, "if he [Olivares] were being forced to go against his will, there would be thousands of us down there protesting." Instead, of course, there were thousands protesting in front of the federal building, not at La Placita or at the Claretian Provincial House, at a time when activists such as Bonpane were focused on ending U.S. military aid to the Salvadoran government after the killing of the Jesuits.[240] Indeed, even parishioners at La Placita seemed also muted in their concerns for the loss of Fr. Olivares. It may be that although many loved and supported their pastor, they did not know how to react or how they could affect the Claretian decision. Some suggested that there probably would be no change and that things would go on as usual at La Placita. One refugee, for example, told *La Opinión* that Olivares's departure would not affect him since he dealt primarily with Fr. Kennedy and other Centro staff members and not directly with the pastor.[241]

But this refugee and other parishioners were mistaken. Things would change; Kennedy and other staff members were aware of this. In April 1990, Kennedy told a reporter that Olivares's departure for Texas would mean that he, too, would be leaving La Placita, since he doubted that a new pastor would keep him on, as he was a Jesuit and not a Claretian. He revealed that he had already been discussing the transfer of Centro Rutilio Grande and its services to the refugees and undocumented immigrants to another parish. He did not reveal which parish, but in a few months Kennedy and the Centro relocated to Dolores Mission, a Jesuit parish in East Los Angeles. "When I first came here, six years ago, my agreement to work here was with Fr. Olivares and with the Centro," he noted. It was already April, he observed, and the Provincial still had not even paid a courtesy visit to La Placita to discuss the transition and so Kennedy saw the writing on the wall about his future and that of the Centro. When interviewed by the same reporter, Olivares stated that it would be regrettable to lose the Centro and its work at La Placita, but that the important thing was that the work with the poor and oppressed continue. What would remain at La Placita, he felt, was how the sanctuary movement had transformed all of those, including himself, who worked on these issues. That could never be taken away. Refugee and Centro staff member Mario Rivas agreed and observed that they could not afford to just wait around to see whether they would continue at La Placita. They had to make arrangements now for the continuity of their work. Rivas added that their efforts would go on with the same spirit that they had displayed in the 1980s, but, at the same time, lamented that Olivares would not be part of this going into the future, or at least not in Los Angeles. "I think," Rivas concluded, "that it will be very difficult to find someone else like him."[242]

By the spring of 1990, it was definite that Olivares would be leaving Los Angeles and moving to Fort Worth. He accepted this, although it still hurt that it had come about in the way it did. Even if he had really tried to mount an effort, which he refused to do, it is not certain that it would have succeeded in restoring him to La Placita. Journalist Rubén Martínez, who covered this last period of Olivares's tenure at La Placita, suggests that part of the problem and the lack of an effective resistance to Olivares's transfer was the fact that Olivares had not effectively organized at the grassroots. He had Kennedy and the Centro staff, a close group, and some parishioners and refugees in small *comunidades de base*, but this did not organize the large number of parishioners into an effective community force, such as Olivares had accomplished at Soledad with UNO. What he had done at La Placita was effective in assisting refugees and immigrants, but it was not UNO and there was no mass organization that could have been mobilized, if Olivares had so desired or if his supporters had, in opposing the Claretian decision to remove him or to make sure that sanctuary continued. Martínez notes that Olivares was a liberationist and a "vanguardist," but he failed to organize an effective community movement at La Placita. Here perhaps he might have borrowed from his UNO experience. But Olivares never believed that his role was to expand UNO at La Placita; instead, his mission became a prophetic, evangelizing one of embracing the refugees and undocumented immigrants, rather than empowering his parish and parishioners. People loved and admired him, but they were not organized to defend him or his programs. "You can make politics that way but it also makes you vulnerable in the end if you don't have a strong base of support," Martínez adds. "It also leaves you vulnerable when another force wants to knock you out." And they did knock him out.[243]

In an interview with Martínez, Olivares in fact agreed with the journalist's assessment and critiqued himself. "Right now, we're in a process of change," he said. "I'm moving out, a new pastor is moving in. If the ministry dies, this ministry that has been so strong and so significant, so powerful for the last seven years or so, if that dies, I really must say that it was mainly my fault, because I did not establish it on a strong grassroots basis." He was concerned that the only way to prevent a new pastor from undoing the work he and others had done would be by a strong grassroots resistance. However, he was not certain that this would occur because of his own failure to organize such a resistance. He did not think this would happen even though the people at La Placita had supported him and his ministry, but mainly as bystanders, not as activists. "Now why am I so threatened by a new pastor coming in?" he said and then, according to Martínez, hugged his pillow. Olivares instinctively knew that his ministry would be unraveled, and it was.[244] After he left La Placita and had to deal with his illness, he again confirmed in an interview with Fr. Juan Romero his failure at effectively organizing the sanctuary movement as a more permanent political force. "I regret that it was not grassroots enough for it to survive on its own," Olivares admitted.[245] And in another interview, he went even further.

> The regret I have is that it [sanctuary movement] outlives me, that it has changed dramatically. In a way, I think that people who establish something bear a responsibility for its continuity by making sure that enough people are on board so that after you are gone it will continue, and that's what we failed to do. We didn't built a base for it. It's ironic, but we didn't put into practice our community organizing principles—I guess because it's a lot of work, and we were so busy day to day.[246]

This unraveling came with the appointment of Fr. Al Vásquez as the new pastor who assumed this position in the summer of 1990. Vásquez was not a stranger to La Placita, having been the pastor for several years prior to Olivares. The Claretians felt that they needed someone like Vásquez who knew the church and parish and would be familiar to many. Moreover,

Vásquez was not charismatic, prophetic, or an oppositional figure such as Olivares. He was someone who would, according to the Claretians, restore order, literally clean up La Placita, and depoliticize it.[247] Mahony welcomed this change and the new pastor. Bishop John J. Ward, later that fall, informed Mahony that under Vásquez political gatherings would no longer be held at La Placita.[248] Mahony himself welcomed the new pastor and informed him that he had the Archbishop's full support "as we attempt to return this Parish to its prior place of honor and respect for both parishioners and for the general public." And in revealing much of his aversion not to the principles of assisting the refugees and immigrants, but in the way that Olivares had done so, Mahony added: "I was astounded to learn what has happened to Parish facilities, and that so many parishioners have abandoned the Parish because of the overly-exaggerated ministry to the undocumented." In effect, now that Olivares was gone, Mahony revealed what others already knew: the archbishop wanted him out and welcomed the change. In doing so, Mahony exaggerated the physical conditions at La Placita, but he was not just addressing these conditions. By "cleaning up" La Placita, Mahony also meant ending the involvement of the parish in controversial issues such as sanctuary.[249] Under Vásquez, no one was allowed to sleep on church property. Instead, they were directed to homeless shelters. Moreover, the new administration did not allow the homeless, immigrant vendors, and day laborers to congregate within church grounds. But it was not just the material changes that affected La Placita after Olivares left. It was the spirit—the spirit of sanctuary that Olivares had created and that was now gone.

X

All of this was bittersweet for Luis Olivares. This is not how he had imagined ending his tenure at La Placita. He felt betrayed and unappreciated by his order and by the archdiocese. He was a man of principles and a man of action. He would miss what he had been doing at La Placita. He would especially miss his comrades in arms, such as Mike Kennedy, Richard Estrada, Lydia López, other Claretian priests who supported his liberationist ministry, his parish staff, the many colleagues and friends he had made in the sanctuary movement and in the Central American oppositional movements. Of course, he would miss his parishioners and those who were special to him, such as the Espinosas and Arvizus. He didn't want to go. He felt fulfilled at La Placita. He had engaged and defined what liberationists refer to as a "prophetic ministry." This was what it meant to be a priest. "As a priest, I have a house all over the world and I don't want for a place to do my work; however, I won't deny that it hurts me very much to leave this place and to leave for another one would be like starting over."[250] He knew that he was entering into a new period of his life. However, he did not realize that this would not involve his going to Texas, but having to literally fight for his life. He never left Los Angeles. His health, not aided by the extra tension of his dismissal, only continued to decline. He was not only sick, he was dying.

TWELVE

¡Presente!

Luis Olivares awoke one morning in early June 1990. He did not feel well, but he got up anyway, showered, and dressed. His dogs and cat all greeted him, as did his birds. This always made him happy even when he wasn't feeling well, either physically or emotionally. After feeding his pets, he cleaned up his room a bit. He bent over to pick up a tank of water for his fish and felt his back buckle on him. Before he knew it, he was falling down face first on the floor. He lay on the wet surface until one of the other priests in hearing his fall went to his room, knocked on the door, and perhaps hearing Olivares moaning, entered and found the fallen pastor. "Luis, what happened" he said. He helped Olivares to his feet.

"Are you alright?"

"I don't feel well. I think I have the flu."[1]

Not taking any chances, the other priests arranged for one of them to drive Olivares to Santa Marta Hospital in East Los Angeles. Santa Marta focused on maternity care, but also provided emergency and critical care, in addition to outpatient surgery. Established as a Catholic hospital in 1924, it was operated by the Sisters of St. Joseph of Carondelet.[2] Olivares had sometimes gone there when he felt sick, and the nuns, who adored him, made special allowances for him. They immediately saw that Olivares did not just have the flu; he was very sick and they called the attending doctors.[3]

I

The fact was that Olivares had always had health problems. As a young boy and as a seminarian, he was frail and underweight. His eating habits were always problematic; he was picky about his food. He differed from his brothers, such as Henry, who was a natural athlete and always robust. Olivares often got colds or the flu. On top of this, he developed diabetes in his adult years and had to take medicine for it. Richard Estrada notes that Olivares was never very healthy. He had, according to Estrada, several bouts

445

of hepatitis, including when he was at Soledad. "I could see him going down physically and getting depressed because of the end of sanctuary at La Placita," Estrada adds.[4] In addition, Olivares had an intestinal ulcer.[5] After Easter in 1990, Estrada observed that Olivares began to get severe headaches. Fr. Luis thought it was a sinus problem and some of the *viejitas* (older women) at the parish gave him home remedies for it, but he didn't take them.[6] Others also recognized that Olivares was not a healthy person. María Valdivia, for example, once picked her pastor up at the airport from one of his trips to El Salvador, and he was sick. She had to pull over so he could throw up.[7] In 1986, Olivares noted that he had recently returned to work after "a serious and long illness."[8] Juanita Espinosa likewise saw this side of the pastor right before he collapsed. He had said the funeral Mass for her nephew. After the Mass, he told her that he didn't feel well enough to go to the cemetery and would have one of the other priests go for him. "That's how I knew," she observes. "I thought he was having the stomach flu because that's what he was saying." Later that week Olivares spent three days in his room without going out, and Espinosa states that this was not like him. "Father Olivares could be sick, but he would still come down. He might be tired and weak and he still came down." But not this time. Something was definitely not right.[9] Estrada says that it was actually a week that Olivares stayed in his room, sleeping a lot, and getting skinnier and skinnier. "He had no *ganas* [motivation] and we couldn't get him to do anything," Estrada notes.

"Louie, are you alright?" Fr. Richard asked.

"Yeah," Olivares mumbled.[10]

At Santa Marta, the attending doctor believed that Olivares might have meningitis but was not sure; they thought it might also be hepatitis, but knew that it was serious. When told by Fr. Martens, the Provincial, that Fr. Luis was at the hospital, Henry and Lillian Olivares immediately drove there. Henry found Luis very sick and in an isolated unit. "He was terrible," he says. "He was a mess."[11] Soon word got out within Olivares's inner circle that he had been hospitalized. Martin Sheen went to the hospital and saw how sick he was. He called Dr. Davida Coady, a friend of his and someone who had been involved in the sanctuary movement as well as in health work in Central America. Dr. Coady specialized in community medicine and was affiliated with the UCLA School of Medicine, although she lived in Berkeley. She had also worked with the UFW. Because of her political involvements, she had met Sheen, Kennedy, and Olivares. It was Coady who gave some activists in Los Angeles going to El Salvador vaccines against various diseases such as hepatitis. This included Kennedy. She offered to do the same for Olivares on his visits to El Salvador, but he refused and said that he would get them from his own doctor. Coady does not believe that he did. These shots were given in one's buttocks and Olivares seemed shy about allowing a doctor, especially a female one, to do this for him.[12] As a result, he came down with a very serious bout of hepatitis on one visit that laid him up for two or three months on returning to Los Angeles.[13] Coady was in Berkeley when she received Sheen's call.

"Davida, Luis is very sick and is in a hospital in East L.A. called Santa Marta. He looks awful. The doctor there thinks it might be meningitis. Can you come down and see him?"

Coady had never heard of Santa Marta Hospital, but agreed to catch the very first flight to Los Angeles. She asked Sheen for the name and number of the attending doctor to call him. At the Oakland Airport before her flight, she reached the doctor. She asked him about Olivares's symptoms. From what she learned, Coady did not believe it was meningitis. "Have you tested him for AIDS?" she asked. "No," was his reply. "He needs to be tested but he has to give his written consent. If he does, can you test him?" Coady asked. The doctor admitted that he did not know how.

"How would you feel about transferring him to another hospital?" Coady inquired.

"I think it would be a good idea," the doctor responded.

"I'm coming down from Oakland. Can you meet me at the hospital?"

"Yes."

"Would you mind if I arrange the transfer?"

"That would be fine."

After hanging up, Coady knew that this doctor was in way over his head. She also knew that Olivares probably had AIDS based on the doctor's description of the symptoms. Her thought was to transfer him to UCLA; however, on the plane she thought of Dr. Larry Heifetz, an oncologist who had more familiarity with AIDS and who worked out of Cedars-Sinai Medical Center in Beverly Hills. After landing at Los Angeles International Airport, she called Heifetz and told him, "Larry, I've got this guy who is very prominent and doing great work. What I need to tell you and ask for has to be kept quiet."

Heifetz had never heard of Olivares, but if Coady worked with him, then he knew that he was a good guy. He listened to Coady's description of Olivares's symptoms.

"He's got AIDS," Heifetz said.

"Yeah, I know that but I can't talk about this right now. Can you take him at Cedars?"

"Yes."

At the airport in Los Angeles, Sheen picked up Coady and drove her to Santa Marta. Olivares was in and out of consciousness. Coady asked Sheen if he could exit Olivares's room so she could talk with him in private.

"Louie," she said. "Are you okay about being moved to another hospital?"

"Yes," he weakly responded.

"I also need your permission to test you for AIDS."

He agreed.

At this point, Coady engaged in a confidential discussion as much as she could with Olivares. She concluded that he had been exposed to AIDS and, in a brief examination, noticed that he had lesions on his legs, which was another symptom of AIDS. At the same time, she knew that the nuns at Santa Marta were not prepared and probably unwilling to do an AIDS test on a Catholic priest. Heifetz had told her what antibiotics to use to treat the meningitis, which he did have, but which was most likely related to AIDS. The hospital administered the drugs. Olivares's condition was not made any easier by his diabetes and intestinal ulcer.[14]

It was now late afternoon and Coady decided it might be best to wait until the morning to transfer Olivares to Cedars in order to not get caught in the awful Los Angeles afternoon commuter traffic. She made arrangements for him to spend the night at Santa Marta, and she went with Sheen to his home. By then, Mike Kennedy had heard about Olivares's condition, after returning from El Salvador. He met Coady the next morning at Santa Marta to assist in the transfer to Cedars.[15]

That morning, an ambulance picked up Olivares and Coady and transferred them to Cedars. They placed him in a private room arranged by Sheen, but in a section, according to Henry Olivares, reserved for AIDS patients. This was the first indication to Henry Olivares that it might be this dreaded disease, but he chose not to think about it.[16] It was touch and go for the next few days for Fr. Luis, due to the severity of the meningitis.[17] That first day Dr. Heifetz, examined Olivares and also brought in Dr. Irving Posalski, an AIDS specialist, to do the test on Fr. Luis. They found him emaciated and very weak, but marginally lucid. The tests conclusively revealed that he had HIV/AIDS and related lymphomatous meningitis which affected the brain and spinal cord. He was partially blind due to the infection. He was near death, and so they immediately treated the meningitis, which was the most immediate threat to his health.[18] As they started treatments, both Coady and Heifetz met privately with Olivares and told him the diagnosis. One can only imagine Olivares's reaction.[19] Valerie Sklarevsky, who spent some time with him at the hospital but did not learn about the diagnosis until later, says that Olivares was mortified about learning he had AIDS.[20] Henry Olivares later learned about it, and witnessed his brother crying "long and hard" about having AIDS.[21] So did Blase Bonpane and his wife when they visited the hospital, although they did not know that he had AIDS. Bonpane recalls that as they entered his room that Olivares began sobbing. Bonpane had never seen Olivares cry before. He did not interpret this as self-pity on the part of the priest. "It's hard to know what was really going on in his mind," Bonpane says.[22]

The evening of the diagnosis, Coady attended a film premier about El Salvador with Sheen and Bonpane. Both inquired about Olivares's condition, but she did not reveal the AIDS diagnosis to them. She did later tell Sheen. She also informed Kennedy, who was devastated.[23]

Over the next two to three weeks, the doctors treated Olivares's meningitis, and he began to recover and feel much better. They could do nothing about the AIDS, since there was no cure for the deadly disease that began to ravage the world in the 1980s, and advanced drugs were not yet available to halt the spread of the AIDS virus in the body. The drug AZT (azidothymidine) was available, and while not very effective, it was administered to Olivares. All the doctors could do was to deal with the other health problems brought on by AIDS, such as meningitis and pneumonia.[24]

Soon after his brother was admitted to Cedars, Henry notified the rest of the family that Luis was gravely ill. They made immediate arrangements to fly to Los Angeles.[25] Teresa, Damaso, Socorro, and Sister Victoria all flew there, where Henry and Lillian picked them up. Arrangements had been made, probably through Richard Estrada, to put all of them up at the Claretian Provincial House. The next day, they visited their brother while he was still undergoing the tests for AIDS, though they were not aware of this. They knew that he had meningitis. At the same time, Teresa recalls that she thought it might be AIDS and told this to the others, but they rejected this possibility.[26] When Olivares awoke he realized that his family was there. Despite his condition, he retained his sense of humor.

"How come everybody is here? Am I dying? Oh, my God, I must be dying because Sister Victoria is also here! She never visits me."

"No, no," one of his sisters replied, "you're not dying. We're here to give you support. We want to see you and make sure you get well."[27]

Others visited as well, including Martin Sheen. Some sent flowers and get-well cards as the word spread that he had been hospitalized. The UFW sent him a big card with a union sign and many signatures.[28] And on one occasion, Archbishop Mahony visited and blessed Olivares, who expressed great thankfulness for this. He later told Henry that even though he was sedated, he felt Mahony pressing very hard on his head in blessing him. Mahony told Olivares: "Luis, whatever you need, let me know and I'll make sure you get it."[29] In sickness, there was no room for animosity.

Two weeks after he entered Cedars and knowing his diagnosis, Olivares insisted on returning to La Placita to say his farewell Sunday Mass, which had been planned prior to his taking ill. Coady and Heifetz opposed this, but could not convince him and felt they could not order him not to go. "I have to go; I have to go," he said.[30] Either on his own but probably in consultation with Kennedy, Olivares decided that he would tell his parishioners that he was dying, but not that he had AIDS. He wanted them to know his condition and not give them false hopes about his future. That Sunday morning, Kennedy picked him up and he was wheeled to the awaiting car that would drive him to La Placita, one of the last times he would go there. On arriving and parking in Olivares's usual spot, Kennedy assisted him into the wheelchair and pushed him into the church filled with parishioners, who, of course, knew that he had been hospitalized but did not know the serious nature of his condition. They had come to bid farewell to their pastor, believing that he was still going to go to Fort Worth. I want to quote liberally from a moving account of what next transpired from Rubén Martínez, who was in attendance at the 11:30 A.M. Mass with his girlfriend.

We enter the church and squirm in through the typical over-capacity crowd. To our surprise, we see Olivares at his usual post, seated beneath the large image of the Virgen de Guadalupe to the left of the altar. His head is bowed with exhaustion, and he still wears a hospital identity bracelet. He cradles his head in pain. Associate pastor Michael Kennedy officiates the Mass, but for the homily he hands the microphone to Olivares, who can barely hold it with his pale, trembling hands. His voice begins in a whisper, but soon he is weaving a powerful and emotional sermon. He confides that the doctors have given him one or two years to live. "But I do not fear death, my brothers and sisters. One must accept the will of God. If He wants me [to] stay on in this, this," he summons a weak, somewhat ironic smile before going on, "vale of tears, then I will stay. If He wishes me to leave, I will leave. One must accept His will."

Father Luis Olivares bids La Placita farewell with these words: "Like John the Baptist was called . . . so each of us, upon being baptized, is called to be a prophet of love and justice. I ask the Lord for a special blessing for this community that has fought so hard for justice, not only here and in Central America, but all over the world. May it continue to do so, to live out the true meaning of the Gospel." He sinks back into the wheelchair, exhausted.

After the recitation of the Lord's Prayer, during the offering of peace, an old Mexicana painfully canes her way up to the altar to touch Olivares. Next, a communion-aged boy does the same. Soon, a crowd of parishioners is tearfully laying hands upon him.[31]

Back at Cedars with his family before they returned to Texas, Olivares decided not to tell them, including Henry, about his AIDS infection. He said goodbye to them, and they hoped they could see him again once he regained his health. However, Henry learned of the diagnosis from Fr. Martens. Olivares confirmed this the next time Henry visited him. When he did so, according to Henry, "He cried long and hard. He just didn't know how he could have been infected with this. 'Why is this happening to me?'" Olivares told Henry that he believed that he had gotten the virus on one of his trips to El Salvador after he got ill and had to get an injection in a rural clinic. He said he was treated with what was probably an infected needle. Henry, in turn, told the rest of the siblings that their brother had AIDS and the account of the infected needle in El Salvador.[32] Teresa told Henry: "I thought about that but I didn't want to say anything to you. But now we know what's wrong." The news was crushing. "We took it very, very hard," Teresa says. "We never expected this to happen to him."[33] Henry told Luis that he had informed the rest of the family. In a later visit to San Antonio when he was still able to travel, Olivares repeated the explanation to them about how he contracted AIDS, but he also said as the siblings tried to control their emotions: "You're going to hear a lot about this. Please forgive me. You're going to hear a lot of things about me, but what I've told you is the truth." His siblings promised that they would pay no attention to rumors, but just wanted and prayed for his health to improve if possible. The family observed that their brother never expressed bitterness about his illness.[34] But they worried about who would take care of Luis.

However, before the siblings had left Los Angeles, Olivares introduced them to Juanita Espinosa, who, over the next three years, would be Olivares's caretaker. He did it with a sense of humor despite the severity of his illness. Olivares in fact had requested that Juanita come to the hospital and stay with him and care for him. Juanita was much honored because she knew that his visits were being restricted and that his family was there with him. On her first visit, Olivares asked her to feed him because he could not see well. Juanita became traumatized by this, because the family was there and she felt that they should be the ones doing this for their brother. Still, Olivares insisted that she feed him. Her hands were shaking as she tried to do so.

"Why are you shaking?" Olivares asked.

Juanita leaned over and whispered to him, "Because you're putting me on the spot. I'm only a parishioner. Your family is in front of you and you're asking me to feed you? What are they going to think about me?"

Olivares whispered back, "Okay, let me clear this up."

He called his siblings to come up to his bedside and said as seriously as he could, although no doubt laughing inside, "Let me introduce you to Juanita. She's my girlfriend. That's why I requested her to feed me."

Juanita was mortified. "I looked at everybody and I was sweating," she says. "I said, 'Let me make this clear. I'm sorry but I'm not Father's girl-friend. I'm a married woman. I have children and I'm only one of a thou-sand friends the Father has in his life. I'm just one of the parishioners. I'm nothing special to the Father.' I was just shaking. I said, 'Father, I should never say anything to you. Next time, I'll keep my mouth shut. It's not going to help cope with the shaking.'"

Olivares, knowing his joke had worked, replied: "No, I want everybody to know."

Juanita then said, "If you're going to say it, say the truth. What's wrong with that?"

Olivares knew the joke was over. He explained to the others that Juanita and her family were dear friends and that she had agreed to help him espe-cially after he would be released from the hospital. The family, one can imagine, was relieved to hear this although they might have been intrigued that perhaps their brother did have a girlfriend.[35]

The account that Olivares told Henry and later his family about how he contracted AIDS became the explanation that Olivares repeated to others after consultation with Coady and Kennedy. In this explanation, Olivares stressed that he believed he had contracted the virus when he had to go to a rural clinic in El Salvador when he became ill. The nature of this illness is not clear because some who repeated the story, like Kennedy, later stated that it was because he had a diabetic attack. Henry Olivares told others that his brother came down with a high fever and flu in El Salvador and that Kennedy, who was with him, told him to go to a local clinic, where he got a shot. In an interview a year later, Olivares himself noted that hygienic con-ditions in El Salvador left a lot to be desired, including clinics, especially in the rural areas. He added that he believed he got AIDS in one of the refugee camps and that the injection he received was not because of his diabetes, but due to a stomach flu and that the needle must have been infected. Novelist Graciela Limón recalls that Kennedy on one occasion went to great lengths to inform her how Olivares contracted AIDS in El Salvador, but she thinks that he mentioned that it was the result of a dental procedure. And during a visit to Olivares at Cedars, journalist Moises Sandoval asked him how he got AIDS, and he repeated the El Salvador account. Sandoval believed that the explanation was plausible, but was not sure. He notes that a secondary source in San Antonio later told him that Olivares's virus might have been contracted in this country, but had no evidence. Sandoval discounted it.[36]

While Olivares was willing to privately tell his family and a few other confidants that he had AIDS, he was reluctant to go public about it. Coady felt otherwise.

"It's going to get out," she told him. "It always does."

"No, no, I'm not going to go public," he responded.

Coady, Heifetz, and Kennedy consulted with each other on whether Olivares should make his illness public. Coady took the lead in these discussions. She expressed concerns that, as she had told Olivares, despite confidentiality with his doctors and the hospital, the news was going to get out about his AIDS. She was concerned that it would be used to smear not only him, but the sanctuary movement. The others agreed that it might be best for Olivares to get ahead of the potential story and make his condition public. They proposed this to Olivares. Reluctantly and no doubt with much fear and trepidation about the fallout of going public, he agreed. However, he insisted that it was not enough to say that he had AIDS, but that it was important to tell the account that he already had told others: he believed that he had gotten it as a result of an infected needle in El Salvador. He believed that this would squelch any rumors about the source of his infection. The others agreed and Coady, with some hesitation, further agreed to substantiate the story from a medical perspective. She believed it was the only humane thing to do.[37]

At the same time a rationale had to be given, they believed, for going public other than the fact that Olivares had AIDS. They proposed that the rationale should be that he was going public to bring awareness to the dangers of AIDS that were afflicting so many others, including children. Olivares agreed to this angle. It was important that the public become better aware of AIDS and the need to combat it. Anyone could get the virus and they should not be abandoned.[38] One of Olivares's sisters believes that the main reason her brother went public was because of the children with AIDS and that few people were aware of this. His family also feels that Fr.

Luis wanted to encourage others with AIDS to not hide their illness, but to openly admit it and work to educate people about this deadly condition and the need for a cure.[39] Juan Romero says that Olivares went public in order to advocate for AIDS victims. Rubén Martínez challenges this explanation by pointing out that after his illness, Olivares was not very active in the AIDS awareness movement. Moreover, Martínez finds it curious that Olivares went public, because he had not been involved in any AIDS awareness activities before he got AIDS. In fact, Olivares had told Martínez that the Latino community was not yet ready to deal publicly with AIDS and that it, or SIDA as it is referred to in Spanish, was a private matter. "Our people aren't ready for that," Martínez recalls Olivares saying. "It's really hard because it's associated with too many things that are difficult for our people." Martínez disagreed, feeling that this was a "vanguardist" attitude on the part of Olivares who assumed that he knew better than the people. However, the fact is that most Latinos, like most other Americans in the 1980s and early 1990s, preferred not to discuss AIDS.[40] Moreover, Olivares did participate, to a degree, in AIDS awareness after his diagnosis.

However, before going public, Olivares had to take into consideration the Claretians and what impact it would have on his order. It is not clear how this was handled with the order and with Archbishop Mahony, if Mahony was indeed involved. Nevertheless, it appears that the Claretians were reluctant to go public about one of their priests having AIDS. Olivares understood their feelings, but in the end concluded that he had to publicize his illness. According to Fr. Luis Quihuis, Olivares might have believed that at some point the order and the archdiocese would be forced to make a statement on his illness and that it would be better for him to make his own statement on his terms before this occurred.[41]

Before going public, Olivares informed other supporters personally so that they would not be taken by surprise. Fr. Richard Estrada was one of these. They had worked together for many years and it was Richard who had made it possible for Olivares to meet César Chávez. Olivares and Kennedy together told Richard. "It was like a numbness," he says. "I didn't know quite what to think of this." They explained the story of how he got AIDS. Of this Estrada remarks, "So what can I say? I knew him too well." (Estrada did not explain this comment to me.)[42]

As he usually did on any issue of major importance, Olivares consulted with attorney Peter Schey. "I was profoundly saddened because he was like almost a partner in the struggle for justice for immigrants and refugees," Schey comments about this shocking revelation. "And to lose a comrade like that, a person who had been a guide and major spokesperson, it was devastating, and not to mention that he was also the president of our board and had become a friend and was a client."

Schey likewise listened to Olivares's proposal to go public. According to Schey, Olivares had at least two concerns. One had to do with the community, meaning his parishioners and the activist community. Schey states:

He did not want the community to become less strong as he became less strong. He did not want the community to lose faith. He did not want the community to feel his loss. I think that was one major concern. I think a second concern was the work of La Placita and how effective would La Placita be as a voice for the dispossessed. I think that was a second concern of his. I think inevitably there was some concern that some would use this in a derogatory way. The only thing he never expressed concern over was his own well-being.[43]

Schey is of the opinion that it was Olivares's decision to go public, and Schey agreed with this decision.[44]

Olivares also told Fr. Frank Ferrante, another close ally in the Claretian order. At the time Olivares was admitted to Cedars, Ferrante left for a scheduled thirty-day retreat in northern California. Sometime after he arrived, he received a call from Fr. Urrabazo that Olivares was in Cedars and wanted to see Ferrante. Urrabazo quoted Olivares that "time is of the essence." Ferrante took a flight to Los Angeles and went to see Olivares with Kennedy. Fr. Luis told Ferrante that he had AIDS and wanted him to know this before he went public. They talked further and Ferrante spent the rest of the day at the hospital with his stricken friend.[45] Within the order, Fr. Lozano states that he knew that Olivares had AIDS a day or two before he announced it, but does not say if he heard it from Olivares or from someone else. As treasurer of the order, Lozano was privy to Olivares's medical bills.[46]

Before going public, however, Olivares had to also talk to César Chávez, his inspiration and personal and spiritual friend. Chávez had learned that Olivares was in the hospital and called Jimmy Rodríguez, who confirmed it to him. César asked Jimmy to go with him to see Fr. Luis. Rodríguez agreed. Arturo Rodríguez, Chávez's son-in-law, accompanied them. When they arrived, Olivares's family was still there. He asked them to give him some time with Chávez and Jimmy Rodríguez. When they were alone, Olivares said to them, "I hope you continue to be my friends after I tell you what I'm going to say."

"There's nothing you can tell us that would keep us from being your friend," César responded.

Olivares then told them that he had AIDS, but did not explain how he had gotten it.

"No, no. You're our friend for life and there's a life after this," Chávez, in a state of disbelief, said.

"Sooner or later I have to go public with this," Olivares added.

"Sure," they replied.

Soon Chávez and Rodríguez left the room after saying goodbye to Olivares. They were both stunned and couldn't believe what they had heard. "It's like a dream," Rodríguez said. He recalls that he was floating as he and the farm-labor leader walked down the hall. It was like he wasn't even walking, or was walking without his feet touching the ground. He mentioned this to Chávez who replied: "I feel the same way."

Soon they both heard the explanation about how Olivares contracted AIDS. What Rodriguez remembers hearing is that Fr. Luis had had a diabetic attack in El Salvador and had to get a shot of insulin immediately from a clinic and that this was how he contracted the virus. "It didn't really matter to me how he did," Rodríguez comments.[47]

How to go public? Olivares discussed this with Kennedy and Coady. A press release could be done. A press conference could be organized. None of these options appealed to Olivares. He finally decided that he would break the news by being interviewed by Marita Hernández of the *Los Angeles Times*, who had interviewed him before and with whom he felt he had good relations. She was called and told that Olivares wanted to talk with her about coming down with AIDS. Hernández, like everyone else, was taken aback at the news and agreed to the meeting. Olivares was a big political and media star, and Hernández felt fortunate that he had chosen her to break the story. Her editors immediately supported her interviewing Olivares. A date was set for late June 1990 for an interview at Cedars. As she prepared for it, her editor told her to ask Olivares if he had contracted AIDS sexually. No doubt uncomfortable with this, still Hernández agreed to do so.[48]

On the appointed day, Hernández arrived at Cedars and went to Olivares's room. Besides Olivares, who was dressed casually and not in bed, Dr. Coady and Kennedy, were present.[49] They both stayed for the interview, and chairs were brought in to accommodate them. Besides taking notes, Hernández taped the interview—a tape that she no longer can find. The atmosphere must have been tense and surreal. Hernández remembers Olivares looking very gaunt and frail, and he did not display his usual sense of humor. He excused himself for not feeling very well. Hernández observed that he spoke very softly, and not with his usual strong voice, which she had become accustomed to from the priest. The interview began, and one of the first questions, and maybe the initial question, that Hernández asked was, "My editor has asked me to ask you if you contracted AIDS by having sexual relations with other men."

"No, I did not," he responded, and proceeded to present the El Salvador account.

Olivares also spoke about the work he had done at La Placita and that he felt good about what he and others had accomplished. He had lived the Gospel rather than just preaching it. He seemed to express anger that he could not continue his work. Hernández also picked up a certain sadness in Olivares.[50] The interview was not long and concluded with both Olivares and Coady making statements. Olivares gave the rationale for going public that he had discussed with Kennedy and Coady. He told the reporter that he was going public to let people "know that anybody can get this disease and not to abandon those who happen to get it, regardless of how they contracted it."[51] Coady then confirmed that it appeared that Olivares had gotten AIDS in El Salvador. She said that she had inquired about several clinics where Olivares had received treatment for various minor maladies related to his health problems including diabetes. Coady added that she was convinced that Olivares had been infected with the AIDS virus six years earlier at one of these clinics, where medication was injected apparently with a contaminated needle. When Hernández asked what other information she had on the clinic or clinics, Coady declined to say, citing confidentiality issues. She did say that she had learned that other people had been infected with the AIDS virus at the same facility. She concluded her statement by saying, "We hope he will have several years of active life." Olivares brought an end to the interview by adding about his diagnosis: "Though it sounds very terminal, I haven't given up. I have a lot of hope."[52]

Hernández returned to her office, briefed her editor, and began to write her story. Before finishing it, she interviewed others. Knowing that Dr. Heifetz was his attending physician at Cedars, but was not at the interview, she interviewed him over the phone. He told her that Olivares had almost fully recovered from the meningitis. "We expect he'll get back to normal before the next manifestation of the HIV (AIDS virus) will hit," he said. He was not quoted in the article as to whether he concurred with Coady about how Olivares had gotten AIDS. It's possible that Hernández did not ask him. However, in my interview with Heifetz, he stated that he was able to say at the time that it was quite likely that Olivares had gotten infected by a blood transfusion in El Salvador, although he probably got sick there because he already had AIDS.[53] In the article, Hernández quotes a source she simply refers to as "doctors," and so it is possible that she included in this both Heifetz and Coady. She wrote: "Doctors said they believe that [Olivares] contracted the disease from contaminated needles while undergoing treatment to other ailments while traveling in Central America." She also included: "Doctors said it is impossible to predict how long Olivares will survive. But they said that once the illness manifests itself in a serious infection, as it has with Olivares, victims generally live from two to six years longer."[54]

Hernández also contacted Fr. John Martens, the Provincial of the Claretians, and Archbishop Mahony for their reactions to her interview with Olivares. Martens simply responded: "We will love and care for Father Louie. He's our brother." Instead of giving an interview, Mahony issued the following statement, reproduced in Hernández's article: "Father Olivares has served the poorest of the poor here in Los Angeles with great commitment and courage, and he has aroused the conscience of us all as we try to understand our responsibilities towards newly arrived peoples and those whose lives are not sheltered by laws and protections."

In her article, Hernández noted that in his statement Mahony had pointed out that he and Olivares "have approached various social issues with different strategies at times," but that nevertheless they had both shared a commitment to "live out the Gospel."[55]

The article appeared on June 28, 1990, under the headline "Activist Priest Says He Has AIDS; Doctors Blame Clinic's Needles." Despite Olivares's well-known status in Los Angeles, the article did not appear on the front page, or even in the front section. Instead, it was published in the Metro section, on pages one and three. It was a short article of only 629 words and was accompanied by a photo of Olivares from the newspaper's files. It contained the key aspects of Hernández's interview with Olivares, the statement by Dr. Coady, and the statement by the other "doctors," as well as those of Martens and Mahony.[56] For those who had not yet heard of Olivares's illness, reading the article must have hit like a bombshell. Mike Kennedy in retrospect believes that Olivares did the right thing in going public. "It was a good move," he says.[57]

One day before the publication of the article, the hospital released Olivares, as he had recovered from the meningitis and regained more of his eyesight. Surviving the meningitis gave him a slight ray of hope. "But I made it," he later said.[58] No longer able to live at La Placita, he instead retreated to Provincial House where his order took him in, and where he would live out the rest of his life.[59]

¡PRESENTE!

The reaction to Olivares's having AIDS was somewhat mixed, although most expressed shock, concern, love, and support for Fr. Luis. Niels Frenzen and Cynthia Anderson-Barker expressed shock. Art Rodríguez felt devastated but was consoled that Olivares came to accept his condition. He recalls Fr. Luis saying to him: "This is my cross; for whatever reason it's been chosen for me and I'm going to continue to do the best that I can while I have the ability to do it." Rev. Don Smith was stunned upon hearing the news. "In my circles," he says, "I think it was something that people didn't want to talk too much about." Labor leader Miguel Contreras likewise was saddened because he knew that AIDS was fatal and also because of how difficult it was for Olivares to admit to having it. Araceli Espinosa notes that she and her family were shocked and deeply saddened about the news, but that the family's relationship with Fr. Luis did not change and, of course, her mother would become his caretaker.[60] And Rubén Martínez, besides his own dismay, expresses the irony involved in Olivares contracting AIDS in El Salvador and contextualizes this historically, given the epidemic of AIDS in the 1980s.

> On a personal level, it seemed like just in keeping with the times we were living in. AIDS was all around us. Just the terrible, cruel irony of what is the official version that he gets it in El Salvador from a contaminated needle because of his diabetes. Just the sheer cruelty of that irony was not lost on anybody. Here's this saint, going down on these missions of absolute deeply felt solidarity and he pays the ultimate price for it.[61]

Clerical reaction ranged from support to silence. Some Catholic clergy chose not to say anything. Others, however, such as members of the Claretians expressed their concerns for Olivares's health. Fr. Ferrante recalls no demeaning comments by anyone in the order. Bishop Thomas Curry, who was in charge of personnel in the archdiocese, observes that there were other priests who had AIDS, but that the difference was that they did not have Olivares's public stature and hence did not go public with their sickness.[62]

Shortly after the *Los Angeles Times* article appeared, the Los Angeles Health Department contacted Dr. Coady to obtain more details about the story of how Olivares had contracted AIDS. Health officials did not seem to believe the explanation. Coady says that she did not respond to their inquiries and did not talk to them.[63]

While most also expressed concern and empathy, some did raise questions about the cause of Olivares's AIDS. Martha Rocha de Zozaya, who worked with Olivares in UNO, notes that when news of his illness became public, some in her parish wondered how he had gotten infected. When he heard about Fr. Luis's condition, former seminarian Pete Gómez also wondered how he had gotten AIDS. "I thought, did he have an affair with somebody? So I went through all these thoughts," he says until he contacted Henry, who told him the story of the infected needle in El Salvador. "So I found out the truth," Gómez states. Manuel De Santos, who had been at Catholic University in Washington, D.C., with Olivares, fully discounted any rumors about how he got AIDS. "Luis was not a homosexual," he comments. "I knew him. He was never that way. He never showed any kind of tendencies in that regard or anything. When I heard about his illness, I couldn't believe it. I said, no, no, there's something else here." Like Gómez, De Santos also came to accept Olivares's account. At the same time, others were skeptical about it. Gloria Kinsler recalls even some friends who were nuns questioning this explanation. She personally dismissed the skepticism. "I'm not against gays and lesbians," she says, "so I was sad because he was such a good man and that's such a terrible death." Lydia López received a couple of anonymous calls saying "we know how he got it." Fr. Chris Ponnet observes that some of Olivares's opponents were quick to use his diagnosis to dismiss his work. Ponnet believes that this was why it was important for Olivares to go public and, in a way, confront those who would want to discredit him. It was especially important that he articulated that his infection was not the result of a sexual encounter, Ponnet believes, and especially important to the Latino community. At the same time, he observed that Olivares was taken aback by some of this negative criticism, which he didn't expect. Of course, it would be hard to believe that Olivares was not aware and concerned, given the nature of his illness, that there would not be some skeptical or negative reaction. For his part, Blase Bonpane does not recall any negative or hurtful comments about Olivares amongst the activists that he worked with.[64]

Still others countered any sexual innuendos about Olivares. Brother Modesto León who had worked with Olivares in UNO believed his account of the infected needle and stresses that, while some questioned Olivares's celibacy, he was in fact committed to his vows of celibacy. Fr. Juan Romero seconded this when he wrote: "I knew Father Olivares to be a person who is neither a drug user or a homosexual." Fr. Rosendo Urrabazo retells the story of how some reporters started investigations to "find some dirt on [Olivares]." One reporter called him and, according to Urrabazo, questioned him very aggressively, but did not find anything and backed off. Urrabazo believed his mentor's account. "When I heard that story," he says, "it's almost too incredible not to be true. My first thought was who's going to believe it?" But Urrabazo believed it, as did many others.[65]

Yet some continued to spread rumors. Ann Kansvaag even heard some of this from people who had ties with CARECEN and El Rescate, and who made jokes "on the heavy side." This didn't surprise her because in her experiences in El Salvador, she found much homophobia. This included a "kind of black sense of humor." She found these jokes and speculation to be nasty.[66]

Then there were conspiracy theories as to how Olivares had gotten infected. Modesto León, for example, believes that the right wing in El Salvador deliberately infected Olivares in one of those clinics. Janis-Aparicio contends that she and others believed the Salvadoran military, in collaboration with the CIA, planted the AIDS virus and gave it to Fr. Luis. Virginia Mejia notes that the U.S. embassy in San Salvador helped Olivares when he got sick there and that some believe that the U.S. government was responsible for infecting him with AIDS.[67] Fr. Romero also promotes the conspiracy theory. He believes that reactionary forces such as the death squads poisoned Olivares with AIDS. In his interviews with Olivares a year or so after his diagnosis, Romero asked him: "Do you think somebody did this? You don't have to tell me if you don't want to."

"I don't know. I don't think so."

However, a few months later, Romero took Olivares out to dinner and asked him again. This time, Olivares said: "No, I don't feel the same. I think it might have been possible."

Romero contends that, in effect, Olivares was assassinated. He asserts: "And for my money, it's a smart way to kill a moral voice of someone who was an advocate for the poor. You don't kill them with a bullet, or you make them a martyr out of them. But if you kill with this kind of stuff and wound him, you will close him off to the minds and hearts of many people for whom he might have been a spokesman. So it was a different kind of assassination."[68]

One expression of support came from the *Los Angeles Times*. It applauded Olivares for revealing his infection as a way of helping others to cope with the disease and to bring awareness and support for AIDS victims. It praised him for his work at La Placita.

Like so many Angelinos, we were particularly moved by the news that Father Luis Olivares . . . has been stricken by the disease. *Padre* [italics in the *Times*] Olivares has made his plaza church more than a sanctuary for Central Americans refugees and undocumented immigrants. He has made it a sanctuary, as well, for those ideals of compassion and justice we all claim, though too seldom practice. . . . It is a place where the poor find both the consolation of faith and the open hand of social justice. . . . As he has for so long, Father Olivares continues to preach "freedom to captives and, to those in sorrow, joy."[69]

Olivares was sensitive to the reactions to his revelation, but he also knew he could not control how others felt. Urrabazo, his former student, suggests that after his mentor went public, Olivares did not care anymore what people believed or didn't believe. "You're dying," Urrabazo underscores. "He had to put his things in order. He continued to be a public person even in the process of death."[70]

III

After his release from the hospital, Olivares was taken to Provincial House, the headquarters of the Claretian order in the western province. Olivares had lived here for his one-year novitiate, and as treasurer had his office there. It was familiar territory for him. It was no longer the novitiate, but served now as a retreat center and the administrative hub for the Claretians. In addition, some of the Claretians, both retired and active priests not assigned to parishes, lived there. Now back at Provincial House, Olivares commented that as treasurer he had begun the structural changes to the building to make it into a retreat center and so he joked that it was, or should be, called "la casa de Luis."[71] In a sense, Olivares was coming home. Despite what tensions he had had with his order, he loved the Claretians and wanted to live out his last days with them. He had given instructions that his care and eventual death should be handled by the order and not by his family. Although it had initially pained him and perhaps still did, he continued to accept what he had been told as a teenager at the seminary— that the Claretians were now his family. "He wanted to die as a Claretian," Richard Estrada stresses.[72]

Olivares had lost a lot of weight in the hospital, and he remained gaunt as a result of his illness and treatments; however, he tried to eat what he could. The house had its own cook and meals were served community-style in the downstairs dining room. If he felt well enough, Olivares would join the other priests for the meals; however, if he did not feel strong enough his meals were taken to him. Sometimes, if he desired something particular, the cook would make it to order.[73] Mostly, Olivares stayed in his room and sometimes had to be coaxed to go downstairs to watch TV or sit in the living room, where books, newspapers, and magazines were available. "Luis, get up, let's go down to the living room and sit," Frank Ferrante, who also lived there, would sometimes encourage him. On occasion, he would walk around the block or in the garden, as he had as a young novice. When he needed a haircut unlike the other priests who went to a barbershop, Olivares had his hair cut at the house by Martin Sheen's barber; Sheen had arranged for him to attend to Fr. Luis. Olivares and the barber actually struck up a bond with each other. On the other hand, his dentist refused to see him because of Olivares's AIDS. In his room, Olivares watched TV such as the news. Although he never fully recovered his eyesight due to the effects of the meningitis, he did read the newspaper and books, some of which visitors brought for him. Toward the end, however, he became almost completely blind due to his high fevers.[74]

Medically, Olivares had to contend with the progression of the AIDS virus and related physical problems, including ones he already had, such as diabetes. For both, he took a good deal of medicine each day, usually with meals. But the strong medications also produced stomach ulcers.[75] He was administered AZT for AIDS although this had side effects. It caused anemia and lowered his blood count. To deal with this, Olivares had to return to the hospital every two weeks for dialysis and blood transfusions. This procedure tired him very much. On other occasions, he had to be hospitalized due to other AIDS-related illnesses.[76] Jimmy Rodríguez notes that while he still had some mobility, Olivares agreed to say the funeral Mass for Rodríguez's father at La Placita. He did this the day after he had dialysis. Rodríguez observed that the priest walked slowly and badly. After the Mass, he told Rodríguez: "I'm really, really tired and very weak and it's raining. I don't think I can make it to the cemetery. Fr. Estrada will carry on from here."[77] Others also commented on Olivares's low energy as time went on. "He was such a dynamic figure," Urrabazo comments, "and he just got wasted away gradually."[78] Some of his treatments also caused him nausea, and he would have to vomit after them.[79] "Honestly," says Kennedy, "he never bounced back, to tell the truth."[80]

At the same time, Olivares still hoped for a cure and agreed to take any experimental drugs that might arrest the virus or destroy it. "He was really praying for a cure," Fr. Lozano, who also lived with him, observed.[81] Some suggested what Dr. Coady refers to as "goofy cures" that raised Olivares's hopes, but which she and Heifetz rejected.[82] Through all of this, the Claretians saw to it that their fellow priest received the best of care. Through their group insurance and perhaps even dipping into their savings, they made sure that the top doctors at Cedars continued to treat him.[83]

Like other AIDS victims, Olivares had to confront the reality of a terminal illness. This was not easy for someone who had been so active and engaged with life such as Olivares. Fr. Chris Ponnet, who worked with AIDS patients, spent some time with him. "I have always been honored by that journey with him," he says. He observes that Fr. Luis had to come to peace with his illness, but that it was difficult at times.[84] Blase Bonpane suggests that, in dealing with AIDS, Olivares responded to it more as a medical problem than a moral one, but does not elaborate on this comment.[85] He taped a radio program about the different views on the origins of AIDS, including linking it to hepatitis.[86] The fact is that Olivares suffered emotionally and psychologically from the realization that he had contracted AIDS. But he seems to have come to terms with the reality that, unless that miracle happened, he was going to die, and soon. He admitted this to Ron Curran of the *LA Weekly*. "The Lord has brought me to this particular situation," he said in an interview in 1991, "where I'm going to die within a year or so, but I've led a very full life. I took some risks in my work and knew there would be some adverse reactions. I'm not angry or bitter toward anyone or anything."[87]

IV

In the three years that Olivares lived after his diagnosis, his main caretaker was unquestionably Juanita Espinosa. His quality of life was immeasurably improved by Juanita's assistance, literally almost every day. She cared for many of his needs and did it willingly and with complete devotion to a man, a priest, her confessor, whom she loved and idolized. He was a saint in her eyes, and she saw her role in ministering to him as part of her faith. Olivares had given so much to her and others; now in his time of need, she needed to give back by caring for him. He had designated her as his caretaker at the hospital when he introduced her to his family. Once at Provincial House, he needed her even more. Juanita still felt uncomfortable and humbled because she did not want to replace his family, or the Claretians for that matter. However, she soon realized that the order could not really care for him in the way he needed to be cared for and no one else seemed to want to volunteer to help him. He was just left to himself and no one gave instructions to the cook about his meals and no one was there to make sure that he took his medicine. She approached Provincial Martens and offered to volunteer to help care for Olivares. "I don't know if it was my instinct

464   ¡PRESENTE!

as a mother," Juanita says. "I asked the person in charge of the Provincial House, 'Do you mind if I stay a little longer so I can give him the medication?'" He also would need special meals, which she could supervise. Realizing that Olivares would only get worse over time, Martens agreed that she could do so.[88] As far as he and the Claretians were concerned, Juanita did not need special permission to assist Olivares; they were happy and probably relieved that she was there. Just in case, however, Juanita told Martens that if at any point the order did not want to care for Olivares, she would take him in to her home. This never happened and Martens even arranged for Juanita to have a small office with a phone where she could set up Olivares's medical appointments and arrange for others to visit him.[89]

Juanita became a fixture at Provincial House. She came every day, usually at 6:30 A.M., and would stay late into the night, sometimes until midnight. She supervised Olivares's meals, medications, treatments, doctor appointments, media requests for interviews, and scheduled his visitors. Sometimes Olivares wanted to eat something special, such as pancakes which he loved even for dinner, and so Juanita would go downstairs to the kitchen and cook them for him. She did not go home to her husband until Olivares fell asleep. She drove him to see his doctors, such as Dr. Heifetz, and returned him back to Provincial House. Sometimes her husband helped her, as did Fr. Castillo, in driving him to his appointments. As his eyesight deteriorated, Juanita read to him. Later, when he needed professional nurses to attend to him, she made sure that they were males in order to protect Olivares's sense of privacy.[90] Sometimes, when his health permitted, she took him home for a home-cooked dinner and at times would invite some of his friends to join them. For one of Fr. Luis's birthdays, Juanita organized a birthday party with eight people for him at Provincial House. This was his last birthday party, on February 13, 1993. Olivares could barely eat.[91]

Seeing each other every day, Olivares and Juanita developed a special relationship. He felt dependent on her, and she was totally committed to him. They would talk either in English or Spanish about a variety of things, sometimes including very private thoughts. This made Juanita uncomfortable, and she once said to him, "I don't think I'm the right person to care for you. You have so many other people and they're being upset because they want to be here."

He replied: "Who's the boss? Are you the boss or am I the boss?"

She never raised this concern again.[92]

These conversations were not really dialogues, but more like monologues by Olivares. He needed to talk to someone and Juanita provided that willing ear. He would talk about his work. He felt he might have done more, but was happy about what he had accomplished. He dreamed that he would get well and resume his work. He would also reminisce about his family in San Antonio, especially about his parents. He missed them and loved them very much, especially Tía Concha, "the love of his life." Juanita does not mention if Olivares cried when he remembered his parents, but more than likely did, as no doubt Juanita also did. She mentions that, over time at Provincial House, Olivares suffered periods of depression and would talk about it with her, even though he was seeing a psychiatrist at Cedars. These were moving reflections that she often felt she should record, but would never do such a thing because these were personal and private thoughts. Juanita, of course, prayed all the time that Olivares might be healed; at one point she confessed to him that she was "negotiating" with God to at least give him more time. Olivares looked at her and said in a stern voice: "You don't ever negotiate with God. You negotiate with a human being, but not God." Olivares also talked to her about dying. She remembers, "He said that dying is a normal thing for people and that all of us have a mission and the secret is for us to find out what's my mission in this world and do the best that we can in our mission. It was very beautiful. I wish I could remember his quotations. He would speak very beautifully."

She believes that Olivares was not afraid of dying. "I think he was ready when it came to his moment."[93]

Juanita Espinosa indeed gave much to Fr. Luis, and it took its toll on her both physically and emotionally. Soon after Olivares died, she became paralyzed and had to be in a wheelchair and lost some of her sight due to a high fever (similar to Olivares) until she recovered.[94]

V

What helped Olivares through these difficult times were the many visitors he had. He didn't have visitors every day and certainly not on the days he had medical appointments, but frequently enough that it helped raise his spirits.[95] Of course, his closest allies, such as Mike Kennedy, Richard Estrada, and Greg Boyle went to see him. No doubt other clergy spent some time with Olivares. Laypeople who had known and worked with him made it a point to visit. Janis-Aparicio observes that she had no difficulty seeing him; she called Juanita and arranged the visit. Former Claretian priest, Al López, who had served with Olivares at Soledad but later left the priesthood, visited with his fiancé. Natalia Hernández and Virginia Mejia, from the sanctuary movement at La Placita, went to see him together. They expressed the hope that when he got better he could return and continue his work. "This work continues with or without me," Olivares told them. "Have you not learned that about me?" It was emotional for these visitors, many believing that they might not see this courageous priest again. This was certainly the sentiment of Miguel Contreras. He remembers calling Olivares to see how he was and how Fr. Luis always wanted to know about the continuing struggle to organize the undocumented workers. "What are you guys doing now?" he would ask. On one and perhaps his only visit to Provincial House, Contreras felt the impact of Olivares's terminal illness: "You knew you were seeing him for almost the last time. But you also saw a man very much at peace with himself and a man who lived a full life." Others who could not visit, such as those who lived outside of Los Angeles, called him on the phone to see how he was. This included his old friend and fellow-seminarian Arnie Hasselwander. In fact, over the years, Arnie had kept in touch, largely via a yearly phone call.[96] Still others wrote him letters, and he would personally write back to them. Olivares kept the letters sent to him, but none seem to still exist, and may have been discarded after his death by the Claretians.[97]

One of the more unexpected visitors that Olivares had was Ernest Gustafson, the INS official whom along with his boss, Howard Ezell, Olivares had battled with over the Central American refugees and undocumented Mexican immigrants. Despite these tensions, Gustafson had always been cordial to Olivares and both men respected each other. Gustafson paid a visit to Provincial House and they chatted in the downstairs foyer. Olivares knew that Gustafson had retired from the INS and had a radio show on one of the Spanish-language stations where he provided useful information on immigration procedures and regulations to listeners. Olivares told Gustafson that he listened to his program and appreciated it.

"There's no difference between you and me," he told the former INS official.

"What do you mean?"

"What I did was the way I did it. What you do is the way you do it. But we're trying to do the same, aren't we? We're helping the same people."

"Sir," Gustafson said with much emotion in his voice, "it's an honor for you to say that."

Olivares gave Gustafson a "big old hug" and said, "We'll see each other in the future."

"I think we will," Gustafson replied.

And with that he said goodbye, knowing it would be the last time he would see him.[98]

Perhaps Olivares's most frequent visitor other than his brother Henry and his sister-in-law Lillian was actor and activist Martin Sheen. They had gotten to know each other in the movement and had developed a close relationship. Sheen admired the Claretian and encouraged other Hollywood figures to contribute to the cause of supporting the refugees and immigrants in addition to opposing U.S. intervention in Central America. Sheen was also a devout Catholic and their common faith also brought the two together.[99]

Archbishop Mahony, who became Cardinal Mahony in 1991, also visited Olivares more than once. They had battled over tactics and over the meaning of the Church and had become personal rivals especially over the leadership of Latino Catholics in Los Angeles, and Mahony had endorsed the removal of Olivares from La Placita. However, Olivares's illness had changed all this. In sickness, they discovered their common faith in God. Juanita sensed this as the two men met in private in Olivares's room. She felt that Mahony admired what Olivares had accomplished and that he now as Cardinal would build on this. Olivares later told her that he and Mahony had prayed together and the Cardinal had blessed him. He felt that others needed to pray and support Mahony.[100] Kennedy notes that on these visits, Mahony treated Olivares with kindness.[101]

César Chávez, of course, visited his dear friend. It appears that he went to Provincial House twice. Art Rodríguez drove César the first time, from the union headquarters in La Paz in the Tehachapi Mountains northeast of Los Angeles. They were taken, probably by Juanita, to Olivares's room where he greeted them. Rodríguez then left to allow César to talk alone with Olivares. Chávez had become very upset about Olivares's illness. This was someone whom he had tremendous respect and admiration for, and who had struggled with the farmworkers and on other social justice causes such as sanctuary. "He was losing a good friend," Rodríguez observes of Chávez, "someone that he believed in." César knew that he couldn't do anything to help Olivares now and that it was just a matter of time. It was sad for the famed farmworker leader to see his confessor physically deteriorate. "It was troublesome for César," Rodríguez acknowledges. Rodríguez, for his part, notes that Olivares was a fighter and that he remained hopeful, but that he also faced reality.[102]

Juanita Espinosa very vividly remembers Chávez's visit and could see how much the two cared for each other. She never forgot that months later, Chávez visited for the second and last time. Before he arrived, Olivares said to her that Chávez would die thirty days after his own death, which actually turned out to be very close to the truth. Chávez died on April 23, 1993, not quite five weeks after Olivares died. Juanita was startled by this prophesy and responded: "Father, you don't play with those things. He's coming to visit you today."

"You'll remember my words after I die."[103]

Helen Chávez accompanied her husband. When they entered the room, Olivares had his eyes closed but Juanita told them: "Don't let Father fool you. Father can hear you; he's awake. You can talk to him and he's listening to you."

She remembers that Chávez cried very profusely at Olivares's bedside. Juanita stepped out to give the Chávezes their time with Fr. Luis. "To me it was beautiful," she says of seeing César and Helen together with their beloved friend. After they left, Olivares told her that he had not mentioned to Chávez his prophesy.[104]

Upon returning to Tehachapi, Chávez told his son Paul how Olivares had reflected on his life and how he felt he had done Christ's work. "I remember my father saying that Fr. Olivares asked for forgiveness," Paul says, "and my dad saying to him 'you don't need my forgiveness.'" Paul explains that it appears that the forgiveness that Olivares was seeking was that he felt that he had not spent his entire life working for poor people. But César reflected to his son that life is a series of conversions and that Fr. Luis had gone through his conversions and had nothing to apologize for. "But I think the understanding of Fr. Olivares's statement," Paul adds, "was that here's a man that you respect and that you felt had given his all and yet he felt that he hadn't given enough."[105]

Henry Olivares and Lillian visited very frequently, either together or just Henry. These were special times for Luis Olivares to have his family with him. Henry and Luis had been special to each other since their seminary years, and that bond continued even as their lives evolved. Damaso Olivares who could not see Luis often because he lived in San Antonio, nevertheless, noticed how strong the relationship was between Henry and Luis when he visited after his brother was first hospitalized. Luis, now more than ever, relied on his big brother for many things, and Henry gave whatever he could as he and Lillian lived with the pain of Luis's terminal illness.[106] The other family members tried to return to Los Angeles when possible and depending on Luis's health. Teresa and Sister Victoria returned at Christmas in 1990 and stayed at Provincial House. Luis was back in the hospital for treatments, but was released while his sisters were still in town. The Arvizus picked up his sisters and drove them to the hospital. After Luis left Cedars, he enjoyed the holidays, shopping and sightseeing with his siblings. On one occasion, they attended dinner at the Arvizus, along with Henry and Lillian. It seemed like old times. At the same time, the sisters expressed concerns among themselves and with Henry about Luis and how much weight he had lost, especially since he had been a slender man to begin with. They noticed that Luis was still trying his best to remain active in the community, but had clearly slowed down. They never talked with their brother about his illness and he did not mention it to them. "I'm feeling much better," is all he would say. Teresa looks back and now wishes they had talked about his condition with him. "Sometimes I wonder why we weren't more open about it," she says with regret.[107]

Teresa returned alone to see Luis almost two years later, in October 1992, only a few months before his death in March. She returned because her brother was back in the hospital due to complications related to AIDS. She and Henry visited him at Cedars. When Luis saw her, he broke down crying. "I have never seen a man cry the way he did," she recalls. "He was just holding very tight on to me and he said what I'll never forget: 'Terry, look what I ended up with. Look how I am.'" When she left later to return to San Antonio, it was very emotional and hard. "When I said goodbye, I knew I wasn't going to see him anymore."[108]

Throughout the entire ordeal of their brother's illness, the siblings were grateful for Henry keeping them updated on Luis's condition. He would phone them to let them know how Luis was doing. Through Henry they felt connected with Luis, but it was hard.[109]

During the first couple of years of his condition, Olivares felt good enough to venture out not only to eat, but to visit others, although it does not appear that he drove himself. For a while he went once a week to Henry's, with either his brother picking him up or Juanita driving him over. He also loved to resume his weekly visits to the Arvizus, which allowed him to see one of his dogs as well. Juanita would drive him after lunch at Provincial House, and during the afternoon, after chatting, he would watch TV and fall asleep. After dinner, Juanita drove him back. On one occasion, he accompanied Fr. Castillo back to the seminary in Compton, where no doubt many memories came back to him. This was where his journey as a priest had started many years before.[110] Of course, he had always loved going to movies, and though it appears that he did not or could not do this as frequently, on one occasion Araceli Espinosa gave her mother a break from caring for Fr. Luis by taking him out to the movies. They went to a Century City multiplex and watched the film version of the hit play *Man of La Mancha*, based on the great novel *Don Quixote*, by Cervantes. "He was really happy," Araceli recalls of this outing. Olivares was being given various awards at this time, and when he felt strong enough to go he did and usually invited the Espinosas to join him.[111]

Olivares's biggest outing, however, was when he felt good enough to go visit his family in San Antonio for Christmas in 1991. He stayed for a week and very much enjoyed seeing his siblings and other relatives although he did not stay with them. Instead, he made accommodations at Immaculate Heart Church, the old barrio church he and his family had attended. Teresa noticed that he had lost more weight and that his coloring had changed and was darker. She thought this might be the results of the transfusions. At the same time, she saw that his appetite was better and that he was enjoying himself. On his visit, they went to a *posada* at the home of one of their aunts, where they celebrated the story of Joseph and Mary seeking shelter. At the same time, his family was reminded of his illness when their brother insisted that they not touch him.

"Stay away, be careful," he told them.

But they refused to do so.

One of his sisters grabbed him and said, "Uh, uh."

"Aren't you afraid?" he said.

"No," his sister replied.

Olivares also insisted that they not do his laundry for fear that they might be contaminated by his clothes; he would do his own wash. But one sister took his laundry anyway and put it in the washing machine. This upset him.

"Aren't you afraid?" he repeated.

"Luis," his sister said, "I've studied this sickness and I don't get it by touching you or your clothes."

Because it was Christmas, Olivares wanted to treat his family, especially his sisters, and so they all went to the shopping mall, and he asked them what they wanted that would be special.

"I want a diamond ring," one of his sisters said.

"No, not that special," he replied. Instead he bought her a bottle of perfume and similarly nice gifts for the other sisters.

After shopping, he treated them to lunch and showed that he still retained his sense of humor. One of the sisters ordered a "quickie lunch." Olivares broke out laughing and said, "Oh, you like quickies, huh?"[112]

This would be Olivares's last visit to his hometown. The *despedidas* (goodbyes) must have been very emotional. "We had no idea how long we were going to have him," Teresa remembers thinking.[113]

VI

Olivares's ability to be somewhat active for a couple of years was not just limited to social events. He still tried to be politically engaged. He returned to Casa Grande in Hollywood to help out by raising funds for the center. Unlike the sanctuary programs that had been discontinued at La Placita, Casa Grande continued because it was under the jurisdiction of the Jesuit order and therefore immune from the ending of sanctuary at La Placita.[114] But he also continued to be invited to participate in fundraisers and other events linked to the Central American support community. People wanted him to speak, including being a keynote speaker. It's not clear how many of these invitations he accepted, but he was still very much in demand and people respected his legacy.[115] One invitation that he accepted was to participate in a fundraiser for the Office of the Americas headed by Blase Bonpane, and which was part of the Central American support groups. He joined Fr. Ernesto Cardenal, the Nicaraguan Minister of Culture and famous poet, on the program. The event was billed as an evening of poetry and music with Cardenal and Olivares, even though Olivares was neither a musician nor a poet. The previous day Provincial House hosted a reception for Cardenal and Olivares, where Cardenal read some of his poetry.[116]

Having contracted AIDS, Olivares turned some of his attention to trying to help out in AIDS prevention activities and to bring support to AIDS patients. He told Henry that people shouldn't go around wondering about why some got AIDS, but that instead they should focus on helping them. "Even then," Henry stresses, "he was thinking of helping other people."[117] Occasionally, he spoke at AIDS fundraisers. His friend Fr. George Regas invited him to speak to his Rector's Forum at All Saints Episcopal Church in Pasadena and to address the issue of AIDS. "We feel such solidarity with you in your struggle with AIDS. It would be such a gift to have you with us for that morning."[118] In his talk, Olivares admitted how hard it was to deal with the affliction. "I'm not afraid to die," he said. "I just don't know how to live with this thing." He later told Marita Hernández for a feature on him in the *Los Angeles Times Magazine*: "The stigma of AIDS, I believe, is part of the rejection and abandonment Our Lord (went through) when he was put on the cross. That's very real to me now."[119] Other invitations to speak on AIDS came from additional churches, such as the Greek Orthodox Church of Saint Athanasius and Saint Paul, which asked Olivares to participate in an AIDS Posada for Christmas in 1990.[120] It does not appear, however, that any Catholic churches extended similar invitations. Perhaps the highlight of his AIDS activities was when he was invited to be the Grand Marshall for the Eastside AIDS-THON sponsored by the AIDS Healthcare Foundation, in the fall of 1990. This was the first multicultural fundraiser for AIDS awareness programs. People could participate by jogging, walking, skating, or biking. Various businesses and community groups cosponsored the event, which was staged in the downtown area and concluded at La Placita Park, adjacent to Olvera Street and La Placita Church. "Father Olivares," wrote Michael Weinstein, the president of the foundation, "you have always been recognized as a man willing to assist those most in need and consequently, we felt a need to solicit your active participation in this effort. We truly feel that [a] man of your stature—especially in the Latino community—will awaken and rally the consciousness which is needed." Olivares accepted, and at a separate dinner, the foundation presented him with its Courage Award. "This Award," Weinstein noted, "symbolizes your own personal courage in the struggle against AIDS through your ministry."[121] On a more personal level, Olivares returned to La Placita to attend a Mass for a young Latino seminarian who had also contracted AIDS.[122]

While Olivares did what he could to bring attention to AIDS including his own battle with it, he was not an AIDS activist in the way some others with AIDS were. He was not part of a conscious and politically engaged AIDS community. He did what he did on his own.[123] In part, this was because, according to Fr. Chris Ponnet, the AIDS community in Los Angeles did not accept him as part of them. They rejected him, Ponnet says, because AIDS was seen as a gay disease and Olivares had said that he had gotten AIDS not because he was gay, but through an infected needle in El Salvador. AIDS activists saw this as a slap in the face. Fr. Ponnet, who headed up the archdiocesan outreach on AIDS, tries to put this rejection, however, in perspective.

> But it was a time when there was some AIDS activists who felt that if you weren't gay and you weren't out about it and you had AIDS that they pretty much said, "thank you, but . . ." And so I would say [Olivares] got silenced on several sides because of this disease. At least I felt that he received some prejudice from within. But it was just because it was such a difficult time for the AIDS community then. They were just looking desperately for public people to support them and Olivares did not fit the bill.[124]

Limited in what he could continue to do publicly as his health began to deteriorate by 1992, Olivares mustered enough energy to participate in his last public appearance in January of that year. The occasion was the celebration of the signing of the peace accords that brought an end to the civil war in El Salvador. After over a decade of conflict, the death of 75,000 people, and a million in exile (25 percent of the nation's total population), the Salvadoran government and the rebel FMLN agreed to a cease-fire and the installation of new democratic procedures to allow the FMLN to participate in open elections. The accords, signed in Mexico City in early January, would go into effect on February 1. In Los Angeles, many of the groups involved in support of the Salvadoran people and for an end to U.S. inter-

Fr. Luis Olivares speaking at celebration of peace accords in El Salvador, MacArthur Park, Los Angeles, January 19, 1992. (Courtesy of Dept. of Special Collections, Charles E. Young Research Library, UCLA)

vention in Central American organized a rally to celebrate the accords in MacArthur Park on January 19. They especially reached out to Olivares to be their principal speaker. Weak and unsure of his ability to give a speech, Olivares agreed to do so. He almost cancelled due to his health, but was able to appear.[125] He was as jubilant as others were, and it was a vindication of his and others' efforts to bring peace and hopefully justice to El Salvador. He put on his collar and his black tailored suit and was driven to the park. When he entered, he was recognized immediately, and a crowd gathered around him and escorted him to the bandstand where the speeches were being given. Others reached out their hands to him. Rubén Martínez was amongst them and wrote in his notes: "He walks slowly, unassisted, although his steps are stiff, awkward, like a baby's. A man reaches his hand out to him: 'Your dream has come true, Father.'"[126]

On a bright, sunny and relatively warm January day, Olivares was introduced. The 5,000 people there gave him a rousing ovation. Whether they knew him personally or not, most knew of him and what he had done at La Placita. They showed their appreciation, respect, and love for him. He was their priest and still their leader. Slowly positioning himself behind the podium and speaking into the microphone, he started remarks that he had thought about but not written down. This was like his homilies; he would speak directly to the people in Spanish. He started slowly and softly but as he continued the historical importance of the moment and what it meant to him personally enveloped him and his voice started to get stronger until it was the old Olivares. It was as if he were back at La Placita and this were a special Sunday Mass with a special homily. Rubén Martínez witnessed this resurrection of Fr. Louie. "He's really back and it's the old Father Olivares," he reminisced many years later. "The voice is strong. Passionate. It must have been quite an effort for him given his condition. It was quite a big event."[127]

Olivares addressed the crowd:

> Thank God for this victorious day, in which the Salvadoran people have achieved a negotiated and just peace, which in many ways is a reflection of His incarnation here on Earth. This is a day to celebrate the resurrection of the Lord. Monseñor [sic] Oscar Arnulfo Romero has been resurrected. The thousands of lives lost in the war have been resurrected with this peace that gives us the possibility of a new El Salvador—an El Salvador that can become an example for the entire world of how a people can achieve a negotiated, just settlement, negating the idea that there are only military solutions to our conflicts.[128]

In his speech, recorded by Martínez, Olivares called on the people to recognize that their challenge now, in order to have peace and justice, was to forgive their oppressors which, he acknowledged, was not easy, but was the Christian thing to do. "I know how hard it will be. How can you look in the face of the one who killed your son? How am I going to extend my hand to the one who took away my husband and my father and my son? How am I going to embrace the one who confronted me and caused physical and emotional injuries? But the Salvadoran have to give the example to the rest of the world that forgiveness is possible and that we can do so without giving up our principles in order to achieve peace and justice." He then spoke very personally and noted that because of his illness, he had not believed that he would live to see this day. "It has been about a year and a half ago that I was told that I would be leaving this world in about a year and a half or two years and that my illness was terminal and that it was very likely I would never see this day, but thanks to God I am here!" He then went on to say that in his and others' struggle for peace and justice in El Salvador, and to protect the refugees, he had himself become "Salvadoran." "If even for a short time, I chose to become Salvadoran, even if I am not, in order to arrive at this day when we can celebrate the resurrection of El Salvador."

When he finished, the people rose in applause and reached out to him. He was exhausted but filled with the old feeling of excitement after knowing he had delivered a strong homily.[129]

Olivares also could take comfort in the fact that in the early 1990s some 500,000 Salvadorans and Guatemalans finally received temporary asylum, one of the goals that Olivares had been working on for years. The federal government agreed to not continue battling a law suit over this issue. In turn, the George H. W. Bush administration agreed to what came to be referred to as Temporary Protective Status, or TPS, for many Salvadorans and Guatemalans, and to discontinue the effort to deport them as "illegal aliens." Under this agreement, the refugees were allowed to stay in the United States with work permits or green cards which could be renewed annually. Moreover, the government agreed to reconsider requests by Salvadorans for political asylum that had been rejected, as well as to consider new requests. In time, many received asylum and were able to become permanent residents.[130]

Olivares seemed to put his efforts on sanctuary and his role in taking on U.S. policies in Central America in perspective when he told a reporter in 1991:

> You have to learn to laugh at yourself and not take yourself so seriously. People have often asked, "Do you really think that you're going to end the war in Central America with what you're doing?" And they're right, it would be ridiculous to think that. But at the same time, if there ever is peace in Central America, I can look back and say that maybe by adding my little grain of sand to the situation, I had something to do with it.[131]

VII

While he received many tributes during his last years that made him feel loved and appreciated, Olivares still had to wrestle with his illness, which led to many mood changes. How could one not, knowing one was going to die? Janis-Aparicio observed that at one point he might feel depressed and abandoned and then at another express hopefulness and reveal his great sense of humor. Some note that his spirits were usually great or good and that he encouraged others to keep up the good fight. Moises Sandoval was impressed with Olivares's attitude; he did not seem to be a person to pity nor did he want to be pitied. To others, he expressed no bitterness about his lot. On the other hand, still others saw Olivares in a state of depression. He seemed lethargic, demoralized and lacked any motivation. "Almost like

Fr. Luis Olivares, two years before his death, September 1991.
(Courtesy of Debra DiPaolo)

what's the use?" he told an interviewer. "I think it's senseless," he told Juan Romero, "I think that you start thinking of all sorts of possibilities." Olivares did not explain what he meant by this, but it reveals someone who is struggling with his condition. Urrabazo felt that Olivares was depressed. Kennedy agrees: "I just think he felt like his life was over. Before life was exciting and he had visibility, like a celebrity. Now he's sitting in a chair and not being able to see very well. You never know if people are visiting to be paternalistic." Rubén Martínez concludes that Olivares had a broken spirit. "He was broken," he says. "More than his body, his spirit was broken. That was my sense of it. It was really sad."[132]

His depression also had to do with feeling lonely and simply being scared. Kennedy believes that this loneliness had to do with a sense of humiliation, because of the stigma of AIDS especially at that time, and his feeling that many did not want to have contact with him anymore.[133] Fr. Lozano saw him looking scared on one occasion, and he tried to offset this feeling by telling Olivares, "Luis, I have to go now, but remember that I love you."

Olivares looked him in the eyes and said, "I love you, too."[134]

Dr. Coady concurs that Olivares suffered from depression because of his AIDS and because he was very sick. She notes that this depression was not constant, but could be very intense.[135]

Psychologically, Olivares had to wrestle with dying. He told Denis Heyck that while he felt fine at the time of the interview, psychologically it was another matter. He had not yet come to terms with dying. "I'm not afraid to die," he said. "It doesn't bother me dying ever. We all have to die eventually and I know that my time will come. It's unbelievable. I just never imagined that I would be in this state of mind."[136] When Sister Patricia Krommer took him out to breakfast, she could see that it was not easy for Olivares to deal with AIDS. "He looked at me and said, 'You know, Pat, if a plane crashed into this building right now, we'd probably both be killed. We know that we all have to die. But you don't know when you're going to die. I do.'" Krommer reached over to him and took his hand and told him how much he was loved.[137] Part of Olivares's emotional reactions had to do also with a sense of guilt over getting AIDS. He felt that he had disappointed others and that he could no longer continue his ministry. "The most devastating thing about the illness," he told Romero in March 1992,

is the psychological effect that it has on your level of motivation. No matter how you try to look at it in a positive view, all is for the good, there's always "why me?" You feel guilty . . . regardless of how you contracted it. You feel you let people down, you know. I thought I had at least another ten, eleven, twelve years left of real activism and here I am in the last stages, basically. Perhaps physiologically, I'm very fortunate in that I haven't gotten seriously ill since the first bout of meningitis about two years ago, but psychologically it's devastating. I'm getting professional help, but it doesn't seem to help much. There is that very, very strong feeling that people have expectations that you are unable to fulfill. Whether it's your fault or not.[138]

Dr. Heifetz notes that Olivares suffered depression and especially a sense of guilt. He felt ashamed and felt he had let his Church down. As a result of his depression, he spent a lot of time with a psychiatrist at Cedars who, Heifetz says, became his confessor.[139]

Because he had his ups and down, some felt that in the good times he was developing a philosophical attitude about his condition. That is, he was coming to terms with it. Here he relied on his faith. He expressed no anger about what had happened to him. "I'm just waiting for the final blow," he said. Romero believed that this involved accepting his infection as "somehow in God's permissive will." After her visit, former UNO colleague Sister Maribeth Larkin felt that, as in most of his life, Olivares was dealing with his illness with much dignity and strength, "just like he did everything else in terms of public life." Rabbi Freehling also saw this philosophical state of mind. He had accepted reality, including "his belief that it was not by accident that he had become infected and this was yet another burden for him to carry on his shoulders. But he never played the martyr. He never manifested the sense that he was a victim. It was another cross for him to bear."[140]

Olivares himself expressed this philosophical attitude. In another interview with Marita Hernández of the *Los Angeles Times*, he said: "The Lord has given me notice so I have enough time to reestablish my priorities as a religious person. Life is worth living. And so, you just hope that you will be able to deal with what comes."[141] He told Rubén Martínez, "People tell me that they are praying for a miracle and they mean that I will be cured. But that's not my prayer. I am ready to die if it is God's will. The miracle that I pray for is that my suffering and my death will somehow hasten the cure so that others will be spared and the world will be rid of this disease."[142]

And in a poignant moment between brothers, Luis confessed to Henry: "I hate to compare myself to Christ but Christ didn't have to die on the cross. It could have been a less cruel way of dying, but he chose the cross and God has chosen this for me. He's teaching me a lesson and I have to accept it."[143]

These different manifestations of his state of mind, his spirit, should not be surprising. Olivares was a complicated individual, and perhaps even a contradictory one, and so his different moods reflect this. Perhaps he accepted his illness but still felt guilty about it. He could accept dying as a man of faith, but as a human being wanted to continue living. There are some, however, who believe that Olivares at the end was at peace with himself and with God. He never blamed God and accepted His will. Perhaps this was the case; one hopes it was.[144]

During the first two years of living with AIDS, Olivares, although physically weaker, experienced relatively decent health. But this was only temporary. By 1992, he began to show more signs of the progression of the infection, though he could still function. However, by early 1993, as Dr. Heifetz says, he began a "nose dive." He now needed full-time care from nurses. He became weaker and weaker. He could barely get out of bed and he found it hard to keep food down. His eyesight deteriorated even more, and he had lost most of his hair due to his treatments and medications. Moreover, he was now in constant pain especially in his stomach. He would say "oh boy, oh boy" as he writhed in pain. The nurses had put a twenty-four hour IV into him, but found it increasingly difficult to insert the needle into his veins. This convinced Heifetz that Olivares could no longer be cared for at Provincial House and had to be hospitalized. He realized that this was now the end. Olivares agreed to be hospitalized and was conscious of being transferred back to Cedars on about March 16. All Heifetz could do was to make sure Olivares was comfortable.[145]

Arriving at Cedars, he was again taken to a private room on the sixth floor. There Heifetz and the medical staff treated him as best they could, and especially tried to relieve his pain. The medications caused him to drift in and out of consciousness, although he recognized visitors who arrived as soon as word went out that he was back in the hospital and that this might be the end. Juanita, who followed him to the hospital, tried to limit the number of visitors because, according to her, Olivares did not want people to see him the way he was. He wanted them to remember him the way he used to be.[146] Still, she did allow some visitors. María Valdivia went and stayed with him, since her mother was not feeling well. The nurses allowed her to sit next to his bed, but Olivares did not say much, only "Hi Chita."

"How are you feeling?" María asked.

"Tired," he weakly responded.[147]

Others also noticed that he could barely talk.[148]

He continued to decline. But up to the day before he died, he still recognized people. Modesto Léon and Richard Estrada visited and they both were taken aback at how weak Olivares was. His energy was drained. But he managed to say, "Mo [Modesto], how are you?" He knew that Léon had recently been sick.[149] Longtime colleague Richard Estrada saw his friend and mentor drifting away. It was hard for Richard to see Olivares this way. "He wasn't the same person," he says. "He didn't know if I was there or not.

It was really hard." This was the last time Estrada saw Fr. Luis alive. He had a sense that Olivares was going to die in a day or so, but he couldn't bring himself to visit again. "I'm a real good one to avoid painful issues," Estrada explains. "I run away from emotional situations."[150]

After three years of suffering physically and emotionally, Father Luis Olivares died on March 18, 1993. He was 59 years old. He had told Henry his death wish when he was still at Provincial House. "When I'm ready I want to die," he said. "When I get sick, I don't want to lie in a sick bed. I want to die."[151]

The morning before he died, Juanita arrived. She had been feeling very weak but didn't know why; and the previous day she had cried and cried, but could not understand why. When she got to the hospital and went to Olivares's room, he was asleep and so she prayed at his bedside. The nurses entered to bathe and change him and Juanita left the room. When she returned, she whispered to Olivares that she was there. He opened his eyes and recognized her. In a very weak voice, he told her that he "was leaving." She knew what this meant.

"Don't leave by yourself," she told him. "You have to hang in there."[152]

At that moment, her daughter walked in. Araceli, who was a teacher now, had a premonition the previous night that Fr. Luis had died. She decided not to go to her school that next day, but to the hospital to be with Olivares. "Come and say goodbye to Father and help us pray because Father is leaving." Olivares didn't say anything to her, but she stayed by his bedside the rest of the day. "I felt so lucky to be there," Araceli fondly remembers. "To say goodbye. I felt so fortunate—so fortunate."[153]

At around 7 P.M., they were joined by Fr. Carlos Castillo. He had worked that day at Queen of Angels Hollywood Presbyterian Hospital, being with patients; however, when he returned to Provincial House, he learned that Olivares was in critical condition. He drove to Cedars to be with him.[154] When Juanita saw Castillo enter the room, she said to him: "Fr. Carlos, help me pray with Fr. Olivares because he's leaving and he's walking through the doors." Castillo approached the bedside. "When he sensed that I was there," he recalls, "he opened his eyes like he was trying to tell me something. I remember that very vividly. Then I came closer and took his hand. We started praying. Juanita and Araceli prayed also." Castillo gave Olivares the last rites, the sacrament of the sick. At approximately 8 P.M., Olivares, according to Juanita, squeezed her hand and died. She closed his eyes. He died peacefully. "It was very spiritual," Juanita affirms.[155] Dr. Heifetz and other medical personnel arrived very soon thereafter to confirm his death. Heifetz does not remember what he listed as the cause of death, but believes it was pneumonia and not AIDS. He knew that Olivares, as most other AIDS patients, would die of complications of the disease.[156]

Juanita, Araceli, and Fr. Castillo remained with Olivares into the night, while the body was prepared to be released to the mortuary where he would lie in state. The Claretians, anticipating the worst, had already made these arrangements with Guerra and Gutiérrez Mortuary in East Los Angeles. Shortly after his death, Castillo and Juanita made phone calls to inform others of Fr. Luis's death. Castillo called Provincial Martens, who notified Henry. Castillo says that he and Juanita also informed the family, meaning Henry. Henry and Lillian, of course, were grief-stricken that Luis had died. Henry had not gone to the hospital that day. However, he still blames Juanita for not calling that day to let him know that it appeared that his brother was dying. "We wanted to be there to say goodbye and we just weren't called." He says that Juanita later told him: "I'm responsible for whoever comes and goes and I didn't think I should have called you." "She was possessive of my brother," Henry says of Juanita.[157] Henry's understanding, according to Juanita, is that after Martens and Ferrante arrived at the hospital, they made the decision as to who should be present to prepare for the body to be transferred to the mortuary and that it did not include him.[158] Juanita did not mention this situation in her interview with me.

Henry, in turn, called his siblings even though it was later in Texas. He reached Teresa and the others. Teresa informed him that Martens had also called. They told Henry that they would make arrangements to fly out within a day or so. Henry warned Teresa that, while she had visited that past October and seen how much Luis had deteriorated, his appearance would be a shock to the others. Teresa herself sensed that her brother's time had come. She had recently talked to her parish priest about Luis and how she was praying for him to somehow recover. The priest in a very kind way told her, "Terry, I think it's time for you to let go and start praying that God takes him. You don't want him suffering anymore." Teresa understood. The day of her brother's death, she went to Mass and believes that she saw the crucifix looking brighter than usual, and she remembers praying, "Lord, it is your wish, but you can take him. I don't want him to suffer." Luis died that night.[159]

Within a day, the media reported Olivares's death. The *Los Angeles Times* and *La Opinión*, along with other newspapers in the Los Angeles area, carried stories of his death and reminded readers of Olivares's work on sanctuary and with Central American refugees and Mexican undocumented workers. *La Opinión* noted the immense loss to the Latino community and observed that Olivares would be hard to replace. The Associated Press likewise circulated the news of his demise.[160] Of course, reaction came from many who knew and had worked with Olivares. They had already paid tribute to him during his illness and so their statement tended to repeat what they had previously said. The Claretians did not put out a statement, but instead a biography of their fellow priest.[161] Individual clergy, Claretian and non-Claretian, issued statements or spoke to the press. Cardinal Mahony again praised Olivares in a written press release and offered his condolences to the family, the Claretians, and to those whose lives he had touched. "I am deeply saddened and share the sense of loss felt at the death of Father Luis Olivares, C.M.F.," the Cardinal wrote. "Even though we knew that Father Olivares was living courageously with acquired immune deficiency syndrome and that AIDS would eventually take his life, nevertheless, we grieve his loss."[162]

Still other clergy, both Catholic and non-Catholic, voiced their sorrow over the death of a man whom they deeply admired. The same came from laypeople, such as those in the Central American activist community, as well as in other community work. Expressing the city of Los Angeles's recognition of his work, the city council passed a resolution extending its sympathy to Fr. Luis's family and friends, and in his memory all council members stood in tribute and reverence to him.[163]

Everyone grieved for Luis Olivares. A word should be said about Juanita Espinosa, his caretaker at Provincial House. Of course, she also grieved but, as noted earlier, she had a physical downturn right after Olivares's death. Some think that she had a stroke, a heart attack, or an emotional breakdown; it's not clear. However, for a period of time she could not walk and was confined to a wheelchair.[164] She remains a controversial figure for some, while others praise her dedication to Olivares. One who did was Kieran Prather, who also contracted AIDS and died some time after Olivares. A member of the Los Angeles Catholic Worker affiliated with Dorothy Day, Prather had known Olivares but never revealed to him that he also had AIDS. He appreciated Juanita's care for Olivares and wrote to her a month after his death expressing his thanks. "A little late," he stated, "I want to personally offer my sympathy to you for Fr. Luis's death. I know how close you were to him, and how much he depended on you. We all feel the loss, but you more than most. . . . I also want to thank you for the care you gave. Fr. Luis was not always easy to be with, but you were faithful, always pleasant, and usually you seemed as happy as could be. Your presence was a gift to Luis—and to us."[165]

According to Juanita Espinosa, Luis Olivares had planned his funeral, or parts of it. It's not clear what he planned, although one can assume that he might have indicated to Juanita and others who he wanted to give eulogies, and that he preferred a mariachi Mass with Los Camperos. What is most certain and acknowledged by others is that he wished his funeral to be at La Placita. This was his parish; this is where he declared sanctuary for both the refugees and immigrants; this was his church and the people there were his parishioners. La Placita also was more centrally located, and many more parish members could attend.[166] Kennedy reinforces this by observing that as Olivares lay dying, he asked for his funeral to be at his former church.[167] Unfortunately, this was not to be. The funeral Mass was not held at La Placita, but at San Gabriel Mission, operated by the Claretians. The Claretians were in charge of the funeral arrangements and Olivares was aware of this before his death, but hoped the order would fulfill his wish. However, Provincial Martens made the final decision to have the funeral at San Gabriel. It would not actually be in the mission because it was too small. Instead the Mass would be at the Chapel of the Annunciation, adjacent to the mission, but which was much larger. The Mass would be on Monday, March 22, with viewing of the body at 1 P.M. and the Mass at 2 P.M.[168]

Why did Martens and the order as a whole insist that the funeral be at San Gabriel and not La Placita? For one, they noted that since Olivares was going to be buried at the mission, it made sense for the Mass to also be there. At the same time, there are some who believe politics and personal issues had perhaps even more to do with the decision as to where the Mass should be. Urrabazo, for example, believes that Martens was concerned about what the reaction would be if the service was held at La Placita, especially in light of the Claretians' removal of Olivares as pastor of La Placita and the subsequent dismantling of sanctuary and other support programs for the immigrants, homeless, and day laborers. He thinks that Martens feared demonstrations.[169] The Olivares family assert that they believe that Martens also was influenced by the riots, or rebellion, in 1992 following the exoneration of the police officers who had beaten up Rodney King, and that the head of the Claretians feared that something like this might happen. "The Claretians didn't want any popular uprising," Henry Olivares states.[170] Moreover, Cully adds that he believes some Claretians still harbored jealousies of or resentments toward Olivares and hence wanted to minimize the funeral and opposed having it at La Placita. "I think there were some people who were fearful of seeing his uniqueness," he says, meaning that there would no doubt be a huge turnout at La Placita if the funeral were held there.[171] "Even in death they did not trust him," one parishioner told Tom Fox of the *National Catholic Reporter*. Fox reported that this reaction echoed that of others who believed that church officials, as well as city officials, "knowing the lightning rod Olivares had been," preferred the funeral away from the city center.[172]

For their part, the Olivares family had their views, but had no role in Martens and the order's decision, which made no sense to them. Henry and the other siblings strongly felt that their brother's funeral should be at La Placita, because he had been pastor there, and the burial at the mission. This, they believed, was his wish, and they felt that the Claretians should have honored this. The family believes the order did not because they did not want to recognize his ministry at La Placita or bring attention to it. Olivares had told them that what would happen to him after he died would be in the hands of his order and not the family. They understood this even if they did not agree with Martens's decision. To this day, the family harbors resentments toward the order for its decision and feels that some sort of conspiracy against the memory of their brother was involved. One of his sisters believes that the order just pushed her brother aside when they did not want him at La Placita anymore. "They're hiding everything," brother Damaso charged. At the same time, they were appreciative of the order's support for their brother while he was ill and of its support for the family. Leaving Texas and arriving in Los Angeles the Saturday after Olivares died, the family once again stayed at Provincial House. Besides the siblings, they were joined by Tía Justa, or Justina Olivares, Olivares's aunt on the paternal side of the family, as well as one of Teresa Garza's daughters and her husband. This created an interesting encounter when they arrived at the house to check in. One of the priests inquired about her daughter: "Is she married to this man?" When Teresa said that of course she was, the priest agreed to put them in the same room.[173]

Monday arrived and the mortuary owners and employees prepared to transfer the casket carrying Luis Olivares to San Gabriel Mission on what Tom Fox of the *National Catholic Reporter* wrote was a balmy afternoon.[174] It was a relatively short drive through surface streets. The family had arrived early at the church to be with the casket. After removing it from the hearse, the mortuary contingent carried the casket to the entrance of the chapel. The family walked behind the casket into the church and to the front of the altar where it would remain for viewing. The casket was opened for people to see Olivares for the last time. As 1 P.M. approached, hundreds of people began to arrive. While many drove to the church, some arrived in chartered buses with many of the parishioners from La Placita and Soledad. One parishioner, Amado Castellanos, who owned his own bus company, transported more than 200 people from La Placita to the mission. He told a reporter: "Fr. Olivares had such compassion for the homeless and for those who came here from the south to work in menial jobs. This is how I show my gratitude and do my part."[175] Soon the church was packed, as people occupied every available pew and crowded in to allow as many people as possible in the pews. Some arrived too late and had to go up to the choir loft where there was limited seating. Still many others had to stand along the side aisles and in the back of the church. Despite the pressure of so many people, they remained orderly, with little conversation as people mourned the beloved priest. Brother Modesto León and Tom Fox from the *National Catholic Reporter* estimate between 2,000 and 2,500 people attended, with some having to stand outside the church.[176] Fox observed this impressive turnout, noting that "inside and outside the church . . . people prayed and sang, many holding back tears."[177]

What impressed many in attendance was the diversity of the people who came to pay their respects to Olivares. There were Olivares's parishioners, Central American activists, labor leaders, union members, political and community leaders, the immigrants, the refugees, the day laborers, street vendors, the poor, the rich, the Hollywood crowd, and, of course, many clergy of various denominations including Catholic, Protestant, and Jewish. They came from all social classes, all having been touched by Olivares. Some of his former seminarian classmates attended as did some of his former students at Claretville. Of this diversity, Rubén Martínez observes: "The usual suspects. Every activist in Los Angeles, from Abraham Lincoln Brigade survivors to young kids returning from El Salvador with a fire in their guts, professors, writers, journalists, the Hollywood crowd, wealthy liberals from the west side." At the same time, Martínez did not see as many refugees or immigrants in attendance and ascribes this to the difficulty of getting to the mission and that the funeral was on a workday.[178] Yet the mixture of people in attendance impressed on many how well Olivares worked with different people of all backgrounds; this was part of his leadership. "He had a heart for everyone," Lisa Martínez emphasizes. "This was Luis," Urrabazo observes of Olivares's ability to reach out to so many varied people. "This was the way he lived and this is the way he died. It was a grand exit."[179]

As people got settled or even as they entered the church, they lined up to view Olivares in the open casket. They saw Fr. Luis with his eyes closed, wearing his favorite simple black cassock and collar. He looked much darker than he had when alive, no doubt due to the ravages of his disease. Every one of all backgrounds, including some children, filed by and viewed the body for a few seconds, many of them blessing themselves as they did or touching the casket as a form of making connection with Olivares.[180] Tom Fox, in witnessing the viewing, wrote later: "The body rested near the altar for more than an hour before the Mass began. Hundreds filed past, touching the coffin. . . . Many, some holding young children, bent over to kiss the body of the priest."[181] As they approached the casket, they noticed that draped over it prominently was the UFW flag that some believe that Olivares had planned before he died. Less prominently on the casket was the red banner of the FMLN, in recognition of Olivares's connection with the Salvadoran refugees and the liberation movement in El Salvador. Of course, on the top of the casket was a crucifix. Two guards stationed themselves on both sides of the casket so that people would not attempt to reach in and pull out a piece of Olivares's hair or a thread from his cassock. However, the guards, as noted in the prologue, allowed people to pin political buttons on Olivares or put them in the casket. Some also left holy cards with the body.[182] Paul Chávez observes that this leaving of *recuerdos* is a Mexican Catholic tradition. "There is nothing more personal than putting a memento of yours in the casket as part of paying tribute to the departed. It tells us about the essence of the person who had passed away."[183] At the same time, few flowers adorned the casket, but various organizations did contribute flower bouquets for the burial.[184]

After the viewing of the body, the funeral Mass commenced. Fr. Frank Ferrante, who had been one of Olivares's strongest supporters within the order and a close friend, was the principal celebrant and was joined by concelebrants Frs. John Martens, Carlos Castillo, and Rosendo Urrabazo. Many other Claretian priests also attended and were considered concelebrants as well. Fr. Brian Cully, stationed at the mission, served as master of ceremonies. Other clergy, both diocesan and religious, likewise chose to attend. However, as had occurred years earlier when Olivares declared sanctuary at La Placita, Cardinal Mahony was not present. Instead, once again Bishop Juan Arzube represented the Cardinal. Mahony allegedly could not attend because he was instead in Washington, D.C., participating at a meeting of the Pro-Life Commission of the U.S. Bishops, of which he was president. He did issue a statement prior to the funeral Mass eulogizing Olivares for feeding the hungry, sheltering the homeless, and for recognizing the dignity of all people.[185] Cully points out that even if Mahony had attended, he would not have been the principal celebrant since this was a Claretian service and the Provincial usually said funeral Masses for deceased members. "For better or worse," Cully says, "Olivares was our own and we're his and we're a part of him."[186]

Mahony's absence, however, again did not sit well with others, who perhaps felt that he could have cancelled or shortened his trip and attended as a way of honoring Olivares. The Olivares family felt this way and still does, as do other close allies of Olivares. Henry Olivares believes that even though in later years, Mahony came closer to his brother's position in defying unjust U.S. immigration laws, that in 1993 Mahony still could not overcome what resentments he had toward Fr. Luis. "At that moment, he [Mahony] was not ready to go that far as to attend the funeral."[187] Blase Bonpane told a reporter that Mahony's absence "resonated in the church; he should have been there." Juan Romero expressed disappointment at Mahony's choice not to attend and says that if rivalry or jealousy with Olivares had anything to do with this, he should have been a bigger man than this. Sister Maribeth Larkin would have been surprised to have seen Mahony at the funeral. At the same time, the Cardinal's absence is defended or explained by others. Ferrante says that if Mahony could have attended, he would have out of respect, but that he can't second guess him. Kennedy perhaps surprisingly notes that Mahony did not need to be at the funeral and does not fault him for not attending. Nevertheless, Mahony's absence, whether justified or not, was noticed by those in the church and by the media.[188]

The Mass was accompanied by the mariachi and religious music provided by Los Camperos de Nati Caño, with special songs sung by Jackson Browne, who had demonstrated with Olivares and whom Kennedy asked to perform at the funeral.[189] Browne sang some funeral songs such as "Wind Beneath My Wings" especially for Olivares. Los Camperos also sang one of Olivares's most favorite songs, "Amor Eterno," by Mexican composer Juan Gabriel.[190] Henry Olivares and Sister Victoria Olivares read the Liturgy of the Word from Job 19 and from the second letter of St. Paul to St. Timothy. Henry read in Spanish and Sister Victoria in English. The readings, especially St. Paul's, seem to capture Olivares's ministry: "The time of my dissolution is near. I have fought the good fight. I have finished the race. I have kept the faith."[191]

Fr. Ferrante and Fr. Urrabazo presented a bilingual reading of the Gospel, with Ferrante reading in English and Urrabazo in Spanish from Luke 4:16–22: "The spirit of the Lord is over me. He has ordained me to bring the good news to the poor to announce to them their liberty."[192] Ferrante then gave his homily in English, and Urrabazo gave his in Spanish. Ferrante spoke about Olivares's work with the poor, the needy, and the undocumented and how he was a wonderful Claretian.[193] In his sermon, Urrabazo said of Olivares: "AIDS consumed his body to his bones and he fought his illness, but he never gave up despite his health his dream and commitment to social justice."[194] The giving of Holy Communion took some time, given the number of people attending. As people lined up for Communion offered by several of the Claretian priests, the mariachis played "Pescador de Hombres" (Fisherman of People); Jackson Browne sang "Wind Beneath My Wings"; and María de Los Angeles Menendez sang a meditation song "Yo No Puedo Callar" (I Will Not be Silenced).[195] At the end of Communion, some spontaneously began to shout out: "¡Viva Luis Olivares! ¡Viva Luis! ¡Luis Olivares! ¡Presente!" Such cries were heard periodically throughout the Mass.[196]

Following Communion, several people delivered eulogies. It's not clear whether Olivares requested them or the Claretians did. It was probably a combination, with others contributing as well. It was a long list of diverse and ecumenical speakers. They included Provincial Martens, Henry Olivares, Martin Sheen, Episcopal Bishop Frederick Borsch, Rabbi Steven Jacobs, Linda Wong, Rev. James Lawson, Mike Kennedy, Congressman Edward Roybal, and César Chávez.[197]

Henry Olivares spoke for the family. He thanked, on behalf of the family, all of the people for being present for his brother's funeral. He especially thanked César Chávez for being present. His eulogy was short, personal, and moving.

My fondest memory of my brother happened on a fall October day on the football field. That memory is engraved because it happened on the least likely place. Louie was not athletically inclined nor built at that time. His frame was more toward the thin, skinny side and so was more . . . musically inclined.

But on that fall day my esteem and bond was established. We were engaged in a touch intramural football game at Dominguez Seminary—the scene of many athletic rivalries. But this was "my" team against another, and we had struggled that afternoon to [a] non-scoring contest. Time was running out, and we had marched the length of the field to the ten-yard line. I called the play to virtually eliminate the defenders by having them cover my receivers deep in the end zone. Louie centered the ball, and I had him drift along the line of scrimmage and just barely penetrate the plane of the end zone. I saw him open and literally drilled the ball that he magnificently and miraculously held on to, to score our only and winning touchdown.

The stock in my brother as a competitor hit the ceiling, and from that day I recognized that when called upon to complete a task he could deliver. The fact that his athletic career went nowhere from there became irrelevant. What mattered is that he came through.

People have asked me how my brother became notable in the field of social justice or how he became a prophet or what is the reason for such an activist stand. My only answer is that there was a need. He perceived a situation that needed a response, an injustice that needed to be corrected, a person that needed support, a wrong that needed to be righted. Just as he saw a ball that needed to be caught to save his brother from an embarrassing loss.[198]

Henry appealed to his brother's supporters to continue Fr. Luis's struggles. "You are now his legs, his arms, his mind and his heart." Henry finished very personally by looking down from the podium to his brother in the casket and saying: "Hasta la vista, carnal" (Until we meet again, my brother).[199] Brian Cully remembers being very impressed with Henry's short but powerful eulogy. "He didn't say many words, but what he said had tremendous impact." Henry's eulogy only further impressed Cully of the strong relationship between the two brothers. "I knew Luis loved Henry," he says, "but there was a bond there that was much deeper than I realized."[200]

Then came the last speaker and the most well-known Chicano figure in the United States and in the world—César Chávez. He had been the leader of the farmworkers movement for thirty years and despite ups and downs had accomplished what had never been done before in the country—the successful organization of farmworkers, most of them of Mexican American descent—*Si Se Puede*! He was a legend among Chicanos. They saw in him their own struggles and their own recognition as important players in American politics. No other figure rivaled Chávez as a living Latino icon. He had arrived in time for the funeral from La Paz, driven down by his son Paul and accompanied by Helen Chávez. On the two-hour drive, Paul recalls how sad his father was. "I remember talking on the way over there and the way back about Father Olivares," Paul recounts. "My dad felt that Father Olivares was a special man. I know that my father's patron saint was St. Frances and I know that one of the reasons St. Francis meant so much to him was because of the opportunities that St. Frances had during his lifetime and he chose the road of being of service and of voluntary poverty to serve people as opposed to enjoying the benefits his parents could give him. And I have to believe that he felt some of that in Father Olivares."[201]

After they arrived at the mission, Chávez, Helen, and Paul walked into the church and sat at the front in the pew reserved for Olivares's family that had yet to arrive. Fr. Cully was the master of ceremonies, and saw them do this, but did not recognize Chávez.

"Those people aren't supposed to sit there," he mentioned to a former altar girl at La Placita who had gone to Harvard.

"Father," she informed him, "that's César Chávez."

Cully did not escort them to another pew and later learned that the Olivares family had requested that César and his family sit with them.[202] Jimmy Rodríguez also sat next to Chávez and noticed that he was not well. He had the flu and walked slowly and, of course, was emotionally affected by Olivares's death. "César wasn't himself," Rodríguez observed. "César was terribly shook up by the loss of Father Olivares, like most of us were. We talked about, 'Who do we have now? Where are we going to find our new leader?'" These were prophetic words that, within a short time, would be applied to Chávez at his death.[203]

When Cully introduced Chávez to deliver his eulogy, the entire congregation rose in a standing ovation for the famed farm-labor leader.[204] Chávez slowly walked to the pulpit. He usually spoke publicly without notes, but this time he had index cards that he referred to and only because of the microphone could his soft voice be heard. Blase Bonpane saw that something was wrong with César. This was not the spontaneous talk that he was used to hearing from Chávez, and this worried Bonpane and, no doubt, others as well. Rodríguez also noticed that Chávez was not in his rhythm when speaking and that this was noticeable.[205] In his eulogy, Chávez extended his condolences to Olivares's family, and he spoke about his friendship with the Claretian priest and said that their friendship would last for eternity. "Luis Olivares was my best friend," he said. He noted that Olivares had been of tremendous support to him and his family and to the farmworkers movement. "He never said no to any request we made of him," Chávez noted. "He joined us in demonstrations, fasted with us, joined us in victory—and he never doubted in the victory and justice of our cause." He stressed how Olivares had given everything to help the poor and oppressed and he challenged everyone there to live their lives as Luis Olivares had lived his. "He had the gift of faith," Chávez concluded, "of knowing what is truly important in this life. He taught us a lot about social justice. We have a responsibility to Father Luis, his memory, to do something for the poor to keep his spirit alive."[206] As Chávez finished and walked back to his pew, Mike Kennedy remembers thinking what a beautiful eulogy this was.[207] Rodríguez, in retrospect, says of César: "Little did we know that he would leave us shortly thereafter."[208] Later on the way back home, Paul Chávez observed that his father, while still sad, felt fulfilled in having not only paid his respects to his friend, but in knowing and working with Olivares and how he had touched his life.[209]

The eulogies over, the Mass came to an end with the final blessing on all by Fr. Ferrante. The service had lasted about three hours.[210] Janis-Aparicio remembers thinking about the funeral Mass that "it was a very un-Luis type of ceremony except for César. It was very solemn as opposed to the dynamic and charismatic way that Olivares celebrated Mass."[211] Before the priests and the congregation followed the casket to the nearby cemetery, the officiating clergy came down to give their personal condolences to family members. This included Bishop Arzube. Many others who attended likewise came up to do the same. Some, especially the women, hugged Olivares's sisters, and the sisters hugged each other. Damaso Olivares recalls people coming up to him and telling him how wonderful his brother was and what Olivares had done for them.[212] Dr. Davida Coady attended the funeral, and some approached her and thanked her for treating Olivares.[213] Many, including the Olivares family, took this opportunity to look one last time at Fr. Luis. The cover of the casket was then closed, and the procession to the burial ground commenced with Jackson Browne's singing "You are My Hero," accompanied by the mariachis. Blase Bonpane noticed the first light moment of the funeral when some of the congregation seemed to be dancing down the aisle to Browne's singing.[214]

They took the casket to the cemetery followed by the clergy, family, and invited guests. Not everyone at the Mass could attend the burial, due to the lack of space at the gravesite. Niels Frenzen, for one, thinks that the full public should have been allowed to attend the internment to pay a final tribute to Olivares. At the gravesite, Fr. Urrabazo led the burial rite that included prayers and the blessing of the casket.[215] Teresa Garza noticed the many other Claretian priests buried there and how beautiful and peaceful the cemetery was. She also noticed that no headstone yet had been created for her brother.[216] After the burial rites, the Claretians invited the family and a few others to attend a reception inside the mission, during which a meal was served. Some, however, chose to stay at the gravesite for a while, such as Fr. Estrada and Fr. Kennedy. Estrada remembers thinking that he was not sure that Olivares would have approved of his funeral, in that he would not have wanted all the fanfare. On the other hand, Fr. Luis as a public figure and even celebrity, might have relished this attention.[217] Natalia Hernández stayed with Kennedy and could feel his pain. "It's hard; it's hard," is all Kennedy could say.[218] Despite their concerns over how the

Claretians had treated their brother and especially about his removal from La Placita, the Olivares family expressed their thanks to the order for the funeral and how it had been arranged.[219]

The funeral was over and everyone was left with their memories of Fr. Louie and thoughts about his legacy.[220]

X

What is Fr. Luis Olivares's legacy, especially to those who knew and worked with him? What is it about him that is important and that people remember? How would he have seen his own life and legacy? There is no question that it was a remarkable life, chiefly characterized by his conversion after meeting César Chávez, although he carried already within him the seeds of that conversion. He had come a long way from the west side of San Antonio and from the boy pretending to be a priest to becoming a real one, and a people's priest at that. He was a complex man whose full complexities we may never know. He was a public figure but a private person who carried with him many feelings, desires, frustrations, and dreams. We will really never know the real Luis Olivares, just as no one will ever really know each of us. Many whose lives he touched have varied views of Fr. Luis's legacy. First and foremost, his family sees him as a true saint who walked this earth. This may be a biased opinion, but it is one that his siblings feel puts their brother the good that he did into the proper context. They don't want to mount an effort for the Catholic Church to declare him a saint, but they want to stress that what their brother accomplished was more than perhaps many other canonized saints ever did. It is not important to them whether others also see him as a saint. "My brother can be considered saintly," Henry Olivares says, "in the fact that he espoused the Gospel of Jesus and if we mean by that that he pursued that Gospel to the end, then I would say yes, he is a saint. In my eyes, he is a saint. I pray to him to give me guidance. Whenever I need support, I ask him to help me."[221]

Friends of Olivares also see saintliness as part of his legacy, although some interpret this in different ways. Juanita Espinosa says that she prays to him like any other saint and knows of others who do also, and some whose wishes have been granted.[222] Mrs. Arvizu calls him a "santo" and prays to him to help her and her family. Araceli Espinosa refers to Fr. Luis as a modern-day saint. She visits his gravesite every year on his birthday and comments: "Who wouldn't want him to be a saint?"[223] Rubén Martínez agrees, but takes this in another direction. "He's my kind of saint," he acknowledges, "a saint that could drink tequila. He was very human. He was earthy in the good sense. He was of this world. He wasn't an ethereal figure.

¡PRESENTE!

The next moment after Mass he was standing right next to you just like anybody else. He was really with us. He wasn't an aloof figure. That was part of his charisma. You could feel close to him without being close to him."[224]

While still others agree to this aspect of Olivares's legacy, one who does not is Presbyterian Rev. Zwerling, not because he is not Catholic, but because he believes that sainthood disguises the complexity of human beings, including their weaknesses and ambivalences. This is how he wants to remember Luis Olivares. "From my point of view, both theologically and personally, I don't really believe in saints. I believe that we are all in some way flawed human beings. To me that makes for a much richer universe. Dorothy Day said, 'Never call me a saint. I don't want to be dismissed that easily.' So I would like to know Luis in the fullest and richest picture of what I'm sure was a very complex human being, as we all are."[225]

But beyond the concept of Olivares being a type of saint as part of his legacy, the views of many who knew him focus on several other, more concrete aspects of his life that they believe are very much a part of the historical Luis Olivares. These include his championing of the poor and oppressed, especially the refugees and undocumented immigrants. Olivares clearly had a preferential option for the poor as espoused by liberation theology. Although he was a liberationist, Olivares was not just someone who preached it; he practiced it. He opened up La Placita to the poor and oppressed. He worked with the farmworkers to help alleviate their poor working conditions. And in UNO, he worked to empower the Mexican American community. This commitment began with his socialization in his family and Abuelita Inez taking in the hungry to her home and feeding them. The roots of Olivares's preferential option for the poor began there and later blossomed after his conversion. Blase Bonpane notes that part of Olivares's legacy was to stress that the Church needed to prioritize the poor.[226] "He was the champion of the voiceless," Fr. Al Vásquez stresses. "He was the champion of those who had no rights. This is how I remember Luis. He used his charisma to defend the poor, the immigrants. I wish he were here today."[227] Al López adds that Olivares "had a radical commitment to the poor, the suffering, the marginated."[228] Peter Schey calls Olivares a "soldier of the dispossessed."[229] Fr. Cully observes that Olivares's commitment to the poor was not just theoretical or even political; it was personal; it was the way he treated them and all people. "He saw he had to do more than speak out for justice," Cully observes. "You had to treat people with justice. Whatever you do to the least of my brothers and sisters. You can't just talk about what the government is doing wrong in a foreign country. You have to treat the person who's in front of you with dignity and respect. If you can do it with a sense of humor as Luis did, so much the better. That's probably what I remember the most, the way he treated the poor and the little ones in front of him."[230]

Olivares's brand of leadership is what some remember the most, and is a major part of what he left behind for others to emulate. He knew that he could not wait for others to lead the struggle for social justice; he had to lead it. This may have been in part his ego, which everyone agrees he possessed, but he used that ego to lead the struggles for the rights of farm-workers, to improve the Mexican American communities, and for the rights and protection of refugees and immigrants. He had the courage to lead even if it meant confronting his own Church leaders. But he was not afraid. He was guided by God's law and not temporal laws that allowed injustice to prevail. He had charisma and knew it, but applied it to inspire others in the struggles. Part of his leadership was his ability to work well with people of different backgrounds. He was not sectarian but ecumenical, and forged ties with people of different ethnic and religious backgrounds, as long as they all were working toward the same goals of achieving justice. Through his courage to lead, to take on the power establishments, whether in Los Angeles, in Washington, or in his own archdiocese, he gave others the courage and perhaps cover to do likewise. And he did it always with a sense of humor, and with class and dignity.

His legacy is also, as some observe, that he worked to redefine what it meant to be a priest. As he said many times, he did not believe that his priestly role was simply to minister to the spiritual needs of his parish-ioners. He did that, but he also believed that a priest should be out with the people, in the barrios, in the community, in the streets, and being part of social movements to take on the social sins that lead to exploitation, racism, nativism, and other forms of oppression and poverty. He was a new type of priest, or perhaps an old type, in that the first priests at the be-ginning of the Church were also with and of the people. Olivares's legacy in this sense was to redefine the meaning of the priesthood and what it meant to be a true Christian. Moreover, by redefining the role of a priest, he was also redefining the role of the Church. This legacy has not been fulfilled, but it remains there as part of moving the Church in this direc-tion. "He helped us to understand that we are called to be prophets on behalf of our people," Urrabazo wrote at the time of Olivares's death. "He showed me that ministry means caring about the day-to-day problems of people and improving the quality of life as well as attending to their spiri-tual needs."[231] Frank Ferrante adds: "He was a kind of icon for me of what it meant to be involved with the needy and doing things that many of us should be doing and could be doing."[232] To Ken Gregorio, Olivares "captured the real essence of what being a Christian is about."[233] Mike Kennedy agrees that what Olivares was doing at La Placita, for example, was redefining the Church, or encouraging it to truly fulfill its mission and that of the Gospel to minister to the needy. "I think it was the Church at its best," he says. "Not only do I think something was being accomplished, but it was thrilling to be part of it. There was a sense that the kingdom of God was being built a little bit because of what we were doing."[234] Fr. O'Connor concludes that Olivares's legacy was to "wake people up that it's not just to say your prayers in private, but to welcome the immigrant, the stranger, the sick, and the poor. Make a bridge between spirituality and social justice." This is what he believes Olivares stood for, but he feels that regrettably "it's not accomplished yet."[235]

These are some of the elements of what some believe to be Olivares's legacy. Those who worked with him have tried to keep this legacy alive, first through their own work with immigrants, the poor, the incarcerated, the homeless, including youth, gang members, and the poor in general. Janice-Aparicio stresses that Olivares inspired a whole new generation of community leaders who worked with him on refugee and immigrant issues and who are still doing this today.[236] Beyond their own lives and work, his followers or apostles, if you will, have tried to keep Olivares's memory alive by commemorating his life and death by holding memorial Masses in his name from time to time, although as the years go by this happens less frequently. Some programs linked with refugees and immigrants have been named after Olivares, although few if any in these programs know who he was.[237] A short side street adjacent to La Placita was renamed Paseo Luis Olivares. Of course, the surviving members of his family and other close friends keep his memory alive in their hearts and prayers, and by sharing his story with others. Catholic journalist Moises Sandoval attempts to put Olivares's historical legacy in perspective, at least in Chicano/Latino history, by observing: "There was only one César Chávez and only one Luis Olivares."[238]

How would Luis Olivares see his legacy? As he said on occasion, he did what he felt he had to do to help people. He did this after his conversion with the farmworkers. He did this through his leadership in UNO. And he certainly did it in the sanctuary movement at La Placita. I think he was most proud of what he accomplished at La Placita because this was something that he initiated and embraced, whereas few other pastors of a Catholic parish would have done the same. This was different from working with Chávez and the UFW, because that movement was already well-organized and had an established leadership. It was also different from UNO, which had its affiliation with the Industrial Areas Foundation. He was proud of his work with both groups and he learned much from these experiences, but sanctuary was his. From the very commencement of the Central American influx into Los Angeles, Olivares embraced the refugees. He had already started programs to help them even before he was approached by Mike Kennedy to do so, and he expanded them with Kennedy's assistance. It was Olivares who declared in 1985 La Placita to be a public sanctuary for the refugees and then two years later did what no other sanctuary movement in the country had done or would do—he expanded sanctuary to undocumented Mexican immigrants. These were the highlights of his ministry, and they were supplemented by his work with other groups protesting U.S. policy in Central America, as well as his expanding his ministry to assist day laborers and to help organize Latino workers into the union movement. This was his ministry and he was proud of it. It was his way to live the Gospel message and to transform what being a priest was all about and what the Church should be all about.

XI

When told by his order prior to the revelation of his illness that he had to leave La Placita, Olivares felt disappointed, frustrated, and even angry that his work would not go on. He blamed himself for not preparing better for the continuation of the movement. It is possible that during his dying days he still felt some of these emotions. But Father Luis was wrong. His influence, his work with the unwanted and the poor, his acceptance of the stranger in our midst, his sheltering of the homeless, protecting the persecuted, promoting of peace and justice, his reminding us that AIDS victims are also God's children, and his courageous effort to transform the Church into one of the people and for the people go on. They go on in the lives of the refugees and immigrants whom he helped; they go on in the work of community activists; they go on even today at La Placita and in new faith-based movements among Latinos and others in Los Angeles. Father Luis still lives in the memories and in the deeds of all these people, directly and indirectly. Father Luis, the prophet, still speaks out. He is still present.

¡LUIS OLIVARES! ¡PRESENTE!

EPILOGUE

After working on the life and times of Fr. Luis Olivares for many years, there is a feeling of accomplishment in completing the biography, but also some sadness in finishing a project that I thoroughly enjoyed and found fulfillment in. I never met Fr. Luis, but I feel that I now know him. I can identify with him at many levels, especially his Catholic education and background, as well as his political progressiveness. I admire him and what he accomplished or set out to accomplish. He fought the good fight and always kept his principles guided by his faith. It was and is a faith steeped in social justice and the biblical call to treat everyone as children of God. I further admire his strong leadership and his ability to articulate his views and his charismatic qualities. He was an elegant man, an intellectual, and, of course, an activist. He possessed a prophetic voice that reached many. I admire all of this. Sometimes when I give what I think is a good lecture, maybe even an excellent lecture, and leave the classroom thinking I had hit it out of the ballpark, I think of how Fr. Luis must have also felt when he delivered his Sunday homilies. At the same time, when he had to leave as pastor of La Placita and deal with rejection, I can also sympathize with him, since we all face rejection from time to time in our own lives. Although I personally never seriously considered the priesthood, I respect those like Olivares who entered it, despite the child abuse scandals that have enveloped the Church in recent times.

Despite his many positive attributes, he was not perfect. Like all of us, he had flaws. He indeed, as most acknowledge, possessed a big ego and a certain self-indulgence that manifested itself in his taste for nice clothes, cars, and restaurants. He did not live a life of poverty, even though he embraced the poor. He struggled with his vows of chastity and celibacy like all priests. He was a human being, perhaps a prophet and maybe even a martyr to his cause, but still a human being. But he was a good priest and a good pastor and he gave everything to the people he worked with and the marginalized that he embraced: the farmworkers, the people of East Los Angeles, the Central American refugees, and the Mexican undocumented immigrants.

My search for Luis Olivares, the priest and the man, has taken me from his childhood in San Antonio to his lengthy training and education as a seminarian in southern California and Washington, D.C., to his ordination back in San Antonio. The search then continued to his early priesthood back in the Los Angeles area and his path to leadership in the Claretian order. As treasurer of the order, Olivares learned to like the good life, but then again as a young boy he was pampered and loved to be treated as a favorite son and grandson. However, his life took a different direction which brought him into history and his own role in making history. Meeting César Chávez changed his life and although his ego and taste for the finer things never left him, he now focused his attention to working with the poor and the oppressed. He became a liberationist priest and embraced the call by liberation theology to have a preferential option for the poor and oppressed. He involved himself with the struggle of the farmworkers, and he became a community priest in his leadership role in UNO. But his greatest challenge and his greatest contribution to the struggle for social justice came with his involvement in the sanctuary movement as pastor of La Placita Church in downtown Los Angeles. He welcomed and supported the Central American refugees fleeing devastating civil wars and he declared La Placita to be a public sanctuary for them. He fed, clothed, and housed them, as well as providing other support. He then did what no other sanctuary movement in the country did. He extended sanctuary to undocumented Mexican immigrants. In all this, he refused to be intimidated by public officials, including the Reagan administration and his own Church hierarchy. He knew he was challenging these authorities and even breaking public laws. But as he often said, he was following a higher law, God's law, and God wanted all of his children, including refugees and undocumented immigrants, to be embraced and welcomed. There were and are no "illegal aliens" for God.

In these struggles, Olivares paid a high price. He was excluded from becoming the Provincial of his order and he ultimately was removed as pastor at La Placita. He received many death threats and navigated ups and downs in his work. But despite these obstacles and challenges, Olivares never wavered in his mission. He showed courage, commitment, and integrity in meeting these challenges. And then there was his wonderful humor, which he used to make others feel at ease and to salve the difficult moments. These same qualities he exhibited in facing death from AIDS. In life and in death, he stood as a symbol of leadership standing up to the forces of repression and exploitation. We need such leadership today and such examples in our own trying times.

I have attempted to be as honest as possible in examining and presenting Luis Olivares's life. It is impossible to reproduce that life in its totality, just as it is impossible for historians to do so for any aspect of history. But we struggle to get as close to the truth as possible, albeit mediated by our own interpretations of history. I hope I have met this challenge in my biography of Olivares. I may have done the research and written this life-story, but it could not have been done without those many others who helped me along the way, especially by opening up informal archival materials and then, of course, the many that allowed me to interview them. Oral history was indispensable in my search for Olivares. Through people's memories, I came to know better who Fr. Luis was. People shared these memories but with the assumption that I would respect them, which I have strived to do.

I stated in my Introduction that, in my opinion, Fr. Luis Olivares needs to be recognized and integrated as one of the most significant religious and political leaders of late-twentieth-century American history, including Chicano/Latino history. My many years of work on this study only have reinforced this view. We need a more integrative American history, and major Chicano/Latino leaders such as Olivares have to be part of this new American history.

I have enjoyed and learned much from my search for Luis Olivares. I feel that I found him, or at least much of him, and in the process, I probably found some of myself as well. I'll never forget that after interviewing Fr. Rolando Urrabazo at La Placita, he said to me: "You remind me of Luis." I was flattered and took this as a great compliment. What I take from this statement and what I take from Fr. Luis Olivares is what I also hope readers will take: an empowerment from his life story to never depart from our commitment to social justice and to have the courage, as he did, to involve ourselves in the struggle to achieve it for everyone, especially for those most excluded in our society, and to do so in the best way we can. This is a scholarly text, but I also wish it to be an inspirational one.

I am pleased that I can share this journey with Fr. Luis with others now, but at the same time I'm saddened that the journey is over. Fr. Luis has been a good companion and a wonderful role model. He, or at least his body, is gone, but his spirit lives on and still speaks to us today. Be not afraid. Life is only worthwhile if it is combined with helping others. In giving, we receive. Fr. Luis is with us in this. ¡Presente!

ACKNOWLEDGMENTS

In writing a full-length biography of an individual such as Fr. Luis Olivares, there are many people to thank. First and foremost is Henry Olivares, Fr. Luis's older brother, who, through these many years of my research and writing of this story, has provided incredible support, both materially and personally. I owe a debt to Henry and his wife Lillian for their encouragement and prayers. I also want to thank the other members of the Olivares family in Texas who assisted through allowing me to interview them. They include the late Damaso Jr., Teresa, Sister Victoria, and Socorro. Oral history was indispensable for this project and those who were kind enough to grant me interviews are listed in the bibliography, but I want to tell them how grateful I am for their time, support, and, in some cases, access to their personal collections related to my research. For giving me access to key archival materials, I want to single out the staff at the Claretian Provincial House in Los Angeles for allowing me to look at Fr. Olivares's collection, which they retained. At La Placita church, I want to thank Fr. Steve Niskanen, C.M.F., the then-pastor, who likewise permitted me to examine the collection of materials that belonged to Fr. Olivares, which were kept at the church. In addition, Fr. Mike Kennedy, S.J., as then-pastor of Dolores Mission in East Los Angeles welcomed me to research the extensive collection of documents related to Fr. Olivares and the sanctuary movement in Los Angeles in their church archives. Furthermore, I am grateful for the assistance I received at the Chancery Archival Collection, Archival Center, Archdiocese of Los Angeles at San Fernando Mission for documents on Fr. Olivares; the Daley Library at the University of Illinois, Chicago, for material related to the United Neighborhoods Organization (UNO); the staff at the Briscoe Center on American History at the University of Texas at Austin for related material on UNO; and the staff at Special Collections in the Hesburgh Library at the University of Notre Dame for materials on Fr. Olivares and PADRES. For photos used in the book, I am grateful to the Department of Special Collections at the Charles E. Young Research Library at UCLA; Henry Olivares; Fr. Juan Romero; Debra DiPaolo; and María Valdivia.

I wish to note and thank the late Fr. Virgilio Elizondo, whose intervention in my life encouraged me to research Chicano Catholic history. I miss him and the many wonderful conversations we had over great food and wine.

I want to acknowledge Darla McDavid, who transcribed most of my audio interviews. Thanks also to my research assistant, Taylor Renteria, for transcribing some of the interviews.

For funding my research, I want to thank the University of California, Santa Barbara (UCSB) Academic Senate; UC MEXUS; and the Chicano Studies Institute at UCSB.

I wish to particularly express my thankfulness to Charles Grench of the University of North Carolina Press for not only his support of this book, but for his collaboration with me over the years on other projects. This is the fifth book that Chuck has worked with me on, both at Yale University Press and now with UNC Press. I am further in gratitude to the anonymous readers of my manuscript, who gave me excellent and supportive suggestions to revise the manuscript, and who enthusiastically endorsed its publication. As with my other two books with UNC Press, I very much want to express my thanks to the editorial staff for their meticulous and professional attention to all of the details that go into publishing a book.

Finally, I am grateful for the support and many discussions over this project with Professor Ellen McCracken, my wife, who has lived with this book over the many years of its development and who always gave me critical and supportive responses to it. She is my best critic and I am better off for it. My children, Giuliana and Carlo, of course, are always in my thoughts and their own hard work and professional commitment only spurs me on to do the best I can in my own endeavors. Lastly, this project began when my mother, Alma Araiza García, who loved me and always encouraged me, was still alive.

I have never rested on whatever laurels I may have accomplished, and I hope my work over all these years encourages young scholars to always maintain their productivity and never be satisfied that we know all about Chicano history. Because we don't.

NOTES

ABBREVIATIONS

LAHE   Los Angeles Herald Examiner
LAT   Los Angeles Times
NCR   National Catholic Reporter

PROLOGUE

1. See *The Tidings*, n.d., Olivares Family Collection; *LAT*, Dec. 16, 1990; Henry Olivares interview; Martínez, *Other Side*, 141–42.

2. Olivares family interview.

3. See Father Luis Olivares, C.M.F., X Anniversary Program, Apr. 7, 2003, Henry Olivares collection.

4. *NCR*, Apr. 2, 1993, 2.

5. Henry Olivares interview.

6. *NCR*, Apr. 2, 1993, 2.

7. Olivares family interview; Henry Olivares interview; also see, *LAT*, Mar. 20, 1993, B-1.

8. Bonpane interview.

INTRODUCTION

1. See Mario T. García, *Blowout!*

2. See Mario T. García, *Latino Generation*.

3. See Mario T. García, *Memories of Chicano History*; Mario García, *Blowout!*; Mario García, *Mexican Americans*; Mario García, *Making of a Mexican American Mayor*; Mario García, *Chicano Liberation Theology*; and Mario García, *Chicano Generation*.

4. See, for example, Blanton, *George I. Sánchez*; Félix D. Almaráz, *Knight Without Armor*; Ignacio García, *Hector P. García*; Fisch, *All Rise: Reynaldo G. Garza*; Limón, *Américo Paredes*; Kreneck, *Mexican American Odyssey*; Busto, *King Tiger*.

5. Carr, *What Is History?*.

6. Mario García, *Católicos*. There has been some significant work on Chicano/Latino Catholic and Protestant history, such as Badillo, *Latinos and the New Immigrant Church*; Hinojosa, *Latino Mennonites*; Mato-

vina, *Guadalupe and Her Faithful*; Matovina, *Tejano Religion and Ethnicity*; Medina, *Las Hermanas*; Pulido, *Sacred World of the Penitentes*; Treviño, *Church in the Barrio*.

7. Djupe and Olson, *Religious Interests in Community Conflict*, 266.

8. Gottlieb, *Joining Hands*.

9. Hondagneu-Sotelo, *God's Heart Has No Borders*.

10. Gutterman and Murphy, *Religion, Politics, and American Identity*, 11; and Burke, "Latino Spirituality," 154. Also see Matovina, *Latino Catholicism*.

11. Gottlieb, *Joining Hands*, xvi.

12. See Smith, *Emergence of Liberation Theology*.

13. Mario T. García, *Católicos*, 131–70, 207–75.

14. Mario T. García, ed., *Gospel of César Chávez*, 31. Also see Dalton, *Moral Vision of César Chávez*. Also see León, *The Political Spirituality of César Chávez*.

15. Slessarev-Jamir, *Prophetic Activism*.

16. Other texts that have influenced my thinking on faith-based movements or on faith and politics include: Marsh, *Beloved Community*; Levitt, *God Needs No Passport*; Foley and Hoge, *Religion and the New Immigrants*; Hagan, *Migration Miracle*; Ebaugh and Chafetz, eds., *Religion Across Borders*; Groody and Campese, eds., *Promised Land, A Perilous Journey*.

17. See Smith, *Resisting Reagan*.

18. Hondagneu-Sotelo, *God's Heart*, 16; Menjivar, *Fragmented Ties*.

19. León, *Political Spirituality of Cesar Chavez*, 89–93.

20. The literature on Chávez is extensive and here I will only reference the following: Levy, *César Chávez*; Griswold del Castillo and García, *César Chávez*; Powell, *Crusades of*

César Chávez; García, *From the Jaws of Victory.*

21. Burke, "Latino Spirituality," 163.

22. Foley and Hoge, *Religion and the New Immigrants*, 13.

23. Warren, *Dry Bones Rattling*, x, 12.

24. Ebaugh and Chafetz, eds., *Religion Across Borders*, 1.

25. Levitt, *God Needs No Passport*, 12.

26. Hagan, *Migration Miracle*, 5.

27. Lash, *Haven in a Heartless World.*

28. Marsh, *Beloved Community*, 6.

29. Carbine, "Beloved Community," 239.

30. See Ignatius Bau, *This Ground Is Holy.*

31. Deck, *Second Wave*; and Mario T. García, *Desert Immigrants.*

32. Gottlieb, *Joining Hands*, 23.

33. Smith, *Resisting Reagan.* Also see Barry, *Roots of Rebellion*; Burns, *At War in Nicaragua*; Walker, *Reagan Versus the Sandinistas*; Coleman and Herring, *Central American Crisis*; Hamilton, et al., *Crisis in Central America.*

34. Marsh, *Beloved Community*, 3.

35. Hondagneu-Sotelo, *God's Heart*, 24.

36. Foley and Hoge, *Religion and the New Immigrants.*

37. Marsh, *Beloved Community.*

38. Interview with Rubén Martínez.

39. Carbine, "Beloved Community," 255.

40. For the Olivares interview, see Denis Lynn Daly Heyck, *Barrios and Borderlands*, 214–28; I want to thank Prof. Heyck for also providing me the transcript of her interview with Olivares. Fr. Juan Romero's interview with Olivares is contained in the PADRES Collection at the University of Notre Dame.

41. Warren, *Dry Bones Rattling*, 16. Warren uses the term "political ethnography."

42. Carr, *What Is History?*

43. Carbine, "Beloved Community," 244–55. For the New Sanctuary Movement, see Louis Sahagun, "L.A. church in forefront of sanctuary movement," *LAT*, Mar. 23, 2007, B-1 and B-10; Louis Sahagun, "Giving shelter from the storm of deportation," *LAT*, May 9, 2007, B-2.

CHAPTER 1

1. See Ruiz, *Great Rebellion.* On early Mexican immigration, see Mario T. García, *Desert Immigrants.*

2. Henry Olivares interview; and Denis Lynn Daly Heyck, "Interview" [with Father

Luis Olivares] in Heyck, *Barrios and Borderlands*, 214–28.

3. Olivares family interview.

4. Olivares interview.

5. Ibid.

6. Olivares family interview.

7. Interview with Luis Olivares by Denis Lynn Daly Heyck, no date, 2; hereinafter cited as Heyck interview. I am thankful to Professor Heyck for use of her transcript of her interview with Olivares.

8. Ibid.

9. Olivares family interview.

10. Henry Olivares interview.

11. See Wikipedia entry on Claretians.

12. "Interview" in Heyck, *Barrios and Borderlands*, 215.

13. Ibid.

14. Olivares family interview.

15. Ibid.

16. Ibid.

17. Ibid.

18. Ibid.

19. Ibid.

20. Henry Olivares interview.

21. See Richard García, *Rise of the Mexican American Middle Class*; on Mexican schools, see González, *Chicano Education in the Era of Segregation*; San Miguel, *"Let All of Them Take Heed"*; Mario T. García, *Desert Immigrants*; Blanton, *Strange Career of Bilingual Education in Texas, 1836–1981*; and Blanton, *George I. Sánchez.*

22. Olivares family interview. Olivares's sister, María del Rosario, later became a Benedictine sister or nun. And her religious name is Sister Victoria Anne.

23. Henry Olivares interview.

24. Olivares family interview.

25. Teresa Garza interview.

26. On the Cristero War, see Bailey, *Viva Cristo Rey!*; Meyer, *Cristero Rebellion.*

27. Henry Olivares interview.

28. "Interview" in Heyck, *Barrios and Borderlands*, 216.

29. Olivares family interview.

30. Henry Olivares interview.

31. Garza interview.

32. Henry Olivares interview.

33. Olivares family interview.

34. Ibid., and Garza interview.

35. Olivares family interview.

36. Ibid.

37. Ibid.

38. Ibid., and Garza interview.

39. Interview with Socorro Nelson, Aug. 28, 2017.

40. Henry Olivares interview.

41. Garza interview.

42. Ibid.

43. Henry Olivares interview.

44. Gil Villanueva interview, Dec. 11, 2004.

45. Olivares family interview.

46. Ibid.

47. Garza interview.

48. Ibid.

49. Olivares family interview.

50. Ibid.

51. Henry Olivares interview.

52. Ibid.

53. Olivares family interview.

54. Garza interview.

55. Ibid.

56. Henry Olivares interview.

57. "Interview" in Heyck, *Barrios and Borderlands*, 216.

58. Garza interview.

59. Heyck interview, 13.

60. "Interview" in Heyck, *Barrios and Borderlands*, 217.

61. Garza interview.

62. Henry Olivares interview.

63. Olivares family interview.

64. Henry Olivares interview.

65. "Interview" in Heyck, *Barrios and Borderlands*, 216.

66. Henry Olivares interview.

67. Garza interview.

68. Ibid.

69. Henry Olivares interview.

70. Olivares family interview.

71. Garza interview; Henry Olivares interview.

72. See my chapter, "Education and the Mexican American: Eleuterio Escobar and the School Improvement League of San Antonio," in Mario T. García, *Mexican Americans*.

73. "Interview" in Heyck, *Barrios and Borderlands*, 216.

74. Ron Curran, "Final Sanctuary: Father Luis Olivares," *LA Weekly*, Sept. 6–12, 1991, 23.

75. Henry Olivares interview.

76. Ibid.

77. Garza interview.

78. Henry Olivares interview.

79. Ibid.

80. Ibid. Gil Villanueva, who attended a different parish in the west side also ministered by the Claretians, recalls a different experience. He notes that the Claretians in his parish were mostly Spaniards who looked down on the Mexicana and were mean and condescending. At the same time, he admits that they still represented role models for boys like him who went on to the Claretian seminary in California; Villanueva interview, Dec. 11, 2004.

81. Henry Olivares interview.

82. Ibid.

83. Olivares family interview.

84. Henry Olivares interview.

85. Olivares family interview.

86. Henry Olivares interview.

87. Ibid.

88. Garza interview.

89. Olivares family interview.

90. Ibid.

91. Ibid.

92. Garza interview.

93. Henry Olivares interview.

94. Garza interview.

95. Henry Olivares interview.

96. Ibid.

97. Olivares family interview.

98. Henry Olivares interview; Heyck interview, 18.

99. Heyck interview, 18.

100. Ibid.

101. Henry Olivares interview.

102. Olivares family interview.

103. Henry Olivares interview.

104. Garza interview.

105. Henry Olivares interview.

106. Olivares family interview.

107. Garza interview.

108. Ibid.; Henry Olivares interview.

109. Olivares family interview.

110. Heyck interview, 40.

111. On Americanization programs, see Sánchez, *Becoming Mexican American*.

112. García, *Mexican Americans*.

113. "Interview" in Heyck, *Barrios and Borderlands*, 222.

114. Heyck interview, 7.

115. Henry Olivares interview; Garza interview.

116. Villanueva interview, Dec. 11, 2004.

117. Henry Olivares interview.

118. Garza interview.

119. Heyck interview, 8.

120. On pachucos and zoot-suiters, see

Luis Alvarez, *Power of the Zoot*; Pagán, *Murder at the Sleepy Lagoon*; Mazón, *Zoot-Suit Riots*; Ramírez, *Woman in the Zoot Suit*.

121. Henry Olivares interview.
122. Garza interview.
123. Curran, "Final Sanctuary," 23.
124. Henry Olivares interview.

CHAPTER 2

1. Garza interview.
2. Henry Olivares interview.
3. Ibid.
4. "Interview," in Heyck, *Barrios and Borderlands*, 219.
5. Henry Olivares interview.
6. Ibid.
7. "Interview," in Heyck, *Barrios and Borderlands*, 218–19.
8. Ibid.
9. Henry Olivares interview.
10. Garza interview.
11. Ibid.
12. Ibid.
13. Villanueva interviews (Dec. 11 and Dec. 14, 2004 and Jan. 12, 2005); Henry Olivares communication to author, Nov. 2013.
14. Ibid.
15. Ibid.
16. Ibid.
17. Ibid.
18. Henry Olivares interview.
19. On Japanese internment, see Dinnon, *Keeper of Concentration Camps*; Robinson, *By Order of the President*.
20. For description of the seminaries, see Villanueva interview, Dec. 11, 2004; Gómez interview; and Zozaya interview.
21. "Interview," 218.
22. Henry Olivares interview; interview with Arthur Zozaya, Dec. 28, 2005; interview with Jesse Flores, Feb. 25, 2006.
23. Ibid.
24. Villanueva interview, Dec. 11, 2004; Gómez interview.
25. Flores interview.
26. Gómez interview; Flores interview.
27. Ibid; Henry Olivares interview; Flores interview.
28. Gómez interview; Henry Olivares email to author, Sept. 23, 2017.
29. Ibid.
30. A. Zozaya interview.
31. Maldonado interview.
32. Henry Olivares interview.

33. Villanueva interview, Dec. 11, 2004.
34. Gómez interview.
35. Ibid; Villanueva interview, Dec. 11, 2004.
36. Gómez interview.
37. A. Zozaya interview; Henry Olivares interview; and Villanueva interview, Dec. 11, 2004.
38. Henry Olivares email to author, Sept. 23, 2017.
39. Gómez interview; Henry Olivares email to author, Nov. 5, 2013.
40. Gómez interview.
41. Villanueva interview, Dec. 11, 2004.
42. Flores interview.
43. Ibid,; Gómez interview.
44. Gómez interview.
45. Henry Olivares email to author, Nov. 5, 2013.
46. Villanueva interview, Dec. 11, 2004.
47. A. Zozaya interview; Villanueva interview, Dec. 11, 2004; Gómez interview.
48. Gómez interview.
49. A. Zozaya interview.
50. Villanueva interview, Dec. 11, 2004.
51. Gómez interview.
52. Villanueva interview, Dec. 11, 2004.
53. Ibid; and Gómez interview.
54. Villanueva interview, Dec. 11, 2004.
55. Gómez interview.
56. Ibid.
57. Henry Olivares interview.
58. Gómez interview.
59. A. Zozaya interview.
60. Gómez interview.
61. Henry Olivares interview.
62. "Interview," in Heyck, *Barrios and Borderlands*, 218.
63. Villanueva interview, Dec. 11, 2004.
64. Gómez interview.
65. Villanueva interview, Dec. 11, 2004.
66. Henry Olivares interview.
67. Ibid.
68. Quevedo interview.
69. Gómez interview.
70. Ibid.
71. Gómez interview.
72. Henry Olivares interview.
73. Gómez interview.
74. Henry Olivares email to author, Nov. 5, 2013.
75. Henry Olivares interview.
76. Ibid.
77. Villanueva interview, Dec. 11, 2004.

78. Henry Olivares interview; A. Zozaya interview.

79. Garza interview. Teresa further notes that many years later, when Henry left the priesthood, Tía Concha expressed her shock at this by discarding Henry's letters and photos.

80. Ibid.

81. A. Zozaya interview; Gómez interview.

82. Olivares family interview.

83. Gómez interview.

84. Ibid.

85. Villanueva interview, Dec. 11, 2004.

86. Ibid.

87. Ibid.

88. Henry Olivares interview.

89. Garza interview.

90. Maldonado interview; Villanueva interview, Dec. 11, 2004.

91. "Interview," in Heyck, *Barrios and Borderlands*, 219.

92. Gómez interview.

93. Maldonado interview.

94. "Interview," in Heyck, *Barrios and Borderlands*, 219.

95. Olivares family interview.

96. A. Zozaya interview.

97. Villanueva interview, Dec. 11, 2004.

98. A. Zozaya interview.

99. For the Mexican American Generation, see Mario T. García, *Mexican Americans*.

100. "Interview," in Heyck, *Barrios and Borderlands*, 23.

101. Gómez interview.

102. Henry Olivares email to author, Oct. 31, 2013.

103. Gómez interview.

104. Henry Olivares interview.

105. Ibid.

106. Gómez interview; Villanueva interview, Dec. 11, 2004.

107. A. Zozaya interview.

108. Gómez interview.

109. Maldonado interview.

110. Villanueva interview, Dec. 11, 2004.

111. Gómez interview.

112. Maldonado interview.

113. Henry Olivares communication to author, Nov. 2013.

114. Gómez interview.

115. Flores interview.

116. Gómez interview.

117. A. Zozaya interview.

118. Gómez interview.

119. Ibid.; A. Zozaya interview.

120. A. Zozaya interview.

121. Gómez interview.

122. A. Zozaya interview.

123. Gómez interview.

124. A. Zozaya interview.

125. Gómez interview.

126. Ibid.

CHAPTER 3

1. Olivares family interview.

2. Henry Olivares interview; Gómez interview; Villanueva interview, Dec. 14, 2004; and Henry Olivares note to author, Jan. 2014.

3. Gómez interview.

4. Henry Olivares interview; Gómez interview; A. Zozaya interview.

5. Henry Olivares interview.

6. Villanueva interview, Dec. 14, 2004.

7. Ibid.

8. Henry Olivares interview.

9. Ibid. and Villanueva interview, Dec. 14, 2004.

10. Villanueva interview, Dec. 14, 2004; Henry Olivares interview.

11. Ibid. and Gómez interview.

12. Villanueva interview, Dec. 14, 2004. Arthur Zozaya recalls two to three in a room; see A. Zozaya interview.

13. Villanueva interview, Dec. 14, 2004. According to Henry Olivares, Father Ellacuria has a group working on his canonization; Henry Olivares note to author, Jan. 2014; also see Wikipedia entry on Claretians.

14. Ibid.

15. Gómez interview.

16. Ibid.

17. Villanueva interview, Dec. 14, 2004.

18. Ibid.

19. Ibid.

20. Henry Olivares interview.

21. Villanueva interview, Dec. 14, 2004.

22. Gómez interview.

23. Ibid.

24. Ibid.

25. Ibid.

26. Gómez interview.

27. Ibid. and Villanueva interview, Dec. 14, 2004.

28. Gómez interview.

29. A. Zozaya interview.

30. Ibid. Arthur Zozaya notes that one had to be twenty-one to receive perpetual vows.

31. Henry Olivares interview; Gómez

interview; Berg interview, Jan. 20, 2005; Arnie Hasselwander to Henry Olivares, Mar. 12, 1999. I want to thank Henry Olivares for sharing Hasselwander's correspondence, plus his diary.

32. Ibid.

33. Hasselwander to Henry Olivares, Mar. 2, 1999; Henry Olivares note to author, Jan. 2014.

34. Berg interview, Jan. 20, 2005.

35. Arnie Hasselwander, unpublished diary, Jan. 10, 1957, in possession of Henry Olivares with copy to author; hereinafter cited as "Hasselwander diary."

36. Ibid.

37. Ibid., Sept. 10, 1956.

38. Henry Olivares interview; Villanueva interview, Jan. 12, 2005.

39. A. Zozaya interview.

40. Ibid.

41. Berg interview, Jan. 20, 2005; also see Gómez interview; Henry Olivares interview; Villanueva interview, Jan. 12, 2005.

42. Hampsch interview.

43. Berg interview, Jan. 20, 2005; Henry Olivares note to author, Jan. 2014.

44. Ibid.

45. Hasselwander diary, Feb. 11, 1957.

46. Berg interview, Jan. 20, 2005.

47. Hasselwander diary, June 24, 1957.

48. Ibid.

49. Ibid., Feb. 13, 1956.

50. Ibid., Jan. 10, 1957, including explanation inserted late 1990s. When Hasselwander gave Henry Olivares a copy of his diary, he added explanations of certain diary notes in which he mentions Luis Olivares. When the information cited comes specifically from Arnie's explanation, I will cite it as "Hasselwander explanation."

51. Al Vásquez interview, May 27, 2005.

52. Villanueva interview, Jan. 12, 2005.

53. Ibid.

54. Villanueva interview, Jan. 12, 2005.

55. Henry Olivares interview.

56. Gómez interview.

57. Hasselwander diary, May 1956.

58. Ibid., Apr. 23, 1956.

59. Ibid.

60. Ibid., June 30, 1958.

61. Ibid., May [probably 1956].

62. Hasselwander to Henry Olivares, Mar. 12, 1999.

63. Hasselwander diary, June 30, 1958.

64. Hasselwander to Henry Olivares, Feb. 1998.

65. Hasselwander explanation of diary entry dated Jan. 18, 1957; Henry Olivares note to author, Jan. 2014.

66. Hasselwander communication to Henry Olivares, late 1990s.

67. Ibid.

68. Ibid.

69. Hasselwander diary, July 12, 1956; Hasselwander to Henry Olivares, Nov. 12, 1999.

70. Hasselwander to Henry Olivares, Feb. 1998.

71. Hasselwander explanation of diary entries dated Jan. 31, 1956 and Feb. 2, 1956.

72. Hasselwander's summary of Luis Olivares to Henry Olivares, Dec. 1, 1997.

73. Henry Olivares interview.

74. Hasselwander explanation of diary dated entry Aug. 1, 1957.

75. Henry Olivares interview; Berg interview, Jan. 20, 2005.

76. Hasselwander explanation of diary entry dated July 8, 1956.

77. Villanueva interview, Jan. 12, 2005.

78. Ibid.

79. Henry Olivares interview.

80. Hasselwander explanation of diary entry dated June 16, 1957.

81. Ibid. of diary entry dated June 18, 1957.

82. Ibid. of diary entry dated July 10, 1957 or 1958.

83. Hasselwander diary, Sept. 3, 1957.

84. Henry Olivares communication to author, Dec. 2, 2013.

85. Ibid.

86. Hasselwander diary, Sept. 3, 1957.

87. Hasselwander to Henry Olivares, Mar. 2, 1999; Hasselwander diary, Feb. 10, 1958; Hasselwander explanation of diary entry dated May, 1958; Hasselwander diary, Feb. 5, 1958; Hasselwander explanation of diary entry dated May 8, 1958.

88. Hasselwander diary, Feb. 7, 1958.

89. Ibid., May 8, 1958; June 5, 1958.

90. On Chavez Ravine, see Normark, *Chavez Ravine, 1949*; Laslett, *Shameful Victory*; Hasselwander diary, Aug. 18, 1958.

91. Henry Olivares communication to author, Dec. 2, 2013.

92. Ibid.

93. Hasselwander diary, Feb. 13, 1958.

94. Ibid., Apr. 4, 1958.

95. Henry Olivares email to author, Dec. 6, 2013.

96. Hasselwander diary, May 2, 1958; Aug. 18, 1958; July 16, 1958.

97. Berg interview, Jan. 23, 2005.

98. Henry Olivares interview.

99. Hasselwander to Henry Olivares, Mar. 12, 1999.

100. Henry Olivares communication with author, Dec. 2, 2013.

101. De Santos interview.

102. Ibid.

103. Ibid.

104. Berg interview, Jan. 23, 2005.

105. Ibid.; de Santos interview; Hasselwander to Henry Olivares, Mar. 2, 1999.

106. Hasselwander diary, June 6, 1959; June 9, 1959; Hasselwander to Henry Olivares, Mar. 2, 1999; de Santos interview.

107. Hasselwander to Henry Olivares, Dec. 1, 1997.

108. Berg interview, Jan. 23, 2005.

109. Hasselwander diary, Feb. 10, 1959; de Santos interview; Hasselwander diary, Aug. 24, 1959, and Feb. 1, 1960.

110. De Santos interview; Hasselwander diary, Sept. 9, 1958, Feb. 9, 1959, and Feb. 11, 1959.

111. Hasselwander diary, July 13, 1959.

112. De Santos interview.

113. Henry Olivares note to author, Jan. 2014.

114. Hasselwander explanation of diary entry dated Feb. 13, 1958. Arnie notes that he would call Luis on his birthday for many years afterwards, until Luis's death in 1993; the only time he missed was Feb. 13, 1986, when Arnie had open heart surgery.

115. De Santos interview.

116. Hasselwander communication to Henry Olivares.

117. De Santos interview.

118. Ibid.

119. Henry Olivares interview.

120. Henry Olivares email to author, Dec. 6, 2012.

121. Olivares family interview; Henry Olivares email to author, Dec. 6, 2013.

122. Hasselwander diary, Feb. 2, 1960; Hasselwander explanation of diary entry dated Feb. 2, 1960.

123. De Santos interview.

124. Ibid.

125. Ibid.

126. Ibid.

127. Henry Olivares interview; Henry Olivares email to author, Dec. 6. 2013.

128. Warren, *Dry Bones Rattling*, 49.

129. Garza interview.

130. Olivares family interview; Henry Olivares note to author, Jan. 2014.

131. Ibid.

132. Garza interview.

133. Henry Olivares note to author, Jan. 2014.

134. Ibid.

135. Ibid.

136. Ibid.

137. Ibid.

138. Henry Olivares interview.

139. Henry Olivares note to author, Jan. 2014.

140. Ibid.

141. Ibid.; Olivares family interview.

142. Garza interview.

143. Ibid.

144. Villanueva interview, Jan. 12, 2005.

145. Henry Olivares note to author, Jan. 2014.

146. Olivares family interview.

CHAPTER 4

1. Henry Olivares interview; Henry Olivares communication to author, May 2014.

2. Olivares family interview.

3. Peterson interview.

4. Fr. Juan Romero interview with Fr. Luis Olivares, Mar. 27, 1992, PADRES Collection.

5. Peterson interview.

6. Ibid.

7. Ibid.

8. Ibid.

9. Ibid.

10. Ibid.

11. Henry Olivares interview.

12. Quevedo interview.

13. "Interview," in Heyck, *Barrios and Borderlands*, 221.

14. Ibid., 219; Henry Olivares interview.

15. "Interview," in Heyck, *Barrios and Borderlands*, 219.

16. Henry Olivares interview.

17. Ibid., and Romero interview with Olivares; Henry Olivares communication to author, May 2014.

18. *Our Sunday Visitor*, Jan. 13, 1991, 10; Henry Olivares email to author, Mar. 27, 2003; *LA Times Magazine*, Dec. 16, 1990, 3; biographical document in Claretian Archives.

19. Garza interview.

20. Ibid.

21. Ibid.

22. Ibid; Henry Olivares communication to author, May 2014.

23. Garza interview.

24. Henry Olivares interview; Henry says that he left the priesthood in 1969.

25. "Interview," in Heyck, *Barrios and Borderlands*, 222; Henry Olivares communication to author, May 2014.

26. Henry Olivares interview.

27. Garza interview.

28. Ibid.

29. Ibid.

30. Ibid.

31. Ibid.

32. Ron Curran, "Final Sanctuary: Father Luis Olivares," *LA Weekly*, Sept. 6–12, 1991, 24.

33. Henry Olivares interview; *Our Sunday Visitor*, Jan. 13, 1991.

34. Lozano interview.

35. O'Connor interview; Henry Olivares interview.

36. Henry Olivares interview.

37. Ibid.; Peterson interview.

38. Curran, "Final Sanctuary," 24.

39. León interview; Ferrante interview.

40. Ferrante interview.

41. O'Connor interview.

42. Henry Olivares interview.

43. Ibid.; Urrabazo interview; Peterson interview.

44. León interview.

45. Ferrante interview.

46. Ibid.

47. Henry Olivares interview.

48. Ferrante interview.

49. O'Connor interview.

50. Lozano interview.

51. Ibid.; Henry Olivares interview.

52. Ferrante interview.

53. Urrabazo interview.

54. León interview.

55. Urrabazo interview.

56. León interview.

57. Henry Olivares interview.

58. *Our Sunday Visitor*, Jan. 13, 1991; Urrabazo interview.

59. *LA Weekly*, no date, 24.

60. O'Connor interview.

61. Garza interview.

62. Peterson interview. Peterson was only a seminarian at the time, and so he must have heard of Olivares's wardrobe from someone else.

63. Ibid.

64. Romero interview (2003).

65. Olivares family interview.

66. León interview.

67. Olivares family interview.

68. *Our Sunday Visitor*, Jan. 13, 1991.

69. Romero interview.

70. De Santos interview.

71. Urrabazo interview.

72. Garza interview.

73. Olivares family interview.

74. Henry Olivares interview.

75. Ibid.

76. Ferrante interview.

77. Urrabazo interview.

78. Ibid.

79. Peterson interview; León interview.

80. Henry Olivares interview.

81. Ibid.; Ferrante interview.

82. Ferrante interview; Henry Olivares interview.

83. Lozano interview; Castillo interview, May 5, 2005.

84. Lozano interview.

85. Ibid.

86. Ibid.; León interview.

87. Lozano interview.

88. Ibid.

89. Ibid.

90. Ibid.; Peterson interview.

91. Peterson interview.

92. Ibid.

93. Lozano interview.

94. Ferrante interview.

95. Castillo interview.

96. Ibid.

97. Lozano interview.

98. Ibid.

99. Castillo interview.

100. Ibid.

101. Ibid.

102. Castillo interview.

103. Al López interview, Oct. 3, 2005.

104. Lozano interview.

105. Ibid.

106. Peterson interview.

107. Lozano interview.

108. Urrabazo interview.

109. Lozano interview.

110. Ibid.

111. Urrabazo interview.

112. Sellers interview. Sellers and his family lived close to Claretville and attended Mass there; he also sometimes hosted seminarians at his home.

113. Interview with Luis Olivares by Denis Lynn Daly Heyck, 30.

114. Urrabazo interview.

115. Ibid.

116. On liberation theology, see Berryman, *Liberation Theology*; Lowy, *War of Gods*; and Gustavo Gutiérrez, *Theology of Liberation*.

117. Lozano interview.

118. Castillo interview.

119. Lozano interview.

120. Ibid.

121. Urrabazo interview.

122. On the Chicano Movement, see Mariscal, *Brown-Eyed Children of the Sun*; Ernesto Chávez, *Mi Raza Primero! (My People First!)*; Mario T. García, *Blowout!*; Mario T. García, ed., *Chicano Movement*; Muñoz, *Youth, Identity, Power*; Oropeza, *Raza Si! Guerra No!*; Ignacio M. García, *United We Win*; Alma A. García, ed., *Chicana Feminist Thought*; Blackwell, *Chicana Power!*.

123. Urrabazo interview; on PADRES, see Richard Edward Martínez, *PADRES*. In 1970 Patricio Flores was appointed the first Mexican American bishop in the U.S. Catholic Church as Auxiliary Bishop of San Antonio. Also see Richard Estrada to Olivares, Feb. 8, 1975, where Estrada noted the establishment of a West Coast Regional Encuentro of Chicano seminarians; La Placita Archives, Los Angeles.

124. Romero interview.

125. Ferrante interview. Ferrante says that Olivares had a "bellow laugh."

126. Urrabazo interview.

127. Ibid.

128. Ibid.

129. Ibid.

130. León interview.

131. Berg interview, Jan. 23, 2005.

132. Ferrante interview.

133. "Interview," in Heyck, *Barrios and Borderlands*, 222.

134. Fr. Juan Romero, "Tension between Cross and Sword," unpublished paper given at CEHILA Symposium, Apr. 24, 1992, 5. I wish to thank Fr. Romero for a copy of this paper.

135. "Interview," in Heyck, *Barrios and Borderlands*, 219–20.

136. Interview with Luis Olivares by Denis Lynn Daly Heyck, 30.

137. "Interview," in Heyck, *Barrios and Borderlands*, 222.

138. Ibid.

139. Curran, "Final Sanctuary," 24.

140. Lozano interview.

CHAPTER 5

1. Urrabazo interview.

2. *Los Angeles Times Magazine*, Dec. 16, 1990; Henry Olivares interview.

3. Interview with Luis Olivares by Denis Lynn Daly Heyck, 43; Henry Olivares interview.

4. O'Connor interview.

5. León interview.

6. Estrada interview.

7. On pachucos, see Alvarez, *Power of the Zoot*; Mazón, *Zoot-Suit Riots*; Pagán, *Murder at the Sleepy Lagon*; Ramírez, *Woman in the Zoot Suit*.

8. O'Connor interview; Juan Romero interview with Olivares, Mar. 27, 1992, in PADRES collection.

9. Berg interview, Jan. 23, 2005.

10. The literature on the farmworkers and César Chávez is extensive; selected texts include: Griswold del Castillo and García, *César Chávez*; Levy, *César Chávez*; Pawel, *Union of Their Dreams*; Bardacke, *Trampling Out the Vintage*; Matt García, *From the Jaws of Victory*; Pawel, *Crusades of César Chávez*; Mario T. García, ed., *Dolores Huerta Reader*; Fuentes, *César Chávez y la Unión*.

11. Ibid.

12. Ibid.

13. Quoted in Mario T. García, ed., *Gospel of César Chávez*, 31. For an excellent study of Chávez's spirituality that encompassed not only his Catholic faith but many other spiritual influences that went beyond Catholicism, see León, *Political Spirituality of Cesar Chavez*.

14. Estrada interview.

15. Urrabazo interview.

16. Estrada interview.

17. Ibid.

18. Romero interview with Olivares.

19. Heyck interview, 32.

20. Estrada interview.

21. Ibid.

22. Henry Olivares interview.

23. Estrada interview.

24. Romero interview with Olivares.

25. Ibid.

26. Ibid.; interview with Luis Olivares by Denis Lynn Daly Heyck, 32.

27. Henry Olivares interview.

28. Estrada interview.

29. Henry Olivares interview.

30. Heyck interview with Olivares, 41.

31. Henry Olivares interview.

32. O'Connor interview.

33. Olivares family interview; Henry Olivares interview.

34. Hartmire interview.

35. Estrada interview.

36. Heyck interview with Olivares, 41.

37. "Interview," in Heyck, *Barrios and Borderlands*, 223; Henry Olivares interview.

38. Urrabazo interview.

39. Al López interview, Sept. 12 and Oct. 3, 2005.

40. Arturo Rodríguez interview.

41. See Fr. Virgilio Elizondo's Foreword in García, ed., *Gospel of César Chávez*, xii.

42. Urrabazo interview.

43. Arturo Rodríguez interview.

44. Romero interview.

45. Hartmire interview.

46. Ibid.

47. Ibid.

48. Estrada interview.

49. Romero interview with Olivares.

50. Estrada interview.

51. Chávez interview.

52. Mondragon interview, Mar. 19, 2005.

53. Henry Olivares interview.

54. Chávez interview.

55. Ibid.

56. Chávez interview.

57. Heyck interview with Olivares, 43.

58. Chávez interview.

59. Mondragon interview.

60. Chávez interview.

61. "Dolores Huerta on Fr. Luis Olivares," in Mario T. García, ed., *Dolores Huerta Reader*, 314.

62. Mondragon interview.

63. Ibid.

64. Al López interview, Sept. 12, 2005; Arturo Rodríguez interview.

65. Arturo Rodríguez interview.

66. Mondragon interview.

67. Lydia López interview.

68. Chávez interview.

69. Urrabazo interview.

70. León interview.

71. Heyck interview with Olivares, 42.

72. "Interview," in Heyck, *Barrios and Borderlands*, 221.

73. Hartmire interview; on Oscar Romero, see Romero, *Voice of the Voiceless*.

74. Estrada interview.

75. Ibid.

76. *Los Angeles Times Magazine*, Dec. 16, 1990.

77. Ibid.

78. Romero interview with Olivares; Fr. Juan Romero, "Tension between Cross and Sword," unpublished paper given at CEHILA Symposium, Apr. 24, 1992, 6.

79. "Interview," in Heyck, *Barrios and Borderlands*, 221.

80. Romero, "Cross and Sword," 6.

81. "Interview," in Heyck, *Barrios and Borderlands*, 222.

82. Urrabazo interview.

83. Al López interview, Sept. 12, 2005.

84. Maldonado interview.

85. Henry Olivares interview.

86. Maldonado interview.

87. Ferrante interview.

88. Henry Olivares interview.

89. Ibid.

90. Romero interview.

91. "Interview," in Heyck, *Barrios and Borderlands*, 221.

92. Heyck interview with Olivares, 32.

93. Al López interview, Sept. 12, 2005.

94. García, ed., *Dolores Huerta Reader*, 319.

95. De Santos interview. Manuel de Santos recalls Olivares introducing him to Chávez; de Santos had left the Claretian Order in 1970 but became a UFW volunteer.

96. Urrabazo interview.

97. Pipes interview.

98. Hartmire interview.

99. Mondragon interview.

100. Heyck interview with Olivares, 36.

101. Hartmire interview.

102. Chávez interview.

103. Arturo Rodríguez interview.

104. Garza interview.

105. Romero interview.

106. Hartmire interview.

107. Ibid.

108. Estrada interview.

109. Mondragon interview.

110. Ibid.

111. Paul Chávez interview.

112. Ibid.

113. Arturo Rodríguez interview.

114. Hartmire interview.

115. "Interview," in Heyck, *Barrios and Borderlands*, 221; Mondragon interview.

116. "Interview," in Heyck, *Barrios and Borderlands*, 223.

117. Chávez interview.

118. Arturo Rodríguez interview.

119. Chávez interview.

120. Urrabazo interview.

121. Mondragon interview.

122. Arturo Rodríguez interview; "Interview," in Heyck, *Barrios and Borderlands*, 223.

123. Ferrante interview.

124. Al López interview, Sept. 12, 2005.

125. Henry Olivares interview.

126. Olivares family interview.

127. Ibid.

128. Henry Olivares interview.

129. Garza interview.

130. Ibid.

131. Arnie Hasselwander to Henry Olivares, Dec. 1, 1997.

132. "Interview," in Heyck, *Barrios and Borderlands*, 220.

133. R.W. Dellinger, "The Radical Conversion of Father Luis Olivares, *Our Sunday Visitor*, Jan. 13, 1991, 10.

134. "Interview," 223.

135. *LA Weekly*, no date, 24.

136. Dellinger, "Radical Conversion," 10.

137. Heyck interview with Olivares, 42.

138. Dellinger, "Radical Conversion," 10. One controversial issue that faced Olivares's relations with Chávez occurred in 1977, when Chávez visited the Philippines under the dictatorship of Ferdinand Marcos. Chávez went to visit with Filipino farm-labor leaders there, but received much criticism from human rights groups in the United States. Olivares defended Chávez and called for this issue not to be used to divide the UFW and the farmworkers' struggle. See Juan Romero, "Chávez and Marcos," *PADRES* 7, no. 4 (Autumn 1977 and Winter 1978): 12, in PADRES Collection.

CHAPTER 6

1. For a comparison of COPS and UNO from a political science perspective, see Skerry, *Mexican Americans*.

2. On Católicos Por La Raza, see chapter 5, "Religion in the Chicano Movement: Católicos Por La Raza," in Mario T. García, *Católicos*, 131–70; and Mario T. García, ed., *Chicano Liberation Theology*.

3. Ibid.

4. Ibid.

5. On PADRES, see Richard Edward Martínez, *PADRES*.

6. On Alinsky and the IAF, see Saul Alinsky, *Rules for Radicals*; Alinsky, *Reveille for Radicals*; Sanford D. Horwitt, *Let Them Call Me Rebel*; Finks, *Radical Vision of Saul Alinsky*; and Robert Bailey, *Radicals in Urban Politics*. For the IAF in Texas, see chapter 4, "Standing for the Whole: The Southwest Industrial Areas Foundation Network," in Márquez, *Constructing Identities*, 48–67.

7. On COPS, see Skerry, *Mexican Americans*.

8. Andrea Sarabia to Bishop Juan Arzube, San Antonio, Mar. 18, 1976, in Industrial Areas Foundation (IAF) Collection, Series VI, Subseries A, Box 98, Fld. 1084.

9. See Warren, *Dry Bones Rattling*.

10. Cortes interview, Feb. 9 and 17, 2004.

11. Frank Del Olmo, "Community Coalition Mobilizing East LA," *LAT*, Dec. 26, 1977.

12. Ibid.

13. Vásquez interview.

14. Warren, *Dry Bones*, x.

15. UNO documents provided to me by Fr. Al Luna; hereinafter referred to as Luna documents.

16. Cortes interview, Feb. 9, 2004; Vásquez interview. Olivares was pastor of Soledad by January 1976; see Rev. Monsignor Clement J. Connolly to Olivares, Jan. 12, 1976, in Chancery Archival Collection.

17. Luna documents.

18. Vásquez interview.

19. Interview with Luis Olivares by Denis Lynn Daly Heyck, 44.

20. Luna interview.

21. See Michael Clements to Olivares, Nov. 3, 1975 in Luis Olivares Collection at La Placita Church, Los Angeles. I want to thank Fr. Steve Niskanen for permission to research this informal collection of Olivares's personal collection.

22. Ibid. Also see Auxiliary Bishop Juan Arzube, "To Whom It May Concern," Nov. 13, 1975, encouraging attendance at meeting, La Placita Archives.

23. Heyck interview with Olivares, 44.

24. Luna interview; Jim Giroud, California Franchise Tax Board to Interreligious Sponsoring Committee, June 17, 1976, approving non-profit status and "By-Laws of the Interreligious Sponsoring Committee," Luna documents.

25. Luna documents.

26. "Proposal for the East Los Angeles Organizing Project," Luna documents.

27. Ibid.

28. Clements interview.

29. Luna interview; "Interview," in Heyck, *Barrios and Borderlands*, 224.

30. Luna interview. Luna recalls first meeting Olivares at Provincial House, where he met with Olivares as treasurer of the Claretians to discuss funding of the committee.

31. "Application for Funding Campaign for Human Development," Luna documents.

32. Luna fax to author, May 22, 2006.

33. Ibid.

34. Manning to [name not clear], Dec. 28, 1977 in IAF, Boc 98, Fld. 1084.

35. Manning to Arzube, Oct. 7, 1976 in Luna Fax to author, May 22, 2006.

36. Skerry, *Mexican Americans*, 196.

37. Ibid., 145.

38. Martínez to Chambers, Los Angeles, Feb. 11, 1976 in IAF, Box 98, Fld. 1084.

39. Ibid. Martínez, in talking with Fr. Pedro Villarroya at Santa Isabel Church, agreed to send him copies of some of Alinsky's books, such as *Rules for Radicals* and *Reveille for Radicals*; see Martínez to Villarroya, Feb. 25, 1976, IAF, Box 98, Fld. 1084.

40. Clements interview; Cortes interview.

41. Garza de Cortes interview.

42. Clements interview; Cortes interview, Feb. 9, 2004; Larkin interview. Larkin believes that Cortes's salary might have also included IAF funds.

43. Cortes interview, Feb. 9, 2004.

44. *LAT*, Dec. 26, 1977.

45. Estrada interview; Al López interview, Sept. 12, 2005.

46. Quoted in *LAT*, Dec. 26, 1977.

47. D'Heedene interview.

48. "Organizing for Family and Congregation," File 4Zd566 in Larry McNeil Papers.

49. Clements interview.

50. Larkin interview; Warren, *Dry Bones Rattling*, 60.

51. Cortes interview, Feb. 9, 2004.

52. Negrete interview.

53. Ibid; Lydia López interview.

54. Luna interview.

55. Ibid.

56. León interview.

57. D'Heedene interview.

58. Larkin interview.

59. DeQuattro interview, Mar. 25 and Apr. 20, 2006.

60. *LAT*, Dec. 26, 1977. The *Times* mentions twenty-five parishes and congregations; however, there were only twenty-two Catholic parishes in East L.A., plus the Episcopalian Church of the Epiphany in Lincoln Heights.

61. Cortes interview, July 2, 2014.

62. Letter of Agreement between the IAF and the IRSC for Sept. 1, 1977 to Aug. 31, 1978, Sept. 1, 1977 in IAF, Box 98, Fld. 1084.

63. Luna interview; Lydia López interview; Cortes interview, July 2, 2014.

64. *LAT*, Dec. 26, 1977.

65. "Progress Report on the East Los Angeles Project," undated, Luna documents.

66. Zozaya interview.

67. See document in IAF, Box 101, Fld. 1154 also in Series VI, Subseries A.

68. "Suggested Budget for an East Los Angeles Project for 1976–77," IAF, Box 98, Fld. 1084.

69. Al López interview, Sept. 12, 2005.

70. Larkin interview; Chambers to Sister Georgiana, Sept. 11, 1978, IAF, Box 98, Fld. 1084; Rocha de Zozaya interview.

71. Clements interview.

72. Al López interview.

73. Luna interview.

74. Ibid.

75. "Progress Report on the East Los Angeles Organizing Project," Luna documents.

76. Peter Martínez memo to Chambers, Feb. 20, 1976, IAF, Box 98, Fld. 1084.

77. Cortes interview, Feb. 9, 2004.

78. León interview.

79. Al López interview, Sept. 12, 2005.

80. *LAT*, Dec. 26, 1977.

81. "Progress Report," Luna documents.

82. See Pawel, *Crusades of César Chávez*.

83. Cortes interview, Feb. 9, 2004.

84. Al López interview, Sept. 12, 2005.

85. León interview.

86. Ibid.

87. Vásquez interview.

88. Warren, *Dry Bones Rattling*, 51.

89. Léon interview.

90. Warren, *Dry Bones Rattling*, 24.

91. Clements interview; IAF to Interreligious Sponsoring Committee, May 9, 1978, IAF, Box 98, Fld. 1084.

92. Larkin interview.

93. Al López interview, Sept. 12, 2005.

94. Wood interview.

95. Larkin interview.

96. Rocha de Zozaya interview; "UNO—When One is Many," *Revista Maryknoll* (March 1981).

97. "Interview," in Heyck, *Barrios and Borderlands*, 223; Cortes interview, Feb. 9, 2004.

98. Heyck interview with Olivares, 44.

99. León interview; Vásquez interview.

100. Clements interview.

101. Larkin interview.

102. Rocha de Zozaya interview.

103. Luna interview.

104. Cortes interview, Feb. 9, 2004.

105. Rocha de Zozaya interview; Wood interview.

106. Oralia Garza de Cortes interview.

107. Cortes interview, Feb. 9, 2004.

108. Vásquez interview.

109. Cortes interview, Feb. 9, 2004.

110. Cortes interview, Feb. 9, 2004.

111. *LAT*, July 27, 1980.

112. Lydia López interview.

113. Clements interview.

114. Negrete interview.

115. "Suggested Agenda," Luna documents.

116. Larkin interview.

117. Rocha de Zozaya interview.

118. Cortes interview, Feb. 9, 2004.

119. "Organizing for Family and Congregations," 22, in Larry McNeil Papers.

120. Larkin interview.

121. "Interview," in Heyck, *Barrios and Borderlands*, 224.

122. Rocha de Zozaya interview.

123. *Our Sunday Visitor*, Jan. 13, 1991, 10.

124. Warren, *Dry Bones Rattling*, 31.

125. León interview.

126. Warren, *Dry Bones Rattling*, 29.

127. Rocha de Zozaya interview.

128. Cortes interview, Feb. 9, 2004.

129. Lydia López interview.

130. Cortes interview, Feb. 9, 2004.

131. Estrada interview.

132. Negrete interview.

133. Juan Romero interview with Olivares, Mar. 27, 1992, in PADRES collection; *LAT*, July 23, 1975.

134. Warren, *Dry Bones Rattling*, 40–71.

135. Larkin interview.

136. León interview.

137. Ibid.

138. Warren, *Dry Bones Rattling*, 21.

139. *LAT*, Dec. 27, 1977.

140. Rocha de Zozaya interview.

141. Vásquez interview.

142. León interview. Fr. Walter D'Heedene does not believe that liberation theology played a large role in UNO because it developed differently in Latin America. Still he notes that, theologically, the concept of working with the poor and oppressed cut across borders; D'Heedene interview.

143. Garza de Cortes interview. Skerry notes that in the late 1980s at IAF training sessions that references were made to papal encyclicals and to theologians such as Reinhold Niebuhr and Karl Rahner; see Skerry, *Mexican Americans*, 165.

144. Cortes interview, Feb. 9, 2004.

145. Ibid.

146. *LAT*, Dec. 26, 1977.

147. Ibid.

148. Ibid., Al López interview, Sept. 12, 2005; Clements interview; Cortes interview, Feb. 9, 2004; Luna interview; D'Heedene interview; Lydia López interview. Also see, "United Neighborhoods Organization, 1979," File 4Zd568, Larry McNeil Papers.

149. "St. Alphonsus, 1979–1980," Larry McNeil Papers.

150. *LAT*, Oct. 15, 1979.

151. Ibid.

152. IAF, Box 109, Fld. 1260, Series VI, Subseries A.

153. *LAT*, Sept. 23, 1981.

154. Ibid., July 27, 1980; IAF, Box 109, Fld. 1260.

155. Rocha de Zozaya interview; *Tidings*, Oct. 19, 1969, Claretian Archives.

156. Ibid.; IAF, Box 109, Fld. 1260. Elected officers were not paid; however, if they traveled on UNO business their expenses were covered by UNO.

157. Skerry, *Mexican Americans*, 177.

158. Romero interview with Olivares.

159. Larkin interview.

160. Rocha de Zozaya interview.

161. Al López interview, Sept. 12, 2005.

162. Vásquez interview.
163. *LAT*, Sept. 23, 1981.

CHAPTER 7
1. Clements interview; Cortes interview, Feb. 9, 2004; DeQuattro interview; Al López interview, Sept. 12, 2005; Negrete interview.
2. Cortes interview, Feb. 9, 2004.
3. Clements interview.
4. "Interview," in Heyck, *Barrios and Borderlands*, 225.
5. Cortes interview, Feb. 9, 2004.
6. DeQuattro interview.
7. Luna interview.
8. Cortes interview, Feb. 9, 2004.
9. Luna interview; Ellen Stern Harris, "A Grass-Roots Victory in East L.A.," *LAT*, July 23, 1978, Part V, 11–12.
10. Cortes interview, Feb. 9, 2004.
11. Clements interview; Cortes interview, Feb. 9, 2004.
12. Interview with Luis Olivares by Denis Lynn Daly Heyck, 46.
13. León interview.
14. "Interview," in Heyck, *Barrios and Borderlands*, 223–24.
15. Larkin interview.
16. León interview.
17. Oralia Garza de Cortes interview.
18. Henry Olivares interview.
19. "Interview," in Heyck, *Barrios and Borderlands*, 224.
20. Larkin interview.
21. D'Heedene interview.
22. Cortes interview, Feb. 9, 2004.
23. Larkin interview; Wood interview; Romero interview, Jan. 18, 2003; Luna interview.
24. Luna interview.
25. León interview.
26. Cortes interview, Feb. 9, 2004; Garza de Cortes interview.
27. Larkin interview; Cortes interview, Feb. 9, 2004; DeQuattro interview.
28. Lydia López interview.
29. Wood interview.
30. Al López interview, Sept. 12, 2005.
31. Leon interview.
32. Ibid.
33. Vásquez interview.
34. Luna interview.
35. León interview; Al López interview, Sept. 12, 2005.

36. León interview.
37. Lydia López interview.
38. Luna interview.
39. Heyck interview with Olivares, 47.
40. Al López interview, Sept. 12, 2005.
41. "Interview," in Heyck, *Barrios and Borderlands*, 224.
42. Lydia López interview.
43. D'Heedene interview.
44. Ibid.
45. Larkin interview.
46. Al López interview, Sept. 12, 2005.
47. Cortes interview, Feb. 9, 2004.
48. Larkin interview.
49. Larkin interview. Al López notes that maybe 1500 attended, but that would not be possible due to seating restrictions; Al López interview, Sept. 12, 2005.
50. Larkin interview.
51. Ibid.
52. Ibid.
53. Cortes interview, Feb. 9, 2004.
54. Ibid.; IAF, Box 111, Fld. 1286.
55. Cortes interview, Feb. 9, 2004.
56. Ibid.
57. Larkin interview.
58. Cortes interview, Feb. 9, 2004.
59. Lydia López interview.
60. Cortes interview, Feb. 9, 2004.
61. Larkin interview; Heyck interview with Olivares, 47.
62. Larkin interview.
63. Ibid.
64. Luna interview.
65. Lydia López interview.
66. Luna interview.
67. *LAT*, Feb. 10 and May 19, 1978.
68. IAF, Box 111, Fld., 1286.
69. *LAT*, Feb. 10, 1978.
70. Larkin interview.
71. Ibid., Cortes interview, Feb. 9, 2004.
72. Larkin interview.
73. IAF, Box 101, Fld. 1154; *LAT*, Sept. 22, 1978. UNO also pressured the state attorney general to investigate redlining; León interview.
74. Lydia López interview.
75. Ibid. Lydia López interview, 2015.
76. *LAT*, July 23, 1978.
77. Wood interview.
78. DeQuattro interview.
79. León interview.
80. Ibid.

81. Vásquez interview.
82. Larkin interview.
83. Wood interview.
84. *LAT*, Feb. 10, 1978.
85. Ibid., Nov. 5, 1977.
86. Larkin interview.
87. IAF Box 101, Fld. 1154; *LAT*, July 23, 1978, Part V, 11.
88. IAF, Box 98, Fld. 1084.
89. Larkin interview.
90. *LAHE*, Feb. 27, 1978, 1 and 14, in IAF, Box 101, Fld. 1154.
91. Ibid.
92. *LAT*, July 23, 1978, Part V, 11–12.
93. Ibid., July 12, 1978.
94. *Wall Street Journal*, July 14, 1978 in IAF, Box 101, Fld. 1154.
95. *LAT*, July 13, 1978 in IAF, Box 101, Fld. 1154.
96. Ibid., July 23, 1978, Part V, 12.
97. Ibid., Jan. 31, 1979.
98. Lydia López interview.
99. Frank Del Olmo, "East L.A. Chicano Group Win Auto Insurance Plan," *LAT*, Jan. 31, 1979, A-3; *LAHE*, Jan. 31, 1979.
100. *LAHE*, Jan. 31, 1979 in IAF, Box 101, Fld. 1154.
101. Ibid.
102. See KNXT news release, Feb. 9 and 12, 1979 in IAF, Box 101, Fld. 1154.
103. "Interview," in Heyck, *Barrios and Borderlands*, 223–24.
104. Clements interview.
105. Lydia López interview.
106. Estrada interview.
107. Larkin interview.
108. As quoted in *Our Sunday Visitor*, Jan. 13, 1991.
109. Wood interview.
110. D'Heedene interview.
111. Wood interview.
112. Henry Olivares interview.
113. León interview.
114. Vásquez interview.
115. Garza de Cortes interview.
116. Wood interview.
117. Al López interview, Sept. 12, 2005.
118. Larkin interview.
119. Urrabazo interview.
120. Lydia López interview.
121. Larkin interview.
122. As quoted in *Our Sunday Visitor*, Jan. 13, 1991.

123. Henry Olivares interview.
124. Olivares to Most Rev. Patrick Flores, Apr. 29, 1980, in La Placita Archives.
125. Cortes interview, Feb. 9, 2004.
126. León interview.
127. Lydia López interview.
128. Luna interview.
129. IAF, UNO Document.
130. See section on Rosalio Muñoz in Mario T. García, *Chicano Generation*.
131. Richard Edward Martínez, *PADRES*, 56. Martínez's study is the most authoritative one on PADRES. Also see unpublished autobiography by Fr. Edmundo Rodríguez, S.J., one of the founders of PADRES. I want to thank Fr. Eduardo Fernández, S.J., for a copy of this manuscript.
132. Ibid., 77.
133. See "The Task Force and the Spanish-Speaking Minorities" (Jan., 1970) in PADRES Collection, Box CPDR Padres, Fld. Padres, 1970; and "Statement and Recommendation of the Subcommittee for the Spanish-Speaking of the Minorities Committee of the Los Angeles Priests's Senate" [no date, but appears to be in early 1970s] in La Placita Archives. This latter material is not organized and hence no specific citations are available.
134. "Interview," in Heyck, *Barrios and Borderlands*, 221–22.
135. Richard Edward Martínez, *PADRES*, 92.
136. Romero interview.
137. Henry Olivares interview.
138. Ibid.; Fr. Juan Romero, "Tension between Cross and Sword," unpublished paper given at CEHILA Symposium, Apr. 24, 1992, 6–7; Romero interview with Olivares.
139. "P.A.D.R.E.S. Report," (circa 1976) in La Placita Archives. Also see "Statement and Recommendation of the Subcommittee for the Spanish-speaking of the Minorities Committee of the Los Angeles Priests's Senate," La Placita Archives.
140. See PADRES report by Fr. Juan Romero, Executive Director, June 24, 1975; report by Pablo Sedillo, Executive Director of Secretariat for the Spanish-Speaking of the National Conference of Catholic Bishops of the U.S. Catholic Conference, Aug. 1975 in La Placita Archives.
141. *LAT*, Mar. 4, 1975.
142. PADRES Board Meeting Minutes, Jan.

24, 1978 in PADRES Collection, Box CMCL, Fld. 7102 PADRES.

143. Stevens-Arroyo interview, Sept. 21, 2005.

144. *Entre Nosotros* 1, No. 3 (1979), 1 in PADRES Collection, Box CPDR Padres, Fld. *Entre Nosotros*, 1978–79.

145. *NCR*, Mar. 9, 1979 in PADRES Collection, Box CPDR Padres, Fld. *National Catholic Reporter* Articles, 1971–1991.

146. *Tidings*, Mar. 2, 1979, clipping in Claretian Archives.

147. *Entre Nosotros* 1, No. 3 (1979), 1 in PADRES Archives, Box CPDR Padres, Fld. *Entre Nosotros*, 1978–79.

148. Ibid., Romero interview with Olivares.

149. Olivares to His Holiness Pope John Paul II, Apr. 25, 1979, in PADRES Collection, Box CMCL-Padres-7102, Fld. CMCL 7102 Padres.

150. Olivares to Most. Rev. Jean Jadot, May 1, 1979, PADRES Collection, Box CMCL-Padres-7102, Fld. CMCL 7102 Padres. Also see Romero interview with Olivares.

151. Olivares to Jadot, Apr. 29, 1980, PADRES Collection, Box CMCL-Padres-7102, Fld. CMCL 7102 Padres.

152. *Entre Nosotros*, Special issue on Flores, 4 in PADRES Collection, Box CPDR Padres, Fld. *Entre Nosotros*, 1978–79.

153. See Box CMCC, Fld. 7102 and *Entre Nosotros* 1, No. 4 (1979) in Box CPDR Padres, Fld. *Entre Nosotros*, 1978–79 in PADRES Collection.

154. Lydia López interview; also see loose folder in La Placita Archives; Bro. Trinidad Sánchez, S.J. to Pablo Sedillo, San Antonio, Apr. 5, 1979 in La Placita Archives.

155. *Time*, Oct. 15, 1979, in La Placita Archives.

156. On liberation theology, see Hennelly, ed., *Liberation Theology*; Berryman, *Liberation Theology*; Gutiérrez, *Theology of Liberation*; Lernoux, *Cry of the People*; Levine, ed., *Religion and Political Conflict in Latin America*; Michael Lowy, *War of Gods*.

157. Richard Edward Martínez, *PADRES*, 79.

158. Material in La Placita Archives.

159. *Entre Nosotros* 1, no. 4 (Summer, 1979) in Box CPDR Padres, Fld. *Entre Nosotros*, 1978–79 in PADRES Collection.

160. Elizondo interview, Mar. 2013. Curiously, Elizondo denied any real influence of liberation theology on U.S. Latino theologians. See Elizondo's writings such as *The Future is Mestizo*.

161. Richard Edward Martínez, *PADRES*, 111.

162. Ibid., 97.

163. Romero, "Cross and Sword," 7–8.

164. Martínez, *PADRES*, 113. At the second National Encuentro, a national conference of Latino Catholics in 1977. The conference stressed recognizing lay leadership. The first National Encuentro was in 1972, and the third and last was in 1985. Also see *San Antonio Express*, Feb. 5, 1975, in La Placita Archives.

165. Richard Edward Martínez, *PADRES*, 84 and 117.

166. Romero, "Cross and Sword," 6–7.

167. PADRES Board Meeting Minutes, Oak Park, Illinois, Apr. 1–3, 1979, in Box CMCL, Fld. 9102 in PADRES Collection.

168. Olivares, "To a Meeting of Hispanic Bishops," Chicago, Apr. 29, 1979, in Box CMCL, Fld. 9102 in PADRES Collection.

169. Richard Edward Martínez, *PADRES*, 126.

170. Ibid., 134.

171. Romero interview with Olivares.

172. Romero interview; Martínez, *PADRES*, 131.

173. Martínez, *PADRES*, 131.

174. Sedillo to Olivares, May 5, 1981, in La Placita Archives.

175. Negrete, Urrabazo, and Clements interviews.

176. Cortes and Larkin interviews.

177. Jimmy Rodríguez interview.

178. "A Barrio Changes Its Political Face," *LAT*, Dec. 28, 1977, in IAF, Box 101, Fld. 1154.

CHAPTER 8

1. Estrada interview.

2. Romero interview, Jan. 18, 2003.

3. Moises Sandoval, "Duermen en Iglesia," *Revista Maryknoll* (Sept. 1986); Raymundo Reynoso, "La iglesia de la Plaza Olvera," *La Opinión*, Aug. 13, 1989, Acceso Section, 1.

4. "City's Oldest Church is 175 Years Old," no publication or date listed, Dolores Mission Archives; Rodolfo Acuña, "History is People, Not Bricks," *LAT*, Apr. 2, 1990; La Placita Church *Boletín*, Sept. 20, 1981, in La Placita

Archives. La Placita is a California Historical Landmark and a Los Angeles Historic-
Cultural Monument.

5. Marita Hernández "The Power and the
Priest," *LAT*, July 7, 1986, Part II, 1 and 6.

6. Vásquez interview; Kennedy interview;
Urrabazo interview; *Boletín*, July 5, 1981, La
Placita Archives. Vásquez was assigned to San
Antonio in 1981.

7. Juanita Espinosa interview, Mar. 27,
2003.

8. Fr. Jack Hencier Report, Apr. 19, 1982,
Group #3 in La Placita Archives.

9. O'Connor interview.

10. Henry Olivares interview.

11. Lozano interview.

12. Garza interview.

13. Romero interview.

14. Tomsho, *American Sanctuary Movement*, 2 and 41.

15. Smith, *Resisting Reagan*, 17.

16. For an excellent account of the Salvadoran war against the Catholic Church in
El Salvador, see Lernoux, *Cry of the People*.
Death squads issued the call: "Be a patriot,
kill a priest!"; ibid., 76.

17. *LAT*, July 16, 1987, clipping in Claretian
Archives.

18. See *Casa Rutilio Grande* newsletter,
Feb., 1989, 2 in Claretian Archives.

19. Mario Rivas, "Who Wants Peace," unpublished and undated document in Dolores
Mission Archives.

20. Interview with Mario Rivas, Nov. 1,
2002.

21. "Congressman Mervyn M. Dymally
on the Sanctuary Movement," Congress of
the United States (no date but issued in Dec.
1985), La Placita Archives.

22. Howard interview.

23. Stephanie Russell, "Millions Mourn
Slain Romero," *NCR*, Apr. 4, 1980, 1 and 4.

24. Excerpt from *Time* magazine, Apr. 7,
1970, Lydia López Private Col.

25. *El Salvador Bulletin* 2, No. 2 (Dec.
1982): 5, La Placita Archives.

26. Jon Sobrino, S.J., "A Powerful Prophet,"
Maryknoll, March 1981, 7.

27. "A Tragic Nuns Tale," unpublished and
undated document provided to me by Graciela Limón; "Way of the Cross in Salvador,"
Maryknoll, March 1981, 20–25 and 63–64.

28. Rubén Martínez interview.

29. Sandoval, "Duermen en Iglesias," 2.

30. Escalante interview.

31. Vásquez interview. For an excellent fic-
tionalized account of Guatemalan refugees,
see Tobar, *Tattooed Soldier*. Also see Smith,
Resisting Reagan, 33–56.

32. Gustafson interview.

33. Howard interview.

34. Kinsler interview, Apr. 30, 2006.

35. Estrada interview.

36. Kennedy interview, Aug. 24, 2002.

37. Mary-Ann Bendel and Timothy Mc-
Quay, "Refugees Fearful after L.A. Attacks,"
USA Today, July 20, 1987, 3A; Rubén Martínez
interview; undated and unreferenced document in Dolores Mission Archives.

38. Jill Stewart, "Mayor Backs Halt on
Deporting Refugees from Central America,"
LAT, July 1, 1986, 3 and 17; Sandoval, "Duer-
men en Iglesias," 12.

39. *El Norte* (Tijuana), Nov. 1989, clipping
in Claretian Archives.

40. Gustafson interview.

41. Ibid.

42. Rivas interview.

43. Statement of USCC on Central
America, Nov. 19, 1981, in La Placita Archives.

44. Quihuis interview.

45. Zwerling interview.

46. Lydia López interview.

47. Cully interview.

48. Quihuis interview.

49. Rubén Martínez interview.

50. Clements interview.

51. Romero interview.

52. Schey interview.

53. León interview.

54. *Boletín*, Sept. 4, 1983, Mar. 23, 1984,
and Oct. 14, 1984, in La Placita Archives.

55. Ibid., April 22, 1984; Romero interview;
Gregorio interview, Mar. 1 and 3, 2006; Cully
interview.

56. Henry Olivares interview.

57. Urrabazo interview; Estrada interview;
Gregorio interview; Cully interview; *Boletín*,
Jan. 26, 1986.

58. Juanita Espinosa interview.

59. Estrada interview.

60. Urrabazo interview.

61. Ibid.

62. Mejia interview.

63. Ibid.

64. Lydia López interview.

65. Lisa Martínez interview.
66. Limón interview.
67. Lisa Martínez interview.
68. Jeff Smith, "Father Michael Kennedy Sees God Where Most of Us Wouldn't Even Look," *Reporter* (San Diego), Aug. 27, 1981, 1, 8, 13, 15.
69. Ibid.
70. Kennedy interview, Aug. 24, 2002; Sandoval, "Duermen en Iglesia, 11.
71. Gregorio interview, Mar. 1 and 3, 2006.
72. Ibid.
73. DeQuattro interview.
74. Kennedy interview, Aug. 24, 2002.
75. Ibid.
76. Ibid.
77. Cully interview.
78. Kennedy interview, Aug. 24, 2002.
79. Ferrante interview, Aug. 24, 2002.
80. Cully interview.
81. Kennedy interview, Aug. 24, 2002.
82. Cully interview.
83. Howard interview.
84. Mejia interview; Valdivia interview.
85. Fr. Juan Romero, "Tension between Cross and Sword," unpublished paper given at CEHILA Symposium, Apr. 24, 1992, 10.
86. Anderson-Barker interview.
87. Howard interview.
88. Lisa Martínez interview.
89. Lydia López interview.
90. Gregorio interview.
91. Howard interview.
92. Mejia interview; Wehrli interview; Anderson-Barker interview.
93. Jimmy Rodríguez interview.
94. Bonpane interview.
95. Kennedy interview, Aug. 24, 2002.
96. Kinsler interview.
97. *Boletín*, June 17, 1984, 3, La Placita Archives.
98. Henry Olivares interview.
99. Rubén Martínez interview.
100. See copies in Dolores Mission Archives.
101. Jimmy Rodríguez interview.
102. Sandoval interview, Feb. 25, 2004.
103. Jimmy Rodríguez interview.
104. Kennedy interview, Aug. 24, 2002.
105. As mentioned in Lydia López interview.
106. Alva interview.
107. Enriquez interview.
108. Cully interview.
109. Jimmy Rodríguez interview.
110. Cully interview.
111. Lisa Martínez interview.
112. Kennedy interview, Aug. 24, 2002.
113. Lisa Martínez interview.
114. Rivas interview.
115. Enriquez interview.
116. Kennedy interview, Aug. 24, 2002.
117. Kinsler interview.
118. Interview in "Sanctuario, una manifestación del Evangelio," *El Mundo*, July 8, 1986, in collections of newspaper articles and other documents in Claretian Archives.
119. Kinsler interview.
120. Estrada interview.
121. Kinsler interview.
122. E-mail Limón to author, June 11, 2002. In 1989, Limón interviewed additional refugees as part of her research for her novel *In Search of Bernabé* (1993). She was able to share three of the interview transcripts with me, and they attest to people leaving El Salvador due to fear of murder, repression, torture, and internal dislocation. They also expressed guilt about leaving family members behind and emotional trauma from being separated from family members. See Graciela Limón to author, Feb. 8, 2006, in author's possession.
123. Enriquez interview.
124. See document from Oficina de Derechos Humanos, Centro Pastoral Rutilio Grande, Iglesia de La Placita in Dolores Mission Archives.
125. Lisa Martínez interview.
126. Rosa María Villalpando, "Concluyen Testimonios en Proceso Sobre Deportaciones de Salvadoreños," *Noticias del Mundo*, Feb. 5, 1987.
127. Lisa Martínez interview.
128. Kennedy interview, Aug. 24, 2002; Araceli Espinosa interview.
129. Enriquez interview.
130. Howard interview; Lisa Martínez interview; Mejia interview.
131. *Boletín*, July 8, 1984, 2, in La Placita Archives.
132. Kennedy interview, Aug. 24, 2002; Jimmy Rodríguez interview; Mejia interview; Henry Olivares interview.
133. Kennedy interview, Aug. 24, 2002; Lisa Martínez interview.
134. Kennedy interview, Aug. 24, 2002.
135. Araceli Espinosa interview.

136. Lisa Martínez interview.

137. Ibid.

138. *Claretian Newsletter*, Feb. 1983, 1–2, La Placita Archives.

139. Ibid., 1.

140. Urrabazo interview; Mejia interview.

141. Janis-Aparicio interview.

142. Alva interview.

143. Villalpando, "Concluyen Testimonios."

144. Janis-Aparicio interview.

145. Marita Hernández, "Immigration Law Chills Central Americans' Hopes," *LAT*, Mar. 9, 1987; also see Marjorie Miller, "Hitching a Ride on the Underground," *LAT*, Mar. 26, 1984, 1 and 3; both in Dolores Mission Archives.

146. Henry Olivares interview.

147. Cully interview.

148. Lozano interview.

149. Kennedy interview, Aug. 24, 2002.

150. Janis-Aparicio interview.

151. Lisa Martínez interview.

152. Estrada interview; Kennedy interview, Aug. 24, 2002; DeQuattro interview.

153. Cully interview.

154. Urrabazo interview.

155. Kinsler interview.

156. Janis-Aparicio interview.

157. Cully interview.

158. Mejia interview. Mejia says that perhaps a majority who slept at La Placita were the homeless and that some Claretians did not like this foot-washing. She further observes that the homeless mostly tended to be Mexican and even a few Anglos.

159. Juanita Espinosa interview.

160. Enriquez interview.

161. Sandoval, "Duermen en Iglesia"; Kennedy interview, Aug. 24, 2002; Romero, "Cross and Sword," 11; Olivares and Kennedy press release, mid-1960s, Dolores Mission Archives; Schey interview; also see, Ron Curran, "Final Sanctuary," *LA Weekly*, Sept. 12, 1991, 23–24, Claretian Archives. Staffer Rosita Enriquez believes that about 300 people slept in the church; Enriquez interview.

162. Jimmy Rodríguez interview; Natalia Hernández interview.

163. Kennedy interview; Henry Olivares interview; Mario Rivas says that the refugees and others did not receive pillows, Rivas interview; Clements interview; Ferrante interview; Hernández interview.

164. Lydia López interview.

165. Ferrante interview.

166. Ponnet interview.

167. Vásquez interview; Kennedy interview; "Interview," in Heyck, *Barrios and Borderlands*, 227.

168. León interview; Cully interview.

169. Ferrante interview.

170. Sandoval, "Duermen en Iglesias," 12.

171. Kennedy interview; Henry Olivares interview; Lisa Martínez interview; Mejia interview.

172. Rivas interview.

173. Mejia interview.

174. Lisa Martínez interview.

175. Natalia Hernández interview.

176. Olivares to Dear [Salutation], Thanksgiving 1990, Claretian Archives.

177. *Casa Rutilio Grande*, Feb. 1989, 4, Claretian Archives.

178. Hernández, "Power and the Priest," *LAT*, July 7, 1986, Part II, 6.

179. *Casa Rutilio Grande*, Feb. 1989, Dolores Mission Archives. Even after La Placita was no longer a sanctuary into the 1990s and Olivares was no longer the pastor, Casa Grande continued for a little longer.

180. Urrabazo interview.

181. Ibid.

182. Kennedy interview, Aug. 24, 2002.

183. Cully interview.

184. Rubén Martínez interview.

185. Regas interview, Mar. 30 and Apr. 19, 2006; Smith interview; Ponnet interview; Krommer interview, Feb. 3, 2003.

186. *LA Weekly*, June 29–July 5, 1990, 12.

187. Romero, "Cross and Sword," 17.

188. *La Opinión*, Aug. 6, 1990, 7.

189. *Noticias del Mundo*, Aug. 13, 1987, 31, in Dolores Mission Archives.

190. Rubén Martínez notes on Olivares. I am thankful to Martínez for sharing these notes with me.

191. "Interview," in Heyck, *Barrios and Borderlands*, 227.

192. Urrabazo interview. At the same time, Urrabazo notes that on matters on doctrine Olivares did not challenge the Church.

193. Clipping from *NCR*, Dec. 22, 1989, in Olivares Family Collection.

194. Olivares family interview.

195. Ibid; *La Opinión*, Aug. 6, 1990, 7.

196. See short biographical document in Claretian Archives.

197. Program for the Commemorative Mass for Father Luis Olivares, Mar. 17, 1995, in Dolores Mission Archives; Henry Olivares Archives.

198. Lydia López interview.

199. Lernoux, *Cry of the People*, 51.

200. Estrada interview.

201. Rubén Martínez, *Other Side*, 46.

202. This term comes from Bishop Pedro Casaldáliga; see Casaldáliga, *In Pursuit of the Kingdom*.

203. *La Opinión*, no date, Olivares Family Archives.

204. *Boletín*, Nov. 4, 1984, La Placita Archives.

205. Regas interview, Mar. 30, 2006.

206. As quoted in *Los Angeles Times Magazine*, Dec. 10, 1990, 5.

207. *La Opinión*, no date, clipping in Olivares Family Col; and ibid., Aug. 6, 1990, 7 in Olivares Family Col. On Boyle, see Celeste Fremon, *G-Dog and the Homeboys*.

208. Henry Olivares interview.

209. George Ramos, "Father Louie's Spirit is Especially Needed Now," *LAT*, Dec. 20, 1993.

210. Casaldáliga, *In Pursuit of the Kingdom*, 4 and 12.

211. Gustavo Gutiérrez, "To Know God Is to Do Justice: A Theology of Hunger," unpublished paper in La Placita Archives.

212. Romero, "Cross and Sword," 8.

213. Coutin, *Culture of Protest*.

214. See document "El Cristiano Es Siempre Forjador De Historia," National Coordinator of the Popular Church, La Placita Archives.

215. Kennedy interview, Aug. 24, 2002.

216. Bonpane interview.

217. Sandoval interview; Gregorio interview.

218. As quoted in *LA Weekly*, June 29–July 5, 1990, 12.

219. Rubén Martínez, "Outgoing Troublemaker," *LA Weekly*, June 29-July 5, 1990.

220. Lozano interview.

221. O'Connor interview.

222. Contreras interview.

223. Rivas interview.

224. Regas interview, Mar. 30, 2006.

225. Kennedy interview, Aug. 24, 2002.

226. Lozano interview.

227. O'Connor interview.

228. Memo from Rev. Bernard O'Connor, C.M.F. to All Professed, Jan. 28, 1983, in Claretian Archives.

229. Cully interview.

230. Sondeo results in document, "Enclosure 1"—Results of 1st Sondeo—Tabulated by Province tellers on Mar. 4, 1983, in La Placita Archives.

231. Berg interview, Mar. 30, 2006.

232. Memo, Provincial Office to All Professed Members, Mar. 10, 1983, in La Placita Archives.

233. Romero, "Cross and Sword," 12.

234. Memo, Mar. 10, 1983, La Placita Archives.

235. Berg interview, Mar. 30, 2006.

236. Lozano interview.

237. Ferrante interview.

238. Lozano interview.

239. Niskanen interview.

240. Lozano interview.

241. Ibid.

242. Ibid.

243. Ibid.

244. O'Connor interview.

245. Ibid; Ferrante interview.

246. Cully interview.

247. Henry Olivares interview.

248. Lozano interview. Lozano believes that Olivares might still have been elected in 1989.

249. León interview.

250. See clipping, "Father Luis Olivares returns from El Salvador," *North East Sun*, July 31, 1986, in Dolores Mission Archives.

251. Howard interview. Howard says that Kennedy was the catalyst for Olivares going to El Salvador.

252. Kennedy interview. Henry Olivares recalls more frequent visits perhaps every four to six months, but that seems inaccurate; Henry Olivares interview. Cully thinks that Olivares also went to Guatemala, but there is no evidence of this; Cully interview.

253. Howard interview.

254. See clipping Michael Kennedy, S.J., "Abuse of Human Rights in El Salvador," *National Jesuit News* (no date), in Dolores Mission Archives.

255. Kinsler interview.

256. Ponnet interview; Krommer interview.

257. Kinsler interview.

258. "Father Luis Olivares Returns from El Salvador," Dolores Mission Archives.

259. Ibid.

260. Henry Olivares interview.

261. Ibid.

262. Ibid.

263. Howard interview.

264. Henry Olivares interview.

265. Ibid.; Quihuis interview.

266. Rivas interview.

267. Anderson-Barker interview, Oct. 8, 2004.

268. Rubén Martínez interview.

269. *Centro Pastoral Rutilio Grande* (no date but perhaps in 1988), in Dolores Mission Archives.

270. *El Mundo*, Nov. 6, 1984, in Dolores Mission Archives.

271. Ibid.

272. Kennedy interview, Aug. 24, 2002.

273. Kinsler interview; Kennedy interview, Aug. 24, 2002.

274. Freehling interview. When I conducted this interview, I failed to note the date; however, it was around the mid-2000s.

275. Howard interview; Anderson-Barker interview.

276. Kennedy interview, Aug. 24, 2002; Arturo López recalls 20,000 letters; Arturo López interview.

277. Arturo López interview. López remembers Olivares's address to Duarte.

278. Ibid. Anderson-Barker remembers Olivares's address to Duarte.

279. Wong interview.

280. León interview.

281. Cully interview.

282. Arturo López interview.

283. Escalante interview.

284. Regas interview, Mar. 30, 2006.

285. Undated clipping from *Noticias del Mundo* in Dolores Mission Archives.

286. Ibid.

287. "Trabajadores Dicen que Patrones Usan ley de Inmigración Para Explotarlos," *La Opinión*, June 15, 1988, in Dolores Mission Archives.

288. Martínez interview with Olivares, Part II (no date), Martinez Collection.

289. DeQuattro interview.

290. Romero interview with Olivares.

291. Cully interview.

292. *Boletín*, Feb. 13, 1983, 2, La Placita Archives.

293. Escalante interview.

294. Cully interview.

295. Ibid.

296. Kennedy interview, Aug. 24, 2002.

297. Henry Olivares interview.

298. "Misa En Memoria De Los Martires En El Salvador," May 28, 1983, in La Placita Archives; Hernández, "Power and the Priest," 6; clipping from *La Opinión*, Aug. 15, 1989, in Olivares Family Col.

299. Ibid.

300. Valdivia interview. Valdivia tells a story of a *borrachito* (drunk) once coming into the church and stealing the statue of St. Anthony Claret. Olivares saw this and chased after him. He stopped the robber, took back the statue, gave him money to eat, and said to him: "Don't steal my statue."

301. Clements interview.

302. On Ortega's visit, see *LAT*, Oct. 5, 1984, 1 and 11; and Oct. 6, 1984, 1.

303. Cully interview.

304. Martínez interview.

305. *Boletín*, Dec. 12, 1986, 2, La Placita Archives.

306. *Noticias del Mundo*, Dec. 13, 1986, 2A, Dolores Mission Archives.

307. For the importance of transnational religious influences, see Ebaugh and Chafetz, ed., *Religion Across Borders*.

308. Kinsler interview.

309. Olivares to Cardinal Mahony, Jan. 7, 1987, in La Placita Archives; CARECEN, "Honoring Father Luis Olivares & Our Lady Queen of the Angeles Church" program, Feb. 15, 1985, in Claretian Archives.

310. On cultural citizenship, see Flores and Benmayor, *Latino Cultural Citizenship*.

311. Quoted from *LAT* synopsis of newspaper articles in La Placita Archives.

312. Kennedy interview, Aug. 24, 2002.

313. Gregorio interview.

314. See clipping from *Noticias del Mundo*, May 25, 1987, in La Placita Archives.

315. Lisa Martínez interview.

316. Romero, "Cross and Sword," 11.

CHAPTER 9

1. Tomsho, *American Sanctuary Movement*, 7–30. For the sanctuary movement, see Cunningham, *God and Caesar at the Rio Grande*; Golden, *Sanctuary*; Coutin, *Culture of Protest*; Crittenden, *Sanctuary*; Davidson, *Convictions of the Heart*; Bau, *This Ground Is Holy*; Nelson and Flannery, "Sanctuary Movement." For an excellent and power-

ful novel of the sanctuary movement, see
Martínez, *Mother Tongue*.

2. Tomsho, *American Sanctuary Movement*, 30.

3. Ibid., 31.

4. Ibid., 26.

5. As quoted in the *Washington Post*, Jan.
27, 1983, A20. For a larger history of the sanctuary, see Rabben, *Sanctuary and Asylum*.

6. Jay Matthews, "Church Sanctuary
Movement for Refugees grows in U.S.," *Washington Post*, Jan. 27, 1983, A20. Three years
later, movement activists claimed that 400
churches had declared sanctuary; see Don A.
Schanche and J. Michael Kennedy, "Sanctuary Movement Encouraged by Pope," *LAT*,
Sept. 14, 1987, Part I, 4. Also see Smith, *Resisting Reagan*, 69.

7. Shawn Hubler and Dan Welkel, "Sanctuary Movement Gaining Force," *Orange
County Register*, Dec. 15, 1985, in Claretian
Archives.

8. Kendall J. Wills, "Churches Debate Role
as Sanctuary," *New York Times*, June 16, 1985,
A35.

9. Smith, *Resisting Reagan*, 70.

10. "Sanctuary Movement Gaining Force,"
Orange County Register, Dec. 15, 1985, in Claretian Archives.

11. Zwerling interview. Also see, Michelle
Markel, "Church Becomes a Sanctuary for
Refugees," *LAT*, Mar. 25, 1983, Metro Section,
1 and 8; "Why U.S. Clergy Open Their Doors
to Latino Refugees," *LAHE*, Feb. 10, 1983, A-2
and A-7. Also see, Philip Zwerling, "Why No
Sanctuary in America for Terror's Refugees?"
LAT, Nov. 26, 1982; Michal P. Roth, "Churches
Giving Sanctuary to 'Deportables," *Guardian*, Apr., 13, 1983; Marie Denunzio and Rose
Arrieta, "The Church as Last, Best Hope
against the Hell of Deportation," *LAHE*, Mar.
25, 1983, A-1 and C-6; "Why U.S. Clergy Open
Doors to Latin Refugees," *LAHE*, Feb. 10,
1983, A-2 and A-7.

12. Bill Billiter, "Students Vow to Expand
Campus Sanctuary Efforts," *LAT*, Feb. 10,
1985, 1 and 27.

13. *NCR*, May 20, 1983, 20; *NCR*, Nov. 26,
1982; Michael McConnell, "Salvadoran Refugees Become Rallying Point for Parish Sanctuary," *NCR*, Feb. 11, 1983, 4.

14. DeQuattro interview.

15. Ibid.

16. Henry Olivares interview.

17. "Interview," in Heyck, *Barrios and
Borderlands*, 226.

18. *NCR*, July 1, 1983, 2.

19. Victor Merina, "Sanctuary: Reviving
an Old Concept," *LAT*, Nov. 17, 1985, 1 and 35;
Dan Welkal, "Cities Defying INS by Passing
Flurry of Sanctuary Statues," *Orange County
Register*, Dec. 16, 1985, 1. New Mexico also became the one and only state that declared
itself a sanctuary state.

20. *LAT*, Feb. 22, 1985, 4.

21. Ronald J. Ostrow, "Clergy, Nuns
Charged with Alien Smuggling," *LAT*, Jan. 15,
1985, 3. Evidence brought forth in the trial revealed that the INS had placed undercover
agents within the movement who tape recorded conversations of activists. The defense objected to this, but the presiding judge
allowed it.

22. Laurie Becklund, "Trial Pitting U.S.
Against Sanctuary Movement, *LAT*, Nov. 18,
1985, 10; Bill Curry, "8 of 11 Activists Guilty in
Alien Sanctuary Case," *LAT*, May 2, 1986, 12;
Tim McCarthy, "Mixed Sanctuary Verdicts
End Controversial Six-Month Trial," *NCR*,
May 9, 1986, 1.

23. Kennedy interview, Aug. 24, 2002.

24. Henry Olivares interview.

25. Ibid.

26. Lydia López interview.

27. Olivares family interview.

28. Henry Olivares interview.

29. Clements interview.

30. Sandoval interview, Feb. 25, 2004.

31. Kennedy interview, Aug. 24, 2002.

32. Ibid.

33. Kinsler interview.

34. Zwerling interview.

35. Ibid.

36. Estrada interview.

37. Lydia López interview.

38. Clements interview.

39. Gregorio interview, Mar. 1, 2006.

40. Lozano interview.

41. Ferrante interview.

42. Ibid.

43. Ibid.; and Romero interview, Jan. 18,
2003.

44. Romero interview. This included
Romero's father, Fr. Tobias.

45. O'Connor interview.

46. Castillo interview, May 5, 2005.

47. Lozano interview.

48. Al Vásquez interview.

49. Cully interview.

50. Kennedy interview, Aug. 24, 2002.

51. Cully interview.

52. Kennedy (Aug. 24, 2002) and Estrada interviews.

53. Schey interview.

54. DeQuattro interview.

55. Jimmy Rodríguez interview.

56. Henry Olivares interview.

57. See David O. Weber, "The Most Reverend Chief Executive," *Executive*, Sept. 1986, 18–22, in Claretian Archives.

58. "Interview," in Heyck, *Barrios and Borderlands*, 226; Ron Curran, "Final Sanctuary: Father Luis Olivares," *LA Weekly*, Sept. 6–12, 1991, 25.

59. Curran, "Final Sanctuary," 25.

60. Fr. Juan Romero interview with Fr. Luis Olivares, Mar. 27, 1992, PADRES Collection.

61. News release, Nov. 18, 1985, Dolores Mission Archive.

62. Pastoral Statement in Dolores Mission Archives.

63. See quote in Jaime Olivares, "Confirman Santuario en Nuestra Señora la Reina de Los Angeles," *Noticias del Mundo*, Dec. 7, 1985, 1; also see press releases from Nov. 18, 1985, and no date, in Dolores Mission Archives.

64. See Jesús Mena, "L.A. Church to Join Sanctuary Movement—with Mahony's Blessings," *LAHE* (no date), clipping in Dolores Mission Archives; also clipping from *Noticias del Mundo*, Dec. 7, 1985, 41, in Dolores Mission Archives.

65. Newsletter, Nov. 18, 1985, in Dolores Mission Archives.

66. Undated news release in Dolores Mission Archives.

67. *LAHE* (no date), in Dolores Mission Archives.

68. John Dart, "Old Plaza Church to Become a Sanctuary," *LAT*, Dec. 6, 1985, Sect. II, 1.

69. See flyer in Dolores Mission Archives.

70. Gregorio interview, Mar. 1, 2006.

71. *Daily News*, Dec. 13, 1985, in Dolores Mission Archives.

72. See program "Santuario, La Placita, 1985" in Dolores Mission Archives. The program also included a partial list of special invited guests.

73. I want to thank Henry Olivares for the translation of this poem.

74. Kinsler, Cully, Gregorio (Mar. 1, 2006), and Kennedy (Aug. 24, 2002) interviews.

75. *Daily News*, Dec. 13, 1985, in Dolores Mission Archives.

76. Davis interview. Davis actually says that Mahony had cussed at Olivares.

77. Gregorio interview, Mar. 1, 2006.

78. Ibid.

79. *NCR*, Dec. 29, 1985.

80. *Noticias del Mundo*, Dec. 13, 1985, 1A and 4A, in Dolores Mission Archives.

81. Romero and O'Connor interviews.

82. As quoted in Juan Romero, "Tension between Cross and Sword," unpublished paper given at CEHILA Symposium, Apr. 24, 1992, 15.

83. Gregorio interview, Mar. 1, 2006.

84. Cully interview.

85. Lydia López interview.

86. *Daily News*, Dec. 13, 1985, in Dolores Mission Archives.

87. Todd Acherman, "'Sanctuary' Comes to Los Angeles," *NCR* (no date but in Dec. 1985), in Dolores Mission Archives.

88. Cully interview.

89. Ibid.

90. Gregorio interview, Mar. 1, 2006.

91. Mejia interview.

92. Juanita Espinosa interview.

93. Gregorio interview, Mar. 1, 2006.

94. *National Catholic Register*, Dec. 29, 1985, in Dolores Mission Archives.

95. *LAT*, Dec. 13, 1985.

96. *Noticias del Mundo*, Dec. 13, 1985, 1A.

97. *National Catholic Register*, Dec. 16, 1985, in Dolores Mission Archives.

98. Peter Kelly, "Sanctuary: L.A.'s Oldest Church Joins the Movement," *Guardian*, Dec. 25, 1985, in Dolores Mission Archives.

99. Janis-Aparicio interview.

100. Kennedy e-mail to author, Sept. 4, 2015.

101. Gregorio interview, Mar. 1, 2006.

102. Henry Olivares interview.

103. Kennedy e-mail to author, Sept. 4, 2015.

104. *LAT*, Dec. 13, 1985; *San Jose Chronicle*, Dec. 13, 1985; *Daily News*, Dec. 13, 1985; *Guardian*, Dec. 25, 1985; *Ventura Star*, Dec.

13, 1985; *Noticias del Mundo*, Dec. 13, 1985; Kinsler interview.

105. Zwerling interview.

106. English and Spanish Declarations of La Placita Public Sanctuary in Dolores Mission Archives.

107. Gregorio interview, Mar. 1, 2006.

108. Kennedy e-mail to author, Sept. 4, 2015.

109. Cully interview.

110. As quoted in *National Catholic Register*, Dec. 16, 1985, in Dolores Mission Archives.

111. As quoted in *Daily News*, Dec. 13, 1985, in Dolores Mission Archives.

112. Untitled and undated clipping in Dolores Mission Archives.

113. *Daily Breeze*, Dec. 13, 1985, in Dolores Mission Archives.

114. Jaime Olivares, "La Placita Se Convirtió en Santuario de Refugiados," *Noticias del Mundo*, Dec. 13, 1985, in Dolores Mission Archives.

115. *Daily Breeze*, Dec. 13, 1985.

116. Cully interview.

117. Kennedy interview, Aug. 24, 2002; also, DeQuattro and Clements interviews.

118. Garza interview.

119. Romero, "Cross and Sword," 16.

120. *Tidings*, Dec. 20, 1985, 6 in Dolores Mission Archives; and *National Catholic Register*, Dec. 29, 1985.

121. Kennedy interview, Aug. 24, 2002; Juanita Espinosa interview.

122. Henry Olivares interview.

123. Flyer in Dolores Mission Archives.

124. Arturo Rodríguez interview.

125. Urrabazo interview.

126. Cully interview.

127. "Interview," in Heyck, *Barrios and Borderlands*, 226.

128. Araceli Espinosa interview.

129. Hartmire interview.

130. Quihuis interview.

131. Kennedy interview, Aug. 24, 2002.

132. Quihuis interview.

133. Jimmy Rodríguez interview.

134. Estrada interview.

135. Romero interview.

136. Romero, "Cross and Sword," 16.

137. Urrabazo interview.

138. Lozano interview.

139. Romero interview; Romero, "Cross and Sword," 16.

140. Alva interview.

141. Lydia López interview.

142. Frenzen interview.

143. Clements interview; Ponnet/Krommer interview; Romero interview.

144. "Interview," in Heyck, *Barrios and Borderlands*, 226.

145. Anderson-Barker interview.

146. Lydia López interview.

147. Regas interview, Mar. 30, 2006.

148. "Interview," in Heyck, *Barrios and Borderlands*, 226.

149. Heyck interview with Olivares, 58.

150. Kennedy interview, Aug. 24, 2002.

151. Cully interview.

152. Bonpane interview.

153. Kennedy interview, Aug. 24, 2002.

154. Lozano interview.

155. Urrabazo interview.

156. Estrada interview.

CHAPTER 10

1. See Ruben Vives, "Return of the Workplace Raid?" *LAT*, Jan. 15, 2017, California section, 1.

2. See Mario T. García, *Memories of Chicano History*.

3. Frenzen interview.

4. Robert Pear, "Immigration Rules Require New Proof from Job Seekers," *New York Times*, Jan. 20, 1987; "Reform Breeds Its Own Crisis," *Business Week*, Mar. 30, 1987.

5. David Maraniss, "Pope Backs Sheltering Immigrants," *Washington Post*, Sept. 14, 1987, A1.

6. Jaime Olivares, "Hispanos Critican Nuevas Regulaciones," *Noticias del Mundo*, Mar. 17, 1987, 1, Claretian Archives.

7. *La Opinión*, July 6, 1986, Claretian Archives.

8. Ibid., Mar. 9, 1986, Claretian Archives.

9. Veronica García, "Non-qualifying Aliens Need Church's Voice," *Southern Cross*, June 5, 1987, Dolores Mission Archives.

10. Ibid.

11. *La Opinión*, June 12, 1983.

12. Ibid., Sept. 21, 1988, Dolores Mission Archives.

13. *LAT*, Dec. 13, 1987, 12.

14. Miguel Jiménez Rivera, "Sacerdotes Ayudarán Más a Indocumentados y Refugiados," *Noticias del Mundo*, Aug. 12, 1987, 3-A, Dolores Mission Archives; Pedro M. Valdivieso, "Los Clérigos Católicos Denunciarán

a E.U. por Abusos Contra Indocumentados Latinos," *El Diario de Los Angeles*, Mar. 23, 1988, Claretian Archives.

15. *Washington Post* (no date), Dolores Mission Archives.

16. *La Opinión*, July 6, 1987, Dolores Mission Archives.

17. Rosa María Villalpando, "Religiosos Denuncian Violaciones Derechos de los Indocumentados," *La Opinión*, Mar. 23, 1988; Kansvaag interview; *La Opinión*, Oct. 31, 1988, Dolores Mission Archives; *El Diario de Los Angeles*, Mar. 23, 1988; *LAT*, Dec. 19, 1988, 4.

18. *Boletín*, May 20, 1984, La Placita Archives.

19. *LAT*, Sept. 12, 1987, 1 and 3, in Claretian Archives; *El Diario de Los Angeles*, Sept. 12, 1987, 1A and 4A, Dolores Mission Archives; *Catholic Review*, Sept. 30, 1987, A-4, Dolores Mission Archives.

20. *LAT*, Sept. 12, 1987, 1 and 3, Claretian Archives; *El Diario de Los Angeles*, Sept. 12, 1987, 1A and 4A, Dolores Mission Archives; *LAT*, Sept. 14, 1987, Claretian Archives.

21. Ethel Pehrson to Olivares, May 9, 1987, in La Placita File, Chancery Archival Collection.

22. Undated audio tape by Olivares of a parish staff meeting; tape courtesy of Henry Olivares.

23. Schey interview.

24. Anderson-Barker interview; Araceli Espinosa interview; Ferrante interview.

25. Olivares to Mahony, June 5, 1987, La Placita File, Chancery Archival Collection.

26. Olivares to Mahony, Nov. 11, 1987, La Placita File, Chancery Archival Collection.

27. Mahony to Olivares, Nov. 23, 1987, La Placita File, Chancery Archival Collection.

28. See document in La Placita File, Chancery Archival Collection .

29. Olivares to Auxiliary Bishop Gilbert Chávez, Nov. 26, 1987; and Mahony to Olivares, Nov. 23, 1987, in La Placita File, Chancery Archival Collection.

30. Olivares to Chávez, Nov. 26, 1987, La Placita File, Chancery Archival Collection.

31. Olivares to Mahony, Nov. 26, 1987, La Placita File, Chancery Archival Collection.

32. *LAT*, Dec. 13, 1987, Part II, 13; Ron Curran, "Final Sanctuary: Father Luis Olivares," *LA Weekly*, Sept. 6–12, 1991, 25–26.

33. Kansvaag interview.

34. Jimmy Rodríguez interview; Alva interview; Rubén Martínez interview; DeQuattro interview; *LAT* (no date), in La Placita archives.

35. Olivares family interview.

36. Schey interview.

37. Curry interview.

38. *La Opinión*, Oct. 6, 1988, Dolores Mission Archives.

39. Juan Romero, "Tension between Cross and Sword," unpublished paper given at CEHILA Symposium, Apr. 24, 1992, 13; Juan Romero interview with Fr. Luis Olivares, Mar. 27, 1992, PADRES Collection.

40. Regas interview, Mar. 30, 2006.

41. Ibid.

42. Schey interview; Garza interview. Garza says that Luis told her that he was always fighting the higher-ups and knew that he was getting in trouble with them.

43. Boyle interview.

44. Ibid.

45. Ferrante interview.

46. Curry interview; DeQuattro interview; Ponnet interview.

47. Romero, "Cross and Sword," 13; Romero interview with Olivares.

48. Curran, "Final Sanctuary," 26; Boyle interview; Lydia López interview; Krommer interview.

49. Marita Hernández, "Mahony Unveils Church Policy on Illegal Aliens," *LAT*, Oct. 6, 1988, Metro Section, Dolores Mission Archives.

50. *LAT*, Sept. 12, 1987.

51. Carlos Alberto González, "INS Llevará a Justicia a Sacerdotes," *La Opinión*, Dec. [?], in Dolores Mission Archives; *El Diario de Los Angeles*, Sept. 12, 1987, Dolores Mission Archives; *Catholic Review*, Sept. 30, 1987, Dolores Mission Archives.

52. Rubén Castañeda, "Activists Demand INS Apologize to Priests," *LAHE*, Sept. 30, 1988, Dolores Mission Archives; *Sunday Press-Telegram*, Oct. 2, 1988, Claretian Archives.

53. Rubén Castañeda and Laureen Lazarovici, "L.A. Priests Investigated in INS Vandalism," *LAHE*, Sept. 24, 1988; Marita Hernández, "INS Investigation 2 Churches That Aid Aliens," *LAT*, Sept. 24, 1988.

54. Castañeda, "Activists Demand"; Marita Hernández and Stephen Braun, "Priests Probed over Alleged Aid to Aliens," *LAT*, Sept. 30, 1988, Metro Section, Dolores Mission Ar-

chives; *La Opinión*, Sept. 30, 1988, Dolores Mission Archives.

55. Rene Lynch, "INS Seeks Restraints on Priests," *Daily News*, Oct. 19, 1988, Dolores Mission Archives.

56. Rubén Martínez, "The INS Targets La Placita," *LA Weekly*, Oct. 21–27, 1988, Martínez Collection.

57. *LAT*, Oct. 2, 1988, Section V, 4.

58. Romero, "Cross and Sword" 13; Wong interview.

59. Rosa María Villalpando, "Arozobispo Repite Compromiso con Indocumentados," *La Opinión*, Oct. 6, 1988, Dolores Mission Archives; Villalpando, "Fieles Agradecen al Arobispo Mahony su Apoyo a Miles de Indocumentados," *La Opinión*, Oct. 20, 1988, Dolores Mission Archives; *Daily News*, Oct. 20, 1988, 19; Timothy Carlson, "Faithful Support 3 priests Under INS fire," *LAHE*, Oct. 20, 1988, Dolores Mission Archives.

60. Curran, "Final Sanctuary," 26.

61. Zwerling interview.

62. Gustafson interview; Lozano interview; Bonpane interview; Kinsler interview; Zwerling interview; Jimmy Rodríguez interview; Tracy Wilinson, "Priests Accuse FBI to Trying to Force Salvadoran to Spy on Church," *LAT*, Apr. 11, 1990 in Lydia López Col.; Jose Luis Sierra, "Acusan al FBI de Pretender Obligar a un Refugiado a Espiar a Sacerdotes," *La Opinión*, Apr. 11, 1990, Lydia López Col.; Lydia López interview. Susan Alva remembers that the INS once went into La Placita but is not sure they arrested anyone; Alva interview. In Orange County, INS officers chased seven Latino undocumented day laborers into La Purisima Catholic Church; see Marita Hernández, "Religious Leaders Join Protest of INS Pursuit of Aliens into Church," *LAT*, Oct. 4, 1988, Part II, 1; Bob Schwartz, "INS Chief Calls Arrests in Church 'Regrettable,'" *LAT*, Sept. 29, 1988, Dolores Mission Archives.

63. Gustafson interview; Zwerling interview.

64. Schey interview.

65. Miguel Jiménez Rivera, "Párroco Olivares Dice Que Ezell Padece de Delirío de Persecusión," *La Opinión*, Mar. 4, 1987, Dolores Mission Archives.

66. Rubén Martínez, "INS Targets La Placita," *LA Weekly*, Oct. 21–27, 1988, Rubén Martínez Collection.

67. Rubén Martínez interview; Clements interview.

68. *LAT*, Sept. 21, 1988, Metro Section.

69. *La Opinión*, Mar. 23, 1988, Dolores Mission Archives.

70. Rosa María Villalpando, "Religiosos Denuncian Violacíones a Derechos de los Indocumentados," *La Opinión*, Mar. 23, 1988, Dolores Mission Archives; Pedro M. Valdivieso, "Los Clérigos Católicos Denunciarán a E.U. por Abusos Contra Indocumentados Latinos," *El Diario de Los Angeles*, Mar. 23, 1988, Claretian Archives.

71. *La Opinión*, June 15, 1988, Dolores Mission Archives.

72. Manuel Aguirre, "Piden que Iglesias Abran Sus Puertas a 'Illegales,'" *Noticias del Mundo*, Aug. 25, 1989, Dolores Mission Archives; George Ramos, "Church Leaders Ask More Pastors to House Illegals," *LAT* (no date, but likely Aug. 25, 1989), Dolores Mission Archives.

73. Kansvaag interview; Wong interview; Alva interview; Frenzen interview.

74. Wong interview.

75. Escalante interview.

76. Ibid.; Wong interview.

77. Alva interview.

78. Kansvaag interview.

79. Frenzen interview. Frenzen would later serve as co-chair and chair.

80. Ibid.; Gustafson, Wong, Kansvaag, Alva, and Escalante interviews; see flyer "Centro Base 'La Placita,'" and *Boletín*, Feb. 8, 1990, 3 in La Placita Archives.

81. DeQuattro interview.

82. "Scitca's 10th Anniversary Dinner Celebration," program in Claretian Archives.

83. Wehrli interview; Zwerling interview.

84. Wehrli, DeQuattro, Zwerling, Kinsler, and Smith interviews.

85. DeQuattro, Zwerling, and Smith interviews.

86. *Episcopal News*, June, 1989, Claretian Archives.

87. Kathleen Hendrix, "A Westside Journey of Conscience," *LAT*, Feb. 26, 1990, View Section, Lydia López Collection.

88. Kennedy interview, Aug. 24, 2002.

89. Henry Olivares interview. Kennedy (Aug. 24, 2002), Schey, Anderson-Barker, and Quihuis interviews. Also see memo from Mario and Sandy to Proyecto Pastoral members (no date), Dolores Mission Archives.

90. Rubén Martínez interview.

91. Other coalition groups that Olivares worked with included the Office of the Americas, directed by Fr. Blase Bonpane.

92. Janis-Aparicio interview.

93. Escalante interview.

94. Kinsler, Mejia, Bonpane, Janis-Aparicio, and Schey interviews; Moises Sandoval, "Duermen en Iglesia," *Revista Maryknoll*, Sept., 1985, 11.

95. Wong and Janis-Aparicio interviews.

96. Kennedy interview, Aug. 24, 2002; Olivares to the Honorable Jim Wright, Speaker of the House, June 28, 1987, Dolores Mission Archives; Venecia Rojas, "500 Ask Pope to Get Together with El Salvador," *LAHE*, Mar. 7, 1983, La Placita Archives.

97. Hartmire interview.

98. Pedro M. Valdivieso, "Misa y Ayuno del Actor Esai Morales en Apoyo a Chávez," *El Diario de Los Angeles*, Dec. 24, 1988, Claretian Archives.

99. Jimmy Rodríguez interview.

100. Ibid.

101. Ibid.

102. Ibid.

103. Ibid.

104. *LAHE*, Dec. 6, 1988, in news summary collection, Claretian Archives.

105. *LAT*, Dec., 1983, Claretian Archives.

106. Martha Hastings, "Protesta ante la Policía de Los Angeles por Arresto de Jornaleros el Jueves Pasado," *La Opinión* (no date), Dolores Mission Archives.; *LAT*, Aug. 13, 1988, in news summary collection, Claretian Archives.

107. *LAT*, July 24, 1988, in news summary collection in Claretian Archives.

108. *LAT*, July 14, 1988.

109. *New York Times*, Jan. 22, 1988, Claretian Archives.

110. *Time*, Aug. 3, 1987, 21.

111. Romero, "Cross and Sword," 13; *La Opinión*, Feb. 21, 1986, Dolores Mission Archives.

112. See copy in La Placita File, Chancery Archival Collection.

113. Cully interview.

114. Miguel Jiménez Rivera, "No Me Intididan las Amenazas Que Puedan Hacer a Mi Vida," *Noticias del Mundo*, July 20, 1987; Laurie Becklund, "Death Squads's Threat Prompts FBI Inquiry," *LAT*, July 18, 1987, Part II, 3; *NCR*, July 31, 1987; *La Opinión*, July 18, 1987; Santiago O'Donnell, "Escuadrones de la Muerte Amenazan al Padre Luis Olivares de La Placita," *La Opinión*, July 17, 1987; Rubén Martínez, "L.A. Hit List," *LA Weekly*, July 24–30, 1987; Mary-Ann Bendel and Timothy McQuay, "Refugees Fearful after L.A. Attacks," *USA Today*, July 20, 1987, 3A; all in Dolores Mission Archives.

115. Bonpane and Escalante interviews.

116. Press Release, July 17, 1987, La Placita File, Chancery Archival Collection.

117. Olivares to Mahony, July 18, 1987, La Placita Archives.

118. José Luis Sierra, "Más Amenazas al Padre Olivares," *La Opinión*, July 27, 1987, Dolores Mission Archives.

119. Olivares to My Very Dear Friends, Aug. 10, 1987, La Placita File, Chancery Archival Collection.

120. Santiago O'Donnell, "Los Angeles No Es Santuario para los 'Escuadrones de la Muerte' Woo," *La Opinión*, Aug. 3, 1987, Dolores Mission Archives.

121. Henry Olivares interview.

122. Clements interview.

123. Kennedy interview, Aug. 24, 2002.

124. Lydia López interview.

125. Schey interview.

126. Cully interview.

127. Garza interview.

128. *Tidings*, July 24, 1987, Dolores Mission Archives.

129. Mahony to Olivares, July 23, 1987, La Placita Archives.

130. Howard, Bonpane, Zwerling, and Freehling interviews.

131. Note in Claretian Archives.

132. *Time*, Aug. 3, 1987, 20.

133. Text in Dolores Mission Archives.

134. Laurie Becklund, "Activists Blame 'Death Squad' for Attack on Woman," *LAT*, July 11, 1987; *NCR*, July 31, 1987; Santiago O'Donnell, "Primera Victima en Los Angeles de los 'Escuadrones de la Muerte' de El Salvador," *La Opinión*, July 12, 1987; Bob Perillo, "Death Squad Terrorists in Los Angeles," *Catholic Agitator*, Oct., 1987, all in Dolores Mission Archives.

135. *NCR*, July 31, 1987; Clara Potes, "Otro Secuestro en Los Angeles," *La Opinión*, July 19, 1987, both in Dolores Mission Archives.

136. Rubén Martínez, "L.A. Hit List," *LA Weekly*, July 24–30, 1987, Dolores Mission Archives.

137. Laurie Becklund, "2nd Abduction Stirs Demands from Activists," *LAT*, July 19, 1987, 3 and 31. Still another abduction later in July involved a man who was not politically active and was found bound and gagged with cloth bearing the signs of an apparent death squad; see Laurie Becklund, "Police Find Inconsistencies in L.A.—Less than Meets the Eye?" *LAT*, Aug. 3, 1987.

138. Jeff Gottlieb, "Bradley Wants Reward Offered for 'Death Squad' Information," *LAHE*, July 23, 1987; Victor Gutíerrez, "Bradley Advierte No Permitirá Caos Que Crean 'Escuadrones de la Muerte,'" *Noticias del Mundo*, July 23, 1987, both in Dolores Mission Archives; Cristina García, "Death Squads Invade California," *Time*, Aug. 3, 1987, 21.

139. Martínez, "L.A. Hit List."

140. Laurie Becklund, "Ezell Terms L.A. Death Squad Threats 'PR,'" *LAT*, July 28, 1987, 3.

141. Becklund, "Congressman Asks Probe of Ezell's View on Death Squads," *LAT*, Aug. 6, 1987, Dolores Mission Archives.

142. *LAHE*, July 30, 1987, Dolores Mission Archives.

CHAPTER 11

1. Rev. Francisco Gómez, C.M.F., "Statement of Reality at Our Lady Queen of Angeles Parish in Los Angeles," Jan. 25, 1982, La Placita Archives; also Cully interview.

2. Olivares to editor, *LAT*, Apr. 8, 1983.

3. Interview with María Valdivia and María Arvizu, Aug., 28, 2004.

4. Cully email to author, July 2, 2005.

5. Ibid.

6. Cully interview.

7. Ibid.

8. Ibid.

9. Araceli Espinosa interview.

10. Cully interview.

11. Rubén Martínez interview.

12. *Boletín*, Sept. 6, 1981, La Placita Archives.

13. Cully interview.

14. Ibid.; *Boletín*, Sept. 6, 1981, La Placita Archives.

15. Cully interview.

16. Rubén Martínez interview.

17. Araceli Espinosa interview.

18. Luz López to John J. Ward, Auxiliary Bishop of Los Angeles, June 13, 1982, La Placita File, Chancery Archival Collection.

19. Ward to Olivares, July 26, 1982, La Placita File, Chancery Archival Collection.

20. Timothy Cardinal Manning to Olivares, Aug. 9, 1982, La Placita File, Chancery Archival Collection.

21. Olivares to Manning, July 20, 1982, La Placita File, Chancery Archival Collection.

22. Cully interview.

23. Garza interview.

24. For transnational religious ties, see Ebaugh and Chafetz, *Religion Across Borders*.

25. Laurie Becklund, "What Began as a Sprinkle Has Turned into a Flood," *LAT*, June 11, 1984.

26. Cully interview.

27. Araceli Espinosa interview; *Boletín*. Sept. 6, 1981; May 12, 1985; Sept. 27, 1981; La Placita Archives.

28. Araceli Espinosa interview. Olivares also supported youth by endorsing Fr. Estrada's work with runaway youth, including opening a house shelter; Estrada interview; and *Boletín*, June 11, 1984.

29. Note by Henry Olivares to author, June 16, 2016.

30. *Boletín*, Dec. 6, 1981, 2; Nov. 16, 1986, 2; Nov. 23, 1986, 3 in La Placita Archives; Jahulé Valuvi, "Concurridas Mananitas a la Virgen de Guadalupe Ayer," untitled news clipping from 1985, Claretian Archives. During Christmas, La Placita organized *Las Posadas* consisting of an eight-day novena; see *Boletín*, Dec. 12, 1981, 3, La Placita Archives. In addition to his parish duties, Olivares would also on occasion make home visits; Estrada interview.

31. Henry Olivares interview; Kennedy interview, Aug. 24, 2002; Cully interview.

32. Kennedy interview, Aug. 24, 2002.

33. Romero interview.

34. Kennedy (Aug. 24, 2002), Vásquez, Estrada, and Lozano interviews.

35. Cully interview.

36. Rubén Martínez interview.

37. Sandoval interview.

38. Howard interview.

39. Jimmy Rodríguez interview.

40. Contreras interview.

41. DeQuattro interview, May 20, 2006.

42. Lozano, Cully, Araceli Espinosa interviews.

43. Estrada interview.

44. Kennedy interview, Aug. 24, 2002.

45. Urrabazo interview.

46. Ibid.
47. Kansvaag interview.
48. Limón email to author, June 11, 2002.
49. Mondragon interview, May 27, 2005.
50. Sandoval interview.
51. Bonpane interview. Kennedy also had refugees speak at his Masses; Howard interview.
52. Rubén Martínez interview.
53. Urrabazo interview.
54. Henry Olivares interview.
55. Maldonado interview.
56. Romero interview.
57. Howard interview.
58. Ferrante interview.
59. Sandoval interview.
60. Ferrante interview.
61. Ponnet interview.
62. Rubén Martínez and Urrabazo interviews.
63. Vásquez interview.
64. Henry Olivares interview.
65. Urrabazo interview.
66. Bonpane interview.
67. Henry Olivares interview.
68. Estrada interview.
69. Cully interview.
70. Martínez interview with Olivares, Part II (no date), Martinez Collection.
71. Transcript in Martínez Collection.
72. Mejia interview.
73. Estrada interview.
74. Cully interview.
75. Juanita Espinosa interview.
76. Mejia interview.
77. Part of being a good pastor included keeping up with his responsibilities as a member of the Claretian order. He attended meetings and retreats of the order and, as Vicar Provincial, still visited and reported on Claretian parishes in the Western Province; see Cully and Castillo interviews; and correspondence as Vicar provincial in La Placita Archives.
78. Bonpane interview.
79. Lydia López, Ponnet, Krommer, Kinsler, and Smith interviews.
80. Escalante interview.
81. Kennedy interview, Aug. 24, 2002.
82. Smith interview.
83. Freehling interview.
84. Vásquez interview.
85. Regas interview, Mar. 30, 2006.
86. Freehling interview.

87. Fr. Juan Romero interview with Fr. Luis Olivares, Mar. 27, 1992, PADRES Collection; Itabari Njeri, "In King's Name, Homelessness Linked to Global Issues," *LAT*, Apr. 3, 1987, Claretian Archives.
88. Freehling interview.
89. Ibid.
90. Zwerling interview.
91. Aracely Domínguez interview; Lydia López notes that Olivares used to like to give nicknames to close friends; he called her "Liz"; Lydia López interview.
92. Lydia López interview.
93. Anderson-Barker interview.
94. Romero and Lydia López interviews.
95. Estrada interview.
96. Ibid.
97. Regas interview, Mar. 30, 2006.
98. Schey interview.
99. Lydia López interview.
100. Garza interview.
101. Contreras interview.
102. Gregorio interview, Mar. 1, 2006.
103. Ibid.
104. Rubén Martínez interview.
105. Lydia López interview.
106. Ibid.
107. Urrabazo interview.
108. Garza interview.
109. Ibid.
110. León interview.
111. Estrada interview.
112. Lydia López interview.
113. Ibid.; Urrabazo, León, and Kennedy (Aug. 24, 2002) interviews.
114. Howard interview.
115. Estrada interview.
116. Lydia López interview.
117. Urrabazo interview.
118. Rubén Martínez interview.
119. Rubén Martínez notes, in Rubén Martínez Collection.
120. Lydia López and Urrabazo interviews.
121. Lydia López interview.
122. Cully and Valdivia interviews.
123. Valdivia interview.
124. Estrada interview.
125. Ibid.
126. Zwerling interview.
127. Kennedy interview, Aug. 24, 2002.
128. Anderson-Barker interview.
129. Valdivia interview.
130. Urrabazo interview; and news summary (undated), Claretian archives.

131. Romero interview.

132. Urrabazo interview.

133. Clipping from *Downtown News*, Mar. 12, 1990, La Placita Archives; also, Garza, Hernández, Mejia, Romero, Araceli Espinosa, Wehrli, Valdivia, and Juanita Espinosa interviews.

134. Krommer and Urrabazo interviews.

135. Lydia López interview.

136. Ibid.; and Urrabazo interview.

137. Cully interview.

138. Ibid.; *Boletín*, Feb. 13, 1983, 3, La Placita Archives.

139. Araceli Espinosa interview.

140. Valdivia interview.

141. Henry Olivares note to author, June 16, 2016.

142. María Valdivia interview.

143. Ibid.

144. Ibid.

145. Ibid.

146. Ibid.

147. Gregorio interview, Mar. 1, 2006.

148. Estrada interview.

149. Valdivia interview.

150. Garza interview.

151. Valdivia interview; see program, "Luis Olivares, C.M.F., Sacerdote, 1961–1986," in Claretian Archives. He celebrated this at a special Mass in San Antonio with his family and some parishioners and friends from Los Angeles, such as the Arvizus.

152. Garza and Urrabazo interviews.

153. Cully interview.

154. Olivares to Ms. Manuela R. Clark, May 16, 1986, La Placita Archives.

155. *NCR*, Nov. 24, 1989, 8; "Martyrs of the UCA in El Salvador," Religious Task Force in Central America, Dolores Mission Archives.

156. Ibid.

157. *LAT*, Nov. 7, 1989; *NCR*, Nov. 24, 199, 8; also see, Philip Bennett, "Burying the Jesuits," *Vanity Fair* (Nov. 1990): 110–23; and Joseph A. O'Hare, "In Solidarity with the Slain Jesuits of El Salvador," *America*, Dec. 16, 1989, 443–46.

158. "The Wednesday Morning Coalition: A Call to Conscience," courtesy of Rev. Don Smith. This was an informal publication.

159. Kennedy interview, Aug. 24, 2002.

160. Wehrli interview; Women of Conscience was established in 1981.

161. Freehling interview.

162. Ponnet interview.

163. Smith interview.

164. *NCR*, Dec. 8, 1989, 7; "Wednesday Morning Coalition"; Ponnet and Krommer interview.

165. Cunningham, *God and Caesar at the Rio Grande*, 100.

166. Wehrli interview.

167. *NCR*, Dec. 8, 1989, 7.

168. Other protests included one with over 700 people in MacArthur Park on Nov. 18, 1989; see *LAT*, Nov. 19, 1989, clipping in Dolores Mission Archives.

169. *LAT*, Jan. 18, 1990, B-3.

170. Transcript of interview with Olivares, Kennedy, and Boyle by Blase Bonpane, Dec. 13, 1989, in author's possession. The interview was part of Bonpane's radio show in Los Angeles.

171. *The Tidings*, Apr. 13, 1990; and Kennedy interview, Aug. 24, 2002.

172. "Wednesday Morning Coalition"; Bonpane interview; *NCR*, Dec. 8, 1989, 7.

173. Bonpane interview.

174. Lisa Martínez interview.

175. Bonpane interview.

176. "Wednesday Morning Coalition."

177. Ibid.

178. Ibid.

179. Ibid.

180. Reference in Blase Bonpane Collection, Box 87, UCLA Special Collections.

181. Bonpane and DeQuattro interviews.

182. Lisa Martínez interview.

183. See YouTube film clip from video "The Faithful Revolution: Vatican II," https://www.youtube.com/watch?v=tErdLefYsbA.

184. Regas, Lisa Martínez, and Lydia López interviews.

185. Ibid.

186. "Wednesday Morning Coalition."

187. Ibid.

188. Bonpane interview.

189. Ibid.; Regas interview; Lydia López interview; *La Opinión*, Mar. 2, 1990, clipping in Lydia López Collection; DeQuattro interview.

190. Bonpane interview.

191. Ibid.

192. DeQuattro interview.

193. Wehrli interview.

194. Ibid.

195. Ponnet interview.

196. *The Tidings* clipping (undated), in Olivares Family Collection.

197. Lydia López interview.

198. Kennedy interview.

199. Lydia López interview; "Wednesday Morning Coalition."

200. Lydia López interview.

201. Bonpane interview.

202. Email from Wehrli to author, Apr. 24, 2003.

203. Bonpane interview.

204. *NCR*, Dec. 8, 1989, 7. Also, transcript of radio interview of Olivares, Kennedy, and Boyle by Blase Bonpane, Dec. 6, 1989, in author's possession.

205. See news summary, *La Opinión*, Nov. 24, 1989; Ibid., Dec. 17, 1989; and Feb. 3, 1990, in Claretian Archives.

206. Lisa Martínez interview.

207. "Wednesday Morning Coalition."

208. Kennedy interview, Aug. 24, 2002.

209. *LA Weekly*, Dec. 16, 1990, 5.

210. Kennedy interview, Aug. 24, 2002.

211. Janis-Aparicio interview.

212. As quoted in "Wednesday Morning Coalition." The protests were carried on for several months, into spring 1990.

213. Demetria Martínez, "Champion of L.A. Hispanics Unhappy to Be Moved," *NCR*, undated clipping, Dolores Mission Archives.

214. Urrabazo interview.

215. *La Opinión*, Sept. 30, 1989.

216. *LA Weekly* undated clipping, 26–27, in Dolores Mission Archives.

217. *L.A. Weekly*, Oct. 29, 1989, in summary of news, Claretian Archives; see Rubén Martínez notes, Rubén Martínez collection.

218. Urrabazo and Kennedy (Aug. 24, 2002) interviews.

219. Estrada interview.

220. *La Opinión*, Sept. 30, 1989.

221. Urrabazo interview.

222. *NCR*, undated clipping.

223. *La Opinión* (undated), Dolores Mission Archives.

224. Olivares interview with Martínez (undated) and Martínez notes.

225. *LA Weekly* clipping, 27, Dolores Mission Archives.

226. Olivares to *LA Weekly*, Dec. 24, 1989, Chancery Archival Collection.

227. See news summary (undated), Claretian Archives.

228. Olivares to *LA Weekly*, Dec. 24, 1989.

229. News summary (undated), Claretian Archives.

230. Hernández and Dart, "Priest Active," *LAT* (undated), Lydia López Collection.

231. News summary (undated), Claretian Archives; *NCR* (undated).

232. *La Opinión*, Oct. 2, 1989, Claretian Archives.

233. Hernández and Dart, "Priest Active."

234. *LA Weekly* (undated clipping), Claretian Archives.

235. As quoted in Rubén Martínez, "The Sacrifice: Luis Olivares, 1934–1993," *LA Weekly* (undated clipping), Henry Olivares Collection.

236. Demetria Martínez, "Champion of L.A. Hispanics," *NCR*, undated.

237. News summary (undated), Claretian Archives.

238. Gregorio interview.

239. Petition in Lydia López Collection.

240. *Downtown News*, Mar. 12, 1990.

241. *La Opinión*, Oct. 1, 1989, Claretian Archives.

242. Jaime Olivares, "Traslado del Padre Olivares Significaría Reubicar También al Centro Rutilio Grande: Kennedy," *La Opinión*, Apr. 2, 1990, Dolores Mission Archives.

243. Rubén Martínez interview; and Rubén Martínez notes in Martínez Collection.

244. Rubén Martínez notes in Martínez Collection.

245. Romero interview, May 11, 2006.

246. "Interview," in Heyck, *Barrios and Borderlands*, 228.

247. Urrabazo interview.

248. Bishop John J. Ward to Mahony, Nov. 7, 1990, La Placita Archives.

249. Mahony to Vásquez, Oct. 6, 1990, La Placita Archives.

250. José Luis Sierra, "Luis Olivares, Ejemplo Claro de Compromiso con su Feligresía," *La Opinión*, Aug. 13, 1989, Section "Acceso," 1–2.

CHAPTER 12

1. Henry Olivares interview.

2. See Santa Marta website: http://santamartahospital.org/history.htm.

3. Henry Olivares interview.

4. Estrada interview.

5. Maria del Pilar, "Lenta Recuperacion del Padre Olivares Preocupa a Amigos," *La Opinión*, June 21, 1990, in news summary, Claretian Archives.

6. Rubén Martínez interview notes with

Estrada, undated, Rubén Martínez Collection.

7. Valdivia interview.

8. Olivares to Ms. Manuela R. Clark, May 16, 1986, La Placita Archives.

9. Juanita Espinosa interview.

10. Martínez interview notes with Estrada. Mario Rivas says that Olivares slept in pain; Rivas interview.

11. Henry Olivares email to author, July 19, 2016.

12. Coady interview.

13. Interview with Luis Olivares by Denis Lynn Daly Heyck, 59.

14. Ibid. Also, *La Opinión*, June 21, 1990, in news survey, Claretian Archives.

15. Kennedy interview, Apr. 26, 2006.

16. Henry Olivares email to author, July 19, 2016.

17. Coady interview.

18. Heifetz interview; Rubén Martínez, "The Sacrifice: Luis Olivares, 1934–1993," *LA Weekly* (undated), Rubén Martínez Collection.

19. Coady and Heifetz interviews.

20. Sklarevsky interview.

21. Henry Olivares interview.

22. Bonpane interview.

23. Coady interview.

24. Heifetz interview.

25. Henry Olivares and Garza interviews.

26. Garza interview.

27. Henry Olivares interview.

28. Lisa Martínez interview.

29. Henry Olivares interview; Henry Olivares note to author, summer 2016; *La Opinión*, June 21, 1990, news survey, Claretian Archives.

30. Rubén Martínez interview.

31. Rubén Martínez, *Other Side*, 68–69; also see, Rubén Martínez, "The Sacrifice: Luis Olivares, 1934–1993," *LA Weekly* (undated clipping), Henry Olivares Collection; Martínez interview; and Rubén Martínez, "Outgoing Troublemaker," *LA Weekly*, June 29–July 5, 1990, Olivares family collection.

32. Henry Olivares interview.

33. Garza interview.

34. Olivares family interview.

35. Juanita Espinosa interview.

36. Kennedy interview, Apr. 26, 2006; Henry Olivares interview; Janis-Aparicio interview; Castillo interview; Limón email

to author, June 11, 2002; Sandoval interview, Dec. 5, 2006.

37. Coady interview; Rubén Martínez interview. Valerie Sklarevsky alleges that Coady came up with the theory that Olivares probably got AIDS in El Salvador with an infected needle; Sklarevsky interview.

38. *LA Weekly*, undated; Olivares family interview.

39. Ibid.

40. Martínez interview; Romero interview.

41. Olivares family interview; Quihuis interview.

42. Estrada interview.

43. Schey interview.

44. Ibid.

45. Ferrante interview. Ferrante says that he had visited Olivares when he first went to Santa Marta Hospital, but no one else mentions this, and so it's possible that he was misremembering and thinking of another occasion prior to Olivares's being diagnosed with AIDS.

46. Lozano interview.

47. Jimmy Rodríguez interview.

48. Marita Hernández interview.

49. Bonpane interview. Bonpane has the impression that Martin Sheen was also in attendance, but that can't be confirmed.

50. Marita Hernández interview.

51. Curran, "Final Sanctuary," 27; *NCR* clipping (no date), Claretian Archives.

52. Marita Hernández, "Activist Priest Says He Has AIDS; Doctors Blame Clinic's Needles," *LAT*, June 29, 1990, Metro Section, 1 and 3.

53. Ibid.; Marita Hernández interview; Heifetz interview.

54. Hernández, "Activist Priest."

55. Ibid.

56. Ibid.

57. Kennedy interview, Apr. 26, 2006.

58. Interview with Luis Olivares by Denis Lynn Daly Heyck.

59. Ron Curran, "Final Sanctuary: Father Luis Olivares," *LA Weekly* Sept. 6–12, 1991, 27.

60. Frenzen, Anderson-Barker, Arturo Rodríguez, Don Smith, Contreras, and Araceli Espinosa interviews.

61. Rubén Martínez interview.

62. Ferrante and Curry interviews.

63. Coady interview.

64. Martha Zozaya, Gómez, de Santos,

Kinsler, Lozano, Ponnet, and Bonpane interviews.

65. León and Urrabazo interviews; Romero, Fr. Juan Romero, "Tension between Cross and Sword," unpublished paper given at CEHILA Symposium, Apr. 24, 1992, 9.

66. Rubén Martínez and Kansvaag interviews.

67. Janis-Aparicio and Mejia interviews.

68. Romero interview.

69. *LAT,* June 30, 1990, B8.

70. Urrabazo interview.

71. *La Opinión,* Aug. 6, 1990, Olivares Family Collection.

72. Estrada and Castillo interviews.

73. Castillo interview.

74. Castillo, Lozano, Ferrante, Wehrli, and Espinosa interviews.

75. Ibid.

76. Juanita Espinosa and Heifetz interviews; Heyck interview with Olivares, 65.

77. Jimmy Rodríguez interview.

78. Urrabazo and Romero interviews.

79. Ferrante interview.

80. Kennedy interview, Apr. 26, 2006.

81. Lozano interview.

82. Coady interview.

83. Lozano interview.

84. Ponnet interview.

85. Bonpane interview.

86. Undated audio tape in Olivares's possessions; courtesy of Henry Olivares.

87. Curran, "Final Sanctuary," 22.

88. Juanita Espinosa interview.

89. Ferrante and Castillo interviews.

90. Ibid.; Juanita Espinosa interview.

91. Juanita Espinosa, Wehrli, Castillo interviews.

92. Juanita Espinosa interview.

93. Ibid.

94. Wehrli and Juanita Espinosa interviews.

95. Araceli Espinosa, Gregorio (Mar. 3, 2006), Coady, Niskanen, Cully, Wood, Gómez, and Peterson interviews.

96. Janis-Aparicio, Al López (Oct. 3, 2005), Natalia Hernández, Contreras, and Maldonado interviews.

97. Juanita Espinosa interview.

98. Gustafson interview.

99. Juanita Espinosa and Castillo interviews.

100. Juanita Espinosa interview; *LAT,* June

28, 1991, 34–35. Mahony was installed as Cardinal in June 1991.

101. Kennedy interview, Apr. 26, 2006.

102. Arturo Rodríguez interview. Chávez and Rodríguez joined Olivares and the other Claretians for lunch that day; Ferrante interview.

103. Juanita Espinosa interview.

104. Ibid.

105. Chávez interview.

106. Olivares family interview.

107. Garza interview.

108. Ibid.

109. Ibid.

110. Juanita Espinosa, Castillo, and María Valdivia interviews.

111. Araceli Espinosa interview.

112. Garza and Olivares family interviews.

113. Garza interview.

114. See fundraising letter by Olivares, dated Thanksgiving 1990, Claretian Archives.

115. See various invitations and correspondence in Claretian Archives.

116. Theresa Bonpane to Dear Friends, Oct. 1990, Claretian Archives.

117. Henry Olivares interview.

118. Regas to Olivares, Nov. 16, 1990, Claretian Archives.

119. *LA Times Magazine,* Dec. 16, 1990, 7.

120. Rev. Philip J. Lance to Olivares, Dec. 4, 1990, Claretian Archives,

121. Michael Weinstein to Olivares, Oct. 1, 1990 (which includes the flyer about the event); Claretian Archives.

122. Cully interview.

123. Rubén Martínez interview.

124. Ponnet interview.

125. Hector Tobar, "Remembering the Fallen," *LAT,* Jan. 20, 1992.

126. Martínez notes, Rubén Martínez Collection; Smith, *Resisting Reagan,* 51. In the 1980s more than 200,000 were killed in Central America due to the civil wars and the low intensity warfare waged by the Reagan administration. An additional 1.8 to 2.8 million Central Americans became refugees; see Smith, *Resisting Reagan,* 52.

127. Rubén Martínez interview.

128. Untitled and undated news clipping in Rubén Martínez Collection.

129. Olivares speech recorded and noted by Martínez, Jan. 19, 1992, Rubén Martínez Collection.

130. Gustafson interview; Jay Mathews, "500,000 Immigrants Granted Legal Status," *Washington Post*, Dec. 20, 1990.

131. Curran, "Final Sanctuary," 27.

132. Janis-Aparicio, Ferrante, Araceli Espinosa, Castillo, Jimmy Rodríguez, Sandoval, Olivares family interviews; Heyck interview with Olivares, 65; Mejia, Romero, Urrabazo, Kennedy (Apr. 26, 2006), and Rubén Martínez interviews.

133. Kennedy interview, Apr. 26, 2006.

134. Lozano interview.

135. Coady interview.

136. Heyck interview with Olivares, 61–62.

137. Krommer interview.

138. Romero interview with Olivares, Mar. 27, 1992, PADRES Collection.

139. Heifetz interview.

140. Heyck interview with Olivares, 61; Romero, Larkin, Freehling interviews.

141. *LA Times Magazine*, Dec. 16, 1990, 7.

142. Martínez notes, Rubén Martínez Collection.

143. Henry Olivares interview.

144. Vásquez and Peterson interviews.

145. Heiftez, Ferrante, Castillo, Juanita Espinosa interviews; *Honolulu Advertiser*, Mar. 21, 1993, Henry Olivares Collection.

146. Juanita Espinosa interview.

147. Valdivia interview.

148. Janis-Aparicio interview.

149. León interview.

150. Estrada interview.

151. Olivares family interview.

152. Juanita Espinosa interview.

153. Araceli Espinosa interview.

154. Castillo interview.

155. Ibid.; Juanita Espinosa interview; *Vida Nueva*, Mar. 26–Apr. 8, 1993, Fr. Juan Romero Collection; Mary Ballesteros, "Fallece el Padre Luis Olivares," *La Opinión*, Mar. 20, 1993, 1 and 10A, Claretian Archives.

156. Heifetz interview. Blase Bonpane and his wife Theresa visited Olivares earlier that day, but left before he died; Bonpane interview.

157. Henry Olivares interview, Oct. 22, 2005.

158. Castillo and Henry Olivares interviews; Henry Olivares's email to author, Aug. 5, 2016.

159. Garza interview.

160. See editorial, "Fin de Una Vida Ejemplar," *La Opinión*, undated, Henry Olivares Collection; Hector Tobar, "Father Luis Olivares, Voice for the Poor, Dies of AIDS," *LAT*, Mar. 20, 1993, B-1 and B-8; Ballesteros, "Fallece el Padre Luis Olivares," *La Opinión*, 1A and 10–12 A; see AP story in clipping of *Honolulu Advertiser*, Mar. 21, 1993, Henry Olivares Collection.

161. Press release, Mar. 18, 1993, in Claretian Archives.

162. "Statement on the Death of Father Luis Olivares, C.M.F.," Mar. 19, 1993, in Rubén Martínez Collection.

163. See resolution in Claretian Archives.

164. Henry Olivares, Cully, and Janis-Aparicio interviews.

165. Prather to Juanita Espinosa, Apr. 16, 1993, Henry Olivares Collection.

166. Juanita Espinosa interview.

167. Kennedy interview, Apr. 26, 2006.

168. Statement on death of Olivares, undated, Claretian Archives; Berg interview; Claretian bio of Olivares, Claretian Archives.

169. Urrabazo interview.

170. Olivares family and Henry Olivares interviews.

171. Cully interview. Cully says that someone at La Placita claimed that they had seen an apparition of Olivares in the church.

172. Tom Fox, "2,000 Gather to Mourn Activist Father Olivares," *NCR*, Apr. 2, 1993, 2.

173. Henry Olivares, Olivares family, and Garza interviews; Henry Olivares email to author, Aug. 16, 2016.

174. Fox, "2,000 gather," 2.

175. Rubén Martínez notes, Rubén Martínez Collection.

176. León interview; Fox, "2,000 gather," 2; also see, María Ballesteros, "Fue Sepultado el Padre Luis Olivares," *La Opinión*, Mar. 23, 1993, Henry Olivares Collection; Arvizu interview; Smith interview; Olivares family interview; Garza interview.

177. Fox, "2,000 gather," 2.

178. Rubén Martínez interview; also, Regas (Apr. 19, 2006), Henry Olivares, de Santos, Peterson, and Ferrante interviews.

179. Lisa Martínez, Urrabazo, and Kennedy (Apr. 26, 2006) interviews.

180. Newsletter of Casa Rutilio Grande (undated), Claretian Archives.

181. Fox, "2,000 gather," 2.

182. *LA Daily News*, Mar. 23, 1993, Olivares file in Chancery Archival Collection; Olivares family, Garza, Wehrli, Urrabazo, Larkin inter-

views; Martínez notes, in Rubén Martínez Collection.

183. Chávez interview.

184. Garza interview.

185. *Vida Nueva*, Mar. 26–Apr. 8, 1993, 2, Fr. Juan Romero Collection; also, Fox, "2,000 Gather," 2.

186. Cully interview.

187. Olivares family and Henry Olivares interviews.

188. Bonpane, Romero, Larkin, Ferrante, Kennedy (Apr. 26, 2006), and Estrada interviews; also, María Ballesteros, "Falese el padre Luis Olivares," *La Opinión*, 1A and 10–12 A.

189. Kennedy interview, Apr. 26, 2006.

190. Martínez notes, in Rubén Martínez Collection.

191. See funeral program in Claretian Archives.

192. Ibid.

193. Ferrante interview.

194. *La Opinión*, Mar. 23, 1993, Henry Olivares Collection.

195. Funeral program.

196. Olivares family interview.

197. Funeral program.

198. Copy of eulogy provided by Henry Olivares.

199. Henry Olivares interview; Martínez notes, Rubén Martínez Collection; Garza interview.

200. Cully interview.

201. Chávez interview.

202. Cully interview.

203. Jimmy Rodríguez interview.

204. News clipping (undated), Claretian Archives.

205. Bonpane and Jimmy Rodríguez interviews.

206. Henry Olivares, Urrabazo, Chavez interviews; undated news clipping in Claretian Archives.

207. Kennedy interview, Apr. 26, 2006.

208. Jimmy Rodríguez interview.

209. Chávez interview.

210. Modesto León believes it was four hours; León interview.

211. Janis-Aparicio interview.

212. Olivares family interview.

213. Coady interview.

214. Funeral program. Bonpane interview; "Activist Priest Mourned," *LAT*, Mar. 23, 1993 in Henry Olivares Collection; Rogelio Stelmanchuck, "El Pueblo Dijo Adios al Padre Olivares," *Vida Nueva*, Mar. 26–Apr. 8, 1993 in Fr. Juan Romero Collection.

215. Frenzen interview; funeral program.

216. Garza interview.

217. Estrada interview.

218. Natalia Hernández interview; Martínez notes, Rubén Martínez Collection.

219. Henry Olivares and Olivares family interviews.

220. Sometime after the funeral, some of Olivares's supporters, such as Martin Sheen, organized a reception at La Placita in memory of Olivares; see Contreras interview. Peter Schey notes that, prior to the funeral, he and others organized a private service with people who had done immigration work with Olivares; Schey interview.

221. Henry Olivares interview.

222. Juanita Espinosa interview.

223. Arvizu and Araceli Espinosa interviews.

224. Rubén Martínez interview.

225. Zwerling interview.

226. Bonpane interview.

227. Vásquez interview.

228. Al López interview, Oct. 3, 2005.

229. Schey interview.

230. Cully interview.

231. Rosendo Urrabazo, "AIDS-infected friend still teaching life's hard lessons," no title of newspaper in San Antonio (undated), Henry Olivares Collection.

232. Ferrante interview.

233. Gregorio interview, Mar. 3, 2006.

234. Kennedy interview, Apr. 26, 2006.

235. O'Connor interview.

236. Janis-Aparicio interview.

237. For example, the Luis Olivares Center for high-risk youth and their families in the Pico-Union district was dedicated on Aug. 6, 1999, as part of the Soledad Enrichment Action, Inc., headed by Brother Modesto León.

238. Sandoval interview.

BIBLIOGRAPHY

ARCHIVAL SOURCES
Al Luna Private Collection
Blase Bonpane Collection, Special
    Collections, UCLA Graduate Library
Chancery Archival Collection, Archival
    Center, Archdiocese of Los Angeles,
    San Fernando Mission, San Fernando,
    California
Claretian Archives, Claretian Provincial
    House, Los Angeles, California
Cynthia Anderson-Barker Private Collection
Dolores Mission Archives, Dolores Mission
    Parish, Los Angeles, California
Don Smith Private Collection
Fr. Brian Cully, C.M.F. Private Collection
Fr. Juan Romero Private Collection
Graciela Limón Private Collection
Henry Olivares Private Collection
Industrial Areas Foundation Collection,
    Daley Library, University of Illinois at
    Chicago
Ken Gregorio Private Collection
La Placita Archives, Los Angeles
Larry McNeil Papers, 1938–1987, Industrial
    Areas Foundation Records, Briscoe
    Center for American History, University
    of Texas at Austin
Lydia López Private Collection
Mary Brent Wehrli Private Collection
Olivares Family Private Collection
PADRES Collection, Special Collections,
    Hesburgh Library, University of Notre
    Dame
Philip Zwerling Private Collection
Rubén Martínez Private Collection

NEWSPAPERS
America
Business Week
Catholic Agitator
Catholic Review

Daily Breeze
Daily News
Downtown News
El Diario de Los Angeles
El Mundo
El Norte
Episcopal News
The Executive
The Guardian
Hispanic Business
Honolulu Advertiser
Los Angeles Herald Examiner
Los Angeles Times
Los Angeles Times Magazine
La Opinión
LA Weekly
Maryknoll
National Catholic Register
National Catholic Reporter
National Jesuit News
New York Times
North East Sun
Noticias del Mundo
Orange County Register
Our Sunday Visitor
Peacemaking
Post-Gazette
Reporter (San Diego)
Revista Maryknoll
San Jose Chronicle
Southern Cross
Sunday Press-Telegram
The Tidings
Time
USA Today
Vanity Fair
Ventura Star
Vida Nueva
Wall Street Journal
Washington Post

ORAL HISTORY INTERVIEWS
All of the following interviews were
  conducted by the author.
Alva, Susan, Nov. 26, 2002.
Anderson-Barker, Cynthia, Oct. 8, 2004.
Arvizu, María, Aug. 28, 2004.
Berg, C.M.F., Fr. Ralph, Jan. 20 and Jan. 23,
  2005.
Bonpane, Blase, Jan. 13, 2003.
Boyle, S.J., Fr. Greg, Nov. 22, 2005.
Castillo, C.M.F., Fr. Carlos, May 5 and 11, 2005.
Chávez, Paul, Feb. 28, 2006.
Clements, Mike, Mar. 23, 2006.
Coady, Dr. Davida, May 13, 2006.
Contreras, Miguel, July 27, 2004.
Cortes, Ernie, Feb. 9 and 17, 2004, and July 2,
  2014.
Cully, C.M.F., Fr. Brian, July 1, 2005.
Curry, Bishop Thomas, May 30, 2003.
Davis, Grace, Aug. 23, 2005.
DeQuattro, Sister Jo'Ann, Mar. 25 and May
  20, 2006.
De Santos, Manuel, Nov. 16, 2005.
D'Heedene, S.J., Fr. Walter, Aug. 17, 2004.
Domínguez, Aracely, Dec. 14, 2002.
Elizondo, Fr. Virgilio, Apr. 1, 2002, and Mar.
  2013.
Enriquez, Rosita, July 9, 2005.
Escalante, Moises, May 11, 2004.
Espinosa, Araceli, Apr. 15, 2005.
Espinosa, Juanita, Mar. 27, 2003.
Estrada, Fr. Richard, Aug. 24, 2002.
Ferrante, C.M.F., Fr. Frank, May 5, 2005.
Flanagan, C.M.F., Msgr. Sean, Mar. 13, 2006.
Flores, Jesse, Feb. 25, 2006.
Freehling, Rabbi Allen, circa 2005.
Frenzen, Niels, June 8, 2004.
Gandara, Bob, Sept. 4, 2005.
Garza, Teresa, Apr. 12–19, 2004.
Garza de Cortes, Oralia, Sept. 23, 2014.
Gómez, Pete, Oct. 24, 2003.
Gregorio, Ken, Mar. 1 and 3, 2006.
Gustafson, Ernest, Feb. 10, 2006.
Hampsch, C.M.F., Fr. John, May 5, 2005.
Hartmire, Rev. Chris, Mar. 11, 2005.
Heifetz, Dr. Laurence, Feb. 10, 2006.
Hernández, Marita, Nov. 3, 2003.
Hernández, Natalia, Sept. 16, 2002.
Howard, Dick, Aug. 6, 2002.
Huerta, Dolores, Apr. 5, 2005.
Janis-Aparicio, Madeline, Mar. 22, 2006.
Kansvaag, Ann, Mar. 9, 2006.
Kennedy, S.J., Fr. Michael, Aug. 24, 2002, and
  Apr. 26, 2006.

Kinsler, Gloria, Apr. 30, 2006.
Krommer, Sister Patricia, Feb. 2, 2003.
Larkin, Sister Maribeth, Jan. 31, 2004.
León, C.M.F., Bro. Modesto, Apr. 7, 2003.
Limón, Graciela, May 29, 2002.
López, Al, Sept. 12 and Oct. 3, 2005.
López, Arturo, Nov. 1, 2002.
López, Lydia, Dec. 14, 2002, and 2015.
Lozano, C.M.F., Fr. Rolando, Apr. 26, 2005.
Luna, Raul, May 22, 2006.
Maldonado, Rudy, May 4, 2004.
Martínez, Lisa, Aug. 29, 2002.
Martínez, Rubén, Nov. 16, 2003.
Mejia, Virginia, Sept. 6, 2002.
Mondragon, Oscar, Mar. 19 and May 27, 2005.
Negrete, Luis, Apr. 7, 2006.
Nelson, Socorro, Aug. 28, 2017.
Niskanen, C.M.F., Fr. Steve, Mar. 9, 2006.
O'Connor, C.M.F., Fr. Bernard, Sept. 14, 2005.
Olivares family, (Damaso, María del Rosario,
  Socorro, Josefina), Mar. 30, 2002.
Olivares, Henry, May 18, 2002.
Peterson, Glen, Apr. 5, 2006.
Pipes, Maggie, Feb. 4, 2005.
Ponnet, Fr. Chris, Feb. 3, 2003.
Quevedo, Eduardo, July 19, 2004.
Quihuis, S.J., Fr. Luis, July 25, 2003.
Regas, Rector George, Mar. 30 and Apr. 19,
  2006.
Rivas, Mario, Nov. 1, 2002.
Rocha de Zozaya, Martha, Dec. 29, 2005.
Rodríguez, Arturo, Feb. 25, 2005.
Rodríguez, Jimmy, Sept. 20, 2005.
Romero, Fr. Juan, Jan. 18, 2003, and May 11,
  2006.
Sandoval, Moises, Feb. 25, 2004, and Dec. 5,
  2006.
Schey, Peter, July 2, 2004.
Sellers, Tom, Mar. 27, 2006.
Sklarevsky, Valerie, Mar. 6, 2006.
Smith, Don, Dec. 6, 2002.
Stevens-Arroyo, Anthony, Sept. 21, 2005.
Urrabazo, C.F.M., Fr. Rosendo, Sept. 8, 2005.
Valdivia, María, Aug. 28, 2004.
Vásquez, C.F.M., Fr. Al, May 27, 2005.
Vásquez-Ramos, Dr. Armando, Sept. 29, 2008.
Villanueva, Gil, June 17, Dec. 11 and 14, 2004,
  and Jan. 12, 2005.
Wehrli, Mary Brent, Oct. 28, 2003.
Wong, Linda, May 21, 2004.
Wood, Fr. Roger, May 13, 2005.
Zozaya, Arthur, Dec. 28, 2005.
Zwerling, Rev. Philip, June 17, 2003.

SECONDARY SOURCES

Alinsky, Saul. *Reveille for Radicals*. New York: Vintage Books, 1969.

———. *Rules for Radicals: A Practical Primer for Realistic Radicals*. New York: Vintage Books, 1972.

Almaráz, Félix. *Knight without Armor: Carlos Eduardo Castañeda*. College Station: Texas A&M University Press, 1999.

Alvarez, Luis. *The Power of the Zoot: Youth Culture and Resistance during World War II*. Berkeley and Los Angeles: University of California Press, 2008.

Badillo, David. *Latinos and the New Immigrant Church*. Baltimore: Johns Hopkins University Press, 2006.

Bailey, David C. *Viva Cristo Rey! The Cristero Rebellion and the Church-State Conflict in Mexico*. Austin: University of Texas Press, 1974.

Bailey, Robert, Jr. *Radicals in Urban Politics: The Alinsky Approach*. Chicago: University of Chicago Press, 1974.

Bardacke, Frank. *Trampling Out the Vintage: César Chávez and the Two Souls of the United Farm Workers*. London and New York: Verso Press, 2011.

Barry, Tom. *Roots of Rebellion: Land and Hunger in Central America*. Boston: South End Press, 1987.

Bau, Ignatius. *This Ground Is Holy: Church Sanctuary and Central American Refugees*. Mahwah, N.J.: Paulist Press, 1985.

Berryman, Philip. *Liberation Theology*. New York: Pantheon Books, 1987.

Blackwell, Maylei. *Chicana Power! Contested Histories of Feminism in the Chicano Movement*. Austin: University of Texas Press, 2011.

Blanton, Carlos Kevin. *George I. Sánchez: The Long Fight for Mexican American Integration*. New Haven: Yale University Press, 2014.

———. *The Strange Career of Bilingual Education in Texas, 1836–1981*. College Station: Texas A&M Press, 2001.

Burke, John Francis. "Latino Spirituality and U.S. Politics: A Communitarianism That Crosses Borders." In *Religion, Politics, and American Identity: New Directions, New Controversies*, ed. David S. Gutterman and Andrew R. Murphy, 151–76. Lanham, Md.: Lexington Books, 2006.

Burns, E. Bradford. *At War in Nicaragua: The Reagan Doctrine and the Politics of Nostalgia*. New York: Harper and Row, 1987.

Busto. Rudy V. *King Tiger: The Religious Vision of Reies López Tijerina*. Albuquerque: University of New Mexico Press, 2005.

Carbine, Rosemary P. "The Beloved Community: Transforming Spaces for Social Change and for Cosmopolitan Citizenship," in Rosemary P. Carbine and Kathleen J. Dolphin, eds. *Women, Wisdom, and Witness: Engaging Contexts in Conversation*. Collegeville, Minnesota: Liturgical Press, 2012.

Carr, Edward Hallett. *What Is History?* New York: Vintage Books, 1962.

Casaldáliga, Bishop Pedro. *In Pursuit of the Kingdom: Writings 1968–1988*. Maryknoll, N.Y.: Orbis Books, 1990.

Chávez, Ernesto. *Mi Raza Primero! (My People First!): Nationalism, Identity, and Insurgency in the Chicano Movement in Los Angeles, 1966–1978*. Berkeley and Los Angeles: University of California Press, 2002.

Coleman, Kenneth, and George Herring, eds. *The Central American Crisis: Sources of Conflict and the Failure of U.S. Policy*. Wilmington, Del.: Scholarly Resources, 1985.

Coutin, Susan Bibler. *The Culture of Protest: Religious Activism and the U.S. Sanctuary Movement*. Boulder: Westview Press, 1993.

Crittenden, Ann. *Sanctuary: A Story of American Consciousness and the Law in Collision*. New York: Weidenfeld and Nicolson, 1988.

Cunningham, Hilary. *God and Caesar at the Rio Grande: Sanctuary and the Politics of Religion*. Minneapolis: University of Minnesota Press, 1995.

Dalton, Frederick John. *The Moral Vision of César Chávez*. Maryknoll, N.Y.: Orbis Books, 2003.

Davidson, Miriam. *Conviction of the Heart: Jim Corbett and the Sanctuary Movement*. Tucson: University of Arizona Press, 1988.

Deck, S.J., Allan Figueroa. *The Second Wave: Hispanic Ministry and the Evangelization of Cultures*. New York: Paulist Press, 1989.

Dinnon, Richard. *Keeper of Concentration Camps: Dillon S. Meyer and American Racism*. Berkeley and Los Angeles: University of California Press, 1989.

Djupe, Paul A., and Laura R. Olson. *Religious Interests in Community Conflict: Beyond the Culture Wars*. Waco: Baylor University Press, 2007.

Ebaugh, Helen Rose, and Janet Saltzman Chafetz, eds. *Religion Across Borders: Transnational Immigrant Networks*. Walnut Creek, Ca.: Altamira Press, 2002.

Elizondo, Virgilio. *The Future is Mestizo: Life Where Cultures Meet*. Rev. ed. Boulder, Co.: University Press of Colorado, 2000.

Escobar, Edward. *Race, Police, and the Making of a Political Identity: Mexican Americans and the Los Angeles Police Department, 1900–1945*. Berkeley and Los Angeles: University of California Press, 1999.

Finks, P. David. *The Radical Vision of Saul Alinsky*. New York: Paulist Press, 1984.

Fisch, Louise Ann. *All Rise: Reynaldo G. Garza: The First Mexican American Federal Judge*. College Station: Texas A&M University Press, 1996.

Flores, William V., and Rina Benmayor. *Latino Cultural Citizenship: Claiming Identity, Space, and Rights*. Boston: Beacon Press, 1997.

Foley, Michael W., and Dean R. Hoge. *Religion and the New Immigrants: How Faith Communities Form Our Newest Citizens*. New York: Oxford University Press, 2007.

Fremon, Celeste. *G-Dog and the Homeboys: Father Greg Boyle and the Gangs of East Los Angeles*. Albuquerque: University of New Mexico Press, 2004.

Fuentes, Victor. *César Chávez y la Unión*. Moorpark, Calif.: Floricanto, 2015.

García, Alma A., ed. *Chicana Feminist Thought: The Basic Historical Writings*. New York: Routledge, 1997.

García, Ignacio M. *Hector P. García: In Relentless Pursuit of Justice*. Houston: Arte Publico Press, 2003.

———. *United We Win: The Rise and Fall of La Raza Unida Party*. Tucson: Mexican American Studies & Research Center, 1989.

García, Mario T. *Blowout! Sal Castro and the Chicano Struggle for Educational Justice*. Chapel Hill: University of North Carolina Press, 2011.

———. *Católicos: Resistance and Affirmation in Chicano Catholic History*. Austin: University of Texas Press, 2008.

———. *The Chicano Generation: Testimonios of the Movement*. Oakland: University of California Press, 2015.

———, ed. *Chicano Liberation Theology: The Writings and Documents of Richard Cruz and Católicos Por La Raza*. Dubuque, Iowa: Kendall Hunt Publishing Co., 2009.

———, ed. *The Chicano Movement: Perspectives from the Twenty-First Century*. New York: Routledge, 2011.

———. *Desert Immigrants: The Mexicans of El Paso, 1880–1920*. New Haven: Yale University Press, 1981.

———, ed. *A Dolores Huerta Reader*. Albuquerque: University of New Mexico Press, 2008.

———, ed. *The Gospel of César Chávez: My Faith in Action*. Lanham, Md.: Sheed & Ward, 2007.

———. *The Latino Generation: Voices of the New America*. Chapel Hill: University of North Carolina Press, 2014.

———. *The Making of a Mexican American Mayor: Raymond L. Telles of El Paso*. El Paso: Texas Western Press, 1998.

———. *Memories of Chicano History: The Life and Narrative of Bert Corona*. Berkeley and Los Angeles: Mexican University of California Press, 1994.

———. *Mexican Americans: Leadership, Ideology & Identity, 1930–1960*. New Haven: Yale University Press, 1989.

———, ed. *Rúben Salazar: Border Correspondent: Selected Writings, 1955–1970*. Berkeley and Los Angeles: University of California Press, 1995.

García, Matt. *From the Jaws of Victory: The Triumph and Tragedy of César Chávez and the Farm Worker Movement*. Berkeley: University of California Press, 2012.

García, Richard A. *Rise of the Mexican American Middle Class: San Antonio, 1929–1941*. College Station: Texas A&M University Press, 1991.

Golden, Renny. *Sanctuary: The New Underground Railroad*. Maryknoll, N.Y.: Orbis Books, 1986.

González, Gilbert G. *Chicano Education in the Era of Segregation*. Philadelphia: Balch Institute, 1990.

Gottlieb, Roger S. *Joining Hands: Politics*

and Religion Together for Social Change. Cambridge, Mass: Westview Press, 2002.

Griswold del Castillo, Richard, and Richard A. García. *César Chávez: A Triumph of Spirit*. Norman: University of Oklahoma Press, 1995.

Groody, Daniel G., and Gioacchino Campese, eds. *A Promised Land, A Perilous Journey: Theological Perspectives on Migration*. Notre Dame: University of Notre Dame Press, 2008.

Gutiérrez, Gustavo. *A Theology of Liberation*. Maryknoll, N.Y.: Orbis Books, 1988.

Gutterman, David S., and Andrew R. Murphy. *Religion, Politics, and American Identity: New Directions, New Controversies*. Lanham, Md.: Lexington Books, 2006.

Hagan, Jacqueline Maria. *Migration Miracle: Faith, Hope, and Meaning on the Undocumented Journey*. Cambridge: Harvard University Press, 2008.

Hamilton, Nora, and Jeffrey Frieden, Linda Fuller, and Manuel Pastor, Jr., eds. *Crisis in Central America: Regional Dynamics and U.S. Policy in the 1980s*. Boulder, Colo.: Westview Press, 1988.

Hennelly, Alfred T., ed. *Liberation Theology: A Documentary History*. Maryknoll, N.Y.: Orbis Books, 1995.

Heyck, Denis Lynn Daly. *Barrios and Borderlands: Cultures of Latinos and Latinas in the United States*. New York: Routledge, 1994.

Hinojosa, Felipe. *Latino Mennonites: Civil Rights, Faith & Evangelical Culture*. Baltimore: Johns Hopkins University Press, 2014.

Hondagneu-Sotelo, Pierrette. *God's Heart Has No Borders: How Religious Activists Are Working for Immigrant Rights*. Berkeley and Los Angeles: University of California Press, 2008.

Horwitt, Sanford D. *Let Them Call Me Rebel: Saul Alinsky—His Life and Legacy*. New York: Alfred A. Knopf, 1989.

Kreneck, Thomas H. *Mexican American Odyssey: Félix Tijerina, Entrepreneur and Civic Leader, 1905–1965*. College Station: Texas A&M University Press, 2001.

Lash, Christopher. *Haven in a Heartless World*. New York: W.W. Norton, 1958.

Laslett, John H. *Shameful Victory: The Los Angeles Dodgers, the Red Scare, and the Hidden History of Chavez Ravine*. Tucson: University of Arizona Press, 2015.

León, Luis D. *The Political Spirituality of Cesar Chavez: Crossing Religious Borders*. Oakland: University of California Press, 2015.

Lernoux, Penny. *Cry of the People: The Struggle for Human Rights in Latin America—The Catholic Church in Conflict with U.S. Policy*. New York: Penguin, 1982.

Levine, Daniel H., ed. *Religion and Political Conflict in Latin America*. Chapel Hill: University of North Carolina Press, 1986.

Levitt, Peggy. *God Needs No Passport: Immigrants and the Changing American Religion Landscape*. New York: The Free Press, 2007.

Levy, Jacques. *César Chávez: Autobiography of La Causa*. New York: W.W. Norton, 1975.

Limón, Graciela. *In Search of Bernabe*. Houston: Arte Publico Press, 1993.

Limón, José E. *Américo Paredes: Culture and Critique*. Austin: University of Texas Press, 2012.

Lowy, Michael. *The War of Gods: Religion and Politics in Latin America*. London: Verso Press, 1996.

Mariscal, Jorge. *Brown-Eyed Children of the Sun: Lessons from the Chicano Movement, 1965–1975*. Albuquerque: University of New Mexico Press, 2005.

Márquez, Benjamin. *Constructing Identities in Mexican American Political Organizations: Choosing Issues, Taking Sides*. Austin: University of Texas Press, 2003.

Marsh, Charles. *The Beloved Community: How Faith Shapes Social Justice, from the Civil Rights Movement to Today*. New York: Basic Books, 2005.

Martínez, Demetria. *Mother Tongue*. New York: Ballantine Books, 1994.

Martínez, Richard Edward. *PADRES: The National Chicano Priest Movement*. Austin: University of Texas Press, 2005.

Martínez, Rubén. *The Other Side: Notes from the New L.A., Mexico City, and Beyond*. New York: Vintage Books, 1991.

Matovina, Timothy. *Guadalupe and Her Faithful: Latino Catholics in San Antonio from Colonial Origins to the Present*. Baltimore: Johns Hopkins University Press, 2005.

———. *Latino Catholicism: Transformation in America's Largest Church*. Princeton: Princeton University Press, 2011.

———. *Tejano Religion and Ethnicity: San Antonio, 1821–1860*. Austin: University of Texas Press, 1995.

Mazón, Mauricio. *The Zoot-Suit Riots: The Psychology of Symbolic Annihilation*. Austin: University of Texas Press, 1989.

Medina, Lara. *Las Hermanas: Chicana/Latina Religious-Political Activism in the U.S. Catholic Church*. Philadelphia: Temple University Press, 2004.

Menjivar, Cecilia. *Fragmented Ties: Salvadoran Immigrant Networks in America*. Berkeley: University of California Press, 2000.

Meyer, Jean. *The Cristero Rebellion: The Mexican People between Church and State, 1926–1929*. Cambridge: Cambridge University Press, 1976.

Muñoz, Carlos, Jr. *Youth, Identity, Power: The Chicano Movement*. London: Verso Press, 1989.

Nelson, Jeffrey, and Mary Ann Flannery. "The Sanctuary Movement: A Study in Religious Confrontation." *Southern Communication Journal* (Summer 1990): 372–87.

Normark, Don. *Chavez Ravine, 1949: A Los Angeles Story*. San Francisco: Chronicle Books, 1999.

Oropeza, Lorena. *Raza Si, Guerra No! Chicano Protest and Patriotism during the Vietnam War Era*. Berkeley and Los Angeles: University of California Press, 2005.

Pagán, Edward Obregón. *Murder at the Sleepy Lagoon: Zoot Suits, Race, and Riot in Wartime L.A.* Chapel Hill: University of North Carolina Press, 2003.

Pawel, Miriam. *The Crusade of César Chávez: A Biography*. New York: Bloomsbury Press, 2014.

———. *The Union of Their Dreams: Power, Hope, and Struggle in César Chávez's Farm Worker Movement*. New York: Bloomsbury Press, 2009.

Pulido, Alberto L. *The Sacred World of the Penitentes*. Washington, D.C.: Smithsonian Institution Press, 2000.

Rabben, Linda. *Sanctuary and Asylum: A Social and Political History*. Seattle and London: University of Washington Press, 2016.

Ramírez, Catherine S. *The Woman in the Zoot-Suit: Gender, Nationalism, and the Cultural Politics of Memory*. Durham, N.C.: Duke University Press, 2009.

Robinson, Greg. *By Order of the President: FDR and the Internment of Japanese Americans*. Cambridge: Harvard University Press, 2001.

Romero, Archbishop Oscar. *Voice of the Voiceless*. Maryknoll, N.Y.: Orbis Books, 1990.

Ruiz, Ramón Eduardo. *The Great Rebellion: Mexico, 1905–1924*. New York: W.W. Norton, 1980.

San Miguel, Guadalupe. *"Let All of Them Take Heed": Mexican Americans and the Campaign for Educational Equality in Texas, 1910–1981*. Austin: University of Texas Press, 1989.

Sánchez, George J. *Becoming Mexican American: Ethnicity, Culture, and Identity in Chicano Los Angeles*. New York: Oxford University Press, 1993.

Skerry, Peter. *Mexican Americans: The Ambivalent Minority*. New York: The Free Press, 1993.

Slessarev-Jamir, Helene. *Prophetic Activism: Progressive Religion Justice Movements in Contemporary America*. New York: Union Press, 2011.

Smith, Christian. *Resisting Reagan: The U.S. Central American Peace Movement*. Chicago: University of Chicago Press, 1996.

———. *The Emergence of Liberation Theology: Radical Religion and Social Movement Theory*. Chicago: University of Chicago Press, 1991.

Tobar, Hector. *The Tattooed Soldier*. New York: Picador, 2014.

Tomsho, Robert. *The American Sanctuary Movement*. Austin: Texas Monthly Press, 1987.

Treviño, Roberto. R. *The Church in the Barrio: Mexican American Ethno-Catholicism in Houston*. Chapel Hill: University of North Carolina Press, 2006.

Walker, Thomas, ed. *Reagan Versus the Sandinistas: The Undeclared War on Nicaragua*. Boulder: Westview Press, 1987.

Warren, Mark R. *Dry Bones Rattling: Community Building to Revitalize American Democracy*. Princeton and Oxford: Princeton University Press, 2001.

INDEX